ON THIS DAY
IN SPORT

First published in 2005
This edition published in 2013 by
New Holland Publishers
London • Sydney • Cape Town • Auckland
www.newhollandpublishers.com

The Chandlery, Unit 114, 50 Westminster Bridge Road, London, SE1 7QY
1/66 Gibbes Street Chatswood NSW 2067 Australia
Wembley Square First Floor Solan Road Gardens Cape Town 8001 South Africa
218 Lake Road Northcote Auckland New Zealand

A catalogue record of this book is available at the British Library and at the National Library of Australia.

ISBN: 9781742574172

10 9 8 7 6 5 4 3 2 1

Managing director: Fiona Schultz
Publisher: Alan Whiticker
Project editor: Kate Sherington
Designer: Kimberley Pearce
Production director: Olga Dementiev
Printer: Toppan Leefung Printing Limited

Follow New Holland Publishers on
Facebook: www.facebook.com/NewHollandPublishers

ON THIS DAY IN SPORT

IAN TRENT

NEW
HOLLAND

CONTENTS

MARCH **68**

APRIL **100**

JULY **194**

AUGUST **226**

NOVEMBER **321**

DECEMBER **352**

JANUARY

1 JANUARY

1908 – Hobbs' Test Cricket debut
Legendary England batsman Jack Hobbs made his Test debut in the second Test against Australia in Melbourne, scoring 83 in his first appearance at the crease. Hobbs became the first Test batsman to score 5,000 runs.

1925 – Layden's College Football treble
Elmer Layden scored 3 touchdowns, as unbeaten national champion Notre Dame beat Stanford 27-10 in the Rose Bowl. Layden was one of an elite corps of Notre Dame receivers known as the 'Four Horsemen', who dominated College Football for 4 seasons. This was their final game together.

1965 – Jets to sign Namath in record NFL deal
Following a 21-17 Orange Bowl defeat to the Texas Longhorns, star Alabama quarterback Joe Namath agreed to sign with the New York Jets in the biggest deal in sports history at that time. Team owner Sonny Werblin organised to pay Namath a package worth $400,000. Namath went on to guide the Jets to Super Bowl III in 1969.

1979 – Cauthen losing streak starts
A disastrous 110-race losing streak at Santa Anita that stretched from New Year's Day to February 8, led to sensational young American jockey Steve Cauthen accepting an offer to ride for British racehorse owner Robert Sangster. He spent the next 14 years mastering the European turf courses. Cauthen was 3 times England's leading jockey and became the first rider to win the world's 4 major derbies: Kentucky, Epsom, French and Irish.

1983 – PGA inaugurates all-exempt tour
The PGA Tour made the top 125 money winners from the previous year fully exempt to play in any PGA Tour tournament the following year. This largely eliminated Monday qualifying and gave many more players in the already deep pool of talent on the PGA Tour the chance to be competitive in tournament play.

2006 – Alexander's NFL TD record
Seattle running back Shaun Alexander set an NFL record with 28 touchdowns in a season, in the Seahawks' 23-17 defeat to the Green Bay Packers at Lambeau Field. Alexander also surpassed the NY Giants' Tiki Barber for the NFL rushing crown.

2007 – Knight's coaching record
Controversial college basketball coach Bob Knight became the leader in NCAA Division I men's victories, as Texas Tech beat New Mexico 70-68 in Lubbock, Texas. The win took Knight past former North Carolina coach Dean Smith, and brought his career record to 880-354.

BIRTHDATES
1857	Baseball Hall of Fame pitcher TIM KEEFE – died 1933
1871	Australian boxer ALBERT GRIFFITHS – died 1927
1899	British rower JACK BERESFORD – died 1977
1902	South African Test fast bowler 'BUSTER' NUPEN – died 1977
1911	Baseball Hall of Fame first baseman HANK GREENBERG – died 1986
1922	American boxer ROCKY GRAZIANO – died 1990
1928	Pakistan Test fast bowler KHAN MOHAMMAD – died 2009
1933	American swimmer FORD KONNO
1943	American golfer JERILYN BRITZ
1944	West Indian Test batsman CHARLIE DAVIS
1945	Belgian auto-racer JACKI ICKX
1946	Brazilian soccer midfielder ROBERTO RIVELINO
1950	Australian rugby league coach WAYNE BENNETT
1955	American golfer MIKE SULLIVAN
1967	NFL defensive end DERRICK THOMAS – died 2000
1969	English golfer PAUL LAWRIE
1972	French soccer defender LILIAN THURAM
1982	Argentine tennis player DAVID NALBANDIAN
1983	South Korean archer PARK SUNG-HYUN
1984	Peruvian soccer striker PAOLO GUERRERO

Bob Knight watches his Texas Tech University basketball players in 2007.

7

1879 – First Test cricket hat-trick

Fearsome Australian fast bowler Frederick Spofforth achieved the first Test match hat-trick in history in the one-off Test against England at the Melbourne Cricket Ground. 'The Demon' dismissed England batsmen Vernon Royle, Francis MacKinnon and Tom Emmett with consecutive balls in the first innings of England's 10-wicket defeat.

1946 – Rani takes first Sydney to Hobart Ocean Classic

The 39ft *Rani* won both line and handicap honours in stormy weather in the inaugural Sydney to Hobart yacht race. The 630-nautical-mile race has become one of the world's premier ocean regattas.

1971 – Football tragedy in Scotland

Sixty-six fans were trampled to death and more than 200 were injured during the New Year's match between Glasgow rivals Rangers and Celtic at Ibrox Park. A large section of the crowd was leaving via a tight stairway when the crush occurred. The tragedy led to the 1975 Safety of Sports Ground legislation.

1978 – Gavaskar's Test triple

Indian opener Sunil Gavaskar became the only batsman to score a century in both innings of a Test match 3 times. Gavaskar hit 182 in the first Test against the West Indies in Calcutta, after compiling 107 in the first innings.

1982 – Tennis rivalry continues

Martina Navratilova beat arch-rival Chris Evert in 3 hard-fought sets to win the Australian Open at Kooyong in Melbourne. Navratilova won the match 6-7, 6-4, 7-5. The pair met in 2 more Australian Open finals, with Evert winning in 1982, and Navratilova in 1985. In all, Navratilova won 3 Australian titles and Evert 2, both from 5 finals appearances each.

1982 – Quarterbacks' day out

The San Diego Chargers scored an amazing 41-38 win over the Miami Dolphins in the AFC divisional playoff game at the Miami Orange Bowl. It was the first time in NFL history that both quarterbacks – Dan Fouts and Don Strock – passed for more than 400 yards.

1983 – Anderson's NFL passing record

Cincinnati Bengals quarterback Ken Anderson completed 20 consecutive passes to set an NFL record for passing accuracy in the Bengals 35-27 win over the Houston Oilers.

1987 – Ramsey's 800th NBA win

Jack Ramsay became only the second coach to claim his 800th NBA victory after his Indiana Pacers beat the Los Angeles Clippers 116-106. The Boston Celtics' Red Auerbach was the first NBA coach to reach the plateau.

2013 – #16 for 'The Power'

52-year-old British darts champion Phil Taylor beat the sport's rising star Michael van Gerwin of the Netherlands 7-4 in the final at the Alexandra Palace in London for an unprecedented 16th world title. Van Gerwin led 2-0 and 4-2 in the race to 7 sets, but could not stay with the irrepressible Taylor, who got stronger as the final progressed.

BIRTHDATES

1870	American boxing promoter TEX RICKARD – died 1929
1886	South African Test batsman BILLY ZULCH – died 1924
1927	Pro Football Hall of Fame defensive end GINO MARCHETTI
1963	Baseball pitcher DAVID CONE
1963	Baseball infielder EDGAR MARTINEZ
1964	American boxer PERNELL WHITAKER
1964	Sri Lankan Test fast bowler RUMESH RATNAYAKE
1967	South African rugby union captain FRANCOIS PIENAAR
1973	American tennis player CHRIS WOODRUFF
1975	New Zealand rugby union captain REUBEN THORNE
1981	Argentine soccer winger MAXI RODRIGUEZ

❸ JANUARY

1943 – Bentley brothers' bliss
In the only time in NHL history that a trio of family members recorded the goal and assists on a scoring play, Max and Doug Bentley assisted on brother Reg's first, and only, NHL goal in the Chicago Blackhawks 3-3 tie against the Rangers in New York.

1949 – Weekes hits fifth straight Test century
West Indian batsman Everton Weekes scored his world-record fifth consecutive Test century when he made 101 in the third Test against India in Calcutta. The century sequence began with 141 against England at Kingston in 1948 and continued with 128 at Delhi, 194 at Bombay and 162 in the first innings at Calcutta.

1983 – Dorsett's NFL record
Dallas running back Tony Dorsett became the only player in NFL history to run 99 yards from scrimmage for a touchdown in the Cowboys' 31-27 loss to the Minnesota Vikings. Dorsett's run broke the NFL record of 97 yards, set by Chicago's Andy Uram in 1939 and tied by Pittsburgh's Bob Gage in 1949.

1981 – Miller's Sun City win
Johnny Miller won golf's first $1m tournament when he beat Spaniard Seve Ballesteros in a playoff in the inaugural Million Dollar World Challenge in South Africa. Later, the tournament was also the first to offer $2 million first prize money.

1992 – 'Chariots' rugby league record fee
Wigan paid Widnes a world record transfer fee of £440,000 for Great Britain winger Martin Offiah. In a 14-year career, 'Chariots', as he was known, scored 501 tries, third to Australia's Brian Bevan and Welshman Billy Boston in the all-time list.

1993 – Bills' NFL record comeback
Frank Reich led the Buffalo Bills to a record 32-point comeback in the AFC Championship game. The Houston Oilers led 35-3 in the third quarter, but Reich threw 4 touchdowns to clinch an improbable 41-38 overtime victory for the Bills.

West Indies cricketer Everton Weekes.

2004 – Quick 5
English League Division 2 football club Plymouth Argyle scored a stunning 5 goals in the first 18 minutes of their match against Chesterfield at Home Park. The Pilgrims won the game 7-0.

BIRTHDATES
1861	English tennis player ERNEST RENSHAW – died 1899
1861	English tennis player WILLIAM RENSHAW – died 1904
1886	Australian Test spinner ARTHUR MAILEY – died 1967
1916	American golfer FRED HAAS – died 2004
1923	NFL coach HANK STRAM – died 2005
1939	Canadian Hockey Hall of Fame forward BOBBY HULL
1941	New Zealand rugby union winger MALCOLM DICK
1944	American swimmer CHRISTINA VON SALTZA
1947	England rugby union prop FRAN COTTON
1962	Scottish rugby union fullback GAVIN HASTINGS
1963	Pakistan Test batsman AAMER MALIK
1964	American basketball player CHERYL MILLER
1966	Indian Test fast bowler CHETAN SHARMA
1969	German auto racer MICHAEL SCHUMACHER
1981	NFL quarterback ELI MANNING

④ JANUARY

1902 – Trumble causes England tumble
Australian off-spinner Hugh Trumble finished England's second innings with the first of his 2 Test hat-tricks, as England crashed to a 229-run, second-Test defeat in Melbourne.

1967 – Speed kills Campbell
Forty-six-year-old British speed ace Donald Campbell was killed on Coniston Water in England, during an attempt to break his own world water-speed record. Campbell's boat, *Bluebird K7*, was travelling at more than 300 miles per hour (483 km/h) when it catapulted 15m into the air after its nose lifted.

1984 – Gretzky's eight-point double
Edmonton's Wayne Gretzky became the first NHL player to score 8 or more points twice in a game. 'The Great One' had 4 goals and 4 assists in the Oilers' 12-8 win over Minnesota.

1986 – NFL rushing record
LA Rams running back Eric Dickerson rushed for an NFL post-season record of 248 yards, in the Rams' 20-0 victory over Dallas in an NFC divisional playoff in Anaheim. Dickerson scored twice and averaged 7.3 yards a carry on his 34 attempts to break the 1964 record of 206, set by the San Diego Chargers' Keith Lincoln.

1991 – Youthful diving champion
Twelve-year-old Chinese diver Fu Mingxia became the youngest world champion in the history of any aquatic event by winning the platform gold medal at the World Championships in Perth, Australia. FINA then passed a rule requiring divers to be at least 14 in an Olympic year. Mingxia beat the requirement by 20 days and won the Olympic platform gold medal in Barcelona in 1992.

2001 – Michael joins exclusive NBA club
Washington's Michael Jordan became the fourth player in NBA history to score 30,000 career points during an 89-83 victory against his former club the Chicago Bulls. Other leading scorers were Kareem Abdul-Jabbar, Wilt Chamberlain and Karl Malone.

Chinese diver Fu Mingxia wins the 1992 Olympic platform gold medal in Barcelona.

2005 – 'Gilly' best keeper
Adam Gilchrist became the most prolific century-scoring wicketkeeper in history when he smashed 113 from just 120 balls in the third Test against Pakistan in Sydney. In his 13th Test century for Australia, Gilchrist hit 14 fours and 5 sixes.

2008 – Over and out for 'Swiss Miss'
The retired Martina Hingis, a five-time tennis Grand Slam winner, was banned for 2 years after an independent tribunal confirmed a doping offence. Hingis denied taking cocaine, but said she would not spend several years fighting officialdom.

BIRTHDATES
1930	NFL coach DON SHULA
1935	American boxer FLOYD PATTERSON – died 2006
1944	New Zealand rugby union lock ALAN SUTHERLAND
1946	England rugby union halfback MALCOLM YOUNG
1949	England soccer defender MICK MILLS
1964	New Zealand squash player SUSAN DEVOY
1965	French tennis player GUY FORGET
1967	Australian rugby union flanker DAVID WILSON
1967	American golfer DAVID TOMS
1978	Slovak tennis player DOMINIK HRBATY
1980	Portuguese soccer defender MIGUEL
1990	German soccer midfielder TONI KROOS

1964 – Lincoln's NFL rumble
San Diego fullback Keith Lincoln ran and received for a total of 329 yards in the Chargers' 51-10 rout of the Boston Patriots in the AFL championship game in San Diego. On just 13 carries, Lincoln ran for a playoff record of 206 yards and caught 7 passes for 123 yards

1967 – 700 for Hockey's Howe
38-year-old Detroit Red Wings right wing Gordie Howe scored 2 goals against the Chicago Blackhawks, becoming the first NHL player to reach 700 career goals

1971 – Cricket's first ODI
After the third Ashes Test in Melbourne was washed out, the inaugural one-day international was played between Australia and England. Ian Chappell's 60 was the highlight of Australia's 5-wicket victory.

1984 – Chappell's fond cricket farewell
Australian captain Greg Chappell scored a fine 182 in his final Test innings during the fifth Test against Pakistan in Sydney. Coincidentally, Chappell scored 182 at the SCG on the same date in 1976.

1988 – Maravich dies on court
At age 40, Pete Maravich, the NCAA's all-time leading scorer, died of a heart attack while playing a pickup game in Pasadena. At LSU, Maravich averaged 44.2 points per game in 3 seasons. In 10 NBA seasons he averaged 24.2 points.

1993 – Lara's Test cricket arrival
Brian Lara scored his maiden century for the West Indies, a swashbuckling 277 in the third Test in Sydney. Lara smashed 38 fours and with Richie Richardson (109) salvaged an important draw.

2001 – NBA triple record
Milwaukee guard Tim Thomas connected on a record 8 3-point shots in the second half of the Bucks' 119-115 win over Portland. The record was equalled by 2 other Bucks players in 2002, Michael Redd and Ray Allen.

2005 – Track and field honours for Holmes
British dual Olympic champion Kelly Holmes was named European Female Athlete of 2004. Holmes, who won the 800m and 1,500m gold medals at the Athens Games, was also made a dame in the New Year's Honours List and took out the prestigious Laureus international award in 2005.

BIRTHDATES

1926	American auto racer PAT FLAHERTY – died 2002
1928	Pakistan Test captain IMTIAZ AHMED
1932	Pro Football Hall of Fame coach CHUCK NOLL
1936	New Zealand rugby union centre TERRY LINEEN
1938	Dutch soccer player PIET KRUIVER – died 1989
1939	British equestrian rider BRIDGET PARKER
1941	New Zealand Test batsman BOB CUNIS – died 2008
1941	American tennis player CHUCK McKINLEY – died 1986
1941	Indian Test captain MANSUR ALI KHAN – died 2011
1945	NFL coach SAM WYCHE
1954	Basketball Hall of Fame forward ALEX ENGLISH
1960	Swedish soccer midfielder GLENN STRÖMBERG
1964	Spanish golfer MIGUEL ANGEL JIMINEZ
1969	American golfer SHAUN MICHEEL
1982	Croatian alpine skier JANICA KOSTELIC

British middle-distance runner Kelly Holmes wins the 1,500m gold medal at the 2004 Athens Olympics.

1930 – Bradman cricket cuts

Twenty-one-year-old Don Bradman smashed 49 fours in a world record first-class score of 452 not out in just 377 minutes, for NSW against Queensland in Sydney. The record stood until Hanif Mohammad's 499 in 1959, and was the highest unbeaten innings before Brian Lara's 501 not out in 1994.

1984 – Cricket greats retire in one hit

Greg Chappell, Dennis Lillee and Rod Marsh retired from Test cricket after Australia thrashed Pakistan by 10 wickets in the fifth Test in Sydney. Master batsman Chappell had scored 24 test centuries with a test average of 53.86; fast bowling ace Lillee had taken a then-record 355 wickets; and wicketkeeper Marsh had a world-record 355 Test dismissals.

1994 – Kerrigan assault

National figure skating champion Nancy Kerrigan was assaulted after a practice session for the US Olympic trials in Detroit. A man struck her with a police baton, bruising her right knee so severely that she was forced to withdraw from the trials. Police arrested Jeff Gillooly, the ex-husband of Kerrigan rival Tonya Harding, as well as Harding's bodyguard Shawn Eckhardt. After the Olympics, Harding was put on 3 years probation and fined $100,000. Kerrigan won the silver medal.

1995 – Wilkens leads NBA coaches

Lenny Wilkens passed Red Auerbach to become the NBA's all-time leader in regular-season coaching victories with 939 as his Atlanta Hawks beat the Washington Bullets 112-90. Before coming to Atlanta in 1993, Wilkens had coached in Seattle, Portland and Cleveland, with the 1978–79 Seattle SuperSonics winning the NBA title.

2002 – Emmitt's 11 straight 1,000-yard seasons

Emmitt Smith of the Dallas Cowboys became the first running back in NFL history to rush for 1,000 yards in 11 consecutive seasons during a 15-10 defeat at Detroit.

2006 – Ponting's world first

Australian captain Ricky Ponting became the first player in Test cricket history to reach triple figures in both innings of his 100th Test during Australia's 8-wicket victory over South Africa in the third Test in Sydney. Ponting scored 120 and an unbeaten 143.

BIRTHDATES

1891	Australian Test fast bowler TED McDONALD – died 1937
1910	Cuban boxer KID CHOCOLATE – died 1988
1921	American golfer CARY MIDDLECOFF – died 1998
1926	Cuban boxer KID GAVILAN – died 2003
1931	Hockey Hall of Fame forward DICKIE MOORE
1935	Australian Test fast bowler IAN MECKIFF
1936	American tennis player DARLENE HARD
1937	College football coach LOU HOLTZ
1939	Australian swimmer MURRAY ROSE – died 2012
1943	English soccer coach TERRY VENABLES
1945	Welsh rugby union fly-half BARRY JOHN
1948	New Zealand Test fast bowler DAYLE HADLEE
1956	England rugby union centre/coach CLIVE WOODWARD
1957	American golfer NANCY LOPEZ
1959	Indian Test fast bowler KAPIL DEV
1960	American golfer PAUL AZINGER
1960	Australian rugby league winger ERIC GROTHE
1961	Pro Football Hall of Fame defensive tackle HOWIE LONG
1961	England rugby union halfback NIGEL MELVILLE
1964	NFL defensive end CHARLES HALEY
1967	New Zealand golfer CRAIG PERKS
1976	South Korean speed skater LEE-KYUNG CHUN
1986	Norwegian cross-country skier PETTER NORTHUG

American figure skater Nancy Kerrigan, taking the silver medal at the 1994 Winter Olympics in Lillehammer, Norway.

⑦ JANUARY

1927 – Globetrotters' debut
The famous Harlem Globetrotters basketball team played their first game. In their early years, they operated in the Chicago area and their first show was in Hinckley, Illinois, 48 miles from Chicago.

1956 – Indian openers' record
Indian batsmen Vinoo Mankad (231) and Pankaj Roy (173) completed a Test record first-wicket stand of 413 in the second Test against New Zealand in Madras.

1980 – Record unbeaten run ends
The Philadelphia Flyers' 35-game unbeaten streak of 25 victories and 10 ties, a pro record, ended in Minnesota. The Flyers came from behind 13 times during the streak to win or tie games. The Flyers scored first, but then Minnesota goalie Gilles Meloche blanked them, the North Stars winning 7-1.

1991 – Rose still paying dues
Baseball's Pete Rose left an Illinois federal prison camp and checked into a halfway house in Cincinnati to complete his sentence for tax evasion. Rose has consistently been refused a nomination for entry into Baseball's Hall of Fame because of allegations that, whilst he was a player and manager, he bet on Major League games.

1992 – Imran departs
Pakistan Test captain Imran Khan played his last day of international cricket in the third Test against Sri Lanka in Faisalabad. In his 88 Tests, Imran scored 3,807 runs at 37.69. He hit 6 Test centuries and took 362 wickets at 22.81, with best bowling figures of 8 for 58.

1994 – Harding's false glory
Tonya Harding won the US Figure Skating Championship in Detroit. She was later stripped of the title and charged with conspiracy when it emerged that her ex-husband and bodyguard was involved in an attack on rival Nancy Kerrigan, who suffered a bruised leg and was forced to withdraw from the event.

Tonya Harding wins the 1994 US Figure Skating title in Detroit, Michigan. She was later stripped of the gold medal.

2011 – Overdue Ashes win for Brits
England clinched its first Ashes victory in Australia in 24 years with an unprecedented third innings victory, this time in Sydney. Alistair Cook was named Man of the Match and of the Series, after his 189 took his tally to 766 runs in 7 innings.

2013 – Messi takes fourth straight award
Lionel Messi strengthened his claim to be considered the greatest footballer of all time, winning a record-breaking fourth consecutive FIFA Ballon d'Or. Barcelona's Argentine forward enjoyed a remarkable 2012, even by his own high standards. He surpassed Gerd Müller's 40-year-old record of 85 goals in a calendar year, finishing with an incredible 91.

BIRTHDATES
1913 Baseball Hall of Fame first baseman JOHNNY MIZE – died 1993
1914 Basketball Hall of Fame guard BOBBY McDERMOTT – died 1963
1916 Canadian Hockey Hall of Fame defenseman BABE PRATT – died 1988
1938 American golfer LOU GRAHAM
1950 England soccer striker MALCOLM MACDONALD
1967 Australian rugby union/league halfback RICKY STUART
1972 Australian cyclist SHANE KELLY
1976 Canadian MLB pitcher ERIC GAGNE
1983 American golfer NATALIE GULBIS
1985 British auto racer LEWIS HAMILTON
1990 Austrian ski jumper GREGOR SCHLIERENZAUER

⑧ JANUARY

1947 – Rookie record goes to Meeker
Howie Meeker of the Toronto Maple Leafs set an NHL record for a rookie by scoring 5 goals in a 10-4 win over the Chicago Blackhawks at Toronto. The mark was tied in 1976 by Don Murdoch of the New York Rangers.

1950 – Hogan returns with courage
In his first tournament since a near-fatal accident 11 months earlier, golfer Ben Hogan showed immense courage to walk damp fairways on his damaged legs and tie with Sam Snead over 72 holes for the Los Angeles Open title. Because of heavy rain, the 18-hole playoff did not take place until January 18 when Snead won 72-76.

1955 – Wildcats' 'unbeaten at home' run ends
Kentucky Basketball's 129 home-game winning streak ended when Georgia Tech upset the Wildcats 59-58 at Memorial Coliseum. Besides stopping the long home-winning streak, the Engineers also ended an overall 32-game winning streak for coach Adolph Rupp's team. Kentucky's last home defeat was to Ohio State in 1933.

1972 – Gould set for gold
Fifteen-year-old Shane Gould took 0.4 seconds off Dawn Fraser's 100m freestyle world record, swimming 58.5 seconds at the Australian Olympic trials in Sydney. At the Games in Munich, Gould was beaten in the 100m by Americans Sandy Neilson and Shirley Babashoff, but won gold in the 200m and 400m freestyle and the 200m individual medley.

1993 – Jordan milestone
Michael Jordan reached the 20,000 point plateau, with a game-high 35 points in Chicago's 120-95 home win over Milwaukee. Jordan achieved the mark in his 620th NBA game, making him the second-fastest player to reach 20,000, behind only Wilt Chamberlain (499 games).

Fifteen-year-old Australian swim star Shane Gould at training for the 1972 Munich Olympics. Gould won 3 gold medals at the Games.

1999 – Expensive youngster
London Premier League club Arsenal paid Notts County £2 million for 15-year-old Jermaine Pennant. Despite his tender age, Pennant was in the County squad for their FA Cup tie with Sheffield United on New Year's Day.

BIRTHDATES

1909	South African Test batsman BRUCE MITCHELL – died 1995
1913	New Zealand Test fast bowler DENNIS SMITH – died 1986
1923	England Test spinner JOHNNY WARDLE – died 1985
1934	French road cyclist JACQUES ANQUETIL – died 1987
1949	West Indies Test batsman LAWRENCE ROWE
1957	NFL receiver DWIGHT CLARK
1959	Australian golfer MIKE HARWOOD
1961	American sprinter CALVIN SMITH
1961	Pakistan Test batsman SHOAIB MOHAMMAD
1963	Japanese golfer HIROMI KABAYASHI
1971	MLB first baseman JASON GIAMBI
1972	American golfer BRANDIE BURTON
1979	Romanian soccer forward ADRIAN MUTU
1981	Chinese badminton player XIE XINGFANG
1986	Spanish soccer midfielder DAVID SILVA
1989	New Zealand rugby fly-half AARON CRUDEN

⑨ JANUARY

1942 – 'Brown Bomber' wins again
Joe Louis knocked out Buddy Baer with just 4 seconds remaining in the first round at Madison Square Garden, to retain his world heavyweight title for the 24th time.

1972 – Lakers' streak ends
The Los Angeles Lakers professional record 33-game winning streak (which still stood in 2013) ended when they suffered a 120-104 home defeat to the Milwaukee Bucks. The Bucks' 24-year-old, 7ft 2in centre Kareem Abdul-Jabbar outplayed Lakers' legend Wilt Chamberlain to set up the win.

1977 – Raiders upset Vikings
The John Madden-coached Oakland Raiders made a mockery of Minnesota quarterback Fran Tarkenton's pre-game 'guarantee' speech, when outstanding blocking enabled the Raiders to run for 266 yards in their 32-14 win in Super Bowl XI in Pasadena. Clarence Davis led Oakland's rushing with 137 yards. Quarterback Ken Stabler completed 12-of-19 passes for 180 yards and a touchdown. Wide receiver Fred Biletnikoff was named MVP with 4 receptions for 79 yards.

1991 – Man U shares, please
Manchester United announced the club would become a publicly traded company listed on the London Stock Exchange. London club Tottenham Hotspur had pioneered the strategy in 1983 with great financial success.

1996 – No free throws for Raptors
The Toronto Raptors established an unwanted NBA record, becoming the first team not to hit a single foul shot during the course of a game. The Raptors were 0-of-3 from the line during a 92-91 loss to the visiting Charlotte Hornets.

2000 – Tiger's 5 straight wins
In Tiger Woods' fifth consecutive PGA Tour victory, he birdied the second playoff hole to defeat Ernie Els in the season opening Mercedes Championships at Kapalua Resort's Plantation Course in Hawaii. Woods

The 'Brown Bomber', World Heavyweight Champion (1937–48) Joe Louis at training.

had won the previous 4 tournaments he'd played, in the 1999 season.

BIRTHDATES
1934	Pro Football Hall of Fame quarterback BART STARR
1935	American sports caster DICK ENBERG
1935	New Zealand rugby union flanker JOHN GRAHAM
1948	Polish soccer goalkeeper JAN TOMASZEWSKI
1958	Scottish golfer SANDY LYLE
1960	American golfer DAVID PEOPLES
1960	Canadian golfer LISA WALTERS
1961	French rugby union fly half DIDIER CAMBERABERO
1965	English soccer manager IAIN DOWIE
1967	South African rugby union number 8 GARY TEICHMANN
1968	West Indian Test captain JIMMY ADAMS
1968	Australian golfer MARDI LUNN
1978	Italian soccer midfielder GENNARO GATTUSO
1980	Spanish golfer SERGIO GARCIA

1911 – Trumper brilliant, but trumped
Australian batting great Victor Trumper scored a majestic 214 before South Africa went on to beat Australia by 38 runs in the third Test in Adelaide. Trumper's double century was the highest score in a Test defeat until Brian Lara's 221 against Sri Lanka in Colombo in 2001–02.

1930 – Kiwis lose inaugural Test match
New Zealand cricket celebrated the start of the country's first ever Test match, against England in Christchurch. Maurice Allom took 4 wickets in 5 balls, including a hat-trick, to help dismiss the hosts for 112, as England went on to win the historic match by 8 wickets.

1982 – 'The Catch'
The San Francisco 49ers beat the Dallas Cowboys 28-27 in the NFC Championship game at Candlestick Park, through the brilliance of champion quarterback Joe Montana and receiver Dwight Clark. Trailing 27-21 with 51 seconds remaining, Montana ran to his right and connected with a leaping Clark in what has been labelled 'The Catch'. Ray Wersching's extra point gave the 49ers a famous victory.

1985 – Shastri does a Sobers
Ravi Shastri emulated Gary Sobers' feat of 1968, when he hit 6 sixes in 1 over in an Indian provincial first-class match. Playing for Bombay in their Ranji Trophy zonal match against Baroda, Shastri hit 200 not out from just 113 balls.

1996 – Barros' three point NBA record
Boston guard Dana Barros sank a three-point field goal in his 89th consecutive game in the Celtics' 113-104 win against the Sacramento Kings. Barros' NBA record streak ended in his next game.

2006 – Huge College gift
Oklahoma State announced billionaire alumnus Boone T. Pickens, Jr had donated $165 million to the university's athletic program. It was the largest single gift ever given to an NCAA program.

World XI wicketkeeper Adam Gilchrist during the World Cricket Tsunami Appeal match against the ICC Asian XI in Melbourne.

2008 – Hockey's Big Deal
In the first $100 million deal in NHL history, Russian forward Alex Ovechkin signed a $124 million, 13-year contract extension with the Washington Capitals.

BIRTHDATES
1895	Australian athletics coach PERCY CERUTTY – died 1975
1903	Australian Test batsman HUGH 'PUD' THURLOW – died 1975
1921	American auto racer RODGER WARD – died 2004
1922	Scottish soccer winger BILLY LIDDELL – died 2001
1937	New Zealand rugby union winger RALPH CAULTON
1938	Baseball Hall of Fame first baseman WILLIE McCOVEY
1938	Hockey Hall of Fame left wing FRANK MAHOVLICH
1949	American boxer GEORGE FOREMAN
1953	American auto racer BOBBY RAHAL
1958	American auto racer EDDIE CHEEVER
1973	Puerto Rican boxer FELIX TRINIDAD
1976	English golfer IAN POULTER

⑪ JANUARY

1959 – Hanif's first-class innings
Pakistan Test batsman Hanif Mohammad scored a then-world-record first-class innings of 499 for Bahawalpar in Karachi, the marathon innings lasting 10 hours 35 minutes.

1973 – Baseball's designated hitter
The American League adopted a rules change allowing a designated hitter, a player who bats for the pitcher throughout the game but never has to play in the field. The National League rules remained unchanged, so in inter-league games and in the World Series, the home team's league rules apply.

1982 – Snooker max on TV
Steve Davis compiled the first televised maximum break of 147 in a match against John Spencer in Oldham, Lancashire.

1987 – 'The Drive'
Denver Broncos quarterback John Elway engineered a famous tying drive in the AFC Championship game against the Browns in Cleveland. Trailing 20-13 with 5 minutes remaining, 'The Drive' culminated in Elway firing a TD bullet to Mark Jackson. Rich Karlis' overtime field goal gave the Broncos a 23-20 victory, sending them to the Super Bowl.

1991 – Chelsea's record fine
The English Football League fined Chelsea a then-record £105,000 for alleged illegal payments to players. Owner and chairman Ken Bates resigned from the Football League management committee as a result of the incident.

2001 – Knicks great 'D'
The New York Knicks held an opponent to under 100 points for an NBA-record 29th straight game in their 76-75 defeat to the Houston Rockets. The streak snapped the 46-year-old NBA record of 28 straight games, set by the Fort Wayne Pistons in 1954–55.

2007 – Big deal for Beckham
In the biggest deal in sports history, former England soccer captain David Beckham agreed to leave Real Madrid and join the Los Angeles Galaxy. Beckham's deal was worth more than US$32 million in salary and much more in commercial endorsements.

2008 – Jail for Jones
Sprinter Marion Jones, having been stripped of the Olympic medals she won in Sydney, was sentenced in a New York court to 6 months' jail for lying about her steroid use and her knowledge of a separate cheque fraud case. In 2000, she had become the first woman to win 5 athletics medals, 3 of them gold, at a single Olympics.

2008 – Everest pioneer passes away
New Zealand mountaineer Sir Edmund Hillary, the first man to scale Mount Everest, died, aged 88.

2010 – McGwire confesses
Baseball player Mark McGwire announced he had intermittently taken steroids for nearly a decade, including the 1998 season when he smashed 69 homers to break the then single season home run record.

BIRTHDATES
1910	New Zealand rugby union hooker ARTHUR LAMBOURN – died 1999
1923	American auto racer CARROLL SHELBY – died 2012
1939	Canadian alpine skier ANNE HEGGTVEIGT
1947	New Zealand rugby union lock HAMISH MACDONALD
1952	American golfer BEN CRENSHAW
1957	England soccer midfielder/manager BRYAN ROBSON
1959	American auto racer BRETT BODINE
1962	England rugby union hooker BRIAN MOORE
1963	American swimmer TRACEY CAULKINS
1963	East German swimmer PETRA SCHNEIDER
1973	Indian test batsman RAHUL DRAVID
1975	England rugby union winger DAN LUGER
1978	England soccer striker EMILE HESKEY

1946 – Cleveland moves West

Less than a month after winning the NFL championship, the Cleveland Rams became the first team in a major professional sports league to locate to the US West Coast. Despite going 9-1 in the regular season and defeating the Washington Redskins in the title game, Cleveland drew only a paltry 77,608 fans in its 4 regular-season home games, an average of only 19,402.

1960 – Windies' legends roar

West Indian batsmen Garry Sobers and Frank Worrell shared a record partnership of 399 in the first Test against England in Barbados. It was the West Indies' highest for the fourth wicket and the highest for any wicket against England. Sobers made 226 and Worrell was unbeaten on 197, having batted for 682 minutes, the longest innings in West Indian test history.

1969 – Jets soar

Despite the New York Jets being 19-point underdogs to the Baltimore Colts, quarterback Joe Namath's pre-game guarantee of a Jets' upset in Super Bowl III in Miami's Orange Bowl came true. Namath guided the Jets to a stunning 16-7 triumph, completing 17-of-28 passes for 206 yards, with George Sauer grabbing 8 receptions for 133 yards.

1986 – NHL quick start

Chicago Blackhawks centre Denis Savard tied the NHL record for the fastest score to start a period. Four seconds into the third period against Hartford at Chicago Stadium, Savard took the puck off the faceoff and quickly moved in for a 35ft blast that tied Montreal's Claude Provost's record set in 1957.

1990 – New Ryder Cup criteria

The PGA of America approved a modification of the guidelines by which the United States Ryder Cup team would be selected. The PGA champion would no longer be an automatic qualifier, but would receive 25 bonus points. In addition, the first 10 members of the team would be determined by the official point standings, the captain selecting the final 2 positions.

1997 – Woods' fast million

Tiger Woods hit his tee shot to within inches of the cup of the first playoff hole to beat Tom Lehman and win the Mercedes Championships in Carlsbad. The victory marked Woods reaching the $1 million mark in career earnings faster than any other player.

2001 – Villa's expensive signing

Aston Villa signed Colombian international Juan Pablo Ángel from Argentine club River Plate for a club record £9.5 million. Family difficulties saw him return to Colombia shortly after his arrival. Fortunately in 2003/04 Ángel was a revelation, scoring 23 goals in 39 games.

2007 – Precise Tom Brady

New England quarterback Tom Brady made 26 completions in 28 attempts, an NFL record 92.9% for regular-season and playoff games, as the Patriots beat Jacksonville 31-20 at Foxborough to advance to the AFC Championship Game for the second straight year. Brady's accuracy record broke the mark of 91.3% (21-of-23) set by Vinny Testaverde with Cleveland in 1993. The Patriots remained perfect at 17-0, matching the 1972 Miami Dolphins, the only team to go unbeaten from the first game through to the Super Bowl.

BIRTHDATES

1894	French boxer GEORGES CARPENTIER – died 1975
1940	New Zealand Test fast bowler DICK MOTZ – died 2007
1940	South African tennis player BOB HEWITT
1944	American boxer JOE FRAZIER – died 2011
1947	NFL kicker TOM DEMPSEY
1952	New Zealand middle distance runner JOHN WALKER
1957	England rugby union fullback MARCUS ROSE
1960	Basketball Hall of Fame forward DOMINIQUE WILKINS
1962	Swedish long jumper GUNDE SVAN
1962	West Indies Test captain RICHIE RICHARDSON
1966	Australian golfer CRAIG PARRY
1968	Brazilian soccer midfielder MAURO SILVA
1969	Croatian soccer midfielder/manager ROBERT PROSINECKI

1962 – Wilt's huge basketball haul
Philadelphia's Wilt Chamberlain scored 73 points, the most ever in a regulation NBA game. He hit 29 field goals and 15 free throws in the Warriors' 135-117 home victory over Chicago. Chamberlain broke Elgin Baylor's record of 71, and his 40 points in the second half was also an NBA record. Less than 2 months later, he made his legendary 100-point haul against the Knicks.

1974 – 'Purple People Eaters' devoured
The Miami Dolphins scored one of the most one-sided victories in Super Bowl history when they beat Minnesota 24-7 in Houston. The Dolphins ran through the Vikings with such ease that quarterback Bob Griese threw only 7 passes. Their offensive line devoured the famous 'Purple People Eaters,' with fullback Larry Csonka rushing for 145 yards and 2 touchdowns.

1979 – Snooker's first maximum break
Englishman John Spencer compiled the first maximum break of 147 in competitive play, in a match against Canada's Cliff Thorburn in the Holsten Lager Tournament in Slough. The television camera crew missed the feat because they were on a tea break.

1995 – America's Cup girls
Mighty Mary became the first all-female crew to win an America's Cup race when they beat four-time champion Dennis Connor in *Stars & Stripes* by 69 seconds in the defenders trials off San Diego. *Stars & Stripes* went on to win the series, but Connor elected to sail *Young America* in the Cup defence, and crashed 5-0 to New Zealand's *Black Magic*.

1999 – MJ gone for a second time
Michael Jordan announced his retirement from professional basketball for a second time. In his last 6 full seasons, Jordan had led the Chicago Bulls to the NBA championship each season, winning Finals MVP each time. In 13 seasons he won a record 10 scoring titles and was NBA MVP 5 times. In 2001 Jordan returned to the court for 2 seasons with the Washington Wizards.

NBA legend Wilt Chamberlain, pictured here in 1959, wearing the uniform of the Harlem Globetrotters.

2005 – Baseball gets 'tough' with steroids
MLB announced a new steroids testing policy after a year of repeated revelations stemming largely from the BALCO steroids scandal. The new policy called for a 10-day suspension for a first-time offender and a one-year ban for a fourth-time offender. The initiatives were criticised for being too lenient.

2009 – Three-point Magic
The Orlando Magic set an NBA-record for completed three-point shots in a 139-107 victory over the Kings in Sacramento. The Magic made 23 of 37 attempts (62%), breaking the old mark of 21 by Toronto in 2005. Orlando rang up its highest point total since scoring 152 at Milwaukee in 1995.

BIRTHDATES
1933	Basketball Hall of Fame forward TOM GOLA
1941	German bobsled driver MEINHARD NEHMER
1957	American golfer MARK O'MEARA
1962	Australian swim coach BRIAN SUTTON
1969	Italian cross-country skier STEFANIO BELMONDO
1969	Scottish snooker player STEPHEN HENDRY
1970	Italian cyclist MARCO PANTINI – died 2004
1972	Belarusian gymnast VITALY SCHERBO
1972	Australian soccer goalkeeper MARK BOSNICH
1977	Korean golfer MI-HYUN KIM
1982	Argentine tennis player GUILLERMO CORIA

1928 – Scot hot-shot
Jimmy McGrory scored a Scottish football top-flight record 8 goals in one game, for Celtic in a 9-0 win against Dunfermline.

1933 – 'Bodyline' drama
The infamous 'Bodyline' cricket series reached its peak on the second day of the third Test in Adelaide. Australian captain Bill Woodfull was repeatedly struck by England's express fast bowler Harold Larwood as all the English bowlers aimed short-pitched deliveries at the bodies of the Australian batsmen. England went on to win the match by 338 runs and go to a 2-1 series lead, amidst calls for the tour to be cancelled.

1954 – Celebrity marriage
The marriage of Joe DiMaggio and Marilyn Monroe at San Francisco City Hall was an amazing union of American celebrities, matching the country's most revered athlete to a beautiful Hollywood star. It was the second marriage for both and ended 9 months later in divorce.

1966 – Home bliss for 76ers
The Philadelphia 76ers, led by Wilt Chamberlain, won the first of what became 36 consecutive home games, then an NBA record, when they defeated the Boston Celtics 112-100. The Celtics broke the mark by winning 38 straight games at home during the 1985–86 and 1986–87 seasons.

1973 – NFL Dolphins perfect season
The Miami Dolphins became the only NFL team to have an unbeaten, untied season, finishing with a 17-0 record, after a 14-7 victory over the Washington Redskins in Super Bowl VII in Los Angeles. Relying on a ball-control offense, with fullback Larry Csonka running for 112 yards on 15 carries, quarterback Bob Griese threw only 11 passes. Miami's defence held the Redskins to 228 yards, and safety Jake Scott made 2 of the Dolphins' 3 interceptions to win MVP honours.

1985 – Martina's tennis ton
Martina Navratilova joined Jimmy Connors and Chris Evert Lloyd as the only professional tennis players

Actress Marilyn Monroe and Baseball superstar Joe DiMaggio after their 1954 marriage in San Francisco.

to win 100 tournaments. Navratilova beat Manuela Maleeva 6-3, 6-2 to win the Virginia Slims event in Washington DC for her 100th victory.

1993 – Eaton blocks into history
NBA star Mark Eaton of the Utah Jazz blocked 2 shots in a 96-89 win over Seattle, becoming only the second player in NBA history, after Kareem Abdul Jabbar, to record 3,000 career blocks. Kareem ended his career with 3,189. Eaton and Kareem were both overtaken by Hakeem Olajuwon, who finished with 3,830 in 2002.

2000 – McGrath's ODI bowling brilliance
In the best one-day bowling performance in Australian history, Glenn McGrath captured 4-8 off 10 overs against India in Sydney. McGrath's 8 runs conceded included 1 no ball and 1 wide. Australia won by 5 wickets after dismissing India for 100.

BIRTHDATES
1892	England soccer defender GEORGE WILSON – died 1961
1936	Russian kayaker LYUDMILA PINAYEVA
1937	England Test fast bowler KEN HIGGS
1941	American golfer GIBBY GILBERT
1944	Australian golfer GRAHAM MARSH
1957	Australian jockey GREG HALL
1969	England Test all-rounder MARTIN BICKNELL
1970	American surfer SUNNY GARCIA
1973	Italian auto racer GIANCARLO FISICHELLA
1978	American sprinter SHAWN CRAWFORD

1965 – Mega NBA trade

In one of the biggest trades in NBA history, the San Francisco Warriors, in the middle of a then-league record 17-game losing streak, traded Wilt Chamberlain to the Philadelphia 76ers. In exchange for the champion centre, San Francisco received Connie Dierking, Lee Shaffer, Paul Neumann and cash.

1967 – Super Bowl I

In what became known as Super Bowl I, the NFL's Green Bay Packers routed the AFL champion Kansas City Chiefs 35-10 at the Los Angeles Memorial Coliseum. The Chiefs trailed 14-10 at halftime, but the Vince Lombardi-coached Packers broke the game open in the second half with 3 unanswered touchdowns. Green Bay quarterback Bart Starr completed 16-of-23 passes for 250 yards to be named MVP.

1985 – England cricket's double-double

Mike Gatting and Graeme Fowler became the first pair of England batsmen to complete double centuries in the same game during the fourth Test against India at Madras. Fowler hit 201 and Gatting 207 as England scored a 9-wicket win. Gatting's score was the then highest by an England batsman in India.

1988 – Dream cricket debut

Nineteen-year-old Indian leg-spinner Narenda Hirwani put up the best bowling figures on debut in Test history when he captured 16 wickets, in a series-levelling, 255-run victory over the West Indies in the fourth Test at Madras. Hirwani took 8 wickets in each innings, and his match figures of 16 for 136 surpassed Australian Bob Massie's 16 for 137 at Lord's.

1997 – Perkins' eight straight threes

Sam Perkins of the Seattle SuperSonics tied Jeff Hornacek's NBA single-game record by connecting on 8 consecutive three-point field goals during the Sonics' 122-78 win over the visiting Toronto Raptors. Seattle also set an NBA record in the game with 27 steals.

1998 – Thorpe starts 400m reign

Fifteen-year-old Sydney schoolboy Ian Thorpe

Teenage Australian swimmer Ian Thorpe during the 400m freestyle final at the 1998 World Championships.

became Australia's youngest ever world champion in swimming when he won the 400m freestyle in Perth. Thorpe swam a time of 3:46.29 seconds and went on to win the event again at the 2001 and 2003 world championships. He was also a member of Australia's winning 4 x 200m relay team in Perth.

2006 – One race, two records for Gebrselassie

Haile Gebrselassie shattered the world half-marathon record by 21 seconds (to record a time of 5855) while running the last half of the Rock 'N' Roll Arizona marathon in Tempe, Arizona. He also passed the 20km point in world record time. It marked the 19th and 20th times the diminutive Ethiopian had broken world records in his career.

BIRTHDATES

1939	British yachtsman TONY BULLIMORE
1943	MLB pitcher MIKE MARSHALL
1949	American golfer HOWARD TWITTY
1950	French soccer defender MARIUS TRESOR
1953	Pro Football Hall of Fame defensive tackle RANDY WHITE
1956	NFL coach MARC TRESTMAN
1965	American boxer BERNARD HOPKINS
1967	American golfer TED TRYBA
1975	French tennis player MARY PIERCE
1976	Scottish rugby union lock SCOTT MURRAY
1979	NFL quarterback DREW BREES
1979	Bulgarian soccer winger MARTIN PETROV
1987	Australian rugby league centre GREG INGLIS

⑯ JANUARY

1916 – The PGA is born
The agenda of the Professional Golfers' Association of America was discussed at a business lunch in New York. Department store magnate Rodman Wanamaker, realising the merchandising potential of a golf association, offered to donate the trophy and the prize money for the first PGA Championship. Prominent golf professionals and amateur players such as Walter Hagen, Francis Ouimet and A.W. Tillinghast attended to discuss the feasibility of forming a national association of professional golfers, similar to the PGA of Great Britain.

1933 – 'Bodyline' turns ugly
Australian wicketkeeper Bert Oldfield was forced to retire on 41 after being flattened by a Harold Larwood bouncer during the third Test of the infamous Bodyline series in Adelaide. Oldfield suffered a fractured skull whilst attempting a hook. The incident followed the battering Bill Woodfull took in the first innings and added fuel to calls for the tour to be cancelled. England went to a 2-1 series lead after taking the match by 338 runs.

1962 – All-Star Basketball records
The West beat the East 150-130 in the annual All-Star game, as 2 significant match records were broken. Wilt Chamberlain of the Philadelphia Warriors scored an All-Star record 42 points and grabbed 24 rebounds to win MVP honours. The West's Bob Pettit had an All-Star record 27 rebounds.

1972 – Cowboys' first Super Bowl win
The Dallas Cowboys won their first Super Bowl, dominating the Miami Dolphins 24-3 in Super Bowl VI at Tulane Stadium in New Orleans. By holding the Dolphins to a lone field goal, the Cowboys set a Super Bowl record that stood for the remainder of the 20th century. Tom Landry's team limited Miami to a total of 185 yards – just 80 rushing and 105 passing. Cowboys quarterback Roger Staubach took MVP honours despite passing for only 119 yards and 2 touchdown passes.

Fearsome England Test fast bowler Harold Larwood in his prime.

1993 – Jordon's second-best tally
Michael Jordan scored 64 points for the Chicago Bulls against Orlando, the second-highest single game total of his career. The Magic was led by rookie centre Shaquille O'Neal, who posted 29 points and 24 rebounds in their 128-124 upset victory.

BIRTHDATES
1902	Scottish sprinter/rugby union winger ERIC LIDDELL – died 1945.
1908	England soccer forward SAMMY CROOKS – died 1981
1911	West Indian Test wicketkeeper IVAN BARROW – died 1979
1935	American auto-racer A. J. FOYT
1945	Dutch soccer defender WIM SUURBIER
1948	Canadian snooker player CLIFF THORBURN
1956	West Indies Test fast bowler WAYNE DANIEL
1956	Dutch soccer manager MARTIN JOL
1964	Canadian golfer GAIL GRAHAM
1966	MLB pitcher JACK McDOWELL
1969	American boxer ROY JONES JR
1969	England rugby union lock NEIL BACK
1971	Spanish tennis player SERGI BRUGERA
1980	Dominican MLB first baseman ALBERT PUJOLS
1985	NFL quarterback JOE FLACCO
1988	Danish soccer striker NICKLAS BENDTNER

1933 – A wicket for 'the Don'
Master batsman Don Bradman captured a rare Test wicket when he bowled the great Walter Hammond for 85, in the second innings of the third Test against England in Adelaide. Bradman took 1 for 23 off 4 overs. It was his second wicket in Test cricket.

1948 – Heavyweights draw record crowd
The match between Manchester United and Arsenal drew a then-League-record crowd of 83,620 at Maine Road. The 1-1 draw was played at Manchester City's ground because of war damage at United's home at Old Trafford.

1971 – 'Blunder Bowl'
The Baltimore Colts beat the Dallas Cowboys 16-13 in Super Bowl V in Miami. The game was labelled the 'Blunder Bowl' after the teams committed a total of 11 turnovers. After Cowboys quarterback Craig Morton threw his third interception, rookie Jim O'Brien nervously kicked a 32-yard field goal with 5 seconds left for the Colts victory.

1995 – Golf Channel goes to air
The Golf Channel debuted on cable television in the United States to a limited audience of roughly 3 million subscribers. One of the first features of the network was an hour-long open-line program with network co-founder Arnold Palmer. The channel is now syndicated internationally.

1997 – Rodman misses games and money
The NBA suspended Chicago Bulls' volatile forward Dennis Rodman for 11 games and fined him $25,000 cash for kicking a cameraman. In a 14-year NBA career (1986–2000) Rodman was a superb rebounding forward and defender. He was also known for his bizarre appearance, dyeing his hair various colours. Rodman led the NBA in rebounding for 7 consecutive years (1992–98); was a member of 5 NBA champion teams with Detroit (1989–90) and Chicago (1996–98); and was twice named defensive player of the year (1990–91).

2000 – Cantona popular
French international striker Eric Cantona won a Manchester United fan poll for the club's Player of the 20th Century. The controversial forward edged out another volatile international, Northern Ireland's George Best.

2005 – Handsome Hoggard
England fast bowler Matthew Hoggard inspired his team to a 77-run victory over South Africa in the fourth Test in Johannesburg. Hoggard's match haul was a career-best 12 for 205. His 7 for 61 on the final day routed the South Africans, who had been set 324 to win after Marcus Trescothick's 180 put England into a commanding position.

2013 – Armstrong comes clean
Disgraced road cyclist Lance Armstrong finally confessed to doping in a television interview with Oprah Winfrey, though he did not implicate any suppliers. He had been banned for life and his titles and records stripped after the USADA had charged him with doping in 2012, something he consistently denied doing throughout his career. During his TV confession, Armstrong admitted to taking banned substances prior to his 1996 cancer diagnosis.

BIRTHDATES
1905	Argentine soccer striker GUILLERMO STÁBILE – died 1966
1925	Pakistan Test captain ABDUL KARDAR – died 1996
1926	West Indian Test batsman CLYDE WALCOTT – died 2006
1929	Canadian Hockey Hall of Fame goalie JACQUES PLANTE – died 1986
1938	Swedish cross country skier TOINI GUSTAFSSON
1940	Kenyan middle distance runner KIP KEINO
1942	American boxer MUHAMMAD ALI
1964	New Zealand rugby union centre JOHN SCHUSTER
1966	English golfer TRISH JOHNSON
1970	Canadian NHL centre JEREMY ROENICK
1973	Australian netball captain LIZ ELLIS
1975	New Zealand rugby union fly-half TONY BROWN
1982	NBA forward DWYANE WADE
1983	Spanish soccer defender ALVARO ARBELOA

1976 – Steelers' Swann MVP
Two weeks after suffering severe concussion, Pittsburgh wide receiver Lynn Swann caught 4 passes for 161 yards to be named MVP of the Steelers' 21-17 victory over the Dallas Cowboys in Super Bowl X in Miami.

1983 – Thorpe medals reinstated
The International Olympic Committee restored American athlete Jim Thorpe's gold medals to his family, 70 years after they were stripped from him after it was found he had played semi-pro baseball. Thorpe won the 10-event decathlon and 5-event pentathlon at the 1912 Games in Stockholm.

1985 – Mary makes amends
Running in competition for the first time since her famed collision with Zola Budd during the 1984 Olympics, Mary Decker broke the world indoor 2,000m record in Los Angeles. Decker recorded a time of 5:34.2. Injuries, and her 1984 disappointment, conspired against Decker ever winning an Olympic medal.

1991 – Boris' marathon match
In the longest-ever match at the Australian Open to that point, Boris Becker of Germany beat Italy's Omar Camporese in a 5-set thriller lasting 5 hours, 11 minutes. Becker won the third-round marathon 7-6, 7-6, 0-6, 4-6, 14-12. He went on to beat Ivan Lendl in 4 sets in the final.

2000 – Cricket shenanigans
There was unprecedented collusion between respective captains, South Africa's Hansie Cronje and England's Nasser Hussain, in the fifth Test at Centurion. It led to innings forfeitures for the first time in Test history, ostensibly because 3 days play had been washed out by rain. South Africa declared at 248 for 8; England declared at 0-0; South Africa forfeited their second innings; and England staged a successful run-chase to win by 2 wickets with 5 balls to spare. The match has since been discredited by the revelation that Cronje received money from a bookmaker to instigate a positive result.

2005 – Overtime joy for Boykins
Denver's Earl Boykins broke the NBA record for points in overtime, scoring 15 of the Nuggets' extra-period 21 points as they beat the Seattle SuperSonics, 116-110. Boykins, a 5ft 5in guard who was the league's smallest player, broke the record of 14 overtime points that had been set by Indiana's Butch Carter in 1984.

BIRTHDATES
1932	Pro Football Hall of Fame linebacker JOE SCHMIDT
1933	New Zealand rugby union centre FRANK McMULLEN – died 2004
1940	Mexican auto racer PEDRO RODRIGUEZ – died 1971
1950	Canadian auto racer GILLIES VILLENEUVE – died 1982
1951	England soccer forward BOB LATCHFORD
1961	England soccer forward PETER BEARDSLEY
1961	Canadian NHL centre MARK MESSIER
1964	American boxer VIRGIL HILL
1967	Chilean soccer striker IVAN ZAMORANO
1971	Brazilian auto racer CHRISTIAN FITTIPALDI
1971	Spanish soccer midfielder/manager PEP GUARDIOLA
1979	Portuguese soccer defender PAULO FERREIRA
1980	NFL defensive end JULIUS PEPPERS
1988	German tennis player ANGELIQUE KERBER

German tennis star Boris Becker.

1974 – Irish end Bruins' winning streak

Notre Dame scored its greatest basketball victory by ending UCLA's record 88-game winning streak. Trailing by 11 points with three-and-a-half minutes remaining, the no. 2 ranked and undefeated Irish scored the game's final 12 points to gain a stunning 71-70 victory. It was the first loss for UCLA since January 23, 1971, when the Bruins were beaten 89-82, ironically by Notre Dame on the same court.

2000 – Michael returns, again

Michael Jordan, who led the Chicago Bulls to 6 NBA championships as a player, returned to the NBA when he joined the Washington Wizards as part owner and president of basketball operations. Jordan also became a partner and investor in Lincoln Holdings, a minority partner in Washington Sports and Entertainment, which owned the Washington Wizards and NHL franchise the Washington Capitals.

2004 – Hookes passes away

Former Australian Test batsman David Hookes passed away in hospital, after being assaulted outside a Melbourne hotel. The coach was involved in an incident with a hotel staff member, hit his head on the ground and never recovered. Hookes played 23 Tests at 34.36. He was best known for hitting 5 consecutive fours off Tony Greig in the Centenary Test in 1977.

2006 – Summitt's 900 victories

The NCAA's all-time winningest women's basketball coach Pat Summitt reached the 900-win milestone, as her top-ranked Tennessee team rallied from its biggest deficit of the season (14) to beat no. 19 Vanderbilt, 80-68, in Nashville. Summitt ran her record to 1,098-208 in 38 seasons at Tennessee.

2006 – Russian skates to record

Twenty-six-year-old Russian Irina Slutskaya won her record seventh European Figure Skating championship title in Lyon, France. She finished with 193.24 points, after taking both the short program and free skate and was more than 15 points ahead of countrywoman Elena Sokolova. Slutskaya surpassed the record of 6 European figure skating titles, previously held by legends Sonia Henie 1931–36 and Katarina Witt 1983–88.

2008 – Test win sequence ends

The Australian cricket team's record-equalling 16-Test winning sequence ended when they were beaten by 72 runs by India, in the third Test in Perth. A frenetic 73-run, ninth-wicket partnership between Mitchell Johnson and Stuart Clark temporarily revived hopes of an Australian victory and a world-record winning streak, but Irfan Pathan's removal of Clark for a fighting 32 effectively ended Australia's resistance, ensuring their first defeat since the Trent Bridge Test of 2005. It had been an amazing unbeaten streak that spanned 22 Tests and more than 2 years.

2013 – Monte Carlo Rally record

Frenchman Sébastien Loeb driving a Citroën, won his record seventh Monte Carlo Rally by 1:39.9 seconds when officials called off the final 2 stages after they were overwhelmed by spectators.

BIRTHDATES

1848	English endurance swimmer MATTHEW WEBB – died 1883
1922	Australian Test batsman ARTHUR MORRIS
1930	South African Test wicketkeeper JOHN WAITE – died 2011
1944	NFL coach DAN REEVES
1949	Irish snooker player DENNIS TAYLOR
1957	NFL running back OTTIS ANDERSON
1960	American triple jumper AL JOYNER
1962	NBA coach JEFF VAN GUNDY
1966	Swedish tennis player STEFAN EDBERG
1969	Australian NBA centre LUC LONGLEY
1969	NFL linebacker JUNIOR SEAU – died 2012
1969	Montenegrin soccer midfielder/manager PREDRAG MIJATOVI
1969	Irish soccer defender STEVE STAUNTON
1973	Russian swimmer YEVGENY SADOVYI
1980	British auto racer JENSEN BUTTON

1970 – Brotherly basketball

Cincinnati's Tom Van Arsdale and Phoenix's Dick Van Arsdale become the first brothers to play in the same NBA All-Star Game. Dick scored 8 points for the West, while Tom netted 5 for the East in their 142-135 win in Philadelphia.

1974 – Miller's golf triple

Johnny Miller beat Ben Crenshaw by 3 strokes to win the Dean Martin Tucson Open. In doing so, he became the first player ever to win the PGA Tour's first 3 events of the year.

1980 – Bradshaw's MVP repeat

Pittsburgh quarterback Terry Bradshaw won MVP honours for the second straight year as the Steelers scored a 31-19 victory over the Los Angeles Rams in Super Bowl XIV in Pasadena. Bradshaw completed 14-of-21 passes for 309 yards and 2 touchdowns. The championship was Bradshaw's and the Steelers' fourth in 6 seasons.

1980 – Devastating Dev

Champion Indian all-rounder Kapil Dev was at his best, taking 7 for 56 to steer India to a 10-wicket win over Pakistan in the fifth Test in Madras. Dev also took 4 wickets in the first innings, and hit 13 fours and a 6 for 84.

1985 – Montana 2-time MVP

San Francisco 49ers quarterback Joe Montana won his second of 3 MVP awards, as SF beat the Miami Dolphins 38-16 in Super Bowl XIX. Montana completed 24 of 35 passes for 331 yards, 2 touchdowns and a 6-yard touchdown run.

1989 – Lemieux's fast fifty

Pittsburgh Penguins centre Mario Lemieux joined Wayne Gretzky as the only players in NHL history to score 50 goals in fewer than 50 games. Lemieux achieved the feat in his 44th game, a 7-3 loss to Winnipeg. In only his fifth NHL season, the 23-year-old Lemieux also became the Penguins' all-time leading scorer with 638 points, passing Rick Kehoe (636).

1994 – Soccer legend passes away

Legendary Manchester United manager Sir Matt Busby died, aged 85. As a player, he won 1 international cap for Scotland (1933) and an FA Cup winner's medal for Manchester City (1934). He was Manchester United manager from 1945–69, winning the European Cup in 1968 in a famous 4-1 defeat of Benfica; the FA Cup in 1948 and 1963; and the FA Charity Shield title in 1952, 1956, 1957, 1965 and 1967.

2006 – Expensive youngster

Arsenal made Theo Walcott the English Premier League's most expensive 16-year-old player, when they signed the teenager from Southampton, for an initial fee of £5 million. The fee rose to £12 million via Walcott's club and international appearances.

2008 – Patriots' 18 straight

The New England Patriots overcame a injury affected San Diego Chargers, pulling out a 21-12 victory at Foxboro that sent them back to the NFL title game for the fourth time in 7 seasons. The win marked the first time in more than 100 years that a team in the 4 major pro sports opened a season with 18 straight victories. The record for wins to start a season was set in 1884 by St Louis in baseball's Union Association.

BIRTHDATES

1874	England soccer midfielder STEPHEN BLOOMER – died 1938
1908	England Test spinner IAN PEEBLES – died 1980
1921	Spanish soccer forward TELMO ZARRA – died 2006
1928	American golfer LIONEL HEBERT – died 2000
1938	Northern Ireland soccer forward DEREK DOUGAN – died 2007
1940	American figure skater CAROL HEISS
1956	American swimmer JON NABER
1968	West Indian Test wicketkeeper JUNIOR MURRAY
1969	New Zealand rugby union flanker BLAIR LARSEN
1977	South African Test spinner PAUL ADAMS

㉑ JANUARY

1911 – First Monte Carlo Rally

The inaugural Monte Carlo Rally commenced, and was won 7 days later by French driver Henri Rougier in a Turcat-Mery. The event is now the first in the World Rally Championship and run over 18 stages. All competitors start and finish in Monaco, with the majority of the action in the mountains in nearby France. Seven-time winner Sébastien Loeb and four-time winners Walter Röhrl of Germany, Italian Sandro Munari and Finland's Tommi Mäkinen have been the most successful drivers of modern times. Frenchman Jean Trévoux also won 4 times, recording victories both pre and post World War II.

1958 – NBA loser wins

Bob Pettit of St Louis became the first member of the losing team to win the All-Star MVP award, scoring 28 points and grabbing 26 rebounds. The East beat Pettit's Western Conference team 130-118.

1979 – Steelers first to 3 Super Bowl titles

The Pittsburgh Steelers became the first team to win 3 Super Bowls, with MVP Terry Bradshaw completing 17-of-30 passes for 318 yards and 4 touchdowns in a 35-31 victory over the Dallas Cowboys in Miami. The Steelers scored 2 touchdowns in the fourth quarter to take a 35-17 lead and held off a late Cowboys' comeback.

1990 – McEnroe theatrics

Volatile American tennis pro John McEnroe became the first player to be expelled from the Australian Open when he threw a tantrum and swore at an official. McEnroe was leading in his match against Mikael Pernfors of Sweden 6-1, 4-6, 7-5, 2-4.

2005 – Clemens an expensive pitcher

Forty-two-year-old pitching ace Roger Clemens signed a one-year $18 million deal with the Houston Astros, at that time the highest salary for a pitcher in baseball history. Clemens retired after pitching for the New York Yankees in the 2003 World Series, but changed his mind and agreed to join his hometown Astros in a one-year deal. He again '99 per cent' retired, but was awarded the record amount in salary arbitration. Clemens is a seven-time Cy Young Award winner and 11-time All-Star.

BIRTHDATES

1888	Australian Test captain HERBIE COLLINS – died 1959
1904	Dutch soccer midfielder PUCK VAN HEEL – died 1984
1925	Pro Football Hall of Fame tackle GEORGE CONNOR – died 2003
1932	Russian gymnast BORIS SHAKHLIN – died 2008
1940	American golfer JACK NICKLAUS
1954	England soccer defender PHIL THOMPSON
1955	American tennis player PETER FLEMING
1959	Scottish soccer defender/manager ALEX McLEISH
1963	New Zealand jockey JIM CASSIDY
1963	German basketball player DETLEF SCHREMPF
1963	Nigerian NBA centre HAKEEM OLAJUWON
1975	England soccer midfielder NICKY BUTT
1975	French rugby union centre THOMAS CASTARGNEDE
1977	England rugby union fullback MATT PERRY
1977	England soccer defender PHIL NEVILLE
1979	Irish rugby union centre BRIAN O'DRISCOLL
1985	English darts player ADRIAN LEWIS

Roger Clemens pitching for the Houston Astros in 2004. Photo: Rdikeman at Wikipedia [CC-BY-SA-3.0], via Wikimedia Commons.

1948 – Laker's 7 against Windies

England spinner Jim Laker captured 7 for 103 in his first Test innings, in the drawn first Test against the West Indies in Barbados. Laker went on to take 193 wickets in 46 Tests at 21.24 and is best remembered for capturing 19 Australian wickets for 90 at Old Trafford in 1956.

1959 – Hawthorne dies in crash

Britain's first Formula 1 world champion Mike Hawthorne died when his Jaguar became out of control on the Guildford by-pass and crashed. The 1958 World Champion had driven in 47 Grand Prix (1952–58) winning 3 races and recording 18 podium finishes. He was just 29.

1968 – Surfing legend passes away

Hawaii's best-known citizen and five-time Olympic swim medallist Duke Kahanamoku died of a heart attack in Honolulu. He was 77. In the 1912 and 1920 Olympics, Kahanamoku won the 100m freestyle, and in 1924 at age 33 finished second to Johnny Weissmuller. He also played a major role in introducing the sport of surfing to the world.

1973 – Foreman 'smokes' Joe

In a battle of unbeaten heavyweights and Olympic gold medallists, George Foreman battered the champion Joe Frazier in 2 rounds in Kingston, Jamaica. Foreman celebrated his 24th birthday by pounding away at his smaller opponent, knocking Frazier down 6 times. After the sixth knockdown, referee Arthur Mercante stopped the fight.

1983 – Borg retires

At just 26, Swedish ace Björn Borg announced his retirement from competitive tennis.
Borg won 11 major events, including 5 consecutive Wimbledon titles (1976–80) and 6 French Open championships (1974–75, 1978–81). He won 64 career titles and had a win-loss record of 608-127. He later played on various senior circuits.

1989 – Walsh's 49ers finale

Bill Walsh coached his final game with the San Francisco 49ers as they recovered from 3 points down, with 3:10 left on the clock, to beat the Cincinnati Bengals 20-16 in Miami, taking their third Super Bowl triumph of the 1980s. Quarterback Joe Montana hurled a 10-yard bullet to John Taylor with 34 seconds remaining. He completed 23-of-36 for a Super Bowl record of 357 yards.

2005 – Wilkens out mid-season

For the first time in his 32-year NBA coaching career, Lenny Wilkens resigned in the middle of a season. The NBA's all-time win/loss leader left after his New York Knicks lost against Houston, their ninth defeat in 10 outings. Wilkens had 2 years and $10 million left on his contract, and ended his one-year run on Broadway with a 40-41 record.

2006 – Kobe's 81

Los Angeles Lakers' star forward Kobe Bryant scored a staggering 81 points against the Toronto Raptors to register the second-highest single-game score in NBA history, in a 122-104 win at the Staples Centre. The 27-year-old Bryant hit 28-of-46 from the floor. Wilt Chamberlain scored 100 points for Philadelphia against the NY Knicks at Hershey in 1962.

BIRTHDATES

1907	England soccer striker DIXIE DEAN – died 1980
1920	England soccer manager SIR ALF RAMSEY – died 1999
1927	Pro Football Hall of Fame fullback JOE PERRY – died 2011
1927	Pro Football Hall of Fame tackle LOU CREEKMUR – died 2009
1938	Brazilian soccer defender ALTAIR GOMES DE FIGUEIREDO
1940	NFL coach GEORGE SEIFERT
1953	American swimmer KAREN MOE
1957	Canadian NHL right-winger MIKE BOSSY
1967	British swimmer NICK GILLINGHAM
1968	French soccer defender FRANK LEBOEUF
1968	Colombian soccer midfielder MAURICIO SERNA
1971	England soccer striker STAN COLLYMORE
1987	NFL running back RAY RICE

㉓ JANUARY

1919 – Liverpool legend is born
Long-serving Liverpool manager Bob Paisley was born. Paisley would go on to join Liverpool as a player in 1939 and stay with the club for 44 years. In 1974, he took over from Bill Shankly, and became the most successful manager in the history of British football. His Liverpool teams won 6 League Championships, 3 League Cups, 1 UEFA Cup and 3 European Cups, and he was Manager of the Year a record 6 times. He died in 1996, aged 77.

1944 – Red Wings thrash Rangers
The Red Wings scored a 15-0 rout of the New York Rangers in Detroit in the most one-sided game in NHL history. The Red Wings also became the first team to score 15 consecutive goals in a game. Syd Howe led the onslaught with a hat-trick as Detroit scored 8 goals in the third period to provide the final margin of victory.

1948 – Bradman's dozen double centuries
Don Bradman hit 21 fours and a 6 for 201 in the first innings of the fourth Test against India in Adelaide. It was Bradman's 12th and final Test double century. Lindsay Hassett also hit 198 in Australia's 674, the third-highest Test score in Australia.

1958 – Ponderous Test knock
Champion Pakistan batsman Hanif Mohammad scored 337 against the West Indies in the first Test in Barbados. It was the longest innings in Test cricket history, taking 16 hours and 10 minutes, having started on January 20.

1998 – Jordan into double figures again ...
Michael Jordan scored in double figures for the 800th consecutive game in the Chicago Bulls' 100-98 overtime win over the Nets in New Jersey.

2005 – Record 51 aces in defeat
Joachim Johansson of Sweden served a record 51 aces in his fourth-round match against Andre Agassi at the Australian Open in Melbourne. It was the highest number of aces ever served in a singles match in a major. Agassi won the match 6-7, 7-6, 7-6, 6-4. The previous record had been 47 served by Gustavo

Swedish tennis player Joachim Johansson.

Kuerton of Brazil in his 2003 Davis Cup playoff defeat to Canada's Daniel Nestor. The current record holder is John Isner with 113 at Wimbledon in 2010.

BIRTHDATES
1919	English soccer defender/manager BOB PAISLEY – died 1996
1930	Australian tennis player MERVYN ROSE
1942	Australian Test fast bowler LAURIE MAYNE
1966	Australian surfer DAMIEN HARDMAN
1968	Czech tennis player PETR KORDA
1969	Canadian NHL winger BRENDAN SHANAHAN
1971	Welsh rugby union centre SCOTT GIBBS
1971	New Zealand Test wicketkeeper ADAM PARORE
1984	Dutch soccer winger ARJEN ROBBEN

1962 – Hanif Pakistan's saviour

Pakistan batsman Hanif Mohammad completed twin-tons and batted for 894 minutes in the match to help save the second Test and draw against England at Dacca. Hannif scored 111 in the first innings and 104 in the second.

1964 – Willie tops earning standings

American jockey Willie Shoemaker topped Eddie Arcaro's career earnings record by riding 4 winners at Santa Anita, California. Shoemaker's total earnings exceeded $30 million.

1981 – Bossy ties 'The Rocket'

Mike Bossy tied 'Rocket' Richard's record of 50 goals in 50 NHL games in a regular season match in a 7-4 home win against the Quebec Nordiques. The New York Islanders' right-wing scored his 49th goal with less than 5 minutes left in the game, and netted his 50th with 1:29 remaining.

1990 – Riley's 500

The Los Angeles Lakers' Pat Riley became the 13th coach to reach the 500-victory plateau, getting there faster than any other coach, as the Lakers beat the Indiana Pacers 120-111. At 500-184, Riley surpassed Don Nelson, who was 500-317 when he reached the milestone.

1992 – Back-to-back in Oz for Seles

Monica Seles, then of Yugoslavia, won her second consecutive Australian Open with a 6-2, 6-3 victory over American Mary Joe Fernandez. Seles had become the youngest Australian Open champion as a 17-year-old the previous year.

1997 – Hingis youngest champion

Sixteen-year-old Swiss tennis star Martina Hingis became the youngest Grand Slam singles champion of the 20th century, with a 6-2, 6-2 win over former champion Mary Pierce to capture the first of 3 consecutive Australian Open titles in Melbourne.

1999 – Duval fires 59

David Duval became only the third player to shoot a sub-60 round in PGA tournament play, posting a 59 in the final round to win the Bob Hope Chrysler Classic at the PGA West course. Duval went out in 31 and came home in 28. He fired 11 birdies and made a 6ft eagle putt on the 18th hole to win by 1 stroke.

2002 – Hendry's century break record

Scottish snooker star Stephen Hendry claimed a record 550th competitive century during the Regal Welsh Open in Cardiff. Hendry achieved the milestone with a break of 101 against Jimmy White.

BIRTHDATES

1913	Australian rugby league forward RAY STEHR – died 1983
1916	American tennis player GENE MAKO
1922	England soccer midfielder NEIL FRANKLIN – died 1996
1947	Japanese golfer MASASHI 'JUMBO' OZAKI
1947	Italian soccer player GIORGIO CHINAGLIA
1949	New Zealand rugby union prop BILLY BUSH
1955	American swimmer JIM MONTGOMERY
1968	American gymnast MARY LOU RETTEN
1970	Australian surfer LUKE EGAN
1970	Zimbabwe Test batsman NEIL JOHNSON

David Duval during his round of 59 in the 1999 Bob Hope Chrysler Classic at the West Palmer Country Club.

1894 – 'Gentleman Jim' first true champion
James Corbett knocked out British champion Charley Mitchell in the third round of their world heavyweight title bout in Jacksonville, Florida. Mitchell was 33 years of age and weighed only 160lbs. He was no match for the silky-skilled Corbett. Given the Transatlantic nature of the fight, it was labelled 'the first true world heavyweight championship' fight.

1924 – Winter Olympics open
The International Winter Sports Week, now known as the first Winter Olympic Games, opened in Chamonix in France. Sixteen nations sent 258 athletes (247 men and 11 women) to compete in 9 sports and 16 events. The big winners of the 11-day competition were Finland and Norway, who took 28 of the 43 medals awarded. Norway won 17 and Finland 11, with the United States and Great Britain winning 4 each.

1957 – Record Test 'dot balls'
South African spinner Hugh Tayfield bowled 137 balls without conceding a run during England's first innings against South Africa in the third Test in Durban. The spell remains the most consecutive dot-balls delivered in Test history. Tayfield's bowling figures were 1 for 21 with 17 maidens, off 24 economical overs.

1960 – Wilt's NBA rookie record
Wilt Chamberlain scored 58 points, an NBA rookie record, as Philadelphia beat Detroit 127-117 in Bethlehem, Pennsylvania. Chamberlain repeated his record achievement less than a month later.

1992 – Backley throws 91m
Britain's Steve Backley became the first man to throw the modified javelin 91.46m at an athletics meet in Auckland, New Zealand, a world record. He was the first British man to win a medal in an athletics event in 3 Olympics, having won bronze in 1992 and silver in 1996 and 2000.

1995 – Catatonic Cantona
Manchester United's French international captain Eric Cantona attacked a spectator after he was sent off in a Premier League match against Crystal Palace at Selhurst Park. Cantona received a record nine-month suspension and was fined a cumulative sum of £20,000 by the FA and his club.

1998 – Celebrity marriage
Soccer superstar David Beckham, then of Manchester United, and *Spice Girl* Victoria Adams (aka Posh Spice), announced their engagement. The couple were married in 1999 and have survived some drama in their private lives to parent four children.

2008 – 'Gilly' gets keeper record
Amidst a form slump, Adam Gilchrist broke the record for Test dismissals by a wicketkeeper during the fourth Test against India in Adelaide. Gilchrist accepted a catch from Anil Kumble to close the Indian first innings, his 414th dismissal in Test cricket (surpassing South Africa's Mark Boucher). In all, Gilchrist had dropped four catches and missed 2 stumping chances in the four Tests against India, and was under fire because of his poor form behind the stumps. The following day he announced his retirement from all forms of cricket.

BIRTHDATES
1879	South African Test all-rounder DAVE NOURSE – died 1948
1942	Portuguese soccer striker EUSEBIO
1947	Spanish motor cyclist ANGEL NIETO
1947	Brazilian soccer forward TOSTÃO
1954	Australian sailor KAY COTTEE
1962	American NHL defenseman CHRIS CHELIOS
1964	American golfer BILLY ANDRADE
1964	Australian cyclist STEPHEN PATE
1967	French soccer midfielder DAVID GINOLA
1971	Australian cyclist BRETT AITKIN
1975	American sprinter TIM MONTGOMERY
1984	Brazilian soccer striker ROBINHO
1987	Russian tennis player MARIA KIRILENKO

1913 – Thorpe loses Olympic medals

American athlete Jim Thorpe relinquished his 1912 Olympic medals after confessing he had played semi-pro baseball, thereby calling into question his amateur status. Thorpe had won the Decathlon and Pentathlon gold medals in Stockholm. The medals were reinstated to his family in 1983.

1924 – Speed skating upset

In his only international meeting, American Charles Jewtraw won the 500m speed skating competition in Chamonix in France, becoming the first-ever gold medallist at the Winter Olympics. Although Jewtraw was the world-record holder over 100 and 220 yards, it was still considered a surprise for him to beat the Finnish and Norwegian favourites.

1986 – Ditka's famous Bears

The Chicago Bears scored a famous 46-10 victory over the New England Patriots in Super Bowl XX in New Orleans. After being 3-0 down, Chicago scored 44 unanswered points and added a safety late in the game. The Bears were loaded with quirky personalities, including coach Mike Ditka, quarterback Jim McMahon and defensive lineman William 'The Refrigerator' Perry.

1993 – Windies close call

The West Indies held the narrowest winning margin in Test history when they scored a 1-run victory over Australia in the fourth Test in Adelaide. Chasing 186 for victory and starting their tenth-wicket partnership at 144 for 9, Tim May (42 not out) and Craig McDermott (18) almost became national heroes before McDermott was controversially given out, caught behind off Courtney Walsh.

1996 – Monica's fourth Oz Open

Monica Seles won her fourth Australian Open crown, beating German Anke Huber 6-4, 6-1 for her ninth major title. It was Seles' first major in 3 years, after having been stabbed by a spectator during a 1993 match in Hamburg.

2000 – Tennis great Budge passes away

Tennis' first grand glam winner Don Budge died in Scranton, Pennsylvania, aged 84. Budge won the US Open and Wimbledon in 1937, before achieving the Grand Slam in 1938. He turned professional in 1939, but a shoulder injury suffered in military training during World War II limited his post-war tennis effectiveness.

BIRTHDATES

1907	English golfer HENRY COTTON – died 1987
1919	English football manager BILL NICHOLSON – died 2004
1922	England soccer goalkeeper GIL MERRICK – died 2010
1935	Pro Football Hall of Fame defensive tackle HENRY JORDAN – died 1977
1954	Australian Test captain KIM HUGHES
1957	Indian Test spinner SHIVLAL YADAV
1961	Canadian Hockey Hall of Fame forward WAYNE GRETZKY
1962	Australian Test spinner TIM MAY
1962	Argentine soccer defender OSCAR RUGGERI
1963	Portuguese soccer manager JOSÉ MOURINHO
1963	Australian Test all rounder SIMON O'DONNELL
1968	New Zealand Test fast bowler CHRIS PRINGLE
1977	American NBA forward VINCE CARTER
1977	American tennis player JUSTIN GIMMELSTOB

American speed skaters, including gold-medal winner Charles Jewtraw, in training for the 1924 Chamonix Winter Olympics.

1964 – Perfect Proteas

South African batsmen Eddie Barlow and Graeme Pollock shared a record partnership of 341 in the fourth Test against Australia in Adelaide. Barlow hit 201, and the 19-year-old Pollock 175, as South Africa won by 10 wickets to square the series 1–1. The Barlow/Pollock partnership remained South Africa's highest for any wicket in Tests for nearly 40 years, until broken by Herschelle Gibbs and Graeme Smith in 2003.

1973 – Brash Barbarians hammer All Blacks

In one of the most thrilling rugby union matches ever played on British soil, the Barbarians beat New Zealand 21–13 at Cardiff Arms Park. The game started at a frenetic pace, with a length-of-the-field try by Barbarians halfback Gareth Edwards. Playing an all-action brand of rugby, the Barbarians led 17–0 at halftime. The All Blacks clawed their way back to 17–11, before a try by J.P.R. Williams sealed the win 5 minutes from fulltime.

1973 – Bruins' Basketball record

Bill Walton's UCLA Bruins beat Notre Dame, 82–63, for their 61st consecutive victory, breaking the NCAA record set in 1956 by Bill Russell's University of San Francisco team. The Bruins' extended the record streak to 88 games without defeat until, ironically, Notre Dame beat them 71–70 in January 1974.

1984 – 'The Great One' takes another record

Wayne Gretzky of the Edmonton Oilers scored a goal against the New Jersey Devils, extending his NHL-record scoring streak to 51 consecutive games. During his run, Gretzky scored 153 points from 61 goals and 92 assists. The sequence was broken by the LA Kings the following night.

1994 – Harding 'in the know'

Tonya Harding admitted post knowledge, but denied conspiracy in the attack on her rival, Nancy Kerrigan, prior to the US Figure Skating Championships. She later pleaded guilty to hindering the investigation and was served a lengthy list of penalties, including 3 years' probation and a $160,000 fine.

2008 – Novak is Serbia's first champ

Twenty-year-old Novak Djokovic became the first Serbian man to win a major when he beat Frenchman Jo-Wilfried Tsonga 4-6, 6-4, 6-3, 7-6 in the Australian Open final in Melbourne. The third ranked Djokovic was the youngest player to win the Australian title since Stefan Edberg in 1985.

2008 – Rally record to Loeb

French world champion Sébastien Loeb won the Monte Carlo Rally, for a record fifth time, in a Citroën C4. Loeb won the event by 2:34.4 from the Ford Focus of Finn Mikko Hirvonen.

2008 – Tiger's quadrella

Tiger Woods finished at 19-under 269 to win the Buick Invitational in San Diego for the fourth consecutive year, tying a PGA Tour record for consecutive wins in a single tournament. Woods was the only player to own such a streak at 2 events, having also won four in a row at Bay Hill.

2013 – 'Joker's' historic treble

Novak Djokovic became the first man in the Open era to win 3 consecutive Australian titles when he beat Andy Murray 6-7, 7-6, 6-3, 6-2 at Rod Laver Arena in Melbourne. He had won four of his 6 major titles there. Only Australians Jack Crawford (1931–33) and Roy Emerson (1963–67) had won 3 or more consecutive Australian championships.

BIRTHDATES

1939	American golfer MIKE HILL
1952	American tennis player BRIAN GOTTFRIED
1959	NFL receiver CRIS COLLINSWORTH
1959	American sports caster KEITH OLBERMANN
1969	New Zealand Test batsman SHANE THOMSON
1970	West Indian Test fast bowler DEAN HEADLEY
1972	Irish rugby union hooker KEITH WOOD
1974	Norwegian biathlete OLE EINAR BJØRNDALEN
1974	Sri Lanka Test fast bowler CHAMINDA VAAS
1979	New Zealand Test spinner DANIEL VETTORI
1980	Russian tennis player MARAT SAFIN
1981	Australian tennis player ALICIA MOLIK
1981	New Zealand rugby union front rower TONY WOODCOCK

㉘ JANUARY

1887 – Low Cricket scores
England was dismissed for an all-time low of 45 in the first Test against Australia in Sydney. Opening bowlers Charles Turner (with 6 for 15) and John Ferris (four for 27) bowled unchanged. Amazingly, England won, when Australia fell 14 runs short of the winning target of 111, with English fast bowlers George Lohmann and Billy Barnes combining for match figures of 14 for 97.

1943 – Blackhawks' Brotherly love
Max Bentley scored four goals and his brother Doug assisted on all of them as the Blackhawks thrashed the New York Rangers 10-1 in Chicago. Doug also scored a goal for a total of 5 points.

1961 – Law's seven of the best
Scottish international striker Denis Law scored all 7 of Manchester City's goals in their FA Cup fourth-round tie against Luton Town at Kenilworth Road – but City lost. The match was abandoned after 69 minutes because of a waterlogged pitch, with City leading 6-2. That score didn't stand and they lost the replay 3-1.

1988 – NBA three-point streak starts
Michael Adams of the Denver Nuggets began a record streak of 79 consecutive games, with at least 1 three-point field goal. The streak, which stretched over 2 seasons, lasted through to January 23 1989. Dana Barros increased the record streak by hitting 89 consecutive during the 1995–96 season.

2005 – Draper in unique dual sport performances
Australian tennis player/pro golfer Scott Draper performed a unique sporting juggling act when he made his pro golf debut in the Victorian Open and on the same day teamed with Samantha Stosur in the semi-finals of the mixed doubles of tennis' Australian Open. Draper missed the cut in the golf, but won the tennis title.

2006 – Top jockey Bailey retires from turf
Jerry Bailey, a two-time Kentucky Derby winner and arguably America's best-ever jockey, retired from

Denis Law following his British record transfer from Huddersfield Town to Manchester City in 1960.

riding. Bailey had 5,893 career victories and more than $295m in North American purse earnings to his credit.

2007 – Woods' magnificent seven
Tiger Woods won the Buick Invitational for the third straight year to stretch his PGA Tour winning streak to seven, the second-longest in tour history behind Byron Nelson's record 11 straight victories in 1945.

BIRTHDATES
1872	Scottish golfer ALEX SMITH – died 1930
1873	Australian Test captain MONTY NOBLE – died 1940
1880	England Test wicketkeeper BERT STRUDWICK – died 1970
1926	American auto racer JIMMY BRYAN – died 1960
1957	Zimbabwe golfer NICK PRICE
1964	England Test fast bowler DAVID LAWRENCE
1969	Italian swimmer GIORGIO LAMBERTI
1972	England rugby union hooker MARK REGAN
1978	Italian soccer goalkeeper GIANLUIGI BUFFON
1978	England soccer defender JAMIE CARRAGHER
1985	Australian swimmer LIBBY TRICKETT

1932 – Grimmett great ... here comes O'Reilly

Australian spinner Clarrie Grimmett ripped through South Africa with 7 for 116 and had 14 wickets for the match as Australia won by 10 wickets in the fourth Test in Adelaide. Leg spinner Bill O'Reilly made his Test debut, taking four wickets.

1985 – Kurri's NHL century

Jari Kurri of the Edmonton Oilers set an NHL record by scoring his 100th point in the 39th game of the season. In a stellar season, the Finn scored career highs of 71 goals (a single-season record by a right-wing) and 135 points.

1988 – Record NBA crowd in 'Motor City'

The Detroit Pistons drew what was, at the time, an NBA regular season record crowd of 61,983 fans to the Pontiac Silverdome for their 125-108 win over the Boston Celtics. Michael Jordan's Chicago Bulls and the Atlanta Hawks broke the attendance record in 1998, drawing 62,046 to the Georgia Dome.

1994 – Chávez loses

Mexican fighter Julio César Chávez suffered his first loss in 91 fights in a split points decision to Frankie Randall, in a WBC super lightweight title fight in Las Vegas. Chávez was also decked for the first time in his career in the 11th round.

1995 – 49ers' Young MVP

San Francisco quarterback Steve Young emerged from Joe Montana's long shadow to take the MVP award in Super Bowl XXIX in Miami. The left-handed Young threw 6 touchdown passes, as the 49ers beat the San Diego Chargers, 49-26.

1998 – Test match abandoned

The first Test between England and West Indies at Sabina Park in Kingston, Jamaica, was abandoned after just 62 deliveries because of the state of the pitch. It was the shortest Test match in history, with England players hit 7 times in the first 10 overs.

2000 – Malone joins NBA 30,000 Club

Karl Malone of the Utah Jazz became only the third player in NBA history to score 30,000 career points when he finished with 35 in a 96-94 away loss to the Minnesota Timberwolves. Malone took his place alongside Kareem Abdul-Jabbar and Wilt Chamberlain.

2006 – Test hat-trick in first over

Indian fast bowler Irfan Pathan became the first man in Test cricket history to capture a hat-trick in the first over, on the first day of the third Test against Pakistan in Karachi. Off the fourth ball of the over, Pathan dismissed Salman Butt and then Younis Khan and Mohammad Yousuf followed.

BIRTHDATES

1923	American golfer JACK BURKE JR
1926	American tennis player BOB FALKENBURG
1932	England Test batsman RAMAN SUBBA ROW
1932	England soccer forward TOMMY TAYLOR – died 1958
1945	American golfer DONNA CAPONI
1950	South African auto racer JODY SCHECKTER
1951	West Indian Test fast bowler ANDY ROBERTS
1957	French rugby union hooker PHILIPPE DINTRANS
1960	American diver GREG LOUGANIS
1964	New Zealand rugby union fullback JOHN GALLAGHER
1965	Czech NHL goaltender DOMINIK HASEK
1965	Swedish tennis player/coach PETER LUNDGREN
1966	Brazilian soccer striker ROMÁRIO
1970	German swimmer JÖRG HOFFMAN
1980	Croatian soccer striker IVAN KLASNI
1988	Australian surfer STEPHANIE GILMORE

Frankie Randall lands a left to the face of Julio César Chávez during their 1994 WBC super lightweight title fight in Las Vegas.

1920 – Malone nets seven in Quebec
Quebec Bulldogs' forward Joe Malone set one of the NHL's longest-standing records by scoring 7 goals in Quebec's 10-6 win over Toronto St Patrick's in Quebec.

1971 – Lillee's devastating debut
Champion fast bowler Dennis Lillee captured 5 for 84 in his Test debut, in the sixth Test against England in Adelaide. The match marked the start of Lillee's fearsome opening bowling combination with Jeff Thomson.

1993 – Seles' tennis triple
Monica Seles came back from a set down to win her third consecutive Australian Open, beating Steffi Graf of Germany 4-6, 6-3, 6-2.

1993 – Curtley unplayable
West Indian fast bowler Curtley Ambrose took 7 for 25 against Australia in the fifth Test in Perth. Ambrose took 7 for 1 in 32 balls as the Australians went from 85-2 to 119 all out. The WACA ground curator was sacked for preparing a tourist-friendly wicket.

1994 – Four Super Bowls for Dallas
The Cowboys won their fourth Super Bowl and the Buffalo Bills became four-time losers, as Dallas won Super Bowl XXVIII 30-13 in Atlanta. Emmitt Smith rushed for 132 yards and 2 touchdowns, and was named MVP.

1996 – 'Magic' returns
Ervin 'Magic' Johnson came out of retirement, helping the LA Lakers to a 128-118 win over Golden State at the Forum. Johnson scored 19 points, took 8 rebounds and made 10 assists. He had last appeared during the 1991 Finals.

1999 – 'Swiss Miss' Oz delight
Switzerland's Martina Hingis claimed her third consecutive Australian Open title with a 6-2, 6-3 win over France's Amélie Mauresmo.

2002 – Another Malone NBA mark
Utah's Karl Malone became the second player in NBA history to register 34,000 career points when he scored 18 in a 90-78 win over Chicago in Salt Lake City. Malone trailed only Kareem Abdul-Jabbar with 38,387 career points.

2005 – Safin victory
Russian Marat Safin beat home favourite Lleyton Hewitt 1-6, 6-3, 6-4, 6-4 to win the Centenary Australian Open at Melbourne Park. It was the first Australian Open final to be played at night and the tournament attracted a record attendance of 543,873.

2012 – Longest Grand Slam final – Novak edges Nadal
Novak Djokovic wore down Rafael Nadal in the longest Grand Slam singles final in history, winning 5-7, 6-4, 6-2, 6-7, 7-5 after 5 hours 53 minutes to claim his third Australian Open title in Melbourne.

BIRTHDATES
1929	South African Test spinner HUGH TAYFIELD – died 1994
1937	Russian chess player BORIS SPASSKY
1950	Australian golfer JACK NEWTON
1955	American golfer CURTIS STRANGE
1957	American golfer PAYNE STEWART – died 1999
1958	Welsh rugby union lock DEREK WHITE
1972	American golfer JILL McGILL
1975	Brazilian soccer midfielder JUNINHO PERNAMUCANO
1977	American swimmer TOM MALCHOW
1981	Bulgarian soccer striker DIMITAR BERBATOV
1981	England soccer striker PETER CROUCH

West Indies' Test fast bowler Curtley Ambrose.

③① JANUARY

1965 – Stein era begins at Celtic
Jock Stein was appointed manager of Scottish soccer club Glasgow Celtic. During his tenure (1965–78) Celtic won 10 Scottish League Championships, 8 Scottish Cups, 6 Scottish League Cups and the European Cup in 1967.

1976 – Gibbs reaches milestone in final Test
West Indian spinner Lance Gibbs became the leading wicket-taker in Test history during the sixth Test against Australia in Melbourne. Gibbs broke Fred Trueman's record of 307 when he dismissed Ian Redpath. It was Gibbs' final Test, and he ended with 309 at an average of 29.09.

1981 – Anfield agony for Reds
Liverpool's 85-match unbeaten home streak, which began 3 years earlier, ended with a 2-1 defeat to Leicester City at Anfield. The run comprised 63 League, 9 League Cup, 7 European competition and 6 FA Cup matches.

1987 – Woods' clean sheet mark ends
Glasgow Rangers' England goalkeeper Chris Woods' British record of 1,196 goalless minutes ended when Rangers crashed 1-0 to Hamilton in a Scottish Cup third-round match at Ibrox Park.

1988 – Redskin ransack
Quarterback Doug Williams led Washington Redskins to a record 35 points on 5 consecutive possessions in the second quarter, for a 42-10 victory over the Denver Broncos in Super Bowl XXII in San Diego.

1992 – Broadcaster Cosell retires
Legendary American sports caster Howard Cosell retired from broadcasting. He was best known as a boxing announcer, and the pot-stirring third man on *Monday Night Football* (1970–83). He died in 1995, aged 77.

1998 – Hingis youngest title defence
Seventeen-year-old Martina Hingis of Switzerland became the youngest player in the Open era to defend a grand slam title, capturing her second Australian

Italian cross-country skier Manuela Di Centa during the 5km event at the 1994 Winter Olympics at Lillehammer, Norway.

Open. Hingis was untroubled in scoring a 6-3, 6-3 victory over Spain's Conchita Martínez.

2004 – United draws an EPL record crowd
An English Premier League record crowd of 67,758 watched Manchester United's 3-2 win over Southampton at Old Trafford.

BIRTHDATES
1914   American boxer JERSEY JOE WALCOTT – died 1994
1916   American tennis player FRANK PARKER – died 1997
1919   Baseball Hall of Fame outfielder JACKIE ROBINSON – died 1972
1920   England soccer goalkeeper BERT WILLIAMS
1930   Swedish auto racer JO BONNIER – died 1972
1931   Baseball Hall of Fame shortstop ERNIE BANKS
1940   South African rugby union coach KITCH CHRISTIE – died 1998
1944   Australian Test all rounder JOHN INVERARITY
1947   Baseball Hall of Fame pitcher NOLAN RYAN
1954   West Indian Test batsman FAOUD BACCHUS
1957   American swimmer SHIRLEY BABASHOFF
1963   Italian cross-country skier MANUELA DI CENTA
1977   South African Test fast bowler DAVID TERBRUGGE

FEBRUARY

1 FEBRUARY

1958 – 'Busby's Babes' final fling
Manchester United's 'Busby Babes' played their last game on British soil, beating Arsenal 5-4 at Highbury. Tommy Taylor and Duncan Edwards were among 7 players killed 5 days later, when the team's charter plane crashed on takeoff at Munich airport.

1960 – 'Rocket' recovery
In an all-Australian final, tennis star Rod Laver recovered from 2 sets down to outlast Neale Fraser in 5 gruelling sets at the Australian Open at Milton. Laver won an epic encounter 5-7, 3-6, 6-3, 8-6, 8-6.

1981 – Underarm is 'not cricket'
Australian captain Greg Chappell was responsible for the infamous 'underarm ball' in the climax of the one-day series final against New Zealand in Melbourne. With 7 runs required off the last ball for New Zealand to win, Chappell instructed his brother Trevor to bowl the final ball underarm, rolling it along the ground. Australia won the match, but the tactic was banned.

1984 – Stern NBA Commissioner
David Stern became the fourth NBA commissioner, replacing Larry O'Brien. Maurice Podoloff, J. Walter Kennedy and O'Brien preceded him. He retains the position today.

1994 – Love gone bad
Jeff Gillooly pleaded guilty to taking part in the attack on figure skater Nancy Kerrigan. In a plea bargain, he confessed to racketeering charges in exchange for testimony implicating his ex-wife Tonya Harding, who was sentenced to 3 years probation, fined $100,000, stripped of the 1994 national championship and banned for life.

1995 – Stockton assists king
Utah Jazz guard John Stockton passed Magic Johnson's all-time NBA assists mark of 9,221, in a 129-98 win over the Denver Nuggets in Salt Lake City. The record breaker came in Stockton's 860th game; Johnson needed 874. Stockton finished a 19-year career in 2003 with an assist record of 15,806.

2005 – Gunners' home streak gone
Arsenal's record 33-game unbeaten streak at home ended when the Gunners went down 4-2 to Manchester United at Highbury. The sequence started with the last home game of 2002–03, included all 19 of 2003–04.

2006 – Miller's high school mark broken
5ft, 9in tall high school senior Epiphanny Prince scored 113 points for Murry Bergtraum HS in a 137-32 win over Brandeis HS, breaking a girls' national prep record previously held by Hall of Famer Cheryl Miller (105).

2008 – Baze cracks 10,000 win barrier
Forty-nine-year-old Canadian jockey Russell Baze rode his 10,000th career winner in the third race at Golden Gate Fields in Albany, California. The milestone win came by the slimmest of margins as Baze, aboard Two Step Cat, prevailed in a 3-horse photo finish.

2009 – Steelers' record sixth Super Bowl
Quarterback Ben Roethlisberger and Santonio Holmes improvised a 6-yard touchdown with 35 seconds left to give the Pittsburgh Steelers a record-setting sixth Super Bowl victory, 27-23, over the Arizona Cardinals in Tampa, Florida.

BIRTHDATES
1915	English soccer winger SIR STANLEY MATTHEWS – died 2000
1938	American golfer JACKY CUPIT
1942	Australian Test spinner DAVID SINCOCK
1966	England soccer midfielder ROB LEE
1968	Canadian NHL right wing MARK RECCHI
1969	Argentine soccer forward GABRIEL BATISTUTA
1971	Indian Test batsman AJAY JADEJA
1972	West Indian Test fast bowler FRANKLYN ROSE
1976	Australian rugby union/league utility MAT ROGERS
1979	Brazilian soccer defender JUAN SILVEIRA DOS SANTOS
1981	South African Test captain GRAEME SMITH
1982	Welsh rugby union utility back GAVIN HENSON

❷ FEBRUARY

1918 – Boxing legend passes away
The last bare-knuckle champion, John L. Sullivan died of heart failure. In 44 fights, Sullivan had 39 wins, 1 loss and 4 draws. His only defeat came in his last fight, when he was KO'd in 21 rounds by Jim Corbett in New Orleans in 1892.

1936 – First baseball HOF votes
First votes for Baseball's Hall of Fame resulted in hits record-holder Ty Cobb receiving 222 of 226 votes from players and writers. Babe Ruth, who bashed 714 home runs, and Honus Wagner tied for second with 215. Also elected were Christy Mathewson and Walter Johnson.

1949 – Hogan dodges death
American golfing great Ben Hogan almost died when a bus collided with his car about 150 miles east of El Paso, Texas. He suffered a broken collarbone, smashed rib, double fracture of the pelvis and a broken ankle, but made a remarkable recovery to win the US Open just 16 months later.

1980 – Esposito second to 700
New York Rangers centre Phil Esposito joined Gordie Howe as the only NHL players to score 700 regular-season goals, with 2 in a 6-3 win over the Capitals in Washington. Esposito finished his 18-year career in 1981 with 717 goals, whilst Howe retired at the end of 1980 with 801.

1995 – Perry passes
Britain's best-ever tennis player, Fred Perry, died aged 85. He won all 4 grand slam singles titles for a career total of 8.

2004 – Federer number one
Roger Federer became the world's no. 1 ranked tennis player, a position he then held for 237 weeks until August 2008 when Rafael Nadal took over.

2005 – Cech's clean sheet record
Goalkeeper Petr Cech set a new record for the longest run without conceding a goal, as Chelsea beat Blackburn Rovers 1-0 at Ewood Park. The 22-year-old beat Peter Schmeichel's 1997 record of 694 minutes.

Babe Ruth was second in votes for baseball's Hall of Fame.

He would play 1,025 goalless minutes until overtaken by Manchester United's Edwin van der Sar in 2009.

2007 – Italian football shut down
All Italian Football League matches were suspended after crowd violence in Sicily. Following the Serie A game between Catania and Palermo, a police officer was killed when a bomb was thrown into his vehicle. It was the second soccer-related death in less than a week. The Italian national team's friendly match against Romania was also cancelled.

BIRTHDATES
1895	Pro Football Hall of Fame end/coach/owner GEORGE HALAS – died 1983
1915	Canadian golfer STAN LEONARD – died 2005
1920	England soccer defender GEORGE HARDWICK – died 2004
1923	Baseball Hall of Fame second baseman RED SCHOENDIENST
1935	American golfer PETE BROWN
1953	Australian golfer PENNY PULZ
1969	Russian soccer midfielder VALERI KARPIN
1974	South African rugby union captain ANDRE SNYMAN
1975	NFL wide receiver DONALD DRIVER

❸ FEBRUARY

1937 – Bradman brilliance
Australian cricket great Don Bradman scored 212 in the fourth Test against England at the Adelaide Oval. Bradman's innings inspired the Australians to a 148-run victory after they had trailed by 42 on the first innings. The win also tied the series 2-2.

1956 – Hello Sailer
Austrian Toni Sailer became the first skier to win gold medals in all 3 alpine events – the slalom, giant slalom and downhill – in the Winter Olympics at Cortina D'Ampezzo in Italy. Sailer credited his success to the innovative coaching methods of team coach Fred Rössner, the first to create training programs for developing explosive strength and speed endurance.

1960 – Spurs' goal glut
Tottenham Hotspur scored the most goals in one half of an FA Cup match during their 13-2 fourth-round replay victory over Crewe Alexandra at White Hart Lane. Spurs led 10-1 at halftime.

1980 – 'Magic' youngest All Star
Ervin 'Magic' Johnson, playing for the West, became the youngest All-Star ever at 20 years, 5 months, in the East's 144-136 overtime victory at the Capital Centre in Landover, Maryland.

1990 – Shoemaker's last ride
Champion 58-year-old American jockey Willie Shoemaker rode his 40,350th and final race at Santa Anita. His mount, Patchy Groundfog, finished fourth in the Legend's Last Ride Handicap, a farewell event that attracted 64,573 fans. Shoemaker retired with a record 8,833 wins, including 4 in the Kentucky Derby, 2 in the Preakness Stakes and 5 in the Belmont Stakes.

1999 – Hoddle gone after gaff
The Football Association sacked England manager Glenn Hoddle after his comments about people with disabilities. Hoddle was quoted in *The Times* newspaper.

2001 – XFL starts
The ill-fated XFL debuted with 2 games. The Vince McMahon owned football league was an off-season complement to the NFL but failed to find an audience. The Las Vegas Outlaws beat the New York/New Jersey Hitmen 19-0 in Whitney, Nevada and the Orlando Rage beat the Chicago Enforcers 33-29 in Las Vegas. The XFL shut down after ' season.

2002 – Pats finally
The New England Patriots won Super Bowl XXXVI, 20-17 over the Los Angeles Rams in New Orleans, Louisiana. It was the first Super Bowl victory for the Patriots. The game ended with a last-second field goal to the Patriots' Adam Vinatieri.

2008 – Giant upset
MVP Eli Manning's 13-yard touchdown pass to Plaxico Burress, with 35 seconds left, boosted the New York Giants to one of the greatest upsets in Super Bowl history, a 17-14 victory over the previously unbeaten New England Patriots in Glendale, Arizona.

2013 – 'Harbaugh Bowl'
In the first Super Bowl to feature brothers as opposing head coaches, John Harbaugh's Baltimore Ravens beat brother Jim's San Francisco 49ers, 34-31, at the Superdome in New Orleans. Ravens quarterback Joe Flacco was named MVP, completing 22 of 33 passes for 287 yards and 3 TDs. A power outage affected half the stadium during the third quarter.

BIRTHDATES
1911 American golfer TOM CREAVY – died 1979
1936 Australian Test captain BOB SIMPSON
1938 American boxer EMILE GRIFFITH
1940 NFL quarterback FRAN TARKENTON
1941 American golfer CAROL MANN
1945 Pro Football Hall of Fame quarterback BOB GRIESE
1949 American golfer JIM THORPE
1960 German soccer coach JOACHIM LÖW
1966 New Zealand Test fast bowler DANNY MORRISON
1967 England soccer goalkeeper TIM FLOWERS
1968 Yugoslav NBA centre VLADE DIVAC
1969 South African golfer RETIEF GOOSEN
1970 Colombian soccer goalkeeper OSCAR CORDOBA
1975 NZ rugby union/Australian rugby league forward BRAD THORN

1987 – Connor's yachting comeback

American helmsman Dennis Connor earned redemption, steering the San Diego Yacht Club's *Stars & Stripes 87* to a 1:59 second victory over Australian yacht *Kookaburra III* in the waters off Fremantle, Western Australia, to complete a 4-0 sweep. Four years earlier, Conner became the first American skipper to lose the America's Cup in the 132-year history of the event. The victory boosted Conner's record to 2-1 in America's Cup sailing.

1990 – Hadlee first to 400 Test scalps

New Zealand fast bowler Richard Hadlee became the first cricketer to take 400 Test wickets when he captured 4 for 69 in the first Test against India in Christchurch. In 86 Tests, Hadlee took 431 wickets at 22.29. He had best bowling figures of 9-52 and captured 10 wickets in a Test on 9 occasions.

1991 – Kiwis' record partnership

New Zealand captain Martin Crowe set a world record Test partnership of 467 with Andrew Jones in the first Test against Sri Lanka in Wellington. In New Zealand's record second innings of 671-4, Jones scored 186 and Crowe was out off the last ball of the day for 299, the highest-ever Test score by a Kiwi.

1996 – Bulls' NBA streak snapped

Mahmoud Abdul-Rauf scored 32 points as the Denver Nuggets beat visiting Chicago 105-99, snapping the Bulls' franchise-record 18-game winning streak. Chicago's 18-game streak tied for the third-longest winning streak in NBA history. The 1971–72 LA Lakers hold the record, at 33.

1996 – Flooded fairways at Pebble Beach

For the first time in 47 years, a PGA Tour event was not completed because rain had flooded the fairways at the AT&T Pebble Beach National Pro-Am in Carmel, California. The 1949 Colonial Classic was the last PGA Tour tournament that had to be cancelled.

2004 – Famous football comeback

In a famous FA Cup comeback, Manchester City trailed Tottenham 3-0 at halftime in a fourth-round replay at White Hart Lane, and were reduced to 10 men after City's Joey Barton was sent off. City went on to win 4-3.

2007 – African-American first

Tony Dungy became the first African-American to coach a Super Bowl winner, as the Indianapolis Colts beat the Chicago Bears 29-17 in Super Bowl XLI in a rain-soaked Miami. It was the Colts' first Super Bowl victory in 36 years, since they moved from Baltimore to Indianapolis.

BIRTHDATES

1912	American golfer BYRON NELSON – died 2006
1926	Australian boxer DAVE SANDS – died 1952
1935	Pakistan Test batsman WALLIS MATHIAS – died 1994
1937	Australian swimmer JOHN DEVITT
1937	Norwegian biathlete MAGNAR SOLBERG
1941	New Zealand rugby union centre RON RANGI – died 1988
1959	NFL linebacker LAWRENCE TAYLOR
1961	Canadian Hockey Hall of Fame centre DENIS SAVARD
1962	New Zealand rugby union centre FRANK BUNCE
1963	American synchronised swimmer TRACIE RUIZ
1963	Swiss alpine skier PIRMIN ZURBRRIGGEN
1967	Russian ice skater SERGEI GRINKOV – died 1995
1973	American boxer OSCAR DE LA HOYA
1987	Czech tennis player LUCIE ŠAFÁROVÁ

Tony Dungy, who coached the Indianapolis Colts to triumph in Super Bowl XLI.

❺ FEBRUARY

1923 – Vics' massive tally
Australian state Victoria became the first team in first-class cricket history to amass a four-figure total of runs. Bill Ponsford scored a first-class world record 429 in the Vic's 1,059 against Tasmania in Melbourne.

1943 – 'Sugar' Ray's first loss
American welterweight boxer 'Sugar' Ray Robinson suffered his first defeat when he was upset by middleweight Jake LaMotta in Detroit. Late in the eighth round, Robinson was saved by the bell when the 'Raging Bull' knocked him through the ropes for a count of nine. LaMotta took a unanimous decision, avenging an earlier defeat to Robinson. Robinson had been 85-0 as an amateur, 40-0 as a pro. They would fight 4 more times, Robinson winning each bout.

1960 – Russell's rebound record
Boston centre Bill Russell became the first player to pull down 50 rebounds in an NBA game when he grabbed 3 in the last 36 seconds of the Celtics home match against the Syracuse Nationals. Russell finished with 51, breaking the NBA mark of 49 he had set in 1957.

1984 – 'Iron Gloves' retires
Australian Test wicketkeeper Rod Marsh announced his retirement from international cricket. Marsh played 96 Tests, taking what was then a world record 355 dismissals from 343 catches and 12 stumpings. He scored 3,633 runs at 26.51 with 3 centuries.

2001 – 'Big' Sam's record deal
Sam Allardyce signed a 10-year contract with the newly promoted English Premier League club Bolton Wanderers, the longest management deal to that point in British football history. Allardyce was later sacked when the club was sold to new American owners.

2011 – Pakistan's cricket trio banned
The ICC banned Salman Butt, Mohammad Amir and Mohammad Asif for spot-fixing during the Lord's Test in 2010. They would be able to return to official, sanctioned cricket by 2015. A London court handed out jail terms to three: Butt for 2 years and 6 months, Asif for 1 year, and Amir for 6 months.

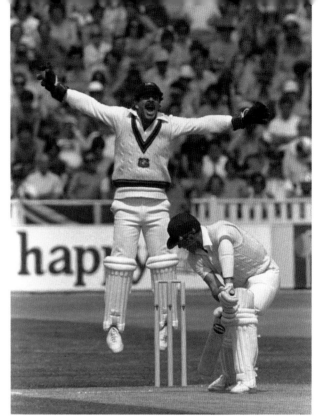

Australian Test wicketkeeper Rod Marsh jumps in the air after catching Geoff Boycott of England at Headingley in Birmingham.

2012 – Eli does it again
Eli Manning and the NY Giants, who had all but given up in mid-December at 7-7, pulled out a fourth-quarter comeback against the New England Patriots to finish a brilliant stretch of play, with a 21-17 victory in Indianapolis for their fourth Super Bowl title.

BIRTHDATES
1889	England Test batsman ELIAS HENDREN – died 1962
1934	Baseball Hall of Fame outfielder HANK AARON
1939	England Test batsman BRIAN LUCKHURST – died 2005
1942	Pro Football Hall of Fame quarterback ROGER STAUBACH
1947	American auto racer DARRELL WALTRIP
1948	Swedish soccer manager SVEN-GÖRAN ERIKSSON
1949	Spanish tennis player MANUEL ORANTES
1960	American golfer JANE GEDDES
1961	New Zealand rugby union player ALBERT ANDERSON
1965	Romanian soccer captain GHEORGE HAGI
1965	Australian boxer JEFF HARDING
1966	Spanish golfer JOSÉ MARÍA OLAZÁBAL
1968	Puerto Rican MLB second baseman ROBERTO ALOMAR
1970	Australian Test batsman DARREN LEHMAN
1984	Argentine soccer forward CARLOS TEVEZ
1985	Portuguese soccer forward CRISTIANO RENALDO

❻ FEBRUARY

1958 – United's Munich air disaster
Eight Manchester United players, 3 club officials and 8 journalists were killed when a British European Airways charter aircraft crashed on takeoff in a blizzard at Munich Airport. United were returning from Belgrade, where they had just beaten Red Star in the European Cup. The United players who were killed included England stars Duncan Edwards, Tommy Taylor, Roger Byrne and David Pegg.

1958 – Williams' big payday
Ted Williams signed a contract with the Boston Red Sox worth $135,000. The deal made him the highest-paid player in Major League Baseball history to that time.

1970 – Pollock's best
South African batsman Graeme Pollock slogged a Test-career best of 274 in the second Test against Australia in Durban. Because of South Africa's sporting isolation in the 1970 and '80s, Pollock played only 23 Tests, scoring 2,256 at 60.97 with 7 centuries.

1990 – First father-son 50
St Louis Blues forward Brett Hull joined father Bobby as the first father-son combination to score 50 goals in a season, when he scored on a breakaway in a 6-4 home win against Toronto. Bobby Hull had scored 50 goals 5 times during a 15-season career with the Chicago Blackhawks (1957–72).

1993 – Tennis loses Ashe
Arthur Ashe, the first African-American to win the US Open (1968), Australian Open (1970) and Wimbledon (1975), died in New York of pneumonia, a complication of AIDS. Ashe contracted the virus through a transfusion of tainted blood during heart surgery in 1983. He was 49.

2000 – Tiger has six straight
Tiger Woods beat Matt Gogel by a stroke in the AT&T Pebble Beach National Pro-Am, taking his PGA winning streak to 6 events.

Arthur Ashe playing at Wimbledon in 1975.

2005 – Pats' back-to-back Super Bowls
The New England Patriots became the eighth team to win consecutive Super Bowls when they beat the Philadelphia Eagles 24-21 in Jacksonville, Florida. The victory moved coach Bill Belichick (10-1) past Vince Lombardi to take the best NFL post-season record.

2012 – Cycling cleans house
Alberto Contador became only the second Tour de France winner to be stripped of his victory, after the Court of Arbitration for Sport slapped a 2-year suspension on the Spaniard for doping in the 2010 race he'd won. Contador joined American Floyd Landis as the only riders at that time to lose their titles. They were followed by Lance Armstrong later that year.

BIRTHDATES
1895	Baseball Hall of Fame slugger BABE RUTH – died 1948
1921	New Zealand rugby union fullback BOB SCOTT – died 2012
1924	England soccer captain BILLY WRIGHT – died 1994
1931	England Test fast bowler FREDDIE TRUEMAN – died 2006
1952	Australian hockey player/coach RIC CHARLESWORTH
1962	Australian jockey GREG CHILDS
1963	England Test batsman DAVID CAPEL
1964	French rugby union flanker LAURENT CABANNES
1970	American golfer TIM HERRON
1983	Australian auto racer JAMIE WHINCUP

➐ FEBRUARY

1949 – Joe's big cheque
Joe DiMaggio signed a contract with the New York Yankees worth $100,000. It was the first six-figure contract in Major League Baseball.

1965 – Clay now Ali
World heavyweight champion Cassius Clay became a Muslim and adopted the name Muhammad Ali. American Islamic movement leader Elijah Muhammad personally named him.

1970 – 'Pistol Pete' scoring record
LSU basketball forward Pete Maravich scored an incredible 47 points in the second half against Alabama to finish with 69, an NCAA record for most points against a Division I opponent. The record lasted 20 years, until Kevin Bradshaw of US International scored 72 against Loyola Marymount in 1991.

1976 – Sutter's NHL 10
Darryl Sutter of the Toronto Maple Leafs created an NHL record of 10 points in 1 regular season game, with 6 goals and 4 assists against the Boston Bruins at Maple Leaf Gardens. Toronto won 11-4.

1994 – MJ tries Baseball
After leading the Chicago Bulls to 3 consecutive NBA Championships, Michael Jordan surprised the sporting world by signing on to play baseball with the Chicago White Sox. He played outfield for the minor league affiliate Birmingham Barons, but never reached the majors. He returned to the Bulls in 1995 and led them to another 3 consecutive NBA titles.

1995 – Mullen first American to 1,000
Joe Mullen of the Pittsburgh Penguins became the first American-born player to score 1,000 points in the NHL. Mullen ended his career with 1,063 career points.

1995 – Gone at the break
English Division 2 soccer club Leyton Orient terminated the contract of defender Terry Howard at halftime, in a 1-0 home loss to Blackpool. Howard's performance was deemed unacceptable.

1997 – McCall meltdown
British heavyweight Lennox Lewis regained the WBC title in a famous Las Vegas rematch with American Oliver McCall, who had stopped him 3 years earlier. Lewis won in the fifth round when McCall suffered a breakdown, crying and refusing to fight.

1999 – Kumble Cricket sweep
Indian spinner Anil Kumble became only the second man, after England's Jim Laker, to take all 10 wickets in a Test innings when he captured 10 for 74 in the second Test against Pakistan at Delhi. All 10 wickets were taken in a devastating spell of 18.2 overs for 37 runs, giving India a 212-run victory, their first win over Pakistan in 20 years.

2005 – Around the World record
Twenty-eight-year-old British sailor Ellen MacArthur crossed the finish line off Ushant to set a new solo, non-stop, round the world record of 71 days, 14 hours, 18 minutes and 33 seconds. The Isle of Wight-based MacArthur, in her B&Q trimaran, took 1 day, 8 hours, 35 minutes, 49 seconds off the previous fastest solo time of Frenchman Francis Joyon in 2004.

2010 – Saints draw big TV crowd
The New Orleans Saints' 31-17 win over the Indianapolis Colts in Super Bowl XLIV became the most watched television program in US history. The game drew 106.5 million viewers, beating the 1983 final of popular TV sitcom M*A*S*H* (105.97 million).

BIRTHDATES
1908	Actor/swimmer BUSTER CRABBE – died 1983
1921	South African Test spinner ATHOL ROWAN – died 1998
1927	Russian distance runner VLADIMIR KUTS – died 1975
1945	Welsh rugby union winger GERALD DAVIES
1949	Brazilian soccer midfielder/coach PAULO CARPEGIANI
1964	American tennis player GRETCHEN MAGERS
1965	American golfer KRISTAL PARKER
1966	East German swimmer KRISTIN OTTO
1968	Czech NHL right wing PETER BONDRA
1968	Canadian swimmer MARK TEWKSBURY
1974	Canadian NBA guard STEVE NASH

Detroit coach Scotty Bowman hoists the Stanley Cup, after his Red Wings swept the 1998 series 4-0 against the Washington Capitals.

1983 – Shergar stolen

1981 English Derby winner Shergar was stolen from the Aga Khan's Ballymany Stud in County Kildare in Ireland. In his career, Shergar had won 6 of 8 races, including a record 10-length win in the Derby. He earned £436,000 for his connections and when Shergar was retired to stud, 34 syndication shares were sold for £250,000 each. Connections failed to pay a £3.9 million ransom demand and the horse was never seen again. It has been speculated the IRA was responsible for the kidnapping. In the absence of a body, insurer Norwich Union refused to pay up.

1994 – Dev delight

Indian fast bowler Kapel Dev became the greatest wicket-taker in Test history when he took his 432nd wicket during the third Test against Sri Lanka in Ahmedabad. Dev had Hashan Tillekeratne caught at short leg by Sanjay Manjrekar to pass the record set by New Zealand fast bowler Richard Hadlee. It was India's ninth consecutive Test win at home.

1997 – Bowman is hockey's best

Scotty Bowman became the first NHL coach to win 1,000 games after the Detroit Red Wings 6-5 overtime victory in Pittsburgh. Bowman retired from coaching in 2002 as the most successful coach in NHL history with 1,244 victories and an astounding .654 winning percentage. His 9 Stanley Cup wins are ranked first. He was inducted into the Hockey Hall of Fame in 1991.

1998 – MJ oldest All-Star

Michael Jordan became the oldest All-Star Game MVP, winning the award 9 days before his 35th birthday. Jordan scored 23 points, grabbed 6 rebounds and also contributed a team-high 8 assists in the East's 135-114 win at New York's Madison Square Garden.

1998 – Ice hockey girls in Olympics

The first-ever female ice hockey game in Winter Olympic history was played at the Nagano Games in Japan. Finland beat Sweden 6-0, and went on to claim the bronze medal behind the United States and Canada.

2000 – Celtic upset defeat

In one of football's biggest upsets, Glasgow Celtic was bundled out of the Scottish FA Cup by First Division part-timers Inverness Caledonian Thistle 3-1 in their third-round match at Parkhead. The defeat led to the sacking of manager John Barnes, along with assistant coach Eric Black. Successful Leicester City manager Martin O'Neill took over and took Celtic to 3 League titles (2001–02, 2004).

2007 – Hockey defenders' record

Colorado Avalanche defenseman Karlis Skrastiņš played his 487th straight game to break the NHL record for consecutive games for a defenseman, during a 6-3 loss to Atlanta in Denver. In 2011, Skrastiņš was killed in the Lokomotiv Yaroslavl air disaster in Russia.

BIRTHDATES

1892	American tennis player ELIZABETH RYAN – died 1979
1929	England soccer defender ROGER BYRNE – died 1958
1959	Swiss tennis player HEINZ GUNTHARDT
1959	Australian equestrian rider ANDREW HOY
1960	Canadian NHL forward DINO CICCARELLI
1963	Indian Test captain MOHAMMAD AZHARUDDIN
1966	Bulgarian soccer striker HRISTO STOICHKOV
1970	NBA centre ALONZO MOURNING
1983	New Zealand rugby winger CORY JANE

❾ FEBRUARY

1952 – Nary's PGA record round
Bill Nary needed just 19 putts, including a PGA Tour record 7 on the back 9 to post a third round of 60 in the El Paso Open. Nary could manage a final-round 74 to finish in 11th place. Cary Middlecoff won with a 269 total.

1963 – British football frozen out
In British football's most weather-affected day, 57 League fixtures, including the entire Scottish programme, were cancelled because of snow and frozen grounds. Only 7 English Football League matches were played.

1979 – Million dollar baby
Trevor Francis became Britain's first £1 million player when he transferred from Birmingham City to Nottingham Forest. Francis made 52 England appearances.

1991 – 'Sugar' Ray pounded by Norris
'Sugar' Ray Leonard lost his WBC light middleweight title, was soundly beaten on points by Terry Norris in New York. Norris floored Leonard in the second and seventh rounds. Leonard announced his retirement after the fight. He made an ill-advised comeback 6 years later in 1997, but was stopped in 5 rounds by Hector Camacho in Atlantic City.

1991 – Shootout record
Craig Hodges of the Chicago Bulls hit 19 consecutive shots to set an All-Star Saturday record in the AT&T Shootout in Charlotte. The streak broke Larry Bird's streak of 11, set in 1986, and helped Hodges capture his second straight shootout title.

1992 – 'Magic' stars after retirement call
Ervin 'Magic' Johnson, playing for the first time since announcing his retirement in November 1991, scored a game-high 25 points and 9 assists to earn his second All-Star Game MVP award. Johnson's Western Conference beat the East 153-113 in Orlando.

1997 – MJ's triple-double
Michael Jordan scored the first triple-double in the history of the NBA All-Star Game, but Glen Rice won the game's MVP award. Rice scored 26 points, a record 24 of them in the second half, to lead the East to a 132-120 victory.

2001 – 'Junior's' ODI record
Mark Waugh hit 16 fours and 3 sixes in an Australian record ODI score of 173, in the second final against the West Indies in Melbourne. The Australians scored an incredible 15th consecutive victory, in a season that had included a 5-0 Test sweep over the West Indies and 10 ODI wins against the Windies and Zimbabwe.

2009 – 'A-Rod' on 'roids
All-Star third baseman Alex Rodriguez, in response to a *Sports Illustrated* report that he failed a drug test, told ESPN he used banned substances while playing with the Texas Rangers from 2001–03 to justify his massive 10-year, $252 million contract.

BIRTHDATES
1905   British hurdler DAVID BURGHLEY – died 1981
1920   New Zealand rugby union captain/coach FRED ALLEN – died 2012
1922   England Test spinner JIM LAKER – died 1986
1928   Dutch football coach RINUS MICHELS – died 2005
1931   Czech soccer midfielder JOSEF MASOPUST
1933   American golfer JO ANN PRENTICE
1946   American golfer BOB EASTWOOD
1949   Scottish golfer BERNARD GALLACHER
1957   Scottish soccer midfielder/manager GORDON STRACHAN
1958   Scottish golfer SANDY LYLE
1961   MLB first baseman JOHN KRUK
1964   England rugby union halfback DEWI MORRIS
1970   Australian Test fast bowler GLENN McGRATH
1971   American golfer MATT GOGEL
1971   Swedish soccer defender JOHAN MJÄLLBY
1972   Hungarian swimmer NORBERT RÓSZA
1975   Dominican MLB outfielder VLADIMIR GUERRERO
1979   Russian figure skater IRINA SLUTSKAYA
1987   German biathlete MAGDALENA NEUNER

⑩ FEBRUARY

1949 – Basketball scoring record
Warriors forward 'Jumpin' Joe Fulks set a new pro scoring record when he accumulated 63 points in a 108-87 win over the Indianapolis Jets in Philadelphia. The previous mark was 48, set by George Mikan. Fulks' record stood for 10 years, until Elgin Baylor scored 64 in 1959.

1983 – Quick three in ice hockey
The Minnesota North Stars and the NY Rangers scored 3 goals in a record 15-second time span during the second period at Minnesota. Mark Pavelich and Ron Greschner scored for the Rangers and Willi Plett replied for the North Stars between 19:18 and 19:33 in Minnesota's 7-5 win.

1992 – Jurisprudence
An Indianapolis jury found former heavyweight champion Mike Tyson guilty of raping an 18-year-old Miss Black America beauty pageant contestant, who said he lured her to his hotel room and overpowered her. The jury also found Tyson guilty of 2 counts of criminal deviate behaviour. He served 3 years of a 6-year sentence.

1999 – Gunners supply 7 for international
Seven Arsenal players featured in the England-France match at Wembley Stadium. Martin Keown, Tony Adams, Lee Dixon and David Seaman started for England, whilst Nicolas Anelka and Emmanuel Petit started for France, and Patrick Vieira substituted for Anelka. France won 2-0, Anelka scoring both goals.

2003 – Zimbabwe protest
Zimbabwe Test batsman Andy Flower and fast bowler Henry Olonga wore black armbands at the start of the World Cup, in a brave protest against President Robert Mugabe's tyrannical regime. Both men were forced into exile and international retirement after the tournament. Flower played Sheffield Shield cricket in Australia and Olonga played county cricket in England.

2011 – Enough Jazz
Basketball Hall of Fame coach Jerry Sloan resigned, after 23 years at the helm of the Utah Jazz. Sloan had a

A statue of one of Arsenal's favourite sons, Tony Adams, stands outside Emirates Stadium. Adams was one of seven players to appear in a 1999 England-France match. Photo: Ronnie Macdonald (Flickr: Arsenal Stadium Tony Adams Statue 2) [CC-BY-2.0], via Wikimedia Commons.

career record of 1221-803, for a winning percentage of 60.3%. He was third all-time among NBA coaches in wins, trailing only Don Nelson and Lenny Wilkens, and was the only coach to win 1,000 games with 1 team.

BIRTHDATES
1893	American tennis player BILL TILDEN – died 1953
1901	American golfer ED DUDLEY – died 1963
1907	New Zealand rugby union hooker BEAU COTTRELL – died 1988
1909	New Zealand rugby union winger GEORGE HART – died 1944
1926	Northern Ireland soccer captain DANNY BLANCHFLOWER – died 1993
1941	England Test batsman JOHN HAMPSHIRE
1950	American swimmer MARK SPITZ
1955	Australian golfer GREG NORMAN
1963	MLB outfielder LENNY DYKSTRA
1964	Canadian swimmer VICTOR DAVIS – died 1989
1967	Australian golfer BRAD HUGHES
1969	South African rugby union captain JAMES SMALL
1970	Moroccan soccer defender NOUREDDINE NAYBET
1972	Australian Test fast bowler MICHAEL KASPROWICZ
1974	England rugby union/NZ league utility back HENRY PAUL
1982	American sprinter JUSTIN GATLIN

⑪ FEBRUARY

1948 – Worrell Test debut
West Indian cricket great Sir Frank Worrell made his Test debut against England at Port-of-Spain. The future Windies captain scored 97 and 28 not out. One of the great gentlemen of cricket went on to play 51 Tests, scoring 3,860 runs at 49.48 with 9 centuries.

1949 – Pep's one-of-four
In a renewal of one of boxing's greatest match-ups, Willie Pep won a 15-round decision from Sandy Saddler in New York to regain the world featherweight title. It was the second of 4 meetings for the pair. Saddler finished with a 3-1 advantage, whilst Pep went on to be one of the sport's best referees.

1973 – Palmer's final PGA victory
Arnold Palmer won his fifth Bob Hope Desert Golf Classic, beating Jack Nicklaus and Johnny Miller by 2 strokes at Bermuda Dunes. It was his 62nd and final win on the PGA Tour.

1976 – British first in figure skating
John Curry became the first British male to win an Olympic figure skating gold medal when he won at the Innsbruck Games.

1984 – First ODI tie
Australia and the West Indies played out the first ever tied match in a limited overs tournament in the second ODI final at the MCG. Chasing the Windies 222-5, the Australians were 213-9 after 49 overs, needing 10 off the final over to win. With the scores level, Carl Rackemann was run out off the last ball for the tie.

1990 – Tyson's first defeat
American fighter James 'Buster' Douglas stunned the boxing world when he knocked out unbeaten Mike Tyson in the 10th round of their heavyweight title fight in Tokyo. Douglas recovered from an eighth-round knockdown to claim *The Ring* magazine's Upset of the Year. However, his reign as heavyweight champion was short-lived. In his first title defence, Douglas was knocked out by Evander Holyfield in the third round in Las Vegas.

Arnold Palmer, pictured in 1961.

1998 – Golf cart OK
A court ruled that professional golfer Casey Martin, the victim of a circulatory problem in his right leg, had won the right to use a golf cart during PGA Tour events. It was the first time the Americans with Disabilities Act had been applied to a professional sport.

2001 – 50th NBA All-Star game
The East came back from a 19-point deficit after 3 quarters to score a dramatic 111-110 victory over the West, in the 50th NBA All-Star Game in Washington D.C. Allen Iverson scored 15 of his game-high 25 points in the fourth quarter to be named MVP.

2011 – Cavs losing streak ends
Antawn Jamison's 3-pointer, with 22 seconds left, helped the Cleveland Cavaliers end an NBA-record, 26-game losing streak with a 126-119 win over the LA Clippers in Cleveland.

BIRTHDATES
1909	American boxer MAX BAER – died 1959
1924	American tennis player BUDGE PATTY
1934	British auto racer JOHN SURTEES
1937	Australian Test captain BILL LAWRY
1938	New Zealand Test all rounder BEVAN CONGDON
1945	Australian middle distance runner RALPH DOUBELL
1959	Brazilian auto racer ROBERTO MORENO
1963	Spanish soccer midfielder/manager JOSE MARI BAKERO
1965	Australian netball captain VICKI WILSON
1972	England soccer midfielder STEVE McMANAMAN
1972	American surfer KELLY SLATER
1974	England soccer winger/manager NICK BARMBY
1982	Australian snooker player NEIL ROBERTSON
1983	Dutch soccer midfielder RAFAEL VAN DER VAART

1908 – Inaugural NY to Paris Rally

The New York-to-Paris auto race got underway with teams from France, Italy and the United States taking part. After driving across North America, cars were taken over the Pacific Ocean by boat, and then driven through Siberia and Europe to reach Paris. The race ended on July 30, with the American team winning.

1964 – Benaud bows out

Australian cricket captain Richie Benaud played the final day of his 63-Test career in the fifth Test against South Africa in Sydney. He bowed out with 14 runs and 4 wickets as Australia squared the series 1-1 with a draw. Benaud finished with 2,201 runs at 24.45, and 248 Test wickets at 27.03. He never captained Australia to a series defeat.

1984 – Yarborough quick at Daytona

Cale Yarborough became the first driver to qualify for the Daytona 500 at above 200 miles per hour. Yarborough went on to win his second consecutive Daytona event ahead of Dale Earnhardt and Darrell Waltrip. He was the first driver since Richard Petty in 1974–75 to win back-to-back 500s.

1989 – Record NBA All-Star crowd

The largest crowd in NBA All-Star history turned out at the Houston Astrodome to watch the West beat the East 143-134. A crowd of 44,735 saw Karl Malone of the Utah Jazz win MVP honours, having scoring a team-high 28 points.

1999 – Waugh 40th Oz Test skipper

Steve Waugh was appointed Australia's 40th Test captain, replacing Mark Taylor. Taylor had captained the side in 50 Tests for 26 wins, 13 losses and 11 draws, and a winning percentage of 52%. Waugh proved to be as tactically astute, but a far more aggressive leader than Taylor, with 41 wins, 9 losses and 7 draws from 57 Tests as captain. He retired in 2004 and was succeeded by Ricky Ponting.

2003 – Youthful Rooney

Wayne Rooney, then of Everton, became England's youngest international when he debuted in a friendly

England's Wayne Rooney above Australian captain Craig Moore, during the Socceroos' 3-1 upset win at Upton Park in 2003.

against Australia at Upton Park, aged 17 years, 111 days. Australia scored an upset 3-1 win.

BIRTHDATES

1926	MLB catcher/sport caster JOE GARAGIOLA
1933	Australian rugby league winger BRIAN CARLSON – died 1987
1934	Basketball Hall of Fame centre BILL RUSSELL
1935	American golfer KEN STILL
1944	American tennis player CHARLIE PASARELL
1949	Australian horse trainer JOHN HAWKES
1949	Indian Test batsman GUNDAPPA VISWANATH
1952	Scotland rugby union centre JIM RENWICK
1953	Irish golfer DES SMYTH
1956	Croatian soccer manager VELIMIR ZAJEC
1963	NFL tight end BRENT JONES
1969	English javelin thrower STEVE BACKLEY
1970	Dutch soccer winger BRYAN ROY
1974	British boxer PRINCE NASEEM HAMED
1976	New Zealand rugby union fullback CHRISTIAN CULLEN
1980	Spanish tennis player JUAN CARLOS FERRERO
1984	American auto racer BRAD KESELOWSKI
1990	NFL quarterback ROBERT GRIFFIN III

⓭ FEBRUARY

1954 – College Basketball ton
Frank Selvy of Furman University scored an even 100 points on 41 field goals and 18 free throws in a 149-95 victory over Newberry College. Selvy's points haul still remains the NCAA Division I record.

1965 – Magnificent Pollock
South African batsman Graeme Pollock became only the second man, after George Headley, to hit 3 Test hundreds before the age of 21, when he smashed 18 fours in 137 in the fifth Test against England at Port Elizabeth. Pollock added 77 not out off 77 balls in the second innings, boosting his average to 53.58 from 11 Tests. Manhood made him an even better player – in 12 further Tests, he averaged 67.

1983 – Aoki first Japanese PGA winner
Isao Aoki became the first Japanese winner on the PGA Tour when he won the Hawaiian Open. Aoki holed out a 128-yard pitching wedge approach for an eagle on the par-5 72nd hole to beat Jack Renner by 1 stroke. In 2004, he became the first Japanese man to be inducted into the World Golf Hall of Fame.

1990 – Bird's free throw streak over
Larry Bird ended the third-highest free throw streak in NBA history, at 71 in the Boston Celtics 107-94 win at Houston. Michael Williams of the Minnesota Timberwolves set the record in 1993, hitting 97 consecutive free throws.

1995 – Amazing Ambrose
West Indian fast bowler Courtney Walsh finished the second Test against New Zealand in Wellington with magnificent match figures of 13 for 55. The Windies went on to thrash the Kiwis by an innings and 322 runs, the fourth-biggest victory in Test history at that time.

2000 – Tall Timber domination
The all-7ft starting frontcourt of the West All-Stars – made up of Shaquille O'Neal, Tim Duncan and Kevin Garnett – combined for 70 points and 33 rebounds in the All-Star game in Oakland. The West held off several strong challenges from the East to score a

Japan's first PGA Tour winner, Isao Aoki.

137-126 victory. O'Neal and Duncan shared MVP honours.

BIRTHDATES
1918	American golfer PATTY BERG – died 2006
1935	American golfer TOMMY JACOBS
1947	American basketball coach MIKE KRZYZEWSKI
1950	Australian Test fast bowler LEN PASCOE
1956	Irish soccer midfielder LIAM BRADY
1971	Swedish ice hockey player MATS SUNDIN
1977	NFL receiver RANDY MOSS
1979	Mexican soccer defender RAFAEL MARQUEZ
1980	German soccer midfielder SEBASTIAN KEHL
1981	Brazilian soccer defender LUISÃO

⑭ FEBRUARY

1896 – Proteas low score

England dismissed South Africa for 30 in the first Test at Port Elizabeth. It was their lowest score in Test history and the second-lowest of all-time. England fast bowler George Lohmann captured 7-38 in the first innings and a remarkable 8-7 in the second, the last 3 wickets falling in consecutive balls for a hat-trick. The match was over inside 2 days.

1951 – Rampaging Robinson

'Sugar' Ray Robinson scored a 13th-round TKO win over Jake La Motta to win the world middleweight title in Chicago. The press dubbed the bout 'The Saint Valentines Day Massacre'. It was the first time a world welterweight champion won the middleweight crown.

1984 – Bolero gold for Torvill & Dean

British ice dancers Jayne Torvill and Christopher Dean performed their famous *Bolero* routine to win the gold medal at the Sarajevo Winter Olympic Games.
The judges awarded them a total of 12 – perfect 6.0 scores – including all 9 for artistic impression.

1988 – 'Elderly' Allison

At age 50, Bobby Allison became the oldest driver to win the Daytona 500. The milestone was achieved in an incredible 195mph final lap, against his 26-year-old son Davey. Bobby won by 2½ car lengths for his third Daytona 500. It was the first time a father and son finished first and second at Daytona, and the first time in any NASCAR race since Lee and Richard Petty finished 1-2 in a minor race in 1960.

1993 – Five-round record

Tom Kite dominated the field with rounds of 67-67-64-65-62 to win the Bob Hope Chrysler Classic by 6 strokes. His total of 325 set a PGA Tour record for low 90-hole scores.

2003 – Vaas ODI hat-trick

Sri Lankan paceman Chaminda Vaas became the first bowler to take a hat-trick with the first 3 balls of a ODI match, against Bangladesh at Pietermaritzburg. Vaas owned the best bowling figures in one-day cricket, 8 for 19 against Zimbabwe.

Jayne Torvill and Christopher Dean during their gold medal winning free dance program at the Sarajevo Winter Olympics in 1984.

2010 – Record NBA crowd

A basketball record 108,713 fans attended the NBA All-Star Game at the new Cowboys Stadium in Arlington, Texas, to watch the East defeat the West 141-139. Dwyane Wade scored a game-high 28 points and won MVP honors.

BIRTHDATES

1923	American golfer JAY HEBERT – died 1997
1931	Canadian Hockey HOF right wing BERNIE GEOFFRION – died 2006
1935	American golfer MICKEY WRIGHT
1943	American golfer BOB MURPHY
1944	Swedish auto racer RONNIE PETERSON – died 1978
1951	England soccer forward KEVIN KEEGAN
1953	Austrian soccer striker HANS KRANKL
1959	England soccer defender RUSSELL OSMON
1960	NFL quarterback JIM KELLY
1962	French rugby union centre PHILLIPPE SELLA
1965	New Zealand rugby union flanker ZINZAN BROOKE
1966	Czech NHL defenseman PETR SVOBODA
1968	England Test all-rounder CHRIS LEWIS
1972	NFL quarterback DREW BLEDSOE
1973	NFL quarterback STEVE McNAIR – died 2009
1983	Australian rugby union captain ROCKY ELSOM
1983	French soccer defender BACARY SAGNA
1988	Argentine soccer winger ANGEL DI MARIA

⑮ FEBRUARY

1921 – Mailey misses perfect haul
Australian spinner Arthur Mailey captured 9-121 off 47 overs in the fourth Test against England in Melbourne. He took 4 for 115 in the England first innings, for match figures of 13 for 236. Australia won by 8 wickets.

1960 – Grout catches 8
Australian Test wicketkeeper Wally Grout set a first-class world record when he caught out 8 batsmen in an innings, in a Sheffield Shield match between Queensland and West Australia in Brisbane. The record now stands at nine, set by Indian wicketkeeper Tahir Rasheed in 1992–93 and equalled by W. R. James in Zimbabwe in 1995–96.

1978 – Spinks upsets Ali
Leon Spinks unseated Muhammad Ali as World Heavyweight Champion when he won on a split-points decision in Las Vegas. Spinks was stripped of the WBC version of the title when he decided to take a big-money rematch with Ali, instead of fighting leading contender Ken Norton. Ali won the rematch in a unanimous points decision.

1978 – First Kiwi win over England
New Zealand fast bowler Richard Hadlee took 6 for 26 off 13 overs, seeing England dismissed for a meagre 64 in the first Test in Wellington. England's 72-run loss was their first-ever Test defeat to the Kiwis.

1989 – Warriors' NBA record
Golden State tied their own NBA record when they picked up 25 steals against San Antonio, in a 133-96 win at the Oakland Coliseum. The Warriors' record was originally set in 1975 in a 139-122 home win over the LA Lakers. The Seattle SuperSonics broke the tie when they tallied 27 steals against Toronto in 1997.

1992 – Gunners' goal glut
Arsenal scored 6 goals in a record 18-minute period of their Division 1 match against Sheffield Wednesday at Highbury. The Gunners scored the 6 between the 71st and 89th minutes in their 7-1 victory.

In 2011, ten years after his tragic death during lap three of the race, fans at the Daytona 500 raise three fingers in the air to honour driver Dale Earnhardt. Photo: US Army (Flickr: 3 Fingers For Dale) [CC-BY-2.0], via Wikimedia Commons.

1998 – Daytona win for patient Earnhardt
In his 20th attempt, 7-time Winston Cup champion Dale Earnhardt won his first Daytona 500. He led 5 times for 107 of the 200 laps, averaging 172.7mph as he ended a 59-race winless streak. In 2001, Earnhardt was tragically killed in a last lap crash at the event.

2008 – Fossett legally dead
American millionaire adventurer Steve Fossett was declared legally dead. The previous September, Fossett took off alone in a single-engine 2-seater plane near Yerington, Nevada. He was scheduled to be back by noon but never returned, subsequent extensive searches revealing nothing.

BIRTHDATES
1929	English auto racer GRAHAM HILL – died 1975
1937	Dutch soccer forward COEN MOULIJN – died 2011
1949	NFL quarterback KEN ANDERSON
1956	West Indian Test batsman DESMOND HAYNES
1960	New Zealand rugby union flanker JOCK HOBBS – died 2012
1960	NFL cornerback DARRELL GREEN
1964	NBA guard MARK PRICE
1965	South African Test fast bowler CRAIG MATTHEWS
1972	Czech NHL forward JAROMIR JAGR
1973	American swimmer AMY VAN DYKEN

1933 – 'Bodyline' series goes to England

England claimed the infamous 'Bodyline' series when they beat Australia by 6 wickets in the fourth Test in Brisbane. England needed 160 on the final day. They also won the fifth Test in Sydney for a controversial 4-1 series win.

1966 – Famous triple ton

Australian batsman Bob Cowper completed his famous innings of 307 in the drawn fifth Test against England in Melbourne. Cowper hit 20 fours in his 727-minute epic.

1968 – Brits win longest doubles match

England's Mark Cox and Bob Wilson beat the American pair Charlie Pasarell and Bob Holmberg at the US Indoor Tennis Championships, in the then longest doubles match in history. Cox and Wilson won 26-24, 17-19, 30-28 in 6 hours, 23 minutes.

1972 – Chamberlain first to 30,000

Wilt Chamberlain became the first player in NBA history to reach 30,000 career points. The Los Angeles Lakers' 7ft 1in centre reached the milestone in a 110-109 loss to the Suns in Phoenix. No other player in the NBA at that point had scored even 25,000. It was his thirteenth year in the League.

1992 – Martina is the 'greatest'

Martina Navratilova became the most successful tennis player of all-time when she beat Jana Novotná 7-6, 4-6, 7-5 in Chicago for her 158th career singles title. Navratilova went on to win 167 singles titles, including 18 Grand Slam victories.

1996 – Kirsten's World Cup best

South African opener Gary Kirsten smashed 188 off 159 balls against the United Arab Emirates in Rawalpindi for the highest ever individual score in World Cup matches, surpassing IVA Richards' 181 against Sri Lanka at Karachi in 1987.

2002 – First Chinese winter gold

Yang Yang won China's first ever Winter Olympics gold medal when she took out the 500m short track speed skating at Salt Lake City. The victory ended more than a decade of frustration for China's winter athletes. In 3 previous Games, China had captured 14 medals, but never managed a gold.

2002 – Corner kick specialist

Wigan Athletic's Northern Ireland international Peter Kennedy scored all 4 goals in the Latics 4-0 win over Cardiff City in the Division 2 match at the JJB Stadium. All 4 of Kennedy's scores were headed from corner-kicks.

2002 – Australian Winter Games first

Stephen Bradbury won Australia's first Winter Olympics gold medal in an amazing 1,000m short track speed skating final in Salt Lake City. Bradbury won when all the other competitors in the race fell, after the leading skaters collided, leaving only Bradbury standing; he had been coming last at the time.

2005 – NHL cancels season

The NHL became the first major professional league in North America to cancel an entire season because of a labour dispute. The sticking point in the negotiation between the Players Association and the NHL owners was the proposed introduction of a salary cap. It was the first time the Stanley Cup was not awarded since a flu epidemic cancelled the finals in 1919.

BIRTHDATES

1902	South African Test spinner CYRIL VINCENT – died 1968
1924	Australian horse trainer COLIN HAYES – died 1999
1934	American golfer MARLENE BAUER HAGGE
1954	West Indies Test fast bowler MICHAEL HOLDING
1958	American golfer JOHN MORSE
1959	American tennis player JOHN McENROE
1964	Brazilian soccer forward BEBETO
1972	NFL running back JEROME BETTIS
1973	Australian middle distance runner CATHY FREEMAN
1979	Italian motorcycle rider VALENTINO ROSSI

⑰ FEBRUARY

1924 – Tarzan's final swim record
American Olympic champion Johnny Weissmuller lowered his own 100m freestyle world record time from 58.6 to 57.4 seconds in Miami. It was the Weissmuller's final world record swim for this distance; the record stood for 10 years.

1973 – Redmond's one and only Test
New Zealand opener Rodney Redmond scored 107 and 56 in his Test debut, in the drawn third Test against Pakistan in Auckland. It was the only Test he ever played. Thereafter he had trouble with contact lenses and his form suffered.

1976 – 'King' Richard prevails
New Zealand fast bowler Richard Hadlee took 7 for 23 in a match-winning spell against India in the third Test in Wellington. It was the Kiwis' first innings victory, Hadlee being dominant with match figures of 11 for 58. The match also marked the final Test for popular wicketkeeper Ken Wadsworth, who was ill with cancer and died later that year.

1994 – Robinson rumble
San Antonio's David Robinson recorded the fifth quadruple-double in NBA history, with 34 points, 10 rebounds, 10 assists and 10 blocks in the Spurs' 115-96 win over visiting Detroit. Other NBA quadruple-doubles had been compiled by Hakeem Olajuwon (1990, twice), Alvin Robertson (1986) and Nate Thurmond (1974).

1998 – US ice hockey Czech-mated
Led by star goal tender Dominik Hašek, the Czech Republic upset the United States 4-1 in a preliminary-round match at the Nagano Olympic Games. Mike Modano scored first for the US, but a 3-0 second period virtually wrapped up the game for the Czechs. Hašek stopped 38 shots. The loss was a blow for the US, who failed to qualify for the medal round, while the Czechs went on to beat Canada 2-1 in the semi-final, and Russia, 1-0 for the gold medal.

Czech goalie Dominik Hašek during his team's gold-medal-winning effort against Russia at the 1998 Nagano Winter Olympics.

2008 – 50th Daytona
Driving for the Roger Penske team, Ryan Newman won the 50th running of the Daytona 500. It was the first restrictor-plate win for Penske Racing.

2010 – Vonn's downhill gold
Lindsey Vonn shook off a shin injury to tear down Whistler Mountain and give the United States its first-ever women's Olympic downhill gold medal. Meanwhile, American speed skater Shani Davis became the first skater to win the 1,000m gold medal twice at the Winter Games.

BIRTHDATES
1916	Australian Test wicketkeeper DON TALLON – died 1984
1919	American tennis player JOE HUNT – died 1945
1931	NFL coach BUDDY RYAN
1936	Pro Football Hall of Fame running back JIM BROWN
1936	Australian Test wicketkeeper BARRY JARMAN
1946	Danish yachtsman VALDEMAR BANDOLOWSKI
1959	American swimmer ROWDY GAINES
1963	Basketball Hall of Fame forward MICHAEL JORDAN
1966	Canadian Hockey Hall of Fame winger LUC ROBITAILLE
1970	French rugby union winger PHILIPPE BERNET-SALLAS
1973	French rugby union captain RAPHAEL IBANEZ
1982	Brazilian soccer forward ADRIANO
1989	British swimmer REBECCA ADLINGTON

⑱ FEBRUARY

1969 – Walters' golden patch
Doug Walters scored 103 in the second innings, following on from his 242 in the first innings, during the fifth Test against the West Indies in Sydney. It was the flamboyant Walters' fourth 100 in 5 innings, leading Australia to a 382-run win and a 3-1 series win.

1978 – Inaugural Hawaiian Iron Man
The first Hawaiian Iron Man Triathlon was run on the island of Kona. Honolulu fitness instructor Gordon Haller was the inaugural race winner, in 11 hours, 46 minutes. The first Ironman Triathlon was contested to settle a debate amongst friends over who was the fittest athlete – a runner, a cyclist or a swimmer. Each discipline existed as a separate event, so to determine who was truly the 'Iron Man', they put all 3 together.

1986 – Basketball's second quad-double
San Antonio shooting guard Alvin Robertson recorded only the second quadruple-double in NBA history with 20 points, 11 rebounds, 10 assists and 10 steals in the Spurs' 120-114 win over Phoenix. Nate Thurmond first achieved the feat in 1974.

2002 – Oz aerial success
Little-known Australian Alisa Camplin nailed both jumps to claim the aerials gold medal in the freestyle skiing section at the Salt Lake City Winter Olympics. Camplin went on to dominate the sport over the next 2 years, winning the World Cup series and World Championships.

2001 – Earnhardt racing tragedy
Seven-time Winston Cup champion Dale Earnhardt died in a 180mph last-lap crash at the Daytona 500 in Florida. Earnhardt was the 27th driver to die at Daytona since the track opened in 1959. He was 49.

2003 – 'Lack' of the Irish
David Healy scored in Belfast to end Northern Ireland's world record for non-scoring in soccer. The Irishmen hadn't scored a goal in 13 international matches, spanning a period of 2 years, 5 days. They lost the Belfast match, 4-1 against Norway.

Australian aerials gold medallist Alisa Camplin at the 2002 Salt Lake City Winter Olympics.

2006 – Davis the first
Twenty-three-year-old Chicago native Shani Davis became the first black athlete to claim an individual gold medal in Winter Olympic history, winning the 1,000m speed skating race in Turin. He duplicated the feat in Vancouver in 2010, becoming the first man to successfully defend the 1000m title.

BIRTHDATES
1898	Italian motor engineer ENZO FERRARI – died 1988
1926	Pro Football Hall of Fame defensive end LEN FORD – died 1972
1927	Pakistan Test fast bowler FAZAL MAHMOOD – died 2005
1931	Pro Football Hall of Fame tackle BOB ST. CLAIR
1933	England soccer manager SIR BOBBY ROBSON – died 2009
1938	England Test all-rounder BARRY KNIGHT
1945	American golfer JUDY RANKIN
1947	Spanish golfer JOSÉ MARIA CAÑIZARES
1947	Portuguese distance runner CARLOS LOPES
1948	Australian Test opener BRUCE FRANCIS
1954	England rugby union prop PAUL RENDELL
1957	German sprinter MARITA KOCH
1959	England rugby union fly-half HEW DAVIS
1960	Canadian NHL goalie ANDY MOOG
1963	England rugby union fly-half ROB ANDREW
1966	England Test fast bowler PHIL DE FREITAS
1967	Italian soccer forward ROBERTO BAGGIO
1969	Russian NHL forward ALEXANDER MOGILNY
1971	Swedish golfer THOMAS BJØRN
1973	French soccer midfielder CLAUDE MAKÉLÉLÉ
1974	Russian tennis player YVGENY KAFELNIKOV
1975	England soccer defender GARY NEVILLE
1981	Russian NBA forward ANDREI KIRILENKO

⑲ FEBRUARY

Striker Alan Shearer (right) in his England debut against France at Wembley Stadium.

1977 – Doug's double ton
Doug Walters and all-rounder Gary Gilmore compiled an Australian record seventh-wicket partnership of 217 in the first Test against New Zealand in Christchurch. Walters finished with 250 and Gilmore 101.

1975 – 'Sir' Gary
West Indian cricket captain Garfield Sobers was knighted by the Queen during her state visit to his native Barbados. Other West Indian cricketers to be knighted include Everton Weekes, Clyde Walcott, Vivian Richards, Frank Worrell, Wes Hall, Conrad Hunte and Learie Constantine.

1980 – 'Beefy's' record
Champion England all-rounder Ian Botham became the first man to score a century and take 10 wickets in a Test during the Golden Jubilee match against India in Bombay. In a stellar all-round performance, Botham took 6 for 58 and 7 for 48, and smacked 114. He also shared a sixth-wicket partnership of 171 with wicketkeeper Bob Taylor. Taylor was also in fine form behind the stumps, taking 10 catches to set a new Test record.

1984 – Alpine brotherly love
Phil and Steve Mahre of the US became the first brothers to win gold and silver medals in one Winter Olympic event. Phil won the gold medal and Steve the silver in the men's slalom at the Sarajevo Olympics in Yugoslavia.

1992 – Shearer scores on debut
Future captain Alan Shearer scored on his England debut against the highly rated France at Wembley Stadium. England won 2-0 as the French crashed to their first defeat in 20 international matches.

1994 – Blair x three gold
American skater Bonnie Blair became the first woman in Winter Olympic history to win the same event at 3 consecutive Games. Blair won her third consecutive 500m sprint at the Lillehammer Games in Norway.

1995 – Marlin repeats at Daytona
Sterling Marlin led for 105 of the 200 laps to become the first driver since Cale Yarborough (1983–84) to win back-to-back Daytona 500s. Except for pit stops, Marlin never lost the lead in the rain-affected race. Amazingly, the 2 Daytona 500 victories were Marlin's only wins in his 310-race Winston Cup career.

2006 – Mac is back
47-year-old John McEnroe completed his ATP Tour comeback, teaming with Jonas Björkman to beat Paul Goldstein and Jim Thomas 7-6, 4-6, 10-7 in the final of the SAP Open in San Jose. It was McEnroe's 78th career doubles victory, and his first ATP final since winning a doubles tournament in Paris with his brother Patrick in 1992.

BIRTHDATES
1916	American jockey EDDIE ARCARO – died 1997
1937	Australian Test batsman NORM O'NEILL – died 2008
1942	Pro Football Hall of Fame defensive back PAUL KRAUSE
1952	New Zealand rugby union number 8 GARY SEEAR
1953	NFL/College Football coach JUNE JONES
1954	Brazilian soccer midfielder SÓCRATES – died 2011
1957	MLB pitcher DAVE STEWART
1961	American golfer ERNIE GONZALEZ
1962	Czech tennis player HANA MANDLIKOVÁ
1966	Belgian soccer midfielder ENZO SCIFO
1966	Dutch tennis player PAUL HAAHUIS
1971	Australian golfer RICHARD GREEN
1977	Italian soccer defender GIANLUCA ZAMBROTTA
1980	NFL linebacker DWIGHT FREENEY
1986	Brazilian soccer forward MARTA

㉜ FEBRUARY

1955 – Four-round record to Souchak
Mike Souchak posted a record 4-round total of 31-under par 257 to win the Texas Open in freezing temperatures at Brackenridge Park in San Antonio. The score remained the 72-hole record on the PGA Tour until 2001. His back 9 of 27 was also a PGA record.

1963 – 'Davo' takes wicket with final ball
Australian all-rounder Alan Davidson took a wicket with his last ball in Test cricket, when he had Alan Smith caught at first slip by Bob Simpson for 1, in the fifth Test against England in Sydney. Davidson played 44 Tests, scoring 1,328 at 24.59. He also took 186 wickets at 20.53, with a Test best 7-93.

1971 – Fast 50 to Esposito
Phil Esposito of the Boston Bruins scored his 50th goal of the season, as the fastest to reach that milestone in NHL history. The feat was achieved on his 29th birthday, and he went on to score an NHL season record of 76 goals.

1995 – Gunners' manager an agent too
The Premier League Commission found Arsenal manager George Graham guilty of taking a cut of the £285,000 transfer fee for Swedish international John Jensen. He was sacked by Arsenal the following day.

1998 – Youthful gold to Tara
Fifteen-year-old Tara Lipinski gave a brilliant freestyle performance to become the youngest-ever Olympic gold medal winner in women's figure skating, at the Nagano Games in Japan. Lipinski was 2 months younger than Sonja Henie had been when she won the first of her 3 Olympic titles in 1928.

1998 – Czech mate
The Czech Republic's ice hockey team shocked the powerful Canadian team 2-1 in an overtime shootout, advancing to the Olympic gold medal game against Russia in Nagano. Robert Reichel scored the winner for the Czechs, who went on to win the gold medal 1-0. Finland won bronze with a 3-2 upset of Canada.

American figure skater Tara Lipinski during her gold-medal free skate routine at the 1998 Nagano Winter Olympics.

1999 – Toronto treasure
The $265 million Air Canada Centre was opened in Toronto, replacing the legendary Maple Leaf Gardens, which was considered too small and rundown for the staging of modern events. The opening NHL game saw the Toronto Maple Leafs take on Canadian rivals the Montreal Canadiens in a 3-2 OT win.

2011 – Bayne youngest Daytona winner
Twenty-year-old Trevor Bayne, in the Wood Brothers throwback no. 21 Ford, became the youngest driver to win the Daytona 500, when he crossed the finish line 0.118 seconds ahead of Carl Edwards.

BIRTHDATES
1934	American auto racer BOBBY UNSER
1937	American auto team owner ROGER PENSKE
1940	England soccer striker JIMMY GREAVES
1942	Canadian Hockey Hall of Fame centre PHIL ESPOSITO
1944	Dutch soccer midfielder/manager WILLEM VAN HANEGEM
1947	English soccer forward PETER OSGOOD – died 2006
1949	England Test spinner EDDIE HEMMINGS
1951	England soccer defender PHIL NEAL
1961	American swimmer STEVE LUNDQUIST
1963	Basketball Hall of Fame forward CHARLES BARKLEY
1963	Swedish tennis player JOAKIM NYSTRÖM
1964	American golfer JEFF MAGGERT
1971	South African rugby union halfback JOOST VAN DER WESTHUIZEN
1977	NBA guard STEPHON MARBURY
1983	MLB pitcher JUSTIN VERLANDER

㉑ FEBRUARY

1924 – Golf blitz
Australian golfer and trick-shot specialist Joe Kirkwood won the Corpus Christi Open by an amazing 16 strokes from Bobby Cruickshank. Kirkwood fired a total 285.

1960 – Wilt's rookie record
Wilt Chamberlain tied his NBA rookie record when he scored 58 points in the Philadelphia Warriors' 129-122 win over the Knicks in New York.

1970 – Football merge = NFL
The American and National Football Leagues officially merged, creating a new 26-team NFL. The Baltimore Colts, Cleveland Browns, and Pittsburgh Steelers joined the 10 former AFL teams in the league's American Football Conference, while the other 13 NFL teams were grouped in the National Football Conference.

1970 – Hull only the third to 500
Bobby Hull became only the third player in NHL history to score 500 career goals, joining Maurice Richard and Gordie Howe in the exclusive club. The 31-year-old, 13-year veteran, scored twice in Chicago's 4-2 win over the NY Rangers. Hull finished his NHL career with 610 goals in 1,063 games.

1993 – First win to lefty Mickelson
Phil Mickelson, arguably golf's best left-handed player ever, won his first PGA Tour event as a professional, capturing the Buick Invitational at Torrey Pines. Mickelson won by 4 strokes over Dave Rummells.

1993 – Jazz pair make history
Utah Jazz pair John Stockton and Karl Malone became the first players to be on the same team and share the All-Star Game MVP award. Malone scored a game-high 28 points and Stockton added 15 assists as the West defeated the East 135-132 in the All-Star game in Salt Lake City.

1994 – Waugh's bowling best
Steve Waugh captured a career-best 5 for 28 to steer Australia to an easy 5-wicket victory over South Africa in the second Test in Cape Town. Best known for his batting (with a 51.06 Test average) and astute

NBA great Wilt Chamberlain, rebounding for the LA Lakers against the Philadelphia 76ers at the Great Western Forum in 1973.

captaincy, Waugh captured 92 Test wickets at a modest 37.44.

1998 – George cracks 15ft mark
Australian pole-vaulter Emma George became the first woman to vault to the 15-feet mark. George cleared an even 15ft at the Robin Tait Classic in Auckland, New Zealand, breaking the world record of 14ft, 11in.

BIRTHDATES
1937	Australian distance runner RON CLARKE
1938	New Zealand rugby union flanker KELVIN TREMAIN – died 1992
1940	English auto racer PETER GETHIN – died 2011
1945	English golfer MAURICE BEMBRIDGE
1949	Swedish soccer goalkeeper RONNIE HELLSTRÖM
1958	MLB shortstop/manager ALAN TRAMMELL
1963	New Zealand golfer GREG TURNER
1967	American sprinter LEROY BURRELL
1969	Austrian alpine skier PETRA KRONBERGER
1970	Australian Test batsman MICHAEL SLATER
1971	Swedish golfer PIERRE FULKE
1972	South African rugby union number 8 MARK ANDREWS
1984	New Zealand rugby union halfback ANDREW ELLIS

1930 – Jones goes out a loser
Bobby Jones suffered the final tournament defeat of his active competitive career, when Horton Smith beat him by a stroke in the Savannah Open.

1936 – Henie skates to 10th straight title
Legendary Norwegian figure skater Sonja Henie won her tenth consecutive and final World Championship in Paris.

1959 – Petty takes inaugural 500 at Daytona
Lee Petty won, in a photo finish with Johnny Beauchamp, in the inaugural Daytona 500 race at the new Daytona International Speedway. Petty's average speed was 135.521mph.

1964 – Bevan ends rugby league career
Spindly Australian winger Brian Bevan played his final top-grade match for English club Blackpool, after an 18-year career that included a world record 834 tries.

1980 – Miracle on ice
The United States ice hockey team, composed mostly of college players, scored one of the biggest upsets in sports history, defeating the Soviet Union 4-3 at the Winter Olympics at Lake Placid. The Americans had just 16 shots for the game, and goalie Jim Craig finished with 36 saves. It was the Soviets' first loss in an Olympic game since 1968.

1981 – Sensational Stastnys
Czech brothers Peter and Anton Stastny shared a unique NHL record, for the most points in a regular season road game, taking 8 each in Quebec's 11-7 win at Washington. Peter had 4 goals and 4 assists, whilst Anton added 3 goals and 5 assists.

2003 – Warne banned for a year
Outstanding Australian leg spin bowler Shane Warne was suspended from cricket for a year, after he was found to have a banned diuretic in his system. Warne claimed the drug had been given to him by his mother to help him lose weight. He returned to his best in 2004, claiming a world record in wickets taken, in an ongoing tussle with Sri Lankan spinner Muttiah Muralitharan.

2006 – Brothers quinella snowboard slalom
Philip and Simon Schochs became the first brothers in more than 20 years to win gold and silver in the same event at the same Winter Olympics, when Philip edged Simon in the final of the Parallel Snowboarding Slalom in Turin. Americans Phil and Steve Mahre had finished first and second in the slalom at the Sarajevo Games in 1984.

2008 – Open-wheel racing merger
The Indy Racing League and the Champ Car World Series signed a deal to unify the 2 American open-wheel circuits, bringing them under the umbrella of the IRL. After 12 years of bitter rivalry, Champ Car agreed to cease operations, giving the surviving IRL the opportunity to rebuild open wheel's lost prestige.

BIRTHDATES
1915	American boxer GUS LESNEVICH – died 1964
1933	England soccer striker BOBBY SMITH – died 2010
1934	Baseball manager SPARKY ANDERSON – died 2010
1937	American golfer TOMMY AARON
1940	NBA forward CHET WALKER
1944	Dutch tennis player TOM OKKER
1949	Austrian auto racer NIKKI LAUDA
1949	Russian tennis player OLGA MOROZOVA
1950	Basketball Hall of Fame forward JULIUS IRVING
1952	American golfer WAYNE LEVI
1956	American golfer AMY ALCOTT
1963	Fijian golfer VIJAY SINGH
1964	Puerto Rican tennis player GIGI FERNANDEZ
1965	American Hockey Hall of Fame centre PAT LaFONTAINE
1965	Irish jockey KIEREN FALLON
1969	Danish soccer winger/analyst BRIAN LAUDRUP
1972	American tennis player MICHAEL CHANG
1972	German speed skater CLAUDIA PECHSTEIN
1973	Brazilian soccer midfielder JUNINHO
1984	Irish rugby union winger TOMMY BOWE
1986	NBA point guard RAJON RONDO

㉓ FEBRUARY

1906 – Tommy Burns takes heavyweight title

Canadian Tommy Burns won 18 of the 20 rounds to beat Marvin Hart for the world heavyweight title in Los Angeles. Hart had won the title in an elimination bout with Jack Root after champion Jim Jefferies' retirement and this was his first title defence. Jeffries refereed the bout. Ironically, Hart had won a 20-round decision over Jack Johnson, the man who eventually beat Burns in his 12th title defence in 1908.

1960 – Amazing Fraser

Australian Olympic champion Dawn Fraser smashed her own 100m freestyle world record when she swam a time of 60.2 seconds at North Sydney Olympic Pool. Fraser was also credited with the world mark for the 110 yards in the same swim. She had to wait another 2 and a half years before she became the first to break the 60-second barrier in Melbourne.

1980 – Heiden's fabulous 5 gold

American speed skater Eric Heiden became the first athlete to win 5 individual gold medals in one Olympics at the Lake Placid Games. He shattered the world record by 6.2 seconds in the 10,000m to finish in 14:28.13. The 21-year-old Heiden produced the most successful individual performance in the history of the Olympics, summer or winter, having already won the 500, 1,000, 1,500 and 5,000m events. American swimmer Mark Spitz won 7 gold medals at the 1972 Munich Olympics, but 3 of them were in relay events.

1986 – Kareem plays record number of games

Los Angeles Lakers centre Kareem Abdul-Jabbar surpassed Elvin Hayes as the NBA's all-time leader in games played when he appeared in his 1,304th game, a 117-111 overtime win at Philadelphia. Abdul-Jabbar went on to play in 1,560 games total, second all-time to Robert Parish, who played in 1,611 games.

2000 – Football great Matthews dead at 85

One of the greats of English football, Sir Stanley Matthews, died aged 85. In a brilliant 33-year career, Matthews played 886 first team matches, including 54 internationals for England, 701 league games

Swimming's sprint queen, Dawn Fraser of Australia, in 1960.

for Blackpool and Stoke City, and 86 FA Cup ties. He scored 95 goals, and in 1965 became the oldest Division 1 player, at 50 years, 5 days.

2010 – Magee passes Knight

Philadelphia University basketball coach Herb Magee won his 903rd career game, moving past Hall of Famer Bob Knight to become the winningest men's coach in NCAA history to that time.

BIRTHDATES

1923	Pro Football Hall of Fame end DANTE LAVELLI – died 2009
1940	Pro Football Hall of Fame tight end JACKIE SMITH
1943	American golfer BOBBY MITCHELL
1943	Pro Football Hall of Fame FRED BILETNIKOFF
1948	England soccer defender TREVOR CHERRY
1951	American tennis player EDDIE DIBBS
1960	American golfer CINDY FIGG-CURRIER
1965	Czech tennis player HELENA SUKOVÁ
1967	American golfer STEVE STRICKER
1969	New Zealand golfer MICHAEL CAMPBELL
1971	Swedish golfer CARIN KOCH
1974	South African Test batsman HERSCHELLE GIBBS
1974	South African rugby union prop ROBBIE KEMPSON
1981	English soccer midfielder GARETH BARRY

1931 – How to play golf, on film

Bobby Jones began filming the first instructional golf motion picture at Warner Brothers studios, entitled *How I Play Golf*. Jones was paid a $250,000 fee for the entire series and worked with celebrities such as W.C. Fields on the project. The slow-motion sequences in the series were revolutionary for the time.

1967 – Accurate Chamberlain

Philadelphia's all-time great Wilt Chamberlain shot 18-for-18 from the field in a 149-118 home win against the Baltimore Bullets, setting an NBA record for field goals, without a miss, in a game. The record still stands.

1980 – US ice hockey gold

The United States beat Finland 4-2 to win the Olympic gold medal at Lake Placid. After their famous upset win over the Soviet Union 2 days earlier, the seventh-seeded Americans needed to beat the Finns to clinch gold; a loss, and the medal would have gone to the Soviets. The Americans trailed 2-1 after 2 periods. Phil Verchota tied the game, McClanahan scored the game-winner and Mark Johnson tacked on a late short-handed goal, to give the US the gold.

1982 – The Great One's goal record

Edmonton's Wayne Gretzky scored his NHL-record 77th and 78th goals of the season, on his way to an incredible season total of 92. Phil Esposito's mark of 76 goals was eclipsed during the Oilers' 6-3 win at Buffalo.

1988 – Nykänen jumps to triple gold

Finnish ski jumper Matti Nykänen won the K120 for an unprecedented treble of Olympic ski jumping gold medals during the Calgary Winter Games. In a brilliant career (1982–90), Nykänen won 19 medals at the Olympics and World Championships. His wild reputation caught up with him in 2004, when he was charged with attempted manslaughter after stabbing a man in southern Finland.

1993 – Football legend Moore passes away

England's legendary World Cup-winning captain Bobby Moore died of cancer at age 51. Moore captained England on 90 occasions in 108 international appearances. West Ham United F.C. paid a record £1.8 million for over 70 items of Moore's football memorabilia.

2004 – Fast hat-trick

James Hayter scored the fastest hat-trick in English Football League history, in Bournemouth's 6-0 win against Wrexham in their Division 2 match at Dean Court. Hayter came on as an 84th minute substitute, and scored in the 86th, 87th and 88th minutes, a span of 2 minutes, 20 seconds.

2010 – First ODI double century

Thirty-six-year-old Indian master batsman Sachin Tendulkar became the first player to score 200 in ODI cricket, during a 153-run win against South Africa in Gwalior. Tendulkar's 200 not out came from just 147 balls, with 25 fours and 3 sixes.

BIRTHDATES

1915	Australian golfer JIM FERRIER – died 1986
1931	England Test captain BRIAN CLOSE
1940	American boxer JIMMY ELLIS
1940	Scottish soccer player DENIS LAW
1942	Australian auto racer COLIN BOND
1947	NBA coach/analyst MIKE FRATELLO
1948	Scottish soccer manager WALTER SMITH
1951	England Test batsman DEREK RANDALL
1955	French auto racer ALAIN PROST
1956	Baseball Hall of Fame infielder EDDIE MURRAY
1959	Australian Test fast bowler MIKE WHITNEY
1963	Canadian NHL goalie MIKE VERNON
1965	NFL offensive tackle PAUL GRUBER
1973	Russian ice hockey right wing ALEXEI KOVALEV
1976	Australian cyclist BRAD McGEE
1976	American golfer ZACH JOHNSON
1977	American boxer FLOYD MAYWEATHER JR
1981	Australian tennis player LLEYTON HEWITT

1935 – Hagan's final fling

Walter Hagen scored the final win of his brilliant career when he finished birdie-birdie, including a 45ft putt at the final hole, to clinch the Gasparilla Open at the Palma Ceia Golf and Country Club in Tampa, Florida. Hagan won by 1 stroke over Clarence Clark.

1964 – Clay is 'the greatest'

Twenty-two-year-old Cassius Clay upset the champion Sonny Liston in a sixth-round TKO in Miami to win the world heavyweight title. Officials had the fight even after 6 rounds, but in the break, a bleeding Liston complained of numbness in his left arm and remained in the corner.

1971 – NHL's fastest three

The Boston Bruins set an NHL record for the fastest 3 goals, scored in an 8-3 win over Vancouver in Boston. In a 20-second time span in the third period, the Bruins scored via John Bucyk, Ed Westfall and Ted Green.

1977 – 'En guard'

New Orleans' Pete Maravich scored 68 points against the New York Knicks, the most ever by an NBA guard. Maravich broke Jerry West's 1962 record of 63 in the Jazz's 124-107 home victory.

2001 – Hendry's snooker record

Stephen Hendry recorded his world-record eighth perfect break in tournament play in the final of the Rothmans Grand Prix at the Hexagon Theatre in Reading.

2001 – Cricket icon dead at 92

Australian cricket's greatest phenomenon, Sir Donald Bradman, died in Adelaide aged 92. To this day, Bradman's batting figures remain unsurpassed. He played 52 Tests, scoring 6,996 runs at the incredible average of 99.94. He scored 29 Test centuries, with a best score of 334. His first-class figures are even more imposing. In 234 matches, he scored 28,067 at 95.14. He hit 117 centuries and 69 fifties, with a high score of 452. Bradman captained Australia in 24 Tests (1936–48) to 15 wins, 3 losses and 6 draws.

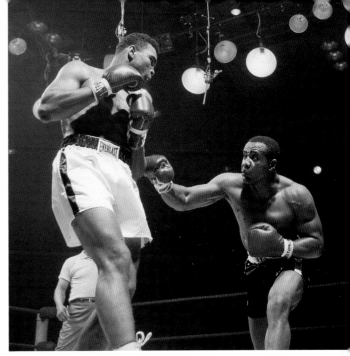

Muhammad Ali, formerly Cassius Clay, in his 1965 rematch with Sonny Liston, where he scored a first-round knockout victory.

2001 – Liverpool start golden run

Liverpool won the first leg of their famous Cup treble when they beat Birmingham City on penalties in the Worthington Cup Final at the Millenium Stadium in Cardiff. The scores were locked at 1-1 after extra time, with Liverpool winning 5-4 on penalties. The Reds went on to score a 2-1 win over Arsenal in the FA Cup Final, and a 5-4 golden goal victory over Spain's Alavés in the UEFA Cup Final.

BIRTHDATES

1918	American tennis player BOBBY RIGGS – died 1995
1928	Danish yachtsman PAUL ELVSTROM
1932	English auto racer TONY BROOKS
1934	American golfer TONY LEMA – died 1966
1938	Australian middle distance runner HERB ELLIOTT
1938	Indian Test wicket keeper FAROKH ENGINEER
1944	French auto racer FRANCOIS CEVERT – died 1973
1949	Pro wrestler 'Nature Boy' RIC FLAIR
1951	Jamaican sprinter DON QUARRIE
1952	Irish motor cycle rider JOEY DUNLOP – died 2000
1954	Australian Test wicketkeeper STEVE RIXON
1958	NFL coach JEFF FISHER
1961	American auto racer DAVEY ALLISON – died 1993
1962	German kayaker BIRGIT FISCHER
1971	Australian Test spinner STUART MacGILL
1971	English golfer HELEN DOBSON
1985	New Zealand rugby league captain BENJI MARSHALL

1935 – Ruth returns to Boston
Babe Ruth signed with the Boston Braves after turning down an offer from the Yankees to become a minor-league manager. However his Braves career was short-lived. On May 25, he belted 3 home runs and retired shortly afterward.

1968 – Africans boycott Olympics
Thirty-two African nations agreed to boycott the Mexico City Olympics because of the presence of South Africa. The IOC eventually excluded South Africa from the Games and the black African nations then agreed to participate.

1980 – Five-century Test
New Zealand fast bowler Richard Hadlee scored 103 against the rampant West Indies pace attack, during the drawn second Test in Christchurch. It was Hadlee's first Test century, coming off only 88 balls. The match featured 4 other centuries, from Kiwi captain Geoff Howarth and the Windies' Desmond Haynes, Lawrence Rowe and Collis King.

1981 – Penalty minutes galore
In an ugly game at Boston Gardens, the Boston Bruins and the Minnesota North Stars shared 406 penalty minutes, the most in a single regular season game in NHL history. Minnesota had a record total of 211 minutes in the penalty box, whilst the teams bashed out a record 67 minutes in the first period.

1983 – Jennings' 1000
Arsenal goalkeeper Pat Jennings made his 1,000th appearance in first-class football in a 0-0 draw with West Bromwich Albion. Jennings ended his 23-year career in 1986 with a total of 1,098 games for Watford, Tottenham, Arsenal and Northern Ireland.

1985 – 'Dr J' third in scoring
Philadelphia's Julius Erving passed Elvin Hayes (27,313 points) as the third leading all-time scorer in NBA history during the 76ers' 116-97 loss at Milwaukee. Erving ended his career with 30,026 points, fifth overall behind Kareem Abdul-Jabbar, Wilt Chamberlain, Karl Malone and Michael Jordan.

1993 – Border rules
Australian captain Allan Border became the highest run-scorer in Test cricket when he hit 88 during the first Test win over New Zealand in Christchurch. Border overtook Indian opener Sunil Gavaskar's world record of 10,122 Test runs. Border played 156 Tests, scoring a record 11,174 at 50.56 with 27 centuries, 63 fifties, 156 catches and 39 wickets.

1994 – Schneider tallies 5 gold
Swiss alpine skier Vreni Schneider won the slalom at the Winter Olympics in Lillehammer in Norway to earn the fifth gold medal of her career. The golden haul was the most of any woman in Winter Olympic history.

2012 – Kobe top All-Star
Kobe Bryant passed Michael Jordan as the leading scorer in NBA All-Star Game history while helping the Western Conference hold on for a 152-149 victory over the East in Orlando, Florida. The LA Lakers' guard, making his 13th All-Star appearance, scored 27 points to pass Jordan's mark of 262 All-Star points with a breakaway dunk during the third quarter and pushed his career total to 271.

BIRTHDATES
1910   England soccer goalkeeper VIC WOODLEY – died 1978
1922   Australian Test fast bowler BILL JOHNSTON – 2007
1931   Scottish soccer winger/manager ALLY MacLEOD – died 2004
1945   Australian auto-racer PETER BROCK – died 2006
1946   England soccer midfielder COLIN BELL
1957   American swimmer KEENA ROTHHAMMER
1957   American Hockey Hall of Fame right wing JOE MULLEN
1958   England rugby union lock PAUL ACKFORD
1973   NFL running back MARSHALL FAULK
1973   Norwegian soccer striker OLE GUNNER SOLSKJAER
1973   American swimmer JENNY THOMPSON
1974   French rally driver SÉBASTIEN LOEB
1982   Chinese tennis player LI NA
1983   Portuguese soccer defender PEPE
1984   Togolese soccer striker EMMANUEL ADEBAYOR
1985   Spanish soccer striker FERNANDO LLORENTE
1986   American mogul skier HANNAH KEARNEY

1959 – Cousy a great helper
Boston playmaker Bob Cousy shattered the NBA record for assists by getting 28 in the Celtics' record-breaking 173-139 victory over the Minneapolis Lakers. The previous mark had been 21, set by the NY Knicks' Richie Guerin. In the next 40 years, only 2 players (Scott Skiles with 30 and Kevin Porter with 29) surpassed Cousy's performance. The Celtics scored the most points ever in a regulation NBA game. The Phoenix Suns tied the record in 1990.

1966 – Haas' lucky break
Fred Haas Jr won the PGA Seniors' Championship at PGA National Golf Club in Palm Beach Gardens, Florida, after being given a lucky reprieve. Haas was set to withdraw, suffering from a virus and a 100-degree temperature, but the first round was postponed because of torrential rain. He recovered in time to become the only player in the field to finish under par, with a 2-under 286 total, to win by 2 strokes from John Barnum and Dutch Harrison.

1996 – Gretzky sings the 'Blues'
Wayne Gretzky, nearing the end of an illustrious career, was traded from the LA Kings to the St Louis Blues. The Kings received Craig Johnson, Patrice Tardif, Roman Vopat, St Louis' fifth-round choice (Peter Hogan) in 1996 Entry Draft and first-round choice (Matt Zultek) in 1997 Entry Draft. Gretzky's stay at St Louis lasted only 5 months. He was signed as a free agent by the New York Rangers in July 1996.

1996 – Brilliant Bulls' 50
The dominant Chicago Bulls defeated Minnesota 120-99 at the United Centre in Chicago to reach a 50-6 record for the season. The Bulls' 50 wins came with the fewest losses in a season of any major professional sports team in the 20th century.

2000 – Foxes' Cup
Matt Elliott scored both goals as Leicester City beat the Division 1 Tranmere Rovers, 2-1 in the final of the League Cup (at that time called the Worthington Cup) at Wembley Stadium. David Kelly netted the consolation goal for Rovers.

2001 – They're not racing …
The British Horse Racing Board and Jockey Club announced the suspension of racing for 7 days due to the outbreak of foot and mouth disease. The disease went on to claim weeks of racing, including one of the highlights of the jump-racing season with the postponement of the annual Cheltenham Festival.

2003 – World Cup wonder
Australia beat Namibia by a record 256 runs during the Cricket World Cup at Potchestroom. Darren Lehmann scored 28 runs in the final over; Glenn McGrath took 7 for 15; and Adam Gilchrist achieved a World Cup record of 6 dismissals.

2008 – LeBron youngest to reach 10,000
At 23 years and 59 days, LeBron James became the youngest player in NBA history to reach the 10,000-point milestone. However, the Boston Celtics got 22 points from Ray Allen to beat James and Cleveland, 92-87.

2011 – World Cup Cricket tie
India and England fought out a classic tie at the World Cup in Bangalore. India piled on 338, courtesy of a Sachin Tendulkar hundred. Andrew Strauss' 158 along with very generous bowling from India, gave England a chance, leaving them chasing 29 off the last 2 overs, then 5 off the last 3 balls. They got 4.

BIRTHDATES
1902	American golfer GENE SARAZEN – died 1999
1902	American swimmer ETHELDA BLEIBTRY – died 1978
1929	Australian rugby league coach JACK GIBSON – died 2008
1933	Pro Football Hall of Fame receiver/coach RAYMOND BERRY
1936	Australian Football League player/coach RON BARASSI
1939	American auto racer PETER REVSON – died 1974
1944	South African Test batsman GRAEME POLLOCK
1958	South African rugby union fly-half NAAS BOTHA
1960	Ecuadorian tennis star ANDREZ GOMEZ
1961	Basketball Hall of Fame forward JAMES WORTHY
1970	American jockey KENT DESORMEAUX
1973	Welsh rugby union captain MARK TAYLOR
1974	American motor-cycle rider COLIN EDWARDS
1976	NFL tight end TONY GONZALEZ
1985	Russian soccer winger DINIYAR BILYALETDINOV

1912 – Trumper's final fifty
The great Victor Trumper scored 50 in his final Test innings during the fifth Test against England in Sydney. The popular Trumper was an elegant batsman who played 48 Tests, scoring 3,163 runs at 39.04, with a Test best of 214 not out. He scored 8 Test centuries, 13 fifties and took 31 catches.

1926 – Hagan dominates Jones
Walter Hagen led Bobby Jones by an astonishing 8-hole margin at the halfway point of their historic 72-hole challenge match at the Whitfield Estates Country Club in Sarasota, Florida. The match moved to Hagen's Pasadena Golf Club, where he cruised to an anti-climactic 12 and 11 win.

1960 – US Hockey gold
Trailing 4-3 after 2 periods, the United States scored 6 goals in a 12-minute span to beat Czechoslovakia 9-4 and capture its first Olympic ice hockey gold medal at Squaw Valley. Roger Christian scored 4 goals and Bob Cleary two, including the game-winner.

1967 – Wilt's streak over, but record remains
Wilt Chamberlain missed his first field goal in 4 games during Philadelphia's 127-107 win over Cincinnati at Syracuse. The miss ended his NBA record of 35 consecutive field goals, a record that still stands.

1971 – Nicklaus' unique feat
Jack Nicklaus become the first player to win all 4 modern major championships twice, after taking out the PGA Championship at the PGA National Golf Club in Palm Beach Gardens, Florida. Nicklaus shot 281 to beat Billy Casper by 2 strokes.

1981 – 78 straight for Murphy
Houston guard Calvin Murphy set a consecutive free throw record when his streak ended at 78. His record lasted 12 years, when Minnesota's Michael Williams set the current record of 97 in 1993.

1999 – Webb's 26-under par win
Karrie Webb beat Janice Moodie by 10 strokes to win the Australian Masters in Queensland. Webb's

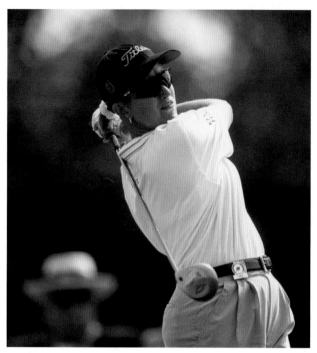

Golfing great Karrie Webb.

26-under par set an LPGA record for the lowest 72-hole score in relation to par.

2010 – Canada takes hockey gold
In one of the greatest ice hockey games in Olympic history, Canada's all-stars held off a young, desperate US team, to whom they had lost the previous week, to win the gold medal 3-2 in overtime in Vancouver.

BIRTHDATES

1890	Canadian Hockey Hall of Fame centre JOE MALONE – died 1969
1931	English golfer/analyst PETER ALLISS
1937	American swimmer JEFF FARRELL
1940	American auto racer MARIO ANDRETTI
1942	Italian soccer goalkeeper DINO ZOFF
1945	NFL defensive end BUBBA SMITH – died 2011
1944	West German soccer goalkeeper SEPP MAIER
1955	Basketball Hall of Fame forward ADRIAN DANTLEY
1957	New Zealand Test wicketkeeper/broadcaster IAN SMITH
1957	Belgian soccer midfielder JAN CEULEMANS
1961	British boxer BARRY McGUIGAN
1970	Algerian middle distance runner NOUREDDINE MORCELI
1973	Canadian NHL centre ERIC LINDROS
1973	New Zealand rugby union centre SCOTT McLEOD
1978	Austrian alpine skier BENJAMIN RAICH
1979	French auto racer SÉBASTIEN BORDAIS
1985	Serbian tennis player JELENA JANKOVIC

㉙ FEBRUARY

1964 – Sprint queen Fraser's career best
Australian sprint queen Dawn Fraser swam the fastest 100m of her brilliant career when she smashed her own world record, with a time of 58.9 seconds at the National Championships at North Sydney Olympic Pool. Fraser, who had won the 100m freestyle gold medals at the 1956 and 1960 Olympics, went on to take an unprecedented treble later that year in Tokyo.

1964 – 40-40 double
Cincinnati Royals teammates Jerry Lucas and Oscar Robertson combined for a rare 40-40 performance, as the Royals defeated the host Philadelphia 76ers, 117-114. League MVP Robertson tallied 43 points and Rookie of the Year Lucas collected a team-record 40 rebounds.

1972 – Aaron's record contract
Future home run leader Hank Aaron became the first Major League Baseball player to sign a contract worth $200,000 a year. Aaron signed a 3-year, $600,000 deal with the Atlanta Braves.

1988 – Greatbatch scores debut century
New Zealand batsman Mark Greatbatch became only the fourth Kiwi to score a century on debut when he hit an unbeaten 107 in the second Test against England in Auckland. The Kiwis held on at 350 for 7 to draw the match.

1996 – Wobbly Windies
The Kenyan cricketers scored a huge upset when they dismissed the West Indies for 93 in a World Cup match in Pune. The Kenyans were dismissed for a moderate 166, but had no trouble routing the Windies. It was the second-lowest score ever by the West Indies. The lowest score by a West Indian team was 87, against Australia in Sydney in 1993.

BIRTHDATES
1908	England Test fast bowler ALF GOVER – died 2001
1932	Australian Test batsman GAVIN STEVENS
1936	Canadian Hockey Hall of Fame centre HENRI RICHARD
1940	American thoroughbred trainer WILLIAM H. TURNER JR.
1952	Russian cross-country skier RAISA SMETANINA
1964	Australian iron man GUY LEECH
1964	Swedish tennis player HENRICK SUNDSTRÖM
1968	NBA forward CHUCKY BROWN
1968	NFL linebacker BRYCE PAUP
1976	Hungarian sprint canoeist KATALIN KOVÁCS
1980	Canadian NHL left wing SIMON GAGNÉ

New Zealand Test opener Mark Greatbatch is bowled for 100 during the second Test against England in Auckland in 1988.

MARCH

1 MARCH

1958 – Sensational Sobers
Gary Sobers set a world record for highest individual Test innings with 365 for the West Indies against Pakistan at Kingston, Jamaica. Sobers' unbeaten innings took 614 minutes and included 38 fours. The record overshadowed Conrad Hunte's magnificent 260 in the Windies total of 760 for 3 declared.

1965 – Dawn dumped
The Australian Swimming Union banned triple Olympic 100m champion Dawn Fraser for 10 years over misbehaviour at the Emperor's Palace during the 1964 Tokyo Games. Fraser was alleged to have stolen a flag at the Palace. She claimed it was a playful prank; the Emperor later gave her the flag.

1969 – Mantle is done
New York Yankees slugger Mickey Mantle announced his retirement from baseball, aged 37. In his injury-marred 18-year career, Mantle was one of the game's shining stars, winning 3 MVP awards, 4 home-run titles and the Triple Crown in 1956 with a .353 average, 52 homers and 130 RBI. His 536 homers trail only Barry Bonds, Hank Aaron, Babe Ruth and Willie Mays.

1977 – New PGA playoff format
The PGA of America announced a sudden-death playoff format for the PGA Championship would be used beginning with this year's tournament. Previously an 18-hole playoff applied when there was a tie after the regulation 72 holes. The PGA later changed the format again, switching to a 3-hole playoff.

1997 – Electric Elvis
Canadian Elvis Stojko hit the first quad-triple combination jump in the history of figure-skating competition, to win the Championship Series final in Hamilton, Ontario. He earned the first perfect 6.0.

1992 – Jenny catches up to drug cheats
American sprinter Jenny Thompson passed one of the most famous drug-tainted East German swim records when she broke Kristen Otto's 1986 100m freestyle world mark. Thompson swam 54.48 in Indianapolis to beat Otto's record by 0.25 seconds.

1996 – Wilkens first to 1,000
Lenny Wilkens became the first NBA coach to reach 1,000 career victories when the Hawks downed the Cleveland Cavaliers 74-68 in Atlanta.

2009 – First US Bobsled win in 50 years
Steven Holcomb was the class of the field in the 4-man competition at the World Bobsled Championships at Mount Van Hoevenberg, piloting the USA-1 sled to the gold medal. It was the first triumph for the US in the 4-man at world championships in 50 years, since Arthur Tyler won at St Moritz in 1959.

BIRTHDATES
1926	MLB Commissioner PETE ROZELLE – died 1996
1943	Japanese gymnast AKINORI NAKAYAMA
1946	Czech tennis player JAN KODEŠ
1952	American golfer DAVE BARR
1952	Australian AFL rover/coach/analyst LEIGH MATTHEWS
1952	Northern Ireland midfielder/manager MARTIN O'NEILL
1958	Australian Test wicketkeeper WAYNE PHILLIPS
1961	NFL running back MIKE ROZIER
1962	New Zealand yachtsman RUSSELL COUTTS
1963	Canadian Hockey Hall of Fame centre RON FRANCIS
1965	Canadian jockey STEWART ELLIOTT
1973	NBA power forward CHRIS WEBBER
1980	Pakistani Test fast bowler SHAHID AFRIDI
1996	Chinese swimmer YE SHIWEN

New York Yankees slugger Mickey Mantle.

❷ MARCH

1986 – Opportunity Knox
Kenny Knox, who'd gained entry as a Monday open qualifier, posted a third-round score of 80, but still won the Honda Classic for his first PGA Tour victory. Knox's 287 total was the highest winning score in PGA tournament history, and remembered as the last time a player shot in the 80s and still won a PGA Tour event.

1997 – Patience is a virtue
Australian batsmen Greg Blewett (214) and Steve Waugh (160) batted for the entire third day of the first Test against South Africa in Johannesburg, to wear the home side down. The South Africans crashed to an innings and 196-run defeat when they were dismissed for 190 in their second innings. Spinners Shane Warne and Michael Bevan each took 4 wickets.

2000 – Team NZ defends Cup
New Zealand became only the second country in 150 years to successfully defend the America's Cup. Team New Zealand comfortably won the fifth and final race by 48 seconds to record a 5-0 clean sweep over the Italian Prada syndicate in the waters off Auckland.

2002 – Sweet ending for Matlala
Forty-year-old South African 'Baby Jake' Matlala ended his 22-year career with a seventh-round TKO win over Columbia's Juan Herrera to retain his WBU junior flyweight title at Carnival City. It was a fitting end to an illustrious career. At 4ft 10in (147cm) Matlala was the shortest-ever world champion. In 68 fights, he had 53 wins, 13 losses and 2 draws, and is the only South African boxer to win 4 world titles.

2011 – Luck of the Irish
Kevin O'Brien smoked the fastest hundred in Cricket World Cup history off a round 50 balls, helping Ireland pull off a legendary upset against England. England racked up 327 and Ireland lost a wicket off the first ball of their chase before slumping to 106 for 4. O'Brien then launched a breathtaking assault, plundering 16 fours and 6 sixes to bring up 113 in 63 balls.

2012 – 'Bountygate'
The NFL confirmed the New Orleans Saints had run

Team New Zealand during the 2000 America's Cup

a bounty program, which gave incentives to players to injure their opposition in violation of league rules, during the 2009, 2010, and 2011 seasons. Coach Sean Payton was suspended without pay for the season, ex-defensive coordinator Gregg Williams indefinitely, and general manager Mickey Loomis for 8 games. The club was fined $500,000 and lost a second-round pick in both 2012 and 2013.

BIRTHDATES
1909	Baseball Hall of Fame outfielder MEL OTT – died 1958
1947	English soccer manager HARRY REDKNAPP
1949	Welsh rugby union fullback J.P.R. WILLIAMS
1955	Australian Test opener STEVE SMALL
1958	South African tennis player KEVIN CURRAN
1962	MLB catcher TERRY STEINBACH
1965	MLB outfielder RON GANT
1966	Austrian tennis player JUDITH WEISNER
1967	French rugby union centre THIERRY LACROIX
1974	Australian swimmer HALEY LEWIS
1975	New Zealand rugby union centre DARYL GIBSON
1977	England Test captain ANDREW STRAUSS
1979	Irish soccer winger DAMIEN DUFF
1985	NFL running back REGGIE BUSH

➌ MARCH

1896 – Lohmann's nine
England fast bowler George Lohmann became the first man to take 9 wickets in a Test when he destroyed South Africa in the second Test at the Old Wanderers Ground in Johannesburg. Lohmann captured 9 for 28 and took 3 more in the second innings, as England won by an innings to take a 2-0 lead in the 3 Test series.

1939 – Slammin' Sam again
Sam Snead beat Henry Picard for the St Petersburg Open title after 25 playoff holes. Snead and Picard had tied on 207 totals after 54 holes of regulation play. The pair posted matching 69s in their scheduled 18-hole playoff, before Snead's birdie 2 at the seventh extra hole clinched the tournament.

1949 – Hogan in hospital
Golf star Ben Hogan, who had been critically injured in a road accident in February, was flown to El Paso for emergency surgery after blood clots were discovered in his abdomen and crushed left leg. Hogan went on to make a full recovery and won the US Open just 16 months after the accident. In all, he won 6 of his 9 major career victories following the near-fatal crash.

1962 – Three hat-trick game
For only the second time in English Football League history, 3 members of a team scored hat-tricks in the same match, when Wrexham thrashed Hartlepool 10-1 in a Division 4 game at the Racecourse Ground. Wyn Davies, Ron Barnes and Roy Ambler each scored 3 goals for the Dragons.

1984 – Olympic expertise for MLB
President of the Los Angeles Olympic Organising Committee, Peter Ueberroth was elected Commissioner of Major League Baseball. His tenure was marked by increased attendances and a significantly improved financial situation. In 1988, Ueberroth's last season, all clubs either broke even or finished in the black. He also negotiated landmark television deals with CBS and ESPN.

2009 – Pakistan future in doubt
Pakistan's status as an international sporting venue

Ben Hogan, suffering complications following a car crash in 1949, went on to win 6 of his 9 major victories after the accident. In 1953, he received a tickertape parade after winning the British Open.

came into question when terrorists attacked the Sri Lankan team bus, on its way to the Gaddafi Stadium in Lahore, on the third morning of the second Test. Six players, including captain Mahela Jayawardene and his deputy Kumar Sangakkara, received minor injuries, while 6 security men and 2 civilians were killed. It was the first time sportsmen had been specifically targeted by terrorists since the 1972 Munich Olympics. The Test was called off and the tour cancelled.

BIRTHDATES
1920	American golfer JULIUS BOROS – died 1994
1935	Australian tennis player MAL ANDERSON
1939	Indian Test batsman MOTGANHALLI JAISIMHA – died 1999
1944	Australian jockey HARRY WHITE
1946	English snooker player/analyst JOHN VIRGO
1953	Brazilian soccer striker/manager ZICO
1954	American golfer KEITH FERGUS
1956	Polish soccer striker/manager ZBIGNIEW BONIEK
1956	New Zealand Test batsman JOHN REID
1962	American heptathlete JACKI JOYNER KERSEE
1962	NFL running back HERSCHEL WALKER
1970	Pakistani Test captain INZAMAM-UL-HAQ
1972	England soccer defender DARREN ANDERTON
1972	Czech NHL forward MARTIN PROCHÁZKA

4 MARCH

1930 – Ten pin's perfect 300
Emma Fahning became the first woman to bowl a perfect 300 game in a sanctioned ten-pin bowling competition in Buffalo, New York. Fahning was relatively new to the game and was never a top-flight bowler. At the time, a 300 game was a huge accomplishment. Modern bowling ball materials and alley finishes have now made it a regular occurrence.

1931 – Windies' first
The West Indies beat Australia for the first time, as Don Bradman was bowled by Herman Griffith for the first duck of his Test career, on the final day of the fifth Test in Sydney.

1967 – Rangers' Wembley upset
Third Division team Queens Park Rangers pulled off a shock 3-2 win over First Division West Bromwich Albion in the first League Cup Final, played at Wembley. Rangers recovered from 2-0 down at halftime with goals from Roger Morgan, Rodney Marsh and the winner from Mark Lazarus in the dying moments.

1977 – Croft's Windies record
In only his second Test, express bowler Colin Croft produced the best-ever figures by a West Indian when he took 8 for 29 in the second Test against Pakistan in Trinidad. The Windies won the match by 6 wickets and took a 1-0 lead in the series.

1990 – Norman's stirring rally
Australian Greg Norman rallied from a 7-stroke deficit, with a final-round 62, to earn a place in a 4-way playoff in the Doral-Ryder Open. The red-hot Norman then chipped-in for an eagle on the first extra hole to beat Paul Azinger, Mark Calcavecchia and Tim Simpson for the title.

1995 – Red Devils devastating
Manchester United created the scoring record for an English Premier League match when they thrashed Ipswich Town 9-0 at Old Trafford. The match also equalled the Premier League record for aggregate score. Andy Cole scored a Premier League record 5 goals for United.

Greg Norman hits out of a sand trap during the 1990 Masters at Augusta National Golf Club, Georgia.

BIRTHDATES

1888	College football coach KNUTE ROCKNE – died 1931
1918	American tennis player MARGARET OSBORNE DuPONT – died 2012
1927	American tennis player DICK SAVITT
1936	Scottish auto racer JIM CLARK – died 1968
1937	New Zealand Test captain GRAHAM DOWLING
1945	Swedish soccer manager THOMAS SVENSSON
1950	American golfer JUDY DICKINSON
1951	Scottish soccer player KENNY DALGLISH
1953	Australian rugby union/league lock RAY PRICE
1954	American golfer PETER JACOBSEN
1954	English snooker player WILLIE THORNE
1961	American boxer RAY 'BOOM BOOM' MANCINI
1966	NBA guard KEVIN JOHNSON
1967	South African Test batsman DARRYL CULLINAN
1969	Italian soccer striker/manager PIERLUIGI CASIRAGHI
1970	Spanish motor cycle rider ÁLEX CRIVILLÉ
1974	Slovak tennis player KAROL KUCERA
1974	Argentine soccer midfielder ARIEL ORTEGA
1974	Australian rugby union front rower BILL YOUNG
1979	Australian swimmer GEOFF HUEGILL
1983	South African rugby union centre JAQUE FOURIE

❺ MARCH

1956 – The Wright way
Mickey Wright earned her first LPGA win in the Jacksonville Women's Open. She was 3 strokes behind Joyce Ziske with 8 holes remaining, but rallied to win. Wright went on to win 82 career titles, second only to Kathy Whitworth's record 88 LPGA Tour victories.

1971 – Six straight for Proctor
South African all-rounder Mike Proctor smashed a world-record sixth consecutive first-class century for Rhodesia against Western Province at Salisbury. It equalled the still-standing record, held by C.B. Fry and Don Bradman. Due to South Africa's sporting isolation, because of its apartheid policies, Proctor was limited to just 7 Tests in which he took 41 wickets at 15.02. But in 401 first-class matches, he scored 21,963 runs at 36.01 with 48 centuries. He took 1,417 wickets at 19.53 with a best 9 for 71. He is now a Test-match referee.

1973 – Wife Swap America
New York Yankees left-handed pitchers Mike Kekich and Fritz Peterson announced at spring training that they had not only swapped wives, but also just about everything else in their lives, including children, houses, cars and dogs. The Yankees wasted little time trading both players. Susan Kekich ended up marrying Peterson, but the Marilyn Peterson/Kekich relationship didn't last.

1993 – Ben banned for life
Disgraced Canadian sprinter Ben Johnson was banned from athletics for life after failing a drugs test for a second time. The IAAF announcement came after Johnson tested positive for a banned substance in Canada in February. Johnson won the 100m at the 1988 Seoul Olympics but was subsequently stripped of his medal after testing positive for performance-enhancing drugs. Returning after a 2-year ban, he failed to regain form and didn't qualify for the final of the Olympic 100m in Barcelona in 1992.

Australian fast bowler Rodney Hogg.

1994 – Drag queen
Rachelle Splatt of Australia became the first woman, and non-American, to make a 300mph pass over a quarter mile in a top-fuel dragster. Splatt was a mother of 2 and ran a leading wheel manufacturing company in Sydney.

1995 – oneAustralia down and out
The America's Cup fourth round robin race saw the sinking of oneAustralia, as the 75ft carbon-fibre boat broke in half in rough seas in San Diego. All 17 crew were rescued.

BIRTHDATES
1876 American tennis player ELISABETH MOORE – died 1959
1936 American golfer DALE DOUGLASS
1940 Australian rugby league winger KEN IRVINE – died 1990
1942 Welsh rugby union fly-half DAVID WATKINS
1951 Australian Test fast bowler RODNEY HOGG
1966 American golfer TRACEY KERDYK
1966 Pro Football Hall of Fame wide receiver MICHAEL IRVIN
1973 Australian tennis player NICOLE PRATT
1976 New Zealand rugby union lock NORM MAXWELL
1982 New Zealand rugby union fly-half DANIEL CARTER

❻ MARCH

1923 – Weissmuller wonderful
American swimmer Johnny Weissmuller became the first to break 5 minutes for 440 yards. Weissmuller, representing the Illinois Athletic Club in a solo swim in New Haven, Connecticut, finished in 4:57 seconds, shaving 11 seconds off his own world record of 5:08. The record was Weissmuller's 47th world mark.

1947 – Fosbury no flop
American high jumper Dick Fosbury was born in Portland, Oregon. Fosbury revolutionised high jumping with his 'Fosbury Flop', whereby he would leap over the bar headfirst and backward. He won the gold medal at the 1968 Mexico City Olympics with a leap of 2.24m.

1974 – Chappells make history
Australia's Chappell brothers created history on the final day of the first Test against New Zealand in Wellington. Ian scored 121 to follow his first innings' 145, whilst Greg added 133 to 247, making the Chappells the first cricketing brothers to score centuries in each innings of the same Test match.

1976 – Dominant Dorothy
Popular American Dorothy Hamill completed figure skating's triple crown by winning the World Championship in Gothenburg in Sweden. She had previously won the United States and Olympic titles.

1984 – Hawerchuk's assists record
Winnipeg centre Dale Hawerchuk made 5 assists in the second period in Los Angeles, to create a new NHL record for assists in one period of a regular season game. The Jets beat the Kings 7-3.

1985 – 'Iron' Mike's pro debut
Mike Tyson began his professional boxing career with the first-round knockout of Hector Mercedes in Albany, New York. By the end of 2004, Tyson's record stood at 50 wins (44 KOs), 5 losses and 2 no contests from 57 fights. The no contests came when Orlin Norris was knocked down after the bell and injured his knee, and when Tyson tested positive for marijuana after his second-round TKO of Andrew Golota.

Dick Fosbury during the AAAU Championships in Oregon in 1972.

1996 – ODI high
Sri Lanka smashed 398 for 5 off 50 overs, the highest total in ODI history, in a World Cup match against Kenya in Kandy. Sanath Jayasuriya and Romesh Kaluwitharana put on an exciting opening stand of 83 in just 6.3 overs. Aravinda de Silva hit a swashbuckling 145 including 14 sixes and 43 fours.

BIRTHDATES

1879	New Zealand rugby union centre JIMMY HUNTER – died 1962
1900	Baseball Hall of Fame pitcher ROBERT 'LEFTY' GROVE – died 1975
1926	American swimmer ANN CURTIS – died 2012
1929	England Test batsman DAVID SHEPPARD – died 2005
1931	Baseball Hall of Fame outfielder WILLIE MAYS
1935	England soccer forward DERECK KEVAN – died 2013
1940	American golfer RICHARD SIKES
1940	Baseball Hall of Fame slugger WILLIE STARGELL – died 2001
1947	American high jumper DICK FOSBURY
1949	Scottish soccer defender MARTIN BUCHAN
1956	England Test batsman PETER ROEBUCK – died 2011
1962	British golfer ALISON NICHOLAS
1962	Swiss alpine skier ERIKA HESS
1965	Welsh rugby union centre ALAN BATEMAN
1972	NBA centre SHAQUILLE O'NEILL
1973	NBA guard MICHAEL FINLEY
1974	American swimmer BRAD SCHUMACHER
1977	South African Test fast bowler NANTIE HAYWARD
1989	Polish tennis player AGNIESZKA RADWA SKA

❼ MARCH

1926 – Heavyweight golfing confrontation
Flamboyant Walter Hagen cruised to a 12 & 11 victory over Bobby Jones in their historic 72-hole match at the Pasadena courses in Sarasota, Florida. Hagen led Jones by an astonishing 8-hole margin at the halfway point, at Jones' home course at the Whitfield Estates Country Club. Promoters had heralded the event as the 'World Championship of Golf', but it turned out to be an anti-climax.

1951 – Charles beat-up, but a winner
World Heavyweight Champion Ezzard Charles took a 15-round unanimous decision from Jersey Joe Walcott in Detroit to retain the title. The result was the same as 21 months earlier, when the pair fought for the title vacated by Joe Louis. Whilst Charles was the clear winner (officials scored 10, 16 and 18-point winning margins), he came out of the fight looking worse than Walcott, whose only wound was a slight cut above his left eye. Charles' left eye was swollen, and his left ear so puffed up that it required surgery the following day to prevent permanent damage.

1954 – Babe brilliant
Babe Zaharias played 27 holes in a single day for the first time since cancer surgery to score a comfortable win in the Sarasota Women's Open in Florida. Zaharias beat Patty Berg and Louise Suggs by 9 strokes.

1970 – Jack's final GP win
Australia's triple World Formula 1 driver's champion, Jack Brabham, won his 14th and final Grand Prix at South Africa's Kyalami Circuit. In a career lasting 15 years, Brabham won 3 Formula 1 Championships (1959–60, 1966).

1988 – Jeff's three titles
Jeff Fenech became only the 11th boxer in history to win world titles in 3 different weight divisions, after he stopped Victor Callejas in the 10th round in Sydney to win the vacant WBC featherweight crown. Fenech had already won the WBC Super Bantamweight and IBF Bantamweight titles.

Australian triple Formula 1 champion Jack Brabham in his Brabham-Repco at Silverstone.

1997 – 'Scud' gives Black a 'serve'
Australian tennis star Mark Philippoussis set a world record for fastest serve during a straight sets quarter-final win over Byron Black in the Templeton Franklin Classic in Scottsdale, Arizona. His serve was a radar-measured 228.5 kph. The mark was bettered by Greg Rusedski in 1998, with a serve of 240 kph at Indian Wells.

2004 – Perfect Parry
Craig Parry of Australia holed a spectacular, 160m, fairway approach shot for an eagle on the first playoff hole against Scott Verplank to win the Ford Classic at Doral. Parry nearly missed the first-round 7:54am tee off when he slept through his alarm; his brother woke him at 7:40am. He went on to post a first-round 1-under par 71 and followed with rounds of 67-65-68 to force the playoff.

BIRTHDATES
1904   Norwegian speed skater IVAR BALLANGRUD – died 1969
1938   American auto racer JANET GUTHRIE
1938   American golfer HOMERO BLANCAS
1950   Pro Football Hall of Fame halfback FRANCO HARRIS
1952   West Indian Test batsman SIR VIVIAN RICHARDS
1952   Pro Football Hall of Fame receiver/sports caster LYNN SWANN
1957   Australian surfer MARK RICHARDS
1959   American golfer TOM LEHMAN
1960   Czech tennis player IVAN LENDL
1965   Swedish golfer JESPER PARNEVIK
1966   Australian rugby union front rower TONY DALEY
1977   Irish rugby union fly-half RONAN O'GARA

⑧ MARCH

1971 – Frazier wins 'Fight of the Century'
World Heavyweight Champion Joe Frazier beat Muhammad Ali in a unanimous points decision at New York's Madison Square Garden. The fight lived up to its hype, in 45 minutes of brutal action that featured only 1 knockdown, when Frazier decked Ali with a sweeping left hook in the 15th round. It was the first of 3 fights between the pair, with Ali winning the next 2.

1983 – 60m mark broken
Australia's Glen Thurlow became the first skier to break the 60m (200ft) barrier, with a jump of 61.57m at the Moomba Masters on Melbourne's Yarra River. In 1993, American Jimmy Siemers jumped a further 10m at the US. Open in Santa Fe, Texas.

1994 – Two four-pointers
Scottie Pippen and Pete Myers of the Chicago Bulls both came up with rare 4-point plays, in a 116-95 home victory over the Atlanta Hawks. It was the first time teammates had achieved the feat in the same game. A 4-point play is a 3-point field goal, followed by a foul shot.

1995 – Paki's clean house
Pakistan captain Saleem Malik and team coach Intikhab Alam were sacked by the Pakistan Cricket Board over bribery allegations, brought forward by Australian team members Tim May and Shane Warne, who alleged Malik offered them money to bowl badly in the first Test in Karachi in 1994. Malik denied the allegations. Intikhab was later reinstated.

2009 – Two-ton Hughes youngest
Playing in only his second Test, Australian opener Phillip Hughes became the youngest batsman in history to score 2 centuries in a Test, on the third day of the second Test against South Africa in Durban. He was 20 years, 98 days old when he broke a 79-year-old record set by West Indian George Headley.

Scottie Pippen, who pulled out a rare 4-point play for the Chicago Bulls in 1994. Photo: Copyright Steve Lipofsky Basketballphoto.com [CC-BY-SA-3.0], via Wikimedia Commons.

2010 – Uconn's 71 straight
The Connecticut Huskies made women's college basketball history when they beat Notre Dame 59-44 in the semi-finals of the Big East tournament in Hartford, Connecticut – it was UConn's NCAA record 71st straight win.

BIRTHDATES
1931	South African Test fast bowler NEIL ADCOCK – died 2013
1939	Russian speed skater LIDIYA SKOBLIKOVA
1945	Australian Test all rounder GRAEME WATSON
1949	Peruvian soccer striker TEOFILIO CUBILLAS
1951	England Test spinner PHIL EDMONDS
1954	British swimmer DAVID WILKIE
1960	Australian swimmer MAX METZKER
1969	Australian surfer LISA ANDERSON
1970	NFL kicker JASON ELAM
1976	NFL wide receiver HINES WARD
1984	New Zealand Test captain ROSS TAYLOR
1990	Czech tennis player PETRA KVITOVÁ

⑨ MARCH

1970 – England skipper comes into the world
World Cup-winning England rugby union captain Martin Johnson was born in Sulihull, England. Johnson was a tough lock who made his England debut at the age of 22, against France, in a 16-15 victory at Twickenham. After 92 internationals, he made his last appearance in the World Cup final against Australia in Sydney, when he captained the side to a dramatic 20-17 victory in sudden-death overtime. After his retirement from international rugby, Johnson continued playing with the Leicester Tigers until his retirement in 2005 and managed the England national team 2008–2011.

1986 – Yan youngest
Wang Yan of China became the youngest female athletics world record holder, when she recorded a time of 21:03.8 seconds in the 5k walk at Jian in China. Yan was 14 years and 334 days old.

1995 – MLB expansion
Major League Baseball owners voted 28-0 to admit 2 new teams, the Tampa Bay Devil Rays and the Arizona Diamondbacks for the 1998 season. Each team paid an expansion fee of $130 million. Whilst the Devil Rays struggled in their formative years but reached the World Series in 2008, the Diamondbacks won the World Series in 2001, on the starting pitching of Randy Johnson and Curt Schilling.

1996 – Champs turn into chumps
Indian batsman Ajay Jadeja smashed 40 off Waqar Younis's last 2 overs, as India knocked out defending World Cup champions Pakistan at Bangalore. Pakistan captain Wasim Akram was a last minute withdrawal from the match with a side strain. Back in Pakistan, his effigies were burned in the streets, and his house was pelted with rubbish. A number of Pakistan fans committed suicide as a result of the match.

1996 – Super Sanath
Sri Lankan opener Sanath Jayasuriya smashed 82 off only 44 balls in a World Cup quarter final against England at Faisalabad. Sri Lanka won with 9 overs to spare and went on to a famous victory over Australia in the final.

England rugby union captain Martin Johnson during the 2003 World Cup Final.

1998 – Tendulkar … again
Indian super-batsman Sachin Tendulkar scored an unbeaten 155 against Australia in the first Test in Chennai. Australia led by 71 on the first innings, but Tendulkar hit 14 fours and 4 sixes off an attack led by leg-spinner Shane Warne to alter the momentum of the series. The tourists crashed to a 179-run defeat and India went on to win the series 2-1.

BIRTHDATES
1887	England Test batsman PHIL MEAD – died 1958
1941	American golfer JIM COLBERT
1944	South African Test batsman LEE IRVINE
1950	American golfer ANDY NORTH
1950	American auto racer DANNY SULLIVAN
1952	England rugby union captain BILL BEAUMONT
1955	Italian auto racer TEO FABI
1960	American tennis player MIKE LEACH
1966	England soccer forward NIGEL CLOUGH
1966	AFL forward TONY LOCKETT
1968	French soccer midfielder YOURI DJORKAEFF
1970	England rugby union captain MARTIN JOHNSON
1975	Argentine soccer midfielder JUAN SEBASTIÁN VERÓN
1975	Dutch soccer striker ROY MAKAAY
1978	Irish jockey FERGAL LYNCH
1984	American alpine skier JULIA MANCUSO
1985	Indian Test wicketkeeper PARTHIV PATEL

⑩ MARCH

1956 – Landy's sporting gesture
John Landy showed inspiring sportsmanship at the Australian Mile Championships in Melbourne. Landy, the second man in history to run a sub-4-minute mile, stopped to help fallen runner Ron Clarke back to his feet, then steamed home to win the race against all the odds. Clarke would go on to break 18 world records, in distances from 2 miles to 20,000m.

1970 – Proteas' last yelp for a while
South Africa completed its last Test for 22 years, with an easy 323-run win over Australia in the fourth Test at Port Elizabeth. Their 4-0 series triumph was also South Africa's first series sweep. Champion opener Barry Richards and Lee Irvine made centuries in their final Test innings and Mike Procter took 9 wickets. The country's policy of apartheid, however, brought about international isolation from sporting competition.

1974 – Rowe rampant
West Indian batsman Lawrence Rowe completed a marathon innings of 302 against England in the drawn third Test in Bridgetown. Rowe's innings included 32 fours and a six. On the same day, Tony Greig laboured gamely for 6 wickets to become the first Englishman to take 5 wickets and score a century in the same Test.

1985 – Motta's 700
Dallas coach Dick Motta became only the fourth NBA coach to win 700 regular-season games when the Mavericks beat the Nets, 126-113 in New Jersey. Red Auerbach, Jack Ramsay and Gene Shue were the other 700-club members.

2003 – Motorcycle legend passes away
British 2-time world 500cc motorcycle champion, Barry Sheene, died of throat and stomach cancer. He was 52. Sheene won the World 500cc championship in 1976 and 1977, but was equally famous for overcoming his numerous crashes on the track. He moved to the warmer climate of the Gold Coast in Australia in the early 1990s and worked as a television commentator. He was awarded an MBE in 1978.

Barry Sheene on a Yamaha during the 1980 British 500cc Motorcycle Grand Prix at Donington.

2007 – Crosby's second 100-point season
Sidney Crosby became the youngest player in NHL history to have two 100-point seasons when he scored in a 3-2 win over the New York Rangers in Pittsburgh. The 19-year-old Crosby scored his 28th goal of the season. He also had 72 assists in 65 games.

2010 – Pakis get tough
Pakistan Cricket Board president Ijaz Butt carried out a deep cull of senior players in the wake of the side's poor performance on the 2009–10 tour of Australia. Younis Khan and Mohammad Yousuf were banned indefinitely, Shoaib Malik and Rana Naved-ul-Hasan for one year, and Shahid Afridi and Umar and Kamran Akmal were fined for various misdemeanors and put on 6-month probations.

BIRTHDATES
1914	American golfer CHANDLER HARPER – died 2004
1928	England Test batsman ARHTUR MILTON – died 2007
1935	Australian AFL ruckman GRAHAM 'POLLY' FARMER
1936	Swiss football executive SEPP BLATTER
1938	Pro Football Hall of Fame tackle RON MIX
1943	American golfer SANDRA PALMER
1956	American golfer JANET ANDERSON
1961	American gymnast MITCH GAYLORD
1969	Australian golfer STEPHEN LEANEY
1972	American auto racer MATT KENSETH
1976	Austrian tennis player BARBARA SCHETT
1977	American gymnast SHANNON MILLER
1979	Australian swimmer ASHLEY CALLUS
1981	Cameroon soccer forward SAMUEL ETO'O

1940 – Mangrum's first PGA win
Lloyd Mangrum edged Byron Nelson by 2 strokes to win the 54-hole Thomasville Open at Glen Arven CC in Thomasville, Georgia. It was the first of Mangrum's 38 PGA Tour victories. He won 1 major, the famous 1946 US Open at Canterbury, where he tied with Vic Ghezzi and Byron Nelson in the 18-hole playoff and went on to win the second playoff by 1 stroke. He also won the Varden Trophy (1951, 1953). Mangrum died in 1973, aged 59.

1945 – Nelson starts win streak
Byron Nelson began his historic 11-tournament winning streak when he teamed with 'Jug' McSpaden to win the Miami Four-Ball Championship at the Normandy Shore Club in Miami, Florida. Nelson and McSpaden posted an easy 8 & 6 victory over Denny Shute and Sam Byrd. It was a stellar year for Nelson, who won a record 18 PGA Tour events, including the PGA Championship. He also won the Varden Trophy for lowest Tour average.

1986 – Another 50 for Bossy
New York Islanders right-wing Mike Bossy became the first player in the NHL to score at least 50 goals in 9 consecutive seasons when he scored in an 8-4 home win against Calgary. Bossy led the Islanders to 4 consecutive Stanley Cup titles (1980–83) and was awarded the Conn Smythe Trophy (for MVP) in 1982. Back injuries forced him to retire prematurely in 1987 and he was inducted into Hockey's Hall of Fame in 1991.

1990 – Seve's Sixtieth
Spanish golfer Severiano Ballesteros won his 60th tour event, the Balearic Open in Majorca. Balleseros won 5 major titles in his career, including 3 British Open Championships (1979, 1984 and 1988) and 2 US Masters (1980 and 1983). He was also the inspiration behind the European revival in The Ryder Cup, scoring 20 points from 37 matches against the United States and captaining Europe in its famous win at Valderrama in 1997. Balleseros was the first player to reach £1 million, £2 million and £3 million in earnings on The European Tour.

1990 – Junior Jen
Jennifer Capriati became the youngest finalist in a professional tennis tournament when, at 13 years and 347 days, she reached the final of the Virginia Slims in Florida. Capriati was beaten 6-4, 7-5 by Argentine glamour girl Gabriela Sabatini.

2000 – 'The Prince' perfect
British fighter Prince Naseem Hamed took his winning streak to 34 when he scored a fourth-round TKO win over the previously unbeaten Vuyani Bungu of South Africa, in their WBO featherweight title bout in London.

2001 – Harbhajan hat-trick
Indian spinner Harbhajan Singh took a rare hat-trick in a brilliant display against Australia in the second Test in Kolkata. Singh dismissed Ricky Ponting, Adam Gilchrist and Shane Warne with consecutive balls on his way to 7 for 123 in Australia's total of 445. He captured another 6 wickets in the second innings for match figures of 13 for 196. Batting heroics from VVS Laxman (281) and Rahul Dravid (180) led India to a famous 171-run victory.

BIRTHDATES
1885	English land/water speed pilot SIR MALCOLM CAMPBELL – died 1948
1915	Indian Test batsman VIJAY HAZARE – died 2004
1921	West Indian Test captain JEFFERY STOLLMEYER – died 1989
1923	American tennis player LOUISE BROUGH
1926	England soccer forward DENIS WILSHAW – died 2004
1929	South African Test captain JACKIE McGLEW – died 1998
1930	American auto racer TROY RUTTMAN – died 1997
1931	Media/sports mogul RUPERT MURDOCH
1943	England rugby union captain COLIN McFADYEAN
1947	Australian squash player GEOFF HUNT
1953	Irish auto racer DEREK DALEY
1958	American motorcycle rider EDDIE LAWSON
1960	New Zealand rugby union centre WARWICK TAYLOR
1961	English golfer ANDREW SHERBORNE
1976	New Zealand rugby union centre PITA ALATINI
1979	NBA forward ELTON BRAND
1980	MLB infielder DAN UGGLA

⑫ MARCH

1940 – Helsinki Games halted
The International Olympic Committee announced the cancellation of the Helsinki Olympic Games, due to the advent of World War II. The Finnish capital later hosted the Games in 1952.

1966 – Hull's Hockey 50
Chicago's Bobby Hull became the first NHL player to score more than 50 goals in a season. Hull's blistering 40ft slap shot beat screened New York Rangers goalie Cesare Maniago, early in the third period of the Blackhawks' 4-2 victory at Chicago Stadium. 3 NHL players had scored 50 goals – Hull (twice), Montreal's 'Rocket' Richard and 'Boom Boom' Geoffrion. Hull's record-breaking 51st goal came in his 56th game of the season.

1989 – Double double-bogey finish
In an unusual finish, Tom Kite and Davis Love III both double bogeyed the 72nd hole to tie in the Nestle Invitational at the Bay Hill Club in Orlando, Florida. Kite went on to beat Love in the sudden death playoff

1991 – Football League's first female official
Wendy Toms became the first woman to officiate at an English Football League match. Toms acted as the fourth official in the Third Division encounter between Bournemouth and Reading.

1996 – Lara ends Proteas' run
South Africa's run of 10 consecutive one-day wins ended, in a World Cup quarter-final against the West Indies at the National Stadium in Karachi. Brian Lara blazed 111 off just 94 balls to lead the Windies to a 19-run victory.

2004 – 500 Warne wickets
Master leg-spinner Shane Warne became only the second man, and the first spin bowler, to reach the 500-Test wickets milestone, on the final day of Australia's come-from-behind first Test victory over Sri Lanka in Gall. Playing in his first Test after a 12-month suspension for failing a drug test, Warne finished with figures of 10-159, as Sri Lanka collapsed to 154 all out in their second innings after the Australians had

NHL legend Bobby Hull in action against the NY Rangers in 1966.

earlier declared on 512 for 8. Warne ended the game with 501 Test victims, chasing Courtney Walsh's all-time record of 519.

2006 – First ODI 400+
Australia became the first team to score more than 400 runs in an ODI, but were beaten by South Africa with just one ball to spare, at the Wanderers Ground in Johannesburg. Ricky Ponting passed 9,000 ODI runs while smashing a personal best 164, in Australia's 434-4. In an improbable run chase, the South Africans followed the Aussies' world-record total with a score of 439. The win gave South Africa the series 3-2.

BIRTHDATES
1923	Norwegian speed skater HJALMAR ANDERSEN – died 2013
1938	American auto racer JOHNNY RUTHERFORD
1949	Irish rugby union captain FERGUS SLATTERY
1954	Japanese golfer HAJIME MESHIAI
1958	Australian road cyclist PHIL ANDERSON
1958	NFL linebacker/executive/analyst MATT MILLEN
1960	West Indian Test all rounder ELDINE BAPTISTE
1962	MLB outfielder DARRYL STRAWBERRY
1963	English golfer PAUL WAY
1963	English soccer manager IAN HOLLOWAY
1965	MLB outfielder STEVE FINLEY
1968	NFL defensive back MERTON HANKS
1970	Swedish golfer MATHIAS GRÖNBERG
1976	Australian triathlete JOANNE KING

1960 – Arnie satisfies his army
Arnold Palmer 1-putted 9 of the last 10 greens to score an incredible win in the Pensacola Open. Palmer made birdie on the 17th and 18th holes to beat Doug Sanders by 1 stroke, for his third consecutive victory and 17th PGA Tour success.

1961 – Floyd gets up to beat rival
After being knocked down twice in the first round, World Heavyweight Champion Floyd Patterson recovered to score a sixth-round knockout over Swedish rival Ingemar Johansson in Miami. Before Patterson agreed to their third fight, he insisted that seating be integrated. The condition was met, and African Americans mixed freely among the predominantly white crowd in Convention Hall. Patterson won the entertaining series against Johansson, with 2 knockout victories to one.

1974 – Terrific Turner
New Zealand opener Glenn Turner became the first Kiwi to score 2 hundreds in a Test match, in the Kiwis first-ever Test cricket victory over Australia at Christchurch. After scoring 101 in the first innings, Turner remained unbeaten at the end, having anchored the chase of 228 with 115. It was a remarkable effort, as only one other New Zealander passed 26 in the match.

1983 – Title fight rounds reduced
The World Boxing Council became the first organisation to cut World Title fights from 15 to 12 rounds. The decision followed the death of Korean lightweight fighter Deuk-Koo Kim after his fight with Ray 'Boom Boom' Mancini in Las Vegas; sadly, within 4 months of Kim's fight, both his mother and the referee, Richard Greene, had committed suicide.

1991 – Ronnie's max
Future snooker legend, Ronnie O'Sullivan, became the youngest player to make a competitive maximum break of 147. O'Sullivan was 15 years and 98 days when he completed the perfect break during the English Amateur Championship at Aldershot, Hants.

1996 – Cricket semi-final abandoned
The World Cup semi-final between India and Sri Lanka had to be abandoned in Calcutta when angry fans set fire to stands and pelted players with water bottles and fruit. Chasing 252, India was struggling at 120-8 when play was stopped. Sri Lanka was awarded the match and went on to win the final.

2000 – Marino memories
Dan Marino, champion Miami Dolphins quarterback, announced his retirement. In a 17-year career, Marino played in 242 games for Miami. He passed for 61,361 yards, 420 touchdowns, and 252 interceptions for an 86.4 efficiency rating, ranking him sixth all-time. Marino held the season touchdown record, with 47 until it was broken by Peyton Manning of the Indianapolis Colts in 2004.

2005 – Record tied from the arc
Donyell Marshall tied an NBA-record with 12 3-pointers, and the Toronto Raptors established a new league mark with 21 as a team, in their 128-110 victory over Philadelphia at Air Canada Centre.

2007 – 'Mush'
Lance Mackey became the first dog musher to complete the 1,000-mile Yukon Quest and the 1,100-mile Iditarod double. Race vets declared Mackey's dog team to be in perfect health at the end of the event. He repeated the feat the following year.

BIRTHDATES
1904	West Indian Test batsman CLIFFORD ROACH – died 1988
1950	Former British boxer 'AUSSIE JOE' BUGNER
1950	West Indian Test all-rounder BERNARD JULIEN
1953	American golfer ANDY BEAN
1955	Italian soccer winger/manager BRUNO CONTI
1959	Australian Test batsman DIRK WELLHAM
1963	NFL receiver VANCE JOHNSON
1964	MLB first baseman WILL CLARK
1967	Colombian soccer defender ANDRÉS ESCOBAR – died 1994
1972	NFL quarterback TRENT DILFER
1973	Dutch soccer midfielder EDGAR DAVIDS
1974	Swedish tennis player THOMAS ENQVIST
1979	Venezuelan MLB pitcher JOHAN SANTANA

⑭ MARCH

1942 – TJ's first finish
Legendary Australian horse trainer T. J. Smith guided the first of more than 7,000 winners to victory, when Bragger won at Rosehill Racecourse in Sydney.

1949 – PGA Championship all-American
The PGA of America decided to keep the PGA Championship, held in Richmond, Virginia, open only to American participants. The PGA Executive Committee voted 8-3 against inviting South African star Bobby Locke to play in one of their marquee events.

1967 – Combined football draft
The American and National Football Leagues conducted a common draft of college players for the first time. Michigan State defensive lineman Bubba Smith was the first player to be drafted to the big leagues, chosen by the Baltimore Colts. It was the first step towards the merger of the Leagues, which took place in 1970.

1969 – Scintillating Seymour
West Indian batsman Seymour Nurse walloped 258 in his final Test against New Zealand at Christchurch. His sixth Test century included 34 fours and a six. The match was drawn, leaving the 3-Test series at 1-1.

1976 – 'The Shoe' wins his 7,000th
Prolific American jockey Bill Shoemaker won his 7,000th race on Royal Derby II at Santa Anita Park. It was Royal Derby II's first win in 3 years.

1987 – Third figure skating title for Witt
Statuesque German Katarina Witt won her third world figure skating championship when she beat both American chances, Debi Thomas and Caryn Kadavy in Cincinnati. Witt had previously won the World Title in 1984 and 1985, and went on to win her fourth world title in 1988. She was the Olympic champion in 1984 and 1988, and was also a 6-time European champion. Witt raised eyebrows when she posed for *Playboy* magazine in 1998.

2001 – Lavish Laxman
On the fourth day of the famous second Test against Australia in Kolkata, during an Indian innings record of 281, V. V. S. Laxman hit 275. Rahul Dravid added 180 as India scored 657, after being forced to follow-on. Spinner Harbhajan Singh took 6 wickets as the Australians crashed for 212, and a 171-run defeat.

Katarina Witt during the 1986 World Figure Skating Championships in Geneva, Switzerland.

2004 – Woeful Windies
After matching England for much of the first Test in Jamaica, the West Indies were blown away for 47 in the second innings, their lowest-ever total in Tests. Steve Harmison's 7 for 12 was the cheapest 7-wicket haul in Test history. England won by 10 wickets, their first of 11 Test wins in 2004.

2008 – Rockets go 21 straight
Tracey McGrady scored 30 points, and the Houston Rockets extended their winning streak to 21 games, in an 89-80 win over Charlotte in Houston. The Rockets owned the NBA's second-longest winning streak, behind only the LA Lakers' 1971–72 run of 33 in a row. The win broke a tie with the 1970–71 Milwaukee Bucks.

BIRTHDATES
1912	England soccer midfielder CLIFF BASTIN – died 1991
1914	American auto racer LEE PETTY – died 2000
1929	American golfer BOB GOALBY
1936	New Zealand golfer BOB CHARLES
1938	Australian Test spinner JOHNNY GLEESON
1946	Basketball Hall of Fame centre/coach WES UNSELD
1963	Australian Test fast bowler BRUCE REID
1969	NBA forward LARRY JOHNSON
1975	Australian pole-vaulter DMITRI MARKOV
1976	England rugby union prop PHIL VICKERY
1977	Australian rugby union hooker JEREMY PAUL
1978	Dutch swimmer PIETER VAN DEN HOOGENBAND
1979	French soccer striker NICOLAS ANELKA

⑮ MARCH

1877 – First Test ton
Australian batsman Charles Bannerman became the first centurion in Test cricket, when he finished the first day of the first-ever Test against England unbeaten on 126. He went on to retire hurt on 165. Australia won the match by 45 runs, the same winning margin seen in the Centenary Test on the same ground in 1977.

1920 – International oldie
Billy Meredith became the oldest player to appear in an international match when he played for Wales against England at Highbury. Meredith was 45 years, 229 days old. Wales won the match 2-1.

1979 – Sarfraz sensational
Pakistan fast bowler Sarfraz Nawaz took an amazing 9 for 36 to skittle Australia for 310 in the first Test in Melbourne. Chasing 382, Australia was cruising at 305-3, when Sarfraz took 7 for 1 in 33 balls.

1987 – Charity hit golfing jackpot
American Dan Pooley recorded a hole-in-one on the 17th hole at the Hertz Bay Hill Classic, earning $1 million ($500,000 for himself and $500,000 for charity). Payne Stewart won the event with a tournament-record 264 and then also donated his prize money of $108,000 to charity.

1988 – Cards off to Phoenix
NFL owners reluctantly, but overwhelmingly, approved the proposed St Louis Cardinals move to Phoenix, Arizona. The City of St Louis had ignored the demands of Cardinals' owner Bill Bidwell for a new, preferably domed stadium, after years of dwindling attendances.

2000 – 'Warnie' Aussie best
Shane Warne became Australia's greatest Test wicket-taker when he passed Dennis Lillee's record of 355 dismissals on the final day of the first Test against New Zealand in Auckland. The record came on the last ball of the Test, when Warne had Paul Wiseman caught behind by Adam Gilchrist. Australia won the match by 62 runs.

Pakistan pace bowler Sarfraz Nawaz during the 1979 World Cup semi-final against the West Indies.

2001 – Cricket winning streak over
Test cricket's longest winning streak of 16 matches came to an end when Australia was beaten by India by 171 runs, in the second Test in Calcutta. After taking 7 for 123 in the first Australian innings, Indian spinner Harbhajan Singh nabbed another 6 as the Australians crashed for 212, and a 171-run defeat. Singh's match figures were 13 for 196. VVS Laxman's second-innings knock of 281 gave him the record for highest Test innings by an Indian batsman.

2008 – Brodeur brilliant
New Jersey goalie Martin Brodeur stopped 24 shots to reach 40 wins for an NHL-record seventh time, in the Devils' 4-2 win over the Colorado Avalanche in Denver. Brodeur broke the league mark in 2007 by earning 48 victories.

BIRTHDATES
1920	Indian field hockey player RANGANANTHAN FRANCIS
1926	Pro Football Hall of Fame quarterback NORM VAN BROCKLIN – died 1983
1931	NFL coach TED MARCHIBRODA
1946	MLB outfielder BOBBY BONDS – died 2003
1947	Australian Test fast bowler DAVID COLLEY
1953	West Indies Test fast bowler COLIN CROFT
1955	Pakistan Test opener MOHSIN KHAN
1957	Spanish soccer midfielder/manager VICTOR MUÑOZ
1962	England rugby union flanker JON HALL
1969	Japanese jockey YUTAKA TAKE
1970	South African rugby union hooker NAKA DROTSKÉ
1972	NFL coach MIKE TOMLIN
1983	Australian Test fast bowler BEN HILFENHAUS

1991 – American 1-2-3

For the first time, American skaters swept all 3 medals at the World Championships in Munich. Kristi Yamaguchi won the gold medal, ahead of Tonya Harding and Nancy Kerrigan.

1991 – Fitch reaches 800 NBA wins

New Jersey coach Bill Fitch earned his 800th career victory, as the Nets beat Washington 110-86 at the Meadowlands.

1996 – Tyson supreme

Mike Tyson scored a third-round TKO win over Englishman Frank Bruno in Las Vegas, regaining the WBC Heavyweight title. It was Bruno's first defence of the title, which he'd won from Oliver McCall in 1995.

1997 – Golf playoff saga

Bob Murphy and Jay Sigel fought out the then longest playoff in Senior PGA Tour history at the Toshiba Classic in Newport Beach, California. Murphy holed an incredible 80ft birdie putt on the ninth extra hole for the victory.

2002 – Alpine ski golden sweep

Australian skier Michael Milton became the first above-the-knee amputee to win all 4 alpine ski events at the same Paralympics, when he won the slalom gold at Salt Lake City. Milton had already won the downhill, the super-G and the giant slalom. In 2003, he was named World Sportsperson of the Year with a Disability at the Laureus World Sports Awards in Monaco.

2004 – Murali's 500

Sri Lankan spinner Muttiah Muralitharan became the youngest and quickest cricketer to take 500 Test wickets, achieving the feat in the second Test against Australia in Kandy. The 31-year-old off-spinner reached the landmark in his 87th Test when he bowled Michael Kasprowicz, leaving him with match figures of 4 for 48.

2007 – Six sixes = Gibbs

In a Group A Cricket World Cup match against the Netherlands in St Kitts, South Africa's Herschelle Gibbs smashed 6 sixes in 1 over. Gibbs was the first player to achieve the feat in a one-day international, although Garfield Sobers and Ravi Shastri had previously done it in first-class cricket. He hammered hapless leg-spinner Daan van Bunge back over his head 4 times, and over the ropes on the on side twice. He faced just 40 balls for his 72, which included 4 fours and 7 sixes. Gibbs's fireworks were worth $1 million to charity, after a sponsor promised to donate the sum in celebration of the feat.

2006 – US out of first Baseball Classic

Oliver Perez and 7 relievers combined to pitch a 3-hitter, leading Mexico past Roger Clemens and Team USA, 2-1, and eliminating the Americans from the inaugural World Baseball Classic in Anaheim.

2008 – Woods third all-time

Tiger Woods posted his 64th career win on the US PGA Tour, when he beat Bart Bryant by 1 shot in the Arnold Palmer Invitational in Orlando, Florida. The total matched the great Ben Hogan in third place on the all-time list, behind only Jack Nicklaus (73) and Sam Snead (82). It was Woods' fifth win in this tournament, making him the first player in Tour history to win 4 tournaments at least 5 times.

BIRTHDATES

1906	England Test batsman MAURICE TURNBULL – died 1944
1908	New Zealand rugby union fullback HERBIE LILBURNE – died 1976
1910	Indian Test batsman NAWAB OF PATAUDI SR – died 1952
1939	Argentine soccer midfielder/manager CARLOS BILARDO
1954	American golfer HOLLIS STACY
1954	Australian Test batsman/coach DAV WHATMORE
1956	NFL tight end/executive OZZIE NEWSOME
1959	Australian Test wicket keeper GREG DYER
1974	Zimbabwean Test captain HEATH STREAK
1989	NBA forward BLAKE GRIFFIN
1989	English soccer forward THEO WALCOTT

⑰ MARCH

1897 – Title fight on film
In the first championship fight recorded on film, Bob Fitzsimmons knocked out Jim Corbett in the 14th round at Carson City, Nevada. The proximity of the fight to the 'wild west', and the nature of the era was emphasised when Sheriff Bat Masterson collected 400 guns from paying customers at the entrance. Another famous sheriff, Wyatt Earp stood in Corbett's corner with a 6-gun as protection.

1923 – Hagen record
Golfing great Walter Hagen fired a then world-record round of 62 as he won the Florida West Coast Championship by 10 strokes at Bellaire, Florida. Hagen's posted a winning total of 276. It was Hagan's third consecutive win in the tournament.

1977 – Centenary Test
Australia won the Centenary Test against England by 45 runs at the MCG – exactly the same margin as in the game's first Test, at the same ground, 100 years before. Chasing 463 to win, Derek Randall scored 174 for England in their total of 417. The great Dennis Lillee captured 5 for 139 for Australia.

1990 – Scots' slam
Scotland upset England 13-7 at Murrayfield to win the rugby union Five Nations Championship and claim an undefeated Grand Slam. The in-form and heavily favoured England side was neutralised by the Scots, who dominated all facets of the game. Winger Tony Stranger scored a try for Scotland and Craig Chalmers kicked 3 penalties.

1996 – Sri Lankan World Cup
Sri Lanka beat Australia by 7 wickets in Lahore to win the Cricket World Cup. Mark Taylor top-scored with 74 in Australia's 7 for 241. After a shaky start, the Sri Lankans took 46-overs to reach 3 for 245. Man of the Match Aravinda de Silva scored 107 not out.

1998 – US girls' ice hockey victory
The United States beat Canada, 3-1 to win the inaugural gold medal for women's hockey in the Winter Olympics at Nagano in Japan. Goalie Sarah Tueting's 22-save performance was key to victory.

1999 – Wilkens' record
Atlanta head coach Lenny Wilkens coached his 2,051st NBA game, surpassing Bill Fitch to become the NBA's all-time leader in games coached. Since 1969, Wilkens had coached in the NBA in Seattle, Portland, Cleveland, Atlanta, Toronto and New York. He guided the Seattle Supersonics to the NBA Championship in 1979 and Team USA to the Olympic gold medal in 1996.

2007 – Ireland's World Cup upset
Inspired by their giant seamer Boyd Rankin, Ireland dismissed defending champions Pakistan for 132 to win by 3 wickets in the Cricket World Cup in Kingston, Jamaica. In another shock, Bangladesh humbled India, winning by 5 wickets in Port of Spain, making it a great day for the underdogs.

2009 – Brodeur #1
Martin Brodeur became the winningest goal-tender in NHL history with 552 career victories, as the New Jersey Devils beat the Chicago Blackhawks 3-2 in Newark, NJ. The 36-year-old Brodeur made 30 saves to pass Hall of Famer Patrick Roy.

BIRTHDATES
1902	American golfer BOBBY JONES – died 1971
1914	Pro Football Hall of Fame quarterback SAMMY BAUGH – died 2008
1915	Australian equestrian rider BILL ROYCROFT – died 2011
1939	Italian soccer coach GIOVANNI TRAPPATONI
1944	MLB manager CITO GASTON
1949	Irish soccer defender/manager PAT RICE
1957	English figure skater ROBIN COUSINS
1959	NBA guard/executive DANNY AINGE
1963	West Indian Test spinner ROGER HARPER
1964	England soccer defender LEE DIXON
1965	South African Test opener ANDREW HUDSON
1969	French moguls skier EDGAR GROSPIRON
1972	American soccer forward MIA HAMM
1976	Uruguayan soccer forward ÁLVARO RECOBA
1981	Australian golfer AARON BADDELEY
1983	Portuguese soccer midfielder RAUL MEIRELES

1945 – 'The Rocket' scores
In the final game of the season, Montreal's star right-wing, Maurice Richard, became the first NHL player to score 50 goals in a season in the Canadiens' 4-2 win in Boston. It would be 36 seasons until another NHL player (Mike Bossy) scored 50 goals in the season's first 50 games.

1964 – Speed skating legend born
American speed skater Bonnie Blair was born in Cornwall, New York. She became the only American woman to win 5 gold medals in Winter Olympic Games competition. She won the 500m in 1988, the 500m and 1,000m in both 1992 and 1994, and added the 1,000m bronze in 1988. She retired from competition as reigning world sprint champion on her 31st birthday in 1995. Blair married Olympic teammate Dave Cruikshank and built a successful career as a motivational speaker and corporate spokesperson.

1986 – Thomson calls it a day
Fast bowling great Jeff Thomson retired from first-class cricket after playing for a beaten Queensland team in the Sheffield Shield Final. Thomson terrified batsmen with his express pace generated from a famous slinging action. He played 51 Tests, taking 200 wickets at 28.0. He formed a lethal opening bowling combination with the great Dennis Lillee.

1993 – Sri Lankan first
Sri Lanka scored their first-ever Test victory over England in the one-off match in Colombo. Trailing by 89 on the first innings, England was dismissed for 228 and a youthful Sanath Jayasuriya, batting at number seven, sealed the win when he smashed the only ball he faced for six. Sri Lankan spinner Jayananda Warnaweera captured 4 wickets in each innings.

1995 – MJ back with the Bulls
Michael Jordan announced his return to the Chicago Bulls after a 17-month retirement. He had spent a largely unspectacular season playing minor league baseball with the Birmingham Barons in the Chicago White Sox organisation. Jordan went on to lead the Bulls to the next 3 NBA Championships.

American speed skating champion Bonnie Blair. Photo: UweFan (Own work) [CC-BY-3.0], via Wikimedia Commons.

2001 – Miller magic
Indiana Pacers guard Reggie Miller became the first NBA player to convert 2,000 3-point field goals. Miller sank a 3-point shot in the third quarter of Indiana's 101-95 home win over the Sacramento Kings. The 3-point field goal was introduced into the NBA in the 1979–80 season.

2007 – Woolmer demise
Bob Woolmer, coach of the Pakistan team that had been knocked out of the World Cup by Ireland, was found unconscious in his hotel bathroom and later died in hospital. He was 58. An inquiry found he had died of natural causes.

BIRTHDATES
1877	Australian Test batsman CLEM HILL – died 1945
1937	American auto racer MARK DONOHUE – died 1975
1938	Finnish rally driver TIMO MÄKINEN
1939	English soccer manager RON ATKINSON
1942	English runner ANN PACKER
1947	England Test batsman DAVID LLOYD
1952	Pro Football Hall of Fame centre MIKE WEBSTER – died 2002
1956	Swedish alpine skier INGEMAR STENMARK
1960	Canadian NHL forward GUY CARBONNEAU
1962	New Zealand Test opener TREVOR FRANKLIN
1964	American speed skater BONNIE BLAIR
1966	Canadian golfer BRIAN WATTS
1967	NFL wide receiver ANDRE RISON
1971	Australian tennis player WAYNE ARTHURS
1980	Russian figure skater ALEXEI YAGUDIN
1981	Norwegian biathlete TORA BERGER
1987	American swimmer REBECCA SONI

⑲ MARCH

1966 – College basketball first
Texas Western became the first NCAA basketball champion to start 5 African Americans, upsetting no. 1 ranked Kentucky's all-white team 72-65 in the final in College Park, Maryland. The Miners took the lead midway in the first half and never relinquished it, though Kentucky came to within a point early in the second half. Texas Western coach Don Haskins received 40,000 pieces of hate mail and a dozen death threats.

1972 – Lakers' big win
The Los Angeles Lakers defeated the Golden State Warriors 162-99 at the Great Western Forum, in what was then the most lopsided victory in NBA history. The 63-point margin lasted as a record for nearly 19 years, until Cleveland beat Miami by 68 points, 148-80, in 1991.

1981 – Sabres' Ice Hockey record
After leading the Toronto Maple Leafs 1-0 after the first period at the Memorial Auditorium in Buffalo, the Sabres broke out for 9 goals in the second period, an NHL record for most goals in a period. Buffalo centre Gil Perreault led the onslaught with a hat-trick as Toronto goaltender Michel Larocque yielded all 9 goals. The Leafs scored 3 goals in the period as the teams set a record of 12 goals in 1 period. The Sabres scored 4 more goals in the third period for a 14-4 rout.

1994 – Brian is brilliant
Champion West Indian batsman Brian Lara hit 25 fours and 2 sixes in a blistering 167 against England in the second Test in Georgetown, Guyana. Jimmy Adams also scored 137 as the Windies won the match by an innings and 44 runs to take a 2-0 lead in the 5-match series.

1995 – Michael rusty after break
After taking 21 months off to play minor-league baseball and golf, Michael Jordan made his comeback at guard for the Chicago Bulls in their 103-96 overtime away loss to the Pacers. Jordan shot only 7-of-28 from the field and scored 19 points in 43 minutes

Michael Jordan, American basketball legend.

on court. The Bulls went on to win the next 3 NBA Championships.

2010 – James reaches quick 15,000-point landmark
LeBron James became the youngest player in NBL history to score 15,000 career points, breaking Kobe Bryant's mark by more than 2 years, as the Cleveland Cavaliers pulled away to beat the Bulls 92-85 in Chicago. James scored 13 of his 29 points in the fourth quarter, bringing him 15,026.

BIRTHDATES
1927	Baseball Hall of Fame outfielder/broadcaster RICHIE ASHBURN – died 1997
1932	American golfer GAY BREWER – died 2007
1936	America's Cup yacht designer BEN LEXCEN – died 1988
1938	College Football Hall of Fame quarterback JOE KAPP
1952	New Zealand Test wicket keeper WARREN LEES
1958	NFL coach ANDY REID
1966	England soccer midfielder ANDREW SINTON
1979	Croatian tennis player IVAN LJUBI I
1981	Ivorian soccer defender KOLO TOURÉ
1988	MLB pitcher CLAYTON KERSHAW

1932 – Phar Lap's US win

Champion Australian thoroughbred Phar Lap won his only start in North America, running a track record in the rich Agua Caliente Handicap over 2,000m. Within a fortnight, the great horse was dead, ostensibly from a mystery virus, but speculation continues that foul play was involved.

1965 – 'Venkat' career best

Indian spinner Srinivas Venkataraghaven captured a career best 8 for 72 in the fourth Test against New Zealand in Delhi. He grabbed another 4 wickets in the Kiwi second innings. 'Venkat' became a respected Test umpire.

1971 – Kareem's first of six

Milwaukee centre Lew Alcindor won the first of his record 6 NBA MVP awards. Alcindor, who later changed his name to Kareem Abdul-Jabbar, played in all 82 games for the Bucks and won the first of back-to-back scoring titles with a 31.7 average. Milwaukee went on to sweep the Baltimore Bullets in the Finals, winning the NBA championship, with Alcindor named the Finals MVP.

1976 – Four for Nicholl

Aston Villa defender Chris Nicholl scored all 4 goals in Villa's 2-2 draw with Leicester City in their Division 1 match at Filbert Street; Nicholl inadvertently scored 2 own goals for the Foxes.

1989 – Reds' Rose researched

Major League Baseball announced Cincinnati Reds manager Pete Rose was under investigation, after reports were received of his alleged gambling activities. In August, he received a life-ban for betting on major league games. Although a 5-page document signed by both parties included no formal findings, MLB Commissioner Bart Giamatti considered Rose's acceptance of the ban to be a no-contest plea.

1990 – Russian football great dies

Legendary Russian goalkeeper Lev Yashin died at the age of 60. He won 78 Soviet international caps in a 20-year career that started in 1950. Yashin played all 20 seasons for his only club, Dynamo Moscow, winning 5 League championships and 3 Cup championships. He is the only goalkeeper to have won the coveted European Player of the Year award (1963). Yashin was famous for always wearing a black strip when he played.

2006 – Lethal Leisel

Leisel Jones became the first woman to break the 1:06 barrier for the 100m breaststroke, with a new world record at the Australian Commonwealth Games Swimming Trials in Melbourne. Jones cruised to the wall in 1:05.71, shaving 0.49 off American Jessica Hardy's world record.

2006 – 'Hawk-Eye'

The NASDAQ-100 Open in Miami became the first ATP event to implement the new Hawk-Eye officiating system. At the time the US Open was the only other event officially committed to the 8-camera system, which featured in-stadium video boards but its use is now commonplace.

BIRTHDATES

1885	Australian Test batsman VERNON RANSFORD – 1958
1933	Australian rugby league captain/coach IAN WALSH – died 2013
1945	Basketball Hall of Fame coach PAT RILEY
1948	Canadian Hockey Hall of Fame defenseman BOBBY ORR
1951	Indian Test fast bowler MADAN LAL
1952	Indian tennis player ANAND AMRITRAJ
1952	Australian auto racer GEOFF BRABHAM
1957	Australian woodchopper DAVID FOSTER
1958	Pro Football Hall of Fame linebacker RICKEY JACKSON
1961	American golfer KATHY GUADAGNINO
1961	Danish soccer winger JESPER OLSEN
1963	American tennis player/coach PAUL ANNACONE
1968	England soccer striker/analyst PAUL MERSON
1969	French rugby union flanker/coach FABIEN GALTHIÉ
1969	England cricket captain KAREN SMITHIES
1973	South African Test spinner NICKI BOJE
1979	New Zealand rugby union hooker KEVEN MEALAMU
1984	Spanish soccer striker FERNANDO TORRES

㉑ MARCH

1935 – Clough comes into the world
Respected English football international and club manager Brian Clough was born in Middlesbrough. A knee injury forced a premature retirement after a successful playing career with Middlesbrough and Sunderland, during which he scored an amazing 251 goals in 274 games. He also won 2 caps for England. As a manager, he took Derby County to the Division 1 title in 1972. Clough moved to Nottingham Forest in 1975, winning promotion in 1977, the Division 1 title in 1978 and the European Cup in 1979 and 1980. He left Forest in 1993. In 2004, he died of stomach cancer, aged 69.

1953 – Cousy's 30 from the line
Celtics guard Bob Cousy scored 50 points (25 in overtime) as Boston outlasted Syracuse 111-105 in 4 overtimes, eliminating the Nationals in the Eastern Division Semi-finals. Cousy made 30 free throws, an NBA playoff record.

1964 – Bruins unbeaten
The John Wooden coached UCLA Bruins became only the third team to go through a season undefeated (30-0) and win the national title when they scored a 98-83 win over Duke in Kansas City. Sharp-shooting guard Gail Goodrich led the offense with a game-high 27 points. It was the first of 10 NCAA basketball titles in 12 seasons for the Bruins. San Francisco in 1956 and North Carolina in 1957 were the first 2 undefeated title winners.

1980 – Americans boycott Moscow Olympics
President Jimmy Carter announced the US would boycott the Moscow Olympic Games scheduled for that summer. The announcement came after the Soviet Union failed to comply with his February 20 deadline to withdraw its troops from Afghanistan. In retaliation for Carter's action, the Soviet Union boycotted the 1984 Olympics held in Los Angeles.

1984 – Cricket comeback
Australian batsman Allan Border survived the final 105 minutes of the match with last man Terry Alderman to save the second Test against the West Indies in Trinidad.

Nottingham Forest manager Brian Clough in 1980.

At the close of play, Border had batted for 279 minutes for his 100 not out. Alderman was unbeaten on 21.

1999 – Spurs' third League Cup
An injury-time header by Danish international Alan Nielsen gave Tottenham Hotspur a 1-0 win over Leicester City in the Football League Cup Final at Wembley. Spurs have now won the trophy 4 times after their win in 2008.

BIRTHDATES
1925	Swiss road cyclist HUGO KOBLET – died 1964
1935	English soccer manager BRIAN CLOUGH – died 2004
1937	NFL coach TOM FLORES
1938	Australian Test batsman GRAHAME THOMAS
1949	West Indian Test batsman ALVIN KALLICHARRAN
1954	NBA coach MIKE DUNLEAVY
1956	Norwegian marathon runner INGRID KRISTIANSEN
1960	Brazilian auto racer AYRTEN SENNA – died 1994.
1961	German soccer striker/manager LOTHAR MATTHÄUS
1963	Dutch soccer defender/manager RONALD KOEMAN
1963	New Zealand rugby union winger TERRY WRIGHT
1966	Australian golfer KAREN LUNN
1966	American NHL defenseman AL IAFRATE
1975	South African rugby union flanker CORNÉ KRIGE
1975	Welsh snooker player MARK WILLIAMS
1985	NFL running back ADRIAN PETERSON

㉒ MARCH

1934 – Inaugural 'Masters' at Augusta
The first US Masters golf event commenced at the famed Augusta National Golf Club in Georgia. Golf administrator Clifford Roberts and player Bobby Jones were the founders. Roberts suggested the name The Masters, but Jones thought it was too presumptuous, so the event was named The Augusta National Invitation Tournament. Horton Smith was the inaugural winner. In 1939, Jones relented, and the name was changed/

1969 – Bruins dominate
UCLA centre Lew Alcindor scored 37 points and grabbed 20 rebounds as the Bruins beat Purdue, 92-72, in the NCAA final in Louisville, becoming the first team to win 5 NCAA titles. It was the third consecutive championship for the Bruins. Alcindor was named the Final Four Most Outstanding Player for the third straight year, the only player to ever achieve the feat.

1974 – Revson killed
Thirty-five-year-old American Formula 1 driver Peter Revson was killed during practice for the South African Grand Prix in Johannesburg, when his car crashed at 160mph and burst into flames. A faulty steering mechanism was blamed for the incident. Revson was renowned for his jet-setting playboy image.

1984 – Boléro
British ice dancers Jayne Torvill and Christopher Dean were awarded a record-breaking 29 maximum scores in the World Figure Skating Championships in Ottawa. After this win, their fourth amateur world ice dancing title, achieved by performing their famous Boléro routine, they announced they were turning professional. After 10 years as professionals, they returned to the amateur arena for the 1994 Lillehammer Olympics, taking bronze.

1992 – Bizarre Cricket finish
England scored a bizarre 19-run win over South Africa in Sydney to advance to the World Cup Final against Pakistan. After a rain delay and slow over penalty, which modified the winning target, the Springboks were left with the impossible task of scoring 22 runs off 1 ball.

Ruud van Nistelrooy controls the ball during a match against Sunderland.

2003 – Ruud starts streak
Manchester United striker Ruud van Nistelrooy started a 10-match scoring streak in the English Premier League when he scored a hat-trick in a 3-0 against Fulham at Old Trafford. The Dutchman scored 13 goals in the final 8 games of the 2002–2003 season and in the first 2 games of 2003–2004.

BIRTHDATES
1908	American tennis player JACK CRAWFORD – died 1991
1928	Basketball Hall of Fame centre ED MACAULEY – died 2011
1940	Canadian Hockey hall of fame centre DAVE KEON
1942	Canadian sports executive DICK POUND
1950	Scottish darts player JOCKY WILSON – died 2012
1952	American sports caster BOB COSTAS
1967	Italian road cyclist MARIO CIPOLLINI
1972	Canadian figure skater ELVIS STOJKO
1974	NBA forward MARCUS CAMBY
1975	Czech tennis player JIRÍ NOVÁK

1934 – Masters' first ace
Canadian amateur C. Ross (Sandy) Somerville shot the first hole-in-one in Masters history, a 145-yard 9-iron ace on the seventh hole, during the second round. Somerville finished with a 78 and 160 total at Augusta National.

1979 – Sliding doors
Philadelphia and New Jersey had to replay the final 17:50 of an NBA game originally played in November 1978 because of a technicality. The 76ers won 123-117. When the game began in 1978, Harvey Catchings and Ralph Simpson played for the 76ers and Eric Money and Al Skinner for the Nets, but they were traded to the opposing teams in the meantime. It's the only time in professional sport a player has appeared for both teams in the same game.

1980 – Border brilliant
Brilliant Australian batsman Allan Border completed innings of 150 not out and 153, in the drawn third Test against Pakistan in Lahore. In the 2 innings, Border smashed 31 fours and 7 sixes.

1994 – 'The Great One' – just that
Wayne Gretzky beat Gordie Howe's record as the NHL's all-time leading goal scorer when he tipped a pass into the Vancouver net at the Los Angeles Forum for his 802nd goal. Gretzky scored his 802 goals in 1,117 games, while it took Howe 1,767 games to notch 801. At a centre-ice ceremony honouring the Los Angeles Kings' centre, NHL commissioner Gary Bettman gave Gretzky a book with a score sheet of every game in which he had scored a goal.

2000 – Parlour's hat-trick
Ray Parlour scored a hat-trick as Arsenal beat Werder Bremen 4-2 to advance to the semi-finals of the UEFA Cup. In a major upset, Arsenal was beaten by Galatasaray of Turkey on penalties, 4-1 in the final.

2003 – Woods' four straight at Bay Hills
Tiger Woods won the Bay Hills Invitational Golf tournament by a whopping 11 strokes for a record fourth consecutive time. Woods was the first player in 73 years to win a PGA Tour event 4 straight years. The great Gene Sarazen won his fourth successive Miami Open in 1930.

2003 – Ponting leads from the front
Ricky Ponting starred with 140 not out as Australia beat India by 125 runs in Johannesburg to win its third World Cup. Ponting shared an unbroken 234-run third-wicket partnership with Damien Martyn in Australia's 359-2. Glenn McGrath captured 3 for 52 in India's 234.

2005 – Miller reaches 25,000-point landmark
Reggie Miller reached the 25,000-point mark in his NBA career, finishing with 21 to lead the Indiana Pacers to a 100-93 victory at home over the San Antonio Spurs.

2007 – Kobe four straight 50-point games
Kobe Bryant scored 50 points in the LA Lakers 111-105 away win against the New Orleans/Oklahoma City Hornets to join Wilt Chamberlain as the only players to score 50 points or more in 4 straight NBA contests.

BIRTHDATES

1921	British land/water speed ace DONALD CAMPBELL – died 1967
1929	British middle distance runner ROGER BANNISTER
1931	Russian speed skater YEVGENY GRISHIN – died 2005
1937	American land speed driver CRAIG BREEDLOVE
1939	England soccer forward TERRY PAINE
1948	Pakistan Test wicket keeper WASIM BARI
1951	NFL quarterback/analyst RON JAWORSKY
1952	New Zealand rugby union prop KENT LAMBERT
1955	Basketball Hall of Fame centre MOSES MALONE
1961	New Zealand rugby union winger CRAIG GREEN
1962	British rower STEVEN REDGRAVE
1968	England Test skipper MIKE ATHERTON
1968	Spanish soccer midfielder FERNANDO HIERRO
1972	Swedish tennis player JONAS BJÖRKMAN
1972	Welsh boxer JOE CALZAGHE
1973	NBA guard JASON KIDD
1973	Polish soccer goalie JERZY DUDEK
1976	Scottish track cyclist CHRIS HOY
1976	Brazilian auto racer RICARDO ZONTA
1979	MLB pitcher MARK BUEHRLE
1983	British middle distance runner MO FARAH

㉔ MARCH

1922 – Carnage at Aintree
Only 4 horses from the field of 32 starters finished an eventful running of the Grand National at Aintree, near Liverpool. The Owen Anthony-trained Music Hall survived the carnage to win.

1936 – Longest NHL game
The Detroit Red Wings beat the Montreal Canadiens, 1-0 in Game 1 of the semi-final Stanley Cup series in Montreal. It was the longest game in NHL history, lasting 176 minutes and 30 seconds. At almost 2.30am, rookie Mud Bruneteau scored in the sixth overtime to give Detroit the victory. Detroit goalie Norman Smith, whom Montreal considered a weak link, made a record 92 saves, whilst his Montreal counterpart Lorne Chabot had 66 saves. The Red Wings went on to win the best-of-five series 3-0, and also beat the Toronto Maple Leafs 3-1 in the Stanley Cup Finals.

1975 – Ali floored before victory
Muhammad Ali was floored in the ninth round before retaining his world heavyweight title with a 15th round TKO of Chuck Wepner, in Richfield, Ohio. Ali recovered from the knockdown to pound Wepner, and referee Tony Perez stopped the fight during the last round.

1985 – Norman finally makes it
England Test spinner Norman Gifford made his one-day international debut against Australia in Sharjah at the advanced age of 44. He captained his team for the 2 matches in the series and never made another one-day international appearance.

1993 – Le Tissier's lone miss
Nottingham Forest goalkeeper Mark Crossley saved a penalty from Southampton's England striker Matthew Le Tissier in a Premier Division match at the Dell. It was the only penalty miss of Le Tissier's career. He netted a record 48 spot kicks out of 49 attempts in the top grade.

2007 – Hayden's World Cup ton
Australian opener Matthew Hayden belted the then fastest ton in World Cup history during Australia's 83-run victory over South Africa in St Kitts. Hayden's ton

Controversial American golfer Tiger Woods.

came in just 66 balls, beating the record of 100 in 67 balls, set by Canadian John Davison against the West Indies in 2003. He was out the following over for 101. Irishman Kevin O'Brien broke Hayden's mark with 100 off just 50 balls against England in Bangalore in 2011.

2008 – Tiger finally beaten
Tiger Woods' 6-month unbeaten streak ended when Australia's former US Open champion Geoff Ogilvy won the CA Championship at Doral. A final round of 1-under 71 was enough for Ogilvy to finish at 17-under, 1 shot better than Retief Goosen, Jim Furyk and Vijay Singh. Woods was fifth at 15-under, losing for the first time in 6 PGA Tour starts and 7 official ones worldwide, not counting his win at the Target World Challenge.

BIRTHDATES
1885	American swimmer CHARLIE DANIELS – died 1973
1915	Pro wrestler 'GEORGEOUS GEORGE' – died 1963
1917	American golfer ED FURGOL – died 1997
1925	French rugby league fullback PUIG AUBERT – died 1994
1936	Mexican tennis player ALEX OLMEDO
1947	NFL coach DENNIS ERICKSON
1949	Dutch soccer defender RUUD KROL
1951	American golfer PAT BRADLEY
1961	Australian Test batsman DEAN JONES
1961	American golfer JIM GALLAGHER
1963	Dutch soccer goalkeeper RAIMOND van der GOUW
1967	American tennis player KATHY RINALDI
1970	Canadian NFL kicker MIKE VANDERJAGT
1975	Swedish tennis player THOMAS JOHANSSON
1976	NFL quarterback PEYTON MANNING
1977	Australian rugby league captain DARREN LOCKYER
1977	American golfer JASON DUFNER
1979	Irish rugby lock DONNCHA O'CALLAGHAN
1984	NBA forward CHRIS BOSH
1987	Brazilian soccer midfielder RAMIRES

1934 – Smith first winner at Augusta
Horton Smith beat Craig Wood by a stroke in the inaugural Augusta National Invitation Tournament in Augusta, Georgia. Event founder and host Bobby Jones finished tied for thirteenth place. The name of the tournament changed to 'The Masters' in 1939.

1945 – Spinner retires
The legendary Australian Test spin bowler Clarrie Grimmett announced his retirement from first-class cricket. In 2,103 matches between 1911 and 1941, Grimmett took 1,424 wickets at 22.28

1958 – Five titles for 'Sugar' Ray
Thirty-six-year-old 'Sugar' Ray Robinson won the world middleweight title for an unprecedented fifth time when he beat champion Carmon Basilio, in a bloody split-points decision in Chicago. Six months earlier, Basilio had beaten Robinson for the crown, but by the seventh round of the rematch, his left eye was almost completely shut. Both judges scored the fight to Robinson, with the referee Frank Sikora voting for Basilio.

1982 – Gretzky first to 200
In only his third NHL season, 21-year-old Wayne Gretzky became the first and only player to crack the 200-point barrier. Two assists put him over the 200 mark in Edmonton's 7-2 win over Calgary. Gretzky finished the season with a record 92 goals and 212 points. He went on to score over 200 points in 3 other seasons, with a high of 215 in 1985–86.

1988 – Browning lands quad
Canada's Kurt Browning became the first skater to land a quadruple jump in competition at the World Figure Skating Championships in Budapest. Browning won 4 world championships (1989–91 and 1993), but the quadruple didn't help in Budapest, where he finished sixth.

1992 – Imran's finale
Pakistan captain Imran Khan scored 72 and took 1 for 43 in his last ODI appearance, in the World Cup Final in Melbourne. Pakistan scored 249 for 6. Wasim Akram and Mushtaq Ahmed both claimed 3 wickets, as England was dismissed for 227.

1993 – 99 unlucky
Pakistani batsmen Majid Khan and Mushtaq Mohammad were both dismissed for 99 in the home side's first innings, in the third Test against England at Karachi. England opener Dennis Amiss was also out for 99.

2006 – Figure skating boilover
Sixteen-year-old American Kimmie Meissner pulled off 1 of the biggest upsets in World Figure Skating Championship history, taking the women's title in Calgary, Alberta. Japan's Fumie Suguri was second and American Sasha Cohen third. Meissner landed 7 triple jumps, including 2 triple-triple combinations.

2012 – Tiger's first win since scandal
Tiger Woods scored his first PGA Tour victory since a sex scandal erupted around him at the end of 2009. Woods closed with a 2-under 70 for a 5-shot win over Graeme McDowell, in the Arnold Palmer Invitational at the Bay Hill Club in Orlando, Florida. He won the event again in 2013.

BIRTHDATES
1918	American sports caster HOWARD COSSELL – died 1995
1926	Hungarian boxer LASZLO PAPP – died 2003
1947	English soccer club owner SIR ELTON JOHN
1953	Pakistan Test batsman HAROON RASHID
1961	American golfer MARK BROOKS
1964	Panamanian jockey ALEX SOLIS
1965	NBA guard/coach AVERY JOHNSON
1966	MLB pitcher TOM GLAVINE
1967	American figure skater DEBI THOMAS
1970	Swedish tennis player MAGNUS LARSSON
1971	American WNBA forward SHERYL SWOOPES
1971	American pole-vaulter STACEY DRAGILA
1974	French rugby union flanker SERGE BETSEN
1976	Russian boxer WLADIMIR KLITSCHKO
1982	American auto racer DANICA PATRICK

1889 – Briggs bags 15 in a day

England spinner Johnny Briggs took 15 wickets in a day as South Africa crashed to an innings and 202-run defeat in the second Test in Cape Town. In reply to England's 292, South Africa was dismissed for 47 and 43. Briggs bowled 14 of his 15 victims, taking 7 for 17 and 8 for 11, for incredible match figures of 15 for 28.

1967 – 26-under for Brewer

Gay Brewer shot a 26-under-262 to win the Pensacola Open. At the time it was the third-best 72-hole score in relation to par in PGA Tour history. His 54-hole score (66-64-61-191) was also a record at the time. Steve Stricker now holds the 54-hole mark at 188.

1972 – Lakers dominate

The Los Angeles Lakers ended the season with a number of NBA records as they routed the Seattle SuperSonics in the Finals, 124-98 for a record-setting 69th victory. The Lakers, who won 69 games to 13 that season, replaced another 'Wilt team' in the record books; Chamberlain's 1966–67 Philadelphia team went 68-13. In 81 of their 82 games, the Lakers had scored at least 100 points, another NBA record, and their road-winning percentage of .816 (31-7) is the NBA's best ever. Inspired by Jerry West, Gail Goodrich and Chamberlain, the Lakers went on to win the NBA Championship for the first time since they moved from Minneapolis in 1960. The Lakers' record of 69 victories lasted until 1995–96, when the Chicago Bulls went 72-10.

1973 – Bruins domination

Bill Walton led UCLA to an 87-66 victory over Memphis State in the NCAA championship game in St Louis, MO. Walton hit 21 of 22 field goal attempts and had 44 points, as UCLA won its seventh consecutive national title and 75th straight game.

1986 – 100 caps for Kenny

Soccer player Kenny Dalglish became Scotland's first 100-cap international, in a 3-0 win against Romania at Hampden Park. Dalglish went on to make 102 international appearances for Scotland.

Liverpool's former midfielder and manager, Kenny Dalglish.

1992 – Jurisprudence

Controversial heavyweight boxing champion Mike Tyson was sentenced to 6 years imprisonment for raping former Miss Black America contestant Desiree Washington. Tyson served 3 years and was released in 1995. He returned to boxing, but his results, like his lifestyle were inconsistent.

BIRTHDATES

1916	England Test batsman BILL EDRICH – died 1986
1925	Pakistan Test batsman MAQSOOD AHMED – died 1999
1940	Panamanian jockey BRAULIO BAEZA
1952	French auto racer DIDIER PIRONI – died 1987
1958	Italian auto racer ELIO DE ANGELIS – died 1986
1960	Pro Football Hall of Fame running back MARCUS ALLEN
1962	Basketball Hall of Fame guard JOHN STOCKTON
1964	Swedish NHL defenseman ULF SAMUELSSON
1969	Dutch golfer ROLF MUNTZ
1971	Australian tennis player RENNAE STUBBS
1973	Australian rugby union centre MATT BURKE
1974	Rumanian tennis player IRINA SPÎRLEA

1902 – 'Cubs' born

Chicago's National League team was first referred to as the 'Cubs'. In its first 26 years in the league, the team wore the nicknames 'the White Stockings,' 'Colts', 'Orphans' and 'the Remnants'. None captured the public's imagination or flattered the team. A *Chicago Daily News* reporter finally labelled them the 'Cubs', but it took several years before the name was commonly used.

1982 – Imran amazing

Great Pakistan all-rounder Imran Khan completed outstanding match figures of 14 for 116 in the third Test against Sri Lanka in Lahore. Imran captured 8 for 58 and 6 for 58, as Pakistan won by an innings and 102 runs, taking the series 2-0.

1988 – Figure skating greats

Germany's Katerina Witt and American Brian Boitano won the individual gold medals at the World Figure Skating Championships in Budapest. The pair also won their respective Olympic gold medals at the 1988 Calgary Winter Games. They then starred together in the television specials *Brian Boitano: Canvas of Ice* (1988) and *Carmen on Ice* (1990), for which both won Emmy Awards. After professionals were admitted into Olympic competition, both returned for the 1994 Games at Lillehammer in Norway, and were unplaced with respectable performances.

1989 – Record five penalties

A record 5 penalty kicks were awarded by referee Kevin Morton in a Division 2 League match between Crystal Palace and Brighton and Hove Albion. Only 2 of the spot-kicks were converted and Palace won 2-1.

1994 – Norman's record low score

Australian golfer Greg Norman was in red-hot form, shooting 4 sub-70 rounds to win the prestigious Players Championship at the TPC at Sawgrass Stadium Course in Florida. Norman's 264 total remains the lowest in tournament history and was 4 better than runner-up Fuzzy Zoeller.

2002 – Irish dynasty

Bournemouth striker Warren Feeney became the third generation of his family to play for Northern Ireland when he was capped in a 0-0 draw against Liechtenstein in Vaduz. Feeney's grandfather James was capped in 1950 and his father Warren Snr. in 1976.

2007 – Americans dominate in swimming

Americans broke 3 world records at the World Swimming Championships in Melbourne, Australia. Michael Phelps became the first man to go under 1:44 in the 200m freestyle, breaking Ian Thorpe's revered world record; Phelps led all the way and touched in 1:43.86, beating Thorpe's mark of 1:44.06, set in 2001. Aaron Peirsol won his third straight world title in the 100m backstroke in 52.98 seconds, beating his previous mark of 53.17, set in 2005. And Natalie Coughlin won the 100m backstroke in 54.44 seconds, bettering her world record of 59.58.

2012 – Dodgers now under 'Magic' spell

The Guggenheim Baseball Management group, led by former Lakers star 'Magic' Johnson, reached an agreement to purchase the Los Angeles Baseball Club from embattled owner Frank McCourt. The deal, a record $2 billion, broke the mark for a North American sports franchise, surpassing the $1.1 billion Stephen Ross paid for the Miami Dolphins in 2009.

BIRTHDATES

1859	Australian Test all-rounder GEORGE GIFFEN – died 1927
1939	American auto-racer CALE YARBOROUGH
1955	American jockey CHRIS McCARRON
1957	English swimmer DUNCAN GOODHEW
1961	Great Britain rugby league captain ELLERY HANLEY
1963	England soccer defender GARY STEVENS
1963	NFL quarterback RANDALL CUNNINGHAM
1970	New Zealand rugby league captain JARROD McCRACKEN
1971	Scottish auto racer DAVID COULTHARD
1972	Spanish golfer IGNACIO GARRIDO
1972	English golfer VAN PHILLIPS
1972	Dutch soccer striker JIMMY FLOYD HASSELBAINK
1975	New Zealand rugby union flanker ANDREW BLOWERS
1987	MLB catcher BUSTER POSEY

1955 – Hutton's last is a NZ low

New Zealand was dismissed for 26, the lowest score in Test history, in the second Test against England at Auckland. Bob Appleyard took 4 for 7, Brian Statham 3 for 9 and Frank Tyson 2 for 10. It was the great Len Hutton's last Test appearance for England. In 79 Tests, Hutton scored 6,971 runs at 56.67, with 19 centuries.

1973 – Chamberlain retires

After a dominating 14-year career, Wilt Chamberlain retired, ending his then-NBA-record streak of 1,045 games without disqualification; he did not foul out of a single game in his career. Moses Malone, who fouled out of only 5 games, later had a string of 1,212 games without fouling out.

1984 – Colts move under cover

To avoid unfavourable publicity and fan backlash, team owners authorised the late-night shifting of the Baltimore Colts equipment to the club's new, relocated home in Indianapolis. The NFL merry-go-round was completed when the Cleveland Browns moved to Baltimore to become the Ravens, and the NFL reinstated a new Browns franchise in Cleveland.

1990 – Jordan's career best

Chicago Bulls superstar Michael Jordan scored a regular-season career high of 69 points during a 117-113 win at Cleveland. Only 4 players in NBA history had previously scored more points in a single game – Wilt Chamberlain, David Thompson, Elgin Baylor and David Robinson.

1999 – Great weekend for the Duvals

Golfing father and son Bob and David Duval won tournaments on their respective tours on the same weekend. Bob won the Emerald Coast Classic by 2-over Bruce Fleisher on the PGA Seniors Tour, then retired to the clubhouse to watch son David win the PGA Tour's Players Championship by 2 strokes over Scott Gump.

2001 – Red Devils in demand

Manchester United equalled Arsenal's record by supplying England with 7 players in the 3-1 World Cup qualifying win against Albania in Tirana. Five Red Devils started, including captain David Beckham, Paul Scholes, Andy Cole, Nicky Butt and Gary Neville, whilst Teddy Sheringham and Wes Brown came on as substitutes.

2008 – Fastest triple ton

In the fastest triple hundred in Test cricket, Indian opener Virender Sehwag hit the second triple century of his career in the first Test against South Africa in Chennai. He finished unbeaten on 309, as India reached 468 for 1 in reply to South Africa's 540, after the third day's play. Sehwag, who also made 309 against Pakistan in 2004, became only the third player ever to achieve the feat, along with Don Bradman and Brian Lara. He was out for 316 the following day.

2009 – Beckham most capped

David Beckham became England's most capped outfield player when he won his 109th cap as a half-time substitute in 4-0 friendly win against Slovakia at Wembley. Beckham beat the previous record of 108 caps, which he shared with the late Bobby Moore, England's 1966 World Cup-winning captain. He also became his country's second-most-capped player of all time, with only goalkeeper Peter Shilton, on 125, making more appearances.

BIRTHDATES

1919	Australian Test cricket umpire TOM BROOKS – died 2007
1926	Indian Test batsman POLLY UMRIGAR – died 2006
1942	Basketball Hall of Fame coach JERRY SLOAN
1944	Basketball Hall of Fame guard RICK BARRY
1945	Australian boxer JOHNNY FAMECHON
1958	American gymnast BART CONNOR
1958	Pro wrestler CURT HENNIG – died 2003
1961	NBA guard/coach BYRON SCOTT
1962	Irish golfer PHILIP WALTON
1965	England soccer forward STEPHEN BULL
1968	England Test cricket captain NASSAR HUSSEIN
1972	American NHL forward KEITH TKACHUK
1975	Spanish soccer midfielder IVAN HEIGUERA
1978	New Zealand rugby league captain NATHAN CAYLESS

㉙ MARCH

1946 – Triple treat
Australian Test greats Keith Miller, Ray Lindwall and Don Tallon all debuted in the first Test between Australia and New Zealand in Wellington. Miller performed best of the 'rookies,' taking 2 for 6 in the Kiwi second innings. Australia won by an innings and 103 runs.

1980 – Failed TV golf experiment
The televised PGA experimented unsuccessfully with live microphones on players during the Heritage Classic. Viewers were treated to Tom Kite's heated criticism of John Schroeder for slow play, and Lanny Wadkins' muttered obscenities. The experiment only lasted the next 2 tournaments.

1988 – Honeyghan regains belt
Lloyd Honeyghan became the first British fighter in 71 years to regain a world title, when he knocked out Mexican champion Joge Vaca in the third round of their WBC welterweight title fight at Wembley.

1994 – Border era ends
Australian Allan Border played his last day of Test cricket against South Africa in Durban. Border, with an unbeaten 42, and Mark Waugh, 113 not out, batted together for almost 4 hours to salvage a draw. Border retired as the most capped Test player to that point in history (156); he had scored the most runs (11,174) and made the most appearances as captain (93).

1998 – Sampras loses top spot
Pete Sampras' 102-week reign as world no. 1 tennis player ended. He had taken over the top spot from Thomas Muster in March 1996. During this tenure at the top, Sampras won the US Open (1996), Australian Open (1997) and Wimbledon (1997). Chilean left-hander Marcelo Rios assumed the prestigious mantle.

2007 – Fabulous Phelps
Michael Phelps set his third world record in as many days at the World Swimming Championships in Melbourne, Australia. He swam the 200m individual medley in 1:54.98, easily bettering his own mark of 1:55.84. The 21-year-old phenomenon had already smashed Australian Ian Thorpe's 6-year-old record

Driver Scott Dixon practising for the 2007 Indianapolis 500. Photo: Carey Akin (Flickr) [CC-BY-SA-2.0], via Wikimedia Commons.

in the 200m freestyle, becoming the first swimmer in history to break 1:44 in that event, and also shattered the 200m butterfly mark by a staggering 1.62 seconds, the biggest margin in 48 years.

2008 – Dixon wins first unified Indy Car event
New Zealander Scott Dixon won the first unified Indy Car Series/Champ Car World Series race, the Insurance Indy 300 at Homestead-Miami Speedway in Florida. None of the newcomers making the transition from the Champ Car World Series to the newly unified Indy Car Series were able to compete with the leaders.

BIRTHDATES
1867	Baseball Hall of Fame pitcher CY YOUNG – died 1955
1879	England Test batsman TOM HAYWARD – died 1939
1921	Australian Test all-rounder SAM LOXTON – died 2011
1937	England soccer midfielder GORDON MILNE
1939	Indian Test batsman HANUMANT SINGH – died 2006
1945	Basketball Hall of Fame guard WALT FRAZIER
1951	New Zealand Test cricket captain GEOFF HOWARTH
1952	Australian rugby union/league fullback/coach RUSSELL FAIRFAX
1952	Cuban boxer TEOFILO STEVENSEN – died 2012
1955	Pro Football Hall of Fame running back EARL CAMPBELL
1962	MLB executive BILLY BEANE
1962	American golfer KIRK TRIPLETT
1972	Portuguese soccer midfielder RUI COSTA
1973	Dutch soccer midfielder MARC OVERMARS
1976	American tennis player JENNIFER CAPRIATI

1954 – Sobers' Test debut
Champion all-rounder Gary Sobers made his debut for the West Indies in the fifth Test against England at Kingston, Jamaica. He made an immediate impact with the ball, taking 4 for 75 in the tourists' first innings.

1969 – Howe's hundred
Forty-year-old Detroit right wing Gordie Howe reached 100 points, for the one and only time in his 26-year NHL career, when he scored 4 points in the Red Wings' season finale, a 9-5 loss to the Chicago Blackhawks. Playing in all 76 games, Howe finished with 103 points from 44 goals and 59 assists. He was third on the scoring list behind Boston Bruins centre Phil Esposito (126 points) and Chicago left wing Bobby Hull (107).

1980 – First F1 win for Piquet
Brazilian driver Nelson Piquet won his first Grand Prix at the US event in Long Beach. It was the first of 23 victories in Piquet's brilliant career (1978–91). He won the World Formula 1 championship in 1981, 1983 and 1987.

1986 – Celtics' home record
The Boston Celtics tied an NBA record by beating New Jersey 122-117 for their 27th consecutive home court victory, matching the single-season mark set by the Minneapolis Lakers in 1950. The Celtics eventually extended their streak to 38 games over 2 seasons, before losing to Washington in Hartford in 1986.

1993 – Cantona spits at fans
Man United's French international striker Eric Cantona was fined £1,000, for spitting at the supporters of his former club, Leeds. Two years later, the volatile Cantona was suspended for 8 months and fined £30,000 for attacking a spectator at Selhurst Park.

2001 – Stockton moves to third
John Stockton of the Utah Jazz played the 1,330th game of his NBA career, a 95-88 win over Cleveland, and moved into third place all-time in NBA games played. Stockton retired in 2003 with 1,504 games, trailing behind only Robert Parish (1,611 games) and Kareem Abdul-Jabbar (1,560).

2002 – Sunline supreme
Sunline scored a gutsy win over Shogun Lodge in the $2.5 million Doncaster Handicap at Randwick Racecourse, to become the first horse in Australasia to win $10 million in stakes. The four-time New Zealand Horse of the Year won 32 races and was the world's highest-ever earning female racehorse.

2006 – Ochoa's best
Twenty-four-year-old Mexican golfer Lorena Ochoa broke the Kraft Nabisco Championship record and matched the best-ever score in a major championship, with a 10-under 62 at the Mission Hills course at Rancho Mirage, California. Ochoa beat Mary Beth Zimmerman's 9-year-old course record by one; she also tied Minea Blomqvist, who shot 62 at Sunningdale in the 2004 Women's British Open. Ochoa lost the title on the first hole of a sudden-death playoff against Australian Karrie Webb.

2007 – Lochte's laughing
American Ryan Lochte pulled off a stunning upset in the 200m backstroke at the World Championships in Melbourne, Australia, beating the supposedly invincible Aaron Peirsol with a world-record time. Peirsol's streak of 3 straight world titles came to an end when Lochte touched in 1:54.32, erasing Peirsol's old mark of 1:54.44.

BIRTHDATES
1912	New Zealand Test fast bowler JACK COWIE – died 1994
1927	Australian Test wicket keeper WALLY GROUT – died 1968
1928	Australian Test cricket umpire COLIN EGAR – died 2008
1940	England Test spinner NORMAN GIFFORD
1940	Basketball Hall of Fame forward JERRY LUCAS
1942	New Zealand rugby union hooker TANE NORTON
1948	Irish auto racer/team owner EDDIE JORDAN
1952	Australian AFL forward/coach PETER KNIGHTS
1958	American golfer JOEY SINDELAR
1960	American alpine skier BILL JOHNSON
1962	Welsh rugby union fullback PAUL THORNTON
1963	American golfer JENNY LIDBACK
1974	Australian Test batsman MARTIN LOVE
1978	Scottish rugby union utility back CHRIS PATERSON
1984	Australian tennis player SAMATHA STOSUR
1984	Croatian tennis player MARIO ANCIC
1986	Spanish soccer defender SERGIO RAMOS

1877 – 'The Demon' unleashed
Legendary Australian fast bowler Frederick 'The Demon' Spofforth made his Test debut against England in Melbourne. Spofforth took 4 wickets, but England won by 4 wickets to square the 2-match series, 1-1. Spofforth terrorised batsmen in his 18 career Tests, taking 94 wickets at a brilliant 18.41.

1931 – Rockne killed in plane crash
Superb 43-year-old Notre Dame football coach Knute Rockne was killed, when his light plane crashed on a trip from Kansas City to Los Angeles. Rockne starred for the Irish as one of the first outstanding receivers, and in 1918 assumed the head coaching position. As coach, he had 5 undefeated seasons and won 3 national titles in 13 seasons. His winning percentage of .881 (105-12-5) remains the best ever in college football.

1973 – Ali ambush
Muhammad Ali suffered a broken jaw in a shock defeat to Ken Norton, a split-points decision over 12 rounds in San Diego. He won the rematch 6 months later, in another controversial split-points decision.

1973 – Fast Flyers
The Philadelphia Flyers scored 8 goals from an astounding 60 shots in the second period in a 10-2 home win against the New York Islanders in Philadelphia.

1980 – Heavyweight bouts on same day
There were almost concurrent heavyweight title fights in the United States. In Las Vegas, Larry Holmes retained his WBC title with an eighth-round TKO of Leroy Jones, whilst Mike Weaver won the WBA title, knocking out John Tate in round 12 of their Knoxville, Tennessee bout.

1983 – First 'goofy foot' champion
Australian surfer Tom Carroll became the first 'goofy footer' (left-footed surfer) to win a world title, when he won 3 consecutive events culminating in the Beaurepaires Open at Cronulla Beach in Sydney, Australia. He also won the 1984 world title.

1991 – Hockey's worst offender
Boston Bruins defenseman Chris Nilan held (and still holds) the dubious distinction of most penalties earned in an NHL regular season game. Playing in a 7-3 win against the Hartford Whalers, Nilan had 6 minors, 2 majors, one 10-minute misconduct and one game misconduct for the record 10 penalties.

1997 – 'Swiss Miss' number one
Swiss tennis star Martina Hingis became the youngest female player ever to lead the world rankings. She was 16 years, 6 months and 1 day old at the time and retained the top ranking for 80 weeks.

2004 – Lenton breaks de Bruin record
Lisbeth Lenton broke Inge de Bruin's 4-year-old world 100m freestyle record with a time of 53.66 seconds at the Australian Olympic trials in Sydney. Later, at the Olympics in Athens, Lenton won a gold medal in the 4 x 100m freestyle relay, but did not qualify for the final of the 100m.

2004 – Celebrations put on hold
NFL owners adopted a 15-yard penalty for excessive celebrations. The penalty was added to the fines already in place for choreographed and multiplayer celebrations. If the infraction was flagrant, the player would be ejected. The previous day, the owners had instituted a modified instant replay system.

BIRTHDATES
1878	American boxer JACK JOHNSON – died 1946
1905	Australian rugby league forward GEORGE TREWEEKE – died 1991
1913	Scottish golfer DAI REES – died 1983
1916	American golfer TOMMY BOLT – died 2008
1928	Canadian NHL centre GORDIE HOWE
1931	American golfer MILLER BARBER
1939	German soccer defender KARL-HEINZ SCHNELLINGER
1952	England rugby union flanker MIKE RAFTER
1960	Scottish golfer ANDREW OLDCORN
1962	NFL receiver JOHN TAYLOR
1965	American NHL goalie TOM BARRASSO
1965	American tennis player PATTY FENDICK
1971	Russian Hockey Hall of Fame right wing PAVEL BURE
1976	English swimmer GRAEME SMITH

APRIL

1930 – Jones' season off and running
Bobby Jones started his Grand Slam season by winning the Southeastern Open by 13 strokes, over Horton Smith, at the Forest Hills-Ricker Course in Atlanta. Later in the year, Jones had won all 4 major championships – the British Open, British Amateur, US Open and US Amateur titles.

1933 – Hammond blasts record score
Walter Hammond set a new world record score for a Test match, with 336 not out in only 318 minutes, in the second Test against New Zealand in Auckland. The innings included 34 fours and a record 10 sixes.

1946 – O'Reilly Retires
Arguably the best spin bowler of all-time, Bill 'Tiger' O'Reilly announced his retirement from first-class cricket. In 27 Tests, O'Reilly took 144 wickets at 22.59. His first-class bowling figures were 774 wickets at just 16.60.

1973 – Three straight for Esposito
Boston Bruins centre Phil Esposito won his third consecutive NHL scoring title, with 130 points from 55 goals and 75 assists. Philadelphia Flyers centre Bobby Clarke, who scored 37 goals and 67 assists for 104 points, finished second. It was the fourth scoring title in 5 years for Esposito.

1985 – Wildcats win
No. 8-seeded Villanova upset the defending national champion Georgetown, 66-64 in the NCAA final in Lexington, with a Final Four field-goal percentage record converting 78.6%. The Wildcats connected on 22 of 28 field-goal attempts, and centre Ed Pinckney outplayed three-time All-American Patrick Ewing, to be named the Final Four MVP.

1990 – 'Golden Bear' wins on senior debut
Jack Nicklaus became only the seventh player to win on his senior PGA debut, when he beat Gary Player by 4 strokes to take out the Tradition Tournament at Desert Mountain.

1995 – Mitchell bows out
Arguably South Africa's best-ever boxer, Brian Mitchell retired as reigning WBA and IBF super featherweight champion, having made 12 successful title defences away from his home base. In his final fight, Mitchell beat Silverio Flores in a non-title bout at Sun City, to take his record to 45 wins, 1 loss and 3 draws.

2007 – Record 7 gold for Phelps
American super swimmer Michael Phelps smashed his own world record for the 400m individual medley by 2.04 seconds, at the World Championships in Melbourne, Australia. The 21-year-old American closed his 8-day run in style, taking a meet record seventh gold medal.

2007 – Pressel youngest LPGA major champ
Eighteen-year-old Morgan Pressel became the youngest major champion in LPGA Tour history, winning the Kraft Nabisco Championship at Rancho Mirage, California. Pressel closed with a 3-under 69, after playing the final 24 holes without a bogey to finish 1 stroke ahead of Catriona Matthew, Suzann Pettersen and Brittany Lincicome.

BIRTHDATES

1922	American yachtsman EMIL 'BUS' MOSBACHER – died 1997
1927	Hungarian soccer midfielder FERENC PUSKÁS – died 2006
1930	New Zealand rugby union fullback DENNIS YOUNG
1939	Baseball Hall of Fame pitcher PHIL NIEKRO
1941	Indian Test captain AJIT WADEKAR
1955	American golfer DAN POHL
1957	England Test captain DAVID GOWER
1957	American golfer DONNIE HAMMOND
1961	Swedish golfer ANDERS FORSBRAND
1964	Canadian Hockey Hall of Fame defenseman SCOTT STEVENS
1965	NBA point guard/analyst/coach MARK JACKSON
1973	New Zealand Test captain STEPHEN FLEMMING
1975	Bulgarian tennis player MAGDALENA MALEEVA
1976	Dutch soccer midfielder CLARENCE SEEDORF
1986	Dutch speed skater IREEN WÜST

② APRIL

1939 – Guldahl wins Masters

The inconsistent Ralph Guldahl shot a 3-under par 69 in the final round for a 279 total to win The Masters by 1 stroke over Sam Snead. It was Guldahl's third and final major championship triumph, but his sixth significant title in 4 years, including back-to-back US Opens (1937–38) and 3 consecutive Western Opens (1936–38).

1974 – Greig's career best

England all-rounder Tony Greig took a career best 8 for 86, in the West Indies first innings, in the fifth Test at Port of Spain. Lawrence Rowe (123) and Roy Fredericks (67) guided the Windies to 305, a 38-run first innings lead. They were dismissed for 199, however, in their second innings, for a 26-run defeat and a 1-1 drawn series.

1995 – UConn girls undefeated

The Connecticut women's college basketball team equalled the 1985–86 Texas team, as the only sides to win the NCAA championship with an unbeaten season since the tournament commenced in 1982. UConn outscored Tennessee 11-3 in the final 2-and-a-half minutes in Minneapolis, to win 70-64, capping a 35-0 season. Rebecca Lobo scored 14 of her game-high 17 points in the second half to spark Connecticut's rally.

1996 – Jayasuriya's jewel

Sri Lankan opening batsman Sanath Jayasuriya hit a world record one-day international century in just 48 balls against Pakistan in Singapore. Jayasuriya's smashed 134 from just 65 balls, including 11 fours and 11 sixes. Sri Lanka won by 34 runs, but Pakistan went on win the series final.

2000 – 'Gilly' gloves ten

Adam Gilchrist took his tenth catch of the match in the third Test against New Zealand in Hamilton, to create an Australian record for dismissals by a wicketkeeper. Gill Langley, Rod Marsh and Ian Healy had shared the previous record of nine. England's Jack Russell set the world record of 11 (all caught) against South Africa in Johannesburg in 1995–96.

2005 – Infighting incident

In a bizarre incident, Newcastle United teammates Kieron Dyer and Lee Bowyer were sent off for fighting each other, in a 3-0 home defeat to Aston Villa at St James Park. The pair was dismissed after 82 minutes; Dyer was suspended for 3 matches and Bowyer for seven. Bowyer was also fined 6 weeks wages, estimated to be £200,000.

2006 – Webb's wondrous wedge

Karrie Webb played arguably one of the greatest shots ever struck in a major championship, when she holed a pitching wedge from 116 yards for eagle on the 18th hole, to close with a 7-under 65. She then made a 7ft birdie putt on the same hole in the playoff to beat Mexico's Lorena Ochoa and capture her seventh career major at the Kraft Nabisco Championship at Rancho Mirage in California.

2011 – India takes second World Cup

India won its second Cricket World Cup, beating Sri Lanka by 6 wickets in the final in Mumbai. Chasing 274, India won with 10 balls to spare. Gautam Gambhir, with 97, and M.S. Dhoni, 91, were the mainstays for the home team.

BIRTHDATES

1896	American golfer JOHN GOLDEN – died 1936
1900	England soccer midfielder ALF STRANGE – died 1978
1926	Australian auto racer SIR JACK BRABHAM
1927	American boxer CARMEN BASILIO – died 2012
1932	Pakistan Test fast bowler MAHMOOD HUSSAIN – died 1991
1940	British motorcycle rider MIKE HAILWOOD – died 1981
1945	Baseball Hall of Fame pitcher DON SUTTON
1946	New Zealand Test fast bowler RICHARD COLLINGE
1951	Japanese golfer AYAKO AKOMOTO
1959	American swimmer BRIAN GOODELL
1959	Finnish rally driver JUHA KANKKUNEN
1960	British sprinter LINFORD CHRISTIE
1966	England soccer striker TEDDY SHERINGHAM
1966	NFL linebacker BILL ROMANOWSKI
1971	Australian tennis player TODD WOODBRIDGE
1976	South African golfer RORY SABBATINI
1981	Australian Test captain MICHAEL CLARKE
1982	Spanish tennis player DAVID FERRER

❸ APRIL

1899 – Sinclair's Test double
South African cricket all-rounder Jimmy Sinclair became the first player to score a century and take 6 wickets in an innings, in the second Test against England at Cape Town. Sinclair's 106 was also South Africa's first ever Test century. England won by 210 runs when South Africa was dismissed for just 35 in the second innings.

1962 – Eddie era ends
After riding in 24,092 races in a 31-year career, American jockey Eddie Arcaro retired from the saddle due to bursitis in his right arm. Arcaro is one of only 2 jockeys to ride 5 Kentucky Derby winners and he won both the Preakness and Belmont Stakes 6 times. He was the only jockey to win the prestigious Triple Crown twice, in 1941 on Whirlaway and in 1948 on Citation. Arcaro's mounts collectively won over $30 million in purses. He died in 1997, aged 81.

1982 – Rugby shock
In one of the biggest upsets in rugby union history, the South American Jaguars beat South Africa 21-12 in Bloemfontein. Having been beaten 50-18 in the first Test in Loftus Versfeld, the composite Jaguars were given no chance. Jaguars' captain and five-eighth Hugo Porta, however, scored all 21 of the Jaguars' points, with a try, 1 conversion, a field goal and 4 penalties for a memorable victory that raised the profile of the sport in South America.

1988 – Lemieux usurps Gretzky
Pittsburgh Penguins centre Mario Lemieux won the NHL scoring title, breaking Wayne Gretzky's 7-year streak as the league's leading scorer. Lemieux finished the season with 168 points, becoming only the fourth player ever to score 70 goals in a season, joining Phil Esposito, Gretzky and Jari Kurri. He also joined Gretzky as the only players to average over 2 points a game, finishing with 168 points in 77 games. After the season, Lemieux won his first Hart Memorial Trophy as the league's MVP, ending another Gretzky record streak of 8 in a row.

1988 – Euro tour low total
Welsh pro golfer David Llewellyn shot a final round of 60 in the AGF Biarritz Open, to record a then-record low for 72 holes in the European Tour. His total of 258 beat the previous best of 259, set by Mark McNulty a year earlier.

1993 – 'The race that never was'
Following a horribly botched start, the Grand National at Aintree was declared void, with $115 million in bets returned to punters. After a false start and a recall, almost the entire field failed to realise that a second false start had occurred. As a result, 7 jockeys did not pull up their mounts until the course was completed.

2012 – Budding star Griner
Brittney Griner had 26 points, 13 rebounds and 5 blocks in the NCAA women's basketball championship game, leading Baylor to a convincing 80-61 victory over Notre Dame in Denver. Baylor became the seventh women's team to run through a season unbeaten and the first in NCAA history to win 40 games.

BIRTHDATES
1897   Australian golfer JOE KIRKWOOD – died 1970
1911   Polish/American sprinter STELLA WALSH – died 1980
1914   English tennis player KAY STAMMERS – died 2005
1916   England Test fast bowler CLIFF GLADWIN – died 1988
1933   American golfer ROD FUNSETH – died 1985
1934   Pro Football Hall of Fame offensive lineman JIM PARKER – died 2005
1937   American golfer SANDRA SPUZICH
1938   American golfer PHIL RODGERS
1945   Canadian Hockey Hall of Fame goalie BERNIE PARENT
1948   British equestrian rider MARY GORDON-WATSON
1953   American boxer JAMES 'BONECRUSHER' SMITH
1967   Australian auto racer MARK SKAIFE
1969   French rugby union prop JEAN-JACQUES CRENCA
1971   American alpine skier PICABO STREET
1972   Scottish rugby winger KENNY LOGAN
1972   French tennis player SANDRINE TESTUD
1976   French tennis player NICOLAS ESCUDÉ
1978   South African rugby union prop JON SMIT
1978   German tennis player TOMMY HAAS

④ APRIL

1930 – First Test triple ton
England opener Andrew Sandham completed the first triple-century in Test history, shortly before the close of the second day of the fourth Test against the West Indies at Kingston, Jamaica. Sandham ended the day on 309 and was dismissed early the next morning for 325. He batted for 10 hours, and his score remained the highest by a no. 2 batsman in Tests for 73 years, until Australia's Matthew Hayden scored a then-highest Test innings of 380 against Zimbabwe at Perth.

1938 – Picard's Masters
Henry Picard posted a final-round 70, defeating Harry Cooper and Ralph Guldahl by 2 strokes to win the Masters at Augusta. Picard led by 1 after the third round, but Cooper and Guldahl could only post 71s in the final round.

1974 – Aaron ties home run record
On Opening Day, Hank Aaron homered off Cincinnati Reds pitcher Jack Billingham at Riverfront Stadium, tying Babe Ruth's all-time home run record of 714. Aaron went on to break the new record just 4 days later. He finished his career with 755 home runs.

1986 – Gretzky domination
Wayne Gretzky broke his own NHL record for points in a season, when he recorded 3 assists in the Edmonton Oilers' 9-3 loss to the Flames in Calgary. This boosted his total to 214 points, 2 more than he'd scored in 1981–82. All 3 Gretzky assists came during Edmonton power plays – 2 on goals by Jari Kurri and 1 by Paul Coffey. Gretzky got an assist in Edmonton's 80th and final game of the season to finish with NHL records of 215 points and 163 assists which still stand.

1993 – Super Swoopes
Texas Tech forward Sheryl Swoopes scored 47 points to lead her team to an 84-82 win over Ohio State in the NCAA women's basketball final in Atlanta, Ga. Swoopes' points haul remains a championship game record for either gender.

1999 – Warne dropped
An out-of-form Shane Warne was dropped from the Australian Test team for the first time in 7 years, missing the fourth Test against the West Indies in Antigua. Warne's replacement, leg spinner Stuart MacGill, captured 5 wickets in the match. Australia won the Test by 176 runs to square the series 2-2.

2005 – Baseball's renamed 'Nats' lose opener
The Washington Nationals, formerly known as the Expos, lost their inaugural season opener to Philadelphia, 8-4. The franchise, which played its initial 36 years in Montreal, became the first team to represent the nation's capital since the Senators left to become the Texas Rangers in 1971.

BIRTHDATES
1913	Australian rugby league centre DAVE BROWN – died 1974
1933	Indian Test all-rounder BAPU NADKARNI
1933	Auto racing executive BILL FRANCE JR – died 2007
1939	American golfer JO ANNE CARNER
1942	MLB manager JIM FREGOSI
1951	Pro Football Hall of Fame guard JOHN HANNAH
1952	Canadian NHL coach/executive PAT BURNS – died 2010
1957	England Test wicket keeper PAUL DOWNTON
1960	English sports caster JONATHAN AGNEW
1963	NFL linebacker/coach JACK DEL RIO
1963	Canadian Hockey Hall of Fame centre DALE HAWERCHUK
1964	England soccer defender PAUL PARKER
1970	Australian tennis player/coach JASON STOLTENBERG
1973	Australian triathlete CHRIS McCORMACK
1973	Italian motorcycle rider LORIS CAPIROSSI
1974	American BMX rider DAVE MIRRA
1976	Brazilian soccer midfielder EMERSON

Hank Aaron, who broke Babe Ruth's home run record in 1974, meets US President Jimmy Carter in 1978.

❺ APRIL

1915 – Willard KO's Johnson in classic bout
Jess Willard knocked out an under-prepared and exhausted Jack Johnson in the 26th round to win the world heavyweight championship in Havana, Cuba. The 37-year-old Johnson was guaranteed $30,000 to fight the 6ft 6in, 250lb Willard. Thereafter Johnson led a chequered life, returning to America, where he was sentenced to jail for 'transporting women across state lines for immoral purposes'. He skipped bail and fled to Europe, but handed himself in 7 years later and was imprisoned for less than a year. Campaigners have since lobbied for a presidential pardon for Johnson. He died in 1946 in a road accident.

1932 – Phar Lap dead in US
Legendary Australian racehorse Phar Lap died at a private ranch near Menlo Park in California. After winning 37 races from 51 starts, dominating Australian racing, Phar Lap won the rich Agua Caliente Handicap in California in a track-record time. A fortnight later, he was struck down by a mystery illness.

1959 – Wall's Masters charge
Art Wall Jr birdied 5 of the last 6 holes to post a final-round 66 and win his only Masters title at Augusta. Wall finished with a 284 total to beat Cary Middlecoff by a stroke. He passed 12 players in the final 6 holes for the victory.

1972 – Baseball strike
The season opener between the Houston Astros and the Cincinnati Reds was cancelled, due to the player strike that had started on April 1. It marked the first time in Major League history that Opening Day was delayed, and 86 games were missed before the labour dispute was settled.

1991 – Terrific twins
Australian batsmen Steve and Mark Waugh became the first twin brothers to play in a Test match, in the third Test against the West Indies at Port of Spain. Mark scored 64 and Steve 26 in the first Australian innings of the drawn match. The pair went on to play in another 104 Tests together.

2006 – Griffey passes legends
With 1 swing, Ken Griffey Jr passed 2 of the greats of baseball in 2 batting categories, during the Reds' 8-6 win over the Chicago Cubs in Cincinnati. Griffey passed Mickey Mantle with his 537th career homer, taking sole possession of 12th place on the career list. The homer also gave Griffey his 1,538th career RBI, breaking his tie with Joe DiMaggio for 31st on the career list.

BIRTHDATES
1893	Finnish speed skater CLAS THUNBERG – died 1973
1911	American golfer JOHNNY REVOLTA – died 1991
1922	England soccer forward TOM FINNEY
1938	South African Test batsman COLIN BLAND
1943	Japanese boxer MASAHIKO 'FIGHTING' HARADA
1948	England soccer defender ROY McFARLAND
1953	Australian cricket coach JOHN BUCHANAN
1958	South African tennis player JOHAN KRIEK
1963	American golfer BILLY RAY BROWN
1964	English darts player STEVE BEATON
1973	Australian rugby union hooker BRENDAN CANNON
1975	Welsh soccer striker JOHN HARTSON
1976	Spanish soccer striker FERNANDO MORIENTES
1978	German swimmer FRANZISKA VAN ALMSICK

Jess Willard in 1915, the year he won the world heavyweight championship over Jack Johnson in Havana, Cuba.

⑥ APRIL

This painting depicts Spyridon Louis, who won the marathon at the 1896 Summer Olympics.

1896 – First Olympics opened
King George I of Greece declared the first Modern Olympic Games open in Athens. There were 245 male athletes from 14 nations, with the largest contingents coming from the host nation Greece, plus Germany and France.

1896 – First Modern Games champ
American James Connolly became the first Olympic champion in 1,527 years, when he won the triple jump (then 2 hops and a jump). The 27-year-old Connolly had dropped out of Harvard University to compete in Athens. He also finished third in the long jump and second in the high jump.

1947 – Masters to Demaret
Jimmy Demaret won his second Masters, beating Byron Nelson and amateur Frank Stranahan by 2 strokes at Augusta National. Demaret carded a 7-under par 281 total to join Nelson and Horton Smith as the only two-time Masters champions to that date.

1980 – Howe bows out a winner
At age 52, the NHL all-time scoring leader, Gordie Howe, played his last regular-season game. Skating for the Hartford Whalers, Howe ended his 32nd season by scoring a goal and an assist in a 5-3 win over the Detroit Red Wings, for whom he played his first 25 years in the NHL. He finished his NHL career with 1,850 points, a record that lasted until 1989, when overhauled by Wayne Gretzky.

1987 – Boxing 'classic'
'Sugar' Ray Leonard came out of retirement after nearly 3 years to beat 'Marvelous' Marvin Hagler, in a split decision for the WBC middleweight title in Las Vegas. For most of the 12 rounds, Leonard circled and countered, confusing the champion. Hagler rallied in the last few rounds, but couldn't overcome Leonard's early lead. It was Hagler's first loss in 11 years.

1991 – Diego out on drugs
Former Argentina captain Diego Maradona was suspended by the Italian Football League for 15 months, after testing positive for cocaine use.

2006 – Bryant's Lakers milestone
Kobe Bryant of the Los Angeles Lakers broke Elgin Baylor's franchise record with his 24th 40-point game of the season, when he scored 42 points in a 2-point overtime loss to the Nuggets in Denver. Baylor had set the previous Lakers' record in 1962–63.

2008 – Like father, like son
Graham Rahal, son of long-time racing star Bobby Rahal, came back from an early spinout to become the youngest winner in major open-wheel history, in the Honda Grand Prix of St Petersburg. At 19 years and 93 days, Rahal broke the age record set in 2006 in Sonoma, California, by Marco Andretti, who was 19 years and 167 days old.

BIRTHDATES
1923	American auto racer HERB THOMAS – died 2000
1930	English soccer manager DAVE SEXTON – died 2012
1937	Australian Test batsman TOM VEIVERS
1943	New Zealand rugby union centre IAN MacRAE
1951	Dutch MLB pitcher BERT BLYLEVEN
1953	Figure skater JANET LYNN
1956	Pakistan Test batsman MUDASSAR NAZAR
1956	Indian Test batsman DILIP VENGSARKAR
1960	New Zealand rugby union prop RICHARD LOE
1965	NFL receiver STERLING SHARPE
1969	MLB infielder BRETT BOONE
1983	English darts player JAMES WADE

❼ APRIL

1935 – 'Shot heard 'round the world'
Gene Sarazen played arguably the most famous shot in golf history, holing a 4-wood from 235 yards for an albatross on the par-5 15th, to keep himself alive in the Masters after trailing by 3 strokes with 4 holes to play. He picked up another stroke to tie Craig Wood at the end of regulation 72 holes, and easily won the 36-hole Monday playoff by 5 strokes.

1963 – Nicklaus youngest Masters champion
Twenty-three-year-old Jack Nicklaus, who weighed 214lbs, became the youngest and heaviest US Masters champion. Nicklaus fired an even par 72 to beat Tony Lema by 1 stroke, for the first of his 6 Masters titles. Tiger Woods went on to become the youngest Masters champion in 1997 at 21 years, 104 days of age.

1968 – Clark killed in crash
Scottish driver Jim Clark was killed in a Formula 2 race at Hockenheim in Germany, when his Lotus left the track and crashed into nearby trees. The accident remains unexplained. Clark had won the Formula 1 World Championship in 1963 and 1965. His dominant 1965 season in the Lotus 33, in which he led every lap of every race he finished, remains unmatched. He won a record 33 Grand Prix pole positions and 25 victories in just 77 starts. Clark was the first driver to go over 160mph at Indianapolis, and he won the 500 in 1965.

1996 – Quick-fire 50
Free-hitting Sri Lankan opener Sanath Jayasuriya hammered 76 off only 28 balls in the Singer Cup Final against Pakistan in Singapore. When his opening partner, Romesh Kaluwitharana, was out for a duck in the sixth over, the score was 70-1. Jayasuriya hit 8 fours and 5 sixes, and his 50 came up in a record 17 balls. Despite the smashing start, Sri Lanka crashed to a 43-run defeat.

Reports of the match-fixing allegations against South African cricket captain Hansie Cronje.

2000 – Cricket fix probe
A Delhi detective stumbled across a taped telephone conversation between South African captain Hansie Cronje and businessman Sanjay Chawla, sparking a controversy that rocked international cricket. Cronje proved to be the central figure in a match-fixing racket, which led to his life ban. Cronje died in a plane crash in May 2002.

2010 – Nelson passes Wilkens' coaching mark
Don Nelson became the NBA's winningest coach, setting the career record for victories in the Golden State's 116-107 win over the Minnesota Timberwolves in Minneapolis. The win took Nelson to a record of 1,333-1,061 in 31 seasons on the bench, surpassing Lenny Wilkens' mark.

BIRTHDATES
1873	Baseball Hall of Fame manager JOHN McGRAW – died 1934
1882	Australian Test spinner BERT IRONMONGER – died 1971
1918	Baseball Hall of Fame second baseman BOBBY DOERR
1943	England Test batsman DENNIS AMISS
1954	Pro Football Hall of Fame running back TONY DORSETT
1960	American boxer JAMES 'BUSTER' DOUGLAS
1964	American golfer JOE DURANT
1967	Pro Football Hall of Fame guard STEVE MISNIEWSKI
1968	Australian swimmer DUNCAN ARMSTRONG
1979	Dominican MLB infielder ADRIAN BELTRÉ
1981	Norwegian golfer SUZANN PETTERSEN
1983	French soccer winger FRANCK RIBÉRY

1951 – Snead implodes – Hogan's first Masters win

Third-round leader Sam Snead blew up with a final-round 80, allowing Ben Hogan to win his first of 2 Masters titles at Augusta. Hogan posted a closing, bogey-less, 4-under 68, to finish with a 280 total, 2 strokes ahead of Skee Riegel.

1972 – Alvin's debut century

West Indian batsman Alvin Kallicharran scored 100 not out in his Test debut, in the fourth Test against New Zealand in Georgetown. The diminutive left-hander played 66 Tests in a 10-year career, scoring 4,399 at 44.43 with 12 centuries, 21 fifties and 51 catches.

1974 – Home run record to Aaron

Hank Aaron broke Babe Ruth's home run record when he ripped a fastball from Los Angeles Dodgers left-hander Al Downing, for his 715th home run in front of a Braves-record crowd of 53,775 fans at Atlanta's Fulton County Stadium. The FBI had investigated death threats prior to the game if Aaron crossed the plate for the record.

1979 – Borg takes over top mantle

Jimmy Connors' 84-week reign as no. 1 tennis player in the world ended. He had held the top spot since August 1977, but Sweden's Bjorn Borg now took over the rankings mantle. Connors was the first player to use a metal racquet and one of the first to make the two-fisted backhand part of the game. He won 8 major titles: US Open (1974, 1976, 1978, 1982–83), Wimbledon (1974, 1982) and the Australian Open (1974).

1990 – Faldo's back-to-back Masters

Englishman Nick Faldo became the first player since Jack Nicklaus (1965–66) to win back-to-back Masters, when he beat Raymond Floyd in a sudden-death playoff. The pair finished on 278, before Floyd found water on the second extra hole. Nicklaus finished sixth on 285 for the best-ever finish by a senior PGA Tour player in a major championship.

1996 – Hornets end Bulls' roll

The Charlotte Hornets ended the Chicago Bulls' NBA-record, regular-season, home winning streak at 44 games, when they won 98-97 at the United Centre. The last time the Bulls had lost in Chicago was March 24, 1995, in Michael Jordan's first home game after coming out of his first retirement.

2006 – Elderly outfield

The Giants fielded the oldest outfield in MLB history, in a 12-6 win over the Atlanta Braves in San Francisco. Left fielder Barry Bonds and centre fielder Steve Finley were both 41, and right fielder Moises Alou was 39. Alou's 299th career homer, a 2-run drive in the first inning, highlighted a fine day for the outfield trio: a combined 5-for-12, with 4 runs, 3 RBIs and 3 walks.

2009 – Cavs unique home record

The Cleveland Cavaliers beat the rival Washington Wizards 98-86 to improve to 38-1 at home. In doing so, they became the first team in NBA history to have two 15-game winning streaks at home in the same season. Cleveland's 38 home wins were a franchise record; they had won 37 in 1988–89.

2012 – Watson's Masters miracle

Left-hander Bubba Watson conjured a miracle shot at the second playoff hole to beat South Africa's Louis Oosthuizen and win the US Masters at Augusta. Watson won as he put a now famous audacious hook 30 yards out of the trees to within 4 yards, whilst Oosthuizen could only bogey.

BIRTHDATES

1912	Norwegian figure skater SONJA HENIE – died 1969
1940	Basketball Hall of Fame guard JOHN HAVLICEK
1946	Baseball Hall of Fame pitcher JIM 'CATFISH' HUNTER – died 1999
1950	Polish soccer striker/coach GRZEGORZ LATO
1954	Baseball Hall of Fame catcher GARY CARTER – died 2012
1955	South African boxer GERRIE COETZEE
1963	England Test captain ALEC STEWART
1963	NBA guard/coach TERRY PORTER
1965	New Zealand rugby union flanker MICHAEL JONES
1966	British auto racer MARK BLUNDELL
1967	West Indian Test fast bowler KENNY BENJAMIN
1974	Australian rugby union number 8 TOUTAI KEFU

1950 – Masters x 3 for Jimmy

Jimmy Demaret became the first three-time Masters champion when he completed a 4-stroke rally to finish on 283, for a 2-stroke victory over Australia's Jim Ferrier. Demaret picked up 6 strokes on par on the par-5 13th hole during the tournament.

1962 – Third Masters for 'Arnie'

Arnold Palmer fired a sensational 31 on the back nine, with 5 birdies in 7 holes, for a 4-under round of 68 to beat Gary Player and Dow Finsterwald in the tournament's first three-man playoff for his third Masters title.

1972 – Kiwi openers shine

New Zealand openers Glenn Turner and Terry Jarvis put on the second-highest opening partnership in Test history when they shared 387 in the fourth Test against the West Indies in Guyana. Turner cracked a mighty 259, and Jarvis 182, his only Test hundred. Turner's innings was the highest by a Kiwi until Martin Crowe's 299 in 1990–91.

1981 – Eight Opens for Hunt

Australian Geoff Hunt won the British Open title for a record eighth time, beating his arch-rival Jahangir Khan of Pakistan 9-2, 9-7, 5-9, 9-7 in the final.

1987 – Gretzky's seven-pointer

Wayne Gretzky scored 7 points in a Stanley Cup game for the third time, as the Oilers thrashed the LA Kings 13-3 in Edmonton. Gretzky scored 1 goal and had 6 assists, whilst Jari Kurri scored 4 goals. The Oilers won the series 4-1 and went on to sweep the Winnipeg Jets 4-0 for the Stanley Cup.

1988 – Shearer's youthful treble

Alan Shearer became the youngest English football player to score a top-flight hat-trick. At 17 years and 240 days, Shearer nailed the treble for Southampton in a 4-2 win against Arsenal at the Dell.

1989 – Faldo first

Nick Faldo became the first Englishman to win the Masters, when he beat American Scott Hoch at the second extra playoff hole. Faldo birdied 4 of the last 6 holes for a final-round 65, to tie Hoch, who missed a 2ft birdie putt at the first playoff hole. Faldo made no mistake with a 25-footer on the second playoff hole for the victory.

1992 – Augusta plays easy

A record 18 golfers scored in the 60s on the opening day of the Masters at Augusta. The previous record had been 12. Fred Couples went on to win by 2 strokes from Raymond Floyd.

2006 – Phil's second Masters

Phil Mickelson won his second Masters, with a 2-stroke victory over South African Tim Clark. It was Mickelson's third major title, with his first Masters in 2004. He shot a final-round 69 for a 7-under par, 4-round total of 281.

BIRTHDATES

1927	New Zealand rugby union flanker TINY HILL
1928	Basketball Hall of Fame forward PAUL ARIZIN – died 2006
1946	England Test wicketkeeper ALAN KNOTT
1952	New Zealand rugby centre BRUCE ROBERTSON
1957	Spanish golfer SEVERIANO BALLESTEROS – 2011
1964	Canadian NHL forward RICK TOCCHET
1965	Swedish golfer HELEN ALFREDSSON
1966	England rugby union prop DARREN GARFORTH
1967	Australian MLB pitcher GRAEME LLOYD
1971	Canadian auto racer JACQUES VILLENEUVE
1975	England soccer striker ROBBIE FOWLER

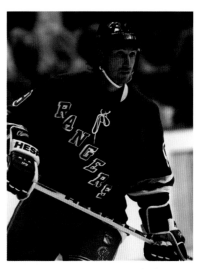

Hockey great Wayne Gretzky in action. Photo: Hakandahlstrom at en.wikipedia [CCBY-SA-3.0], from Wikimedia Commons.

1896 – Louis first marathon winner
Twenty-four-year-old Greek shepherd Spiridon Louis won the marathon at the inaugural Athens Olympic Games. Louis took the lead 4km from the Panathenaic Stadium and won the race by more than 7 minutes, ahead of countryman Charilaos Vasilakos.

1949 – 'Slammin' Sammy's Masters
Sam Snead won the first of his 3 Masters titles with a 6-under 282, 3 strokes ahead of Johnny Bulla and Lloyd Mangrum. Snead became the first Masters champion to be presented with the now-traditional green jacket.

1960 – Start to finish Masters for Arnie
Arnold Palmer became only the second player to lead the Masters from start to finish. His 282 total was 1 stroke ahead of Ken Venturi. Other wire-to-wire champions have included Craig Wood (1941), Jack Nicklaus (1972) and Raymond Floyd (1976).

1961 – Player first foreign Masters champ
South Africa's Gary Player became the first international Masters champion when he beat Arnold Palmer and amateur Charles Coe by a stroke at Augusta. Player made a memorable recovery from a greenside bunker on the 18th hole, to salvage par. Palmer's approach landed him in the same bunker, but he stumbled to a closing double-bogey six.

1990 – Career best for Curtley
West Indian fast bowler Curtley Ambrose captured a career best 8 for 45 on the final day of the fourth Test against England in Barbados. Chasing 356, England was dismissed for 191 to crash to a 164-run loss. Ambrose captured 10 wickets for the match.

1994 – Eight of the best for Angus
England fast bowler Angus Fraser took a career best 8 for 75, as the tourists upset the West Indies by 208 runs in the fourth Test in Barbados. The Windies won the series 3-1.

2005 – Four Masters to Woods
Tiger Woods sank a 15ft birdie putt to beat Chris DiMarco on the first playoff hole and win his fourth Masters title. The pair finished on a total of 12-under par 276, 7 shots ahead of Retief Goosen and Luke Donald. Woods had previously won the tournament in 1997, 2001 and 2002.

2005 – Indian women in final
India became the first Asian side to play in the final of the women's Cricket World Cup, when they met Australia in Centurion. Australia lifted the tournament for the fifth time in a heavily one-sided affair, thanks to Karen Rolton's rampant 107 not out. They won by 98 runs.

2011 – Schwartzel takes Masters
First the first time, no American held a major golf title. This followed a dramatic final day at Augusta, when South African Charl Schwartzel became the first Masters champion to close with 4 straight birdies. His 6-under 66 was the best closing round at the Masters in 22 years, giving him a 2-shot victory over Australians Adam Scott and Jason Day. Irishman Graeme McDowell (US Open), German Martin Kaymer (US PGA) and Luis Oosthuizen of South Africa (British Open) were the other major champions at that time.

BIRTHDATES
1914	Australian Test batsman JACK BADCOCK – died 1982
1921	MLB player/actor CHUCK CONNORS – died 1992
1923	South African Test all-rounder JOHN WATKINS
1929	British auto racer MIKE HAWTHORNE – died 1959
1936	NFL coach JOHN MADDEN
1938	NFL quarterback/analyst DON MEREDITH – died 2010
1942	England soccer midfielder IAN CALLAGHAN
1945	Australian swimmer KEVIN BERRY – died 2006
1948	Pro Football Hall of Fame quarterback MEL BLOUNT
1950	MLB outfielder KEN GRIFFEY SNR
1969	Australia lawn bowler STEVE GLASSON
1972	Australian Test all-rounder IAN HARVEY
1973	Brazilian soccer midfielder ROBERTO CARLOS
1980	American auto racer KASEY KAHNE

⑪ APRIL

1965 – Nine-stroke Masters to Nicklaus
Twenty-five-year-old Jack Nicklaus won his second Masters title at Augusta, achieving two long-standing records. His final-round 69 gave him a 17-under par 271 and a 9-stroke victory; both records would stand for 32 years. Nicklaus took only 123 putts in the 4 rounds, and his total beat Ben Hogan's 1953 record of 274.

1976 – Everybody loves Raymond
Raymond Floyd became only the fourth player to lead from start to finish in the Masters. Floyd tied Jack Nicklaus's tournament record of 271 to win by 8 strokes over Ben Crenshaw.

1989 – Goalie's delight
Ron Hextall of the Philadelphia Flyers sent a clearing pass all the way into Washington's empty net, becoming the first NHL goalie to score in the Stanley Cup playoffs. The Flyers won the game, 8-5 and the series 4-2, before taking the Stanley Cup 4-3 against Pittsburgh.

2000 – Cronje out as bribe scandal hits
The South African Cricket Board sacked skipper Hansie Cronje after he admitted to dishonesty and accepting bribes to fix matches. The SACB and the International Cricket Council subsequently handed down a life ban to Cronje from all forms of cricket.

2001 – Football tragedy
Forty-three died and 155 were injured as fans tried to get into an already packed Ellis Park in Johannesburg, prior to the Premiership derby between rival Soweto teams, the Kaizer Chiefs and the Orlando Pirates. It was the second occasion on which the teams had been involved in a crowd tragedy, the first occurring in 1991 at Oppenheimer Stadium in Orkney, when 42 fans were killed in a crowd crush.

2001 – Socceroos record
In qualifying rounds for the 2002 FIFA World Cup, Australia's Socceroos set a world scoring record when they hammered American Samoa 31-0, in Coffs Harbour, New South Wales. Striker Archie Thompson

Jack Nicklaus during the 1965 Masters at Augusta, Georgia.

scored 13 goals, an individual scoring record in an international football match.

2010 – Phil's third Masters
Behind a final-round 67, Phil Mickelson claimed his third Masters title and a fourth major overall, rolling in a birdie at the 18th for a 5-under 67. That gave him a 3-stroke win over third-round leader Englishman Lee Westwood.

BIRTHDATES
1856	England Test batsman ARTHUR SHREWSBURY – died 1903
1951	England rugby union fly-half JOHN HORTON
1963	New Zealand Test cricket umpire BILLY BOWDEN
1964	MLB pitcher BRET SABERHAGEN
1971	New Zealand rugby union lock MARK COOKSLEY
1973	French rugby union flanker OLIVER MAGNE
1974	Spanish tennis player ÀLEX CORRETJA
1980	MLB first baseman MARK TEIXEIRA
1982	England Test batsman IAN BELL
1983	Canadian moguls skier JENNIFER HEIL
1991	Australian swimmer JAMES MAGNUSSEN

⑫ APRIL

1930 – Rhodes oldest
At 52, Wilfred Rhodes became the oldest man to play Test cricket for England. He announced his retirement after playing the fourth Test against the West Indies in Kingston, Jamaica. Rhodes played 58 Tests, taking 127 wickets at 26.96. He also had a Test batting average of 30.90, with 2 centuries.

1965 – Indoor MLB
The first indoor Major League Baseball regular season game was played, when the hometown Houston Astros went down to the Philadelphia Phillies, 2-0 at the Astrodome.

1981 – 'Brown Bomber' passes away
Former world heavyweight boxing champion Joe Louis died of a heart attack, aged 66, in Las Vegas. His championship reign from 1937–49 remains the longest of any title-holder in any division. Louis defeated all 25 of his world title challengers, another record. He was buried in Arlington National Cemetery at the request of President Ronald Reagan. His professional record reads: 71 fights – 68 wins with 54 knockouts and 3 losses.

1987 – Famous wedge shot sinks Norman
Larry Mize sank a famous 50-yard wedge on the second playoff hole, defeating Greg Norman and Seve Ballesteros for the Masters title. Ballesteros 3-putted the first playoff hole to drop out, after the trio had tied on 285 in hot conditions with lightning fast greens.

1989 – 'Sugar' Ray dead at 67
Former world welterweight and middleweight champion 'Sugar' Ray Robinson died aged 67, suffering from Alzheimer's disease and diabetes. The skilful and resilient Robinson was 85-0 as an amateur, then won his first 40 professional fights before losing to Jake LaMotta, whom he beat in their 5 other bouts. He was welterweight champion in the late 1940s and middleweight champion a record 5 times in the 1950s. Robinson's professional record reads: 200 fights – 173 wins with 108 knockouts, 19 losses and 6 draws.

2004 – Bonds equals May's HR record
San Francisco Giants slugger Barry Bonds tied his godfather Willie Mays' career home run total of 660, when he hit Milwaukee's Matt Kinney out of SBC Park in San Francisco. The homer put Bonds equal third in the all-time standings, behind Babe Ruth (714) and Hank Aaron (755). He went on to hit a record 762 homers before retiring in 2007.

2004 – Lara first quad century
West Indian captain Brian Lara became the first man to score 400 in a Test match, when he reached the landmark in an unbeaten innings during the fourth Test against England in Antigua. In an innings lasting 773 minutes, Lara faced 582 balls and hit 43 fours and 4 sixes. Lara's innings beat the record of 380, set by Australian opener Matthew Hayden against Zimbabwe in Perth in 2003.

2009 – Argentine Masters first
Kenny Perry imploded on the final 2 holes, to allow Angel Cabrera to become the first Argentine to win the Masters at Augusta National. Perry bogeyed 17 and 18 to force a three-way playoff with Cabrera and Chad Campbell. Cabrera won on the 10th hole when Perry missed the green badly to the left and made yet another bogey.

BIRTHDATES
1883 Australian rugby league centre DALLY MESSENGER – died 1959
1917 Indian Test batsman VINOO MANKAD – died 1978
1924 American auto racer CURTIS TURNER – died 1970
1930 Australian middle distance runner JOHN LANDY
1939 Australian rugby league lock JOHNNY RAPER
1941 England soccer captain BOBBY MOORE – died 1993
1942 Argentine auto racer CARLOS REUTEMANN
1948 Italian soccer manager MARCELLO LIPPI
1952 New Zealand rugby union flanker LEICESTER RUTLEDGE
1962 Spanish rally driver CARLOS SAINZ
1966 NFL running back LORENZO WHITE
1983 Australian tennis player JELENA DOCKIC

⑬ APRIL

1936 – No Payne for Joe
Joe Payne scored 10 goals in 1 match for Luton against Bristol Rovers, setting a Football League goal-scoring record.

1979 – Final day of World Series Cricket
The fifth Super Test between West Indies and Australia in Antigua petered out into a tame draw on the final day of the controversial World Series Cricket, the breakaway Test series devised by media mogul Kerry Packer. After this day, top-line international cricket returned to the establishment, as Packer settled his differences with the Australian Cricket Board.

1985 – Four goals in one NHL period
Tim Kerr created a record for most goals scored in a single period of a Stanley Cup playoff match, when he netted 4 for Philadelphia against the New York Rangers at Madison Square Garden. Three of Kerr's scores were power play goals, also a record. The Flyers won the game, 6-5.

1986 – Senna by a touch
In the closest finish in Formula 1 history, Brazilian Ayrton Senna, in a Lotus/Renault, beat English Williams driver Nigel Mansell in the Spanish Grand Prix at Jerez – by just 0.014 seconds. Mansell started third on the grid, behind Senna in pole position. He recorded the fastest lap of the race before being edged out by the smallest margin, in a frenetic finish.

1986 – 'Golden Bear' oldest Masters winner
Forty-six-year-old Jack Nicklaus became the oldest man to win the Masters title (his sixth), with a popular 1-stroke victory over Greg Norman and Tom Kite at Augusta National. Trailing by 4 strokes on the final nine, Nicklaus finished with a brilliant 30, to shoot a 65 for a total 279. His rivals made crucial mistakes at the 18th hole, with Kite missing a 12ft birdie putt and Norman recording a bogey.

1997 – Tiger youngest Masters winner
Twenty-one-year-old Tiger Woods became the youngest ever Masters champion and the first African American to win one of the 4 major championships.

Woods shot a final-round 69 for a Masters record 18-under par 270, breaking the mark of 271 shared by Nicklaus (1965) and Raymond Floyd (1976). His 12-stroke victory over Tom Kite was the largest major championship margin in the 20th century, 3 better than the Masters record of 9 set by Nicklaus in 1965.

2008 – Immelman's green jacket
Trevor Immelman, after a final-round 3-over 75, matched the highest final round by a Masters champion and became the first South African to earn a green jacket in 30 years, when he beat Tiger Woods by 3 shots at Augusta.

2011 – Bonds drugs impasse
Following a 12-day trial, Major League Baseball's home-run record holder, Barry Bonds, was found guilty of obstruction of justice. A jury failed to reach a verdict on 3 other counts as to whether he had lied to a grand jury in 2003, when he specifically denied knowingly using steroids and human growth hormone. It was a messy end to a case that put the slugger in the spotlight for more than 3 years. Bonds was sentenced to probation and fined.

BIRTHDATES
1929	American golfer MARILYNN SMITH
1931	American auto racer DAN GURNEY
1948	England rugby union lock NIGEL HORTON
1955	Mexican boxer LUPE PINTOR
1960	German soccer striker RUDI VÖLLER
1963	Russian chess player GARY KASPAROV
1964	American golfer DAVIS LOVE III
1968	NFL nose tackle TED WASHINGTON
1971	French swimmer FRANCK ESPOSITO
1975	Canadian snowboarder JASEY JAY ANDERSON
1978	Spanish soccer defender CARLES PUTOL
1979	American tennis player MEGHANN SHAUGHNESSY
1983	Chilean soccer goalie CLAUDIO BRAVO
1983	South African rugby flanker SCHALK BURGER
1988	Brazilian soccer midfielder ANDERSON

1910 – Baseball tradition born
United States President William Howard Taft inaugurated the season by throwing out the first ball to Walter Johnson before the Washington Senators' home game against Philadelphia. The act began a baseball tradition that Taft's successors have continued. The Senators won the game 3-0.

1962 – Baylor's playoff record
Elgin Baylor set an NBA playoff record by scoring 61 points in the Lakers' 126-121 win over the Boston Celtics, in Game 5 of the Finals. In breaking the record of 56 points, set by Philadelphia's Wilt Chamberlain 3 weeks earlier, Baylor hit on 22 of 46 field-goal attempts and 17 of 19 free throws. The record was broken by Michael Jordan with 63 points, in a 1986 playoff game that went to 2 overtime periods.

1968 – Roberto out on technicality
After tying with Bob Goalby on 11-under 277, Argentina's Roberto De Vincenzo withdrew from the Masters for signing an incorrect scorecard. De Vincenzo missed a playoff with Goalby, when playing partner Tommy Aaron incorrectly (and inadvertently) marked his card. DeVicenzo didn't notice the error and signed the scorecard. The blunder resulted in scoring tents being set up behind the 18th green in future Masters, to ensure players had ample opportunity and privacy to check scorecards.

2009 – 'Golden Boy' bows out
Thirty-six-year-old Oscar De La Hoya retired from boxing after a 17-year pro career. 'The Golden Boy' had 45 fights (39-6), won 10 titles in 6 weight classes, had appeared in a record 19 pay-per-view fights and 32 HBO telecasts, and generated just shy of $US700 million in pay-per-view revenue, also a record.

2010 – Durant's scoring title
Kevin Durant became the youngest ever NBA scoring champion, with a 31-point haul in Oklahoma's 114-105 win against Memphis in Oklahoma City. The 21-year-old Durant finished with an average of 30.1 points, just .4 ahead of LeBron James and supplanting 22-year-old Max Zaslofsky of the 1947–48 Chicago Stags.

Elgin Baylor of the Los Angeles Lakers during an NBA game against the New York Knicks at Madison Square Garden in 1962.

2013 – Scott first Aussie Masters winner
Adam Scott became the first Australian to win the Masters when he beat Argentine Ángel Cabrera on the second playoff hole at Augusta. The pair had tied at 9-under par 279 before Scott birdied at the 10th hole in the playoff.

BIRTHDATES
1870	Australian Test captain SYD GREGORY – died 1929
1923	Argentine golfer ROBERT DE VINCENZO
1931	West Indian Test batsman BRUCE PAIRAUDEAU
1936	American golfer BOBBY NICHOLS
1941	MLB utility/manager PETE ROSE
1947	Australian Test fast bowler BOB MASSIE
1958	South African rugby union centre DANNIE GERBER
1958	Australian yachtsman IAIN MURRAY
1960	South African Test spinner PAT SYMCOX
1963	WNBA guard CYNTHIA COOPER
1963	American golfer MEG MALLON
1965	Australian Test fast bowler/coach CRAIG McDERMOTT
1966	MLB pitcher GREG MADDUX
1966	MLB outfielder DAVID JUSTICE
1970	Dutch tennis player JAN SIEMERINK
1979	England rugby union winger IAN BALSHAW

1947 – Robinson makes MLB history
Twenty-eight-year-old Jackie Robinson became the first African-American to play Major League Baseball in the 20th century, when he batted second and played first base for the Brooklyn Dodgers at Ebbets Field in their season opener against the Boston Braves. It was a breakthrough for equal opportunity in professional sport in the United States, and helped to change the attitudes of many Americans. Robinson went hitless in 3 at-bats, but scored the winning run in the Dodgers' 5-3 victory.

1964 – Best's international debut
The controversial Manchester United star George Best made his debut for Northern Ireland, in their 3-2 win over Wales at Swansea. Best went on to represent his country on 37 occasions, scoring 9 international goals.

1969 – Punters say 'Moore please'
Champion jockey George Moore set a record for most winners at a major racing carnival in Australia. Moore rode an amazing 15 winners out of 29 races at the AJC Autumn Carnival in Sydney.

1973 – Wright's final victory
Mickey Wright won her 82nd and final LPGA Tour tournament, when she took out the Colgate Dinah Shore Winner's Circle title by 2 strokes ahead of Joyce Kazmierski at the Mission Hills Golf & Country Club in Rancho Mirage, California. Wright's career total comes in second only to Kathy Whitworth, with 88 tour victories.

1986 – Quick ton for Viv
The great Vivian Richards hit a Test century off just 56 balls in the fifth Test against England on his home ground, the Antigua Recreational Ground in St John's. Richards went on to score 110 off 58 balls, including 7 fours and 7 sixes. The West Indies won the Test by 240 runs, for a 5-0 sweep of the series.

1989 – Hillsborough disaster
Ninety-six Liverpool supporters died and 766 were injured in the worst disaster in British sports history, in a crowd crush at the start of the Reds' FA Cup semi-final against Nottingham Forest, at Hillsborough Stadium, Sheffield. Most were trapped at the perimeter fencing at the Leppings Lane end during the opening minutes of the game. The match was abandoned without score after 6 minutes play.

1990 – Windies openers' record
Gordon Greenidge and Desmond Haynes put on a West Indian record opening partnership of 298, in the fifth Test against England in Antigua. In his 100th Test, Greenidge made 149, and Haynes hit 167 as the West Indies won by 32 runs to wrap up the series 2-1.

2013 – Boston bombings
Nearly 3 hours after the winners crossed the Boston Marathon finish line, 2 explosions occurred about 180m apart on Boylston Street, in the last 205m of the course. The race was halted, with 3 spectators killed and 264 people injured. After images of the suspects, 2 brothers, were released, they killed an MIT police officer, carjacked an SUV, and exchanged gunfire with the police in Watertown, Massachusetts. During the bedlam, an MBTA police officer was critically injured, and one of the suspects, Tamerlan Tsarnaev, was killed. His brother Dzhokhar was injured, but escaped. An unprecedented door-to-door manhunt ensued and Dzhokhar was captured.

BIRTHDATES
1875	American boxer JAMES J. JEFFRIES – died 1953
1901	English snooker/billiards player JOE DAVIS – died 1978
1956	NBA guard/coach MICHAEL COOPER
1957	American sprinter EVELYN ASHFORD
1958	New Zealand Test spinner/coach JOHN BRACEWELL
1963	Indian Test all-rounder MANOJ PRABHAKAR
1964	South African rugby union fullback ANDRÉ JOUBERT
1965	American golfer MICHELLE REDMAN
1965	NHL right wing KEVIN STEVENS
1967	American swimmer DARA TORRES
1968	England rugby union fullback BEN CLARKE
1971	French rugby union halfback PHILIPPE CARBONNEAU
1972	Canadian boxer ARTURO GATTI – died 2009
1983	Russian NHL left wing ILYA KOVALCHUK

1922 – Annie can shoot

Legendary cowgirl Annie Oakley, at age 62, set a US trapshooting record hitting 100 consecutive clay targets at Pinehurst North Carolina. Oakley had set numerous trap-shooting records, having honed her skills as the star attraction of Buffalo Bill Cody's famous Wild West Show. She died in 1926, aged 66.

1940 – Opening day no-hitter

Twenty-one-year-old Cleveland Indians right-hander Bob Feller became the first pitcher in history to fire a no-hitter on Opening Day, when he beat the White Sox 1-0 in Chicago. Feller struck out 8 and walked five. The Indians scored the game's only run on Jeff Heath's single and catcher Rollie Hemsley's 2-out triple in the fourth inning, off Edgar Smith.

1949 – Leafs take three

The Toronto Maple Leafs became the first NHL team to win 3 consecutive Stanley Cups when they scored a 3-1 victory over the Detroit Red Wings to complete a 4-game sweep in the finals. The Leafs dominated the finals, beating the second-place Boston Bruins in 5 games in the semi-finals, and with goalie Turk Broda allowing Detroit just 5 goals in the 4 Stanley Cup games. It was the eighth Stanley Cup title for the Leafs and the fifth for their coach Hap Day.

1965 – Five of the best for Dear

Brian Dear scored the quickest 5 goals in English Football League history. Playing for West Ham United in their Division 1 match against West Bromwich Albion at Upton Park, Dear struck for 5 in a 20-minute time span either side of half time. The Hammers won the match 6-1.

1992 – Souness in shock move

Manager Graeme Souness shocked Glasgow Rangers Football Club by quitting to take over the managers' job from Kenny Dalglish at his old club Liverpool. After a period of poor health, requiring triple heart by-pass surgery, and poor results Souness was sacked in 1994. He has since managed at Galatasaray, Southampton, Torino, Benfica, Blackburn Rovers and Newcastle United.

1996 – Bulls bag 70

The Michael Jordan-inspired Chicago Bulls became the first NBA team to win 70 games in a season, after an 86-80 victory in Milwaukee. Jordan scored 22 points as the Bulls 70-9 record beat the 1971–72 Lakers' mark of 69-13. Chicago finished the regular season 72-10 and went on to win the championship, the first in their second three-peat of the '90s.

2009 – Madden out of SNF

Popular NFL analyst and Pro Football Hall of Fame coach, John Madden, announced his retirement from broadcasting. The 73-year-old Madden left midway through a 6-year contract with NBC's *Sunday Night Football*.

BIRTHDATES

1878	England cricket and soccer captain R.E.'TIP' FOSTER – died 1914
1940	West Indian Test all-rounder DAVID HOLFORD
1943	Australian Test spinner JOHN WATKINS
1947	Basketball Hall of Fame centre KAREEM ABDUL JABAR
1952	NFL coach BILL BELICHICK
1955	MLB manager BRUCE BOCHY
1960	Spanish soccer manager RAFAEL BENÍTEZ
1963	Pakistan Test batsman SALEEM MALIK
1971	Australian rugby union front rower CAMERON BLADES
1971	Belarus tennis player NATASHA ZVEREVA
1972	Spanish tennis player CONCHITA MARTINEZ
1973	Swedish golfer CARLOTTA SÖRENSTAM

American rodeo star and sharpshooter Annie Oakley in 1899.

⑰ APRIL

1939 – 'Brown Bomber' retains crown
Joe Louis retained his world heavyweight title with a first-round knockout of Jack Roper in Los Angeles. The fight lasted just 2:20. It was the sixth defence of his title; he made another 19, until beaten on points by Ezzard Charles in 1950.

1953 – Zaharias' surgery
Golfing great Babe Zaharias underwent cancer surgery in Beaumont, Texas. Doctors believed the talented athlete would be able to return to top-level sport, and Zaharias went on to make a comeback in 1954, winning the US Open, her tenth major victory. However, her cancer reappeared in 1955 and she passed away in 1956. Under her maiden name of Didrikson, she first came to national attention as a track and field star, winning a record 5 gold medals at the 1932 LA Olympics. When she turned to golf, her national notoriety brought a new level of awareness to the women's game.

1972 – Women OK for Boston
Women were invited to run in the prestigious Boston Marathon for the first time despite having unofficially participated since 1966. The first official winner of the Women's Open was New York's Nina Kuscsik, in a time of 3:10.26.

1979 – Celebrity Marriage
Chris Evert, American tennis star, married English tennis player John Lloyd in Fort Lauderdale, Florida. The union lasted 8 years. She later married, and divorced from, downhill skier Andy Mill and Australian golfer Greg Norman.

1987 – 'Dr. J' joins 30,000 club
In his final regular season home game before he retired, Philadelphia 76ers forward Julius Erving joined Kareem Abdul-Jabbar and Wilt Chamberlain as the only players to score 30,000 career points. In the third period of a 115-111 loss to the Indiana Pacers, Erving hit a fade-away jumper for points 29,999 and 30,000. He finished the game with a season-high 38 points. Erving scored 18,340 points in 11 seasons with the 76ers and 11,662 during his 5 years in the ABA.

2000 – Closest ever Boston jog
Kenyans Elijah Lagat and Catherine Ndereba won the closest Boston Marathon (men's and women's divisions) in the race's 104-year history. Lagat won the men's division, recording the same time as runner-up Gezahenge Abera of Ethiopia; Ndereba, meanwhile, beat three-time champion Fatuma Roba in the women's division by only 16 seconds.

2006 – Crosby youngest to 100 points
In his rookie season, 18-year-old Sidney Crosby became the youngest player in NHL history to score 100 points in a season, setting up 3 goals in the Pittsburgh Penguins' 6-1 victory at home over the NY Islanders. Crosby's 3-point night gave him 62 assists, to go with 38 goals, and tied Mario Lemieux (1984–85) for the team rookie scoring record of 100 points.

2009 – Todd aces same hole in 2 days
Brendon Todd made Nationwide Tour history by making a hole-in-one at the same hole 2 days in a row, at the Athens Regional Foundation Classic. The former Georgia All-American aced the 147-yard, 17th hole for the second straight day, using an 8-iron, during the second round at the Jennings Mill Country Club course.

BIRTHDATES
1852	Baseball HOF infielder/manager ADRIAN 'CAP' ANSON – died 1922
1954	Italian auto racer RICARDO PATRESE
1954	Canadian pro wrestler 'ROWDY' RODDY PIPER
1956	American boxer 'SUGAR' RAY LEONARD
1961	England Test fast bowler NORMAN COWANS
1961	NFL quarterback/analyst BOOMER ESIASON
1967	New Zealand rugby union lock IAN JONES
1968	New Zealand Test batsman ROGER TWOSE
1972	Sri Lanka Test spinner MUTTIAH MURALITHARAN
1977	American speed skater CHAD HEDRICK
1978	Scottish rugby utility forward JASON WHITE
1985	French tennis player JO-WILFRIED TSONGA

1923 – Yankee Stadium opens

The famous Yankee Stadium opened in the Bronx, with a capacity crowd of 74,000 in attendance. The *New York Times* reported that the gates were closed half an hour before the start of the game and that 25,000 fans were turned away. Babe Ruth christened the venue with its first home run, a 3-run shot in the third inning, in the Yankees' 4-1 victory over the Boston Red Sox. The new stadium cost $2.4 million to build.

1942 – Unique Ice Hockey comeback

The Toronto Maple Leafs became the only team in any major league sport to win a championship after being down 3-0 in the final series. Down 1-0 to the Detroit Red wings with 13 minutes remaining in Game 7 of the Stanley Cup Finals, 'Sweeney' Schriner scored twice and Pete Langelle once to clinch a 3-1 victory at Maple Leaf Gardens for a 4-3 series win.

1983 – Benoit brilliant in Boston

Twenty-five-year-old Joan Benoit smashed the women's world record when she finished the Boston Marathon in a time of 2.22:43. The freakish time was 2:45.7 seconds better than Grete Waitz's run the previous day in London. It was Benoit's second Boston victory, and her time was almost 13 minutes faster than when she won the marathon 4 years earlier.

1994 – Lara betters Sobers' Test mark

Champion West Indian batsman Brian Lara scored a then-world-record 375 in the fifth Test against England in Antigua. Lara's innings took 766 minutes off 538 balls, and he hit 45 fours in beating countryman Garfield Sobers' mark of 365. The record lasted 9 years, before Australian opener Matthew Hayden hit 380 against Zimbabwe in Perth in 2003.

2005 – Catherine 'the Great'

Catherine Ndereba of Kenya became the first woman to win 4 Boston Marathon titles, beating Elfenesh Alemu of Ethiopia by 1:50. Hailu Negussie of Ethiopia captured the men's crown.

2008 – Knight Riders take first IPL match

Following an extravagant opening ceremony in

Toronto Maple Leafs player scoring goal against Detroit Red Wings, Stanley Cup Playoffs, 1942.

Bangalore, the Kolkata Knight Riders thrashed the Bangalore Royal Challengers by 140 runs in the first match of the revolutionary Indian Premier League Twenty20 cricket series. Kiwi Brendon McCullum stole the show with a crowd-pleasing 158 not out, off just 73 balls.

2012 – Summitt retires at the top

Iconic women's basketball coach Pat Summitt stepped down as head coach of the Tennessee Lady Vols. The 59-year-old Summitt, the most successful coach ever in women's college basketball, had been diagnosed with early onset dementia. Her career ended with an imposing 1,098-208 record. During her time, Tennessee never failed to reach the NCAA tournament.

BIRTHDATES

1926	England Test batsman DOUG INSOLE
1942	Austrian auto racer JOCHAN RINDT – died 1970
1949	American auto racer GEOFF BODINE
1962	Australian rugby union captain NICK FARR JONES
1963	West Indies Test batsman PHIL SIMMONS
1966	Russian NHL left wing VALERI KAMENSKY
1969	Swedish soccer midfielder/manager STEFAN SCHWARZ
1970	German swimmer HEIKE FRIEDRICH
1973	Ethiopian runner HAILE GEBRSELASSIE
1971	England rugby union prop GRAHAM ROUNTREE
1976	Australian tennis player ANDREW ILIE
1983	Venezuelan MLB third baseman MIGUEL CABRERA

1987 – Slow double ton
Sri Lankan wicketkeeper-opener Brendon Karuppu became only the third batsman to score a double century on his Test debut, in the first Test against New Zealand in Colombo. Kuruppu's 201 was the slowest double-hundred in first-class history, taking 777 minutes. It was his first first-class century, and his last Test century.

1989 – No error Elster
New York Mets shortstop Kevin Elster played his 73rd consecutive errorless game in a 4–2 win over the Philadelphia Phillies at Shea Stadium. Elster's mark broke Ed Brinkman's major-league record for shortstops, set in 1972 when Brinkman was playing for the Detroit Tigers.

1991 – Holyfield too good for Foreman
Evander Holyfield retained his undisputed world heavyweight title with a unanimous points decision over former champion George Foreman in Atlantic City. It was Holyfield's first defence of his title.

1997 – Celebrity Marriage
Andre Agassi married actress Brooke Shields in Monterey, California. Shields' father gave Agassi a medal that Brooke's grandfather, Frank Shields, had been awarded as a member of the 1930 US Davis Cup team. The union lasted 2 years and the couple were divorced in 1999.

1998 – Three straight for Irwin
Hale Irwin won his third consecutive PGA Seniors' Championship when he beat Larry Nelson by 7 strokes at the Palm Beach Gardens Club in Florida. Irwin posted a 13-under par 275 total.

2000 – Real take United's crown
Manchester United's reign as European champions ended, when they were beaten 3-2 by Spanish giants Real Madrid in their Champions League second leg match at Old Trafford. The first leg in Madrid was a 0-0 draw; Roy Keane scored an own goal for Real with Raul adding another two, whilst David Beckham and Paul Scholes replied for United.

2006 – Gillespie double ton
On his 31st birthday, Jason Gillespie became the highest-scoring nightwatchman in Test history, with 201 not out in the second Test against Bangladesh in Chittagong. Gillespie had never previously scored a century in any form of the game.

2008 – Calzaghe unbeaten
Welshman Joe Calzaghe, the reigning WBC, WBA and WBO super-middleweight champion, made a successful foray to the United States, winning a split decision over American veteran Bernard Hopkins in a 12-round light-heavyweight bout in Las Vegas. Calzaghe survived a first-round knockdown to take his record to 45-0.

2009 – 'Rafa' likes Monte Carlo
Spanish tennis ace Rafael Nadal became the first tennis player to win the Monte Carlo Masters on 5 straight occasions. Nadal overcame the third-ranked Serbian, Novak Djokovic 6-3, 2-6, 6-1. He went on to win the event 8 times.

BIRTHDATES

1873	England Test fast bowler SYDNEY BARNES – died 1967
1933	English Test cricket umpire HAROLD 'DICKIE' BIRD
1936	NFL linebacker/coach JACK PARDEE – died 2013
1952	Nicaraguan boxer ALEXIS ARGÜELLO – died 2009
1954	England soccer midfielder TREVOR FRANCIS
1956	English tennis player SUE BARKER
1956	England rugby union winger MIKE HARRISON
1960	MLB pitcher FRANK VIOLA
1962	American auto racer AL UNSER JR
1966	Australian Test fast bowler/umpire PAUL REIFFEL
1967	French rugby union winger/coach PHILIPPE SAINT-ANDRE
1970	British middle distance runner KELLY HOLMES
1972	Brazilian soccer player RIVALDO
1973	Australian rugby union captain GEORGE GREGAN
1975	Australian Test fast bowler JASON GILLESPIE
1975	Finnish soccer goalkeeper JUSSI JÄÄSKELÄINEN
1981	NFL strong safety TROY POLAMALU
1982	New Zealand rugby winger SITIVENI SIVIVATU
1983	MLB catcher JOE MAUER
1987	Russian tennis player MARIA SHARAPOVA
1987	English soccer goalkeeper JOE HART

1910 – Joss' gem
Addie Joss of the Cleveland Indians threw his second no-hitter to beat Chicago 1-0 at South Side Park. He died less than a year later and was kept out of the Baseball Hall of Fame for years because he'd failed to meet the requirement of 10 years in the major leagues.

1939 – One time only, Williams v Gehrig
Two of the greats of baseball Ted Williams and Lou Gehrig played against each other for the first and only time on Opening Day at Yankee Stadium. For the 20-year-old Williams, it was his debut major league game, playing right field and batting sixth for Boston, and for the Yankees' Gehrig, his 2,124th consecutive game. Williams struck out twice and went 1-for-4 against Red Ruffing who shut out Boston, 2-0. Gehrig, batting fifth, was 0-for-4 against Lefty Grove, including a low liner that Williams caught with 2 runners on base. Gehrig played only 6 more games before illness forced him to retire.

1969 – Heavyweight golf clash
In a head-to-head battle between the 2 top players in women's golf, Kathy Whitworth defeated Mickey Wright on the first playoff hole to win the Lady Carling Open at the Pine Ridge Golf Course in Timonium, Maryland. It was Whitworth's fourth consecutive LPGA Tour victory, tying Wright's all-time record.

1981 – Davis dynasty starts
Steve Davis won the first of his 6 World Snooker titles, beating Doug Mountjoy, 18-12 in the final in at the Crucible Theatre in Sheffield.

1986 – Playoff record for MJ
Michael Jordan scored a playoff-record 63 points in the Bulls' 135-131 2OT loss to the Celtics in Boston Garden. In breaking the 24-year-old playoff record (61 points, set by Elgin Baylor), Jordan shot 22 of 41 from the field and 19 of 21 from the foul line. He also had 6 assists and 5 rebounds. Boston superstar Larry Bird scored 36 points with 12 rebounds and 8 assists.

1994 – ODI Paki partnership
Pakistan batsmen Aamer Sohail and Inzamam-ul-Haq shared a then-record one-day international partnership, for any wicket, of 263 against New Zealand in Sharjah. Sohail scored 134 and Inzamam 137.

2008 – Danica wins Indycar
Twenty-six-year-old Danica Patrick became the first female victor in IndyCar history, winning the Indy Japan 300 in her 50th career start. She finished 5.8594 seconds ahead of Hélio Castroneves, having taken the lead in the 198th lap of the 200-lap race,

BIRTHDATES
1851	Scottish golfer YOUNG TOM MORRIS – died 1875
1927	American auto racer PHIL HILL – died 2008
1938	Australian sprinter BETTY CUTHBERT
1945	NFL/College Football coach STEVE SPURRIER
1954	Australian Test batsman PETER TOOHEY
1957	England Test opener GRAEME FOWLER
1958	Russian NHL defenseman VIACHESLAV FETISOV
1960	Australian hurdler DEBBIE FLINTOFF KING
1961	MLB first baseman/manager DON MATTINGLY
1964	NFL kicker JOHN CARNEY
1964	Figure skater ROSALYNN SUMNERS
1967	Dutch darts player RAYMOND VAN BARNEVELD
1968	Russian cross-country skier YELENA VÄLBE
1971	Australian golfer JOHN SENDEN
1971	NBA guard/executive ALLAN HOUSTON
1976	Irish soccer goalkeeper SHAY GIVEN

Baseball's Addie Joss, pictured in 1910.

1909 – Rare triple hat-trick
For the first time in English Football League history, 3 members of a team scored hat-tricks in the same match, when Nottingham Forest played Leicester Fosse in a Division 1 match at the City Ground. Billy Hooper, Alfred Spouncer and Enoch West scored 3 goals apiece in Forest's 12-0 romp.

1959 – Big fish
Victorian market gardener Alf Dean set the IGFA recognised world record for the biggest great white shark caught, with the monster weighing 1,208.4kg (2,664lbs), caught off Ceduna in South Australia. The shark was caught with a rod and reel and was 16ft 10in long.

1974 – Elder earns Masters invite
Thirty-eight-year-old African-American Lee Elder won his first PGA Tour event and put an end to the all-white Masters' policy of the Augusta National Country Club in Georgia. Elder birdied the final 2 holes of the Monsanto Open in Pensacola, Florida to force a playoff with Englishman Peter Oosterhuis at 10-under par 274. He won on the fourth extra hole to earn automatic entry into the previously by-invitation-only Masters.

1977 – Random selection works
NY Yankees manager Billy Martin, facing a 2-8 slump, drew his line-up out of a hat for a home game against Toronto. The ploy worked for the unconventional Martin, with the Yankees winning 8–6.

1980 – Rogers takes fourth Boston Marathon
Thirty-three-year-old American Bill Rodgers won his third consecutive, and fourth overall Boston Marathon in a time of 2:12.11. Rodgers also won the New York Marathon 4 times. In all, he ran 57 marathons, completing 28 of them in less than 2 hours and 15 minutes.

1986 – Hat-trick v different keepers
England defender Alvin Martin scored 3 goals against different goalkeepers during West Ham's 8-1 thrashing of Newcastle, in their Division 1 match at Upton Park. Martin scored against regular keeper Martin Thomas before he injured a shoulder and was replaced, in turn, by field players Chris Hedworth and Peter Beardsley.

1987 – Hadlee bags Kiwis' 100th Test ton
Champion New Zealand all-rounder Richard Hadlee made the larger of his 2 Test career hundreds, with an unbeaten 151 against Sri Lanka in Colombo. Hadlee's 240-ball innings was also the 100th Test century to be scored by a New Zealander. He added a Kiwi record 246 for the sixth wicket, with captain Jeff Crowe.

1991 – Ten Opens for Khan
Squash legend Jahangir Khan of Pakistan won the British Open for a record 10th consecutive time, beating compatriot Jansher Khan 2-9, 9-4, 9-4, 9-0 in the final in London. Jansher went on to win the next 6 Open titles.

2013 – Rafa's Monte Carlo streak ends
Rafael Nadal's 8-year reign at the Monte Carlo Masters finally ended as the Spaniard lost 6-2, 7-6 to top-ranked Novak Djokovic in the final. Nadal had won his 46 previous matches at Monte Carlo. His 8 straight titles were an ATP record for 1 tournament.

BIRTHDATES
1922	England Test all-rounder ALLAN WATKINS – died 2011
1932	English tennis player ANGELA MORTIMER
1943	American golfer JIM JAMIESON
1945	Indian Test cricket sinner/umpire SRINIVAS VENKATARAGHAVAN
1953	American golfer ED FIORI
1956	American swimmer RICK DE MONT
1960	Canadian Hockey Hall of Fame left wing MICHEL GOULET
1964	Canadian swimmer ALEX BAUMANN
1965	Canadian NHL goalie ED BELFOUR
1965	American boxer OLIVER McCALL
1975	New Zealand swimmer DANYON LOADER
1977	Canadian pairs figure skater JAMIE SALÉ
1980	NFL quarterback TONY ROMO
1980	Canadian NHL forward VINCENT LACAVALIER

1970 – 19 Ks for Seaver

New York Mets pitcher Tom Seaver struck out the last 10 San Diego batters at Shea Stadium, equalling the Major League strikeout record of 19 in a game. It was also the first time in the 20th century a pitcher had struck out 10 consecutive batters. The Mets won the game, 2-1.

1976 – Schultz PIM record

Dave Schultz of the Philadelphia Flyers set a record for most penalty minutes in a Stanley Cup playoff game when he racked up an amazing 42 minutes against the Maple Leafs in Toronto. Shultz was charged with 1 minor, 2 majors, one 10 minute misconduct and 2 game misconducts. Despite Schultz's lengthy absences, Toronto won 8-5. The record was later beaten by Randy Holt with 67 minutes, but Schultz still holds the record for most career penalty minutes at 472.

1983 – Greg's last day in charge

Greg Chappell played his 48th and final match as Australian cricket captain, in the inaugural Test against Sri Lanka in Kandy. He was an astute captain, winning 21, losing 13 and drawing 14. Australia won the one-off Test by an innings and 38 runs, with Kepler Wessells (141) and David Hookes (143 not out) in form in the Australian first innings of 514 for 4. Spinners Tom Hogan and Bruce Yardley did the rest on a wearing pitch.

1994 – Moorer upsets Holyfield

Evander Holyfield lost his WBA and IBF heavyweight titles to Michael Moorer in an upset points decision in Las Vegas. Moorer recovered from a second-round knockdown to earn a majority decision. Two of the judges gave the fight to Moorer and one judge scored it a draw. Holyfield won a rematch 3 years later by TKO in the eighth round in Las Vegas.

2003 – O'Sullivan to the max ... again

Champion snooker player Ronnie 'The Rocket' O'Sullivan became the first player to make 2 maximum breaks in the World Championships, when he made a 147 in 6:30 in the seventh frame of his first-round match against Marco Fu of Hong Kong. Fu won by 10 frames to six.

2007 – Sox smash four straight dingers

The Boston Red Sox hit 4 straight home runs in a 7-6 win against the New York Yankees at Fenway Park, tying a major league record. Manny Ramirez, J. D. Drew, Mike Lowell and Jason Varitek connected in a span of 10 pitches, during the third inning against Chase Wright. The Red Sox became the fifth team in MLB history to hit 4 consecutive homers.

2010 – Big money for rugby

SANZAR, the southern hemisphere's rugby body, confirmed new broadcast rights agreements for professional rugby competitions across Australia, New Zealand and South Africa from 2011 to 2015. Agreements were concluded with SuperSport (South Africa), Fox Sports (Australia) and Sky Television (New Zealand), as well as for the UK market. The deal was valued at US$437m, a 35% increase on the comparable components of the existing US$323m 5-year agreement.

2013 – Red Devils' 20th League title

Manchester United captured the club's record 20th English League title with a 3-0 win over Aston Villa in the Premier League match at Old Trafford. Dutch international Robin van Persie fired in 3 first half goals to clinch the title with 4 games still to play. Veteran midfielder Ryan Giggs and manager Sir Alex Ferguson had been involved in all 13 of the club's titles since the start of the Premier League era in 1993.

BIRTHDATES

1935	New Zealand rugby union number 8 DICK 'RED' CONWAY
1944	American adventurer STEVE FOSSETT – died 2007
1949	NBA forward SPENCER HAYWOOD
1952	New Zealand rugby union captain DAVID LOVERIDGE
1959	Sri Lankan Test batsman RANJAN MADUGALLE
1959	MLB manager TERRY FRANCONA
1960	British boxer LLOYD HONEYGHAN
1961	NFL quarterback JEFF HOSTETLER
1961	MLB pitcher JIMMY KEY
1968	Australian Test fast bowler JO ANGEL
1969	England soccer striker DION DUBLIN
1971	Swedish tennis player NICKLAS KULTI
1972	Belgian tennis player SABINE APPELMANS
1972	Australian rugby union back rower OWEN FINEGAN
1975	Spanish road cyclist CARLOS SASTRE

㉓ APRIL

1963 – Naish is born

Pioneering windsurfer and kite surfer Robby Naish was born in San Diego. He won his first overall world championship in windsurfing aged 13, and took 8 more in his career, plus 3 PWA world championships. In the 1990s, he entered the emerging sport of kite surfing, with great success.

1983 – Snooker first

Cliff Thorburn of Canada made the first maximum break of 147 in the history of the World Professional Snooker Championship, in a second-round match against Terry Griffiths at the Crucible Theatre, Sheffield.

1983 – Buster Crabbe dead at 75

American swimmer and actor Buster Crabbe died in Scottsdale, Arizona, at age 75. Crabbe learned to swim in Hawaii and the great Duke Kahanamoku became his idol. He was successful at the AAU National Championships and beat the French world record holder, Jean Taris, for the 1932 Olympic 400m freestyle gold medal. He went on to appear in 175 movies, the most notable being serial roles in *Buck Rogers* and *Flash Gordon*.

1991 – Greenidge is great

West Indian opener Gordon Greenidge smashed 226 in the fourth Test against Australia in Barbados. It was Greenidge's fourth Test 2 hundred, and included 32 fours. It was also a welcome return to form for the aggressive opener, who had made only one 50 in his last 24 innings. The Windies strolled to 536 for 9 declared, and Australia was well beaten by 343 runs and 2-0 down in the series.

2001 – Ruud a Red Devil

Manchester United completed the record £19 million signing of Dutch international centre forward Ruud van Nistelrooy. In his first season at Old Trafford (2000–01), van Nistelrooy broke a Premiership record by scoring in 8 consecutive matches. He was also the top scorer in the Champions League competition and became one of the few United forwards to score more than 20 goals in a season. In his second season in England, he scored 44 goals in all competitions (25

American windsurfer and kite surfer Robby Naish.

in the Premiership), including 12 penalties and 3 hat-tricks. Injuries, however, curtailed that blazing goal-scoring pace, and Nistelrooy announced his retirement in 2012.

2003 – Long wait followed by flood

After 10 years in Test cricket, champion West Indian batsman Brian Lara scored his maiden Test century on his home ground of Queen's Park Oval at Port of Spain in Trinidad. Lara's 122 came in the second Test against Australia, after 9 Tests and 19 innings in Trinidad. He also scored 91 in the first innings, but the Windies went down by 118 runs and trailed 2-0 in the 4-Test series.

BIRTHDATES

1921	Baseball Hall of Fame pitcher WARREN SPAHN – died 2003
1943	Basketball Hall of Fame guard GAIL GOODRICH
1943	Japanese boxer MASAHIKO 'FIGHTING' HARADA
1943	Canadian NHL goalie TONY ESPOSITO
1960	American golfer JODIE MUDD
1963	American windsurfer ROBBY NAISH
1969	Russian gymnast YELENA SHUSHUNOVA
1972	Australian golfer RACHEL HETHERINGTON
1977	American pro wrestler JOHN CENA
1977	MLB outfielder ANDRUW JONES
1979	Finnish Nordic combined skier SAMPPA LAJUNEN
1983	Slovak tennis player DANIELA HANTUCHOVÁ
1986	Dutch speed skater SVEN KRAMER

1937 – Scots like their Football
A record crowd for a Scottish FA Cup Final, of 146,433 attended Hampden Park in Glasgow for the Celtic-Aberdeen clash. Celtic won the match 2-1.

1960 – Four Grand Slams in one day
A record 4 home run grand slams (in which a home run is hit when bases are loaded, and so scores the maximum 4 runs) were hit in Major League Baseball. The Baltimore Orioles' Albie Pearson and Billy Klaus both completed grand slams against the Yankees in New York; Detroit's Lou Berberet hammered the White Sox at Tiger Stadium; and Philadelphia's Jimmie Coker slammed Cincinnati at Shibe Park.

1979 – Packer wins
The Australian Cricket Board granted media magnate Kerry Packer the exclusive right to show matches organised by them, for the next 10 years. His company, PBL, was also granted marketing rights to the sport in Australia. The completion of the negotiation meant the end of World Series Cricket, an alternative contest that had attracted the top 60 players in the world.

1981 – 8,000 wins for Shoemaker
Champion American jockey Willie Shoemaker won his 8,000th race, 2,000 more than any other jockey in the US. Considered to be the most successful jockey in history, he won his first race at 18 and by the time he retired in 1990, had won 8,833 races, including 4 Kentucky Derbies, 5 Belmont Stakes, and 3 Preakness Stakes. He was the first jockey to win over $100 million in purses. The one American trophy that eluded Shoemaker was the prestigious Triple Crown of Thoroughbred Racing.

1994 – Scoring title to 'The Admiral'
San Antonio Spurs centre David Robinson scored 71 points against the LA Clippers to tie the seventh-highest career total in NBA history. Robinson also clinched the season scoring title.

1994 – Second-best all-time from the line
Denver Nuggets' guard Mahmoud Abdul-Rauf finished the 1993–94 season by hitting 219 of 229 free throw attempts for a 95.6% free throw percentage, the second-highest in NBA history, behind Calvin Murphy's mark of 95.8% in 1980–81.

1996 – All in the family football
Thirty-five-year-old Iceland international Arnór Gudjohnsen and his 17-year-old son, Eidur, created football history when they were both capped on the same day. During Iceland's 3-0 win over Estonia in Tallin, Arnor was substituted by Eidur in the 62nd minute, for a unique father-son occurrence.

2003 – Hendry plays well in Sheffield
Scottish snooker player Stephen Hendry set a record when he became the first player to achieve 100 century breaks in competitive snooker in one venue. Hendry compiled a break of 115 in the seventh frame of his second-round World Championship match, against Drew Henry at the Crucible Theatre, Sheffield.

BIRTHDATES
1868	Scottish golfer SANDY HERD – died 1944
1916	Pro wrestler LOU THESZ – died 2002
1925	England soccer midfielder JIMMY DICKINSON – died 1982
1939	New Zealand rugby union fullback FERGIE McCORMICK
1940	England Test fast bowler DAVID LARTER
1945	American golfer BOB LUNN
1954	NFL quarterback VINCE FERRAGAMO
1955	New Zealand rugby union centre BILL OSBORNE
1962	England soccer defender/manager STUART PEARCE
1962	Australian rugby league front rower/analyst STEVE ROACH
1967	Venezuelan MLB shortstop OMAR VIZQUEL
1970	Australian Test fast bowler DAMIEN FLEMING
1971	Sri Lankan Test spinner KUMAR DHARMASENA
1972	MLB infielder CHIPPER JONES
1973	Indian Test batsman SACHIN TENDULKAR
1973	British golfer LEE WESTWOOD
1977	Puerto Rican MLB outfielder CARLOS BELTRÁN
1981	American tennis player TAYLOR DENT
1989	American diver DAVID BOUDIA
1997	New Zealand golfer LYDIA KO

1872 – England all-rounder born

Charles Burgess Fry, arguably England's greatest all-round sportsman, was born. Fry was a dual international, playing both cricket and football for England. On the cricket field, Fry played 26 Tests, scoring 1,223 runs at 32.18, with 2 centuries. In football, he was an accomplished fullback and was capped 26 times. He also played in a winning FA Cup final side for Southampton in 1902. Fry also set the world long jump record of 23ft, 5in in 1892; the record stood for 21 years. He later stood as a Liberal candidate for Parliament and became a successful journalist and author. He died in 1956, aged 84.

1950 – NBA colour line broken

Duquesne small forward Chuck Cooper became the first African-American to be drafted into the NBA when he was taken in the second round by the Boston Celtics. He played 4 seasons in Boston, before being traded to the Milwaukee Hawks and then ending his career with the Ft. Wayne Pistons. During his NBA career, Cooper played a total of 409 games.

1974 – NFL rule changes

The NFL changed 2 significant rules that stand to this day. One sudden death overtime period (15 minutes) was added to all regular season games; if no team scored in this period, the game would result in a tie. In addition, the goal posts were to be moved from the goal line to the end line, where they were in 1932. This was to reduce the number of games being decided by field goals; to increase their difficulty as well as to reduce the risk of player injuries.

1989 – Eight points to 'Super Mario'

Pittsburgh Penguins NHL centre Mario Lemieux tied Patrik Sundström's record for the most points scored in a Stanley Cup playoff match, when he recorded 8 against the Philadelphia Flyers in Pittsburgh. Lemieux scored 5 goals and had 3 assists in the Penguins' 10-7 victory. Four of his goals were scored in one period. Sundström had scored 3 goals and had 5 assists in the New Jersey Devils' 10-4 playoff win over Washington in 1988.

1993 – Penguins playoff streak ends

The Pittsburgh Penguins' record 14-game winning streak in Stanley Cup playoff matches ended when they were beaten 4-1 at New Jersey. The Penguins did not lose a game in 4 series, including a 4-game sweep of the Chicago Blackhawks in the 1992 Finals.

2001 – Schmeichel era over

Outstanding Danish goalkeeper Peter Schmeichel announced his retirement from international football after 129 appearances. His final game was Denmark's 3-0 win over Slovenia in Copenhagen. On an international level, Schmeichel starred for Denmark in their 1992 European Championship victory; he also played 5 World Cup matches in 1998. Schmeichel earned Champions League, League, FA Cup and League Cup winners' medals in an 8-year career with Manchester United. He also won the Danish League and Cup with Brøndby and the Portuguese League with Sporting Lisbon.

BIRTHDATES

1872	England Test batsman and soccer player C. B. FRY – died 1956
1882	Scottish golfer FRED McLEOD – died 1976
1916	American golfer JERRY BARBER – died 1994
1929	New Zealand long jumper YVETTE WILLIAMS
1947	Dutch soccer midfielder JOHAN CRUYFF
1952	French soccer manager JACQUES SANTINI
1953	Australian Test batsman GARY COSIER
1955	Argentine soccer midfielder/manager AMÉRICO GALLEGO
1955	British tennis player BUSTER MOTTRAM
1957	British darts player/analyst ERIC BRISTOW
1963	Scottish soccer manager DAVID MOYES
1964	Australian cricket batsman/coach JAMIE SIDDONS
1967	American swimmer ANGEL MARTINO
1969	Sports caster JOE BUCK
1969	NFL safety DARREN WOODSON
1973	German tennis player BARBARA RITTNER
1976	NBA forward TIM DUNCAN
1976	German tennis player RAINER SCHÜTTLER
1976	South African rugby union winger BREYTON PAULSE
1980	Spanish road cyclist ALEJANDRO VALVERDE
1981	Brazilian auto racer FELIPE MASSA
1981	Swedish alpine skier ANJA PÄRSON
1989	Dutch darts player MICHAEL VAN GERWEN

㉖ APRIL

Australian boxer Jeff Fenech during an eighth-round TKO against Tialano Tovar in 1995.

1931 – Technicality beats Gehrig
New York Yankees first baseman Lou Gehrig missed out on the outright home run title after a bizarre incident in Washington. Gehrig's drive into the stands bounced back and was caught by centre fielder Harry Rice. According to the rules, it was a home run. Gehrig's on-base teammate Lyn Lary, however, thought it was the final out of the inning, and headed for the dugout after crossing third base. Gehrig was called out and credited for a triple instead of a homer. As a result, he ended the season tied for the title with Babe Ruth.

1952 – Berg fires 64
Three-time Vare Trophy winner Patty Berg set a new 18-hole LPGA record with a 6-under par 64 in the opening round of her victory at the Richmond Open in California. Her front 9 of 30 also set the 9-hole record and her rounds of 64-74-72 for a 210 total set a women's record for 54 holes.

1964 – Smith defends Championship
Marilynn Smith successfully defended her LPGA Titleholders Championship, in a playoff triumph over Mickey Wright. Smith hit a memorable 3-iron to within a foot of the 18th hole for a birdie and victory.

1966 – 'Red' retires
Arnold 'Red' Auerbach retired as Boston coach after guiding the Celtics to 8 consecutive NBA Championships. The Celtics surrendered a 3-1 advantage, allowing the Los Angeles Lakers to force a deciding Game 7 in Boston. The Celtics gave Auerbach his desired send-off with a nail-biting 95-93 victory. It was also the Celtics' ninth title in 10 years.

1985 – Early title for 'Mauler'
After just 6 professional fights, Australian Jeff Fenech won the IBF bantamweight title, beating Japan's Satoshi Shingaki in a ninth-round TKO at Sydney's Hordern Pavilion. 'The Marrickville Mauler' went on to become the first undefeated boxer to win world titles in 3 different weight divisions. His other successes were in the WBC super-bantamweight and the WBC featherweight divisions. Fenech retired in 1996 and became an accomplished fight trainer and promoter. He was inducted into the International Boxing Hall of Fame in 2002.

1991 – Maradona arrested
Argentina and Napoli football superstar Diego Maradona, whilst serving a 15-month suspension for testing positive to cocaine use in Italy, was arrested at Buenos Aires airport for possession of illegal narcotics.

1996 – Pollock four from four in County debut
Former South African Test captain Shaun Pollock took 4 wickets with 4 consecutive balls in his debut in County Cricket for Warwickshire against Leicestershire at Edgbaston. At one stage Pollock's figures were 5 for one, and he ended with a more than respectable 6 for 21.

BIRTHDATES
1909   England Test all-rounder DICK HOWARTH – died 1980
1918   Dutch sprinter FANNY BLANKERS-KOEN – died 2004
1937   French auto racer JEAN PIERRE BELTOISE
1940   Great Britain rugby league front rower CLIFF WATSON
1947   American swimmer DONNA DE VERONA
1961   American golfer NANCY SCRANTON
1963   Canadian NBA centre BILL WENNINGTON
1966   Hungarian tennis player ANDREA TEMESVÁRI
1985   American tennis player JOHN ISNER

㉗ APRIL

1929 – Britain rules Ryder Cup
Golf's British team captain George Duncan beat Walter Hagen, 10 & 8, on the way to a 7-5 victory over the US in the Ryder Cup at the Moortown Golf Club in Leeds, England. Other big-name Americans to lose their singles matches were Gene Sarazen, Jim Turnesa and Johnny Farrell.

1956 – 'Brockton Blockbuster' retires
After a 4-year undefeated reign as World Heavyweight Champion, Rocky Marciano announced his retirement from the ring. He won the heavyweight title when he knocked out Jersey Joe Walcott in 13 rounds in 1952. He retired with a record of 49 fights for 49 wins, and his walk-up, no-nonsense style contributed to 43 knockouts. He died in a plane crash in Iowa, aged 45.

1983 – Ryan rules
Houston Astros' ace Nolan Ryan struck out Montreal's Brad Mills, moving one ahead of Walter Johnson to become baseball's all-time leader at 3,509. It was a seesawing race for the record, with Philadelphia's Steve Carlton leading at 3,709 by the end of the season, and Ryan finishing at 3,677. Ryan went on to top Carlton on the all-time list.

1991 – Wigan's 3 straight titles
Ellery Hanley captained Wigan to a third consecutive Challenge Cup finals victory at Wembley Stadium, with a 13-8 win over St Helens. The knockout competition in British rugby league is the equivalent to the FA Cup in football.

1996 – Celebrity marriage
Romanian Olympic gymnastics champion Nadia Comaneci married another Olympic champion, American Bart Connor. In 1976, at age 14, Comaneci won 3 gold medals and scored 7 perfect 10 scores at the Montreal Olympics. Connor was America's most decorated male gymnast, having won 2 gold medals at the LA Olympics in 1984. The Connors operate a successful gymnastics academy in Oklahoma.

1998 – 'Thorpedo' era begins
Fifteen-year-old Australian pool prodigy Ian Thorpe broke countryman Duncan Armstrong's 10-year-old Commonwealth 200m freestyle record at the Australian Championships in Melbourne. Thorpe went on to become one of the greatest middle distance swimmers in history, winning gold medals in the 400m, 4 x 200m relay and 4 x 100m relay at the Sydney Olympics, and the 200m/400m double at the Athens Games in 2004.

2007 – Record EPL fine
West Ham United was fined a record £5.5 million by a Premier League panel, on charges of breaching ownership rules over the signings of Argentines Carlos Tevez and Javier Mascherano. The fine was the biggest in English football history, dwarfing the old record of £1.5 million, imposed on Tottenham in 1994 for financial irregularities. The case centred on the issue of third-party ownership of the 2 players, who were signed from Brazilian club Corinthians, and the club's failure to disclose details of the deals.

2008 – Rafa's fourth Monte Carlo
Spanish tennis star Rafael Nadal defeated world no. 1 Roger Federer 7-5, 7-5 to win the prestigious Monte Carlo Masters for a record fourth consecutive year. For a second straight year, the Spaniard did not drop a set. Nadal went on to win the event on 8 occasions.

BIRTHDATES
1875	England Test batsman FREDERICK FANE – died 1960
1899	American golfer LEO DIEGEL – died 1951
1932	NFL coach CHUCK KNOX
1945	England soccer forward MARTIN CHIVERS
1946	Australian Test wicketkeeper JOHN MacLEAN
1952	Finnish rally driver ARI VARTANEN
1952	Basketball Hall of Fame forward GEORGE GERVIN
1954	NFL coach/analyst HERM EDWARDS
1956	England rugby union prop JEF PROBYN
1966	Australian Test spinner PETER McINTYRE
1972	Italian tennis player SYLVIA FARINA ELIA
1973	Canadian tennis player SÉBASTIEN LAREAU
1975	MLB pitcher CHRIS CARPENTER
1986	Russian tennis player DINARA SAFINA
1988	Russian NHL goalie SEMYON VARLAMOV

1923 – FA Cup record crowd
A record crowd for an FA Cup final – 126,047 – attended the first final to be held at Wembley Stadium. Officials delayed the start of the Bolton-West Ham match for 40 minutes as the crowd invaded the ground. It was estimated that a realistic attendance figure would have been higher, at 150,000–200,000. Bolton won the match 2-0.

1934 – Double play misery
Future Baseball Hall of Fame outfielder Goose Goslin, of the Detroit Tigers, grounded into double plays in 4 consecutive trips to the plate against Cleveland at Tiger Stadium. Despite Goslin's misfortune, the Tigers won 4-1.

1967 – Ali stripped of title
Muhammad Ali was stripped of his world heavyweight title after he refused to be drafted into the US army for service in Vietnam. After 3 years, the Federal Court rescinded a decision to imprison Ali. He returned to the ring in October 1970, in a third-round TKO of Jerry Quarry. He later regained his title against George Foreman in 1974's 'Rumble in the Jungle'.

1984 – Century of Tests for 'Black Cat'
Clive Lloyd became the first West Indian to play 100 Test matches, as the fifth Test against Australia got underway in Kingston, Jamaica. Coincidentally, it was also the 100th Test to be played in the Caribbean. The West Indies cruised to a 10-wicket win, which gave them a 3-0 series victory.

1996 – Double ton for Adams
West Indian all-rounder Jimmy Adams scored an unbeaten 208 in the drawn second Test against New Zealand in Antigua. Adams hit 31 fours and a 6 in and took his average up to a spectacular 68.33. The Windies took the series 1-0.

2001 – Saints rugby league treble
The St Helens rugby league club beat the Bradford Bulls, 13-6, in the Challenge Cup final at Twickenham, for a unique treble. The Saints had won the English Super League Premiership and World Club title against the Brisbane Broncos (20-18) earlier in the year.

2007 – 'Gilly' leads the way
Australia made it a hat-trick of World Cup wins with a 53-run victory over Sri Lanka in Barbados. Adam Gilchrist led the way with a stunning 149 off 104 balls as Australia posted 281 for 4 in a rain-restricted 38 overs, and although SL made a flying start, they were always behind the clock.

2008 – Riley resigns
Pat Riley resigned as Miami Heat coach, ending a 25-year career. He remained team president and led them to the NBA title in 2012. Riley finished with 1,210 victories, the third-most in NBA history, behind Don Nelson and Lenny Wilkens. He won 7 championships – 5 as a head coach, one as an assistant and one as a player – and was voted into the Hall of Fame in 2008.

2012 – Black Caviar's world best 20 straight
Superstar racehorse Black Caviar easily won the Robert Sangster Stakes at Morphettville, for a world-best 20th consecutive victory. Always in second gear, Black Caviar defeated Sistine Angel by 4 lengths. The old record of 19 straight had been jointly held by Desert Gold and Gloaming in Australasia, and Zenyatta in the United States. Black Caviar went on to win 25 straight races and was retired in 2013.

BIRTHDATES
1908	Australian Test batsman JACK FINGLETON – died 1981
1930	West Indian Test spinner ALF VALENTINE – died 2004
1942	England Test captain MIKE BREARLEY
1953	England soccer midfielder BRIAN GREENHOFF
1958	American golfer HAL SUTTON
1960	Italian soccer goalkeeper WALTER ZENGA
1964	American golfer STEPHEN AMES
1964	MLB shortstop BARRY LARKIN
1966	American golfer JOHN DALY
1967	NFL kicker PETE STOYANOVICH
1968	Zimbabwe Test batsman ANDY FLOWER
1970	Swedish NHL defenseman NICKLAS LIDSTRÖM
1970	Argentine soccer midfielder DIEGO SIMEONE
1970	Australian tennis player RICHARD FROMBERG
1973	New Zealand rugby union five-eighth ANDREW MEHRTENS

㉙ APRIL

1970 – First FA Cup replay
Chelsea beat Leeds 2-1 after extra time at Old Trafford, winning in the first replay of an FA Cup Final since 1912. The teams had drawn 2-2 after extra time in the first final at Wembley Stadium on April 11.

1986 – 20 Ks for Clemens
Boston Red Sox pitcher Roger Clemens struck out 20 batters in a 3-1 win over the Seattle Mariners at Fenway Park, breaking the major-league record of 19 shared, which had been shared by Nolan Ryan, Steve Carlton and Tom Seaver. Clemens allowed just 3 hits, didn't walk a batter, and tied the American League record with 8 consecutive strikeouts.

1990 – Youngest snooker champ
Aged 21 years and 106 days, Scotsman Stephen Hendry became the youngest World Professional Snooker champion. Hendry beat Englishman Jimmy White 18-14 in the final in Sheffield. It was the first of 7 world titles for Hendry; White lost the next 4 consecutive World Championship finals.

1997 – De Silva delight
Sri Lankan batsman Aravinda de Silva became the first man to score 2 unbeaten hundreds in a Test match, in the drawn second Test against Pakistan in Colombo. De Silva's 138 and 103 were the second and third of 6 consecutive hundreds in Test innings in his own country. All were scored on various grounds in Colombo.

2000 – Lewis retains title
Lennox Lewis retained his heavyweight title when he landed a devastating right uppercut to knockout the previously unbeaten Michael Grant, in the second round at Madison Square Garden in New York.

2005 – Rare pitching match-up
In a rare MLB match-up of 300-game winners, Greg Maddux beat Roger Clemens, as the Chicago Cubs edged the Houston Astros 3-2 at Minute Maid Park. The last such showdown had occurred in 1987, when Angels' hurler Don Sutton defeated Twins southpaw Steve Carlton.

Spanish tennis star Rafael Nadal.

2007 – One-day high score
Surrey smashed the existing first-class, limited-overs record score, making 496 for 4 in 50 overs against Gloucestershire at the Oval. Ali Brown led the way, smashing 176 off 97 balls.

2012 – Nadal scores unique double
Rafael Nadal became the first player in open era of tennis to win 2 tournaments 7 times, after beating David Ferrer 7-6, 7-5 in the Barcelona Open final. The second-ranked Nadal's 21st straight victory on clay followed his eighth consecutive win, achieved in Monte Carlo.

BIRTHDATES
1927　England soccer midfielder BILL SLATER
1934　Venezuelan Baseball Hall of Fame shortstop LUIS APARICIO
1940　Australian Test wicketkeeper BRIAN TABER
1941　British squash player JONAH BARRINGTON
1942　Russian cross-country skier GALINA KULAKOVA
1944　England soccer forward FRANCIS LEE
1947　American golfer JOHNNY MILLER
1947　American middle distance runner JIM RYUN
1951　American auto racer DALE EARNHARDT – died 2001
1960　American golfer BILL GLASSON
1966　England Test spinner PHIL TUFNELL
1967　Australian squash player MICHELLE MARTIN
1967　Canadian NHL goalie CURTIS JOSEPH
1970　American tennis player ANDRE AGASSI
1978　American tennis player BOB BRYAN
1978　American tennis player MIKE BRYAN
1983　NFL quarterback JAY CUTLER

1939 – Gehrig's MLB record

Lou Gehrig set a Major League Baseball record when he played his 2,130th consecutive game for the New York Yankees. Gehrig, however, went 0-4 against Washington's Joe Krakauskas and was in a major form slump, batting an out of character .143 with just 1 RBI. He voluntarily benched himself for the next game and never played again. He made his famous farewell speech on June 2 at Yankee Stadium, and died in June 1941 of what has become known as *Lou Gehrig's Disease*. He was 37.

1976 – Ali's worst fight

Muhammad Ali beat Jimmy Young in a controversial unanimous points decision in Landover, Maryland, to retain his world heavyweight title. In what is regarded to be the worst fight of his career, Ali was under-prepared and failed to take Young seriously, and the crowed booed when the decision fell in his favour. Ali's trainer Angelo Dundee criticised Ali for his attitude and sub-standard performance.

1983 – Greenidge tragedy

West Indian Test openers Gordon Greenidge and Desmond Haynes compiled 296 in the fifth Test against India in Antigua, when Greenidge had to retire to visit his sick daughter in hospital. Sadly, she died 2 days later. Greenidge was eventually adjudged to have retired not out on 154, the only such scorecard entry in Test history.

1993 – Seles stabbed courtside

World no. 1 ranked tennis player Monica Seles was stabbed in the back during a match against Magdalena Maleeva, in Hamburg, Germany. During a break on court, Günter Parche, a 38-year-old deranged fan of Seles' chief rival, Steffi Graf, ran onto courtside and stabbed Seles, who was seated during a break in play. Although she recovered, Seles did not play competitively again for more than 2 years. During her layoff, she became a US citizen. She won the Australian Open in 1991, 1992, 1993, and 1996; the French Open in 1990, 1991, and 1992; and the US Open in 1991 and 1992.

1995 – Record haul for Lynagh

In rugby union, Michael Lynagh scored 28 points in a 53-7 thrashing of Argentina in Brisbane to set a then Australian record for an international match. He retired from international rugby after the 1995 World Cup, having played 72 internationals, scored 17 tries, and kicked 177 penalties, 140 conversions and 9 field goals, for a then-world-record 911 points. Lynagh continued to play club rugby for the big-spending Saracens in England until 1998.

1996 – Longest regulation MLB game

The New York Yankees and the Baltimore Orioles played the longest 9-inning game in Major League Baseball history. The game took 4 hours and 21 minutes. The Yankees won 13-10 at Camden Yards after the Orioles blew a 5-run lead.

BIRTHDATES

1922	South African Test all-rounder ANTON MURRAY – died 1995
1940	Australian rugby union/league winger MICHAEL CLEARY
1942	England rugby union flanker BOB TAYLOR
1944	England rugby union flanker PETER DIXON
1946	American swimmer DON SCHOLLANDER
1949	MLB second baseman/manager PHIL GARNER
1961	Basketball Hall of Fame guard ISIAH THOMAS
1963	American auto racer MICHAEL WALTRIP
1963	NFL wide receiver AL TOON
1964	Australian Test wicketkeeper IAN HEALY
1975	American auto racer ELLIOTT SADLER
1981	Irish soccer defender JOHN O'SHEA

Monica Seles during the 1998 French Open in Paris.

MAY

1 MAY

1948 – Arcaro first to 4 Derby winners
American jockey Eddie Arcaro became the first jockey to ride 4 Kentucky Derby winners when 2-5 equal favourite Citation scored a three-and-a-half-length win over co-favourite Coaltown in front of nearly 100,000 at Churchill Downs. Citation's trainer, Ben Jones, tied the record for trainers by saddling his fourth Derby winner. Citation went on to win the Preakness and Belmont Stakes, becoming only the fourth horse to win the Triple Crown in the 1940s.

1977 – Littler's last
Sweet swinging Gene Littler won his 29th and final PGA Tour event, when he scored a 3-stroke win over Lanny Wadkins in the Houston Open. The pair played off for the PGA Championship later in the year, with Wadkins winning his lone major title.

1981 – Out of the cupboard
Billie Jean King shocked the tennis world by admitting to a lesbian affair dating back to 1971, whilst she had still been married to her husband, Larry King. In becoming the first high-profile American female athlete to acknowledge a homosexual relationship, King admitted to an affair with her long-term secretary, Marilyn Barnett, after Barnett sued her, alleging that King had promised to support her for life.

1991 – Henderson new steals king
Rickey Henderson passed Lou Brock as all-time steals leader when he stole second base against Yankees pitcher Tim Leary in the fourth inning in Oakland. It was his 939th steal in 13 seasons, compared to Brock's 938 in 18.

1994 – Senna F1 tragedy
Thirty-four-year-old Brazilian F1 driver Ayrton Senna was killed during the San Marino Grand Prix at Imola. While leading on the fifth lap, Senna's Williams FW16, travelling at a speed of 309 kph, ran off the track at the sharp Tamburello Corner and crashed into a cement wall. The previous day Senna had gained his record 65th Grand Prix pole position. In his career, he had won 41 Grand Prix and was the World Formula 1 champion in 1988, 1990 and 1991.

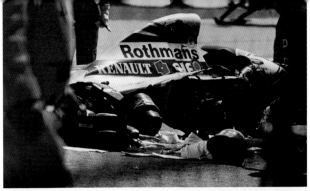

Ayrton Senna was killed on this day in the 1994 San Marino Grand Prix.

2010 – Borel's third Derby, Pletcher's first
Jockey Calvin Borel steered Super Saver through the mud to win his third Kentucky Derby at Churchill Downs in 4 years. The win also ended trainer Todd Pletcher's Derby drought; Pletcher came into the race 0 for 24. Borel won on 50-1 long shot Mine That Bird in 2009 and took his first Derby in 2007, aboard Street Sense.

BIRTHDATES
1925	Pro Football Hall of Fame linebacker CHUCK BEDNARIK
1934	New Zealand rugby union number 8 NEV MacEWAN
1939	American golfer FRANK BEARD
1947	American golfer JERRY HEARD
1951	West Indian Test batsman GORDON GREENIDGE
1954	Pakistan Test wicketkeeper TASLIM ARIF – died 2008
1957	Australian Test batsman RICK DARLING
1959	British golfer ROGER CHAPMAN
1961	American jockey STEVE CAUTHEN
1963	American tennis player ROBERT SEGUSO
1964	Dutch speed skater YVONNE VAN GENNIP
1966	German soccer midfielder/coach OLAF THON
1971	Australian golfer STUART APPLEBY
1973	NFL running back CURTIS MARTIN
1973	German soccer striker OLIVER NEUVILLE
1975	Russian soccer midfielder ALEKSEY SMERTIN
1979	Italian rugby flanker MAURO BERGAMASCO
1982	Spanish tennis player TOMMY ROBREDO
1986	Ecuadorian soccer striker CHRISTIAN BENÍTEZ

1929 – Murt clears the table
New Zealander E. J. (Murt) O'Donoghue became the first snooker player to clear the table from the break in competition. Playing in Auckland, New Zealand, he broke, fluked a red, and sunk the lot to make a break of 134.

1939 – Gehrig' career over
Lou Gehrig's amazing streak of playing in 2,130 consecutive games ended when he removed himself from the Yankees' lineup before the game in Detroit, because of an unexplained weakness and sluggishness. Gehrig never played again. An examination revealed he had ALS, a form of infantile paralysis. The illness went on to be referred to as 'Gehrig's disease'. He died in 1941.

1971 – Portent of Gould gold
Fourteen-year-old swim sensation Shane Gould stamped herself as a gold medal contender for the 1972 Munich Olympics, with a world record swim in the 200m freestyle in London. Gould swam a time of 2:06.5 at Crystal Palace. She went on to win gold medals for Australia in the 200m and 400m, and the 200m individual medley in Munich, all in world record time. She is the only swimmer, male or female, to have simultaneously held all freestyle world records from 100m to 1,500m. She retired early at the age of 16.

1980 – 'Chappelli' retires
Australian captain Ian Chappell retired from Test cricket. The always outspoken and controversial Chappell scored 5,345 runs in 75 Tests at 42.42. He scored 14 Test centuries, took 105 catches and captured 20 wickets.

1988 – Trouble follows Rose
Cincinnati Reds manager Pete Rose was suspended for 30 days for pushing an umpire. Known for his volatile temper, the former MLB hits leader got into a shoving match with umpire Dave Pallone. Rose was later barred for life, for betting a minimum of $10,000 a day on 52 Reds' games in 1987.

1990 – Simon says, 'Slog'
Australian all-rounder Simon O'Donnell thrashed a one-day international record 50 off 18 balls against Sri Lanka at Sharjah. O'Donnell eventually smashed 74 not out off just 29 balls, in an innings that included 6 fours and 4 sixes.

2003 – Waugh beats 'The Don's' century mark
Australian captain Steve Waugh scored 115 in the third Test against the West Indies in Bridgetown, to surpass Sir Donald Bradman as the most prolific Australian Test century scorer, with 30. Waugh would go on to score 32 Test hundreds before he retired in early 2004. He played 168 Tests compared to Bradman's 52.

2005 – Cash for comment!
Houston Rockets head coach Jeff Van Gundy received a $100,000 fine from the NBA, for comments made to the media regarding NBA officiating, accusing referees of being biased. It was the largest fine ever issued against a coach.

2009 – Shock Derby result
In the second-biggest upset in 135 years of the Kentucky Derby, 50-1 shot Mine That Bird pulled away in the stretch to score a six-and-three-quarter-length victory at Churchill Downs. His margin was the largest since Assault had won by 8 lengths in 1946. On a sloppy dirt track, the gelding paid $103.20 to win, the second-largest payout in Derby history behind Donerail's $184.90 in 1913.

BIRTHDATES
1901	England Test batsman BOB WYATT – died 1995
1935	Spanish soccer manager LUIS SUÁREZ
1958	Irish soccer defender/manager DAVID O'LEARY
1960	England rugby union flanker GARY REES
1960	Sri Lankan Test fast bowler RAVI RATNAYEKE
1961	Australian tennis player PETER DOOHAN
1962	English snooker player JIMMY WHITE
1967	England soccer midfielder DAVID ROCASTLE – died 2001
1969	West Indian Test batsman BRIAN LARA
1972	American synchronised swimmer JILL SAVERY
1972	Pro wrestler/actor DWAYNE JOHNSON 'THE ROCK'
1975	England soccer captain DAVID BECKHAM
1985	American auto racer KYLE BUSCH

❸ MAY

1936 – DiMaggio debut
Twenty-one-year-old New York Yankees rookie Joe DiMaggio was an instant hit in his long-awaited Major League debut, in a 14-5 thrashing of St Louis at Yankee Stadium. In 6 at-bats DiMaggio registered 2 singles and a triple, scored 3 runs and drove in one. He went on to have a sensational rookie season, batting .323 with 29 homers, 132 runs and 125 RBI.

1952 – Geordies' successive Cups
Newcastle beat Arsenal 1-0 to become the first team in the 20th century to have back-to-back FA Cup success at Wembley Stadium. Jorge Robledo scored the Geordies' winner in the 84th minute. They had beaten Blackpool 2-0 in 1951.

1978 – Riot mars Test
The final day's play in the fifth Test between the West Indies and Australia in Jamaica was abandoned when a riot erupted. Windies pace bowler Vanburn Holder was given out caught; he refused to leave, and the match was called a draw.

1986 – Willie oldest Derby winning jockey
Fifty-four-year-old jockey Willie Shoemaker became the oldest rider to win a Kentucky Derby, when he rode outsider Ferdinand for his fourth win in the classic race. Ferdinand won by two-and-a-quarter lengths ahead of Bold Arrangement. Shoemaker's last Derby winning ride had been 21 years earlier, on Lucky Debonair.

1992 – Three straight to Trevino
Lee Trevino posted a 10-under 206 to edge Orville Moody by 1 stroke and win the Las Vegas Senior Classic, his third consecutive individual tournament victory.

1995 – Rare series win in the Caribbean
Paul Reiffel and Shane Warne each took 4 wickets, as Australia dismissed the West Indies for 213 to win the fourth Test in Jamaica by an innings and 53 runs, and take the series 2-1. It was Australia's first series win in the Caribbean since 1973.

2005 – Three figure city
West Indian batsman Dwayne Bravo's maiden Test century was an historic highlight of the final day of the drawn fifth Test against South Africa in Antigua. Bravo's 107 was the eighth three-figure score of the match – a new world record – as the Windies were dismissed for 747. Other century-makers in the match were South Africans A. B. de Villiers (114), Graeme Smith (126), Jacques Kallis (147) and Ashwell Prince (131) for South Africa; and Chris Gayle (317), Ramnaresh Sarwan (127) and Shivnarine Chanderpaul (127) for the Windies.

2009 – Crawford steals six
Tampa Bay outfielder Carl Crawford tied the modern major league record for stolen bases in a game, with 6 in the Rays 5-3 home victory over the Boston Red Sox. He joined Eddie Collins, Otis Nixon, and Eric Young as the only players to do so.

2011 – Rose new MVP
Twenty-two-year-old Chicago Bulls star Derrick Rose was named the NBA's MVP, becoming the youngest player in league history to win the award. He ended the 2-year MVP reign of LeBron James.

BIRTHDATES
1905	Baseball Hall of Fame pitcher CHARLES 'RED' RUFFING – died 1986
1918	English soccer manager TED BATES – died 2003
1921	American boxer 'SUGAR' RAY ROBINSON – died 1989
1934	English boxer HENRY COOPER – died 2011
1936	Puerto Rican boxer JOSÉ TORRES – died 2009
1943	Mexican boxer VICENTE SALDIVAR – died 1985
1948	English golfer/analyst PETER OOSTERHUIS
1952	Scottish sprinter ALLAN WELLS
1955	Australian Test batsman DAVID HOOKES – died 2004
1957	American NHL defenseman ROD LANGWAY
1961	English soccer manager STEVE McCLAREN
1963	NBA guard JEFF HORNACEK
1964	Canadian NHL goalie RON HEXTALL
1965	Danish soccer midfielder JOHN JENSEN
1968	Australian rugby union flanker WILLIE OFAHENGAUE
1977	MLB pitcher RYAN DEMPSTER

④ MAY

1957 – Bill's blunder
Champion American jockey Bill Shoemaker committed one of the sport's greatest blunders in the Kentucky Derby. Shoemaker was riding Gallant Man to apparent victory, but he thought the 1/16 pole was the finish line and stood up in the stirrups, allowing Iron Liege to win.

1966 – Shilton era commences
Peter Shilton made his Football League debut for Leicester City in a 3-0 home win against Everton. The England goalkeeper went on to set a league record of 1,005 appearances. Shilton passed a century of league games for his first 5 clubs: Leicester City, Stoke City, Nottingham Forest, Southampton and Derby County. He also played for Plymouth Argyle, Bolton Wanderers and Leyton Orient, before retiring in 1996. He earned a record 125 caps for England, retiring from international football after the 1990 World Cup.

1973 – 20 innings and out
The Philadelphia Phillies outlasted the Atlanta Braves 5-4 in a 20-inning marathon at Veterans Stadium in Philadelphia. Dick Ruthven started for the Phillies, and reliever Jim Lonborg earned the victory over Ron Reed.

1985 – Aussies star in Cup Final
Four Australians – Peter Sterling and John Muggleton for Hull, and Brett Kenny and John Ferguson for Wigan – played in what is regarded as the best-ever British Challenge Cup final at Wembley. Wigan won the match 28-24. Kenny won the Lance Todd Trophy as the man of the match.

1990 – Akram hat-trick specialist
Pakistan left-arm fast bowler Wasim Akram became the only man to take 2 hat-tricks in both Test matches and one-day internationals in the Sharjah final against Australia. He captured his second ODI hat-trick in 6 months when he bowled Merv Hughes, Carl Rackemann and Terry Alderman with consecutive deliveries to set up Pakistan's 36-run win.

Leicester City and England goalkeeper Peter Shilton.

1994 – Gunners' triumph
Arsenal beat Italian club Palma 1-0 in Copenhagen to win the European Cup Winners Cup. Striker Alan Smith scored the Gunners' winner in the 20th minute.

BIRTHDATES
1928	German auto racer WOLFGANG VON TRIPS – died 1961
1928	American golfer BETSY RAWLS
1946	Irish auto racer JOHN WATSON
1949	American drag racer JOHN FORCE
1957	Australian Test spinner PETER SLEEP
1957	Canadian alpine skier KATHY KREINER
1959	American golfer BOB TWAY
1960	England Test batsman MARTYN MOXON
1964	Australian surfer JODY COOPER
1970	New Zealand Test spinner PAUL WISEMAN
1970	American WNBA guard/coach DAWN STALEY
1971	Australian triathlete MILES STEWART
1974	Irish jockey TONY McCOY
1987	Spanish soccer midfielder CESC FÀBREGAS
1989	Irish golfer RORY McILROY

1963 – 'Golden Bear' wins Tournament of Champions

Jack Nicklaus captured the first of his 5 Tournament of Champions titles, beating Tony Lema and Arnold Palmer by 5 strokes, with a total of 273. The tournament has now reverted to the season-starting Mercedes Championship in Hawaii.

1973 – 'Big Red' first leg of Triple Crown

The 1972 Horse of the Year, Secretariat, captured the first leg of the famed Triple Crown and became the first horse to break 2 minutes when he won the Kentucky Derby. Ridden by Ron Turcotte, 'Big Red' blitzed the final quarter in 23.2 seconds to finish two-and-a-half lengths ahead of Sham in a winning time of 1:59.4. Secretariat went on to win the Preakness and Belmont Stakes, becoming the first horse in 25 years to take the Triple Crown.

1978 – Rose fastest to hit milestone

In his 16th season with the Cincinnati Reds, 37-year-old Pete Rose reached the 3,000-hit milestone quicker than anybody in baseball history. Rose singled in his second and third at-bats in a 4-3 loss to the Expos in Montreal, joining 12 others in the prestigious 3,000-hit club.

1992 – Football stand collapse

Eighteen fans died and an estimated 2,300 were injured when a temporary stand collapsed during the French Cup semi-final between Bastia and Marseille in Corsica. The match was cancelled and the winner of the other semi-final, Monaco, was permitted to play in the 1993 European Cup Winners' Cup.

2003 – Hat-trick over 2 innings

West Indian fast bowler Jermaine Lawson completed a rare and unusual hat-trick during the third Test against Australia in Barbados. Lawson took the wickets of Brett Lee and Stuart MacGill with the final 2 balls of the first innings, and struck with his first ball of the second innings when he trapped Justin Langer lbw. Australia won the match, however, to take an unbeatable 3-0 lead in the series. Lawson's promising career was limited to 13 Tests, after coming under scrutiny from the International Cricket Council because of his suspect bowling action.

2004 – Catchers' HR record to Piazza

New York Mets catcher Mike Piazza set the record for home runs by a catcher in an 8-2 win against the San Francisco Giants at Shea Stadium, passing the old mark of 351 he had shared with Carlton Fisk.

2007 – 'Pretty Boy' beats 'Golden Boy'

In a high profile fight, Floyd Mayweather Jr (37-0) earned a 12-round split decision to beat Oscar De La Hoya for the WBC light middleweight title in Las Vegas.

2013 – LeBron takes fourth MVP award

Miami Heat star LeBron James was named the NBA's Most Valuable Player for the fourth time after collecting 120 of the 121 first-place votes, with Carmelo Anthony of the New York Knicks picking up the lone remaining top choice.

BIRTHDATES

1889	South African Test captain HERBIE TAYLOR – died 1973
1923	American golfer WILLIAM C. CAMPBELL
1933	West Indian Test batsman O'NEIL 'COLLIE' SMITH – died 1959
1944	Swedish soccer striker BO LARSSON
1950	American golfer REX CALDWELL
1965	Australian auto racer GLENN SETON
1969	South African rugby union centre PIETER MULLER
1972	Slovak NHL right wing ZIGGY PÁLFFY
1972	Swedish NHL right wing MIKAEL RENBERG
1976	Argentine soccer defender JUAN PABLO SORIN
1980	Israeli soccer midfielder YOSSI BENAYOUN

⑥ MAY

1915 – First of many for 'the Babe'
Twenty-year-old Babe Ruth smashed his first MLB home run for the Boston Red Sox in a 4-3 loss to the New York Yankees at the Polo Grounds. In the third inning, Ruth ripped a drive off Jack Warhop into the upper tier of the right-field grandstand. He also hit 2 singles. As starting pitcher, Ruth had a 1-run lead with 2 outs in the ninth, but couldn't close the victory. He had an 18-8 season record as a pitcher and went on to hit 713 more homers in his career, a record that remained unbroken until 1974.

1954 – Four-minute mile barrier broken
Twenty-five-year-old English doctor Roger Bannister became the first man to break the 4-minute mile, in a time of 3:59.4, at the Iffley Track in Oxford. Watched by 3,000 spectators, Bannister was assisted by 2 pacemakers, Chris Brasher and Chris Chataway. Later in the year, Bannister beat John Landy of Australia in a showdown at the 1954 British Empire and Commonwealth Games, in the first race in which 2 runners broke the 4-minute mark. Bannister then retired to concentrate on his medical studies, and was knighted in 1975.

1961 – Spurs' Cup double
Tottenham became the first club in the 20th century to win the English FA Cup/League double, when they beat Leicester 2-0 in the FA Cup final at Wembley, with Bobby Smith and Terry Dyson scoring. The previous Wednesday, Tottenham had finished on top of the Division 1 table on 66 points, 8 points ahead of Sheffield.

1978 – Cauthen's winning Derby debut
In his first ride in the Kentucky Derby, 18-year-old jockey Steve Cauthen steered second-favourite Affirmed to victory. Affirmed was close to the lead all the way and held off 6-5 favourite Alydar to win by a length. Cauthen followed aboard Affirmed to wins in the Preakness and Belmont Stakes to take the Triple Crown, with Alydar finishing second in all 3 races.

1981 – First leg of UEFA win to 'Tractor Boys'
Ipswich Town beat AZ'67 of the Netherlands, 3-0, in

Roger Bannister breaks the 4-minute mile in a time of 3:59.4 in 1954.

the first leg of the final of the UEFA Cup at Portman Road. John Wark, Frans Thijssen and Paul Mariner scored for Ipswich. The unlikely champions went on to lose the second leg 4-2 in Amsterdam, to take the trophy 5-4 on aggregate.

2006 – 'Golden Boy' is back
Fighting for the first time in 20 months, Oscar De La Hoya dominated Ricardo Mayorga, knocking down the Nicaraguan brawler in the first round before finally stopping him in the sixth to claim the WBC super light middleweight title in Las Vegas. De La Hoya (38-4, 30 KOs) clearly hadn't lost his passion for the ring since Bernard Hopkins stopped him in 2004.

BIRTHDATES
1907	Pro Football Hall of Fame coach WEEB EWBANK – died 1998
1931	Baseball Hall of Fame slugger WILLIE MAYS
1937	American boxer RUBIN 'HURRICANE' CARTER
1946	American golfer GRIER JONES
1947	American high jumper DICK FOSBURY
1969	Irish soccer midfielder/manager JIM MAGILTON
1972	Canadian NHL goalie MARTIN BRODEUR
1977	Australian diver CHANTAL NEWBERRY
1978	NFL defensive end JOHN ABRAHAM
1980	American swimmer BROOKE BENNETT
1982	NFL tight end JASON WHITTEN
1983	Brazilian soccer defender DANI ALVES
1989	Slovak tennis player DOMINIKA CIBULKOVÁ

⑦ MAY

1950 – Hogan ties Nelson record
Ben Hogan tied Byron Nelson's 72-hole PGA scoring record on a par-70 course, winning the Greenbrier Spring Festival in White Sulphur Springs, West Virginia. Hogan posted rounds of 64-64-65-66 for a 259 total.

1959 – Baseball crowd record
The largest crowd in the history of baseball (93,103) jammed into the Los Angeles Coliseum to watch an exhibition game held to honour Roy Campanella, the former Brooklyn Dodgers catcher who had been paralysed in a road accident. It was estimated that at least 15,000 additional people were turned away. Campanella received $60,000 to aid in his rehabilitation. The Yankees beat the Dodgers 6-2 in the exhibition game.

Roy Campanella in 1961. The baseball player was paralysed in 1959.

1968 – Craig Wood dead at 67
1941 US Open and 1942 Masters champion Craig Wood died in Palm Beach, California, aged 67. Wood was the first player in history to lose playoffs in all 4 of the modern major championships. He still holds the record for the longest drive ever hit in major championship play – 430 yards on the fifth hole, at St Andrews in the British Open.

1977 – Seattle Slew takes first leg of Triple Crown
Seattle Slew beat Run Dusty Run and Sanhedrin to win the Kentucky Derby on his way to the Triple Crown of American racing. Seattle Slew is the only horse to win the Triple Crown with an undefeated record. He died aged 28, in 2002.

1982 – NFL's Raiders off to LA
The Oakland Raiders announced the franchise would be moving to Los Angeles for the 1983 season, making their new home base the Olympic Stadium. The club spent 13, mainly unsatisfying years in LA, although they did win Super Bowl XVIII in 1983. The Raiders moved back to Oakland in 1995, after the City approved a massive overhaul to the old Oakland Alameda County Coliseum.

1999 – Doohan smashed in crash
Australia's five-time 500cc motorcycle world champion Michael Doohan broke his leg, shoulder and wrist when he crashed his Honda in practice for the Spanish Grand Prix at Jerez. The 33-year-old Doohan underwent 3 operations following the crash, and officially retired from racing in December 1999. In 11 Grand Prix seasons Doohan rode to 54 victories.

2003 – Gunners' double treble
The only English Premiership double hat-trick to date occurred in Arsenal's match against Southampton at Highbury. Robert Pires and Jermaine Pennant scored 3 goals apiece in the Gunners' 6-1 victory.

BIRTHDATES
1896	English tennis player KATHLEEN McKANE GODFREY – died 1992
1933	Pro Football Hall of Fame quarterback JOHNNY UNITAS – died 2002
1977	Australian rugby union five-eighth ELTON FLATLEY
1962	NBA forward TONY CAMPBELL
1964	NFL running back RONNIE HARMON
1964	NFL defensive end LESLIE O'NEAL
1965	Irish soccer striker NORMAN WHITESIDE
1969	Bulgarian tennis player KATERINA MALEEVA
1984	NFL quarterback ALEX SMITH

⑧ MAY

1937 – First Derby at 'Churchill Downs'

War Admiral beat Pompoon and Reaping Reward to win the 63rd Kentucky Derby, heading for the Triple Crown. It was the first year the Louisville Jockey Club incorporated the track name 'Churchill Downs'.

1959 – Perfect game to 'Catfish'

Oakland Athletics' 22-year-old right-hander Catfish Hunter became the first American League pitcher to throw a perfect game in the regular season in 46 years, when he dominated the Minnesota Twins in Oakland. Hunter struck out 11 in a 4-0 victory.

1970 – Knicks' first NBA title

The NY Knicks won their first NBA title in the club's 24-year history, when they beat Wilt Chamberlain's LA Lakers 113-99 in Game 7 at Madison Square Gardens. Knicks centre Willis Reed, playing with an injured leg, lasted 27 minutes and kept Chamberlain to 21 points, winning the Finals' MVP award.

1980 – Soviets boycott LA Olympics

Just 3 months before their scheduled start, the Soviet Union announced it was boycotting the Los Angeles Olympic Games. As expected, most of the Eastern Bloc followed suit. The Soviets blamed US commercialisation of the Games and a lack of security measures as primary reasons for the boycott. However it was a transparent payback to the US for leading more than 60 countries in the 1980 boycott of the Moscow Olympics in protest to the Soviet invasion of Afghanistan.

1982 – Villeneuve killed in crash

Popular Canadian driver Gilles Villeneuve was killed in practice for the Belgian Grand Prix at Zolder. Villeneuve's Ferrari hit the rear of German driver Jochen Mass' March at an estimated 160mph and was tossed high into the air. Villeneuve was thrown 30m across the track, breaking his neck. He died in hospital that evening. Known for a risky, all-or-nothing style, Villeneuve won 6 Grand Prix in 13 podium finishes (1978–82). His son, Jacques, won the Formula 1 World Championship in 1997.

1984 – MLB's longest day

The Chicago White Sox beat the Milwaukee Brewers, 7-6 at home, in the longest timed game in Major League history. The match lasted 25 innings and went for 8 hours and 6 minutes.

2011 – 'Zen Master' bows out

Hall of Fame coach Phil Jackson ended an illustrious NBA career on a sour note, as Jason Terry tied an NBA postseason record with nine 3-pointers, and the Mavericks matched a league playoff mark with 20 threes, on their way to a 122-86 victory over the LA Lakers in Dallas. The win gave the Mavs a sweep of their second-round series against the most successful coach in NBA history and his two-time defending champions. Jackson retired with a record 11 titles.

2013 – Sir Alex bows out at United

After 27 years managing Manchester United, Sir Alex Ferguson announced he would retire at the end of the season, but would remain at the club as a director and ambassador. The 71-year-old Scot won 38 trophies during his reign at Old Trafford, including 13 league titles, 2 Champions League crowns, 5 FA Cups and 4 League Cups. Everton's David Moyes succeeded Ferguson as manager.

BIRTHDATES

1893	American golfer FRANCIS OUIMET – died 1967
1910	England soccer defender GEORGE MALE – died 1998
1932	American boxer SONNY LISTON – died 1970
1935	England soccer defender JACK CHARLTON
1938	Pakistan Test batsman JAVED BURKI
1942	England spinner ROBIN HOBBS
1942	American jockey ANGEL CORDERO JR.
1942	Irish soccer defender/manager TERRY NEILL
1951	NBA coach MIKE D'ANTONI
1957	NFL coach BILL COWHER
1958	NFL coach LOVIE SMITH
1959	Pro Football Hall of Fame linebacker RONNIE LOTT
1960	Italian soccer defender FRANCO BARESI
1962	Scotland rugby union captain DAVID SOLE
1964	American auto racer BOBBY LABONTE
1969	New Zealand rugby union/league centre JOHN TIMU
1970	Australian Test batsman MICHAEL BEVAN
1978	Brazilian soccer defender LÚCIO
1981	Italian soccer defender ANDREA BARZAGLI

❾ MAY

1914 – Gelding takes Derby
Old Rosebud became the first gelding in 26 years to win the Kentucky Derby, in a record-breaking performance. In a field of 7 3-year-olds, Old Rosebud, ridden by jockey John McCabe, beat Hodge by 8 lengths in a Derby and track-record time for the one-and-a-quarter-mile race at Churchill Downs. His time of 2:03.4 on a slow track lasted 17 years, until Twenty Grand won the race in 2:01, in 1931.

1970 – Famechon disillusioned
Australia's world featherweight boxing champion Johnny Famechon retired from the sport in disgust, after he lost the title in a controversial points decision to Mexican southpaw Vincente Saldivar in Rome. Saldivar had only fought once in the past 2 years. In retirement, Famechon started running marathons, but was tragically hit by a car whilst training in Sydney in 1991, suffering serious and long-lasting injuries. He was inducted into the Boxing Hall of Fame in 1997.

1977 – WSC leaked
London tabloid newspaper the Daily Mail revealed Australian TV magnate Kerry Packer's plans for World Series Cricket. It was reported that Packer's most significant signing was influential England captain Tony Greig, who had also persuaded the stars of world cricket to join. These included Vivian and Barry Richards, Dennis Lillee and the Chappell brothers. World Series Cricket lasted only 17 months, before Packer and the ACB negotiated broadcast rights for Test cricket in Australia. World Series innovations such as coloured clothing and night games, however, revolutionised cricket.

2001 – Ghana stadium tragedy
In the worst recorded stadium disaster in African history, 129 football fans died at the Accra Sports Stadium in Ghana as a stampede followed a controversial decision with Accra's Hearts of Oak leading Assante Kotoko 2-1 with 5 minutes left in the game. Assante supporters began throwing bottles and chairs onto the field. Police then fired tear gas, creating panic in the stands and the resulting crush.

Australian media Mogul Kerry Packer (centre)

2004 – Canada's World Hockey title
Jay Bouwmeester and Matt Cooke each scored third-period goals as Canada rallied to win the gold medal, with a 5-3 win over Sweden at the World Hockey Championships in Prague.

2010 – Blues win in style
Chelsea reclaimed the Barclays Premier League title as they thrashed Wigan 8-0 at Stamford Bridge. The victory was the biggest in their 105-year history and also saw them break the record for the most league goals in an EPL season with 103. The previous best was the 97 by Manchester United scored in 1999/2000.

BIRTHDATES
1870	English golfer HARRY VARDON – died 1937
1907	West Indian Test captain JACKIE GRANT – died 1978
1928	American tennis player PANCHO GONZALES – died 1995
1928	Canadian figure skater BARBARA ANN SCOTT – died 2012
1932	West Indian Test batsman CONRAD HUNTE – died 1999
1939	American long jumper RALPH BOSTON
1939	Australian land/water speed pilot KEN WARBY
1939	Romanian tennis player/manager ION TIRIAC
1948	American golfer JOHN MAHAFFEY
1948	Basketball Hall of Fame guard CALVIN MURPHY
1959	New Zealand Test batsman ANDREW JONES
1959	Sri Lankan Test fast bowler ASHANTHA DE MEL
1960	Baseball Hall of Fame outfielder TONY GWYNN
1965	Canadian Hockey Hall of Fame centre STEVE YZERMAN
1968	French sprinter MARIE-JOSÉ PÉREC
1979	MLB pitcher BRANDON WEBB
1980	Australian swimmer GRANT HACKETT
1984	MLB first baseman PRINCE FIELDER

1929 – Fourth Open to Hagan
American golfer Walter Hagen successfully defended his British Open title at Muirfield in Scotland. In his fourth and final Open victory, Hagan posted a total 292, beating 1928 US Open champion Johnny Farrell by 6 strokes.

1970 – Spectacular Stanley Cup winner
Twenty-two-year-old Boston defenseman Bobby Orr scored one of the most acrobatic goals in NHL history, as the Bruins beat the Blues 4-3 at home, clinching their first Stanley Cup in 29 years. Early in overtime of Game 4 in Boston, Orr slipped the game-winner past goalie Glenn Hall just before he was sent flying, courtesy of a full-fledged leg trip by Noel Picard. The dramatic goal was caught on camera and the image of Orr in the air was used in hockey promotion for decades to come.

1970 – Wilhelm throws in 1,000th
Forty-six-year-old Atlanta Braves knuckleballer Hoyt Wilhelm became the first in MLB history to pitch in 1,000 games. However the day ended badly for Wilhelm who was credited with the Braves 6-5 home loss to St Louis, after allowing 3 runs in relief. Wilhelm finished his career in 1972 with 1,070 appearances, with a 143-122 mark 2.52 earned run average and 227 saves. His appearances record lasted until 1998, when Dennis Eckersley pitched in his 1,071st game.

1978 – Reds' trophy
Liverpool beat Club Brugge of Belgium, 1-0 to win the European Cup at London's Wembley Stadium. Scottish international Kenny Dalglish scored the winner in the 64th minute for the Reds.

1980 – Cup Final junior
Paul Allen, at 17 years and 256 days old, became the youngest man to play in an FA Cup Final, when West Ham upset Arsenal 1-0 at Wembley. Trevor Brooking scored one of his rare headed goals in the 13th minute to give the Hammers victory.

1986 – Merseyside Cup to Reds
Liverpool scored 3 second-half goals to beat Everton 3-1 in the all-Merseyside FA Cup final at Wembley. Gary Lineker scored a 27th-minute goal to put Everton ahead, before Ian Rush (2) and Craig Johnston scored for the Reds.

1995 – Gunners beaten in Cup Winners final
Arsenal was beaten 2-1 by Spain's Real Zaragoza, in the final of the European Cup Winners Cup in Paris. The score was 1-1 at fulltime, before Nayim scored the winner for Real in extra time.

2005 – Chelsea bags most Premier points
Chelsea beat Manchester United 3-1 at Old Trafford to create a new Premiership record of 94 points in a season. The tally was a monumental 20 more than United, with 1 match remaining. Chelsea ended the season as champions on 95 points; United had set the previous record of 92 in 1994.

BIRTHDATES
1927   American golfer MIKE SOUCHAK – 2008
1930   American sports caster PAT SUMMERALL – died 2013
1937   Russian discus thrower/shot putter TAMARA PRESS
1938   Spanish tennis player MANUEL SANTANA
1953   NFL quarterback/coach JIM ZORN
1955   Sports caster CHRIS BERMAN
1957   American alpine skier PHIL MAHRE
1957   American alpine skier STEVE MAHRE
1958   Pakistan Test spinner TAUSEEF AHMED
1959   NBA forward DANNY SCHAYES
1960   Jamaican sprinter MERLENE OTTEY
1965   Lebanese NBA centre RONY SEIKALY
1965   Australian swimmer GREG FASALA
1966   English triple jumper JONATHAN EDWARDS
1969   Dutch soccer striker DENNIS BERGKAMP
1972   German alpine skier KATJA SEIZINGER
1973   South African rugby prop OLLIE LE ROUX
1973   Australian tennis player/analyst JOSH EAGLE
1974   French soccer striker SYLVAIN WILTFORD
1975   Brazilian auto racer HÉLIO CASTRONEVES
1977   German auto racer NICK HEIDFELD
1981   Chilean soccer striker HUMBERTO SUAZO
1995   Swimmer MISSY FRANKLIN

1900 – Jeffries KOs Corbett

Jim Jeffries retained his world heavyweight title when he knocked out his mentor, 'Gentleman' Jim Corbett, in the 23rd round at Coney Island in Brooklyn. After being badly outboxed by the 33-year-old former champion, Jeffries landed a devastating left hook to the jaw that flattened Corbett, who remained unconscious for 5 minutes. Three years earlier, Jeffries had been a sparring partner for Corbett who knocked out the mighty John L. Sullivan in 1892.

1966 – Real 'unreal'

Real Madrid beat Partizan Belgrade 2-1 to win the European Cup Final at the Heysel Stadium in Brussels. Vasovic put Partizan ahead in the 55th minute, before Amancio and Serena scored within 6 minutes of each other to seal the Real victory.

1978 – Peterson killed in crash

Flashy Swedish Formula 1 driver Ronnie Peterson was killed when his Lotus crashed in a fiery multi-car pileup at the start of the Italian Grand Prix at Monza. Peterson suffered 27 fractures to his legs and died later in hospital, bone marrow having entered his bloodstream and caused a fat embolism. As a result of the accident, it became compulsory for an ambulance to follow grand prix cars on the first lap so that injured drivers could receive immediate medical help. In a 9-year Formula 1 career, Peterson gained 14 pole positions and won 10 Grand Prix.

1985 – Bradford disaster

Fifty-six fans were killed, and 265 were injured, when fire destroyed the main stand at the Valley Parade football ground in Bradford. Bradford City was playing its last game of the season and had been presented with the Third Division Championship. The fire broke out just before half time and took only 5 minutes to engulf the 77-year-old stand.

1994 – Border bows out

Allan Border announced his retirement as Australia's Test captain. He is remembered for bringing Australian cricket out of one of its bleakest periods into one of its greatest. In 156 Tests, Border scored a world record 11,174 runs, at 50.56. He scored 27 centuries, took 156 catches and captured 39 wickets.

2005 – Rare consecutive walk-off win

The Red Sox ended a game for the second consecutive day by hitting a walk-off home run off the same pitcher. The Oakland A's closer, Octavio Dotel, who also gave up Kevin Millar's decisive blast the previous day, was victimised by Boston catcher Jason Varitek, who hit a ninth-inning homer to beat Oakland 6-5.

2009 – Tallest MLB match-up

In the tallest pitching match-up in baseball history, 6ft 10in Randy Johnson gave up 8 hits and 4 runs while out-duelling 6ft 9in Daniel Cabrera, as the Giants beat the Washington Nationals 11-7 in San Francisco.

2013 – Latics shock FA Cup win

Wigan Athletic secured one of the biggest upsets in modern FA Cup history after beating Manchester City 1-0 in the final at Wembley. Ben Watson's powerful header a minute into added-time saw Wigan win the Cup for the first time and also clinch the first major trophy in the north-west club's 91-year history. 72 hours later the Latics were relegated from the Premier League after going down 4-1 to Arsenal.

BIRTHDATES

1854	Australian Test wicketkeeper JACK BLACKHAM – died 1932
1895	French tennis player JACQUES BRUGNON – died 1978
1924	England soccer forward JACKIE MILBURN – died 1988
1941	Australian Test batsman IAN REDPATH
1941	English snooker player GRAHAM MILES
1943	Canadian alpine skier NANCY GREENE
1944	Australian Test batsman JOHN BENAUD
1951	England rugby union winger MIKE SLEMAN
1958	Australian rower PETER ANTONIE
1962	NFL quarterback STEVE BONO
1963	American boxer MARK BRELAND
1964	English snooker player JOHN PARROTT
1977	American golfer KELLI KUEHNE
1977	Uruguayan soccer midfielder PABLO GARCIA
1981	Australian basketball forward LAUREN JACKSON
1984	Spanish soccer midfielder ANDRÉS INIESTA
1989	NFL quarterback CAM NEWTON

1927 – Davis wins first World Snooker title
Joe Davis beat T.A. Dennis, 20 frames to 11 in the final of the inaugural World Professional Snooker Championship at Camkin's Hall in Birmingham. Davis went on to win the next 14 consecutive world titles.

1979 – Evert's clay streak stopped
Tracey Austin beat Chris Evert in 3 sets at the Italian Open in Rome, ending Evert's record 125-match winning streak on clay courts. Austin won the semi-final against the top-seeded Evert, 6-4, 2-6, 7-6. She went on to win the final against Sylvia Hanika of Germany in 3 sets. Austin was one of only 4 players who had a positive win-loss record against Evert. In 16 head-to-head meetings, Austin held a 9-7 advantage.

1984 – Cruyff bows out in style
Dutch superstar Johan Cruyff played his last competitive game, guiding Feyenoord to a 2-1 win over PEC Zwolle '82 and the Dutch League title. Cruyff dominated European football in the 1970s, taking 3 Footballer of the Year awards and leading Ajax to 6 Dutch League titles, 3 European Cups and 4 Dutch FA Cups. As a coach, he guided Barcelona to the 1992 European Cup and 4 Spanish League titles, in a 9-year stint.

1985 – Last win for Whitworth
Kathy Whitworth collected her 88th and final LPGA victory, winning the United Virginia Bank Classic at the Sleepy Hole Golf Course, Suffolk, Virginia. Whitworth joined the LPGA Tour in 1959, and her 88-career tournament wins remain an all-time record for both men's and women's US Tours. She was the leading money-winner on the LPGA Tour 8 times, Player of the Year 7 times and winner of the Vare Trophy 7 times. Whitworth became the first LPGA player to record $1 million in career winnings in 1981. She won 6 majors: the LPGA Championship (1967, 1971, 1975), the Western Open (1967) and the Titleholders Championship (1965–66).

1995 – Sexist comments not Wright
English CBS commentator Ben Wright sparked an international controversy with his remarks about the LPGA. Wright was quoted by the Wilmington Delaware News Journal saying a lesbian image hurt the LPGA. The network subsequently fired him.

1997 – Maroney's ocean swim
Susie Maroney of Australia became the first woman to swim non-stop from Cuba to Florida. In her second attempt, 22-year-old Moroney completed the 112-mile swim from Havana in Cuba to Key West in Florida, in just over 24 hours. She retired in 2003, having crossed the English Channel twice and holding the Manhattan Island race record in New York. She also completed swims from Mexico to Cuba (1998) and Jamaica to Cuba (1999).

2000 – Petty tragedy
Nineteen-year-old NASCAR driver Adam Petty was killed when his car crashed into a wall at New Hampshire International Speedway. He was a fourth-generation NASCAR driver, following his great-grandfather Lee, grandfather Richard, and father Kyle. He had been practising for the following day's Busch series race.

2006 – Evans' 400m mark finally beaten
Olympic champion Laure Manaudou of France broke Janet Evans' 18-year-old world 400m freestyle record, finishing in 4:03.03 at the French Championships in Tours. Manaudou beat the time of 4:03.85 set by Evans at the 1988 Seoul Olympics.

BIRTHDATES
1867   Australian Test spinner HUGH TRUMBLE – died 1938
1925   Baseball Hall of Fame catcher 'YOGI' BERRA
1935   MLB manager FILIPE ALOU
1939   Australian rugby league captain REG GASNIER
1945   England soccer midfielder ALAN BALL – died 2007
1951   NBA coach GEORGE KARL
1960   Australian marathon runner LISA MARTIN
1962   American golfer AMY BENZ
1968   American skateboarder TONY HAWK
1970   Scottish golfer ANDREW COLTART
1970   American golfer JIM FURYK
1970   Canadian golfer MIKE WEIR
1975   New Zealand rugby union winger JONAH LOMU
1983   French tennis player VIRGINIE RAZZANO

⓭ MAY

1958 – Musial fastest to 3,000

Thirty-seven-year-old St Louis Cardinals batter Stan Musial became the fastest man to reach 3,000 hits, beating Ty Cobb's pace by more than 3 months playing time. He was not scheduled to start against the Cubs in Chicago, after his 2,999th hit a day earlier, but management wanted to attract a big crowd in St Louis the following day. He was called in to pinch hit in the sixth inning, with St Louis trailing 3-1, and duly lined a run-scoring double into the left-field corner, sparking the Cardinals to a 4-run inning and a 5-3 victory.

1973 – Riggs takes first 'Battle of the Sexes'

Fifty-five-year-old Bobby Riggs beat Australia's Margaret Court in straight sets, in a much-publicised 'Mother's Day challenge' match in Ramona, California. It's been suggested Riggs 'psyched out' Court when he presented her with a huge bouquet of flowers. He won a one-sided match 6-2, 6-1.

1977 – Packer announces World Series Cricket

Following weeks of newspaper speculation and rumours, Australian media magnate Kerry Packer officially announced the signing over 60 of the world's best players to World Series Cricket. Packer had been frustrated in his attempts to gain television broadcast rights from the Australian Cricket Board, so decided to conduct his own televised international competition. The innovative WSC was a huge hit and within 18 months Packer and the ACB had reached a long term rights agreement.

1992 – Ajax cleans up

Ajax of Amsterdam drew 0-0 with Italy's Torino at home, to clinch the UEFA Cup. The first-round match ended in a 2-2 draw in Turin, with Ajax claiming the Cup on the away goals rule.

1995 – Kiwis take America's Cup

New Zealand won the America's Cup for the first time, when *Black Magic* beat Dennis Connor's *Young America* 5-0, off San Diego. Led by syndicate head Peter Blake and helmsman Russell Coutts, the Kiwis showed finesse in concept, organisation, details and sailing skill to dominate the veteran Connor.

Margaret Court at the net in 1970. Photo: Koch, Eric / Anefo neg. stroken, 1945–1989, 2.24.01.05, item number 923-7230 (Nationaal Archief Fotocollectie Anefo) [CC-BY-SA-3.0-nl], via Wikimedia Commons.

2005 – Tiger's cuts streak over

Tiger Woods saw his streak of 142 consecutive cuts come to an end, as he struggled to a 2-over 72 at Cottonwood Valley, and missed the weekend at the EDS Byron Nelson Championship.

BIRTHDATES

1914	American boxer JOE LOUIS – died 1981
1950	MLB infielder/manager BOBBY VALENTINE
1951	NFL coach/analyst MIKE MARTZ
1961	NBA forward DENIS RODMAN
1963	Australian tennis player WALLY MASUR
1965	Dominican MLB pitcher JOSÉ RIJO
1972	Canadian NHL defenseman/coach DARRYL SYDOR
1978	NBA guard MIKE BIBBY
1978	MLB pitcher BARRY ZITO
1983	Ivorian soccer midfielder YAYA TOURÉ
1986	South Korean golfer EUN-HEE JI
1993	Belgian soccer striker ROMELU LUKAKU

1966 – Famous pitch invasion
Everton fought back from a 2-0 deficit to level the FA Cup Final against Sheffield Wednesday at Wembley. The anticipation of winning the Cup for the first time in more than 30 years was too much for Toffees fan Eddie Kavanagh, who staged a solo pitch invasion. After he was eventually captured, Derek Temple scored Everton's winner with 16 minutes remaining.

1972 – Mays scores for Mets
In his first game for the New York Mets, 42-year-old Willie Mays hit the game-winning home run to beat his former club, the San Francisco Giants, 5-4 at Shea Stadium. Mays retired in 1973 with 3,283 hits and 660 home runs. His totals include 17 seasons of 20 or more home runs. The impressive numbers earned him a spot in Baseball's Hall of Fame in 1979.

1977 – Bobby Moore's final fling
England's 1966 World Cup winning captain, Bobby Moore, played his last competitive match for Fulham, a 1-0 loss at Blackburn. Moore played 108 matches for England (1962–74), 90 as captain. He made 642 appearances for West Ham United and 150 for Fulham. He died of colon cancer in 1993, aged 51.

1995 – Burridge oldest Premier League player
Manchester City goalkeeper John Burridge became the oldest player to play in the English Premier League, in a 3-2 loss to QPR at Maine Road. Burridge was 43 years, 5 months and 11 days old.

1996 – 'Magic' retires for good
After a 32-game comeback attempt for the LA Lakers, Ervin 'Magic' Johnson announced his final retirement. He first retired in 1991, after learning he was HIV-positive. Johnson played on 5 Lakers NBA Championship teams (1980, 1982, 1985, 1987–88); he was NBA MVP 3 times (1987, 1989–90); he was a nine-time All-NBA First Team member (1983–91); and an Olympic gold medallist (1992). In 2002, he was inducted into the Basketball Hall of Fame.

2000 – Thorpe's ninth world record
Australian swimmer Ian Thorpe recorded his tenth world record, at the Olympic trials in Sydney. Thorpe won the 200m freestyle in a time of 1:45.51. He later took the silver medal behind Dutchman Peter van den Hoogenband at the Sydney Games, but broke the record twice more in 2001 and came back to win the event in Athens in 2004.

2008 – Henin goes out on top
Twenty-five-year-old world no. 1 tennis player Justine Henin of Belgium shocked the sporting world by announcing her retirement, effective immediately. Henin attributed her decision to burn-out. She became the first woman to quit the sport while atop the WTA rankings. In addition to 4 French Open titles, Henin had won the Australian Open in 2004, and the US Open in 2003 and 2007.

2013 – Latics go down after FA Cup triumph
Wigan became the first FA Cup winners to be relegated from the English Premier League in the same season, when they were beaten 4-1 by Arsenal at Emirates Stadium. Just 72 hours after they beat Manchester City 1-0 in an FA Cup final shock at Wembley, Wigan joined Reading and Queens Park Rangers in relegation to the second-tier Championship for 2013–14.

BIRTHDATES
1883	New Zealand rugby union flanker CHARLIE SEELING – died 1956
1910	South African Test batsman KEN VIJOEN – died 1974
1948	England Test batsman BOB WOOLMER – died 2007
1955	South African Test batsman PETER KIRSTEN
1955	Nicaraguan MLB pitcher DENNIS MARTINEZ
1959	West Indian Test batsman CARLISLE BEST
1960	New Zealand golfer FRANK NOBILO
1967	NFL defensive tackle TONY SIRAGUSA
1973	England rugby union prop JULIAN WHITE
1977	MLB pitcher ROY HALLADAY
1980	South African rugby union flanker JOHANN VAN NIEKERK
1983	Zimbabwe Test captain TATENDA TAIBU
1983	NFL running back FRANK GORE
1984	Australian AFL midfielder GARY ABLETT JR
1987	South African rugby utility FRANCOIS STEYN

1948 – 721 in a day

Australia scored a first-class world record – 721 runs in 1 day – in a tour match against Essex. The massive haul was achieved in just 129 overs. Don Bradman's contribution was a slashing 187 in 123 minutes, including 33 fours. The following day, the tourists dismissed Essex for 83 and 187, wrapping up an early innings victory.

1953 – Rocky's first title defence

Rocky Marciano knocked out the former champion, Jersey Joe Walcott, in the first round in Chicago, to retain his world heavyweight title. It was Marciano's first title defence since he knocked out Walcott 7 months earlier, in 13 rounds in Philadelphia. Marciano retired in 1955 with a perfect 49-0-0 record, with 43 knockouts. He retired as the only undefeated champion in any weight division in history.

1963 – Spurs first Brits to win in Europe

Tottenham Hotspur became the first British winners of a European trophy when they beat Athlético Madrid 5-1 in Rotterdam to win the European Cup Winners Cup. Jimmy Greaves and Terry Dyson scored 2 goals each and John White 1 for Spurs.

1981 – Perfect game for Barker

Cleveland Indians right-hander Len Barker became only the ninth pitcher to record a perfect game in the 20th century, and the first since 'Catfish' Hunter 13 years earlier. Barker threw 60 devastating curve balls from his 103 pitches, in a 3-0 victory over the Toronto Blue Jays. He struck out 11 and never threw more than 2 balls to any batter.

1994 – Six-way golf playoff

Neal Lancaster made PGA Tour history when he won a record 6-way playoff to claim the GTE Byron Nelson Classic. Lancaster birdied the first playoff hole to beat David Ogrin, Mark Carnevale, Yoshinori Mizumaki, David Edwards and Tom Byrum, for his only PGA Tour victory.

2004 – Gunners unbeaten season

Arsenal beat Leicester City 2-1 at Highbury and became the first side to go through a league season unbeaten since Preston had achieved the feat in 1888–89. Leicester threatened to stop the Gunners entering the history books, with Paul Dickov heading after 25 minutes. But Thierry Henry scored a penalty in the 46th minute, and Patrick Vieira made it an invincible season with a 66th minute winner.

2004 – Tarver KOs Jones

In a high-profile contest, Antonio Tarver stopped Roy Jones in the second round, to win the unified light-heavyweight title at the Mandalay Bay Casino in Las Vegas.

2006 – Flutie finished

Doug Flutie ended an illustrious 21-year career in football, during which the undersized Heisman Trophy winner had spent 12 seasons in the NFL. He also played in the Canadian Football League and the USFL. He won the CFL Most Outstanding Player award 6 times and the League's Grey Cup championship 3 times. Flutie's next job was as a college football analyst with ABC and ESPN.

BIRTHDATES

1901	Argentine/Italian soccer midfielder LUIS MONTI – died 1983
1917	Australian Test wicketkeeper RON SAGGERS – died 1987
1924	England Test batsman DON KENYON – died 1996
1931	American golfer/analyst KEN VENTURI – died 2013
1935	England Test captain TED DEXTER
1940	Basketball Hall of Fame coach DON NELSON
1945	American boxer JERRY QUARRY – died 1999
1950	American golfer JIM SIMONS – died 2005
1950	German sprinter RENATE STECHER
1953	Baseball Hall of Fame third baseman GEORGE BRETT
1965	Brazilian soccer midfielder RAÍ
1967	MLB pitcher JOHN SMOLTZ
1969	NFL running back EMMITT SMITH
1970	Dutch soccer defender FRANK de BOER
1970	Dutch soccer midfielder RONALD de BOER
1975	NFL linebacker RAY LEWIS
1982	Jamaican sprinter VERONICA CAMPBELL-BROWN
1987	Scottish tennis player ANDY MURRAY

⑯ MAY

1954 – Curruthers retires unbeaten
Australia's world bantamweight champion Jimmy Carruthers announced his retirement from the ring, as the first world title-holder to retire undefeated (though he later made an unsuccessful comeback in 1961). He is best known for his title win over South African Vic Toweel in Johannesburg, where he threw an estimated 147 punches in a bout that lasted just 139 seconds.

1955 – A Lindwall lash
Champion Australian fast bowler Ray Lindwall scored 118 while batting at number 8, in the drawn fourth Test against the West Indies at Bridgetown, Barbados. Lindwall smashed 16 fours and 2 sixes in Australia's 668. Australia held an unbeatable 2-0 lead in the five-Test series.

1956 – Laker's precursor to history
England Test spinner Jim Laker captured an incredible 10 for 88 for Surry, in a tour match against Australia at the Oval. Ten weeks later, Laker took 10 for 53 in the second innings of the fourth Test at Old Trafford, for match figures of 19 for 90.

1982 – Islanders' third straight Cup
The New York Islanders became the first US-based ice hockey team to win a third consecutive Stanley Cup, when they beat the Vancouver Canucks 3-1 in Game 4, for a series sweep. Islanders' right wing Mike Bossy scored 7 goals in the series, tying him with Jean Béliveau of the Montreal Canadiens in 1956 for most goals in the finals.

1982 – Whitworth's record
Kathy Whitworth scored her record 83rd LPGA Tour career victory, breaking Mickey Wright's previous mark. Whitworth beat Barbara Moxness and Sharon Barrett by 4 strokes in winning the Lady Michelob event. She went on to win 88 Tour events, which remains the LPGA record.

1994 – Capriati captured
Young tennis star Jennifer Capriati was arrested by Florida police in Coral Gables and charged with possession of marijuana. The tennis star settled the misdemeanour charge by agreeing to attend drug counselling.

2009 – Rare female success at Preakness
Rachel Alexandra became the first filly in 85 years to win the Preakness Stakes, the second leg of the Triple Crown. With jockey Calvin Borel aboard, Rachel Alexandra shot to the front and wasn't seriously challenged until a late surge by Kentucky Derby-winner Mine That Bird; she won by a length.

2010 – An England first
England saw their first global tournament win in the West Indies-hosted Cricket World Cup. England took just 17 overs to chase Australia's 148 in Barbados. Ryan Sidebottom took 2 for 26 and Craig Kieswetter hit 63 off 49 balls.

2011 – Americans disappear from top 10
For the first time in the 38-year history of tennis rankings, no American appeared in the top 10, after Serena Williams dropped out because of ongoing injury. Williams hadn't competed since winning Wimbledon in 2010. Former no. 1 Andy Roddick sat 12th in the men's standings.

BIRTHDATES
1906	Australian Test fast bowler ERNIE McCORMICK – died 1991
1918	England soccer forward WILFRED MANNION – died 2000
1925	Brazilian soccer defender NILTON SANTOS
1928	MLB manager BILLY MARTIN – died 1989
1955	Russian gymnast OLGA KORBUT
1955	MLB pitcher JACK MORRIS
1957	American marathon runner JOAN BENOIT
1966	Pro Football Hall of Fame running back THURMAN THOMAS
1970	Argentine tennis player GABRIELA SABATINI
1971	Great Britain rugby league captain PHIL CLARKE
1972	French rugby union prop CHRISTIAN CALIFANO
1972	New Zealand Test spinner MATTHEW HART

⑰ MAY

1875 – First Kentucky Derby
The Kentucky Derby was run for the first time, the winner, Aristides, ridden by African-American jockey Oliver Lewis. A crowd of 10,000 attended the inaugural Derby, with a field of 15 3-year-olds contesting the event over a one-and-a-half mile course.

1895 – 100 centuries for W. G.
English cricket great W. G. Grace scored his 100th first-class century, in a county match for Gloucestershire against Somerset at Bristol. It took Grace 1,113 innings to reach the milestone; he scored 124 hundreds and 251 fifties in a 43-year career.

1964 – Inaugural World Surfing titles
The first officially recognised world championships in surfing were run at Manly Beach in Sydney, in front of 60,000 spectators. Australian Bernard 'Midget' Farrelly won the men's title and compatriot Phyllis O'Donnell took out the inaugural women's championship.

1970 – Aaron reaches 3,000 hits
Thirty-six-year-old Atlanta Braves slugger Hank Aaron became only the ninth player to reach 3,000 hits, but the first to reach that milestone while hitting more than 500 home runs. Aaron recorded the 3,000th off Cincinnati's Wayne Simpson in a 15 inning, 7-6 defeat at Crosley Field. In his next at-bat, also against Simpson, Aaron smashed his 570th homer.

1983 – Islanders claim 4 straight Cups
The New York Islanders beat the Edmonton Oilers 4-2 in Game 4, clinching their fourth consecutive Stanley Cup. That record was second only to the 5 consecutive Cups won by the Montreal Canadiens (1956–60). Islanders' goalie Billy Smith allowed only 6 goals in the series and won the Conn Smythe Trophy.

1990 – Ferguson's first United trophy
Now-legendary manager Sir Alex Ferguson won his first trophy as Man United manager, with a 1-0 win over Crystal Palace in the FA Cup final replay at Wembley Stadium. He joined United in 1986 from Aberdeen, where he'd won 3 championships, 4 Scottish Cups and the European Cup Winners' Cup in 6 years.

W. G. Grace, 'The Father of Cricket', pulling a ball in 1897.

1996 – Indy tragedy
IndyCar veteran Scott Brayton won pole position in the Indianapolis 500, but was killed after a tyre deflation caused a crash during practice. Brayton was the 40th driver to be killed at the sport's most famous track. He was just 40 years old.

2000 – 'Madame Butterfly' breaks Mary T's mark
Susie O'Neill broke the longest-standing world record in swimming when she won the 200m butterfly at the Australian Olympic trials in Sydney. The 26-year-old O'Neill beat Mary T. Meagher's 18-year-old record by 0.15 seconds, recording a time of 2:05.81.

BIRTHDATES
1888   England Test spinner ALFRED FREEMAN – died 1965
1924   England soccer midfielder ROY BENTLEY
1932   Australian Test batsman PETER BURGE – died 2001
1945   Indian Test spinner SUBRAMANIAM CHANDRASEKHAR
1945   Australian tennis player TONY ROCHE
1952   NFL coach NORV TURNER
1956   American boxer 'SUGAR' RAY LEONARD
1963   British horse trainer KARL BURKE
1966   Australian tennis player MARK KRATZMANN
1971   Australian rugby union lock MARK CONNORS
1985   NFL quarterback MATT RYAN

1975 – Final fling for Casper

Billy Casper scored his 51st and final PGA Tour win, beating Englishman Peter Oosterhuis by 2 strokes in the First NBC New Orleans Open. Casper won 3 major championships: the US Open (1959, 1966) and the Masters (1970). He is best remembered for his 1966 Open victory, in which he trailed Arnold Palmer by 7 shots with 9 holes to play, before a barnstorming finish. Casper represented the United States in 8 Ryder Cup teams between 1961 and 1978.

1990 – Record fee for Baggio

Italian international striker Roberto Baggio was transferred from Fiorentina to Juventus for a then-world-record £8 million. Following the transfer, there were full-scale riots on the streets of Florence where fifty people were injured. Baggio spent 5 seasons at Juventus, where he won the Serie A Championship, Italian Cup and UEFA Cup, as well as being voted World and European Player of the Year in 1993. He went on to have a long and celebrated career, playing for a number of Italian clubs and as a popular star in international matches, before his retirement in 2004.

1994 – Milan's title

AC Milan won the Champions League, defeating Barcelona 4-0 in Athens. Massaro scored 2 first-half goals before Savicevi and Desailly netted in the second half to complete the rout for Milan.

1996 – Day rides to third straight Preakness

Jockey Pat Day won his third consecutive Preakness Stakes and his fifth Preakness overall, after riding Louis Quatorze to victory. For trainer Nick Zito, the win broke the Triple Crown win-streak of trainer D. Wayne Lukas, which had extended to six, beginning with the 1994 Preakness win by Tabasco Cat.

1998 – Husband and wife team

Trainer Aimee Hall saddled 4 winners from 5 starters at Suffolk Downs, with all of the winners being ridden by her husband, Jose Caraballo. The wins are believed to be the first involving a married couple as jockey and trainer.

2000 – McGwire passes Mantle

St Louis slugger Mark McGwire passed Mickey Mantle, moving to eighth on the all-time home run list, when he smashed 3 homers in the Cardinals' 7-2 win over the Phillies in Philadelphia. The home run treble brought McGwire's career total to 539. It was also his 64th multi-homer game, passing the great Willie Mays' total and taking him to second all-time, behind Babe Ruth with 72.

BIRTHDATES

1909	British tennis player FRED PERRY – died 1995
1905	England Test spinner HEDLEY VERITY – died 1943
1924	American sports caster JACK WHITAKER
1942	England soccer defender NOBBY STILES
1946	Baseball Hall of Fame outfielder REGGIE JACKSON
1951	Australian golfer RODGER DAVIS
1956	Japanese golfer JOE OZAKI
1959	England Test fast bowler GRAHAM DILLEY – died 2011
1960	French tennis player YANNICK NOAH
1960	Finnish Hockey Hall of Fame right wing JARI KURRI
1967	Austrian auto racer HEINZ HAROLD FRENTZEN
1968	French rugby union flanker PHILIPPE BENETTON
1970	Australian rugby union centre TIM HORAN
1971	American soccer goalkeeper BRAD FRIEDEL
1977	England soccer defender DANNY MILLS
1978	Portuguese soccer defender RICARDO CARVALHO
1979	Polish soccer midfielder MARIUSZ LEWANDOWSKI
1980	French tennis player MICHAËL LLODRA
1993	Australian sailor JESSICA WATSON

Mark McGwire in 2001. Photo: Rick Dikeman (Own work) [CC-BY-SA-3.0], via Wikimedia Commons.

⑲ MAY

1909 – Johnson retains title
Jack Johnson retained his heavyweight title in a 6-round no-decision against classy light-heavyweight Jack O'Brien in Philadelphia. There was an agreement that no decision was to be rendered if both men were on their feet at the scheduled end of the fight.

1935 – NFL brings in the Draft
The NFL adopted Bert Bell's proposal to hold an annual draft of college players, to begin in 1936. Teams were to select players in an inverse order of their season finish.

1965 – Hammers' Cup
West Ham United won the famous London club's only European triumph with a 2-0 win over Germany's 1860 Munich in the Cup Winners Cup final at Wembley Stadium. Alan Sealey scored both Hammers' goals.

1973 – Secretariat's on the way
Secretariat won the second leg of the Triple Crown by capturing the Preakness Stakes at the Pimlico Race Track in Baltimore, Maryland. The famed horse later went on to win the Belmont Stakes in New York, earning the Triple Crown with jockey Ron Turcotte on board.

1976 – Reds win in Europe
Liverpool claimed the UEFA Cup, after a Kevin Keegan equaliser earned them a 1-1 away draw against Club Bruges. The Reds had won the first leg 3-2 at Anfield.

1984 – Islanders' era over
The Edmonton Oilers, led by superstar centre Wayne Gretzky, ended the New York Islanders' 4-year reign as Stanley Cup champions with a 5-2 win in Game 5 in Edmonton. In only their fifth season in the NHL, the free-scoring Oilers netted 19 goals in the final 3 games of the series, convincingly eliminating the champions. Edmonton tallied a record 446 goals in the regular season. Gretzky scored the game's first 2 goals in the clincher, but teammate Mark Messier was awarded the Conn Smythe Trophy as playoff MVP, after scoring 26 points.

1994 – Tennis teen in trouble
18-year-old American Jennifer Capriati checked into a drug rehabilitation centre after being arrested for possession of marijuana. She had also been arrested for shoplifting. After 5 largely unproductive years, Capriati made a comeback, winning the Australian Open twice (2000–1) and the French Open (2001).

BIRTHDATES
1874	England Test batsman GILBERT JESSOP – died 1955
1908	Canadian sprinter PERCY WILLIAMS – died 1982
1910	South African Test batsman ALAN MELVILLE – died 1983
1922	Australian boxer TOMMY BURNS – died 2011
1928	Basketball Hall of Fame forward DOLPH SCHAYES
1934	NBA coach BILL FITCH
1946	French pro wrestler ANDRÉ THE GIANT – died 1993
1949	NFL quarterback ARCHIE MANNING
1957	NBA centre/coach BILL LAIMBEER
1964	American golfer MIKE STANDLY
1973	Scottish auto racer DARIO FRANCHETTI
1974	Australian rugby league captain ANDREW JOHNS
1979	Argentine soccer striker DIEGO FORLÁN
1979	Italian soccer midfielder ANDREA PIRLO

Kevin Keegan (right) in action against QPR in a 1975 League Division 1 match at Loftus Road.

1964 – Mathis beats Frazier for Olympic berth

Buster Mathis beat Joe Frazier in the US Olympic trials to earn a place in the team for the Tokyo Games. Mathis, however, suffered a broken knuckle in training and withdrew. As his replacement, Frazier won the gold medal.

1970 – Bobby's final England goal

Bobby Charlton scored his record 49th and final goal for England in a 4-0 World Cup warm-up win against Columbia in Bogota. Charlton made 106 appearances for England between 1958 and 1970.

1983 – Heavyweight title bouts on same card

For the first time ever, 2 heavyweight world champions defended their titles on the same day at the same place. Larry Holmes beat Tim Witherspoon in a controversial split-points decision to retain his WBC title. On the same card at the Dunes Hotel in Las Vegas, Michael Dokes retained his WBA title, with a draw against Mike Weaver.

1989 – Tight Preakness

In the closest ever Preakness Stakes, Kentucky Derby winner Sunday Silence edged Derby runner-up and 3-5 favourite Easy Goer by a nose, after the horses travelled cheek to cheek for the final quarter-mile. The win followed Sunday Silence's two-and-a-half-length victory over Easy Goer in the Derby a fortnight earlier.

1990 – Graf streak undone

Monica Seles ended Steffi Graf's record of 66 consecutive victories when she beat her in straight sets in the final of the German Open in Berlin. On the slow clay surface, Seles won 6-4, 6-3.

2000 – Youngest female at Indy

Nineteen-year-old Sarah Fisher became the youngest, and only the third, woman to qualify for the Indianapolis 500. She recorded a 4-lap qualifying average of 220.237mph.

2007 – Nadal's clay streak ends

Rafael Nadal's 81-match winning streak on clay courts ended when he was beaten by Roger Federer in the final of the Hamburg Masters. Federer won 2-6, 6-2, 6-0. Nadal had been unbeaten on clay since April 2005, a run that included 13 titles.

2006 – Bonds ties Babe

San Francisco slugger Barry Bonds tied Babe Ruth for second place, with 714, on the MLB all-time career home run list. In doing so, he ended a 9-game slump, during the Giants' 4-2 inter-league victory at Oakland.

2006 – Barbaro tragedy

America's no. 1 racehorse Barbaro fell and shattered a leg near the start of the Preakness, ending his career and eventually taking the champion thoroughbred's life. Barbaro was the odds-on favourite to remain undefeated and win the Preakness, but a few hundred yards out of the starting gate, he took a bad step. His leg flared out grotesquely and he veered sideways, before jockey Edgar Prado pulled the powerful colt to a halt. After 6 surgeries Barbaro was eventually euthanised in January 2007.

2009 – Harsh penalties in NASCAR

NASCAR handed out the largest penalty in the sport's history when it fined crew chief Charles Swing $200,000. Driver Carl Long was suspended for 12 Sprint Cup races and docked a NASCAR-record 200 points, and both were placed on probation until December 31, 2009. The car's owner Danielle Long, Carl's wife, was suspended for 12 races, docked 200 owner points and placed on probation. The team used an engine that was too big for NASCAR's specifications at Lowe's Motor Speedway.

BIRTHDATES

1926	American auto racer BOB SWEIKERT – died 1956
1937	American golfer DAVE HILL – died 2011
1940	Canadian Hockey Hall of Fame centre STAN MIKITA
1942	South African tennis player FREW McMILLAN
1942	Pro Football Hall of Fame running back LEROY KELLY
1943	West Indies Test wicket keeper DERYCK MURRAY
1952	Cameroon soccer striker ROGER MILLA
1966	Swedish golfer LISELOTTE NEUMANN
1972	French rugby union winger CHRISTOPHE DOMINICI
1977	Australian rugby union centre STIRLING MORTLOCK
1981	Spanish soccer goalkeeper IKER CASILLAS
1982	Czech soccer goalkeeper PETR CECH
1983	Paraguayan soccer striker ÓSCAR CARDOZO

1926 – Seven base hits
Chicago White Sox first baseman Earl Sheely equalled Elmer Smith's 1921 record of 7 consecutive base hits in a series. Against the Boston Red Sox, Sheely had doubled in each of his last 3 at-bats the previous day in a 13-4 win, before starting the new day with 3 doubles and a home run in an 8-7 loss. The 6 consecutive doubles also equalled an MLB record.

1966 – Defence #4 for Ali
In the fourth defence of his world heavyweight title, Muhammad Ali stopped England's Henry Cooper, in the sixth round at Highbury Football Stadium in London. Having decked Ali during their first fight 3 years earlier, Cooper was hopeful of a good showing, but was past his prime and succumbed to a cut eye.

1971 – Cup Winner's Cup replay
Chelsea beat Real Madrid 2-1 to win a replay of the European Cup Winners Cup final in Athens. John Dempsey and Peter Osgood scored for Chelsea, whilst Sebastián Fleitas replied for Real. The teams had drawn 1-1 in the first match, 2 days earlier.

1977 – Seattle Slew's Preakness
Kentucky Derby winner Seattle Slew captured the eighth race of his unbeaten career, holding off Iron Constitution to win the Preakness Stakes in record time, by one-and-a-half lengths at Pimlico. Seattle Slew went on to win the Belmont and become the first horse to be undefeated Triple Crown champion.

1997 – Anwar amazing
Pakistan opener Saeed Anwar smashed the highest score in ODI history, with a blistering 194 off only 146 balls against India, in the Independence Cup at Chennai. Saeed hit 22 fours and 5 sixes in the innings, which lasted only 206 minutes. He blazed 3 consecutive sixes off champion spinner Anil Kumble. Pakistan's 327 for 5 was enough, Aaqib Javed taking 5 for 61 and India dismissed for 292.

2008 – All English Champions League final
Edwin van der Sar saved the 14th penalty of a shootout to give Manchester United a 6-5 win over Chelsea, after a 1-1 draw in the first all-English Champions League final in Moscow. It was United's third Champions League title.

2011 – Hopkins oldest champ
Forty-six-year-old Bernard Hopkins became the oldest man to win a boxing world title when he defeated Canadian Jean Pascal by unanimous decision in Montreal, to claim the WBC and IBO light-heavyweight belts. Hopkins eclipsed the achievement of George Foreman, who was 45 when he knocked out Michael Moorer to win the heavyweight title in 1994.

BIRTHDATES
1893	England Test captain ARTHUR CARR – died 1963
1930	New Zealand rugby union halfback KEITH DAVIS
1941	MLB manager BOBBY COX
1942	Australian swimmer JOHN KONRADS
1946	Australian equestrian rider WAYNE ROYCROFT
1952	NFL coach DAVE WANNSTEDT
1960	Russian swimmer VLADIMIR SALNIKOV
1970	Australian surfer PAULINE MENCZER
1973	American golfer STEWART CINK
1975	Australian boxer ANTHONY MUNDINE
1977	South African soccer midfielder QUINTON FORTUNE
1985	Norwegian swimmer ALEXANDER DALE OEN – died 2012
1994	British diver TOM DALEY

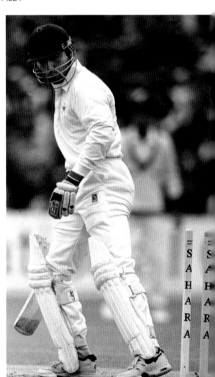

Pakistan Test batsman Saeed Anwar, looking at the stumps after having been bowled.

1907 – 2 hat-tricks for Trott
Albert Trott became the first man to take 2 hat-tricks in an innings in a first-class match, during his benefit match for Middlesex against Somerset at Lord's. After his first run of 3 wickets in successive deliveries, Trott made it 4 in 4 to finish with figures of 7 for 20.

1930 – Home run feast
The New York Yankees and the Philadelphia Athletics combined for a double-header total of 14 home runs, as the Yankees prevailed 10-1 and 20-13 at Shribe Park in Philadelphia. In the second game Lou Gehrig smashed 3 homers and drove in 8 runs for the Yankees. Tony Lazzeri was 4-for-4 and scored 5 runs, whilst Babe Ruth hit 1 homer to add to his 2 in the first game. Jimmie Fox hit 2 homers and drove in 6 runs for the As.

1963 – Cup to Milan
AC Milan of Italy beat Portuguese club Benfica 2-1 in the European Cup Final at Wembley Stadium. Milan's Brazilian star José Altafini scored both goals whilst Eusébio replied for Benfica.

1977 – Homer heaven
The Boston Red Sox and the Milwaukee Brewers combined for a major league record, equalling 11 home runs, as the Red Sox won 14-10 at Fenway Park. Each of the homers was a solo shot, scoring just 1 run.

1977 – First female Indy qualifier
After being the first woman to officially enter the Indianapolis 500 a year earlier, Janet Guthrie also became the first to qualify for the prestigious event, with a 4-lap average of 188.403mph in the no. 27 Lightning-Offenhauser. The 39-year-old physicist-turned-racer did more than 191mph before hitting the wall in qualifying.

1988 – Bird's amazing quarter
In one of his most memorable performances, Larry Bird scored 20 points in the fourth quarter, hitting 9 of 10 shots from the field to outduel Atlanta's Dominique Wilkins and lead the Celtics to a 118-116 win in Game 7 of the Eastern Conference Finals at Boston Garden. Wilkins scored a phenomenal 47 points, including 16 in the fourth quarter, but couldn't match the sharp-shooting Bird in the final period.

1990 – Graziano dead at 68
Former world middleweight champion Rocky Graziano died of heart failure, aged 68. Graziano is best known for his trilogy of fights with Tony Zale (1946–48); the 3 contests lasted a combined 15 rounds and there were 7 knockdowns. Graziano's record reads 83 fights for 67 wins, 10 losses and 6 draws, with 52 knockouts. The movie *Somebody Up There Likes Me* is based on his life.

2003 – Annika takes on the men
Annika Sörenstam became the first woman to compete in a PGA Tour event in 58 years when she carded an opening-round 1-over par 71 at the Bank of America Colonial in Fort Worth, Texas. Sörenstam carded a second-round 74 to miss the cut. Babe Didrikson Zaharias was the last woman to tee off against the men in the 1945 Los Angeles Open.

BIRTHDATES
1879	Australian Test captain WARWICK ARMSTRONG – died 1947
1908	American golfer HORTON SMITH – died 1963
1927	New Zealand Test wicket keeper ERIC PETRIE – died 2004
1940	Indian Test spinner E. A. S. PRASANNA
1943	Baseball Hall of Fame pitcher TOMMY JOHN
1946	Irish soccer player GEORGE BEST – died 2005
1946	English soccer midfielder/manager HOWARD KENDALL
1953	England soccer striker PAUL MARINER
1959	American golfer OLIN BROWNE
1962	American golfer ANDREW MAGEE
1968	American golfer BRENT GEIBERGER
1970	Brazilian auto racer PEDRO DINIZ
1977	Irish jockey PAT SMULLEN
1981	Austrian tennis player JÜRGEN MELZER
1982	American speed skater APOLO ANTON OHNO
1987	Chilean soccer midfielder ARTURO VIDAL
1987	Serbian tennis player NOVAK DJOKOVIC

1918 – Compton comes into the world

Hugely popular English cricketer Denis Compton was born. Compton was a talented and aggressive batsman, a fine fielder, and a dangerous, unorthodox left-arm spinner. In 78 Tests, Compton scored 5,807 runs at 50.06, with 17 centuries. He had a Test career-high score of 278, against Pakistan at Trent Bridge in 1954. Compton is credited with the fastest triple-century in first-class history, scored in just 181 minutes for the MCC against North East Transvaal, at Benoni in 1948–49. He died in 1997, aged 79.

1944 – 'Newc' born

Australian tennis great John Newcombe was born in Sydney. Newcombe won 7 major singles titles: Wimbledon (1967, 1970–71); the US Open (1967, 1973); and the Australian Open (1973, 1975). He also formed one of history's best doubles combinations with Tony Roche, winning 17 major titles. He was ranked the world's no. 1 player in 1970–71, and was inducted into the Tennis Hall of Fame in 1986. As Davis Cup captain in 1999, he led Australia to a 3-2 triumph over France.

1948 – Joe's 3-from-3 homers

New York outfielder Joe DiMaggio hit an amazing 3 home runs in consecutive at-bats for the Yankees, in a 6-5 win over the Indians at Cleveland Stadium. The first 2 homers were off Indians future Hall of Fame starter Bob Feller.

1977 – Nicklaus in the money

Jack Nicklaus became the first player to earn $3 million in official PGA Tour events, after winning his own sponsored event, the Memorial Tournament at Muirfield Village near his hometown of Columbus, Ohio. He beat Hubert Green by 2 strokes to earn $45,000 and reach $3 million overall.

2000 – Martina is back

After a 5-year layoff, nine-time Wimbledon champion Martina Navratilova returned to doubles competition with Mariaan de Swardt at the Madrid Open where they beat Japan's Rika Hiraki and American Meghann Shaughnessy 6-3, 7-5. Navratliova eventually capped off her career by winning the mixed doubles title at the 2006 US Open with Bob Bryan, her 41st Grand Slam doubles title (31 in women's doubles and 10 in mixed doubles) and 177th overall. At the time, she was just over a month away from her 50th birthday.

2003 – Annika misses cut in men's event

Annika Sörenstam of Sweden posted a second-round 4-over par 74 to miss the cut by 4 strokes at the PGA Tour's Bank of America Colonial event at Fort Worth, Texas. In the LPGA leader's much publicised entry into a male tournament, Sörenstam had a first-round 71, for a 5-over 36-hole total 145.

2005 – No magic for Myskina

Anastasia Myskina of Russia became the first defending champion, male or female, to be defeated in the first round of the French Open in Paris. Myskina's game collapsed in the deciding set and Spaniard Sanchez Lorenzo pounced for a 6-4, 4-6, 6-0 upset.

BIRTHDATES

1918	England Test all-rounder DENIS COMPTON – died 1997
1944	Australian tennis player JOHN NEWCOMBE
1946	Australian golfer DAVID GRAHAM
1947	New Zealand rugby union fly-half DOUG BRUCE
1951	Russian chess player ANATOLIY KARPOV
1954	American boxer 'MARVELOUS' MARVIN HAGLER
1956	New Zealand rugby union flanker MARK SHAW
1963	West Indian Test fast bowler TONY GRAY
1965	Spanish soccer sweeper MANOLO SANCHIS
1965	Indian Test batsman WOORKERI RAMAN
1966	England Test batsman GRAEME HICK
1966	Canadian NHL left wing GARY ROBERTS
1967	American golfer STEVE FLESCH
1972	Brazilian auto racer RUBENS BARRICHELLO
1984	Portuguese soccer striker HUGO ALMEIDA
1986	Australian swimmer ALICE MILLS
1988	American golfer MORGAN PRESSEL

㉔ MAY

1935 – A night at the Baseball
The Reds edged Philadelphia 2-1 at Cincinnati's Crosley Field, in the first-ever night game in MLB history. The original plan was that the Reds would play 7 night games each season, 1 against each visiting club. Night baseball quickly found acceptance in other Major League cities and eventually became the norm; the term 'day game' was subsequently coined to designate the increasingly rarer afternoon contests.

1964 – Football riot in Peru
After a disputed goal during an Olympic qualifying match between Peru and Argentina, 320 fans died and 500 more were taken to hospital when a riot erupted at the National Stadium in Lima, Peru.

1987 – Unser oldest to win at Indy
Forty-seven-year-old Al Unser Sr became the oldest driver to win the Indianapolis 500, beating Roberto Guerrero by 4.496 seconds. It was Unser's fourth Indy 500 victory, tying A.J. Foyt's record. His 17-year span between first and final victories (1970–87) is the longest ever at Indianapolis.

1989 – Milan majestic
Before 97,000 fans at the Nou Camp Stadium in Barcelona, AC Milan beat Romania's Steaua Bucharest 4-0 to win the European Cup. Dutchmen Ruud Gullit and Marco Van Basten scored 2 goals each for Milan.

1992 – Closest Indy finish
Al Unser Jr maintained the family tradition when he beat Canadian Scott Goodyear by 0.043 seconds, in the closest-ever finish of the Indianapolis 500. It was the first time a father and son had won the prestigious event. Al Snr won in 1970–71, 1978 and 1987, whilst Al Jr won in 1992 and 1994.

2000 – Spanish delight
In an all-Spanish final, Real Madrid humbled Valencia 3-0 to win the Champions League final in Paris. Morientes, McManaman and Raúl scored for Real. The final marked the first time that both finalists in the competition had come from the same country.

2009 – Aces record
Ivo Karlovic of Croatia set a record for aces in a tour-level match, serving 55 in his upset 5-set loss to Australian Lleyton Hewitt in the first round of the French Open. The old mark for aces in a French Open match was 37, set by American Andy Roddick in 2001.

2009 – Danica first woman on Indy podium
Danica Patrick came in third, in the best Indianapolis 500 finish by a woman. Hélio Castroneves clinched his third Indy 500 title, ahead of English driver Dan Wheldon. Patrick is the only woman ever to lead an Indy 500.

2010 – Two nine-darters for 'The Power'
Professional darts player Phil Taylor became the first to hit two 9-dart finishes in a single match, during the Premier League final against James Wade. These were his seventh and eighth 9-dart finishes.

BIRTHDATES
1899	French tennis player SUZANNE LENGLEN – died 1938
1910	American golfer JIMMY DEMARET – died 1983
1935	NFL coach JIM MORA SNR
1942	South African Test batsman/administrator ALI BACHER
1942	Finnish rally driver HANNU MIKKOLA
1946	New Zealand rugby union flanker IAN KIRKPATRICK
1962	Puerto Rican boxer HÉCTOR CAMACHO – died 2012
1963	Basketball Hall of Fame guard JOE DUMARS
1964	Scottish middle distance runner LIZ McCOLGAN
1964	English swimmer ADRIAN MOOREHOUSE
1964	Canadian NHL right wing PAT VERBEEK
1965	Paraguayan golfer CARLOS FRANCO
1966	French soccer striker ERIC CANTONA
1972	Australian surfer LAYNE BEACHLEY
1973	Czech soccer striker VLADIMIR ŠMICER
1976	Australian netball shooter CATHERINE COX
1979	NBA forward TRACY McGRADY

1935 – Owens outstanding
American sprinter Jesse Owens broke 5 world records and equalled a sixth in the space of 45 minutes, whilst competing at the Big Ten Track & Field Championships at Ann Arbor, Michigan. Between 3.15pm and 4.00pm, Owens set new world marks in the long jump, 220-yard sprint (with a 200m record on the way), and the 220-yard low hurdles (and the 200m hurdles mark). He also tied the world 100-yard record.

1935 – Final 3 for Ruth
At age 40, Babe Ruth, playing for the Boston Braves at Forbes Field, slammed the final 3 home runs of his illustrious career in an 11-7 loss to Pittsburgh. It was the fourth time Ruth had hit 3 homers in a game. A week later, Ruth announced his retirement from baseball, with a career total of 714 home runs, a record that stood for 39 years.

1947 – Fastest England score
Chelsea's Tommy Lawton scored the fastest-ever England goal, after just 17 seconds against Portugal in Lisbon. England won 10-0 with Lawton and Stan Mortenson each scoring 4 goals.

1967 – Celtic's British first
Glasgow Celtic became the first British club to win the European Cup final, beating Inter Milan 2-1 in Lisbon. Mazzola gave Inter a seventh-minute lead, before Gemmell and Chalmers scored in the second half for Celtic.

1980 – Rutherford's third Indy
Johnny Rutherford became the first driver in Indianapolis 500 history to win twice from pole position. It was Rutherford's third Indy win in 7 years. He finished more than a mile ahead of runner-up Tom Sneva, having led for 118 of the 200 laps.

2005 – Magic figure is 42 years
The Seattle Mariners battery consisted of a pair of 42-year-olds, as Jamie Moyer threw to backstop Pat Borders in a 3-1 loss against the Baltimore Orioles. According to the Elias Sports Bureau, it marked the first time in MLB history that 2 players aged 42 years or older had been the starting pitcher and catcher for a team.

2007 – Four top-of-the-order tons
In the first instance in Test cricket of the first 4 batsman scoring centuries in an innings, Wasim Jaffer, Dinesh Karthik, Rahul Dravid and Sachin Tendulkar all smashed centuries for the visitors in the second Test between India and Bangladesh in Dhaka.

2009 – 'Rafa' rampage
Top-seeded Spaniard Rafael Nadal eclipsed the French Open men's record for consecutive wins, beating Marcos Daniel of Brazil 7-5, 6-4, 6-3 for his 29th straight win, on the red clay at Roland Garros. Nadal's win bettered the French Open record held by Bjorn Borg, who won 28 straight from 1978–81.

2013 – All-German final
Arjen Robben, who missed a penalty in the last year's final, scored a late goal to give Bayern Munich the Champions League title with a 2-1 victory over Borussia Dortmund at Wembley. After a goalless first half, Mario Mandzukic put the Bavarians ahead from close range, but a clumsy foul by Dante on Marco Reus allowed Ilkay Gundogan to level the scores from the penalty spot. But with 1 minute remaining, Robben squeezed the ball over the line, to ensure that Bayern took home the trophy that eluded it in 2010 and 2012.

BIRTHDATES
1897	Australian Test batsman ALAN KIPPAX – died 1972
1897	American boxer GENE TUNNEY – died 1978
1932	Basketball Hall of Fame guard/coach K.C. JONES
1936	Indian Test spinner RUSI SURTI – died 2013
1944	England rugby union lock CHRIS RALSTON
1948	Australian golfer BOB SHEARER
1953	American golfer D.A.WEIBRING
1953	Argentine soccer defender DANIEL PASSARELLA
1953	Italian soccer defender GAETANO SCIREA – died 1989
1967	French golfer JEAN LOUIS GUEPY
1970	England spinner ROBERT CROFT
1970	England rugby union flanker STEVE OJOMOH
1978	NFL linebacker BRIAN URLACHER
1979	England rugby union fly-half JONNY WILKINSON
1988	South African swimmer CAMERON VAN DER BURGH

1923 – Le Mans is born

The prestigious 24 Hours of Le Mans car race was run for the first time, over a 17.262km circuit through public roads around Le Mans. The first winner was the French team of André Lagache and René Léonard, for Chenard and Walcker Sport. They covered 2,209.536km.

1955 – Ascari killed at Monza

Italian driver Alberto Ascari was killed whilst testing a Ferrari sports car, crashing on one of the Monza track's tight corners. His death remains mysterious. The corner where the accident happened now bears his name, known as 'the Variante Ascari'.

1966 – You can't beat experience

At 54 years of age, veteran Australian jockey Arthur 'Scobie' Breasley won his second English Derby, on Charlottown, only 24 hours after being hurt in a race fall. Breasley first won the Derby in 1964 on Santa Claus, having previously won the 1958 Prix de L'Arc de Triomphe on Ballymoss.

1982 – Villa's Cup

Big striker Peter Withe scored the only goal of the game in the 67th minute, as Aston Villa beat Bayern Munich 1-0 in Rotterdam to win the European Cup. Villa goalkeeper Nigel Spink starred as the Cup stayed in England for the sixth consecutive year.

1991 – Mears joins select club

Thirty-nine-year-old Rick Mears beat Michael Andretti to join A. J. Foyt and Al Unser Sr. as the only drivers to have won the Indianapolis 500 4 times. Mears outdrove Andretti to win by 3.1 seconds in his Penske-Chevrolet, at an average speed of 176.46mph. He had previously won the classic race in 1979, 1984 and 1988.

1999 – United in OT

Manchester United beat Bayern Munich of Germany, 2-1, in the Champions League final in Barcelona. Basler gave Bayern a sixth-minute lead before Teddy Sheringham and Ole Gunnar Solskjær both netted in injury time, for a dramatic United victory.

1999 – Indian WC revolution

Indian batsmen Sourav Ganguly and Rahul Dravid shared a record 318 for the second wicket, in a World Cup match against Sri Lanka at Taunton. Ganguly smashed 183 off 147 balls, and Dravid 145 off 129. Dravid was also involved when the record was broken in 2000. He added 331 with Sachin Tendulkar, against New Zealand at Hyderabad.

2001 – Brumbies breakthrough

Australia's ACT Brumbies became the first non-New Zealand team to win the rugby union Super 12 title, when winger Joe Roff scored 2 tries and Andrew Walker kicked 21 points, in a 36-6 home win over South Africa's Coastal Sharks at Bruce Stadium in Canberra. The Brumbies also won the title in 2004.

2002 – Dramatic back-to-back at Indy

Defending champion Hélio Castroneves of Brazil became the fifth driver in history to repeat at the Indianapolis 500. In one of the most controversial races in Indy history, second-placed Paul Tracy attempted to pass Castroneves for the lead. At the same time, a crash occurred on another part of the track, bringing out the caution flag. Officials ruled that the yellow came out before Tracy completed the pass, and Castroneves was declared the winner.

BIRTHDATES

1909	Scottish soccer manager SIR MATT BUSBY – died 1994
1920	South African Test captain JACK CHEETHAM – died 1980
1921	England soccer striker STAN MORTENSON – died 1991
1939	American sports caster BRENT MUSBURGER
1941	South African tennis player CLIFF DRYSDALE
1947	New Zealand Test batsman GLENN TURNER
1958	American golfer RONNIE BLACK
1958	England rugby union centre PAUL DODGE
1960	Australian weightlifter DEAN LUKIN
1961	American golfer STEVE PATE
1963	English golfer JAMIE SPENCE
1966	South African runner ZOLA BUDD
1974	Swedish swimmer LARS FRÖLANDER
1977	Italian soccer striker LUCA TONI

㉗ MAY

1873 – Inaugural Preakness
One of America's famed 'Triple Crown' events of horse racing, the Preakness Stakes, was run for the first time with 7 starters at the Pimlico track in Maryland. 11-1 outsider Survivor was the inaugural winner by 10 lengths. The race was named in honour of the horse, Preakness, the winner of a major stakes race on the day the track opened in 1870.

1933 – Billiards breakthrough
Australian Walter Lindrum became the first non-English player to win the world professional billiards title, when he beat 4-time champion Joe Davis by 694 points in the final.

1961 – First Cup Winners Cup Final
Italian club Fiorentina beat Glasgow Rangers 2-1 in Florence, in the second leg of the inaugural European Cup Winners Cup Final, claiming the trophy after a 2-0 first leg win at Hampden Park. Milan put Fiorentina ahead in the 13th minute, before Scott equalised in the second half. Hamrin scored the winner with just 4 minutes remaining.

1981 – Reds score Cup
Liverpool scored a 1-0 win over Spanish giants Real Madrid to win the European Cup at the Parc des Princes in Paris. Alan Kennedy scored the 82nd-minute winner for the Reds. Liverpool manager Bob Paisley became the first manager to win the competition 3 times.

1989 – Rare ODI tie
Australian wicketkeeper Ian Healy scampered for a bye when Carl Rackemann missed the last ball from Phil DeFreitas, leading to only the second tie in one-day international history. Allan Lamb hit 100 not out in England's 226-5, before Healy's 26 not out in 226 for 8 off 55 overs.

1997 – Sammy still 'Slamming' at 85
Seven-time major winner Sam Snead beat his age on his 85th birthday, posting a 78 in the company of old friend Johnny Bulla, at his home course, The Greenbrier Resort in White Sulphur Springs, West Virginia. Snead died in 2002 aged 89.

American golfer Sam Snead, born on this day in 1912

2012 – Knights win IPL
The Indian Premier League's The Kolkata Knight Riders won their first IPL title by beating the defending champions, Chennai Super Kings, by 5 wickets. Manvinder Bisla added 136 with Jacques Kallis, as the Knight Riders chased 191.

2013 – Griner debut features 2 dunks
Phoenix centre Brittney Griner became the first player to dunk twice in a WNBA game during her league debut as the Mercury lost 102-80 to the Chicago Sky. The no. 1 overall draft pick finished the game with 17 points.

BIRTHDATES
1887	England Test all-rounder FRANK WOOLEY – died 1978
1906	England soccer goalkeeper HENRY HIBBS – died 1984
1912	American golfer SAM SNEAD – died 2002
1956	NFL kicker NICK LOWERY
1957	American swimmer BRUCE FURNISS
1957	English swimmer DUNCAN GOODHEW
1962	Indian Test all-rounder RAVI SHASTRI
1965	Australian tennis player PAT CASH
1967	England soccer midfielder PAUL GASCOIGNE
1972	NFL receiver ANTONIO FREEMAN
1973	New Zealand rugby union centre TANA UMAGA
1975	Australian Test batsman MIKE HUSSEY
1977	Sri Lankan Test batsman MAHELA JAYAWARDENA
1987	Ivorian soccer forward GERVINHO

1912 – Matthews' double hat-trick
Spin bowler Jimmy Matthews led Australia to victory in the Triangular Test match against South Africa in Manchester, with an incredible double hat-trick, one in each innings. Amazingly, no fielders were involved in any of the 6 wickets. Australia won the match by an innings and 88 runs.

1934 – Hobbs' final ton
Fifty-one-year-old English batting icon Sir Jack Hobbs scored his 199th and last first-class cricket century, playing for Surrey against Lancashire at Old Trafford. In 834 first-class matches (1905–34) Hobbs scored a massive 61,760 runs at 50.70.

1956 – Consecutive game homer record
Thirty-year-old Pittsburgh Pirates' first baseman, Dale Long, became the first player to homer in a record 8 consecutive games when he hit Brooklyn's Carl Erskine into the lower right-field stands at Forbes Field. He finished the year with a career-high 27. Don Mattingly (1987) and Ken Griffey Jr (1993) tied Long's record.

1957 – West Coast move approved
The National League club owners meeting in Chicago unanimously approved the historic relocation of the Brooklyn Dodgers to Los Angeles and the New York Giants to San Francisco. Both ownerships had failed to get new stadiums built in New York and were upset with falling attendances, antiquated ballparks and lack of parking.

1980 – Forest win Euro Cup
With Brian Clough at the helm, Nottingham Forest beat Hamburg 1-0 in the European Cup final in Madrid. A crowd of 50,000 at the Bernabéu Stadium saw John Robertson score the Forest winner in the 20th minute.

2003 – All-Italian Final
In an all-Italian Champions League final at Old Trafford in Manchester, AC Milan beat Juventus 3-2 on penalties, after the scores were locked at 0-0 after extra time. Both teams missed 2 out of their first 3 penalties, before Paolo Montero made the fateful error for Juventus.

2006 – Bonds moves past Ruth for second all-time in HRs
Forty-one-year-old San Francisco Giants slugger Barry Bonds smashed his 715th career home run to move past Babe Ruth into sole possession of second place on the career list, behind Hank Aaron (755). Bonds homered off Colorado's Byung-Hyun Kim in the fourth inning of a 6-3 loss to the Rockies, in front of his home fans at AT & T Park. He still holds the record, with 762 career homers.

2011 – Super Kings win IPL
The Chennai Super Kings beat the Royal Challengers Bangalore by 58 runs in a one-sided IPL final in Chennai. M. Vijay (95) with Michael Hussey (63) scored more than two-thirds of Chennai's 205 for 5. Bangalore lost all hope when Chris Gayle was out for a duck in the first over, struggling to 147 for 8.

BIRTHDATES
1888	American athlete JIM THORPE – died 1953
1911	South African Test fast bowler BOB CRISP – died 1994
1938	Basketball Hall of Fame guard JERRY WEST
1949	American golfer SHELLEY HAMLIN
1956	West Indies Test wicket keeper JEFF DUJON
1957	MLB outfielder/manager KIRK GIBSON
1964	Australian boxer JEFF FENECH
1966	Australian Test spinner GAVIN ROBERTSON
1967	NBA guard GLEN RICE
1971	Russian figure skater EKATERINA GORDEEVA

1963 – Moore England's youngest skipper
Bobby Moore became England's youngest-ever football captain, against Czechoslovakia in Bratislava. He was 22 years and 47 days old. England won 4-2.

1968 – United's Cup
Manchester United won the European Cup at Wembley Stadium, beating Benfica of Portugal 4-1 after extra time. Bobby Charlton put United ahead with a rare header, before Graça netted for Benfica. Charlton, George Best and Brian Kidd added extra-time goals for United.

1977 – Guthrie historic qualifier
Janet Guthrie, who qualified at 188mph, became the first woman to race in the Indianapolis 500. Mechanical problems forced her car out of the race after only 27 laps. Race winner A.J. Foyt became the first driver to take out the prestige event 4 times.

1985 – Heysel disaster
Thirty-nine fans were crushed to death and 600 were injured when a retaining wall collapsed prior to the final of the European Cup between Liverpool and Juventus, at the Heysel Stadium in Brussels. Liverpool fans were blamed for the tragedy; English clubs were banned from European competition for 5 years and Liverpool for six. Juventus won the match 1-0.

1990 – Ricky AL stolen base leader
Oakland Athletics' outfielder Rickey Henderson broke Ty Cobb's 62-year-old American League record for stolen bases, when he swiped his 893rd in the sixth inning of the A's 2-1 home loss to Toronto. The following year, Henderson gained the MLB record too, stealing his 939th base to break Lou Brock's mark.

2000 – Adams' patient knock
West Indian cricket captain Jimmy Adams made a laborious 48 not out in almost 6 hours to guide his team to a memorable 1-wicket victory over Pakistan, in the series decider in Antigua. Adams did not hit a single four in the match-saving innings.

2005 – Danica leads at Indy
Twenty-three-year-old Rookie of the Year, Danica Patrick became the first woman to lead the Indianapolis 500, getting out front 3 separate times for a total of 19 laps. Dan Wheldon passed her with just 7 of the 200 laps remaining, and became the first Englishman to win Indy since Graham Hill in 1966. Patrick came in fourth.

2006 – Nadal ultimate clay specialist
Spain's tennis champ Rafael Nadal broke the Open-era record for consecutive victories on clay courts when he beat Robin Soderling of Sweden 6-2, 7-5, 6-1 in a first-round match at the French Open in Paris. Nadal overtook Guillermo Vilas' mark of 53 straight victories on clay courts and took the record to 81.

2010 – Halladay perfect
Philadelphia Phillies ace Roy Halladay threw the 20th perfect game in MLB history, beating the Florida Marlins 1-0 in Miami. It was the first time in the modern era that a pair of perfect games was thrown in the same season, after Dallas Braden against Tampa Bay on May 9. Halladay struck out 11 and didn't need any great defensive work in his gem.

BIRTHDATES
1904	Australian cyclist SIR HUBERT OPPERMAN – died 1996
1913	American boxer TONY ZALE – died 1997
1922	American auto racer JOE WEATHERLY – died 1964
1939	American auto racer AL UNSER SR
1949	England soccer striker/coach BRIAN KIDD
1950	Pakistan Test batsman TALAT ALI
1964	Wallaby front rower MARK HARTHILL
1966	French golfer JEAN VAN DE VELDE
1974	Australian rugby union five-eighth STEVE LARKHAM
1978	French tennis player SÉBASTIAN GROSJEAN
1981	Russian soccer striker ANDREI ARSHAVIN
1984	NBA small forward CARMELO ANTHONY

1902 – Rhodes destroys Aussies

Australia was dismissed for a record low score of 36 in the first innings of the first Ashes Test against England at Edgbaston. England slow left-arm bowler Wilfred Rhodes destroyed the Australian innings, taking 7 for 17 off 11 overs. Fast bowler George Hirst complemented Rhodes with 3 for 15. Bad weather intervened and the match was drawn.

1937 – Back-to-back PGA titles for Shute

Denny Shute won his second consecutive PGA Championship, going 37 holes in the final match to defeat Harold 'Jug' McSpaden at Pittsburgh Field Club. Shute was the last player to win back-to-back PGA Championships until Tiger Woods in 1999–2000.

1979 – Forest's trophy

Nottingham Forest beat Malmö FF of Sweden 1-0 to win the final of the European Cup in Munich. Trevor Francis scored the Forest winner in the 45th-minute.

1981 – RSA first black rugby rep

Thirty-one-year-old fly-half Errol Tobias became the first black player to start a Test match for South Africa's rugby union team, in a 23-15 win over Ireland at Newlands in Cape Town. South Africa won each of the 6 Tests in which Tobias played. He retired in 1984, having played 15 games for the Springboks.

1984 – Reds' treble

Liverpool won the European Cup in Rome to complete a unique treble, having won the League title and League Cup trophy. The Reds beat Roma 4-2 on penalties, after Neal for Liverpool, and Puzzo for Roma had netted to lock the score at 1-1 after extra time.

1985 – Oilers second straight Cup

The Oilers beat the Philadelphia Flyers 8-3 in Game 5 in Edmonton, for their second consecutive Stanley Cup triumph. Led by Wayne Gretzky, the Oilers set an astounding 24 records during the playoffs. Jari Kurri scored 19 goals to tie former Flyer Reggie Leach; the team won its 16th consecutive playoff game at Northlands Coliseum and Paul Coffey set records for most goals (12), assists (25) and points (37) by a defenseman. Gretzky scored 17 goals and 30 assists for a record 47 points in just 18 games, to win his first Conn Smythe Trophy for playoff MVP.

1987 – Tyson supreme

Mike Tyson stopped Pinklon Thomas in 6 rounds in Las Vegas to retain his WBC and WBA heavyweight titles. The fight marked Tyson's second defense of his title and the 27th knockout of his unbeaten career.

2010 – Ganassi's unique double

Chip Ganassi became the first team owner to win the Indianapolis 500 and NASCAR's Daytona 500 in the same year, when Scotsman Dario Franchitti won his second Indy. Franchitti worked the gas pedal perfectly to stretch his final fill-up for the last 37 laps and edge out the 2005 champion Dan Wheldon of England.

2012 – Roger has most major wins

Sixteen-time Grand Slam champion Roger Federer earned his record-breaking 234th victory at Grand Slam tournaments with his second-round win at the French Open. Federer beat Adrian Ungur of Romania in 4 sets to break a tie with Jimmy Connors. Federer's record stood at 234-35 in tennis' top 4 tournaments, a .870 winning percentage.

BIRTHDATES

1879	England Test spinner CHARLIE BLYTHE – died 1917
1895	England Test all-rounder MAURICE TATE – died 1956
1909	West Indian Test captain GEORGE HEADLEY – died 1983
1943	Pro Football Hall of Fame running back GALE SAYERS
1949	England Test captain BOB WILLIS
1949	NBA coach P.J. CARLESIMO
1953	Australian surfer PETER TOWNEND
1957	Australian golfer MIKE CLAYTON
1965	Australian rugby union flanker TROY COKER
1967	Australian hockey captain RACHELLE HAWKES
1976	Swedish tennis player MAGNUS NORMAN
1980	England soccer midfielder STEVEN GERRARD

1942 – Snead breaks through with PGA win
Sam Snead won his first major title when he holed a 60ft chip to beat Jim Turnesa, 2 & 1, for the PGA Championship at the Seaview CC in Atlantic City, New Jersey. Snead had received an extension of his military induction date so he could compete in the Championship.

1965 – Clark first foreign winner at Indy
Scottish driver Jim Clarke became the first foreigner to win the Indianapolis 500 since 1920 when he crossed the finish line with an average speed of 150.686mph. It was considered a foreign invasion when Englishman Graham Hill won the following year. Other overseas drivers to win the classic race are Dutchman Arie Luyendyk (1990, 1997), Brazilians Emerson Fittipaldi (1983, 1989) and Hélio Castroneves (2001–02), Canadian Jacques Villeneuve (1995), Columbian Juan Pablo Montoya (2000) and Englishman Dan Wheldon (2005, 2011).

1967 – A. J. quick at Indy
A. J. Foyt recorded the fastest-ever average speed in winning the third of his 4 Indianapolis 500s. The race took 2 days to complete, after the previous day's racing had been postponed by rain, with Parnelli Jones leading after 18 laps. After leading for 171 laps, Jones was forced to retire with gearbox problems, allowing Foyt through to first-place. He averaged a record 151.207mph in a Coyote Ford.

1972 – Cruyff guides Ajax to Cup
Dutch champions Ajax won the European Cup, defeating Inter Milan 2-0 before 61,354 fans in Rotterdam. Johan Cruyff netted just after halftime before sealing the win in the 76th minute.

1984 – 'Master Blaster' supreme
West Indian batting icon Vivian Richards hit 21 fours and 5 sixes in a slashing one-day record of 189 not out off 170 balls, against England in Manchester. In one of the great innings of all-time, Richards guided the Windies from 102-7 to 272-9, and a 104-run victory.

Ajax coach George Knobel (left) and player Jan Mulder (right) in 1973. Photo: Nationaal Archief, Den Haag, Rijksfotoarchief: Fotocollectie Algemeen Nederlands Fotopersbureau (ANEFO), 1945–1989, [CC-BY-SA-3.0-nl], via Wikimedia Commons.

2009 – Söderling upsets Nadal
Robin Söderling of Sweden pulled off one of the biggest upsets in Grand Slam tennis history, ending Rafael Nadal's perfect French Open record with a 6-2, 6-7, 6-4, 7-6 fourth-round victory. Nadal had never lost at Roland Garros, heading into the match with a 31-0 record and 4 titles.

BIRTHDATES
1924   South African Test wicketkeeper RUSSELL ENDEAN – died 2003
1928   Indian Test batsman PANKAJ ROY – died 2001
1943   Pro Football Hall of Fame quarterback JOE NAMATH
1946   West Indian Test cricket umpire STEPHEN BUCKNOR
1955   American golfer LAURA BAUGH
1958   Australian swimmer STEVE HOLLAND
1959   Italian auto racer ANDREA DE CESARIS
1966   Sri Lanka Test batsman ROSHAN MAHANAMA
1972   Norwegian cross-country skier FRODE ESTIL
1973   Belgian tennis player DOMINIQUE VAN ROOST
1973   Scottish golfer JANICE MOODIE
1974   American golfer CHAD CAMPBELL
1975   Finnish ski jumper TONI NIEMINEN

JUNE

1 JUNE

1899 – W. G.'s last hurrah
The 'Father of Cricket' W. G. Grace began the last of his 22 Tests at the age of 50, in England's draw against Australia at Trent Bridge. He scored 28 and one. Two young debutants with big futures had mixed starts. For England, Wilfred Rhodes took 7 wickets. For Australia, Victor Trumper began with a duck, but became one of the game's finest batsmen.

1954 – Zátopek's freakish three days
Amazing Czech distance runner Emile Zátopek ran a time of 28:54.2 in Brussels to break the 10,000m world record. Two days earlier in Paris, Zátopek had broken the 5,000m world mark in a time of 13:57.2. It was the first time that a runner had broken the 5,000m and 10,000m world record over a 3-day period since Hannes Kolehmainen at the 1912 Olympics.

1979 – First title for Seattle
The city of Seattle had its first-ever pro sports champion team, when the SuperSonics beat the Washington Bullets 97-93 in Game 5 to clinch the NBA Championship.

1985 – 'Master Blaster' runs rampant
Vivian Richards became the first West Indian to make 300 first-class runs in a day, when he smashed a Somerset-record 322 against Warwickshire at Taunton. He reached 300 off only 244 balls, and went from 100 to 300 in just 130 deliveries, belting 8 sixes and 42 fours.

1986 – Bradley makes golf history
Pat Bradley sank a 12ft birdie putt on the 18th hole at the Jack Nicklaus Sports Centre in Mason, Ohio, winning the LPGA Championship by 1 stroke from Patty Sheehan. Bradley became the first woman to win all 4 major championships. She had won the US Open in 1981, the Canadian Open in 1980 and 1985, and the Dinah Shore and now the LPGA in 1986.

2002 – Cronje killed in plane crash
Disgraced former South African cricket captain Hansie Cronje was killed in a plane crash outside the city of George, about 500km east of Cape Town. In 2000,

Czech legend Emil Zátopek, in the lead during the 5,000m race at the 1952 Helsinki Olympics.

Cronje had been banned for life from all forms of cricket, after admitting to taking money to fix matches involving South Africa. He was 32.

2008 – Royals win IPL off last ball
The first Indian Premier League cricket series ended with a cliffhanger final, as the Rajasthan Royals (164/7) beat the Chennai Super Kings (163/5) off the final ball in Mumbai. It came down to 1 off the last one. Sohail Tanvir pulled to short mid-on, by which time batting partner Shane Warne had already scrambled halfway down the pitch.

BIRTHDATES
1930	New Zealand Test batsman MATT POORE
1932	New Zealand Test fast bowler FRANK CAMERON
1948	American auto racer TOM SNEVA
1959	English auto racer MARTIN BRUNDLE
1961	American golfer JOHN HUSTON
1961	Canadian Hockey Hall of Fame defenseman PAUL COFFEY
1965	Russian cross-country skier LARISA LAZUTINA
1973	Belgian swimmer FRÉDÉRIK DEBURGHGRAEVE
1979	NFL wide receiver SANTANA MOSS
1981	Venezuelan MLB pitcher CARLOS ZAMBRANO
1982	Belgian tennis player JUSTINE HENIN

❷ JUNE

1941 – Gehrig dead at 37
One of the greats of baseball, Lou Gehrig, died of ALS (amyotrophic lateral sclerosis) at his home in Riverdale, New York, exactly 16 years to the day since he became the Yankees' regular first baseman. Known as 'the Iron Horse', Gehrig worked as a member of the New York City Parole Commission following his retirement from baseball. He was 37 when he passed away from the chronic disease that would be named after him.

1954 – First Epsom Derby to Piggott
Champion English jockey Lester Piggott, at just 18, won his first Epsom Derby on 33-to-1 shot Never Say Die. In a spectacular career that spanned 4 decades, Piggott went on to ride 9 Derby winners, 3 Prix de l'Arc Triomphes, eleven English Championships, 465 group races and over 5,300 winners in the UK and 27 other countries. He became a trainer in 1990.

1970 – McLaren killed in crash
New Zealand-born racing car driver, designer and team owner Bruce McLaren was killed at the Goodwood circuit in England, testing a new car. Driving his newest Cam-Am challenger, the M8D, McLaren hit an earthen bank when the rear end of the car broke away at speed. In 1958, at age 22, McLaren had become the youngest driver to win a Formula 1 race when he took out the US Grand Prix. He drove in 100 F1 Grand Prix and in 1965 started his own Grand Prix team. The McLaren Racing Team remains one of Formula 1 racing's most successful organisations.

1978 – Gower's England debut
Future England captain David Gower hit a 4 off his first ball in Test cricket, in the first Test against Pakistan at Edgbaston. England's new woolly-haired left-hander went on to make 58 on debut. He scored 8,231 Test runs, second among English batsmen only to Graham Gooch.

1985 – Easy for Lopez
Nancy Lopez opened with a 7-under par round of 65, and finished her weekend with another 65, to post a resounding 8-stroke victory over Alice Miller in the McDonald's LPGA Championship at the Jack Nicklaus Sports Centre in King's Island, Ohio. Lopez carded a 15-under par total 273.

2005 – 9,000 wins for Baze
Canadian/American Hall of Fame jockey Russell Baze rode his 9,000th career winner aboard Queen of the Hunt in the eighth race at Golden Gate Fields. Only Laffit Pincay Jr, who registered 9,530 wins during his racing career, had more victories than Baze at that time.

2009 – Yankees' errorless streak over
The New York Yankees' record-setting errorless streak ended at 18 games, when catcher Jorge Posada threw the ball into centre field on Elvis Andrus' fourth-inning steal of second base, in a 12-3 win against Texas. New York broke the previous major league mark of 17 games, set by the Boston Red Sox in 2006.

BIRTHDATES
1865	England Test fast bowler GEORGE LOHMAN – died 1901
1914	American golfer JOHNNY BULLA – died 2003
1939	American golfer JOHN SCHLEE – died 2000
1951	Canadian Hockey Hall of Fame defenseman LARRY ROBINSON
1953	American golfer CRAIG STADLER
1955	Australian boxer BARRY MICHAEL
1957	Republic of Ireland soccer defender MARK LAWRENSON
1960	American auto racer KYLE PETTY
1965	Australian Test batsman MARK WAUGH
1969	American tennis player DAVID WHEATON
1981	Russian tennis player NIKOLAY DAVYDENKO
1988	Argentine soccer forward SERGIO AGÜERO

Champion English jockey Lester Piggott aboard Minstrel in 1977.

3 JUNE

1932 – Big day for Lou
New York Yankees first baseman Lou Gehrig became the first player in the 20th century to hit 4 home runs in a game in the Yankees 20-13 win over the Athletics in Philadelphia. Gehrig homered on his first 4 plate appearances, with drives in the first, fourth, fifth and seventh innings. He tied Ty Cobb's American League record of 16 total bases and the Yankees set a major league mark with 50 total bases.

1981 – Shergar sensational
Champion racehorse Shergar won the Epsom Derby by a massive 10 lengths, the biggest winning margin in the race's long history. In 1983, the stallion was kidnapped from the Ballymany Stud in County Kildare, Ireland. A nationwide hunt failed to find any trace of the horse, valued at £10 million by Lloyds of London. An ex-IRA police informer said the IRA had kidnapped Shergar to raise funds to buy weapons, but this is just one of many theories about the still unsolved mystery.

1984 – Two straight for Patty
Patty Sheehan, boosted by a third-round 9-under par 63, cruised to her second consecutive LPGA Championship, easing past Beth Daniel and Pat Bradley by 10 strokes at the Jack Nicklaus Sports Centre, King's Island, Ohio. Sheehan's total was 16-under par 272. A year earlier, Sheehan had beaten Sandra Haynie by 3 strokes.

1992 – MJ on target
Michael Jordan set an NBA Finals record by hitting 6 three-pointers (from 9 attempts) in the first half, as his Chicago Bulls beat Portland 122-89 in Game 1 of the Finals in Chicago. Jordan set another Finals record with 35 points in the first half, making 14 of 21 field-goal attempts in 19 minutes. He finished the game with 39 points and 11 assists.

1993 – Desjardins NHL history
Éric Desjardins became the first NHL defenseman to score a hat-trick in the Stanley Cup Finals. His third goal of the game at 0:51 of overtime gave Montreal a 3-2 win over the Kings at home in Game 2, in the Canadiens eighth straight overtime win.

Baseball Hall of Fame first baseman Lou Gehrig in 1939.

2012 – Tiger ties 'Golden Bear'
Tiger Woods tied Jack Nicklaus for career PGA Tour victories (73) at the tournament Nicklaus hosted, the Memorial at Dublin, Ohio. Woods birdied 3 of his last 4 holes to close with a 5-under 67, turning a 2-shot deficit into a 2-shot win over Rory Sabbatini and Andrés Romero. It was Woods' fifth Memorial victory. Sam Snead still holds the PGA Tour record with 82 wins.

BIRTHDATES
1879	England soccer striker VIV WOODWARD – died 1954
1906	England Test all-rounder WALTER ROBINS – died 1968
1921	Australian swim coach FORBES CARLILE
1928	New Zealand Test captain JOHN REID
1936	New Zealand rugby union lock COLIN MEADS
1943	Basketball Hall of Fame forward/coach BILLY CUNNINGHAM
1945	American golfer HALE IRWIN
1945	English golfer BRIAN BARNES
1956	Scottish soccer defender/manager GEORGE BURLEY
1957	South African rugby union coach PETER DE VILLIERS
1960	Australian Test fast bowler CARL RACKEMANN
1966	Pakistan Test captain WASIM AKRAM
1975	New Zealand rugby union lock SIMON MALING
1977	American tennis player JAN-MICHAEL GAMBILL
1978	England rugby union captain STUART ABBOTT
1982	Russian pole-vaulter YELENA ISINBAYEVA
1986	Spanish tennis player RAFAEL NADAL
1992	German soccer midfielder MARIO GÖTZE

④ JUNE

1913 – Principle kills suffragette
Suffragette Emily Davison died after throwing herself in front of King George V's horse Anmer during the running of the Derby at Epsom. As the field rounded Tattenham Corner, Davison, wearing a suffragette flag tied around her waist, ducked under the railings and made an unsuccessful grab at the reins of the oncoming Anmer, ridden by Herbert Jones. Davison was struck head-on and lifted into the air as horse and jockey tumbled to the ground. She died from her injuries.

1927 – First Ryder Cup to Americans
The United States dominated the inaugural Ryder Cup, beating an undermanned Great Britain 9½ to 2½ at the Worcester CC in Massachusetts.

1961 – Magnificent Middlecoff
Cary Middlecoff won his 40th and final PGA Tour title, a 5-stroke win over Gardner Dickinson and Mike Souchak in the Memphis Open at the Colonial CC. Middlecoff won 37 events after World War II, including the US Open (1949, 1956) and the Masters (1955).

1977 – Rampaging Scots
Following a 2-1 win over England, an estimated 20,000 Scotland fans invaded the famous Wembley turf, destroying the goalposts and advertising hoardings.

1987 – Holy Moses!
Champion American hurdler Edwin Moses lost his first 400m hurdles race in nearly 10 years, when 21-year-old Danny Harris ran a personal best time of 47.56 seconds in Madrid, Spain. Harris led from the fifth hurdle and his winning margin was 0.13 seconds. Before the race, his winning streak stood at 122 races.

1993 – 'Ball of the century'
Australian leg spinner Shane Warne bowled England batsman Mike Gatting with what has been labelled the 'ball of the century', and his first ball in an Ashes Test. On the second day of the first Test at Old Trafford, the famous delivery drifted lazily onto leg stump, spun back a yard and clipped the top of Gatting's off-stump, much to his amazement. Australia won by 179 runs and took the series 4-1.

1995 – Rugby union record
New Zealand created a world record score for a rugby international when they thrashed Japan 145-17 in a World Cup match in Bloemfontein, South Africa. The All Blacks scored 21 tries to 2. Centre Marc Ellis crossed for 6 tries, and fly-half Simon Culhane kicked 20 conversions.

2005 – Good day for Castro
Jockey Eddie Castro set a North American record for most wins by a jockey in a single day at one racetrack, by winning 9 races on the 13-race card at Miami's Calder Race Course.

2008 – Lidström a winner
Swedish defenseman Nicklas Lidström made ice hockey history, becoming the first European captain to hoist the Stanley Cup after the Detroit Red Wings beat the Penguins 3-2, in Game 6 in Pittsburgh. The victory gave Lidström his fourth Stanley Cup in 5 chances.

2011 – First Chinese major winner
Li Na became the first Chinese player to win a Grand Slam singles title, beating defending champion Francesca Schiavone of Italy 6-4, 7-6 in the French Open final at Roland Garros.

BIRTHDATES
1915	New Zealand Test captain WALTER HADLEE – died 2006
1943	American golfer SANDRA HAYNIE
1948	Canadian golfer SANDRA POST
1948	English jumps jockey BOB CHAMPION
1949	Scottish soccer midfielder/manager LOU MACARI
1965	Australian motorcycle rider MICK DOOHAN
1963	New Zealand rugby union captain SEAN FITZPATRICK
1963	NFL offensive tackle JIM LACHEY
1965	American tennis player ANDREA JAEGER
1970	Australian rugby union flanker DANIEL MANU
1970	Italian alpine skier DEBORAH COMPAGNONI
1983	Ivorian soccer defender EMMANUEL EBOUÉ
1983	Ivorian soccer midfielder ROMARIC
1985	German soccer forward LUKAS PODOLSKI

❺ JUNE

Russian tennis star Anastasia Myskina during the 2005 Wimbledon Championships.

1925 – Eyewear makes no difference
Scottish golfer Willie MacFarlane became the first US Open winner to wear eyeglasses, upsetting amateur Bobby Jones in a 2-round playoff, 147 to 148, at the Worcester CC in Massachusetts. The pair had tied with 4-over par 75's after the first playoff round. MacFarlane posted a record 4-under par 67 in the second round of regulation play.

1964 – First sub-four-minute mile by the field
For the first time in history, a mile race was run in which all 8 finishers recorded times below 4 minutes. Dyrol Burleson won the race at Compton, California, in a time of 3:57.4. Jim Ryan, a 17-year-old high school student destined for bigger things, finished fifth with a time of 3:59 after being bumped during the race. He went on to become one of the greatest middle distance runners of all-time.

1983 – Couples' first win
Twenty-three-year-old Fred Couples scored his first PGA Tour victory when he won the Kemper Open in a 5-way playoff featuring T.C. Chen, Barry Jaeckel, Gil Morgan, and Scott Simpson. Couples' only major victory has been the 1992 Masters.

1988 – Cottee first solo female
Australian Kay Cottee sailed into Sydney after a 189-day voyage, becoming the first woman to singlehandedly circumnavigate the globe non-stop. Cottee's 11.2 metre yacht, *First Lady,* had set out from Sydney on November 29, 1987.

2004 – Oh, those Russians
Anastasia Myskina defeated fellow Russian Elena Dementieva 6-1, 6-2 to win the 2004 French Open, in the first ever all-Russian Grand Slam final. She also became the first Russian woman to win a Grand Slam singles title.

2004 – Unprecedented interest in Smarty Jones
Smarty Jones' journey to become horse racing's 12th Triple Crown winner ended when he was upset by Birdstone, a 36-1 long-shot, by a length, in front of a record Belmont Park crowd of 120,139. NBC Sports' telecast of the race was the highest-rated program of any kind for the week.

2010 – Italy's #1 girl
Francesca Schiavone became Italy's first female champion at a Grand Slam tournament when she beat Australia's Samantha Stosur 6-4, 7-6 to win the French Open title in Paris.

2011 – Six French titles for 'Rafa'
Spain's Rafael Nadal equalled Björn Borg's record of 6 singles titles at Roland Garros and earned his 10th career major championship with a 7-5, 7-6, 5-7, 6-1 victory over Roger Federer. It was Nadal's fourth win against Federer in a French Open final.

BIRTHDATES
1912   England Test spinner ERIC HOLLIES – died 1981
1916   Australian Test batsman SID BARNES – died 1973
1938   Australian jockey ROY HIGGINS
1955   Brazilian soccer defender EDINHO
1959   Australian rugby union five-eighth MARK ELLA
1961   Indian tennis player RAMESH KRISHNAN
1974   West Indian Test fast bowler MERVYN DILLON
1974   Australian tennis player SCOTT DRAPER
1975   Lithuanian NBA centre ZYDRUNAS ILGAUSKAS
1978   Portuguese soccer midfielder FERNANDO MEIRA
1992   Australian swimmer EMILY SEEBOHM

❻ JUNE

1946 – BAA established
Team owners and arena managers met in New York to establish the 11-team Basketball Association of America. In 1949, the BAA merged with the National Basketball League to form the NBA.

1976 – Kite's first PGA win
Tom Kite claimed his first PGA Tour victory, defeating Terry Diehl on the fifth extra hole to win the IVB Philadelphia Classic. Kite had turned professional in 1972 and before he joined the Champions Tour in 2000, he won 19 PGA Tour events, including the 1992 US Open. He was the US Ryder Cup captain in 1997.

1992 – Murray RBI leader
Eddie Murray of the New York Mets became baseball's all-time RBI leader among switch-hitters, when he drove in 2 runs to pass Mickey Mantle. Murray claimed the mark with a run-scoring single off Dennis Lamp in the Mets' 15-1 thrashing of the Pirates in Pittsburgh. Murray's career total of 1,510 RBIs included 404 homers.

1994 – Lara's 501
West Indian batsman Brian Lara achieved cricket immortality by smashing an unbeaten 501 for Warwickshire against Durham, the highest score in first-class cricket history. In all, Lara faced only 427 balls, hammering 62 fours and 10 sixes. His mark surpassed Hanif Mohammad's 499 for Karachi against Bahawalpur at Karachi in 1959.

1997 – England jags Ashes series lead
England batsman Nasser Hussain hit 38 fours in a dominating 207, on the second day of the first Test against Australia, at Edgbaston. Hussain's knock, along with Graham Thorpe's 138 and Andy Caddick's 5 for 50 in the Australian first innings, led England to a 9-wicket win and an unlikely 1-0 series lead. The Australians won the series 3-2.

1999 – 'Plugger' record
Australian football's Sydney Swans full-forward Tony Lockett kicked his 1,300th career goal at the Sydney Cricket Ground against Collingwood, eclipsing Gordon Coventry's long-standing VFL/AFL record. Lockett retired after the 1999 season, and after a brief comeback, finally retired at the end of the 2002 season at the age of 36, with 1,360 goals from 281 games.

2007 – Ducks' first Cup
Travis Moen's pair of goals and Jean-Sèbastien Giguére's 11 stops paced the Anaheim Ducks as they clinched the first Stanley Cup in team history, with a 6-2 victory over the Ottawa Senators, in Game 5 of the Finals in Anaheim.

2010 – Fifth Open for Nadal
Spanish clay court king, Raphael Nadal, won his fifth French Open title, avenging his lone Roland Garros defeat by beating Sweden's Robin Söderling 6-4, 6-2, 6-4. The victory ended his longest Grand Slam drought since he won his first major title in Paris in 2005.

2011 – USC break rules, lose title
The University of Southern California's football team was stripped of the 2004–05 National Championship trophy. The NCAA penalised the Trojans for numerous improper benefits that running back Reggie Bush had received during his final year at the school.

BIRTHDATES
1884	Scottish golfer JOCK HUTCHISON – died 1977
1930	England Test fast bowler FRANK TYSON
1940	South African Test all rounder HERBERT 'TIGER' LANCE – died 2010
1940	Irish rugby union number 8 WILLIE JOHN McBRIDE
1943	Pakistan Test all rounder ASIF IQBAL
1944	American sprinter TOMMIE SMITH
1954	New Zealand rugby union fullback ALLAN HEWSON
1956	Swedish tennis player BJÖRN BORG
1957	England Test captain MIKE GATTING
1962	New Zealand rugby union fly-half GRANT FOX
1966	Ghanaian soccer striker TONY YEBOAH
1970	Indian Test spinner SUNIL JOSHI
1983	New Zealand rugby union winger JOE ROKOCOKO
1985	Swedish soccer defender SEBASTIAN LARSSON
1988	New Zealand rugby utility back ISRAEL DAGG

❼ JUNE

1932 – Vardon's farewell
Six-time British Open champion Harry Vardon played his final round of championship golf while trying to qualify for the Open. Only 2 spectators were on hand as he turned in disappointing scores in the 80s. Vardon won the British Open championship 6 times – in 1896, 1898, 1899, 1903, 1911, and 1914. He also won the US Open in 1900, among 62 other career tournaments. A PGA trophy, awarded annually for low-average scoring, is named after him. He died in 1937.

1941 – Final pre-war Open
Craig Wood won the final US Open to be held until 1946 (due to World War II), when he beat Denny Shute by 3 strokes at the Colonial CC in Fort Worth, Texas. Wood was in pain throughout the Championship because of a back injury and he wore a corset for support. He had considered withdrawing before the Open began. Wood was the first golfer to lose a playoff in all 4 of the modern major championships.

1941 – Triple Crown to Whirlaway
Whirlaway became the fifth horse to win the famed Triple Crown, by scoring an easy 3-length win over Robert Morris in the Belmont Stakes. Ridden by jockey Eddie Arcaro, Whirlaway recorded the slow time of 2:31 minutes for the one-and-a-half miles.

1952 – Woeful start to Test
In the worst start to an innings in Test cricket history, it took England just 14 balls to have India 0 for 4 in the first Test at Leeds. The chief destroyer was England's 21-year-old debutant fast bowler Fred Trueman, who took 3 of the wickets; Alec Bedser also took one. India recovered to accumulate a total of 165, but lost the match by 7 wickets.

1967 – Moore's rare treble
Australian jockey George Moore rode the Noel Murless-trained, 7-4 favourite, Royal Palace, to victory in the Epsom Derby, completing a unique treble in English racing – Moore had also won the 2,000 Guineas Stakes on Royal Palace, and the 1,000 Guineas on Fleet, in one season.

1981 – Borg's fifth French
Björn Borg won a record sixth French Open singles title when he beat Ivan Lendl in 5 gruelling sets 6-1, 4-6, 6-2, 3-6, 6-1 in Paris. It was his 11th (and last) career Grand Slam title.

1989 – Nine Harts for the 'Great One'
Ice Hockey legend Wayne Gretzky won his ninth Hart Trophy in 10 years, as the National Hockey League's Most Valuable Player. Gretzky had played his first season with the LA Kings and the team finished with the most improved record in the NHL (42-31-7). Gretzky finished second in League scoring with 168 points (54-114-168).

1998 – No Bull in thrashing
The Chicago Bulls defeated the Utah Jazz, 96-54, in the most lopsided game in the history of the NBA Finals. The 54 points by the Jazz was also an NBA record for fewest points in a game since the inception of the 24-second shot clock.

2004 – First Cup to Lightning
Ukrainian winger Ruslan Fedotenko scored a pair of goals as the Tampa Bay Lightning captured their first Stanley Cup ice hockey title, with a 2-1 victory over the Calgary Flames in Game 7 of the finals, at the St Pete Times Forum.

BIRTHDATES

1905	American boxer JAMES J. BRADDOCK – died 1974
1928	English boxer RANDY TURPIN – died 1966
1938	Scottish soccer forward/manager IAN ST. JOHN
1945	England rugby union fullback TONY BUCKNALL
1955	American auto racer TIM RICHMOND – died 1989
1964	Sri Lankan Test spinner GRAEME LABROOY
1966	New Zealand rugby union halfback ANT STRACHAN
1967	Australian rugby union hooker MICHAEL FOLEY
1970	Brazilian soccer defender CAFU
1975	NBA guard ALLEN IVERSON
1975	New Zealand Test fast bowler SHANE BOND
1981	Russian tennis player ANNA KOURNAKOVA
1986	American golfer KEEGAN BRADLEY
1990	American swimmer ALLISON SCHMITT

8 JUNE

Jacqui Frazier-Lyde (left) and Laila Ali exchange punches during their women's Super Middleweight fight in 2001 Verona, New York. Ali won the fight on points in the eigth rond.

1958 – Wright-on major
Mickey Wright claimed her first major championship, defeating Fay Crocker by 6 strokes in the LPGA Championship at Churchill Valley in Penn Hills, Pennsylvania. Arguably the greatest player in LPGA history, Wright joined the Tour in 1955 and scored 82 victories in her amazing 26-year career. She won the 1958, 1959, 1961 and 1964 US Open Championship, sharing the record of 4 titles with Betsy Rawls. In the 10-year span from 1959–68, Wright captured 79 of her 82 victories, averaging an incredible 7.9 victories per year. She is the only woman in LPGA history to have won the LPGA Championship 4 times.

1966 – NFL born
The National Football League and the American Football League agreed to merge into a single league of at least 26 teams in 25 cities by the year 1970. It was decided that the unified schedule would not take place until 1970, because of separate, existing multi-million dollar television contracts. Interim plans included a championship game in January 1967 between the 1966 champions of each league, inter-league exhibitions starting in 1967, and a common draft of college players.

1968 – Drysdale scoreless mark
LA Dodgers right-hander Don Drysdale created baseball history when he broke Walter Johnson's 55-year-old consecutive scoreless streak record, of 55 and two-third innings. Drysdale had pitched shutouts in his past 6 starts and reached 58 and two-third innings, before the Philadelphia Phillies scored in the fifth inning of a 5-3 Dodgers victory. Ironically the streak was snapped by a player who had scored only 1 run that year with pinch-hitter Howie Bedell hitting a sacrifice fly to send Tony Taylor home in the fifth.

2001 – Chips off the blocks
The daughters of 2 of boxing's greatest rivals fought a well-publicised 8-round bout in Verona, New York. Leila Ali, daughter of Muhammad Ali, beat Jacqui Frazier-Lyde, daughter of Joe Frazier, in a majority points decision. The fight attracted a crowd of 8,000 and drew more than 100,000 pay-per-view buys

2008 – Roger's worst defeat
Rafael Nadal inflicted Roger Federer's worst loss in 173 career Grand Slam matches, as he became the first player since Björn Borg to win 4 consecutive French Open titles. Nadal totally outplayed Federer, winning 6-1, 6-3, 6-0. It was the third consecutive French final the pair had played, with Nadal having won all of them.

2013 – Serena supreme
Serena Williams won her second French Open title, 11 years after her first triumph, defeating title-holder Maria Sharapova 6-4, 6-4 at Roland Garros. It was the 31-year-old American's 16th Grand Slam title win, taking her to within 2 of Chris Evert and Martina Navratilova who are tied for fourth on the all-time list.

BIRTHDATES
1932	England Test captain RAY ILLINGWORTH
1939	Pro Football Hall of Fame cornerback HERB ADDERLEY
1942	Welsh snooker player DOUG MOUNTJOY
1945	England Test spinner DEREK UNDERWOOD
1946	Australian Test wicketkeeper RICHIE ROBINSON
1962	French rugby union flanker ÉRIC CHAMP
1964	American sprinter BUTCH REYNOLDS
1976	American tennis player LINDSAY DAVENPORT
1979	New Zealand netball wing attack ADINE WILSON
1982	Russian tennis player NADIA PETROVA
1983	Belgian tennis player KIM CLIJSTERS
1984	Argentine soccer midfielder JAVIER MASCHERANO

1899 – Jeffries' heavyweight title
Heavy-hitting James J. Jeffries won the world heavyweight title when he knocked out champion Bob Fitzsimmons in the 11th round at Coney Island in New York. Fitzsimmons couldn't keep up with Jeffries, who was 13 years his junior and outweighed him by 70lbs.

1934 – Sick Dutra wins Open
Olin Dutra won his second major title when he left his sick bed in hospital to beat Gene Sarazen by 1 stroke in the US Open at the Merion Cricket Club in Ardmore, Pennsylvania. Dutra was suffering from a stomach complaint and after uninspiring opening rounds of 76 and 74, trailed by 8 strokes. He finished with rounds of 71 and 72 for a 13-over par 293. His comeback from that deficit remains a record, only equalled by Arnold Palmer in 1960.

1967 – Typical Boycott innings
England opener Geoff Boycott lived up to his stodgy reputation in scoring his highest Test score of 246 not out against India at Headingley. His marathon innings took just short of 10 hours. Even though England went on to win by 6 wickets, he was dropped from the next Test, reportedly due to selfish (rather than slow) batting.

1973 – Triple Crown to Secretariat
Secretariat scored a stunning 31-length victory in the Belmont and wrap up the famed Triple Crown of American racing. In front of a crowd of 69,138 and guided by jockey Ron Turcotte, Secretariat blitzed a small field, finishing the last quarter of a mile in an amazing 25 seconds to set a world-record of 2:24. The chestnut colt, known as 'Big Red', beat Gallant Man's Belmont mark by an incredible 2.6 seconds.

1983 – Zimbabwe's first ODI an upset
In their first-ever ODI match, Zimbabwe began the third World Cup with one of the biggest upsets in cricket history. Inspired by their 34-year-old captain Duncan Fletcher, Zimbabwe stunned Australia with a 13-run victory at Trent Bridge. Fletcher cracked 69 not out and then took 4-42, as Australia spluttered to 226 for 7.

1990 – Teen bliss
Yugoslavia's Monica Seles beat Steffi Graf of Germany in straight sets 7-6, 6-4 in the final of the French Open, to become the youngest winner of a Grand Slam event in over 100 years. Seles was 16 years, 6 months old.

2010 – Blackhawks win Cup
Patrick Kane snuck the puck past Michael Leighton, 4:06 into overtime, to stun the Philadelphia Flyers and lift the Chicago Blackhawks to a 4-3 overtime win in Game 6, for their first Stanley Cup championship since 1961. The win ended the longest active championship drought in the NHL.

2012 – Pacquiao controversially beaten
Tim Bradley ended Filipino legend Manny Pacquiao's remarkable 7-year unbeaten run, when he controversially won the WBO Welterweight title in Las Vegas. Bradley won 115-113 on 2 scorecards, while losing on the third by the same margin. Associated Press had Pacquiao winning, 117-111. Promoter Bob Arum blasted the decision.

2013 – 'King of Clay'
Rafael Nadal became the first man to win 8 titles at the same Grand Slam tournament when he beat fellow Spaniard David Ferrer in the French Open final, 6-3, 6-2, 6-3. Nadal broke the men's record for match wins at Roland Garros, where he improved to 59-1, with his lone defeat against Robin Söderling in 2009. He came into the final with a 16-match winning streak on clay against Ferrer who was a big underdog playing in his first major final at age 31.

BIRTHDATES
1898	Italian auto racer LUIGI FAGIOLI – died 1952
1931	MLB outfielder/manager BILL VIRDON
1959	Australian golfer PETER FOWLER
1969	Australian triathlete MICHELLIE JONES
1973	NFL linebacker TEDY BRUSCHI
1975	Australian Test batsman ANDREW SYMONDS
1978	German soccer striker MIROSLAV KLOSE
1984	Dutch soccer midfielder WESLEY SNEIJDER
1985	New Zealand rugby winger RICHARD KAHUI

1829 – Rowing rivalry commences
The first of the famous Oxford-Cambridge boat races for heavyweight eights was rowed on the River Thames in England with Oxford running out easy winners. The race between the 2 premier universities is conducted over a course from Putney to Mortlake, measuring 4 miles and 374 yards. It has been run annually since 1856, except in war years.

1934 – Italy's World Cup at home
In an atmosphere of pre-war Fascism, Italy won a controversial second-ever World Cup at home in Rome, when they beat Czechoslovakia 2-1 after extra time. Defending champions Uruguay boycotted because of the lack of European support for the first World Cup, which they'd hosted, and Argentina, the 1930 runners-up, had seen 3 of their best players poached by Italy and sent a virtual 'C' team in protest. One of those players, Orsi, scored a freakish goal to level the match for Italy before Schiavio got the extra time winner.

1977 – Geiberger breaks 60
Al Geiberger became the first PGA Tour player to break 60 in an official PGA Tour event, recording a 13-under par 59 in the second round of the Danny Thomas Memphis Classic at the par-72 Colonial CC. During the historic round, Geiberger went out in 29 and came home with 30. He had 6 birdies and an eagle in an irresistible 7-hole stretch. He eventually won the event by 3 strokes from Jerry McGee and Gary Player.

1978 – Triple Crown for Affirmed
Affirmed, the 3-5 favourite, became the 11th winner of the famed Triple Crown when he beat arch-rival Alydar by a neck in the one-and-a-half-mile Belmont. Ridden by Steve Cauthen, Affirmed once again edged out Alydar in a tight finish, having won the Kentucky Derby by one-and-a-half lengths and the Preakness by a nose. It was the first time there had been successive Triple Crown winners after Seattle Slew's triumph a year earlier.

1989 – Spanish first
Seventeen-year-old Arantxa Sánchez Vicario became the first Spaniard to win a Grand Slam singles title when she beat Steffi Graf 7-6, 3-6, 7-5 in the final of the French Open. She went on to win 2 more French Open titles (1994, 1998).

2006 – Hopkins over Tarver on points
Bernard Hopkins capped an 18-year career with a commanding unanimous decision over Antonio Tarver for the IBO light-heavyweight title in Atlantic City. All 3 officials scored the fight to Hopkins, 118-109. The 41-year-old Hopkins dominated the middleweight division for 12 years, making a division record 20 consecutive successful title defences.

2007 – First black F1 winner
The 22-year-old English Mercedes McLaren driver, Lewis Hamilton, already the first black driver in Formula 1 history, added his first F1 victory to an already remarkable start by winning a crash-filled Canadian Grand Prix at the Circuit Gilles Villeneuve in Montreal. Apart from losing the lead when he made his first of 2 pit stops, he led all the way and was never challenged.

2012 – Tino is Best #11
Tino Best made the highest score by a number 11 in Test cricket, with an entertaining 95 in the drawn third Test at Edgbaston. It helped West Indies to their first 400-plus total in their England tour.

BIRTHDATES
1927	Hungarian soccer forward/manager LÁSZLÓ KUBALA – died 2002
1951	Pro Football Hall of Fame quarterback DAN FOUTS
1959	Italian soccer midfielder/manager CARLO ANCELOTTI
1962	Canadian NHL centre BRENT SUTTER
1966	England soccer midfielder DAVID PLATT
1968	American skeleton racer JIMMY SHEA
1969	Norwegian soccer defender RONNY JOHNSEN
1970	English soccer manager CHRIS COLEMAN
1982	American figure skater TARA LIPINSKI
1985	Estonian tennis player KAIA KANEPI

⑪ JUNE

1950 – Hogan definitely a hero
Ben Hogan won his second US Open at the Merion Club near Philadelphia in a three-way playoff, just 16 months after having been involved in a road accident that almost claimed his life. In only his seventh tournament since the accident, a tired Hogan had battled difficult weather conditions to bogey 2 of the last 4 holes of regulation play, to tie with Lloyd Mangrum and George Fazio at 7-over 287. Rejuvenated by 2 baths and a good night's sleep, Hogan then fired a 1-under 69 in the playoff to beat Mangrum by 4 and Fazio by six.

1955 – Le Mans tragedy
In the worst accident in motor racing history, 83 spectators were killed at the Le Mans 24 Hour Race in France, marring the most prestigious event on the sports car calendar. The Mercedes of Pierre Levegh collided with Lance Macklin's Austin Healy, catapulting over an earth bank into a teeming spectator enclosure. Levegh and 83 spectators were killed, with 120 more injured. In the aftermath, all motor racing was banned in France, Mexico, Spain and Switzerland. The bans were eventually lifted, except in Switzerland, where motor racing still remains restricted.

1990 – Nolan no-hitter
Forty-three-year-old Texas Rangers hurler Nolan Ryan became the oldest pitcher to throw a no-hitter in a 5-0 win over the A's in Oakland. Ryan struck out 14 and walked just 2 while pitching his 59th shutout. It was his sixth no-hitter, extending his major-league record. He retired with 7 no-hitters to his credit.

1999 – Saqlain WC hat-trick
Pakistan spinner Saqlain Mushtaq became only the second bowler to claim a World Cup hat-trick as Pakistan thrashed Zimbabwe by 148 runs at the Oval. Saqlain joined teammate Wasim Akram as the only bowlers to take 2 hat-tricks in ODIs.

2000 – 'Woodies' best doubles team
Australian pair Todd Woodbridge and Mark Woodforde became the most successful doubles team in history when they won their 58th title at the French Open, beating Paul Haarhuis and Sandon Stolle 7-6, 6-4. They won 11 Grand Slam doubles titles together: Australian Open (1992, 1997); Wimbledon (1993–97, 2000); US Open (1995–96); and French Open (2000). They were ATP Doubles Team of the Year (1992, 1995–97, 2000) and won the Olympic gold medal in Atlanta in 1996.

2006 – Third LPGA title to Pak
Se Ri Pak of South Korea captured the McDonalds LPGA Championship for the third time, with a birdie on the first playoff hole against Australian Karrie Webb. Pak also won the event in 1998 and 2002.

2012 – First Cup for Kings
The LA Kings won the Stanley Cup for the first time, with a 6-1 victory over the New Jersey Devils in Game 6 in Los Angeles. Jeff Carter and Trevor Lewis scored 2 goals apiece, whilst playoff MVP Jonathan Quick made 17 saves in a stellar performance. The Kings became the first eighth-seeded playoff team to win the league title.

2012 – 'Rafa's' magnificent seven
Rafael Nadal won his record seventh French Open title, in rain affected 6-4, 6-3, 2-6, 7-5 victory over Novak Djokovic. Nadal broke the record he shared with Björn Borg, improved to 52-1 at the French Open, and beat the man who had defeated him in the last 3 Grand Slam finals.

BIRTHDATES
1902	Pro Football Hall of Fame running back ERNIE NEVERS – died 1976
1913	NFL coach VINCE LOMBARDI – died 1970
1925	New Zealand rugby union lock RICHARD 'TINY' WHITE – died 2012
1939	Scottish auto racer JACKIE STEWART
1942	New Zealand rugby union prop JAZZ MULLER
1951	West Indian Test all rounder COLLIS KING
1954	Australian Test opener JOHN DYSON
1956	Pro Football Hall of Fame quarterback JOE MONTANA
1962	Brazilian soccer manager MANO MENEZES
1964	French auto racer JEAN ALESI
1966	American swimmer TIFFANY COHEN
1967	New Zealand rugby union halfback GRAEME BACHOP
1971	New Zealand Test opener MARK RICHARDSON
1977	Australian golfer GEOFF OGILVY

⑫ JUNE

1930 – Schmeling wins title via DQ
Germany's Max Schmeling became the only man to be crowned world heavyweight boxing champion via a disqualification. In against American Jack Sharkey and in front of 79,222 fans at Yankee Stadium in New York, Schmeling won in the fourth round when Sharkey was charged with a low blow. In January 1931, Schmeling was stripped of the title for failing to agree to a rematch with Sharkey.

1937 – Guldahl's Open scoring record
Ralph Guldahl set a new US Open scoring record with a 7-under par 281, winning by 2 strokes from Sam Snead at the Oakland Hills CC in Bloomfield Hills, Michigan. Snead's first Open appearance marked the first of 4 disappointing runner-up finishes in the only major championship he never won.

1939 – Baseball Hall of Fame opens
Major League Baseball's Hall of Fame opened in Cooperstown, New York, on the 100th anniversary of the sport. Ten of the eleven living Hall members attended: Connie Mack, Honus Wagner, Tris Speaker, Nap Lajoie, Cy Young, Walter Johnson, George Sisler, Eddie Collins, Grover Cleveland Alexander and Babe Ruth. Ty Cobb arrived late, as he was ill. The 14 deceased members were Christy Mathewson, Wee Willie Keeler, Cap Anson, Morgan Buckley, Alexander Cartwright, Henry Chadwick, Charles Comiskey, William Cummings, Buck Ewing, Ban Johnson, John McGraw, Hoss Radbourne, A.G. Spalding and George Wright.

1948 – Hogan's first Open victory
The great Ben Hogan carded a tournament record score of 276 to win the first of his 4 US Open titles at the Riviera CC in Pacific Palisades, California. Hogan beat his great rival Jimmy Demaret by 2 strokes.

1991 – Bulls' era begins
The Chicago Bulls won their first NBA championship with a 108-101 victory over the LA Lakers in Game 5 at the Great Western Forum. Finals MVP Michael Jordan led the way with 30 points and 10 assists, whilst guard John Paxson scored 10 of his 20 points after the Lakers had tied the game at 93. The Bulls went on to win 6 NBA titles in the 1990s.

1997 – MLB inter-league begins
In the first-ever regular-season inter-league game, the visiting San Francisco Giants beat the Texas Rangers 4-3 at Arlington, behind the pitching of Mark Gardner. Giants' outfielder Darryl Hamilton got the first inter-league hit, outfielder Stan Javier hit the first home run, and Rod Beck earned the first save. Glenallen Hill has the distinction of being the first National League designated hitter to play in a regular season game.

2011 – Mavs first NBA title
The Dallas Mavericks won their first NBA title, taking Game 6 of the Finals in Miami 105-95, celebrating on the Heat's home floor. The Mavericks won 4 of the series' last 5 games. Dirk Nowitzki, who had 21 points, took Finals MVP honors, whilst Jason Terry led Dallas with 27 points.

BIRTHDATES

1901	New Zealand rugby union flanker RUBEN McWILLIAMS – died 1984
1930	English auto racer INNES IRELAND – died 1993
1930	Australian Test batsman JIM BURKE – died 1979
1935	Australian Test captain IAN CRAIG
1945	Irish soccer goalkeeper PAT JENNINGS
1956	Australian Test fast bowler/analyst TERRY ALDERMAN
1957	Pakistan Test captain JAVED MIANDAD
1959	Pakistan Test fast bowler/coach JALAL-UD-DIN
1960	American golfer MARK CALCAVECCHIA
1969	American NHL defenseman MATHIEU SCHNEIDER
1976	Danish soccer goalkeeper THOMAS SØRENSEN
1978	England rugby union flanker LEWIS MOODY
1983	South African rugby winger BRYAN HABANA

1912 – Mathewson first to 300

New York Giants right-hander Christy Mathewson became the first pitcher to win 300 games in the 20th century, in a 3-2 win over the Chicago Cubs at the Polo Grounds. Between 1901–14, Mathewson won at least 20 games 13 times. He retired in 1916 with 363 victories.

1953 – Hogan's Open blitz

In one of golf's greatest achievements, Ben Hogan beat Sam Snead by 6 strokes to win the US Open at the Oakmont CC in Pennsylvania. It was 1 of only 6 events Hogan entered during a year. Incredibly, he won 5 of them including The US Masters and the British Open.

1953 – Bedser brutal

England fast bowler Alec Bedser took match figures of 14-99 for England against Australia in the first Test at Nottingham, in Test cricket's best ever performance by a bowler whose team did not win. Bedser took 7-55 in the first innings, and 7-44 in the second, but with England on course for victory, rain washed out all of the fourth day and most of the fifth.

1985 – Open albatross

T. C. Chen scored the only albatross in US Open history at the Oakland Hills CC in Birmingham, Michigan. Chen hit his second shot on the 527-yard second hole into the cup from 255 yards. He finished in a three-way tie for second place.

1999 – Gibbs' famous gaffe

In a famous World Cup gaffe, South African opener Herschelle Gibbs dropped Australian captain Steve Waugh at midwicket, seemingly in a premature celebration of the catch. Waugh had come to the crease with Australia struggling at 48-3, chasing 272 – and went on to score 120 not out. The dropped catch put Australia above South Africa in the Super 6 stage, an incidental detail at the time, but one of huge significance when the rivals tied in the semi-final 4 days later. Waugh is reputed to have said to Gibbs, 'How does it feel to drop the World Cup?' Australia went on to beat Pakistan in the final.

2004 – Le Mans domination

Danish driver Tom Kristensen teamed with Seiji Ara of Japan and Italian Rinaldo Capello in an Audi R8 to win a record fifth consecutive Le Mans 24 Hour Classic. Kristensen also equalled Jacky Ickx's 6 victories in the sports car race, having completed a record 379 laps and 5,169km.

2012 – Armstrong charged

The US Anti-Doping Agency officially charged seven-time Tour de France champion Lance Armstrong with doping and trafficking of drugs and suspended him from competing. In July, Armstrong filed a lawsuit in the federal court in Texas against USADA, which was dismissed. He didn't take the case to arbitration, and was stripped of all results dating back to August 1, 1998, as well as being banned from competitive cycling for life. He later admitted to doping throughout his career.

2012 – Cain perfect

Matt Cain pitched the 22nd perfect game in MLB history, the first for the Giants, by striking out a career-high and record-equalling 14, getting help from 2 spectacular catches by outfielders Melky Cabrera and Gregor Blanco, and beating the Houston Astros 10-0 in San Francisco.

BIRTHDATES

1897	Finnish distance runner PAAVO NURMI – died 1973
1903	Pro Football Hall of Fame halfback RED GRANGE – died 1991
1915	American tennis player DON BUDGE – died 2000
1955	Scotland soccer defender/analyst ALAN HANSEN
1961	Swedish tennis player ANDERS JÄRRYD
1964	Lithuanian NBA guard SARUNAS MARCIULIONIS
1965	Pakistan Test spinner MANINDER SINGH
1970	New Zealand Test all-rounder/analyst CHRIS CAIRNS
1974	Australian golfer MATTHEW GOGGIN
1974	Russian NHL winger VALERI BURE
1980	England soccer forward DARIUS VASSELL
1980	French soccer midfielder FLORENT MALOUDA
1982	Ethiopian long distance runner KENENISA BEKELE

1949 – 'The Natural'
The event that would inspire Bernard Malamud's novel *The Natural* took place in Chicago, when Philadelphia Phillies first baseman Eddie Waitkus was lured into a deranged female fan's hotel room and shot. The 29-year-old Waitkus recovered after surgery and resumed his career. The fan, 19-year-old typist Ruth Steinhagen, was judged to be insane and committed to Kankakee State Hospital until 1952. *The Natural* later became a successful movie starring Robert Redford.

1994 – Stanley Cup drought ends
The New York Rangers edged the Vancouver Canucks 3-2 in Game 7 at Madison Square Garden to win their first Stanley Cup in 54 years, the longest championship drought in NHL history. Long-suffering NY hockey fans were relieved with goals from Brian Leetch, Adam Graves and Mark Messier, while goaltender Mike Richter put on a stellar performance. Leetch became the first American-born player to be awarded the Conn Smythe Trophy as playoff MVP.

1999 – Olympic scandal
In a pre-Olympic scandal, veteran administrator Phil Coles resigned from the board of the Sydney Olympics event organising committee (SOCOG), accused of allowing dossiers on IOC members to fall into the hands of Salt Lake City Winter Games officials. It was a delicate issue, the bid organisers having been charged with overzealous lobbying to gain IOC approval.

1999 – Garry who?
Star Australian Rules footballer Garry Hocking was re-named 'Whiskas' by deed poll. The marketing ploy linked Hocking to a cat food brand, as well as the Geelong Football Club, whose nickname is 'The Cats'. The cash-strapped club was paid over $100,000.

2003 – Wilkinson England's saviour
Jonny Wilkinson kicked England to a 15-13 victory over NZ in a one-off Test at Westpac Stadium in Wellington. Wilkinson landed 4 penalties and a drop goal, whilst his All Black counterpart Carlos Spencer had an off night with the boot, kicking 2 penalties and converting Doug Howlett's try. Spencer had the chance to win the game for the home side, but missed with a penalty attempt late in the game.

2005 – Powell – fastest man on earth
Twenty-two-year-old Jamaican Asafa Powell broke the world 100m record with a 9.77, during the Super Grand Prix meeting in Athens. Powell shaved 0.01 seconds off Tim Montgomery's record of 9.78.

2007 – Crosby youngest MVP
Nineteen-year-old Pittsburgh captain Sidney Crosby became the NHL's youngest MVP since Wayne Gretzky, polling 91 first-place votes and 1,225 points in a survey of Professional Hockey Writers' Association members. Gretzky won his first of 9 Hart Trophies when he was 5 months younger than Crosby. Crosby led the NHL with 120 points (36 goals, 84 assists), earning him the Ross Trophy and making him seventh in NHL history to win the Hart, Pearson and Ross.

BIRTHDATES
1951	American golfer DANNY EDWARDS
1952	Basketball Hall of Fame coach PAT SUMMITT
1956	American golfer FRED FUNK
1961	NBA centre SAM PERKINS
1969	German tennis player STEFFI GRAF
1969	Canadian NHL defenseman ÉRIC DESJARDINS
1977	South African Test batsman BOETA DIPPENAAR
1977	England rugby union flanker JOE WORSLEY
1984	Russian swimmer YURY PRILUKOV

Garry Hocking changed his name by deed poll to a cat food brand for seven days.

Formula 1 driver James Hunt died of a heart attack on this day, in 1993.

⑮ JUNE

1938 – NY baseball at night ends in history
In the first-ever major league night game to be played in New York, Cincinnati Reds left-hander Johnny Vander Meer became the only pitcher ever to throw consecutive no-hitters. Four days earlier, the hard-throwing 23-year-old held the Boston Braves hitless. 38,748 attended Ebbets Field for the novelty of the inaugural night game, but witnessed history in Vander Meer's 6-0 win over the Brooklyn Dodgers, as he struck out 7 and walked 8 for the unique achievement.

1955 – Five centuries in an innings
A Test-record 5 individual hundreds from Colin McDonald (127), Neil Harvey (207), Keith Miller (109), Ron Archer (128) and Richie Benaud (121) highlighted Australia's 758 for 8 in the fifth Test against the West Indies in Jamaica, their highest Test total. Benaud's hundred came in just 78 minutes, and for the first time in Test history, 5 bowlers conceded 100 runs and a sixth (Garry Sobers) went for 99. Australia went on to win the match by an innings and 82 runs.

1968 – Catchpole chicken-winged
The brilliant international career of Australian halfback Ken Catchpole was cruelly brought to an end in a 27-11 defeat against New Zealand in Sydney. Catchpole was considered to be the premier halfback in world rugby, but appeared to be targeted by the All Black forward pack, and ripped a groin under a savage ruck. He was forced to retire after having played 27 Tests for the Wallabies.

1993 – Hunt dead at 45
Britain's 1976 World Formula 1 Drivers Champion James Hunt died aged 45 from a heart attack suffered at his Wimbledon home. In 92 Grand Prix starts, Hunt had gained 14 pole positions and won 10 races. After retiring, he became a controversial and entertaining commentator for the BBC, partnering Murray Walker.

2003 – Bentley wins at Le Mans
The classic motor brand Bentley won the Le Mans 24 Hour race for sports cars, for the first time in 73 years. The driving team of Tom Kristensen from Denmark, Englishman Guy Smith and Italian Renaldo Capello completed a record 377 laps of the 13.84km circuit. Bentley had returned to competing in the race in 2001, after a lapse of 71 years.

2011 – Thomas stars in Bruins' triumph
The Boston Bruins beat the Vancouver Canucks 4-0 in Game 7 in Vancouver, clinching the Stanley Cup. Thirty-seven-year-old Bruins goalie Tim Thomas held the Canucks to 8 goals in 7 finals games, winning MVP honors. He also won the Vezina Trophy. Thomas then set a new record for total post-season saves, surpassing Vancouver goalie Kirk McLean's 1994 total.

BIRTHDATES
1948   NFL coach MIKE HOLMGREN
1949   MLB manager DUSTY BAKER
1954   Australian swimmer BEV WHITFIELD – died 1996
1958   Baseball Hall of Fame first baseman WADE BOGGS
1959   Scottish soccer forward/analyst ALAN BRAZIL
1964   Danish soccer midfielder/manager MICHAEL LAUDRUP
1969   French tennis player CEDRIC PIOLINE
1969   German soccer goalkeeper OLIVER KHAN
1972   American golfer JUSTIN LEONARD
1972   MLB pitcher ANDY PETTITTE
1973   Norwegian soccer striker TORE ANDRÉ FLO
1980   Australian rugby union flanker DAVID LYONS
1984   MLB pitcher TIM LINCECUM

⑯ JUNE

1924 – Protea low
Chasing an imposing England total of 438 in the first Test at Edgbaston, South Africa collapsed to be dismissed for a dismal 30, equalling their lowest Test total. England captain Arthur Gilligan had the ridiculous figures of 6-7, and followed up with 5-83 in the second innings. South Africa salvaged some dignity in the defeat, with Bob Catterall making 120 in their second-innings 390.

1956 – Middlecoff edges Hogan
Ben Hogan fell just 1 stroke short of winning his fifth US Open at the Oak Hill CC in Rochester, New York, when Cary Middlecoff edged him by 1 stroke. Hogan had a chance to force a tie but missed a short par putt on the 17th hole.

1979 – Mick's mark
Australian rugby league centre Michael Cronin created a record for goals kicked in an Ashes Test, with 10 from 11 attempts, in Australia's 35-0 thrashing of Great Britain in Brisbane.

1996 – MJ's fourth MVP award
Michael Jordan became the first player to win the NBA Finals MVP 4 times, when he led the Chicago Bulls to an 87-75 win over the Supersonics, in Game 6 in Seattle. It was Jordan and the Bulls' fourth NBA Championship, and Jordan's first since returning from his 'retirement.' Dennis Rodman was dynamic on the boards in the clincher, with 19 rebounds, including tying a Finals single-game record with 11 offensive rebounds.

1999 – Greene quickest
American sprinter Maurice Greene set a new 100m world record with a 9.79 second run in Athens, equalling disgraced Canadian Ben Johnson's drug-assisted effort at the 1988 Seoul Olympics. Greene's mark beat the existing record of 9.84 seconds set by Donovan Bailey at the 1996 Atlanta Olympics.

2008 – Tiger's third Open
Tiger Woods won the US Open in a 19-hole playoff over Rocco Mediate, at Torrey Pines near San Diego,

Brilliant American sprinter Maurice Greene in action during 2005.

for his 14th career major title. One shot behind after a collapse, Woods birdied the 18th hole to force sudden death. Mediate put his tee shot in the bunker at no. 7 and bogeyed, whilst Woods, although inconvenienced by a knee injury, only needed a 2-putt par to win the Open for the third time.

BIRTHDATES
1906	Australian Test all-rounder ALAN FAIRFAX – died 1955
1927	England Test batsman TOM GRAVENEY
1941	English golfer TOMMY HORTON
1942	Italian motorcycle rider GIACOMO AGOSTINI
1946	NBA coach RICK ADELMAN
1949	Brazilian soccer midfielder CAJU
1951	Panamanian boxer ROBERTO DURAN
1960	Australian rugby league halfback PETER STERLING
1961	Australian Test opener ROBBIE KERR
1965	England rugby union winger CHRIS OTI
1966	Czech javelin thrower JAN ZELEZNY
1966	Australian surfer MARK OCCHILUPO
1966	French rugby union back rower OLIVER ROUMAT
1970	American golfer PHIL MICKELSON
1976	Ecuadorian soccer midfielder EDWIN TENORIO
1977	MLB pitcher KERRY WOOD
1984	Canadian NHL right wing RICK NASH

1954 – Rocky on points
In his third heavyweight title defence, Rocky Marciano beat former champion Ezzard Charles in a 15-round unanimous points decision at Yankee Stadium in New York. Three months later, at the same venue, Marciano saw off Charles' final challenge for the title; he knocked him out in 8 rounds when the champion was in danger of being stopped because of facial cuts.

1945 – Seven straight for Nelson
Byron Nelson birdied 5 of the last 6 holes to beat Harold 'Jug' McSpaden by 1 stroke in the Philadelphia Inquirer Invitational, his seventh consecutive PGA Tour win in his record 18-victory season.

1962 – 'Golden Bear' youngest Open winner
Twenty-two-year-old rookie Jack Nicklaus became the youngest US Open winner since Bobby Jones in 1923, when he beat Arnold Palmer by 3 strokes in a playoff at the Oakmont CC in Pennsylvania.

1999 – Best ODI ever
Australia and South Africa sensationally tied for the Cricket World Cup at Edgbaston in what has been labelled the greatest ODI in history. The match was tied at 213 and Australia went through to the final because of their superior run-rate in the earlier Super Six stage. In an unbelievable finish, with 2 balls to spare and 1 run required, Lance Klusener set off on a fateful run, only to find Allan Donald was less decisive, and was run out.

2007 – 30th La Liga title for Real
Real Madrid won the Spanish league title for the 30th time, with a 3-1 comeback win over Real Mallorca in Madrid. Former England captain David Beckham played his final game for Real and Brazilian star Roberto Carlos also played his final game at the Bernabéu, after 11 years, more than 500 games, 4 league titles and 3 European Cups.

2007 – Second Puma Open winner
Ángel Cabrera gave Argentina its first major championship in 40 years when he held off Tiger Woods and Jim Furyk by a stroke at the US Open at a brutal Oakmont CC in Pennsylvania. Cabrera shot a 1-under par final-round 69 for a total 5-over 285. The only other Argentine to win a major was Roberto De Vicenzo in the 1967 British Open at Hoylake.

2008 – 'Celts' nab 17th championship
The Boston Celtics won their 17th NBA title with a stunning 131-92 blowout of the LA Lakers in Game 6 in Boston. The Celtics' 39-point win surpassed the NBA record for the biggest margin of victory in a championship clincher (Boston beat LA 129-96 in Game 5, 1965). Boston's big 3 dominated as Kevin Garnett scored 26 points/14 rebounds, Ray Allen scored 26 and Finals MVP Paul Pierce added 17 as the Celtics wrapped up their first title since 1986.

2009 – 'Pudge' leads catchers
Houston Astros catcher Ivan Rodriguez became MLB's all-time leader in games caught, passing Carlton Fisk in a 5-4 defeat to the Texas Rangers at Arlington, Texas. It was Rodriguez's 2,227th game behind the plate.

2010 – Lakers rally for 16th title
The LA Lakers won their 16th NBA championship, dramatically rallying from a fourth-quarter deficit to beat the Boston Celtics 83-79 in a Game 7 classic at the Staples Centre in Los Angeles. Finals MVP Kobe Bryant scored 23 points to earn his fifth title with the Lakers.

BIRTHDATES
1881	Canadian boxer TOMMY BURNS – died 1955
1929	American sports writer BUD COLLINS
1930	England Test batsman BRIAN STATHAM – died 2000
1940	Pro Football Hall of Fame linebacker BOBBY BELL
1945	Belgian road cyclist EDDIE MERKX
1956	England Test spinner NICK COOK
1956	Scottish rugby prop IAIN MILNE
1958	French rugby union halfback/coach PIERRE BERBIZIER
1964	England Test wicketkeeper STEVE RHODES
1964	German swimmer MICHAEL GROSS
1965	American speed skater DAN JANSEN
1973	Indian tennis player LEANDER PAES
1980	American tennis player VENUS WILLIAMS
1981	Australian Test all-rounder SHANE WATSON
1988	Australian swimmer STEPHANIE RICE

⑱ JUNE

1941 – Louis connects with Conn
Heavyweight champion Joe Louis was severely tested by former light-heavyweight champion Billy Conn in front of 54,487 fans at the Polo Grounds in New York. Conn gave up 25½lbs to Louis but, after the 12th round, was ahead on 2 officials' cards. He then ignored corner instructions and reverted to slugging it out with the champion in the 13th round. The tactical change backfired and a hard right from Louis sent Conn sprawling for the full count.

1963 – Clay down, but not out
Britain's Henry Cooper put Cassius Clay on the canvas in the fourth round in their heavyweight bout at Wembley Stadium. Clay hit back to win by TKO in the fifth round in his final fight before successfully challenging for Sonny Liston's world heavyweight title the following year.

1983 – Dev-astating
Kapil Dev singlehandedly assured India's qualification for the World Cup semi-finals when he smashed 16 fours and 6 sixes for 175 not out, off 138 balls, against Zimbabwe at Tunbridge Wells. Kapil came to the crease with India at 9-4, and left at 226-8. Seven days later, the Indians were world champions..

1990 – Irwin Open champ at 45
At 45, Hale Irwin became the oldest US Open champion when he beat Mike Donald on the 19th hole of a playoff, at the Medinah CC in Illinois.

1995 – A bulldozer called Lomu
Towering All Black winger Jonah Lomu scored 4 bulldozing tries as New Zealand qualified for the Rugby World Cup final, with a 45-29 victory over England at Newlands in Cape Town. The All Blacks were upset 15-12 by South Africa in the final in Johannesburg.

2003 – Becks to Madrid
Spanish giants Real Madrid agreed to a fee of £24.5 million for England captain David Beckham to transfer from Manchester United. Beckham had helped United win 6 of its 8 league titles in 11 years, and the European Champions Cup in 1999.

British heavyweight fighter Henry Cooper during his 1963 title bout against Cassius Clay in London.

2005 – Ashraful attack
Mohammad Ashraful smashed 100 off 101 balls, spearheading Bangladesh to one of the biggest upsets in cricket history, a 5-wicket one-day international win over Australia in Cardiff.

2006 – Ogilvy's Open
Geoff Ogilvy took advantage of a Phil Mickelson meltdown to become the first Australian since David Graham in 1981 to win the 106th US Open at Winged Foot, New York. Ogilvy finished at 5-over 285, the first time a US Open champion finished over par since Andy North in 1978. It was the highest score by a winner since Hale Irwin shot 287, also at Winged Foot in 1974.

BIRTHDATES
1924	Basketball Hall of Fame forward GEORGE MIKAN – died 2005
1939	Baseball Hall of Fame outfielder LOU BROCK
1946	Italian soccer midfielder/manager FABIO CAPELLO
1963	NFL defensive end BRUCE SMITH
1966	Canadian figure skater KURT BROWNING
1969	Australian yachtsman CHRIS NICHOLSON
1975	Canadian NHL right wing MARTIN ST. LOUIS
1980	NFL tight end ANTONIO GATES
1983	Australian rugby league fullback BILLY SLATER
1983	Australian rugby league hooker CAMERON SMITH
1986	French tennis player RICHARD GASQUET
1990	Romanian gymnast SANDRA IZBASA

⑲ JUNE

1914 – Six of the best for Harry
Forty-four-year-old Harry Vardon won his sixth British Open Championship, beating his great rival J. H. Taylor by 3 strokes, at Prestwick in Scotland.

1938 – Three wins for Azzurri
Italy successfully defended their World Cup title when they beat Hungary 4-2 in the final in Paris. The match was virtually over when the Italians led 3-1 at halftime, with 2 goals from Colaussi and 1 from Piola. Though Sárosi pulled 1 back for the Hungarians, Piola sealed the win for Italy, 8 minutes from time. It was Italy's third consecutive major trophy, after they also won the intervening Olympics.

1984 – Bulls 'stuck' with Jordan!
The Chicago Bulls selected the sport's greatest prize when they drafted Michael Jordan with the third pick in the NBA Draft – even though they didn't really want him. They had been coveting a big centre, specifically the University of Houston's 7ft tall Akeem Olajuwon, but he was taken by the Houston Rockets in the first selection. The Portland Trail Blazers then took Kentucky centre Sam Bowie and the Bulls were 'stuck' with Jordan, who went on to become arguably the best player in history, with 10 NBA scoring titles and leading the Bulls to 6 championships!

1992 – Larry's last challenge
Evander Holyfield beat former champion Larry Homes in a unanimous points decision to retain the undisputed heavyweight title in Las Vegas. It was Holmes' final challenge for the undisputed title.

2002 – First-class records
English county teams Surrey and Glamorgan combined for a massive aggregate 867 in a C&G Trophy match at the Oval. Ally Brown pounded 268 from 160 balls in Surrey's 438-5, both world first-class records. Glamorgan replied with 429.

2005 – US GP farce
Michael Schumacher won a farcical US F1 Grand Prix at Indianapolis, when only 6 cars competed following the withdrawal of all teams who drove on Michelin tyres. Following several tyre failures in practice, Michelin advised its 7 customer teams that tyres provided for the race were not safe to use for the entire race.

2006 – Panthers earn first Cup
In ice hockey, Cam Ward made 22 saves and Frantisek Kaberle netted the game-winning goal in the second period, as the Carolina Hurricanes captured both Game 7 and their first Stanley Cup with a 3-1 victory over the Edmonton Oilers at RBC Centre in Raleigh.

2011 – McIlroy magnificent
Four days of flawless golf ended with 22-year-old Rory McIlroy of Northern Ireland polishing off a 2-under 69 at Bethesda, shattering US Open records. The combined scores of the last 10 US Open champions were 14-under par; McIlroy was 16-under. He finished 8 shots ahead of Australian Jason Day, whose score of 8-under 276 would have been enough to win 26 of the last 30 US Opens. Among the major records McIlroy set were the 72-hole record at 268; the 54-hole record at 199; the 36-hole record at 131; most under par at any point at 17-under ; and quickest to reach double digits under par – 26 holes when he got to 10-under in the second round. McIlroy tied Tiger Woods' record for a 6-shot lead at the halfway point, and joined Lee Janzen (1993) and Lee Trevino (1968) as the only players to post all 4 rounds in the 60s.

BIRTHDATES
1903	Baseball Hall of Fame first baseman LOU GEHRIG – died 1941
1903	England Test captain WALTER HAMMOND – died 1965
1958	Russian NHL right wing SERGEI MAKAROV
1960	American golfer PATTI RIZZO
1962	English tennis player JEREMY BATES
1963	England rugby union winger RORY UNDERWOOD
1967	Norwegian cross-country skier BJØRN DÆHLIE
1971	England soccer striker CHRIS ARMSTRONG
1972	American soccer striker BRIAN McBRIDE
1978	German NBA forward DIRK NOWITZKI
1979	Brazilian soccer midfielder KLÉBERSON
1982	Russian NHL left wing ALEXANDER FROLOV
1982	Australian motor-cycle rider CHRIS VERMEULEN

⓴ JUNE

1910 – First three-way Open playoff
In the first three-way playoff in US Open Championship history, Alex Smith beat his brother Macdonald by 6 strokes and Johnny McDermott by 4 at the St Martins Club at the Philadelphia Cricket Club in Chestnut Hill, Pa.

1958 – Lock destroys Kiwis
England spinner Tony Locke finished with sensational match figures of 9-27, as New Zealand, following-on after being dismissed in their first innings for 47, were bundled out for 74 in the second Test at Lord's.

1980 – Boxing classic
Panama's Roberto Duran took the WBC welterweight title from 'Sugar' Ray Leonard in Montreal, in a famous unanimous points decision. After a torrid struggle, 2 judges had Duran winning by just 1 point, and the other by two. It was the first bout of a famous trilogy, with Leonard regaining the title 5 months later with an eighth-round TKO in New Orleans, and winning the WBC super middleweight crown 9 years later in a unanimous points decision in Las Vegas.

1982 – Six Le Mans wins for Ickx
Jacky Ickx of Belgium teamed with Englishman Derek Bell in a Porsche 956 for his record sixth victory in the Le Mans 24 Hour race for sports cars. It was the third time Ickx and Bell had won the classic event. Ickx had previously won in 1969, 1975–77 and 1981.

1987 – All Blacks take inaugural World Cup
New Zealand's All Blacks beat France 29-9 in front of 48,350 fans in Auckland to win rugby union's inaugural World Cup. The David Kirk-captained All Blacks scored 3 tries to 1, and super-boot fly half Grant Fox kicked 4 penalties, a conversion and a field goal.

2006 – MVP Wade lifts Heat to first NBA title
Dwyane Wade led the Miami Heat to their first NBA title, as they beat the Mavericks 95-92 in Dallas for an historic 4-2 comeback series win. The Heat became just the third team to overcome a 0-2 deficit to win the Finals, joining the 1969 Boston Celtics and 1977 Portland Trail Blazers. The win marked a return to the top for Pat Riley, who won his fifth title as a coach.

2009 – Spain claim football record
Spain set a football world record by beating South Africa 2-0 in Bloemfontein for their 15th consecutive win. Goals from David Villa and Fernando Llorente were enough to tame the Confederations Cup hosts and ensure the European champions top their group. The win surpassed the old record of 14 held by Australia, Brazil and France.

BIRTHDATES
1915	Australian AFL midfielder DICK REYNOLDS – died 2002
1921	Ecuadorian tennis player PANCHO SEGURA
1925	American tennis player DORIS HART
1935	Pro Football Hall of Fame quarterback LEN DAWSON
1939	England rugby union flanker BUDGE ROGERS
1939	Indian Test fast bowler RAMAKANT DESAI – died 1998
1953	Mexican tennis player RAUL RAMIREZ
1954	England Test batsman ALLAN LAMB
1956	English soccer midfielder/manager PETER REID
1969	Portuguese soccer defender/manager PAULO BENTO
1969	American tennis player MALIVAI WASHINGTON
1971	New Zealand rugby union flanker JOSH KRONFIELD
1975	Spanish tennis player JOAN BALCELLS
1978	England soccer midfielder FRANK LAMPARD JR
1979	American golfer CHARLES HOWELL III

New Zealand rugby captain David Kirk gets some help from winger John Kirwan in scoring a try during the All Blacks 29-9 win over France in Auckland in 1987.

㉑ JUNE

1954 – Landy breaks Bannister mile mark
Australian John Landy broke Roger Bannister's world mile record when he ran a time of 3:57.9 seconds in Turku, Finland. Bannister had broken the elusive 4-minute mile barrier 46 days earlier at Oxford University, with a time of 3:59.4. Later that year, both men broke 4 minutes in the so-called 'Mile of the Century' at the Empire Games in Vancouver, with Bannister prevailing.

1964 – Bunning double
Philadelphia's Jim Bunning became the first pitcher to record no-hitters in both the National and American Leagues with a 6-0 road-victory over the New York Mets.

1970 – Brazil's World Cup
In the culmination of the soccer World Cup, Brazil beat Italy 4-1 in front of 107,412 fans at the Azteca Stadium in Mexico City. After the score was locked 1-1 at halftime, Brazil took over with a brilliant brand of flashy football. In scoring Brazil's third goal, Jairzinho became the only player to have scored in every round of a World Cup.

1970 – Rare English win at Open
Tony Jacklin became the first Englishman in 50 years to win the US Open when he mastered windy conditions and the rugged Hazeltine National layout in Chaska, Minnesota. Jacklin was the only player in the field to finish under par, with a 7-under 281, 7 strokes ahead of Dave Hill.

1975 – Windies win first World Cup
The West Indies won the inaugural Cricket World Cup when they beat Australia by 17 runs at Lord's. Sent into bat, Windies' skipper Clive Lloyd (102) and Rohan Kanhai (55) held the innings together to finish 291-8. Dennis Lillee took 5 for 48. The Australians were dismissed for 274 in an innings that featured 4 run outs. Ian Chappell top-scored with 62, whilst Keith Boyce captured 4 for 50.

2002 – Top jockey Eddery second all-time
Pat Eddery won his 4,494th race to move ahead of

John Landy leading Roger Bannister during the mile race at the 1954 Vancouver Empire Games. Bannister took the lead in the final lap to win the race, with both men breaking the 4-minute barrier.

Lester Piggott on the jockeys winning list in Britain. Only Sir Gordon Richards was ahead of Eddery, on 4,870 wins. Eddery finished his riding career with 4,632 winners.

2009 – Pakistan win Twenty20 title
Three months after an horrific terrorist attack on Sri Lankan cricketers in Lahore, Pakistan, the two teams met in the final of the World Twenty20 at Lord's. Mohammad Amir dismissed Sri Lanka's Tillakaratne Dilshan for a duck in the first over and Abdul Razzaq picked out Sanath Jayasuriya for 17. Shahid Afridi led the 139-run chase with a masterful unbeaten 54.

BIRTHDATES
1937	England Test batsman JOHN EDRICH
1942	NFL coach DAN HENNING
1947	NFL coach WADE PHILLIPS
1948	Australian boxer LIONEL ROSE – died 2011
1952	New Zealand Test captain JEREMY CONEY
1956	MLP pitcher RICK SUTCLIFFE
1959	NBA forward TOM CHAMBERS
1960	English golfer BARRY LANE
1965	Australian rugby union front rower EWEN McKENZIE
1972	South African/New Zealand netball shooter IRENE VAN DYK
1978	American golfer MATT KUCHER

㉒ JUNE

1938 – 'Brown Bomber' smashes German
In one of the most famous fights in history, Joe Louis took just over 2 minutes to exact revenge on the German World Heavyweight Champion Max Schmeling in front of 70,000 fans at Yankee Stadium. Two years earlier, Schmeling had knocked out Louis for the title. The re-match was an anti-climax, with Louis knocking Schmeling to the canvas 3 times. After just 124 seconds, he was counted out.

1962 – Total bases record to Musial
Forty-one-year-old St Louis Cardinals cleanup hitter Stan Musial passed Ty Cobb's record for most total bases when he connected twice in the second inning in Philadelphia. In his 21st year in the majors, Musial reached 5,864 bases with a home run and a 2-run single.

1965 – Trueman exits Test arena
Outstanding England fast bowler Fred Trueman's 67-Test career came to an end as England scored a 7-wicket win over New Zealand at Lord's. He finished the match with 2 for 40 and 0 for 69, taking his career wickets total to 307, which remained a world record for just over 10 years until beaten by the West Indian spinner Lance Gibbs.

1994 – Houston's first title
For the first time, a team representing Houston captured a major league sports championship, when the NBA Rockets beat the visiting New York Knicks, 90-84, in Game 7 of the Finals. Seven-foot centre Hakeem Olajuwon was dominant with 25 points, 10 rebounds and 7 assists, taking out the Finals MVP award to add to his regular season MVP recognition.

2006 – World record RL fee for Fielden
Bradford Bulls star front rower Stuart Fielden joined Wigan after the English Super League club shattered the rugby league transfer record to sign the Great Britain international on a 4-year deal. Wigan paid the Bulls almost £450,000 ($1.13 million) to sign Fielden. The deal comfortably eclipsed the previous transfer record, set in the 1990s, when Wigan paid Widnes £440,000 for winger Martin Offiah.

Outstanding England fast bowler Fred Trueman in 1949.

2009 – Mickelson five times unlucky
Unlikely major champion Lucas Glover snapped a 4-year victory drought by winning the 109th US Open at wind-whipped Bethpage Black, NY, forcing compatriot Phil Mickelson to come in second for a record fifth time. Glover struggled to a 3-over 73 final round to finish 72 holes on 4-under par 276, defeating Mickelson, Ricky Barnes and David Duval by 2 strokes.

BIRTHDATES
1903   Baseball Hall of Fame pitcher CARL HUBBELL – died 1988
1914   England soccer defender BERT SPROSTON – died 2000
1947   Basketball Hall of Fame forward PETE MARAVICH – died 1988
1959   Irish jockey MICHAEL KINANE
1962   Basketball Hall of Fame forward CLYDE DREXLER
1963   Spanish soccer forward EMILIO BUTRAGUEÑO
1966   Australian cyclist DEAN WOODS
1971   NFL quarterback KURT WARNER
1972   Australian jockey DAMIEN OLIVER
1978   NFL cornerback CHAMP BAILEY
1978   English auto racer DAN WHELDON – died 2011
1979   French road cyclist THOMAS VOECKLER
1984   American golfer DUSTIN JOHNSON

㉓ JUNE

1894 – IOC kicks off
The International Olympic Committee was founded at the Sorbonne, Paris, on the initiative of Baron Pierre de Coubertin.

1922 – American first as Hagan wins Open
Walter Hagen became the first American to win the British Open when he beat George Duncan and Jim Barnes by a stroke to take the title at Royal St George's in Sandwich, England. It was the 29-year-old Hagan's first of 4 Open victories in the 1920s.

1947 – Protea bowlers punished
England batsmen Bill Edrich and Denis Compton, in the midst of a purple patch in form, punished a modest South Africa attack at Lord's, with a record 370-run partnership. Compton compiled 208 and Edrich 189. At the time, it was the highest partnership for the third wicket in a Test. It remains England's highest for the third wicket, and is the highest for any wicket in a Lord's Test.

1968 – Nicklaus couldn't win in Canada
New Zealand left-hander Bob Charles beat Jack Nicklaus by 2 strokes to win the Canadian Open at St Georges in Toronto, Ontario. It was the second of what would be an incredible 7 runner-up finishes by 'The Golden Bear', in an event he would never win.

1969 – Joe 'smoking'
In *The Ring* magazine's Fight of the Year, Joe Frazier scored an eighth-round TKO win over Jerry Quarry at New York's Madison Square Garden. Referee Arthur Mercante stopped the fight after round 7 because of a bad cut to Quarry's eye. Eight months later, Frazier won the world heavyweight title with a fifth-round TKO of Jimmy Ellis.

1979 – Windies repeat in World Cup
The West Indies retained their World Cup crown with an emphatic 92-run victory over England at Lord's. Sent in to bat, the Windies scored 286 for 9 with Vivian Richards scoring a regal 138, including 11 fours and 3 sixes. Geoff Boycott and Mike Brearley laid a platform with an opening partnership of 129, but the home side crumbled from 183-2 to be dismissed for 194. Giant Windies fast bowler Joel Garner wrapped the innings up in blistering style, with a spell of 5 for 4 in 11 balls.

1989 – Curtis' back-to-back Opens
Curtis Strange became the first player in 38 years to win back-to-back US Open titles, at the Oak Hill CC in Rochester, New York. Strange's 278 total beat Welshman Ian Woosnam, Chip Beck, and Mark McCumber by a stroke. The great Ben Hogan had been the last to achieve the feat (1950–51).

1996 – Lindwall passes away at 74
One of the great all-rounders in Test cricket history, Australian Ray Lindwall, died aged 74. In 61 Tests, Lindwall took 228 wickets with a career best 7-38 against India in 1947–48. He hit 2 Test centuries and five 50s at 21.15. Lindwall was also an accomplished rugby league footballer, having played 31 first grade matches for St George in the NSWRL premiership.

2003 – First Twenty20 ton
In the first season of England's Twenty20 Cup, Ian Harvey smashed an unbeaten 100 off 50 balls for Gloucestershire, as they chased Warwickshire's 134 in just 13.1 overs at Edgbaston. Seventy-six of Harvey's runs came off boundaries (in 17 balls). It was the first first-class Twenty20 century in history.

BIRTHDATES
1904	South African Test spinner QUINTIN McMILLAN – died 1948
1910	American golfer LAWSON LITTLE – died 1968
1916	England Test captain SIR LEONARD HUTTON – died 1990
1932	New Zealand Test batsman BOB BLAIR
1940	American sprinter WILMA RUDOLPH – died 1994
1941	England soccer defender KEITH NEWTON – died 1998
1955	French soccer midfielder/manager JEAN TIGANA
1957	Zimbabwe Test captain DAVE HOUGHTON
1963	British golfer COLIN MONTGOMERIE
1965	Australian golfer PETER O'MALLEY
1971	Canadian NHL goalie FÉLIX POTVIN
1972	French soccer midfielder ZINEDINE ZIDANE
1975	British golfer DAVID HOWELL
1976	French soccer midfielder PATRICK VIEIRA
1979	NFL running back LaDAINIAN TOMLINSON
1980	West Indian Test batsman RAMNARESH SARWAN
1980	Italian tennis player FRANCESCA SCHIAVONE

㉔ JUNE

1913 – Taylor's fifth Open
J. H. Taylor joined rivals and members of 'The Great Triumvirate,' Harry Vardon and James Braid, as a five-time British Open champion, winning by 8 strokes from Ted Ray at Hoylake in England.

1952 – Arcaro's 3,000th winner
Thirty-six-year-old Eddie Arcaro became the first American-born jockey to ride 3,000 winners when he guided 2 winners at Arlington Park in Chicago. No. 3,000 was a 2-year-old filly, Ascent. Arcaro had already ridden 5 Kentucky Derby winners, including Triple Crown champions Whirlaway and Citation. At the time, he was the world's leading jockey in money earned by his mounts, at $12,265,455. 2 jockeys, Johnny Longden and Gordon Richards, had won more than 4,000 races, but they were both born in England.

1960 – First Protea hat-trick
In his second and final Test match, fast bowler Geoff Griffin became the first South African to take a Test hat-trick. He dismissed M. J. K. Smith, Peter Walker and Fred Trueman with consecutive deliveries, but was no-balled for throwing 11 times, having previously been called 17 times in a tour match. He played no further Tests and did not bowl again on the tour. It remains the only Test match hat-trick taken at Lord's.

1974 – India's low score
Following on, 327 runs behind England in the second Test at Lord's, India made just 42 for their lowest ever Test score, and the lowest ever total in a Lord's Test. England quicks Geoff Arnold and Chris Old grabbed 4 for 19 and 5 for 21 respectively.

1995 – No tries; Springboks win
South Africa took its first Rugby World Cup with a 15-12 win over New Zealand in front of a crowd of 63,000 at Ellis Park, Johannesburg. In the first World Cup final to be devoid of tries, Proteas' fly-half Joel Stransky kicked 3 penalties and 2 field goals to out-duel his All Black counterpart Andrew Mehrtens, who landed 3 penalties and a field goal. The match ushered in a new professional era in rugby, with the IRB signing huge broadcasting deals with satellite television barons.

2000 – Wilkinson on target
Fly-half Jonny Wilkinson scored all of England's points, as the tourists beat South Africa 27-22 in Bloemfontein. Wilkinson landed an England rugby Test record of 8 penalties and a drop goal.

2001 – Career grand slam for Karrie
Twenty-seven-year-old Australian Karrie Webb became the youngest female player to complete a career grand slam when she won the LPGA Championship with a 14-under 270, beating Laura Diaz by 2 strokes at the DuPont CC in Wilmington, Delaware. Webb is 1 of only 6 women to win each 1 of the 4 major tournaments during their career. The others were Julie Inkster, Pat Bradley, Mickey Wright, Louise Suggs and Annika Sörenstam.

BIRTHDATES
1895	American boxer JACK DEMPSEY – died 1983
1911	Italian auto racer JUAN MANUEL FANGIO – died 1995
1912	England Test batsman/commentator BRIAN JOHNSTON – died 1994
1924	Australian rugby league winger BRIAN BEVAN – died 1991
1931	American golfer BILLY CASPER
1933	Basketball Hall of Fame guard SAM JONES
1938	New Zealand rugby union prop KEN GRAY – died 1992
1941	Australian Test fast bowler GRAHAM McKENZIE
1951	Australian sprinter RAELENE BOYLE
1954	Australian tennis player MARK EDMONDSON
1955	American golfer LOREN ROBERTS
1960	American golfer JULI INKSTER
1964	American NHL defenseman GARY SUTER
1972	Australian road cyclist ROBBIE McEWEN
1978	Argentine soccer midfielder JUAN ROMÁN RIQUELME

Jockey Eddie Arcaro, pictured in formal attire, in 1957.

1932 – Sarazen wins Open at 'home'

British Open champion Gene Sarazen won his second major title of the year when he won the US Open at Fresh Meadow in Flushing, New York. Sarazen posted a final-round 4-under 66 to beat Bobby Cruickshank and Philip Perkins by 3 strokes. Curiously, between 1925 and 1931, Sarazen was the head professional at the club, and never carded a score lower than 67 while employed at the course.

1934 – 14 wickets in a day

England spinner Hedley Verity took 14 for 80 in one day, in Australia's only defeat in a Lord's Test match during the 20th century. Verity's match figures were an incredible 15 for 104 with 7 for 61 and 8 for 43. Verity died as a prisoner of war in Italy in 1943, aged 38.

1948 – 'Brown Bomber' goes out swinging

Joe Louis knocked out Jersey Joe Walcott in 11 rounds at New York's Madison Square Garden in the record 25th and final defence of his world heavyweight title. 'The Brown Bomber' retired from the ring 8 months later, whilst Walcott went on to beat Ezzard Charles for the title in 1951, before losing it to Rocky Marciano in 1952.

1968 – Bonds Snr hits grand slam on debut

San Francisco Giants outfielder Bobby Bonds (father of home run king Barry Bonds) became the first player in the 20th century to hit a grand slam in his major league debut in a 9-0 home win over the LA Dodgers.

1969 – Longest Wimbledon match

Pancho Gonzales and Charles Pasarell played the then longest match in Wimbledon history as their 5-set, first-round encounter encompassed 2 days. The 41-year-old Gonzales prevailed 22-24, 1-6, 16-14, 6-3, 11-9 in a match that lasted a record 5 hours and 12 minutes over a total of 112 games. The first 2 sets took 2 hours 20 minutes, but the match was interrupted by bad light and resumed the following day.

1978 – Kempes clinches Cup for Argentina

Striker Mario Kempes played the game of his life as Argentina claimed the World Cup, with a 3-1 win over the Netherlands after extra time in Buenos Aires. The score was locked at 1-1 at fulltime after Kempes had put the home team ahead and the substitute Nanninga equalised for the Dutch. Kempes then scored the winning goal after a dazzling run in overtime, and made the clincher for Bertoni.

1982 – World Cup fix

West Germany beat Austria 1-0 in a contrived World Cup result at Gijón in Spain. Both teams needed that exact result to advance, eliminating Algeria, whose protest failed. All final group games have since been played concurrently.

1983 – First Indian World Cup

India scored a sensational upset win over the West Indies at Lord's to claim the World Cup for the first time. Sent into bat, India was dismissed for 183 in 54.4 overs, Kris Srikkanth top-scoring with only 38. The Windies were bundled out in 52 overs for a meagre 140. Vivian Richards blazed 33 off 28 balls and wicket keeper Jeff Dujon chipped in for 25. Man of the match Mohinder Amarnath, and Madan Lal each captured 3 Windies' wickets for the unlikely victors.

BIRTHDATES

1942	Basketball Hall of Fame forward WILLIS REED
1949	French auto racer PATRICK TAMBAY
1953	Australian Test batsman IAN DAVIS
1955	England Test spinner VIC MARKS
1960	Australian soccer player CRAIG JOHNSTON
1960	French rugby union number 8 LAURENT RODRIGUEZ
1963	Canadian NHL centre DOUG GILMORE
1964	English auto racer JOHNNY HERBERT
1964	Australian Test wicketkeeper PHIL EMERY
1966	Nigerian NBA centre DIKEMBE MUTOMBO
1968	South African rugby union prop ADRIAN GARVEY
1971	Australian rugby union centre/analyst ROD KAFER
1973	England international midfielder JAMIE REDKNAPP
1975	Spanish tennis player ALBERT COSTA
1976	Welsh rugby union/league utility back IESTYN HARRIS
1981	Swiss ski jumper SIMON AMMANN

㉖ JUNE

1937 – Hutton's scratchy debut
England batting icon Len Hutton made an uninspiring Test debut against New Zealand at Lord's. The 21-year-old Hutton was thrown in, and made 0 and 1, each time falling to Kiwi pace bowler Jack Cowie. Hutton retained his place in the team and scored 100 in his next innings. He went on to score 6,971 runs at 56.67 in 79 Tests.

1954 – World Cup goal glut
The highest-scoring match in the final stages of soccer's World Cup was played in the quarter-finals in Lausanne, when Austria beat host-nation Switzerland, 7-5. Hat-tricks were scored by Theodor Wagner for Austria and Josef Hügi for the Swiss, with all 12 goals coming in the space of an hour.

1959 – Johansson in fight upset
Twenty-six-year-old Swedish challenger Ingemar Johansson stunned a big Yankee Stadium crowd by knocking out heavyweight champion Floyd Patterson and capturing the title. A booming right knocked Patterson to the canvas in the third round. It was the first of 7 knockdowns before referee Ruby Goldstein stopped the fight at 2:03 of the round. The pair fought twice more, with Patterson knocking out Johansson on both occasions.

1976 – Fijians walk off in referee protest
In international rugby union, the Fijian team staged a famous 15-minute walk-off during the third Test against Australia, at the Sydney Cricket Ground. The tourists were incensed with the performance of the Australian referee and left the field in protest. On the Fijians' return, the Wallabies won the match, 27-17.

1995 – Cork's dream debut
Fast bowler Dominic Cork took 7 for 43 in the West Indies second innings at Lord's, the best figures in history by an English Test debutant. Cork's performance and 2 majestic innings (61 and 90) from Robin Smith inspired England to a memorable 72-run victory.

2003 – Foe dies during international
Cameroon midfielder Mark Vivien Foé became the first

Ingemar Johansson knocks out Floyd Patterson in 1959.

football player to die during an international match, when he collapsed during the FIFA Confederation's Cup semi-final against Columbia in Lyon in France. The 28-year-old Foe was later found to have a heart condition. Whilst playing for Manchester City, he was the last player to score at the old Maine Road ground.

2003 – LeBron drafted by home-town Cavs
The much-maligned Cleveland Cavaliers hit the jackpot when they selected Akron high school forward LeBron James first in the NBA draft. The signing of James completely turned the club's fortunes around, with an increase in attendances, sponsorship, merchandising and on-court results. James moved to the Miami Heat in 2010, winning his first NBA title in 2012.

BIRTHDATES
1936 Basketball Hall of Fame guard HAL GREER
1946 Swedish rally driver PER EKLUND
1951 Australian Test all rounder GARY GILMORE
1952 Scotland soccer defender GORDON McQUEEN
1961 American road cyclist GREG LeMOND
1962 NBA forward JEROME KERSEY
1964 Finnish rally driver TOMMI MÄKINEN
1966 NHL goalie KIRK McLEAN
1967 American thoroughbred trainer TODD PLETCHER
1968 NFL tight end SHANNON SHARPE
1968 Italian soccer defender PAOLO MALDINI
1971 Italian motor-cycle rider MAX BIAGGI
1974 MLB shortstop DERECK JETER
1980 NFL quarterback MICHAEL VICK
1987 French soccer midfielder SAMIR NASRI

㉗ JUNE

1939 – Headley's 2 tons at Lord's
West Indian batting great George Headley became the first to score 2 centuries (106 and 107) in a Lord's Test, although the Windies still went down by 8 wickets to England. It was the second time in his career that Headley had made 2 centuries in a Test, making him only the second batsman (after Herbert Sutcliffe) to do so.

1985 – White's unconventional tennis attire
American Anne White flouted Wimbledon convention by wearing a full-length, skin-tight white body stocking during her match against Pam Shriver on an outside court. Play was suspended by the weather at one-set all, and when they reappeared the next day, White was dressed in more orthodox gear. She lost the match. Tournament officials deemed the body stocking 'not traditional tennis attire' and had asked the Californian to wear something a little more demure.

1999 – Hawk does a 900
Tony Hawk pulled off the Holy Grail of skateboarding – the 900 (two-and-a-half spins) – on the Summer X Games' vertical ramp. Once considered unattainable, much like the 4-minute mile, Hawk attempted the trick for 10 years, finally nailing it on his 11th try.

2006 – Roger perfect on grass
Roger Federer won his record 42nd straight grass-court match, beating Richard Gasquet 6-3, 6-2, 6-2 to open his bid for a fourth consecutive Wimbledon championship. The top-ranked Federer broke the record he had shared with Björn Borg.

2006 – Ronaldo World Cup scoring leader
With one swift move in the fifth minute of Brazil's 3-0 drubbing of Ghana, superstar Brazilian striker Ronaldo overtook Germany's Gerd Müller as the greatest scorer in World Cup history. Ronaldo's strike helped spoil Ghana's scrappy debut and put defending champion Brazil into its fourth straight quarterfinal.

2004 – Drag accident leads to change
Drag racer Darrell Russell was fatally injured during eliminations at the Sears Craftsman Nationals in Madison, Illinois, when his dragster broke up and burst

American tennis player Anne White in her controversial body suit during the 1985 Wimbledon Championships.

into flames after he crossed the finish line. He died of severe head injuries. After the accident, the NHRA required all top fuel cars to switch to improved tyres; to use fuel with reduced nitro-methane content (90% to 85%); to change the maximum rear wing angle; and to install a thick titanium shield on the portion of the roll-cage behind the driver's head.

BIRTHDATES
1913   American pocket billiards player WILLIE MOSCONI – died 1993
1918   American swimmer ADOLF KEIFER
1924   England Test spinner BOB APPLEYARD
1939   Australian Test fast bowler NEIL HAWKE – died 2000
1945   French golfer CATHERINE LACOSTE
1967   Australian rugby union hooker PHIL KEARNS
1967   Canadian synchronised swimmer SYLVIE FRECHETTE
1969   Ukrainian figure skater VIKTOR PETRENKO
1977   Spanish soccer forward RAÚL
1980   English Test batsman KEVIN PIETERSEN
1983   South African Test fast bowler DALE STEYN
1985   Russian tennis player SVETLANA KUZNETSOVA

1915 – Trumper's premature passing

Australia's legendary batsman, Victor Trumper died of Bright's Disease at the age of 37. The popular Trumper was considered Australia's finest batsman of the era. His funeral was attended by an estimated 250,000. In 48 Tests, Trumper scored 3,163 runs at 39.04 with a career high of 214.

1958 – Mickey does it easy for first Open title

Mickey Wright with a 2-under par total 290, won her first of 4 US Open titles, beating Louise Suggs by 5 strokes at Forest Lake in Detroit, Michigan.

1971 – Ali conviction overturned

By an 8-0 vote, the US Supreme Court overturned Muhammad Ali's 1967 conviction for draft evasion. He went on to regain the title against George Foreman in the famous 'Rumble in the Jungle'.

1990 – Football off-side rule amended

In a much-debated decision, FIFA made the first change in football's off-side law in 65 years. The new rule stated that players who were level with defenders when a through ball was played would be on-side.

1997 – 'Hungry' Tyson's infamous disqualification

In one of boxing's most infamous fights, Mike Tyson was disqualified in the third round in Las Vegas for biting off part of champion Evander Holyfield's ear during a clinch. Referee Mills Lane penalised Tyson 2 points and let the fight continue, after an incident that left Holyfield minus part of his right ear. In another clinch, Tyson took a bite of Holyfield's left ear. Lane then disqualified Tyson. Holyfield underwent a 20-minute procedure to have his right ear repaired.

2005 – Bogut first Australian top NBA draft pick

The Milwaukee Bucks selected 213cm centre Andrew Bogut first in the NBA Draft. He became the first Australian, and only the second foreigner after Yao Ming, to be no. 1 pick.

2006 – First European #1

Twenty-year-old, 7ft tall Italian Andrea Bargnani became the first European chosen with the top selection in the NBA draft, when he was named by the Toronto Raptors.

2007 – Allen traded

Just prior to the much anticipated choice of Texas star Kevin Durant at number 2 in the NBA draft, the Seattle SuperSonics pulled of a stunning trade, sending seven-time All-Star Ray Allen to Boston. In return for their most popular player and leading scorer, the SuperSonics received Wally Szczerbiak, Delonte West and the no. 5 pick. Boston selected Georgetown forward Jeff Green for Seattle with the fifth pick. Portland chose imposing Ohio State centre Greg Oden first overall.

2008 – Celebrity wedding

Former American tennis star Chris Evert married Australian golfer Greg Norman at Paradise Island in the Bahamas. A host of celebrities attended the lavish wedding, including former US presidents Bill Clinton and George Bush Sr., singer Gwen Stefani and her husband Gavin Rossdale, Kenny Loggins, comedian Chevy Chase and tennis players Lleyton Hewitt, Anna Kournikova, Lindsay Davenport, Martina Navratilova and Ms Evert's former fiancé Jimmy Connors. The union lasted 15 months.

BIRTHDATES

1928	South African Test fast bowler PETER HEINE – died 2005
1931	American auto racer JUNIOR JOHNSON
1934	West Indian Test fast bowler ROY GILCHRIST – died 2001
1937	Canadian golfer GEORGE KNUDSON – died 1989
1945	Scottish boxer KEN BUCHANAN
1946	England rugby union winger DAVID DUCKHAM
1949	MLB coach DON BAYLOR
1960	NFL quarterback JOHN ELWAY
1964	New Zealand rugby union centre BERNIE McCAHILL
1965	South African rugby union flanker TIANN STRAUSS
1970	Pakistan Test spinner MUSHTAQ AHMED
1971	French soccer goalkeeper FABIEN BARTHEZ

1903 – Anderson takes another Open in a playoff

Scotland's Willie Anderson became the first to win the US Open twice in playoffs. Anderson beat David Brown 82 to 84 at the Baltusrol GC in Springfield, New Jersey after the pair tied at 307 in regulation.

1950 – Football World Cup shock

In one of the biggest upsets in World Cup history, England was beaten 1-0 in their second preliminary match in Belo Horizonte, Brazil, by a United States team made up of part-timers. The winning goal was scored by Joe Gaetjens in the 39th minute. England then lost 1-0 to Spain and failed to qualify for the final round.

1950 – Windies claim first Test in England

In a landmark day for West Indian cricket, they won their first Test in England, a 326-run thrashing at Lord's. Youthful spinners Sonny Ramadhin and Alf Valentine starred for the Windies, both having played only 2 first-class matches before the tour. Valentine's match figures were 7 for 127 – his 75 maidens are still a Test record. Ramadhin captured 11 for 152. The Windies batting hero was Clyde Walcott, with a slashing innings of 168.

1958 – Brazil score first 'away' World Cup win

Brazil became the first country to win the World Cup outside their own continent when they dominated home team Sweden 5-2 in Stockholm. The Brazilians played spectacular football, a 17-year-old Pelé stealing the show in the second half, with 2 goals. In a celebrated move in the 56th minute Pelé collected possession on his chest in the penalty area, flicked the ball over the head of a defender, rounded the man and, the ball having bounced once, shot Brazil into a match-winning 3-1 lead.

1986 – Argentina edge Germany for World Cup

Argentina beat a brave German team 3-2 in the World Cup final, in front of a crowd of 114,600 at the Azteca Stadium in Mexico City. The Argentines looked to be cruising to an easy victory after Brown and Valdano gave them a 2-0 lead 11 minutes into the second half. The Germans levelled, however, through Rummenigge and Völler, before Diego Maradona manufactured the winner for Argentina via midfielder Burruchaga.

1990 – Two no-no's on same day

For the only time in the modern era, Oakland's Dave Stewart and the Dodgers' Fernando Valenzuela became the only 2 pitchers to record no-hitters on the same day. Both veterans had been struggling, losing 5 of their last 6 starts. In Toronto, though, Stewart overcame a shaky start, walking the first 2 batters before retiring 26 straight in a 5-0 win. In Los Angeles, Valenzuela had little trouble in a 6-0 gem against the St Louis Cardinals.

1996 – Burke points scoring machine

Matt Burke created an Australian individual rugby union Test record of 39 points in the Wallabies' 74-9 thrashing of Canada in Brisbane. Burke scored 3 tries, and kicked 9 conversions and 2 penalties.

2007 – Teldulkar's 15,000

Sachin Tendulkar became the first player to reach 15,000 runs in one-day internationals, while steering India to a 6-wicket win over South Africa, in the Future Cup in Belfast. Tendulkar thumped 93, sharing an opening partnership of 134 with Saurav Ganguly (42), to help India reach their target of 227 with 5 balls to spare, levelling the three-match series 1-1.

BIRTHDATES

1890	Scottish golfer WILLIE McFARLANE – died 1961
1936	Baseball Hall of Fame slugger HARMON KILLEBREW – died 2011
1939	Australian Test fast bowler ALAN CONNOLLY
1949	NFL offensive tackle/broadcaster DAN DIERDORF
1954	Brazilian soccer midfielder JÚNIOR
1954	MLB pitcher/coach RICK HONEYCUTT
1958	Portuguese marathon runner ROSA MOTA
1965	England Test fast bowler PAUL JARVIS
1966	Canadian darts player JOHN PART
1968	NHL right wing THEO FLEURY
1973	American road cyclist GEORGE HINCAPIE

㉚ JUNE

1911 – Vardon takes fifth Open
Harry Vardon defeated Arnaud Massy for his record-tying fifth British Open Championship at Royal St George's. Vardon and Arnaud Massy tied on 303 after regulation. Vardon won when Massy conceded on the 35th hole of the 36-hole playoff. J. H. Taylor and James Braid were the other members of 'The Great Triumvirate' to win 5 Opens.

1916 – Evans' Open record
Amateur Charles Evans Jr posted a record total of 286 to win the US Open at Minikahda in Minneapolis, Minnesota. The mark stood for 20 years. Evans also won the US Amateur title later that year. He won 54 tournaments over a career spanning 4 decades. He retained his amateur status and used his golf earnings to establish the Charles Evans Jr Trust in 1928, to assist caddies.

1929 – Jones' third Open in a playoff
Bobby Jones won his third US Open title, when he comfortably beat Al Espinosa 141-164 in a 36-hole playoff at the Winged Foot Club's West Course in Mamaroneck, New York. Jones took two 7s in his final round and had to hole a 12ft putt on the last green to tie Espinosa at 6-over par 294 and earn the playoff.

1930 – 'The Don' likes Lords
Australian batting master Don Bradman smashed a glorious 254 in his first Test innings at Lord's. He led Australia to 6-720, the highest total in any first-class match at the famous ground and, ultimately, to a 7-wicket victory. Lord's was not Bradman's favourite ground – his career average there was a relatively paltry 78.

1994 – Harding banned for life
The US Figure Skating Association stripped Tonya Harding of her national title and banned her for life for her role in the attack on rival Nancy Kerrigan, a month before the Winter Olympics. The board decided Harding knew about the January 6 attack before it had happened. It was the first time an official body had come to that conclusion in the case.

2002 – Ronaldo brace earns Brazil World Cup
The genius of Ronaldo was the deciding factor as Brazil beat Germany 2-0 in the World Cup final in Yokohama, Japan. Ronaldo's 2 second-half goals gave the Brazilians their fifth FIFA World Cup championship and firmly put the ghosts of the France '98 final (when they were thrashed 3-0 by the home team) to rest.

2006 – Sox errorless streak ends
The Boston Red Sox played their 17th consecutive errorless game, a 5-2 loss to the Marlins in Miami, which stopped their winning streak at 11. The accomplishment established a new big league mark, surpassing the Cardinals, who played 16 straight error-free games in 1992.

BIRTHDATES
1927	American tennis player SHIRLEY FRY
1933	England Test captain MIKE SMITH
1938	American middle distance runner BILLY MILLS
1941	South African Test fast bowler PETER POLLOCK
1951	American golfer ROGER MALTBIE
1965	England soccer defender GARY PALLISTER
1965	NBA guard MITCH RICHMOND
1966	American boxer MIKE TYSON
1969	Sri Lankan Test opener SANATH JAYASURIYA
1975	German auto racer RALF SCHUMACHER
1985	American swimmer MICHAEL PHELPS

Ronaldo during the 2002 World Cup Final against Germany.

JULY

1 JULY

1920 – Lenglen Wimbledon sweep
France's Suzanne Lenglen won the women's singles, women's doubles, and mixed doubles titles to become the first female player to win 3 championships at Wimbledon in the same year. In her second consecutive singles title, Lenglen beat Dorothea Chambers 6-3, 6-0. She went on to win 5 straight Wimbledon singles championships (1919–23).

1961 – Third Open win for Wright
Twenty-six-year-old American Mickey Wright won her third US Open in 4 years, despite a disastrous second-round 8-over par 80 at the Baltusrol Golf Club's Lower Course in Springfield, New Jersey. On a challenging layout, Wright's total of 5-over 293 was good enough to beat Betsy Rawls by 6 strokes, with Ruth Jessen a stroke further back in third place. Wright played the final 36 holes in 3-under 141, to pull away from the field.

1973 – Crampton passes $1m mark
Australian Bruce Crampton became the first golfer from outside the US to win more than $1 million in his career by finishing fourth at the Western Open. At the time Crampton was the fifth overall to crack the mark.

1974 – NFL strike
Players went on strike after negotiations with team owners broke off in a stalemate. The players sought a bigger voice in free agency on the expiration of contracts. Their major gripe was the 'Rozelle Rule', which allowed NFL commissioner Pete Rozelle to set compensation when a player played out his option and signed with another team. The owners refused to participate in collective bargaining, believing they could win in court. By August 11, there was still no agreement and in frustration, the players called off the strike and took the battle to the courts. The ensuing standoff lasted through the 1974–76 seasons.

1996 – Incredible all-rounder
Hampshire's Kevan James became the only man to take 4 wickets in 4 balls – and then score a century in a first-class match. In a tour match at Southampton, India had stormed to 207 for 1. James then removed

French tennis player Suzanne Lenglen in action in 1922.

Vikram Rathour, Sachin Tendulkar, Rahul Dravid and Sanjay Manjrekar in consecutive balls. The tourists declared at 362 for 5. James' bowling figures were 5 for 74. He then went on to compile 103 in the Hampshire first innings of the drawn match.

BIRTHDATES
1941	Canadian Hockey Hall of Fame right wing ROD GILBERT
1942	Canadian NHL coach DOUG CARPENTER
1954	American golfer MIKE REID
1956	MLB executive BRIAN SABEAN
1961	American sprinter CARL LEWIS
1964	French rugby union halfback/coach BERNARD LAPORTE
1966	American tennis player PATRICK McENROE
1976	Dutch soccer forward PATRICK KLUIVERT
1976	Dutch soccer striker RUUD van NISTELROOY
1977	Canadian NHL right wing JEROME IGINLA
1982	Swedish tennis player JOACHIM JOHANSSON
1989	Australian auto racer DANIEL RICCIARDO

② JULY

1938 – Wills-Moody claims eighth Wimbledon
American Helen Wills Moody took advantage of an injury to her rival Helen Jacobs to win the Wimbledon women's singles title for an unprecedented eighth time. Jacobs suffered a strained right Achilles tendon with the score tied at 4-4 in the first set and didn't win another game in the final. Moody won 6-4, 6-0.

1963 – Giants 1-0 in the 16th
Willie Mays homered to end an incredible game between the San Francisco Giants and the Milwaukee Braves in the 16th inning at Candlestick Park. Future Hall of Fame starting pitchers, the Giants' Juan Marichal and the Braves' Warren Spahn fought out a scoreless 15 innings. Mays' homer gave SF a memorable 1-0 victory.

1967 – Lacoste's Open records
Twenty-two-year-old French player Catherine Lacoste became the first foreign, first amateur, and youngest winner of the US Women's Open at The Homestead, Virginia. She won by 2 shots from Beth Stone and Susie Maxwell with a score of 294. Lacoste's father, Rene, was the well-known French tennis champion.

1989 – Moody's Senior Open
Orville Moody beat Frank Beard by 2 strokes at the Laurel Valley GC, Ligonier, Pa to win the US Senior Open, 2 decades after capturing the US Open.

1994 – Football retribution?
Columbian soccer defender Andrés Escobar was gunned down outside a Medellin nightclub after a heart-breaking World Cup loss to the United States 10 days earlier. During the game, Escobar inadvertently nudged the ball into his own net, a gaffe that contributed to the 2-1 American upset. Escobar was shot 12 times in the face by 3 men.

2006 – ODI record opening stand
Sri Lanka's Upul Tharanga and Sanath Jayasuriya's compiled a world record ODI opening stand of 286 as Sri Lanka scored a crushing 8-wicket victory in the fifth ODI against England at Headingley. Set an imposing 322, Sri Lanka finished on 324 for 2 with 12 overs

Colombian defender Andrés Escobar during the 1994 World Cup.

to spare. Jayasuriya, playing a world record-equalling 362nd ODI, scored 152 and Tharanga 109.

2006 – Michael magnificent in the US too
Michael Schumacher won the US Formula 1 Grand prix for the fifth time and became the first driver in any series to win 5 races at the Indianapolis Motor Speedway. The seven-time F1 world champion won for the fourth straight time on the 2.6 mile, 13-turn road course at the famed Brickyard. The only other drivers to win as many as 4 at Indy are A. J. Foyt, Al Unser and Rick Mears, all in the Indianapolis 500 and Jeff Gordon in the Allstate 400.

2008 – SuperSonics move to OKC
The ownership group reached a final settlement, with the city of Seattle allowing the former SuperSonics NBA franchise to move to Oklahoma City. An overall payment of about $75 million was made to Seattle to get out of the final 2 years of a lease at KeyArena.

BIRTHDATES
1904	French tennis player JEAN RENÉ LACOSTE – died 1996
1937	American auto racer RICHARD PETTY
1957	Canadian Pro wrestler BRET HART
1964	MLB outfielder JOSE CANSECO
1964	Scottish rugby union/league fullback ALAN TAIT
1969	England rugby union flanker TIM RODBER
1971	Scottish rugby union halfback BRYAN REDPATH
1975	Australian swimmer DANIEL KOWALSKI
1975	South African rugby union winger STEFAN TERBLANCHE
1979	Canadian NHL centre JOE THORNTON
1979	American auto racer SAM HORNISH JR

❸ JULY

1920 – First American to win Wimbledon
Bill Tilden became the first American to win the Wimbledon men's singles title when he beat Australian defending champion Gerald Patterson in 4 sets. Tilden used his famous array of sliced shots to perfection to take advantage of Patterson's vulnerable backhand and win the match 2-6, 6-3, 6-2, 6-4.

1954 – Courageous Zaharias
Only 14 months after undergoing radical surgery for colon cancer, Babe Zaharias won the US Women's Open at the Salem CC in Massachusetts. In her comeback tournament, Zaharias finished with 291, 12 strokes ahead of Betty Hicks. Her courage earned her the respect of her colleagues and the admiration of the American public. She died in 1956.

1966 – Pitcher's 2 Grand Slams
Atlanta Braves pitcher Tony Cloninger became the first National League player to hit 2 grand slams in a game and is the only pitcher to ever accomplish the feat. Cloninger also knocked in another run to set a modern major league record for pitchers with 9 RBI during the Braves' 17-3 rout of San Francisco.

1994 – Tennis great passes away
One of the greats of tennis, Lew Hoad died in Fuengirola, Spain aged 59. In all, Hoad won 5 Grand Slam singles titles and was a member of the Australian team that won the Davis Cup 4 times between 1952 and 1956. He was inducted into the International Tennis Hall of Fame in Newport, Rhode Island in 1980.

2005 – Wimbledon hat-trick for Roger
Swiss world no. 1 Roger Federer won his third consecutive Wimbledon singles title when he beat American Andy Roddick 6-2, 7-6, 6-4.

2007 – Swiss back-to-back
Alinghi retained the America's Cup with a thrilling photo finish victory over *Team New Zealand*, squeaking across the finish line 1 second ahead to take the best-of-9 series 5-2 off the waters of Valencia in Spain. The Swiss joined the United States and New Zealand as having successfully defended their titles in yachting's

Wimbledon champ Roger Federer.

most prestigious race. *Alinghi* swept defending winner *Team New Zealand* in Auckland in 2003.

2010 – Lucky 13 for Serena
Serena Williams captured her 13th Grand Slam title when she overpowered 21st seeded Russian Vera Zvonareva 6-3, 6-2 in a one-sided Wimbledon final. Williams added to the Wimbledon titles she won in 2002–3 and 2009.

BIRTHDATES

1911	England Test batsman JOE HARDSTAFF JR – died 1990
1916	Basketball Hall of Fame coach JOHN KUNDLA
1940	American swimmer LANCE LARSON
1947	Dutch soccer forward ROB RENSENBRINK
1947	American swimmer MIKE BURTON
1950	New Zealand Test fast bowler EWEN CHATFIELD
1951	New Zealand Test all-rounder SIR RICHARD HADLEE
1952	Pakistan Test batsmen WASIM RAJA – died 2006
1954	England rugby union fly-half LES CUSWORTH
1964	American surfer TOM CURREN
1966	MLB outfielder MOISÉS ALOU
1967	MLB executive BRIAN CASHMAN
1970	Finnish NHL right wing TEEMU SELÄNNE
1976	Zimbabwe Test fast bowler HENRY OLONGA
1980	Indian Test spinner HABHAJAN SINGH
1980	South African swimmer ROLAND MARK SCHOEMAN
1984	Irish road cyclist NICOLAS ROCHE
1987	German auto racer SEBASTIAN VETTEL
1988	New Zealand soccer defender WINSTON REID

④ JULY

1919 – 'Mauler' takes heavyweight title
Jack Dempsey captured the world heavyweight title when he demolished champion Jess Willard in 3 rounds in Toledo, Ohio. In a brutal exhibition, Dempsey knocked Willard down 7 times in the first round, breaking his jaw with one of the first punches of the bout. Willard, with both eyes closed, 4 teeth missing, his nose smashed and 2 cracked ribs, failed to come out for the fourth round. Dempsey was 5in shorter and 58lbs lighter than the giant 6ft 6in, 245lb Willard.

1987 – Six on the trot for Martina
Martina Navratilova defeated Steffi Graf 7-5, 6-3 to claim her record sixth consecutive Wimbledon singles title. In all, Navratilova won the singles crown at Wimbledon 9 times (1978–9, 1982–7, 1990). Graf went on to beat Navratilova in 3 sets in the following 2 finals and win 7 Wimbledon titles in her career (1988–9, 1991–3, 1995–6).

1999 – Six-woman playoff
South Korean defending champion Se Ri Pak rolled in a 3-metre birdie putt on the first extra hole of the Jamie Farr Kroger Classic to win the most crowded playoff in LPGA history. Pak was joined by Australians Karrie Webb and Mardi Lunn, Sweden's Carin Koch and Americans Sherri Steinhauer and Kelli Kuehne in the playoff after the group had finished on 8-under 276.

2001 – Goalie record fee
Italian Serie A club Juventus signed Italian international goalkeeper Gianluigi Buffon from Parma for a fee of £32.5 million. The transfer fee was a world record for a goalkeeper.

2004 – Portugal's Greek tragedy
Greece scored a major upset over host nation Portugal, winning the European Championship final 1-0 in Lisbon. Charisteas grabbed a 57th minute winner to give Greece its first-ever major tournament trophy. The victory made them the biggest pre-tournament outsiders (80-1) to win a major international football event.

2005 – NFL innovator Stram passes away
Coaching legend Hank Stram died aged 82 of complications from diabetes. Stram coached the Kansas City Chiefs to a Super Bowl win in 1970. He was known as an innovator, and was the first to wear a microphone in a Super Bowl.

2006 – ODI record total
Sri Lanka shattered the one-day world record by piling up 443-9 in their 195-run win over the Netherlands in Amstelveen. Chasing the Dutch total of 248, Sanath Jayasuriya hit 157 off 104 balls and Tillakaratne Dilshan 117 not out as they beat South Africa's record of 438-9 against Australia set in 2006.

2009 – McNair shot dead
Four-time Pro-Bowl quarterback Steve McNair was shot multiple times and the body of a 20-year-old woman was found dead with him in a downtown condominium in Nashville, Tennessee. McNair led the Tennessee Titans to within a yard of forcing overtime in Super Bowl XXXIV, which they lost 23-16 to the St Louis Rams in 2000.

2009 – Williams' double
Serena Williams wrapped up a 7-6, 6-2 victory over her sister, five-time champion Venus, for a third Wimbledon singles championship and an 11th major title overall. The sisters later successfully defended their doubles title with a 7-6, 6-4 win over Australians Samantha Stosur and Rennae Stubbs.

BIRTHDATES
1918 American auto racer JOHNNIE PARSONS – died 1984
1918 England Test spin bowler ALEC BEDSER – died 2010
1922 Indian Test spinner GHULAM AHMED – died 1998
1926 Argentine/Spanish soccer forward ALFREDO DI STÉFANO
1928 Italian soccer forward GIAMPIERO BONIPERTI
1929 NFL coach/owner AL DAVIS – died 2011
1948 French auto racer RENE ARNOUX
1951 Australian tennis player JOHN ALEXANDER
1959 England Test batsman JAN BRITTIN
1962 American tennis player PAM SHRIVER
1963 French Tennis player HENRI LECONTE
1972 New Zealand Test batsman CRAIG SPEARMAN

⑤ JULY

1907 – No Englishmen on Wimbledon dias
Australian businessman Norman Brookes became the first non-British player and left-hander to win the Wimbledon singles title. Brooks beat Arthur Gore 6-4, 6-2, 6-2 in the final.

1957 – Graveney's famous double century
England's Tom Graveney carved out a famous 258 in the drawn third Test against the West Indies at Trent Bridge but was denied victory by Frank Worrell's unbeaten 191 and Collie Smith's 168.

1958 – Thomson's fourth Open win
Australian Peter Thomson won his fourth British Open Golf title in 5 years, beating Welshman David Thomas by 4 strokes, 139-143 in a 36-hole playoff at Royal Lytham & St Annes. Thompson had won 3 consecutive Open titles 1954–6 and had to wait until 1965 to capture his fifth and final Championship at Royal Birkdale.

1975 – Ashe with 'feeling'
Arthur Ashe became the first African-American to win the Wimbledon men's singles crown when he beat defending champion Jimmy Connors in 4 sets in the final. In a match laced with feeling, Ashe scored a famous 6-1, 6-1, 5-7, 6-4 triumph. Two weeks earlier, Connors had issued a $5 million libel suit against Ashe for his criticism of Connors' refusal to join the US Davis Cup team. Connors had previously filed 3 other suits for a total of $20 million against the Association of Tennis Professionals, of which Ashe was President.

1980 – Borg takes 5
Björn Borg won his fifth consecutive Wimbledon singles title in an epic encounter with volatile American John McEnroe. The 24-year-old Swede won the match 1-6, 7-5, 6-3, 6-7, 8-6. The fourth set tie break went for over 22 minutes, producing 34 contested points, a record for a Wimbledon final.

1997 – Hingis a youthful winner
Martina Hingis, at age 16, became the youngest Wimbledon winner in 110 years when she beat Jana Novotná 2–6, 6–3, 6–3 in the women's final.

2008 – Williams' double Wimbledon act
Venus Williams beat sister Serena 7-5, 6-4 for her second consecutive Wimbledon singles title and seventh major overall. It was also Venus' fifth Wimbledon singles Championship. The sisters then teamed to win their seventh Grand Slam and third Wimbledon doubles title, beating Lisa Raymond and Samantha Stosur 6-2, 6-2.

2009 – 'Fed Express' claims Slam record
Roger Federer won his record 15th Grand Slam title, outlasting Andy Roddick for his sixth Wimbledon championship in a match that went to 30 games in the final set. Federer served a career-high 50 aces and overcame the resilient American 5-7, 7-6, 7-6, 3-6, 16-14 to break the record of major titles he shared with Pete Sampras.

BIRTHDATES
1879	American tennis player DWIGHT DAVIS – died 1945
1910	New Zealand runner JACK LOVELOCK – died 1949
1923	Australian jockey GEORGE MOORE – died 2008
1929	Australian boxer JIMMY CARRUTHERS – died 1990
1929	England Test spinner TONY LOCK – died 1995
1943	French rugby union fullback PIERRE VILLEPREUX
1952	German soccer midfielder/manager ULI HOENEß
1954	New Zealand Test opener JOHN WRIGHT
1954	Basketball Hall of Fame forward/coach ALEX ENGLISH
1955	Australian tennis player PETER McNAMARA
1956	NFL receiver JAMES LOFTON
1965	Welsh soccer midfielder/actor/analyst VINNIE JONES
1966	Italian soccer striker/manager GIANFRANCO ZOLA
1969	Canadian NHL left wing JOHN LeCLAIR
1975	Japanese tennis player Ai SUGIYAMA
1977	German tennis player NICHOLAS KIEFER
1979	French tennis player AMÉLIE MORESMO
1982	Croatian alpine skier JANICA KOSTELIC

❻ JULY

1907 – Billiards marathon
Tom Reece took 5 weeks to compile the highest break recorded in a match, a huge 499,135, which he completed at Soho Square in London. Reece's 'cradle' cannon scoring method was banned after his feat.

1931 – Playoff format change for Open
The playoff format of the US Open reverted to 18-holes after Billy Burke and George Von Elm took 72 extra holes at the Inverness Club in Toledo, Ohio. Burke won the second 36-hole playoff by a stroke.

1957 – First African-American Wimbledon win
Twenty-nine-year-old Althea Gibson became the first African-American to win a Wimbledon singles title when she beat compatriot Darlene Hard 6-3, 6-2 in the final. The pair then teamed to win the women's doubles title, defeating Mary Hawton and Thelma Long 6-2, 6-1.

1933 – Inaugural All-Star game
NY Yankees slugger Babe Ruth was the star attraction at the inaugural All-Star game in Chicago. The event was labelled 'The Game of the Century' and was held in conjunction with the World's Fair. Ruth did not disappoint, with a 2-run homer in the third inning of the American League's 4-2 victory over the National League before 49,200 fans at Comiskey Park.

1997 – Twin tons to Waugh
Australia's Steve Waugh became the first batsman in 50 years to score twin centuries in an Ashes Test against England at Old Trafford. Australia was 1-0 down in the series and 160 for 7 – but Waugh kept them alive with a brilliant 108. He then frustrated England with a ruthlessly drawn out 116 on a difficult pitch.

2000 – Hammers shell out for Moore
West Ham United paid a record £1.8 million for 79 items once belonging to former captain Bobby Moore. Amongst the memorabilia were Moore's 1966 World Cup medal, and his FA Cup and European Cup Winners Cup medals. Moore made a record 642 League and Cup appearances for West Ham and earned 108 caps for England.

2005 – London's Games
London beat Paris 54 votes to 50 for the right to host the 2012 Summer Games as IOC nations voted in Singapore. London had not hosted the Games since 1948, while Paris was frustrated with a third failed bid in 20 years.

2007 – Celebrity wedding
NBA Finals MVP Tony Parker married *Desperate Housewives* star Eva Longoria in a civil ceremony in Paris, the prelude to a star-studded weekend wedding bash. The couple divorced in 2011.

2008 – Nadal new Wimbledon king
Rafael Nadal ended Roger Federer's five-year reign at Wimbledon, holding off a comeback by the champion from 2 sets down to prevail 6-4, 6-4, 6-7, 6-7, 9-7. The loss snapped Federer's All England Club winning streak at 40 matches. The rain-delayed match ended in near darkness after 4 hours, 48 minutes of play.

BIRTHDATES

1877	French golfer ARNAUD MASSY – died 1950
1886	Australian swimmer ANNETTE KELLERMAN – died 1975
1890	England Test batsman ANDREW SANDHAM – died 1982
1938	England Test batsman/broadcaster TONY LEWIS
1943	Australian swim coach TERRY BUCK – died 2005
1954	MLB second baseman WILLIE RANDOLPH
1956	American golfer JACK RENNER
1960	American golfer LAURI MERTEN-PETERSON
1960	American athlete VALERIE BRISCO-HOOKS
1977	South African Test fast bowler MAKHAYA NTINI
1980	Spanish NBA centre PAU GASOL SAEZ

Australian cricket captain Steve Waugh.

1948 – Paige signs

Forty-two-year-old starting pitcher Satchel Paige signed with the Cleveland Indians to become the first African-American to pitch in Major League Baseball. A Negro League ace for years, Paige was the fourth black player in the majors, following Jackie Robinson, Larry Doby and Roy Campanella. In his rookie season, he went 6-1 with a 2.48 ERA to help the Indians win the pennant, then the World Series.

1981 – 'Beefy' booted

England captain Ian Botham bagged a pair against Australia at Lord's and then resigned, after a reign that encompassed no wins in 12 Tests. Chairman of selectors Alec Bedser later announced Botham would have been sacked if he had not resigned. Such was the poor treatment handed out to the champion all-rounder by Lord's members that Botham vowed never to raise his bat to them again.

1985 – Boris arrives

Boris Becker became the youngest man to win the Wimbledon men's final when he beat Kevin Curren of South Africa 6-3, 6-7, 7-6, 6-4. The 17-year-old Becker was also the first unseeded player and the first German ever to win the coveted Wimbledon crown.

1990 – Martina first to nine

Martina Navratilova became the first player to win 9 Wimbledon singles titles when she thrashed Zina Garrison 6-4, 6-1 in a 75-minute final. The 33-year-old Navratilova improved her Wimbledon singles record to 99-9, and broke her tie with Helen Wills Moody who had also won 8 Championships.

2001 – Rolton record

Karen Rolton smashed an unbeaten 209 to set the record for highest score in a women's Test and become the first woman to score a Test double century at Headingley. Her teammate Michelle Gonsko had jointly shared the mark with New Zealand's Kirsty Flavell with innings of 204. Rolton held the record for a year before it was passed, first by India's Mithali Raj (214) and then by Pakistan's Kiran Baluch (243).

2003 – Tour day out for Aussies

For the first time, Australians were in possession of both the coveted yellow and green jerseys in the Tour de France. Brad McGee held the overall lead and Robbie McEwen the sprint lead after the second stage. Another Australian, Baden Cooke, won the second stage and went on to take the sprint title.

2006 – MLB Grand Slam record

With his fifth grand slam, Cleveland's Travis Hafner broke the MLB record for grand slams in a season. The Indians' designated hitter had shared the record with Al Rosen, who hit 4 bases full home runs for Detroit in 1951.

2012 – Andy makes Britain proud

Scottish tennis star Andy Murray won his first Wimbledon singles title with a hard-fought victory over no. 1 seeded Novak Djokovic 6-4 7-5 6-4. The 26-year-old ended the 77-year wait for a British men's singles champion.

BIRTHDATES

1906	Baseball Hall of Fame pitcher SATCHEL PAIGE – died 1982
1909	German tennis player GOTTFRIED von CRAMM – died 1976
1921	American boxer EZZARD CHARLES – died 1975
1933	New Zealand middle distance runner MURRAY HALBERG
1936	Swiss auto racer JO SIFFERT – died 1971
1944	British golfer TONY JACKLIN
1952	American boxer MIKE WEAVER
1954	Australian surfer SIMON ANDERSON
1959	Italian auto racer ALESSANDRO NANNINI
1960	Basketball Hall of Fame centre RALPH SAMPSON
1965	England rugby union centre JEREMY GUSCOTT
1967	Danish auto racer TOM KRISTENSEN
1968	MLB infielder CHUCK KNOBLAUCH
1969	Canadian Hockey Hall of Fame forward JOE SAKIC
1970	German road cyclist ERIK ZABEL
1972	American WNBA centre LISA LESLIE
1975	South African rugby union fly-half LOUIS KOEN
1976	New Zealand rugby union number 8 RON CRIBB
1980	American figure skater MICHELLE KWAN

1889 – Last bare-knuckle title fight

The last bare-knuckle world heavyweight title fight took place in Mississippi with the legendary John L. Sullivan beating Jake Kilrain over 75 brutal rounds. Kilrain, whose second was famed western lawman Bat Masterson, was worn down in the 2 hour, 16 minute bout. Thereafter, all official boxing was fought with gloves under Queensberry rules.

1912 – American 800m quadrella

The first 4 runners in the 800m final of the Stockholm Olympics were all American and all broke the World record. The winner was James 'Ted' Meredith whose time of 1:51.9 stood as a world best for the next 14 years. He continued running after the regulation finish to set a new world 880-yard record of 1:52.5.

1924 – Hubbard first black to win gold

William DeHart Hubbard became the first black athlete to win an individual Olympic gold medal when he won the long jump in Paris. The feat was overshadowed by compatriot Robert LeGendre, who had failed to qualify for the US long jump team. LeGendre set a world record of 25ft 5¾in while competing in the pentathlon.

1967 – King's Wimbledon treble

Billie Jean King completed an amazing Wimbledon sweep by winning the women's singles, doubles and mixed doubles titles. King scored a comfortable 6-3, 6-4 over Ann Hayden Jones for her second singles title. She then teamed with Rosie Casals to outlast Mario Bueno and Nancy Richey 9-11, 6-4, 6-2. She won the mixed doubles with Australian Owen Davidson, beating Ken Fletcher and Bueno 7-5, 6-2.

1984 – Easy Wimbledon for Mac

Temperamental American left-hander John McEnroe won his third Wimbledon singles crown in 4 years, beating countryman Jimmy Connors in the most one-sided Wimbledon men's final in 46 years. It took him only 80 minutes to dispose of two-time champion Connors 6-1, 6-1, 6-2.

1995 – Sweet 6 for Steffi

Steffi Graf grabbed her sixth Wimbledon singles title, taking out Arantxa Sánchez Vicario, 4-6, 6-1, 7-5 in the final.

2006 – Bryans crack Wimbledon

Top seeded American twins Bob and Mike Bryan broke through for their first Wimbledon doubles title. The Bryans beat Frenchman Fabrice Santoro and Nenad Zimonjic of Serbia 6-3, 4-6, 6-4, 6-2 in the final.

2010 – The LeBron Show

NBA superstar LeBron James announced on a live ESPN special that he would be playing for the Miami Heat for the 2010–11 season. The program drew high ratings, along with criticism for the prolonged wait until the actual decision and the spectacle of the show itself.

2010 – Goydos' 59

Paul Goydos needed just 22 putts to become the fourth player in PGA Tour history to shoot a 59, during the first round of the John Deere Classic. He rolled in 12 birdies at the par-71 TPC Deere Run. It was the first 59 on the PGA Tour since David Duval in 1999.

2012 – Fed wins seventh Wimbledon title

Roger Federer came back to beat Andy Murray 4-6, 7-5, 6-3, 6-4 indoors on Centre Court for a record-tying seventh singles championship at Wimbledon. The victory also increased Federer's record total to 17 major titles and clinched a return to the top of the ATP rankings after an absence of 2 years.

BIRTHDATES

1911	England Test fast bowler KEN FARNES – died 1941
1940	New Zealand rugby union flanker WAKA NATHAN
1952	Pro Football Hall of Fame linebacker JACK LAMBERT
1957	West Indian Test fast bowler CLYDE BUTTS
1960	Australian rugby league centre MAL MENINGA
1970	American tennis player TODD MARTIN
1971	Welsh rugby union fly-half NEIL JENKINS
1972	Indian Test cricket captain SOURAV GANGULY
1976	British sailor ELLEN MACARTHUR
1980	Irish soccer striker ROBBIE KEANE
1981	Russian tennis player ANASTASIA MYSKINA

9 JULY

1877 – Wimbledon's first Championship
The first Wimbledon Lawn Tennis Championship began at the All England Lawn tennis and Croquet Club with 22 competitors. The only title being played for, the men's singles, was won by Spencer Gore who beat his fellow Briton W.C. Marshall 6-1 6-2 6-4.

1908 – Swahn oldest Olympic winner
Swedish shooter Oscar Swahn became the oldest man to win an individual event at a modern Olympics when, at the age of 60, he beat 14 rivals to take out the single-shot running deer shoot in London.

1922 – 'Tarzan' breaks swim sprint barrier
Johnny Weissmuller became the first man to swim 100m in less than a minute at Neptune Beach, Alameda, in California. Swimming freestyle with a revolutionary 6-beat kick, he recorded a time of 58.6 seconds, smashing Duke Kahanamoku's 1920 world record by 1.8 seconds.

1966 – 'Golden Bear' has full set
Jack Nicklaus joined Gene Sarazen, Ben Hogan and Gary Player as the only players at that time to have won all 4 modern majors when he captured the British Open at Muirfield. Nicklaus birdied the par-5 17th hole to edge Doug Sanders and Dave Thomas with 2-under 282. Tiger Woods joined the 'club' when he won the British Open in 2000.

1982 – Botham's best
England all-rounder Ian Botham made his highest Test score, a swashbuckling 208 against India, in the third Test at the Oval. It was the then fastest-recorded Test double century, in terms of balls faced (220).

2001 – Cashed-up Real spend big
Spanish giants Real Madrid completed the signing of Juventus' French international Zinedine Zidane for a world record transfer fee of £45.8 million. The 4-year contract was worth £3.6 million per season.

2005 – Lions humbled
The British and Irish Lions slumped to their first series wipe-out in 22 years when beaten 38-19 in the third

American swimmer, and later star of the Tarzan movies, Johnny Weissmuller, in 1922.

Test in Auckland. Tana Umaga scored 2 tries as the All Blacks followed up their 21-3 win in Christchurch and 48-18 victory in Wellington.

2006 – Azzurri take fourth Cup
Italy won the FIFA World Cup for a fourth time, defeating France 5-3 on penalties in Berlin after the scores were level at 1-1 AET. In a famously ugly incident, Zinedine Zidane was banned for 3 games after being sent off for headbutting Italian defender Marco Materazzi.

2006 – Montoya switch
Columbian driver Juan Pablo Montoya announced he would leave the McLaren-Mercedes F1 team, re-uniting with team owner Chip Ganassi to drive in NASCAR's Nextel Cup Series. It was the first time in history a F1 driver had defected to NASCAR.

BIRTHDATES
1930	South African Test batsman ROY McLEAN – died 2007
1947	NFL running back/actor O.J. SIMPSON
1950	Italian tennis player ADRIANO PANATTA
1955	England soccer forward/manager STEVE COPPELL
1959	American pro wrestler KEVIN NASH
1964	American golfer SCOTT VERPLANK
1968	Italian soccer striker/manager PAOLO DI CANIO
1969	Indian Test spinner VENKATAPATHY RAJU
1970	NFL quarterback TRENT GREEN
1975	Welsh rugby union flanker CRAIG QUINNELL
1985	England soccer winger ASHLEY YOUNG

1924 – One hour – 2 gold for Nurmi
Finnish runner Paavo Nurmi put on an incredible exhibition to win 2 gold medals in just over an hour at the Paris Olympic Games. He easily won the 1,500m, and 55 minutes later he returned to the track and won the 5,000m. Nurmi won 5 gold medals at the games to follow the 3 that he won in Antwerp in 1920.

1926 – Jones' golf double
American amateur prodigy Bobby Jones became the first golfer to win the US Open and British Open in the same year when he captured the US Open at the Scioto Country Club in Columbus, Ohio. Jones finished with a 73 to win by a stroke over Joe Turnesa.

1951 – Famous Turpin upset
Underdog Englishman Randy Turpin scored a major upset by beating Sugar Ray Robinson in a 15-round decision to win the world middleweight title in London. It was only the second loss for Robinson in 133 professional bouts. Two months later, in the rematch in New York, he stopped Turpin in the 10th round.

1978 – Snooker icon passes away
Fifteen-time World Professional Snooker champion Joe Davis died aged 77. Davis was instrumental in the establishment of the first World Professional Championship in 1929, when he beat T.A. Dennis in the final, 20-11. He won the next 14 titles in a row, and is also credited with the first perfect break of 147 in 1955.

1984 – Gooden youngest All-Star
At 19 years, 7 months and 24 days, New York Mets starter Dwight Gooden became the youngest pitcher to appear in an All-Star game. He struck out 3 hitters in the sixth inning of the National League's 3-1 victory.

1990 – Hadlee's last hurrah
Champion Kiwi all-rounder Sir Richard Hadlee played his last day of Test cricket in the third Test against England at Edgbaston. His last ball produced a wicket in a fine final performance of 5 for 53 in the second innings to give the Kiwis a winning chance, but England won the match by 114 runs.

1991 – Proteas back from purgatory
After 21 years, the South African cricket team was readmitted into the International Cricket Council. This followed the end of the RSA government's policy of apartheid, a policy that led them to play only against the white nations (England, Australia, New Zealand), and field only white players.

2006 – WNBA record
Phoenix Mercury guard Diana Taurasi scored a WNBA record 47 points in a 111-110 3OT victory over the Houston Comets.

2007 – 10 straight MLB All-Star games to AL
The American League won its 10th consecutive All Star game in matches played to a decision with a 5-4 victory over the National League in San Francisco. The game was highlighted by Ichiro Suzuki's first inside-the-park home run in All-Star Game history. The only longer streak was when the NL took 11 straight 1972–82.

2012 – Giants' day out
San Francisco sluggers Melky Cabrera and Pablo Sandoval keyed a 5-run blitz against Justin Verlander in the first inning to power the NL to an 8-0 romp over the AL in the MLB All Star Game in Kansas City. Cabrera homered and won the MVP award; Sandoval got a triple, whilst Giants starter Matt Cain got the win in the NL's most lopsided All-Star victory.

BIRTHDATES
1899	Swiss road cyclist HEIRI SUTER – died 1978
1900	South African Test batsman BOB CATTERALL – died 1961
1921	American boxer JAKE LA MOTTA
1927	England soccer manager DON REVIE – died 1989
1935	New Zealand rugby union prop WILSON WHINERAY – died 2012
1940	Australian Test batsman KEITH STACKPOLE
1943	American tennis player ARTHUR ASHE – died 1993
1945	British tennis player VIRGINIA WADE
1949	Indian Test captain SUNIL GAVASKAR
1954	MLB outfielder ANDRE DAWSON
1960	Pro Football Hall of Fame running back ROGER CRAIG
1965	American golfer SCOTT McCARRON
1968	Algerian middle distance runner
1976	Brazilian soccer defender EDMÍLSON

⑪ JULY

1916 – Harness Racing legend dies
Dan Patch, arguably the greatest pacer ever, died aged 20 in Savage, Minnesota. Dan Patch was undefeated in races in his 10 years (1900–09) on the track. He set 9 world records and drew vast crowds throughout rural America. His best performance was his 1:55 mile at the Minnesota State Fair Track in 1906.

1930 – 'The Don' at his best
Australian batting icon Don Bradman hit the quickest double century in Test history when he smashed an unbeaten 309 in Australia's 458 for 3 on the first day of the third Test at Headingly. Bradman's triple-ton took just 214 minutes and he remains the only man to make 300 in a day.

1982 – Azzurri take Cup
In front of a crowd of 90,000 at Madrid's Bernabéu Stadium, Italy beat West Germany 3-1 to claim the Football World Cup. Rossi, Tardelli and Altobelli scored second-half goals to give the Italians a 3-0 lead, before Breitner replied for the Germans, becoming only the third player after Vava and Pelé to score in 2 World Cup finals.

1985 – Ryan first to 4,000 Ks
At age 38, Houston ace Nolan Ryan became the first pitcher to ever reach 4,000 strikeouts during the Astros' 4-3 win over the New York Mets. Ryan continued to pitch through the 1993 season and retired with a record 5,714 strikeouts on his way to the Hall of Fame.

2010 – Spain wins first World Cup
Spain won the Football World Cup title for the first time, with a 1-0 win over the Netherlands in extra time at Soccer City in Johannesburg. A 116th minute goal to Andrés Iniesta settled a grinding, niggly affair, decided by a goal that was shrouded in controversy. Referee Howard Webb blew 46 fouls and issued 12 yellow cards and 1 red in an ugly game. John Heitinga was sent off in the 109th minute for the Dutch whose strongarm tactics ultimately backfired.

2010 – All cream for Paula
Twenty-three-year-old Paula Creamer shed the title

Strikeout king Nolan Ryan pitching for the Texas Rangers. He now owns the club.

of being the best women's golfer to not win a major, with a 4-shot victory in the US Women's Open at Oakmont, Pa. Creamer made it look easy, finishing the tournament with a 3-under 281. Na Yeon Choi of South Korea shot a 5-under 66 to tie Suzann Pettersen of Norway for second place at 1-over 285.

2011 – South Koreans dominate Open
In an unprecedented all-South Korean playoff, 21-year-old So Yeon Ryu won the US Women's Open at the Broadmoor GC, Colorado Springs. Ryu first birdied the 18th, tying Hee Kyung Seo, then put on a shot-making clinic over a 3-hole playoff to win by 3 shots. It was Ryu's first major and her first LPGA victory.

BIRTHDATES
1928	American boxer CARL 'BO BO' OLSON – died 2002
1930	New Zealand Test spinner JACK ALABASTER
1950	Australian Test spinner JIM HIGGS
1953	American boxer LEON SPINKS
1955	American golfer MIKE DONALD
1963	England rugby union number 8 DEAN RICHARDS
1963	Canadian NHL defenseman AL MacINNIS
1965	England soccer striker TONY COTTEE
1972	New Zealand auto racer STEVEN RICHARDS
1975	Spanish soccer midfielder RUBÉN BARAJA
1978	Italian swimmer MASSIMILIANO ROSSOLINI
1990	Danish tennis player CAROLINE WOZNIACKI

1912 – First Olympic swim gold
Australian Fanny Durack won the first Olympic women's swimming gold medal with victory in the 100m at the Stockholm Games. The New South Wales Amateur Swimming Association only voted to send Durack and teammate Mina Wylie if they paid their own way to Sweden. Durack swam a winning time of 1:22.2 and Wylie took the silver medal.

1930 – Grand Slam looming
Bobby Jones captured the third leg of the Grand Slam, winning the US Open at Interlachen CC in Edina, Minnesota. Jones appeared to have the tournament won with 2 holes left but a double-bogey on the 17th cut his lead to one. On the final hole he sank a 40ft birdie putt for his fourth US Open title. Scotsman Macdonald Smith finished 2 strokes back in second place. Jones had already won the British Amateur at St Andrews and his third British Open at Hoylake. He went on to win his fifth US Amateur title and complete the Grand Slam.

1930 – Bradman's best
After scoring 309 on the first day of the third Test against England at Headingley, Don Bradman was dismissed for 334 creating an Australian Test record. The mark was equalled in 1998 when Mark Taylor declared Australia's innings closed at 599 for 4 when he was 334 not out during the second Test against Pakistan in Peshawar.

1975 – Gooch pair
England opener Graham Gooch became the first batsman to bag a pair in an Ashes Test in the 20th century when he was dismissed for 0 in both innings during the first Test against Australia at Edgbaston.

1996 – MJ highest paid NBA star
Michael Jordan agreed to a one-year contract with the Chicago Bulls, worth $25–30 million. The new salary made the NBA's 1995–96 MVP the highest paid player in the league, surpassing New York Knicks centre Patrick Ewing, who earned $18.7 million the previous season.

1998 – Pak sets LPGA records
South Korean rookie Se Ri Pak won the Jamie Farr Kroger Classic by 9 strokes. Her first round 61 was an LPGA record, as was her winning total 261 for 72 holes.

2005 – Abreu smashes Derby records
Phillies outfielder Bobby Abreu shattered 3 records at the Home Run Derby in Detroit. He set marks for a single round (24), the championship round (11) and the grand total for all 3 rounds by hitting 41 dingers into every part of Comerica Park.

BIRTHDATES
1908 American golfer PAUL RUNYAN – died 2002
1932 American sprinter OTIS DAVIS
1938 New Zealand rugby union flanker STAN MEADS
1941 American auto racer BENNY PARSONS – died 2007
1942 Australian rugby league halfback BILLY SMITH
1943 New Zealand Test all-rounder BRUCE TAYLOR
1943 NBA coach PAUL SILAS
1944 England soccer defender TERRY COOPER
1946 England Test batsman GRAHAM ROOPE – died 2006
1947 Welsh rugby union halfback GARETH EDWARDS
1948 American fitness trainer RICHARD SIMMONS
1949 American golfer MARK HAYES
1962 Mexican boxer JULIO CÉSAR CHÁVEZ
1963 French tennis player THIERRY TULASNE
1965 Indian Test batsman SANJAY MANJREKAR
1969 England Test fast bowler ALAN MULLALLY
1971 Australian golfer ROBERT ALLENBY
1971 American figure skater KRISTI YAMAGUCHI
1973 Italian soccer striker CHRISTIAN VIERI
1986 South African rugby winger JP PIETERSEN
1988 South Korean golfer INBEE PARK
1995 American gymnast JORDYN WIEBER

⓭ JULY

1934 – 'The Babe' reaches 700 homers
Babe Ruth hit the 700th home run of his career as the New York Yankees beat the Detroit Tigers, 4-2, at Navin Field. Ruth's homer was the match-winner.

1974 – Player improvises for Open win
South Africa's Gary Player played a memorable 18th hole to highlight his third British Open victory at Royal Lytham & St Annes. During the final round, Player's approach on the 18th hit the clubhouse wall and landed in an awkward position. He then hit left-handed with the back of his putter, landing the ball on the green. He 2-putted for a 4-shot victory over Englishman Peter Oosterhuis. Jack Nicklaus was a further stroke back in third place.

1979 – Gower hits double century
Stylish England batsman David Gower scored an unbeaten 200 in the first Test against India at Edgbaston. Gower hit 24 fours off only 279 balls.

1980 – Alcott's scoring record
Amy Alcott won the US Women's Open at the Richland CC in Nashville, Tennessee setting the 72-hole scoring record with 280, 9 strokes ahead of Hollis Stacey.

1994 – Harding's ex in jail
Figure skater Tonya Harding's ex-husband Jeff Gillooly was sentenced to 2 years in prison for his role in an attack on fellow skater Nancy Kerrigan prior to the Winter Olympics in Lillehammer, Norway. He was also fined $100,000. Gillooly joined Shawn Eckardt, Shane Stant and Derrick Smith in prison. They were sentenced to 18 months. Harding pleaded guilty to conspiracy to hinder prosecution and was placed on 3 years' probation and fined $160,000.

1996 – Cigar ties record
Champion American racehorse Cigar tied Citation's record streak of 16 consecutive wins at the Arlington International Racecourse, near Chicago. With jockey Jerry Bailey aboard, the 3-10 favourite easily took out the $1.05-million Arlington Citation Challenge by 3½ lengths over runner-up Dramatic Gold. Cigar's 16th consecutive victory came almost 2 years after the first,

Drew Brees playing for the New Orleans Saints. Photo: dbking (originally posted to Flickr as _MG_5421) [CC-BY-2.0], via Wikimedia Commons.

the streak spanning 8 tracks, including a trip to Dubai. The streak ended at 16, however, with the six-year-old colt being beaten in the Pacific Classic at Del Mar on 10 August.

2012 – Brees in the money
All-Star quarterback Drew Brees and the New Orleans Saints reached an agreement on a 5-year, $100 million contract that included a first-year take in 2012 of $40 million. The guaranteed money was considered, by all parties involved, to be an NFL record $60 million.

BIRTHDATES
1901 New Zealand rugby union fly-half MARK NICHOLLS – died 1972
1908 English tennis player DOROTHY ROUND LITTLE – died 1982
1914 American auto racer SAM HANKS – died 1994
1918 Italian auto racer ALBERTO ASCARI – died 1955
1929 Russian gymnast SOFIA MURATOVA – died 2006
1937 American golfer CHARLES COODY
1944 Australian Test fast bowler ERIC FREEMAN
1945 Australian Test spinner ASHLEY MALLETT
1953 West Indies Test batsman LARRY GOMES
1954 Australian Test spinner RAY BRIGHT
1956 American boxer MICHAEL SPINKS
1957 Belgian auto racer THIERRY BOUTSEN
1960 England rugby union winger SIMON HALLIDAY
1961 Swedish tennis player ANDERS JÄRRYD
1970 Australian tennis player SANDON STOLLE
1972 New Zealand rugby union hooker MARK HAMMOTT
1973 British boxer DANNY WILLIAMS
1974 Italian auto racer JARNO TRULLI
1981 Hungarian swimmer ÁGNES KOVÁCS
1982 Puerto Rican MLB catcher YADIER MOLINA

⑭ JULY

1951 – Citation tops $1m
Champion American horse Citation topped $1 million in career earnings when he won his final race, the Hollywood Gold Cup. Connections then retired Citation to stud. In 45 starts, Citation finished out of the money only once and won a total $1,085,760.

1964 – Fifth Tour de France win for Anquetil
French time trial specialist Jacques Anquetil won an unprecedented fifth Tour de France in racing to his record fourth consecutive Classic victory. Anquetil beat countryman Raymond Poulidor by just 55 seconds to become only the second man to claim the Giro d'Italia–Tour de France double.

1965 – One race – 2 world marks
Australian Ron Clarke broke 2 world records in one race in Oslo. He became the first man to go under 28 minutes for 10,000m, in 27:39.4, and on the way broke the 6-mile record in 26:47 seconds. From 1963 to 1970, Clarke set 19 world records in races from 2 miles to 20,000m. He also carved huge chunks from other 'lesser' distances such as 3 and 6 miles. Strangely, he never won an Olympic gold medal; his best Olympic result was a bronze in the 5,000m in Rome in 1960.

1984 – Marauding Marshall
West Indian fast bowler Malcolm Marshall captured 7 for 53 as England collapsed from 104 for 2 to be dismissed for 159 during the third Test at Headingley. Marshall was operating with his left thumb in plaster. He also batted bravely, shielding Larry Gomes to a century.

1997 – Maccabiah Games bridge tragedy
Four Australian athletes died and 64 were injured when a 65ft long, 25ft high bridge over the Yarkon River collapsed prior to the opening ceremony of the Maccabiah Games in Tel Aviv in Israel.

2001 – First for Wallabies
In rugby union, Australia claimed their first ever series win over the British Lions, with a 29-23 victory in the deciding third Test in Sydney. Two penalties

England batting star David Gower during his record-breaking double century in the first Test against India at Lord's in 1979.

from Matthew Burke in the final 12 minutes made the difference. Centre Daniel Herbert scored 2 tries and Burke kicked 5 penalties and 2 conversions for Australia. Lions' Jason Robinson and Jonny Wilkinson crossed for tries, Wilkinson also landing 3 penalties and 2 conversions. The Lions had won the first Test in Brisbane 29-13, while the Wallabies took the second Test 35-14 in Melbourne.

2005 – SF first to 10,000 MLB games
The Giants become the first team to win 10,000 games as an MLB franchise by edging historical rivals the Dodgers in LA, 4-3. The Giants, who started as the New York Gothams in 1899, had posted a 10,000-8,511 record during the club's 123 seasons in the National League.

2004 – NBA super-stars on the move
In the first of two huge transactions, the LA Lakers sent centre Shaquille O'Neal to the Miami Heat for Caron Butler, Lamar Odom, Brian Grant and a first round draft pick. The Phoenix Suns scored a coup when they signed point guard Steve Nash to a 5-year, $65 million contract. Nash had been with the Dallas Mavericks.

BIRTHDATES
1916 American golfer CLAUDE HARMON – died 1989
1928 Australian distance runner DAVE POWER
1932 NFL defensive lineman 'ROSEY' GREER
1934 American golfer LEE ELDER
1967 Sri Lanka Test batsman HASHAN TILLAKARATNE
1967 MLB third baseman/manager ROBIN VENTURA
1973 Turkish weightlifter HALIL MUTLU
1976 England Test wicketkeeper GERAINT JONES
1980 Australian rugby flanker GEORGE SMITH
1981 Australian motor-cycle rider ROBBIE MADDISON

⑮ JULY

1912 – Thorpe's Olympic double
Twenty-five-year-old American Jim Thorpe completed the pentathlon-decathlon double at the Stockholm Olympics. Thorpe dominated the 10-event decathlon to such an extent that his world record points total of 8,413 would have won the silver medal at the 1948 Games. In 1913, however, he was stripped of his medals and stricken from the record books after it was revealed he had infringed his amateur status by playing semi-professional baseball. Thorpe went on to play Major League Baseball and professional football until 1928. The IOC reinstated his medals and records in 1983.

Jim Thorpe, a champion all-round athlete, took out the pentathlon/decathlon double at the Stockholm Olympics in 1912.

1912 – Kohlemainen's first of three
Hannes Kohlemainen of Finland completed an incredible gold medal treble in long-distance running at the Stockholm Olympics when he won the 12,000m cross-country race. In the space of 7 days, Kohlemainen also won the 5,000m and 10,000m, and broke the world 3,000m record in the team race.

1922 – Sarazen's first major
Gene Sarazen won his first of 7 major golf titles, finishing with a 68 to capture the US Open by 1 stroke over John Black and Bobby Jones at the Skokie CC in Glencoe, Illinois. Sarazen recovered form 5 shots down during the final round.

1923 – Jones claims first Open
Twenty-one-year-old amateur Bobby Jones showed all the hallmarks of a champion in his first US Open victory at the Inwood CC, New York. Tied on the 18th hole of an 18-hole playoff against Bobby Cruickshank, Jones boldly lofted a 2-iron approach shot from the rough over water to within 8ft. He 2-putted for the victory 76-78 after Cruickshank made bogey.

1938 – Two double centuries for Fagg
Arthur Fagg became the only man in history to score 2 double centuries in a first-class match, when he cracked 202 not out in Kent's second innings against Essex at Colchester. Fagg had already scored 244 on the first day of the match.

2000 – Huge rugby crowd
A crowd of 109,874 saw New Zealand beat Australia 39-35 in their Bledisloe Cup match at Stadium Australia in Sydney. It was the biggest attendance for a rugby union match in history.

2005 – Nicklaus' last major
Sixty-five-year-old Jack Nicklaus played his final round in a major when he posted par-72 in the British Open at St Andrews. The 'Golden Bear' missed the cut by 2 strokes.

2005 – Conte guilty as charged
Victor Conte, who founded the Bay Area Laboratory Co-Operative (BALCO), pleaded guilty to steroid distribution along with two other men in a deal with federal prosecutors. The deal avoided an embarrassing trial and Conte spent 4 months in prison.

BIRTHDATES
1856	South African Test captain OWEN DUNELL – died 1929
1939	Pakistan Test spinner HASEEB AHSAN – died 2013
1950	Australian Test fast bowler ALAN HURST
1952	NFL receiver JOHN STALLWORTH
1954	Argentine soccer striker MARIO KEMPES
1958	American golfer DAN FORSMAN
1962	Australian swimmer MICHELLE FORD
1963	Canadian NHL right wing STEVE THOMAS
1969	American golfer DICKY PRIDE
1977	South African Test fast bowler ANDRÉ NEL
1978	England rugby union hooker STEVE THOMPSON
1982	New Zealand rugby front rower NEEMIA TIALATA

JULY

1909 – Baseball stalemate

Detroit and Washington played 18 innings at Bennett Park in the longest scoreless game in American League history. Tigers' starter Ed Summers pitched the complete game, holding the Nationals to 7 hits, 2 walks, while striking out 10. Washington's 30-year-old rookie, Bill Gray, allowed only 1 hit before leaving with an injury after 8 innings, replaced by Bob Groom. Bad light stopped play.

1932 – Dominant Didrikson

Twenty-one-year-old Babe Didrikson dominated the US Olympic track and field trials in Evanston, Illinois. Didrikson competed in 8 of 10 events and scored 30 points as the sole representative of the Employers Casualty Company of Dallas, 8 more than the runner-up team, the 22-athlete strong University of Illinois. In a span of 3 hours, she won 5 events outright and tied for first in a sixth. She set world records in the javelin, 80m hurdles, high jump and baseball throw. She was also won the shot putt and long jump.

1950 – Uruguay's World Cup

The largest crowd in sporting history, comprising 199,854 people, saw Uruguay upset Brazil 2-1 in the World Cup final at the Maracaña Stadium in Rio de Janeiro. Hot favourites Brazil went ahead early in the second half through Friaça, before Schiaffino and Ghiggia stunned the massive crowd and the over-confident Brazilians. It was Uruguay's second World Cup triumph from 2 attempts, while Brazil had entered all 4 without success.

1988 – 'Flo Jo' flies

American sprinter Florence Griffith-Joyner ran a world record time of 10.49 seconds for the 100m at the US Olympic Trials in Indianapolis. Griffith-Joyner took 0.27 seconds off Evelyn Ashford's world mark set in 1984. The record still stands, although there has always been speculation that she was drug-assisted. A triple gold medallist at the 1988 Seoul Olympics, she died at the age of 38 of a heart seizure in Mission Viejo, California.

1995 – Annika's first major

Sweden's Annika Sörenstam captured her first major title when she won the US Women's Open at the Broadmoor Golf Club, Colorado Springs. The 25-year-old Sörenstam beat Meg Mallon by 1 stroke. Later in the year she became only the second international player to be named LPGA Player of the Year.

2006 – Michael's record eighth French GP

Michael Schumacher won the French Grand Prix at the Nevers Circuit to become the first driver in F1 history to win the same Grand Prix on 8 different occasions. Schumacher also achieved his 22nd career hat-trick (pole position, win and fastest lap at the same race), also a record. He finished 10.131 seconds ahead of world champion Fernando Alonso.

2011 – Celebrity marriage

Russian tennis star Elena Dementieva married ice hockey player Maxim Afinogenov in Moscow. Afinogenov had spent 10 seasons in the NHL, mainly with the Buffalo Sabres. Dementieva won the Olympic gold medal in Beijing in 2008 and reached the final of the French and US Opens in 2004.

BIRTHDATES

1887	MLB outfielder 'SHOELESS' JOE JACKSON – died 1951
1910	Australian Test batsman STAN McCABE – died 1968
1912	England soccer forward LEN GOULDEN – died 1995
1928	American auto racer JIM RATHMAN – died 2011
1930	American boxer JOEY GIARDELO – died 2008
1942	Australian tennis player MARGARET COURT
1943	NFL coach JIMMY JOHNSON
1946	Pro Football Hall of Fame offensive tackle RON YARY
1959	NFL kicker GARY ANDERSON
1963	Swedish tennis player MIKAEL PERNFORS
1964	Spanish road cyclist MIGUEL INDURAIN
1967	South African rugby union fly-half JOEL STRANSKY
1968	NFL running back BARRY SANDERS
1969	Australian netball captain KATHRYN HARBY
1973	South African Test captain SHAUN POLLOCK
1974	Australian rugby union/league winger WENDELL SAILOR
1980	Australian golfer ADAM SCOTT
1989	Welsh soccer winger GARETH BALE

⑰ JULY

1941 – Joe's hitting streak ends
NY Yankees slugger Joe DiMaggio's record hitting streak ended at 56 in front of an MLB record crowd for a night game (67,468) in Cleveland. Two outstanding plays by Indians third baseman Ken Keltner and shortstop Lou Boudreau prevented any advance to the record. During the streak DiMaggio hit .408 (91-of-223) with 15 homers, 55 RBI and 56 runs.

1979 – Coe on fire in mile record run
British runner Sebastian Coe ran a world record time of 3:48.95 for the mile in Oslo. It was part of a magic 41 days for Coe. He also broke the 800m record in Oslo and the 1,500m in Zurich, making Coe the first man in more than 50 years to set world records at both 800 and 1,500m. The following July, he added the 1,000m record, making him the holder, for a short time, of 4 simultaneous world records.

1994 – Price is right
Zimbabwe's Nick Price holed an incredible 50ft eagle putt on the 17th hole of the final round to win the British Open at Turnberry. Price posted a total 268 to beat Sweden's Jesper Parnevik by 1 stroke.

1999 – Heyns at her peak
Champion South African breaststroker Penny Heyns broke 4 world records in 2 days during the Janet Evans meet in Los Angeles. Heyns broke Rebecca Brown's 5-year-old world 200m record in the heats with a time of 2:24.69. She beat the mark in the final by a further 0.18 seconds. Heyns repeated the feat the following day with her own 100m record, becoming the first woman to go under 1:07 seconds with a 1:06.99 swim in the heats and 1:06.95 in the final

2011 – Monumental soccer upset
Japan won the Women's Soccer World Cup 3-1, stunning the United States in a penalty shootout, after coming from behind twice in a 2-2 tie in Frankfurt, Germany. The Americans missed 3 penalties and squandered dozens of chances throughout the game, blowing a lead just 6 minutes from winning their third World Cup title. Japan became the first Asian team to win the World Cup, doing so with their first win against the US in 26 tries.

2011 – Youngest surf world champion
18-year-old Hawaiian Carissa Moore became the youngest woman in history to be crowned ASP World Champion after finishing runner-up to defending champion Rebecca Gilmore of Australia in the Roxy Pro in Biarritz, France. Moore was also the first Hawaiian in 30 years to take the world surfing title.

BIRTHDATES
1919	New Zealand Test spinner ALEX MOIR – died 2000
1932	NBA forward/coach JOHNNY KERR – died 2009
1933	South African Test batsman TONY PITHEY – died 2006
1941	England Test wicketkeeper BOB TAYLOR
1942	Basketball Hall of Fame forward CONNIE HAWKINS
1944	New Zealand Test batsman MARK BURGESS
1949	American golfer LON HINKLE
1949	Russian swim coach GENNADI TOURETSKI
1960	Dutch soccer defender/manager JAN WOUTERS
1963	Finnish ski jumper MATTI NYKÄNEN
1963	MLB pitcher BOBBY THIGPEN
1966	American golfer MICHAEL BRADLEY
1972	Dutch soccer defender JAAP STAM

British runner Sebastian Coe completing the 1979 Dubai Golden Mile in Oslo, Norway.

⑱ JULY

1927 – 'Georgia Peach' reaches 4,000 hit milestone

The legendary Ty Cobb reached the 4,000 hits mark at his former club's home ground, Detroit's Navin Field. In his first year with the Philadelphia A's after 22 seasons at Detroit, Cobb doubled off former teammate Sam Gibson in the first inning of a 5-3 defeat to the Tigers. He retired in 1928 season with 4,191 hits. Cobb's mark was beaten by Pete Rose in 1985.

1951 – Walcott oldest champion

Thirty-seven-year-old Jersey Joe Walcott became the oldest fighter to win the world heavyweight title when he knocked out the heavily favoured champion Ezzard Charles in the 7th round at Forbes Field in Pittsburgh. In his fifth attempt at the title, Walcott decked Charles with a stinging left hook.

1988 – Seve's third Open

Spaniard Seve Ballesteros captured his third British Open and fifth major championship with a 273 total at Royal Lytham and St Annes in England. He finished 2 strokes ahead of Zimbabwe's Nick Price.

1999 – Golf suicide

In one of the most bizarre endings to any major championship, Scotland's Paul Lawrie beat Frenchman Jean van de Velde and American Justin Leonard in a four-hole playoff to win the British Open at Carnoustie. Van de Velde found the rough, water and bunker to blow a 3-stroke lead by making a triple bogey on the 72nd hole, forcing the playoff. Lawrie had been 10 strokes behind after the third round

2007 – Dog's life for Vick

Star Atlanta Falcons quarterback Michael Vick was charged with crimes relating to his involvement in competitive dog-fighting. He served 21 months in prison and 2 months in home confinement before returning to the NFL with the Philadelphia Eagles in 2009.

Ty Cobb (left), pictured with fellow MLB legend Joe Jackson, in 1913.

BIRTHDATES

1848	England's Test captain W. G. GRACE – died 1915
1925	Australian sprinter SHIRLEY STRICKLAND – died 2004
1927	New Zealand Test batsman ZIN HARRIS – died 1991
1929	American figure skater/commentator DICK BUTTON
1935	American figure skater TENLEY ALBRIGHT
1938	England soccer forward JOHN CONNOLLY – died 2012
1940	MLB manager JOE TORRE
1942	Italian soccer defender/executive GIACINTO FACCHETTI – died 2006
1943	American golfer CALVIN PEETE
1949	Australian Test fast bowler DENNIS LILLEE
1951	American golfer BRUCE LIETZKE
1957	British golfer/analyst NICK FALDO
1963	Luxemburg alpine skier MARC GIRARDELLI
1966	American decathlete DAN O'BRIEN
1968	Australian rugby union/league forward SCOTT GOURLEY
1971	NBA guard AFERNEE 'PENNY' HARDAWAY
1978	Irish rugby winger SHANE HORGAN
1979	NFL wide receiver DEION BRANCH

🟦19 JULY

1877 – Gore first Wimbledon champion
Englishman Spencer Gore won the first men's singles championship at Wimbledon, beating his countryman W. Marshall in straight sets 6-1, 6-2, 6-4.

1903 – Garin takes inaugural Tour de France
The first Tour de France Cycle Classic was won by Frenchman Maurice Garin. The 32-year-old won in 94 hours, 33 minutes and 14 seconds ahead of countrymen Lucien Pothier and Fernand Augereau.

1910 – Young reaches 500-win mark
The Cleveland Naps' Cy Young became the first and only pitcher to win 500 major league games. The 43-year-old right-hander notched the milestone victory in a 5-2 defeat of Washington. He retired after the 1911 season with a 511-316 record. Major League Baseball still honours Young by naming the annual award for the best pitcher in both the National and American Leagues after him.

1976 – Gymnastics first for Comaneci
Fourteen-year-old Romanian Nadia Comaneci became the first gymnast in Olympic history to receive perfect 10.00 scores, whilst competing in the team's event in Montreal. She scored 10.00 on the balance beam and uneven bars as the Romanians finished second to the powerful Soviet Union. By the end of the competition, Comaneci earned 7 perfect 10.00 scores whilst her Soviet rival Nellie Kim gained two. Comaneci won 5 medals – 3 gold, 1 silver and 1 bronze.

1980 – Olympic boycott mars Games
The 22nd Summer Games opened in Moscow with 65 countries supporting a US-led boycott in protest of the Russian invasion of Afghanistan. Some did not officially send teams, but took no action against athletes who did participate. Medal winners were greeted by the Olympic hymn and flag, rather than their national anthem and flag. In the most lopsided Olympics since 1904, the Soviet Union won 80 gold medals in a total of 195.

11993 – Botham swansong
Champion England all-rounder Ian Botham played

Romanian gymnastics superstar Nadia Comaneci winning gold at the 1976 Montreal Olympics.

his last day of first-class cricket for Durham in a tour match against Australia at Durham University. After terrorising Australia for 15 years, 'Beefy' was now less awesome, scoring 32 and going wicket-less.

2009 – Cink never sunk
Stewart Cink sank a 15ft birdie putt on the final hole of regulation, then after the 59-year-old, five-time champion Tom Watson bogeyed the same hole, he crushed him in their 4-hole playoff to win the British Open. The pair tied at 2-under 278, Watson then coming unglued, with 4-over in the 4 extra holes, while Cink went 2-under for his first major title.

BIRTHDATES

1923	Basketball Hall of Fame coach ALEX HANNUM – died 2002
1946	Romanian tennis player ILIE NASTASE
1947	German soccer striker HANS-JÜRGEN KREISCHE
1955	Indian Test all rounder ROGER BINNY
1958	Ghanaian boxer AZUMAH NELSON
1964	American WNBA forward THERESA EDWARDS
1968	Czech soccer striker PAVEL KUKA
1971	Ukrainian boxer VITALI KLITSCHKO
1972	Danish soccer striker EBBE SAND
1974	American tennis player VINCE SPADEA
1974	Irish rugby second rower MALCOLM O'KELLY
1977	Sudanese soccer midfielder HAITHAM MUSTAFA
1980	Belgian tennis player XAVIER MALISSE

㉔ JULY

1924 – Weissmuller wins Paris 100
American Johnny Weissmuller won the first of 3 medals on this day when he took out the 100m freestyle final at the Paris Olympics. Weissmuller beat the legendary Hawaiian surf icon Duke Paoa Kahanamoku by 2.4 seconds. He also won a gold medal in the 4 x 200m freestyle relay and a bronze medal as part of the US water polo team.

1958 – Stroke play PGA to Finsterwald
American Dow Finsterwald captured the first PGA Championship contested at stroke play at the Llanerch CC in Havertown, Pennsylvania. Finsterwald finished at 4-under 276 for a 2-stroke margin over Billy Casper.

1976 – Aaron home run king
In a 6-2 win over the Angels, Milwaukee Brewers designated hitter Hank Aaron sent a Dick Drago fastball over the left-field fence at County Stadium for his tenth homer of the season and a history making record 755th of his illustrious career. It was the last home run Aaron ever hit.

1981 – Botham brilliance
Ian Botham scored 145 of his famous innings of 149 not out to give England an outside chance of beating Australia after following-on in the third Test at Headingley. Prior to Botham's innings England's odds slipped out to 500-1. It was a price Australia's punting duo of Dennis Lillee and Rod Marsh couldn't refuse, and a bet that put them under scrutiny following England's unlikely victory.

1986 – Norman wins first major
Despite years of dominating the PGA and European Tours, Australian Greg Norman won his first major championship in the British Open at Turnberry in Scotland. Norman was never challenged, defeating Gordon Brand Jr by 5 strokes.

1996 – Luck of the Irish
Ireland's Michelle Smith won the 200m IM at the Atlanta Olympics to become only the second woman in Olympic history to win 3 gold medals in Summer Games.

Sri Lankan opener Sanath Jayasuriya with the ball during the first Test against South Africa in Galle in 2000.

2000 – A Jayasuriya gem
Opener Sanath Jayasuriya was at his scintillating best as he set Sri Lanka on the way to their first ever Test victory over South Africa on the first day of the first Test at Galle. Jayasuriya smashed 148 off only 156 balls, including 96 in the morning session.

2002 – Rio to United
Manchester United agreed to a British record transfer fee of £30 million for Leeds' England defender Rio Ferdinand. It was Ferdinand's second record transfer for a defender after his £18.5 million move from West Ham to Leeds in 2000.

BIRTHDATES
1900	England Test batsman MAURICE LEYLAND – died 1967
1909	South African Test batsman ERIC ROWAN – died 1993
1921	American tennis player TED SCHROEDER – died 2006
1930	NBA coach CHUCK DALEY – died 2009
1933	English snooker player REX WILLIAMS
1938	England soccer forward ROGER HUNT
1943	New Zealand auto racer CHRIS AMON
1950	Canadian NHL defenseman/coach TERRY MURRAY
1956	Cameroon soccer goalkeeper THOMAS N'KONO
1972	Czech NHL centre JOZEF STÜMPEL
1973	Swedish NHL forward PETER FORSBERG
1973	West Indian Test fast bowler NIXON McLEAN
1975	NBA guard RAY ALLEN
1988	MLB pitcher STEPHEN STRASBURG

㉑ JULY

1934 – Vicious Voce uses 'leg theory'
England fast bowler Bill Voce was taken out of the attack after bowling 4 overs of 'Bodyline' in Nottinghamshire's county match against Lancashire at Old Trafford. During Voce's vicious spell, Lancashire's Jack Iddon was struck twice and carried off the ground. It was the last occasion in first-class cricket when 'leg-theory' was used so blatantly.

1968 – Boros oldest PGA champion
Forty-eight-year-old American Julius Boros became the oldest winner of the PGA Championship and the oldest player to win a major championship. Boros parred the 72nd hole to edge Arnold Palmer and New Zealander Bob Charles by a stroke at Pecan Valley in San Antonio, Texas.

1973 – Aaron joins 700 club
Hank Aaron joined the legendary Babe Ruth as one of only two men to hit 700 major league home runs. Aaron smacked a fastball off Philadelphia starter Ken Brett in the third inning at Atlanta-Fulton County Stadium for the milestone. He broke Ruth's record by hitting his 715th home run on 8 April 1974, and set the major league record of 755 on 20 July 1976.

1974 – Merckx wins fifth Tour
After missing the 1973 event, Eddie Merckx of Belgium won his fifth Tour de France in 5 starts. Merckx had won a record-equalling 4 consecutive Tours (1969–72), tying Jacques Anquetil. In winning 8 stages, Merckx showed he was the complete rider, able to sprint, climb, descend and time trial with the best. He beat Frenchman Raymond Poulidor by 8:04.

2007 – Hopkins still has it
Forty-two-year-old Bernard Hopkins earned a stunning victory in the twilight of his career, ending 'Winky' Wright's 7½-year unbeaten streak with a unanimous decision in their IBO light-heavyweight title fight in Las Vegas. Hopkins opened a gash over Wright's left eye with a head-butt in the third round and spent the night picking at it while Wright scrambled and counterpunched. Hopkins had retired in 2006 after a career highlighted by 21 straight middleweight

Belgian cyclist Eddie Merckx during the 1977 Tour de France.

title defences but abandoned retirement for a shot at Wright.

2007 – 'Becks' part of the Galaxy
Former England soccer captain David Beckham made his debut for the LA Galaxy in a friendly against Chelsea in front of a capacity crowd in Los Angeles. The 32-year-old Beckham came on as a 78th minute substitute in Chelsea's 1-0 win.

BIRTHDATES
1908	American golfer HAROLD 'JUG' McSPADEN – died 1996
1934	Indian Test all-rounder CHANDU BORDE
1945	South African Test opener/analyst BARRY RICHARDS
1945	English darts player JOHN LOWE
1947	Indian Test batsman CHETAN CHAUHAN
1950	Argentine soccer goalkeeper UBALDO FILLOL
1953	New Zealand rugby union winger BERNIE FRASER
1959	Australian rugby league second rower/analyst PAUL VAUTIN
1964	German ski jumper JENS WEIßFLOG
1977	English golfer PAUL CASEY
1979	WNBA forward TAMIKA CATCHINGS
1980	MLB pitcher CC SABATHIA
1981	Spanish soccer winger JOAQUÍN

㉒ JULY

1923 – 'Big Train' first to 3,000 Ks

Washington hurler Walter Johnson became the first pitcher to strike out 3,000 batters when he fanned 5 in a 3-1 victory over the Indians in Cleveland. He went on to retire after the 1927 season, with 3,508 career strikeouts.

1963 – Second mismatch

Former heavyweight champion Floyd Patterson suffered a second one-round humiliation at the hands of Sonny Liston in a title bout mismatch in Las Vegas. Ten months earlier, Liston took Patterson's title in a first-round knockout in Chicago. The rematch lasted a mere 4 seconds longer, with Patterson floored 3 times.

1973 – Birthday present for Susie

Susie Maxwell Berning celebrated her 32nd birthday by easily winning her third US Open Championship at the Rochester CC, New York. Maxwell Berning finished with a total of 2-over 290, 5 strokes ahead of Gloria Ehret and Shelley Hamlin.

1980 – Sizzling Salnikov

Russian swimmer Vladimir Salnikov broke the elusive 15-minute barrier in the 1,500m at the Moscow Olympics. His time of 14:58.27 beat American Brian Goodell's world record by 4.1 seconds.

2001 – Huge Bombers' recovery

Essendon staged the greatest comeback in Australian Football League history, overhauling North Melbourne at the Melbourne Cricket Ground. The Bombers trailed the Kangaroos by a massive 69 points into the second quarter, only to storm home and win by 12.

2005 – NHL back on

The National Hockey League's Board of Governors ensured the 2005–06 season would go ahead by ratifying the terms of the Collective Bargaining Agreement negotiated with the Players' Association. The agreement ended a 310-day work stoppage that had encompassed the entire 2004–05 season.

2005 – Yelena clears 5m

Russian pole vault champion Yelena Isinbayeva became the first woman in history to clear 5m. Competing at a Grand Prix meeting in London, it was the 23-year-old's fourth world mark of the month and the 17th of her career.

2007 – Celebrity marriage

Twenty-nine-year-old four-time super-middleweight champion Laila Ali and retired NFL star Curtis Conway were married in Los Angeles.

2010 – Murali reaches 800 wickets

Thirty-eight-year-old Sri Lankan spinner Muttiah Muralitharan reached the astonishing 800-wicket mark with his final ball in Test cricket, when he dismissed Pragyan Ojha to bring India's second innings to an end, in the first Test at Galle.

2012 – Wiggins first Brit to win Tour

Bradley Wiggins became the first British cyclist to win the Tour de France. He also helped Sky teammate Mark Cavendish to earn his fourth straight sprint victory. Wiggins secured his win with a dominating performance in the final time trial to extend his already commanding lead.

BIRTHDATES

1935	England soccer goalkeeper RON SPRINGETT
1936	England Test fast bowler HAROLD 'DUSTY' RHODES
1941	American golfer SUSIE MAXWELL BERNING
1941	Canadian jockey RON TURCOTTE
1949	Finnish middle distance runner LASSE VIRÉN
1951	England rugby union halfback STEVE SMITH
1954	New Zealand rugby union winger/analyst STU WILSON
1963	Spanish soccer striker EMILIO BUTRAGUEÑO
1965	Pro wrestler SHAWN MICHAELS
1966	NFL receiver TIM BROWN
1972	NFL receiver/analyst KEYSHAWN JOHNSON
1980	New Zealand auto racer SCOTT DIXON
1980	Dutch soccer striker DIRK KUYT
1982	Sri Lanka Test fast bowler NUWAN KALASEKARA
1982	Russian high jumper ANNA CHICHEROVA
1983	NFL running back STEVEN JACKSON
1984	English soccer defender STEWART DOWNING

1934 – Another Bradman triple ton
Master Australian batsman Don Bradman hit 43 fours and 2 sixes in an innings of 304, his second triple century in a Headingley Test match. On his favourite English ground, Bradman faced 430 balls in an innings of 473 minutes. He also shared a stand of 388 with Bill Ponsford, who hit 181 in the drawn fourth Test.

1960 – Four Opens to Betsy
American Betsy Rawls became the first woman to win 4 US Open Championships with her victory at the Worcester CC, Massachusetts. Rawls closed with a 3-over par 75 for a total of 292 to beat Joyce Ziske by a stroke.

1966 – Eusébio scores remarkable four
Portuguese superstar Eusébio sparked a remarkable comeback during the World Cup quarter-final at Goodison Park, Liverpool. With Portugal trailing North Korea 3-0, Eusébio scored 4 goals, including 2 penalties, in a remarkable 5-3 victory.

1995 – 'Big Mig' wins fifth Tour
Spanish cyclist Miguel Indurain won an unprecedented fifth consecutive Tour de France, beating Alex Zülle of Switzerland by 4:35. He achieved the feat without winning a single road stage, his only stage wins were being time trials. In his fifth victory, he won the final 46.5km time trial by almost a minute.

1995 – Daly's Open
John Daly won the British Open at St Andrews in bizarre fashion. Italy's Costantino Rocca forced a 4-hole playoff by chunking a chip at the 18th green, then holing a monstrous 65ft birdie putt from the famous 'Valley of Sin'. Daly easily won the four-hole playoff by 4 strokes.

1996 – Strug's courage wins team gold
Eighteen-year-old American Kerri Strug completed her second vault at the Atlanta Olympics, despite having badly torn her ankle ligaments during the first attempt. Strug's score clinched the gold medal, wiping out the US team's low score. She was unable to compete in any individual events.

2006 – Landis 'wins' Tour
Floyd Landis won the Tour de France and kept cycling's most prestigious title in American hands for the eighth straight year. The 30-year-old's win was made possible thanks to a 'once-in-a-lifetime ride' in stage 18 in the Alps, one day after a disastrous ride dropped him from first to 11th, more than 8 minutes back. A failed drug test led to Landis being stripped of the race win in 2008.

2012 – Penn State in disgrace
As punishment for covering up the Jerry Sandusky scandal, the NCAA hit Penn State football with a four-year post-season ban, the loss of 40 scholarships over 4 years, and a $60 million fine. The Freeh Report, an independent review of the scandal, found that former coach Joe Paterno had knowledge of Sandusky's sexual abuse of young boys going back to 1998. All Penn State wins from 1998–2011 were declared void; with this vacating of wins, Florida State's Bobby Bowden became all-time FBS wins leader. It was also ruled that the team was ineligible for the Big Ten championship game, and would not share in the conference's bowl game revenue for the next 4 years, amounting to an estimated $13 million loss.

BIRTHDATES
1936	MLB pitcher DON DRYSDALE – died 1993
1941	American auto racer RICHIE EVANS – died 1985
1949	South African Test all rounder CLIVE RICE
1950	Australian Test opener ALAN TURNER
1953	England Test captain GRAHAM GOOCH
1958	American golfer KEN GREEN
1960	Australian rugby union centre GARY ELLA
1963	Yugoslavian tennis player SLOBODAN ŽIVOJINOVI
1966	NBA guard MICHAEL WILLIAMS
1968	NBA player GARY PAYTON
1973	MLB shortstop/analyst NOMAR GARCIAPARRA
1974	American sprinter MAURICE GREENE
1981	Finnish tennis player JARKKO NIEMINEN
1983	American swimmer AARON PIERSOL
1991	Australian gymnast LAUREN MITCHELL

1908 – Dramatic marathon finish

In a dramatic conclusion to the marathon at the London Olympics, Italian Dorando Pietri was the first man to enter the stadium, but collapsed from exhaustion 5 times before being carried across the finish line by officials. American John Hayes finished second under his own steam, and US officials immediately lodged a protest, which was upheld. The incident set off a worldwide marathon craze.

1952 – Zátopek family double gold

In a unique double, Czech runner Emile Zátopek and his wife Dana won gold medals on the same day at the Helsinki Olympics. Having earlier defended the 10,000m, Emile scored a 5-yard win in the 5,000m. Later in the day, Dana triumphed in the javelin final.

1960 – Hebert brothers, one major each

Jay and Lionel Hebert became only the second combination of brothers to win a major title, when Jay won the PGA Championship by a stroke from Australian Jim Ferrier at Firestone CC in Akron, Ohio. Lionel was 1957 PGA champion.

1966 – Lema dies in plane crash

Thirty-two-year-old American golfer Tony Lema had his promising career cut tragically short when he and his pregnant wife Betty were killed in a plane crash. The 1964 British Open champion was flying in a small chartered plane bound for a charity exhibition when it crashed on a golf course near Chicago.

1969 – Ali convicted

World Heavyweight Champion Muhammad Ali's appeal was turned down. He was convicted for refusing induction into the US Army and sentenced to 5 years in prison, although as a conscientious objector, he didn't go to jail. In 1971, the Supreme Court upheld his draft appeal and he made a successful comeback to the ring, regaining his title against George Foreman in the famous 'Rumble in the Jungle'.

2005 – Armstrong's 7th Tour 'win'

Texan Lance Armstrong completed a record seventh consecutive winning Tour de France campaign, and

Disgraced cyclist Lance Armstrong during the 2005 Tour de France.

reconfirmed his retirement from the sport. The 33-year-old cancer survivor finished 4:40 ahead of Italian Ivan Basso. He was later stripped of his titles after failing to contest drugs charges.

2007 – Jackson ties WNBA scoring mark

Centre Lauren Jackson tied the WNBA all-time scoring record with 47 points for the Seattle Storm in a 97-96 OT loss to the Mystics in Washington DC. Jackson was 18 from 28 in field goal attempts and also had 14 rebounds. She tied the WNBA scoring mark of Phoenix's Diana Taurasi in 2006.

BIRTHDATES

1897	American aviatrix AMELIA EARHART – died 1939
1917	Australian Test batsman JACK MORONEY – died 1999
1933	American golfer DOUG SANDERS
1939	Basketball Hall of Fame centre WALT BELLAMY
1947	Pakistan Test batsman ZAHEER ABBAS
1947	French rugby halfback/coach JACQUES FOUROUX – died 2005
1952	Australian surfer IAN CAIRNS
1958	Scottish soccer goalkeeper JIM LEIGHTON
1963	NBA player KARL MALONE
1963	French rugby union prop LOUIS ARMARY
1963	American jockey JULIE KRONE
1964	Baseball slugger BARRY BONDS
1966	England soccer defender MARTIN KEOWN
1971	Italian soccer midfielder DINO BAGGIO
1974	England rugby union halfback ANDY GOMERSALL
1975	Welsh rugby winger DAFYDD JAMES
1978	American surfer ANDY IRONS – died 2010

1914 – Farwell W. G.
At the age of 66, W. G. Grace, 'the father of cricket', played his last innings in club cricket, scoring 69 not out for Eltham against Grove Park. He died in 1915.

1976 – Like father, like son
Hungarian javelin thrower Miklos Németh became the first son of a track and field Olympic gold medallist to win a gold of his own when he threw a world record of 94.58m in Montreal. His father, Imre, had won the hammer throw in London in 1948.

1976 – Magnificent Moses
American hurdler Edwin Moses burst onto the international scene at the Montreal Olympics with a world record performance. Moses scored a stunning 8m win over teammate Mike Shine in the 400m hurdles final in a record time of 47.63. Over a period of nearly 10 years, Moses collected 122 straight victories including the gold medal at the 1984 LA Olympics and the first 2 World Championships.

1980 – Dityatin gym genius
Aleksandr Dityatin of the Soviet Union won a bronze medal in the floor exercises at the Moscow Olympics, making him the only man to win 8 medals at a single Games. Dityatin won 3 gold medals (including the all-around event), 4 silver and 1 bronze. He also became the first male gymnast to score a perfect 10.00 in Olympic competition, with his vault on the long horse.

1981 – Rugby called off after pitch invasion
The Springbok rugby tour match in Hamilton, New Zealand, was called off after 350 anti-apartheid protesters invaded the field. Police felt they could not control the crowd and, following reports that a light plane piloted by an inmate from a mental institution was approaching the stadium, cancelled the match.

1999 – Armstrong's first Tour
Lance Armstrong 'won' his first Tour de France, 33 months after he was diagnosed with life-threatening cancer that had spread to his lungs and brain. He recovered after invasive brain surgery and chemotherapy. Riding for the US Postal Team, Armstrong won 3 stages and beat Alex Zülle of Switzerland by 7:37 seconds. In 2012, he was stripped of his Tour wins as a result of doping charges.

2010 – McMurray NASCAR double
Jamie McMurray became just the third driver in NASCAR history to win the Brickyard 400 and Daytona 500 in the same year, when he took out the former at the Indianapolis Motor Speedway. The win was huge for Earnhardt-Ganassi Racing, with Chip Ganassi becoming the first team owner to win the Daytona 500, Indianapolis 500 and Brickyard 400 in the same season.

2011 – NFL lockout over
Four-and-a-half months after the NFL's first work stoppage in 24 years, Commissioner Roger Goodell and the NFL Players Association announced their agreement on a 10-year deal. Owners gained a higher percentage of all revenue, one of the central issues; they got 53%, and players 47%, whilst teams committed to changes to offseason and in-season practice rules designed to make the game safer.

2011 – 2,000th Test
The 2,000th Test match – England versus India at Lord's – promised much, but delivered little. Matt Prior's 100 set India a target of 458. They were bowled out 196 short, soon after tea on the final day.

BIRTHDATES
1908	England medium pace bowler BILL BOWES – died 1987
1914	American decathlete/NFL end/actor WOODY STRODE – died 1994
1941	Basketball Hall of Fame centre NATE THURMOND
1954	Pro Football Hall of Fame running back WALTER PAYTON – died 1999
1956	Australian golfer PETER McWHINNEY
1962	MLB pitcher DOUG DRABEK
1964	NHL right wing/coach TONY GRANATO
1969	NBA guard/analyst JON BARRY
1971	MLB pitcher BILLY WAGNER
1973	England soccer striker KEVIN PHILLIPS
1974	Welsh rugby union winger GARETH THOMAS
1975	Russian NHL goalie EVGENI NABOKOV
1985	Colombian soccer forward HUGO RODALLEGA

1920 – Swahn oldest Olympic medallist
Seventy-two-year-old Swede Oscar Swahn became the oldest Olympic medallist ever when he won the silver medal in the team double shot running deer event at the Antwerp Games. Swahn won his first gold medal at the age of 60 at the 1908 London Games and repeated the feat in 1912 in Stockholm.

1952 – Mathias' repeat gold
American decathlete Bob Mathias completed the largest winning margin in Olympic history as he became the first man to win 2 gold medals in the gruelling event at the Helsinki Games. The 21-year-old beat countryman Milt Campbell by 912 points in scoring a world record 7,887. Mathias' performance came despite a painful leg injury and beat his career bests in the javelin and 1,500m. He retired after the Games.

1952 – Sprint double to Jackson
Australian Marjorie Jackson broke the long-standing 200m world record in the semi-final at the Helsinki Olympics. Jackson ran a time of 23.4 seconds to break Stanislawa Walasiewicz's 17-year-old mark by 0.2 seconds. She won the final by 4 yards to become the first Australian ever to win an Olympic sprint double. She had won the 100m final in equal world record time of 11.5 seconds.

1993 – England cricket disaster
For the second time in the series, Australia won a Test in which they lost only 4 wickets, regaining the Ashes with an innings victory at Headingley. Allan Border scored an unbeaten 200 in Australia's 653 for 4. An inspired 8-wicket haul from seamer Paul Reiffel sealed the victory. England captain Graham Gooch resigned after the match, with Mike Atherton his replacement.

1996 – Perkins guts out a golden victory
In the greatest triumph of an illustrious career, Australian Kieren Perkins won the gold medal in the 1,500m at the Atlanta Olympics after qualifying eighth to reach the final. The world record holder, in a deep form slump, only qualified by 0.25 seconds and had to start the final from the outside lane 8. However, Perkins swam the first 100m in a sizzling 55.3 and

American decathlete Bob Mathias throwing the discus during the 1952 Helsinki Olympics.

continued to dominate the field for the remainder of the race.

2010 – US tops in Softball
The United States beat Japan 5-1 in Oklahoma City to win its fourth consecutive World Cup of Softball title. It was the final game for champion pitcher Jenny Finch who didn't allow a run in 18 innings in the World Cup.

BIRTHDATES
1858	Australian Test batsman TOM GARRETT – died 1943
1922	Baseball Hall of Fame pitcher HOYT WILHELM – died 2002
1922	Indian Test all-rounder G.S.RAMCHAND – died 2003
1931	Brazilian soccer winger/manager TELÊ SANTANA – died 2006
1934	Pro Football Hall of Fame receiver TOMMY McDONALD
1939	Pro Football Hall of Fame defensive tackle BOB LILLY
1939	Australian Test batsman/broadcaster KEN CUNNINGHAM
1954	American tennis player VITAS GERULAITIS – died 1994
1956	American figure skater DOROTHY HAMILL
1957	Australian golfer WAYNE GRADY
1965	Australian surfer PAM BURRIDGE
1967	Australian golfer DAVID McKENZIE
1974	New Zealand rugby union front rower KEES MEEUWS
1977	Danish soccer defender MARTIN LAURSEN
1981	Brazilian soccer defender MAICON
1983	American snowboarder KELLY CLARK

㉗ JULY

1952 – Incredible treble to Zátopek
Czech runner Emile Zátopek won the marathon at the Helsinki Olympics, becoming the only person to win the 5,000m, 10,000m and marathon treble at one Olympics. Zátopek had never run a marathon before.

1956 – Greatest Test bowling figures to Laker
England spinner Jim Laker took 9 for 37 in the first innings against Australia in the fourth Test at Old Trafford. The Australians offered little resistance and were dismissed for a paltry 84. Later in the match, Laker went on to take all 10 Australian second innings wickets for 53, and record incredible match figures of 19 for 90.

1976 – Diving treble to Dibiasi
Italian Klaus Dibiasi comfortably beat American Greg Louganis by 23.52 points to win an unprecedented third consecutive Olympic platform gold medal in Montreal. Dibiasi was the first Italian to win an Olympic gold medal in swimming or diving.

1984 – Rose singles record
Montreal first baseman Pete Rose broke Ty Cobb's all-time singles record of 3,052 as the Expos beat Phillies, 6-1, in Philadelphia.

1986 – LeMond, first American Tour victory
Twenty-five-year-old American Greg LeMond became the first non-European to win the Tour de France. LeMond beat five-time winner Bernard Hinault of France by 3:10. LeMond went on to win the Tour twice more, in 1989 and 1990.

1996 – Bailey brilliant
Canada's Donovan Bailey showed tremendous mental strength to run a world record in the 100m final at the Atlanta Olympics. There were 3 false starts, 1 from Ato Bolden of Trinidad and 2 from Great Britain's Linford Christie, resulting in his disqualification. Christie made an angry spectacle with officials in pre and post race theatrics. Bailey broke Leroy Burrell's world mark by 0.01 seconds, running a time of 9.84 ahead of Frankie Fredericks of Namibia and Bolden.

Champion Italian diver Klaus Dibiasi on his way to gold in the 10m platform event at the 1972 Munich Olympics.

2006 – Pavin's record nine
Corey Pavin set the PGA Tour's scoring record for 9 holes, shooting a 26 on the front 9 in the US Bank Championship at the par-70 Brown Deer Park GC in Milwaukee. Pavin, who was 8-under at the turn and finished his bogey-free round at 9-under 61, broke the mark of 27 set by Mike Souchak (1955) and matched by Andy North (1975), Billy Mayfair (2001) and Roberts Gamez (2004). The 46-year-old Pavin birdied the first 6 holes, pared the seventh and rebounded with birdies on 8 and 9.

BIRTHDATES
1899	Australian Test spinner PERCY HORNIBROOK – died 1976
1905	MLB manager LEO DUROCHER – died 1991
1915	Australian Test spinner JACK IVERSON – died 1973
1933	Australian AFL ruckman TED WHITTEN – died 1995
1942	American tennis player DENNIS RALSTON
1948	American figure skater PEGGY FLEMING
1955	Australian Test captain ALLAN BORDER
1958	English figure skater CHRISTOPHER DEAN
1962	Australian swimmer NEIL BROOKS
1965	Paraguayan soccer goalkeeper JOSÉ LUIS CHILAVERT
1967	New Zealand rugby union prop MARK ALLEN
1969	South African Test batsman JONTY RHODES
1973	Australian rugby league captain GORDEN TALLIS
1975	MLB shortstop ALEX RODRIGUEZ
1979	Mexican boxer JOGE ARCE

1936 – Windies legend born

Garry Sobers was born in Barbados. Regarded as the greatest all-rounder in history, Sobers was one of the Wisden Five Cricketers of the Century. In 93 Tests, he scored 8,032 runs at 57.78. He also took 235 wickets at 34.03. He was just 21 when he converted his maiden Test century into a colossal 365 not out against Pakistan at Kingston in 1957–58, which remained the Test record for 36 years, until beaten by Brian Lara. Playing for Nottinghamshire against Glamorgan at Swansea in 1968, Sobers became the first batsman to hit 6 sixes in an over in first-class cricket. He retired in 1974, and was knighted shortly afterwards.

1937 – Two triple tons in one day

For the first time in first-class cricket, 2 triple hundreds were scored on the same day. Playing English County Cricket Eddie Paynter hit 322 for Lancashire against Sussex at Hove, whilst Richard Moore scored 316 for Hampshire against Warwickshire at Bournemouth.

1968 – Lombardi-Packers no more

After 9 seasons, Vince Lombardi announced his resignation as coach of the Green Bay Packers. Lombardi guided the Packers to 5 NFL championships and the first 2 Super Bowls. He remained as general manager for a year before going to the Washington Redskins in 1969.

1979 – Wallabies – finally

Australia scored its first rugby union win over New Zealand at home in 45 years, with a 12-6 victory at the Sydney Cricket Ground. Fullback Paul McLean kicked 3 penalties and a field goal to complete the Wallabies' scoring.

1993 – Eight straight dingers to Griffey Jr

Seattle Mariners outfielder Ken Griffey Jr tied the MLB record by hitting a home run in his eighth consecutive game. Griffey belted a solo homer off Minnesota's Willie Banks in the seventh inning. Dale Long of Pittsburgh set the record in 1956 and Don Mattingly of the Yankees had tied it in 1987.

1994 – Lefty Rogers throws perfect game

Kenny Rogers became the first American League left-hander to pitch a perfect game as the Texas Rangers beat the California Angels 4-0 in Arlington, Texas.

2011 – First WR without suits

Ryan Lochte edged Michael Phelps for gold in the 200m IM at the world swimming championships in Shanghai, setting the first world record since high-tech bodysuits were banned at the start of 2010. Lochte touched in 1:54.00, improving on his old mark of 1:54.10 set at the Worlds in Rome in 2009, when polyurethane suits were still in use. Phelps settled for silver in 1:54.16.

2012 – US first for Lochte, no medals for Michael

Ryan Lochte notched the United States' first gold at the London Olympic Games, dominating the 400m IM in a time of 4:05.18 to win the race by more than 4 seconds. Michael Phelps came in fourth, the first time since the 2000 Sydney Games that he hadn't won at least a bronze in an Olympic race.

BIRTHDATES

1924	Italian auto racer LUIGI MUSSO – died 1958
1925	Uruguayan soccer forward JUAN SCHIAFFINO – died 2002
1931	Australian Test spinner JOHNNY MARTIN – died 1992
1934	England soccer midfielder RON FLOWERS
1936	West Indian Test captain SIR GARFIELD SOBERS
1938	Spanish soccer striker/manager LUIS ARAGONÉS
1943	Basketball Hall of Fame forward BILL BRADLEY
1946	Australian cricket administrator DAVID RICHARDS
1951	NBA coach DOUG COLLINS
1951	England soccer defender RAY KENNEDY
1955	Russian cross-country skier NIKOLAY ZIMYATOV
1969	American golfer FRANK LICKLITER
1970	Zimbabwe Test spinner PAUL STRANG
1977	Argentine NBA guard MANU GINÓBILI
1978	New Zealand Test all-rounder JACOB ORAM
1981	England soccer midfielder MICHAEL CARRICK
1984	American NHL left wing ZACH PARISE

1976 – Magnificent seven to Szewinska
Poland's Irena Szewinska won her seventh Olympic medal in her fifth event when she broke her own world record to win gold in the 400m at the Montreal Games. Szewinska ran a time of 49.29 seconds. It was her third Olympic gold medal in a career that included medal-winning performances in the 100m and 200m, the 4 x 100m relay and the long jump.

1996 – Four straight long jump titles to Lewis
Carl Lewis leaped 27ft 10¾in into a stiff headwind to win his fourth straight Olympic gold medal in the long jump in Atlanta. Lewis joined American discus thrower Al Oerter as the only track and field athlete to win the same event in 4 consecutive Olympics. It was Lewis' ninth Olympic gold medal, tying him with US swimmer Mark Spitz, Finnish long-distance runner Paavo Nurmi and Soviet gymnast Larysa Latynina.

1996 – Johnson on way to double
American super runner Michael Johnson won the first leg of a unique double in the 400m at the Atlanta Olympics. Johnson extended a 7-year winning streak in overwhelming Britain's Roger Black by 10m. He went on to join France's Marie-Jose Perec as the only athletes to have completed the 200m/400m double in a boycott-free Olympics.

2001 – Masakadza's records
At 17 years and 352 days old, Zimbabwe's Hamilton Masakadza became the first black African to score a Test century, and the youngest player to debut with a century, scoring 119 during the second Test against the West Indies in Harare.

2006 – Record Test partnership
Sri Lankan captain Mahela Jayawardene fell for 374, 26 short of Brian Lara's Test record, but did share in a new landmark on an amazing third day of the first Test against South Africa in Colombo. Jayawardene set a new partnership record of 624 with Kumar Sangakkara, who hit 35 fours in 287. Sri Lanka won by an innings and 153 runs.

2007 – Watson claims third Senior Open
Tom Watson fired his tee shot into a fairway bunker at the last hole, but survived a double bogey to win his third Senior British Open in 5 years at Muirfield in Scotland. The five-time Open winner who also won 2 Masters titles and 1 US Open, captured his fifth senior major with an even par total 284, 1 ahead of Mark O'Meara and Australian Stuart Ginn.

2012 – Medals in 5 straight Games for Rhode
Skeet shooter Kim Rhode became the first American with individual medals in 5 straight Olympics, after taking gold in a near perfect performance in London. Rhode won in double trap at Atlanta as a teenager in 1996, took bronze in that event 4 years later at Sydney, re-claimed the gold at Athens in 2004 and won the silver in skeet at Beijing in 2008.

2012 – First sub-56 'fly to Vollmer
American swimmer Dana Vollmer won the 100m butterfly gold medal in world record time at the London Olympics. Vollmer touched in 55.98 seconds, becoming the first woman to break the 56-second mark in history.

BIRTHDATES
1925	Canadian Hockey Hall of Fame left wing TED LINDSAY
1933	American pro wrestler/manager 'CAPTAIN' LOU ALBANO – died 2009
1943	English snooker player DAVID TAYLOR
1944	New Zealand Test batsman TERRY JARVIS
1948	Irish thoroughbred trainer DERMOTT WELD
1957	Russian gymnast NELLIE KIM
1958	England soccer defender ALVIN MARTIN
1962	Australian golfer CORINNE DIBNAH
1963	Pakistan Test fast bowler AZEEM HAFEEZ
1966	British hurdler SALLY GUNNELL
1971	Australian triathlete EMMA CARNEY
1971	American golfer HARRISON FRAZAR
1980	Chilean tennis player FERNANDO GONZÁLEZ
1981	Spanish auto racer FERNANDO ALONSO

③⓪ JULY

1930 – Uruguay wins first World Cup
Uruguay defeated Argentina 4-2 in the final to claim soccer's first World Cup Final in Montevideo. Playing in front of a home crowd of 93,000 at the Centenario Stadium, Uruguay trailed 2-1 at half time. However, second half goals from Cea, Iriarte and Castro sealed the historic victory.

1960 – Billiards legend dead at 61
Billiards champion Walter Lindrum died, aged 61. Considered to be the most dominating champion of any sport, the Australian was world billiards champion from 1933 to 1950. His record break of 4,137 was made in 175 minutes and consisted of an estimated 1,900 consecutive scoring shots. The rules of the game were altered on several occasions to try to curb Lindrum's prolific scoring. He established 57 world records, none of which were broken, except by himself.

1966 – Famous Hurst hat-trick
Geoff Hurst scored a hat-trick, and his West Ham teammate Martin Peters added another goal, as England beat West Germany 4-2 in extra time in the World Cup final at Wembley Stadium. England's go-ahead goal in extra-time remains a talking point. Hurst slammed the ball onto the underside of the bar and down to the goal line. After consulting the linesman, the referee awarded the contentious goal.

1976 – Virén dominates the distances
Just 4 days after winning the 10,000m, Finland's Lasse Virén captured his fourth Olympic gold when he took out the 5,000m in Montreal. The win was controversial, as Virén had been questioned about blood boosting, a method whereby blood is extracted from the body, frozen, then unfrozen close to an event and reinjected to increase the haemoglobin level and oxygen-carrying capability of the blood. Virén denied he had engaged in the practice and beat New Zealand's Dick Quax by just 0.4 seconds in a frenzied finish. Virén had completed the 5,000m–10,000m double twice and became the first runner to repeat in the 5,000m.

1984 – Lamb lovin' it
England batsman Alan Lamb scored his third

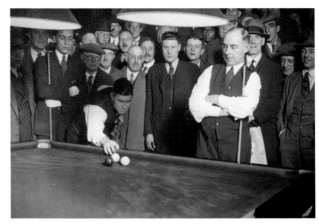
The great Walter Lindrum in action during a 1929 billiards match against England's Willie Smith at the Memorial Hall in London.

consecutive hundred (100 no) as the home team headed for an embarrassing 4-0 series deficit in the fourth Test against the West Indies at Old Trafford.

1995 – Cork's hat-trick
Fast bowler Dominic Cork became the first England player to take a Test hat-trick in 38 years during the first over of the fourth morning of the fourth Test against the West Indies at Old Trafford. Cork dismissed Windies captain Richie Richardson, Junior Murray and Carl Hooper with consecutive deliveries.

2002 – Thorpe in the groove
Australian super-swimmer Ian Thorpe broke his own world 400m freestyle record for the fifth time at the Manchester Commonwealth Games. Thorpe was in dominating form, with a time of 3:40.08.

BIRTHDATES
1890   MLB outfielder/manager CASEY STENGEL – died 1975
1946   American auto racer NEIL BONNETT – died 1994
1947   Austrian body builder/actor/politician ARNOLD SCHWARTZENEGGER
1950   New Zealand rugby union prop/coach BRAD JOHNSTONE
1957   NBA centre/coach BILL CARTWRIGHT
1958   British decathlete DALEY THOMPSON
1959   French rugby union number 8 MARC CÉCILLON
1963   Basketball Hall of Fame guard/analyst CHRIS MULLIN
1963   England soccer midfielder NEIL WEBB
1964   German soccer striker JÜRGEN KLINSMANN
1966   Australian rugby league halfback ALLAN LANGER
1974   England rugby union/league winger JASON ROBINSON
1979   Irish golfer GRAEME McDOWELL
1980   English golfer JUSTIN ROSE
1981   American motor-cycle rider NICKY HAYDEN
1982   England Test fast bowler JAMES ANDERSON

㉛ JULY

1928 – First women's Olympic track event
American sprinter Elizabeth Robinson won the 100m in Amsterdam, the first women's track event to be run at an Olympic Games. Robinson equalled her own world record of 12.2 seconds to beat Canadians Fanny Rosenfeld and Ethel Smith who dead-heated with 12.3 seconds.

1943 – Verity dies at war
England's slow left-arm bowler Hedley Verity died in a prisoner of war camp in Italy during World War II. Verity had played in 40 Tests, taking 144 wickets at 24.37. He was the only player to have taken 14 wickets in a day in a Test match – against Australia at Lord's in the second Test in 1934, when he took 15 for 104. With Wilfred Rhodes, he shares the honour of taking most wickets in an England–Australia Test. He also set a first-class world record by taking 10 for 10 for Yorkshire against Nottinghamshire.

1954 – Adcock hits 4 dingers
Milwaukee Braves first baseman Joe Adcock became only the third player in the 20th century to hit 4 homers in a 9-inning game (Lou Gehrig and Gil Hodges were the others) in a 15-7 win over the Brooklyn Dodgers at Ebbets Field. The 6ft 4in Adcock saw only 7 pitches. He also doubled, giving him an MLB record 18 total bases.

1961 – Barber wins PGA with putter
Jerry Barber beat Don January 67 to 68 in a playoff to win the PGA Championship at Olympia Fields CC in Illinois. Barber made spectacular 40ft and 60ft putts on the 71st and 72nd holes, to come from behind to tie and then beat January.

1999 – Harrington repeats in darts Match Play
Englishman Rod Harrington became the first man to retain the World Darts Matchplay crown. He beat Peter Manley 19-17 in a nail-biting final in Blackpool. Harrington is now a well-respected television darts analyst. Phil Taylor later won the tournament from 2000 through 2004, and 2006 through 2012.

English darts champion Rod Harrington during the 1999 PDC Grand Prix in Rochester, England.

2007 – Huge trade for KG
The Boston Celtics, who had gone without a championship for more than two decades, obtained former MVP and 10-time All-Star Kevin Garnett in a 7-for-1 deal with Minnesota, the NBA's biggest ever trade for one player. Boston sent the Timberwolves forwards Al Jefferson, Ryan Gomes and Gerald Green, guard Sebastian Telfair and centre Theo Ratliff, two first-round draft picks and cash.

2012 – Phenomenal Phelps
Michael Phelps became the greatest medal winner in Olympic history when he and his teammates – Ryan Lochte, Ricky Berens and Conor Dwyer – easily won gold in the 4 x 200m relay in London, giving Phelps his 19th career Olympic medal and his 15th overall gold. He passed Russian gymnast Larissa Latynina in the former.

BIRTHDATES
1902	England Test all-rounder GUBBY ALLEN – died 1989
1912	Australian Test batsman BILL BROWN – died 2008
1919	Indian Test batsman HEMU ADHIKARI – died 2003
1931	American tennis coach NICK BOLLETTIERI
1941	Australian squash player HEATHER McKAY
1951	Australian tennis player EVONNE CAWLEY
1953	South African Test batsman JIMMY COOK
1959	Australian golfer PETER SENIOR
1965	NBA guard/coach SCOTT BROOKS
1980	New Zealand rugby union fullback MILS MULIAINA
1982	Spanish tennis player ANABEL MEDINA GARRIGUES
1986	Russian NHL centre EVGENI MALKIN
1989	Belarusian tennis player VICTORIA AZARENKA

AUGUST

1 AUGUST

1961 – Famous Benaud spell
Australian captain Richie Benaud captured 5 for 12 in a famous spell, bowling around the wicket on the final day of the fifth Test against England at Old Trafford. Chasing a winning target of 256, England was dismissed for 201. Benaud finished with 6 for 70 off 32 overs. Australia won the series and retained the Ashes.

1976 – Lauda badly burnt in crash
Austrian Formula 1 driver Niki Lauda was seriously burned in a high-speed crash during the German Grand Prix at Hockenheim. Lauda missed the remainder of the season after he had looked certain to retain his world championship. However the 1975 world champion showed immense courage to recover and win the 1977 world title. He also won in 1984.

1987 – Tyson undisputed champ
Mike Tyson beat IBF titleholder Tony Tucker in a unanimous points decision in Las Vegas to become the first undisputed heavyweight champion since Leon Spinks in 1978.

1992 – Christie oldest 100m winner
Jamaican born Linford Christie, representing Great Britain, became the oldest man to win an Olympic 100m final at the Barcelona Games. The 32-year-old Christie was 4 years older than Scotsman Allan Wells when he won in Moscow in 1980. Second placed Frankie Fredericks of Namibia became the first black African to win a medal in the 100m.

1992 – Davers takes 5-woman blanket finish
American sprinter Gail Devers won the 100m in a five-woman photo finish at the Barcelona Olympics. In an incredibly tight race, the 5 runners were within .06 seconds of Devers' winning time of 10.82. Devers' win came barely 18 months after her feet were almost amputated as a result of radiation treatment for Graves' disease.

1996 – Perec wins 200m/400m double
French sprinter Marie-Jose Perec became just the second woman in history to win the gold medal in both the 200 and the 400-metres sprints at the same Olympics after taking out the 200-metres final in Atlanta. Perec joined American Valerie Brisco-Hooks, who won both the 200 and 400 races in 1984 in Los Angeles.

2012 – 'Missile' shot down
Twenty-three-year-old American swimmer Nathan Adrian defeated Australian favourite James Magnussen by one 100th of a second in the 100m freestyle at the London Olympics, with a speed of 47.52. He had never swam under 48 seconds prior to his London races.

BIRTHDATES
1921	American tennis player JACK KRAMER – died 2009
1924	West Indian Test captain SIR FRANK WORRELL – died 1967
1931	South African Test all rounder TREVOR GODDARD
1934	New Zealand Test batsman JOHN BECK – died 2000
1947	Scotland soccer manager ANDY ROXBURGH
1961	American golfer BRAD FAXON
1962	South African boxer JAKE MATLALA
1963	England soccer defender MARK WRIGHT
1969	England Test batsman GRAHAM THORPE
1970	England soccer goalkeeper DAVID JAMES
1976	Nigerian soccer striker NWANKWO KANU
1978	NFL running back EDGERRIN JAMES
1989	MLB pitcher MADISON BUMGARNER

Linford Christie, qualifying for the 200m at the 1996 Atlanta Olympic Games.

② AUGUST

1912 – Back-to-back Opens for McDermott
Johnny McDermott successfully defended his US Open title at the Country Club of Buffalo in Williamsville, New York. Despite a bogey on the last hole, McDermott carded a 71 for a 294 total, 2-shots ahead of fellow American Tom McNamara.

1952 – Patterson's gold
Seventeen-year-old future heavyweight champion Floyd Patterson won the middleweight gold medal at the Helsinki Olympics, when he knocked out Romanian Vasile Ti in the first round of the final.

1980 – Three straight for Stevenson
Cuban super-heavyweight Teófilo Stevenson became the first fighter to win 3 Olympic gold medals in the same division when he scored a 4-1 points decision over Pyotr Zayev of the Soviet Union in Moscow.

1992 – Back-to-back heptathlons
American Joyner-Kersee became the first athlete to win consecutive gold medals in the gruelling heptathlon when she won the 7-event competition at the Barcelona Olympics. Going into the final 3 events, Joyner-Kersee led by 129 points. She expanded her advantage after the long jump, javelin and 800m for a total of 7,044 points and a winning margin of 199 over Irina Belova of the Soviet Union.

1992 – Six gold for Scherbo
Vitaly Scherbo of Belarus became the first gymnast to win 6 gold medals at an Olympics during the Barcelona Games. The 20-year-old was also the first to win 4 gold medals in one day when he won the the parallel bars, long horse vault, rings and pommel horse. Scherbo had already won the prestigious all-around gold medal, as well as the team event.

2003 – Smith leads the way
Twenty-two-year-old rookie cricket captain Graeme Smith hit 34 fours in a South African record 259, in the second Test against England at Lord's.

2009 – Funk's Senior record
Fred Funk set a tournament record by finishing

Vitaly Scherbo of Belarus on the rings, one of his 6 gold medal events at the 1992 Barcelona Olympics.

20-under par in winning the Senior US Open at Crooked Stick in Carmel, Indiana. Funk finished with a 7-under par 65 to beat Hale Irwin's record, set in 2000, by 3 strokes.

2012 – Phelps, Soni trumps in pool
Michael Phelps won an unprecedented third straight gold medal in the 200m IM in 1:54.27 at the London Olympics. Also at the pool, Rebecca Soni became the first swimmer in the history of the 200m women's breaststroke to win the event twice when she blazed to a world-record time of 2:19.59.

BIRTHDATES
1887	South African Test wicketkeeper TOMMY WARD – died 1936
1917	American boxer IKE WILLIAMS – died 1994
1932	NFL owner LAMAR HUNT – died 2006
1945	Australian AFL forward ALEX JESAULENKO
1958	Irish soccer player SAMMY McILROY
1965	American golfer J.P.HAYES
1966	MLB pitcher TIM WAKEFIELD
1967	American tennis player AARON KRICKSTEIN
1968	German soccer player STEFAN EFFENBERG
1970	West Indian Test batsman PHILO WALLACE
1970	NHL right wing TONY AMONTE
1973	Australian swimmer SUSIE O'NEILL
1979	Kenyan Runner REUBEN KOSGEI

❸ AUGUST

1921 – 'Black Sox' banned
Commissioner Kenesaw Mountain Landis issued lifetime bans to 7 former Chicago White Sox players accused of throwing the 1919 World Series. The bans came a day after the players were acquitted by a jury on charges of conspiring to defraud the public. Landis was adamant that the players, including legendary 'Shoeless' Joe Jackson, had not told the club of events promptly, and would never play professional baseball again.

1932 – Auto-timing and photo finishes for track
Official automatic timing and the photo-finish camera was used for track events for the first time at the LA Olympics. The technology was instrumental in changing the result of the 110m hurdles final. American Jack Keller was awarded the bronze medal, but the review of race film showed British hurdler Donald Finley had actually finished third.

1984 – Mary Lou's American first
Mary Lou Retton became the first American woman to win an Olympic gymnastics medal when she won the individual all-around gold in Los Angeles. She needed a maximum score of 10 in her final event to win outright and the 16-year-old responded with a perfect vault.

1984 – Sieben's shock win
Seventeen-year-old Australian Jon Sieben scored a huge upset and swam a world record in beating German favourite Michael Gross in the final of the 200m butterfly at the LA Olympics. Sieben swam a time of 1:57.04 after turning seventh at 100m.

1996 – Pro cycling comes to the Olympics
The opening of the Olympics to professional athletes gave 5-time Tour de France winner Miguel Indurain the opportunity to compete for Spain in Atlanta. Indurain was convinced to ride by compatriot and IOC President Juan Antonio Samaranch. He took the gold medal in the 52.2km road time trial in a time of 1.04:05, 12 seconds ahead of countryman Abraham Olano.

1997 – A serious Charity Shield!
Manchester United beat Chelsea 4-2 on penalties to win the Charity Shield, after a bad-tempered 1-1 draw at Wembley. Mark Hughes put Chelsea ahead after halftime and Ronnie Johnsen equalised for United just 6 minutes later.

1997 – Walker's first win in 52 starts
In her 52nd major championship start, Colleen Walker won her first major, the du Maurier Classic at Glen Abbey CC in Oakville, Ontario. Walker posted a 14-under 278 to win by 2 strokes from Sweden's Liselotte Neumann.

1999 – Henry a bargain for Gunners
London club Arsenal completed a signing coup when they snapped up ace French striker Thierry Henry for a bargain £11 million from Juventus of Italy. Henry went on to dominate the EPL for the next 8 years until he transferred to Barcelona in 2007.

2006 – Oh deer!
Outstanding 32-year-old Brazilian Champ Car driver Cristiano da Matta needed surgery to remove a ruptured blood vessel in his head after his race car collided with a deer on the track during testing at Road America, Elkhart Lake, Wisconsin. CT scans revealed a subdural hematoma.

2012 – All-America night at pool
In his final Olympic individual race, Michael Phelps took his all-time gold medal tally to a record 17 when he won the 100m butterfly in 51.21 in London.

BIRTHDATES
1916	Argentine soccer forward JOSE MANUEL MORENO – died 1978
1925	NFL coach MARV LEVY
1940	Pro Football Hall of Fame receiver LANCE ALWORTH
1950	German marathon runner WALDEMAR CIERPINSKI
1951	Canadian Hockey Hall of Fame centre MARCEL DIONNE
1953	Argentine soccer midfielder OSSIE ARDILES
1960	American tennis player TIM MAYOTTE
1963	New Zealand rugby union fly-half FRANO BOTICA
1963	Australian rugby union five-eighth DAVID KNOX
1964	NBA forward/coach NATE McMILLAN
1977	NFL quarterback TOM BRADY
1984	American swimmer RYAN LOCHTE
1985	New Zealand rugby utility SONNY BILL WILLIAMS

4 AUGUST

1945 – 11th straight PGA win for Nelson
Byron Nelson beat Herman Barron by 4 strokes to win the Canadian Open at the Uplands and Thornhill CC, Ontario to notch his record 11th consecutive tournament victory. In a stellar year, Nelson won a record total of 18 PGA titles and maintained a scoring average of 68.3.

1957 – Fangio wins fifth World F1 title
Argentinian Maserati driver Juan Manuel Fangio clinched his record fifth World Formula 1 title and his fourth consecutive championship when he won the German Grand Prix at the Nürburgring. It was his fourth win of the 8-race season. Fangio's records were finally beaten by Michael Schumacher, in the next century.

1982 – Joel, 2 clubs, 2 hits, one day
Joel Youngblood became the only major leaguer to get hits for different teams in two different cities on the same day. He singled the winning run for the New York Mets in the afternoon before being traded to Montreal. He flew to Philadelphia for a night game, joined the Expos in the fourth inning, and singled again.

1984 – Lewis claims 100m in LA
Carl Lewis won his first gold medal in the 100m at the Los Angeles Olympic Games. In the biggest winning margin in Olympic history – 8ft – Lewis recorded a time of 9.9 seconds to beat fellow American Sam Graddy by 0.2 seconds. Lewis went on to win another 3 gold medals in the 200m, 4 x 100m relay and long jump to emulate the performance of Jesse Owens in Berlin in 1936.

2000 – Stewart, 100 in 100th Test
England wicketkeeper Alec Stewart became the fourth batsman to score a century in his 100th Test, against the West Indies in Manchester. The other players to achieve the feat were Colin Cowdrey, Javed Miandad and Gordon Greenidge.

2005 – Jockey Day retires
Fifty-two-year-old Hall of Fame jockey Pat Day announced his retirement after 32 years in the saddle.

His 8,803 career wins included the Preakness Stakes 5 times, the Belmont Stakes 3 times and 12 Breeders' Cup wins. Day rode just one Kentucky Derby winner – in 1992 aboard long shot *Lil E. Tee*. He also won 4 Eclipse Awards as the nation's best jockey and retired as thoroughbred racing's career money leader with purses totalling $297,941,912.

2007 – Bonds ties Aaron's HR record
San Francisco slugger Barry Bonds homered off Clay Hensley in the second inning of a 3-2 loss to San Diego to tie Hank Aaron's 33-year-old career home run record of 755.

2012 – Phelps finishes on top
Michael Phelps wrapped up his Olympic career in London as a member of the victorious US 4 x 100m medley relay team. It was his 18th gold medal and the 22nd medal of his career. The US took out the medley relay double with the women's team recording a world record time of 3:52.05, slicing 0.14 off the previous mark set by China in 2009 at the height of the high-tech bodysuit era. Elsewhere, Serena Williams destroyed Maria Sharapova 6-0, 6-1 to capture Olympic tennis gold for the first time in singles.

BIRTHDATES
1904	English golfer HARRY COOPER – died 2000
1913	Australian tennis player ADRIAN QUIST – died 1991
1921	Canadian Hockey Hall of Fame wing MAURICE RICHARD – died 2000
1931	Indian Test wicketkeeper NARENDRA TAMHANE – died 2002
1949	Pro Football Hall of Fame running back JOHN RIGGINS
1956	England rugby union winger PETER SQUIRES
1956	American boxer GERRY COONEY
1958	American middle distance runner MARY DECKER-SLANEY
1962	MLB pitcher ROGER CLEMENS
1967	American sprinter MIKE MARSH
1968	American golfer DUDLEY HART
1971	American auto racer JEFF GORDON
1973	Brazilian soccer goalkeeper MARCOS
1976	England rugby union prop TREVOR WOODMAN
1978	American auto racer KURT BUSCH
1985	Ecuadorian soccer winger ANTONIO VALENCIA

1973 – Holland's new 1,500m mark
Fifteen-year-old schoolboy Stephen Holland took a massive 14.78 seconds off the world record for the 1,500m swim in Brisbane. Holland swam a time of 15:37.8, smashing American Mike Burton's mark.

1978 – First all-seat stadium opened
The first all-seater football stadium in Britain opened in Aberdeen, Scotland. The new Pittodrie Stadium was inaugurated with a friendly between Aberdeen and London club Tottenham Hotspur.

1982 – Floyd's all the way win
Raymond Floyd opened the PGA Championship at Southern Hills Country Club in Tulsa, Oklahoma by tying the 18-hole tournament record with 9-under par 63. Floyd led from start to finish to win his second PGA Championship. He won his first PGA title in 1969.

1984 – Moses still the hurdles king
American super-hurdler Edwin Moses won the 400m hurdles gold medal at the Los Angeles Olympics. It was his 105th consecutive victory, including 90 in finals.

1989 – Hambletonian tie
For the only time in history, the third and final heat of harness racing's Hambletonian ended in a dead heat, between Park Avenue Joe and Probe. Park Avenue Joe, who had finished second and first in the 2 previous heats, was declared winner of the series. In 1990 an administrative law judge declared Park Avenue Joe and Probe co-winners, but allowed the owners of Park Avenue Joe to keep 50 per cent of the purse, and owners of Probe 25 per cent.

2005 – Great start to Pujols' great career
Albert Pujols became the first player to connect for 30 home runs in each of his first 5 MLB seasons. The then Cardinals first baseman had hit 190 homers during this 5-year span from the start of career.

2006 – Over the 'Moon' for Warren
Warren Moon became the first black quarterback to be inducted into the Pro Football Hall of Fame. In an emotional ceremony at Canton, Ohio, Moon was joined by Troy Aikman, John Madden, Rayfield Wright, Harry Carson and the late Reggie White.

2006 – 11 straight 30 save seasons
For the 11th time in his career, Padres closer Trevor Hoffman recorded 30 or more saves in a season to conclude a 6-3 home win against Washington. The milestone established a major league record, surpassing the mark set by Lee Smith, baseball's all-time saves leader.

2012 – Williams sisters take Olympic doubles
Serena and Venus Williams won the women's doubles title at the London Olympics, with Serena adding to the singles gold she won at Wimbledon a day earlier. They beat Andrea Hlaváá ková and Lucie Hradecká of the Czech Republic 6-4, 6-4.

2012 – London gold for Bolt
Jamaica's Usain Bolt ran the second-fastest 100m in history, an Olympic-record 9.63 seconds, to give him the gold at the London Games. It was the second straight gold for Bolt in this event, and by winning, he became the only man besides Carl Lewis to defend the title of Fastest Man in the World at back-to-back Olympics. Bolt's Jamaican teammate, Yohan Blake, took silver in 9.75 seconds and Justin Gatlin won bronze with 9.79.

BIRTHDATES
1866 Australian Test captain HARRY TROTT – died 1917
1874 American golfer HORACE RAWLINS – died 1940
1930 American auto racer RICHIE GINTHER – died 1989
1937 NHL coach HERB BROOKS – died 2003
1944 Australian rugby league forward BOB McCARTHY
1946 NFL coach BRUCE COSLET
1948 England soccer goalkeeper RAY CLEMENCE
1962 NBA centre PATRICK EWING
1968 Scottish rally driver COLIN McRAE – died 2007
1969 Indian Test fast bowler VENKATESH PRASAD
1972 England rugby union winger JON SLEIGHTHOLME
1972 Pakistan Test fast bowler AAQUIB JAVED
1973 New Zealand rugby union halfback JUSTIN MARSHALL
1980 England soccer player WAYNE BRIDGE
1985 Ivorian soccer forward SALOMON KALOU
1986 American golfer PAULA CREAMER
1988 Italian swimmer FEDERICA PELLEGRINI

❻ AUGUST

British Formula 1 driver Sterling Moss during the 1955 British Grand Prix at the Aintree Circuit in Liverpool

1926 – Ederle conquers Channel
American Gertrude Ederle, aged 20, became the first woman to swim the English Channel, achieving the feat in a record time for a man or woman. She made the swim from Cape Gris-Nez, France to Kingsdown Beach in England in 14 hours, 39 minutes – 1 hour, 52 minutes faster than the previous record.

1948 – Mathias youngest track & field winner
Seventeen-year-old American Bob Mathias became the youngest winner of a men's track and field Olympic event when he won the decathlon in London. Mathias won the gold medal with just 3 months experience in the event. He won again in 1952 in Helsinki, by a record margin.

1961 – Moss powers to final GP win
British driver Sterling Moss scored his final Formula 1 victory in the German Grand Prix. In a 67-race career (1951–61), Moss won 15 Grand Prix. He never won a world championship but finished in second place 4 times and third place on 3 occasions.

1966 – Ali KO's London
Muhammad Ali knocked out English challenger Brian London in 3 rounds at Earl's Court in London to retain his undisputed world heavyweight title. Boxing was undergoing a resurgence in the UK and the fight generated huge interest.

1972 – Recovery shot key to Player's PGA
South African Gary Player played one of the greatest shots in history on his way to the PGA Championship at Oakland Hills CC in Bloomfield Hills, Michigan. During the final round on the par-4 16th hole, Player executed a near-impossible 9-iron recovery shot over a willow tree and pond to within 4ft of the cup for a birdie. He finished on 281 total to win by 2 strokes from Tommy Aaron and Jim Jamieson.

1978 – Comeback victory to Mahaffey
John Mahaffey became the best comeback winner in PGA Championship history when he won at the Oakmont CC in Pennsylvania. Mahaffey trailed Tom Watson by 7 with 14 holes to play but posted a final round 5-under 66 to tie with Watson and Jerry Pate on 8-under 276 in the first 3-way playoff in tournament history. Mahaffey won on the second playoff hole with a 12ft birdie putt.

1997 – Biggest Test score in history
Sri Lanka stormed to 952 for 6, the highest score in Test history, in the first Test against India in Colombo. Opening batsman Sanath Jayasuriya hit 36 fours and 2 sixes in an innings of 340. He batted with Roshan Mahanama (225) through two full day's play in a record partnership for any Test wicket of 576.

22006 – Tiger youngest to 50 wins
Thirty-year-old Tiger Woods became the youngest player to compile 50 PGA Tour victories with a 3-shot victory at the Buick Open at Grand Blanc, Michigan. He was the seventh player to win 50 tournaments and the youngest, ahead of Jack Nicklaus (33).

BIRTHDATES
1919	American tennis player PAULINE BETZ – died 2011
1922	American golfer DOUG FORD
1933	Indian Test batsman KRIPAL SINGH – died 1987
1934	Great Britain rugby league winger BILLY BOSTON
1938	American golfer BERT YANCEY – died 1994
1946	New Zealand rugby union lock POLE WHITING
1947	Australian Test fast bowler TONY DELL
1953	Pakistan Test spin bowler IQBAL QASIM
1965	NBA centre DAVID ROBINSON
1966	American golfer BILLY MAYFAIR
1969	New Zealand Test fast bowler SIMON DOULL
1973	Australian cyclist STUART O'GRADY
1983	Dutch soccer striker ROBIN VAN PERSIE

1932 – 'Babe' takes silver despite record
Twenty-one-year-old American athlete Mildred 'Babe' Didrikson earned her second world record of the LA Olympics in the high jump – but didn't win the gold medal. Didrikson tied with teammate Jean Shiley during the rounds and in a jump-off. Officials then ruled Didrikson's western roll style was illegal and awarded Shiley the gold medal, although Didrikson was given the silver and a share of the world record. Didrikson also won gold, set the world record in the 80m hurdles and won gold in the javelin.

1948 – Fanny blanks opposition
Eighteen-year-old Dutch athlete Fanny Blankers-Koen completed a haul of 4 gold medals as a member of the winning 4 x 100m relay team at the London Olympics. She had already won the 100m/200m sprint double as well as the 80m hurdles. Prior to the Games, she held 6 world records, but Olympic rules permitted her to enter only 4 events. She become the only woman to win 4 track and field gold medals at one Olympics.

1948 – Coachman first
American Alice Coachman became the first black woman to win an Olympic gold medal in the high jump in London. She beat Dorothy Odam of Great Britain on a countback, the second consecutive Olympics Odam had lost in a tie.

1954 – Mile 'classic' to Bannister
In an athletics classic, Englishman Roger Bannister beat Australia's John Landy in the mile at the Empire Games in Vancouver. Bannister, the first man to break the 4-minute barrier, seized the lead with 70 yards to the finish and Landy could not respond. In the first race in which 2 men ranmile in less than 4 minutes, Banister ran 3:58.8 and Landy 3:59.6.

1966 – Brabham first to F1 double
Australian Jack Brabham became the first man to win the Formula 1 World Drivers and Constructors Championship in the same year when he won the German Grand Prix at the Nürburgring. Driving his Brabham/Repco BT19, Brabham beat John Surtees by 44.4 seconds for his fourth consecutive race success.

1987 – First Paki to 6,000
Javed Miandad become the first player to score 6,000 Test runs for Pakistan in completing one of his six Test double centuries with 260 during the drawn fifth Test against England at the the Oval.

2005 – England by 2
In the closest Ashes Test in history, England beat Australia by 2 runs in the second Test at Edgbaston. Needing 107 runs to win with 2 wickets in hand, Australia's tail-enders almost got an unlikely win only for no. 10 Michael Kasprowicz to be controversially caught out by 'keeper Geraint Jones for 20. Brett Lee remained unbeaten on 43.

2007 – Bonds takes Aaron HR record
San Francisco Giants slugger Barry Bonds broke Hank Aaron's storied 33-year-old MLB career home run record, with one out in the fifth inning, hitting a full-count, 84mph pitch from Washington's Mike Bacsik at AT&T Park. The 43-year-old Bonds sent the ball 435ft into the right-centre field seats for his 756th career homer. Aaron had held the top spot for 12,173 days after connecting for no. 715 to pass Babe Ruth on 8 April 8, 1974.

BIRTHDATES
1928	Ethiopian marathon runner ABEBE BIKILA – died 1973
1929	MLB pitcher DON LARSEN
1937	England Test spinner DON WILSON
1942	Argentine boxer CARLOS MONZÓN – died 1995
1945	Pro Football Hall of Fame defensive tackle ALAN PAGE
1948	Australian Test captain GREG CHAPPELL
1952	Irish golfer EAMONN DARCY
1957	Russian gymnast ALEXANDR DITYATIN
1958	American marathon runner ALBERTO SALAZAR
1961	Irish jockey WALTER SWINBURN
1965	Canadian figure skater ELIZABETH MANLEY
1968	Australian iron man TREVOR HENDY
1971	England Test fast bowler DOMINIC CORK
1982	Argentine rugby utility JUAN MARTIN HERNÁNDEZ
1982	Ukrainian swimmer YANA KLOCHKOVA
1987	Canadian NHL centre SIDNEY CROSBY

⑧ AUGUST

1900 – First Davis Cup played in Boston
The first Davis Cup tennis competition began at the Longwood Cricket Club in Boston with the US beating Great Britain 3-0. Malcolm Whitman, Dwight Davis and Holcombe Ward comprised the American team, and the British side included Arthur Gore, Herbert Roper Barrett and Earnest Black. The competition was named after Davis, who donated the Cup.

1966 – Gibbs dominates England
West Indian off-spinner Lance Gibbs took 6 for 39 in the fourth Test against England at Headingley to spearhead the tourists' innings victory and a winning 3-0 series lead. Gibbs was the first spinner to pass 300 Test wickets. In 79 Tests, he took 309 wickets.

1982 – Everybody loves Raymond
Raymond Floyd set records aplenty as he led from start to finish to win his second PGA Championship at the Southern Hills CC in Tulsa, Oklahoma. Floyd opened with a record-tying 63, never 3-putted in 72 holes, set a 36-hole scoring record (132), a 54-hole mark (200) and his 8-under 272 total was a stroke higher than Bobby Nichols' 72-hole record. Lanny Wadkins finished 3 strokes back in second.

1990 – Rose in jail
Forty-nine-year-old Pete Rose began his 5-month sentence for tax evasion at a minimum-security prison camp in Marion, Illinois. Baseball's all-time hits leader, who was banned from the game for betting on games, had been convicted for failing to report $354,000 in income.

1992 – Basketball 'Dream Team' takes gold
America's first Dream Team cruised to the gold with an easy 117-85 victory over Croatia in the final at the Barcelona Olympics. It was the first time professional players had been permitted to compete in the Games. The team included Magic Johnson, Larry Bird and Michael Jordan and was coached by Chuck Daly. The Americans trailed 25-23 after 10 minutes, but came back to lead 56-42 at halftime. Jordan finished with a team-high 22 points and Charles Barkley scored 17 as 7 US players reached double figures.

Ervin 'Magic' Johnson in action for the original 'Dream Team' at the 1992 Barcelona Olympics.

1992 – 'Golden Boy' takes Olympic gold
Oscar De La Hoya pre-empted a successful professional career when he won the gold medal in the lightweight division at the Barcelona Olympics. He beat Germany's Marco Rudolph of Germany on points after decking him in the third round.

2011 – Twenty20s first six-wicket haul
Sri Lankan spinner Ajantha Mendis claimed 6-16 against Australia in Kandy, for the first 6-wicket haul in international Twenty20 cricket. Australia made 149-9 to fall just short of a victory target of 158 and lose the Twenty20 series 2-0.

BIRTHDATES
1889	Australian Test batsman JACK RYDER – died 1977
1921	American swimmer/actress ESTHER WILLIAMS
1930	College basketball coach JERRY TARKANIAN
1940	Indian Test batsman DILIP SARDESAI – died 2007
1947	Hockey Hall of Fame goalie KEN DRYDEN
1953	British auto racer NIGEL MANSELL
1960	Australian surfer CHEYNE HORAN
1965	England Test fast bowler ANGUS FRASER
1970	South African rugby union winger CHESTER WILLIAMS
1978	French soccer striker LUIS SAHA
1981	Swiss tennis player ROGER FEDERER
1985	English rugby utility back TOBY FLOOD

⑨ AUGUST

1936 – Four gold for Owens
Jesse Owens won his fourth gold medal of the Berlin Olympics when he teamed with Ralph Metcalf, Foy Draper and Frank Wykoff to run a world record time of 39.8 seconds in the 4 x 100m relay. The record stood for 20 years. Owens had already won the 100m/200m sprint double and the long jump.

1984 – Thompson's back-to-back decathlons
British decathlete Daley Thompson successfully defended his Olympic title and equalled the world record at the LA Games. Thompson scored 8,798 points to tie German Jürgen Hingsen's world record.

1987 – Nelson's PGA best total
In oppressive heat, Larry Nelson's final-round 72 produced the highest winning score (1-under 287) in PGA Championship history. Nelson won his third major and became the 15th multiple winner of the Championship when he beat Lanny Wadkins on the first playoff hole at PGA National in Palm Beach Gardens, Florida.

1988 – 'The Great One' traded!
Edmonton Oilers team owner Peter Pocklington, citing financial troubles, traded super-star Wayne Gretzky, along with Marty McSorley and Mike Krushelnyski, to the LA Kings for Jimmy Carson, Martin Gelinas, 3 first round draft picks and an estimated $15 to 20 million.

1992 – Gower bows out
Former England captain David Gower played his last day of Test cricket in the fifth Test against Pakistan at the Oval. The stylish left-hander played 117 Tests and scored 8,231 runs at 44.25, with a career best of 215. He made 18 Test centuries.

2002 – 600 dingers for Bonds
Giants slugger Barry Bonds hit his historic 600th career home run in a 4-3 loss to the Pirates at Pac Bell Park in San Francisco. The 38-year-old Bonds smashed a 421ft homer off Pittsburgh's Kip Wells over centre-field for the milestone. Bonds hit his 700th homer in late 2004.

2005 – Lenton first under 52
Australian Libby Lenton became the first woman to ever go under 52 seconds for the short course 100m freestyle at the Australian swimming championships in Melbourne. Lenton swam a time of 51.7 seconds to beat her heat time by 0.21 seconds. She had broken Therese Alshammar's world mark of 52.17 the previous night.

2012 – 'Lightning' Bolt
Usain Bolt beat Jamaican teammate Yohan Blake in the 200m final at the London Olympics to become the first sprinter in history to win back-to-back gold medals in the Olympic 100m and 200m events. Easing up, Bolt ran a time of 19.32, two 100ths of a second shy of the Olympic record. He was also the first athlete to win the 200m title in 2 Olympics.

2012 – American treble in soccer
The US women's soccer team won its third straight Olympic gold medal beating Japan 2-1 in a rematch of the 2011 World Cup final and avenging the most painful loss in its history. Carli Lloyd scored early in both halves.

BIRTHDATES

1911	American boxing trainer EDDIE FUTCH – died 2001
1914	English soccer midfielder/manager JOE MERCER – died 1990
1926	West Indian Test batsman DENIS ATKINSON – died 2001
1928	Basketball Hall of Fame guard BOB COUSY
1935	New Zealand rugby union halfback DES CONNOR
1938	Australian tennis player ROD LAVER
1943	American boxer KEN NORTON
1944	French auto racer PATRICK DEPAILLER – died 1980
1947	English soccer defender/manager ROY HODGSON
1955	NFL quarterback DOUG WILLIAMS
1961	American tennis coach BRAD GILBERT
1963	Australian surfer BARTON LYNCH
1964	NHL forward BRETT HULL
1967	NFL/MLB player DEION SANDERS
1970	NHL centre ROD BRIND'AMOUR
1973	Italian soccer striker FILIPPO INZAGHI
1977	French soccer defender MIKAËL SILVESTRE

⑩ AUGUST

1954 – Champion jockey Richards retires
Champion English jockey Sir Gordon Richards retired from the saddle. His 4,870 career wins were only surpassed in 2002, by jumps jockey Tony McCoy. Richards was English champion jockey 26 times and in 1947 rode a record 269 winners. In 1933, he also rode a record 12 consecutive winners. He had a career total of 14 classic wins but only one Derby winner, Pinza, in 1953. Richards pursued a successful training career until 1969.

1984 – Famous collision
The famous collision between American Mary Decker and Zola Budd, the 18-year-old South African who represented Britain, took place during the 3,000m at the Los Angeles Olympics. With 3 laps remaining, Decker's right foot became tangled with the left foot of Budd, who was leading. Decker fell, tried to get up, and collapsed in tears. A distraught Budd continued, but faded badly to finish seventh. Decker blamed Budd for the collision, though not all analysts agreed.

1989 – Taylor/Marsh bat all day
Future Australian Test captain Mark Taylor, and future coach Geoff Marsh, batted the entire first day of the fifth Test at Trent Bridge. Australia ended the day at 301 without loss with Taylor on 219 and Marsh 138. They went on to make 329 for the first wicket, still the highest stand for any wicket in a Trent Bridge Test.

2002 – Rugby referee attacked
Burly Pieter van Zyl rushed onto the pitch and grabbed Irish referee David McHugh in a headlock during New Zealand's 30-23 Tri Nations win over South Africa in Durban. McHugh had to retire with a dislocated shoulder and the SARU banned van Zyl for life.

2012 – Mega NBA trade
In a mega-four team NBA trade, star Orlando Magic centre Dwight Howard moved to the LA Lakers along with Chris Duhon and Earl Clark. The Magic received Arron Afflalo, Nicola Vucevic, Al Harrington, Josh McRoberts, Moe Harkless, Christian Eyenga, a conditional Lakers' first-round pick, a conditional 2015 second-round pick, the lower of the Denver

Mary Decker (leading) with Zola Budd on her right shoulder during the famous 3,000m at the 1984 LA Olympics. The pair crashed, leaving Decker distraught.

Nuggets' two 2014 picks, a 2013 second-round pick, and a protected pick from the Philadelphia 76ers. The Nuggets received Andre Iguodala, and the Sixers received Andrew Bynum and Jason Richardson.

2012 – Long term relay record smashed
The United States women won gold and set a new world record in the 4 x 100m relay final at the London Olympics. The previous record stood for 27 years. Tianna Madison, Allyson Felix, Bianca Knight and Carmelita Jeter ran a blistering time of 40.82 seconds.

BIRTHDATES
1911   Greek footballer LEONIDAS ANDRIANOPOULOS – died 2011
1928   Australian boxing referee and actor GUS MERCURIO – died 2010
1947   England rugby union captain JOHN SPENCER
1956   Australian tennis player DIANNE FROMHOLTZ
1958   England Test wicket keeper JACK RICHARDS
1958   American boxer MICHAEL DOKES – died 2012
1960   American golfer KENNY PERRY
1965   American jockey MIKE E. SMITH
1967   American boxer RIDDICK BOWE
1970   Australian Test fast bowler BRENDON JULIAN
1971   Irish soccer captain ROY KEANE
1972   England rugby flanker LAWRENCE DALLAGLIO
1972   South African rugby union hooker JAMES DALTON
1973   American tennis player LISA RAYMOND
1973   Argentine soccer midfielder JAVIER ZANETTI

⑪ AUGUST

1977 – Boycott record
England opening batsman Geoff Boycott became the first player to hit his 100th first-class century in a Test match. Boycott went on to make 191 at Headingley as England beat Australia by an innings in the fourth Test to regain the Ashes.

1984 – Fourth gold to Lewis
Carl Lewis won his fourth gold medal of the LA Olympics as a member of the winning US 4 x 100m relay team. Lewis had won the 100m/200m sprint double and the long jump. Lewis duplicated Jesse Owens' performance in Berlin in 1936.

1986 – Famous Tway shot sinks Norman
Bob Tway holed out from a greenside bunker for a famous birdie-3 on the 72nd hole to beat Greg Norman by 2 strokes in the PGA Championship in Toledo, Ohio. Norman, the British Open champion, faltered in the final round carding a 5-over 76.

1991 – Daly wins PGA after late call-up
John Daly won the PGA Championship at Crooked Stick in Carmel, Indiana without a practice round and after a 7-hour drive. He made the field when Nick Price withdrew. In the most memorable exhibition by a rookie, Daly averaged 303 yards per drive to finish 3 strokes ahead of Bruce Lietzke at 12-under 276.

2005 – Warne first to 600
Shane Warne became the first bowler to take 600 Test wickets during the drawn third Test against England at Old Trafford. The victim was Marcus Trescothick who scuffed the ball with the back of his bat, and Adam Gilchrist completed a juggling catch as the ball bobbled up off his thigh.

2008 – Americans' relay WR
Jason Lezak produced an amazing come-from-behind anchor leg to touch out Frenchman Alain Bernard for a US gold medal in the 4 x 100m freestyle relay at the Beijing Olympics. The team of Lezak, Michael Phelps, Garrett Weber-Gale and Cullen Jones swam a world record time of 3:08.24, nearly 4 seconds better than the mark they set in the previous night's prelims.

John Daly during the 1991 US PGA Championship in Indianapolis.

2012 – US dominance
The US women's basketball team won an unprecedented fifth straight Olympic title, beating France 86-50 in the final at the London Games. Candace Parker top scored with 21 points, making it 41 straight victories in Olympic play. Meantime, DeeDee Trotter, Allyson Felix, Francena McCorory and Sanya Richards-Ross won the US's fifth straight gold medal in the 4 x 400m relay.

BIRTHDATES
1870	England Test fast bowler TOM RICHARDSON – died 1912
1920	Canadian hockey Hall of Famer CHUCK RAYNER – died 2002
1953	Pro wrestler TERRY 'HULK' HOGAN
1954	Indian Test batsman YASHPAL SHARMA
1958	New Zealand rugby union centre STEVEN POKERE
1964	New Zealand golfer GRANT WAITE
1966	England soccer goalkeeper NIGEL MARTYN
1974	Australian cyclist DARRYN HILL
1978	American boxer JERMAIN TAYLOR
1986	Venezuelan MLB infielder PABLO SANDOVAL

1936 – Gestring youngest to win Olympic gold
American diver Marjorie Gestring became the youngest-ever Olympic individual gold medallist in any sport when she won the springboard event in Berlin. Gestring was just 13 years, 9 months old

1960 – Boston breaks Owens jump barrier
American Ralph Boston broke Jesse Owens' 25-year-old world long jump record with a leap of 8.21m at Walnut, California. The leap beat Owens' 1935 mark by 0.08m. Boston took the record to 8.28m in 1961.

1972 – Chappell bros score tons
Australia's captain Ian Chappell and his brother Greg became the first pair of brothers to score centuries in the same Test innings in the fifth Test at the Oval. Ian scored a patient 118 whilst Greg contributed 113. Australia won by 5 wickets to square the series 2-2.

1973 – 'Golden Bear' – twelve majors
Jack Nicklaus captured his 12th major title and third PGA Championship with a 4-stroke victory over Bruce Crampton at the Canterbury GC near Cleveland, Ohio. Nicklaus finished at 7-under 277. Crampton had been runner-up to Nicklaus in 3 major events, including the US Open and Masters.

1974 – Ryan equals K record
Nolan Ryan equalled Tom Seaver and Steve Carlton's MLB strikeout record of 19, in California's 4-2 win over the Boston Red Sox at Anaheim Stadium.

1991 – Sad end to trio's Test career
Three giants of West Indies cricket – Vivian Richards, Malcolm Marshall and Jeff Dujon – played their last day in Test cricket as the Windies crashed to a 5-wicket defeat to England in the fifth Test at the Oval. Richards hit 60 to keep his Test batting average over 50; Marshall finished with 376 wickets at 20.94 each; and Dujon had a Windies' record 272 dismissals.

2007 – Major #13 for Tiger
Tiger Woods won his 13th career major when he captured his fourth PGA Championship at Southern Hills in Tulsa, Oklahoma. Woods closed with a 1-under 69 for an 8-under total 272 and a 2-shot victory over Woody Austin.

2008 – Gold medal #9 for Phelps
Michael Phelps's ninth career gold in the 200m freestyle in Beijing tied him with Mark Spitz, Carl Lewis, Soviet gymnast Larysa Latynina and Finnish runner Paavo Nurmi for the most in Olympic history. Phelps was under world-record pace the whole way and pulverised his own world mark, clocking 1:42.96.

2012 – US take basketball gold
The United States fended off another huge challenge from Spain, pulling away in the final minutes for a 107-100 victory and their second straight Olympic basketball title in London. Kevin Durant scored 30 points and LeBron James had 19 on a day when he joined Michael Jordan as the only players to have won the NBA title, regular-season MVP, NBA Finals MVP and Olympic gold in the same year.

BIRTHDATES

1880	Baseball hall of fame pitcher CHRISTY MATHEWSON – died 1925
1891	American golfer JOHNNY McDERMOTT – died 1971
1906	Australian Davis Cup captain HARRY HOPMAN – died 1985
1921	American jockey STEVE BROOKS – died 1979
1923	West Indian Test batsman JOHN HOLT – died 1997
1924	England Test medium pace bowler DEREK SHACKLETON – 2007
1933	American auto racer PARNELLI JONES
1939	Australian hurdler PAM KILBORNE
1940	South African Test batsman EDDIE BARLOW
1956	Sri Lankan Test batsman SIDATH WETTIMUNY
1956	Australian horse trainer LEE FREEDMAN
1960	England Test fast bowler GREG THOMAS
1960	French road cyclist LAURENT FIGNON – died 2010
1971	American tennis player PETE SAMPRAS
1977	Croatian tennis player IVA MAJOLI
1981	French soccer striker DJIBRIL CISSÉ

⓭ AUGUST

1919 – Man o'War misses start, only defeat
Champion American race horse Man o' War missed the start and suffered the only defeat of his 21-race career in the Sanford Memorial Stakes at Saratoga. He was beaten by a horse he'd trounced on 6 other occasions, ironically named Upset.

1932 – Kitamura youngest Olympic winner
Fourteen-year-old Kusuo Kitamura of Japan became the youngest male ever to win an individual Olympic event when he won the 1,500m freestyle in LA.

1981 – Mary T. sets long standing mark
Mary T. Meagher set one of the longest standing world records ever when she broke her own 200m butterfly mark at Brown Deer, Wisconsin. Meagher swam a time of 2:05.96. The record stood for 18 years until broken by 0.15 seconds in 2000 by Susie O'Neill at the Australian Olympic trials in Sydney.

1990 – Edberg takes #1 ranking
Sweden's Stefan Edberg broke Ivan Lendl's 80-week monopoly as tennis' world no. 1. Lendl had been at the top since January 1989 and prior to that had held the ranking for nearly 3 years from 1985 to 1988. Edberg remained no. 1 for 24 weeks before being usurped by German Boris Becker.

1995 – Legendary slugger passes away
At age 63, former NY Yankees slugger Mickey Mantle died of liver cancer. In an 18-year career, Mantle hit 536 home runs and set a World Series record with 18 homers. He won 3 MVP awards and helped the Yankees to 7 World Series and 12 pennants.

1999 – Graf retires
German tennis champion Steffi Graff announced her retirement. Graf won 22 grand slam singles titles including 7 Wimbledon; 5 US Opens; 4 Australian Opens; and 6 French Open titles. In 1988 she became only the third woman, after Maureen Connolly and Margaret Court, to win the Grand Slam. Graf held the no. 1 ranking for a record 377 consecutive weeks and her career earnings totalled $21.8 million. In 200, she married Andre Agassi, and they have 2 children.

German tennis star Steffi Graf during the 1994 French Open in Paris.

2008 – Phelps most successful Olympian
Michael Phelps won his 10th and 11th Olympic gold medals to become the most successful Olympian ever during the Beijing Games. A day after etching his name alongside Mark Spitz, Carl Lewis, Paavo Nurmi and Larysa Latynina with gold no. 9, Phelps claimed the record all to himself when he won the 200m butterfly. An hour later, he swam leadoff in a runaway world record victory by the US 4 x 200m freestyle relay team.

2011 – England top team
With an innings victory over India in the third Test at Edgbaston, England became the no. 1 Test side for the first time since rankings were established in 2003.

BIRTHDATES
1860	American shooter ANNIE OAKLEY – died 1926
1898	French tennis player JEAN BOROTRA – died 1994
1912	American golfer BEN HOGAN – died 1997
1949	Canadian Hockey Hall of Fame centre BOB CLARKE
1955	American golfer BETSY KING
1958	Irish golfer DAVID FEHERTY
1959	England Test wicketkeeper BRUCE FRENCH
1970	England soccer striker ALAN SHEARER
1975	Pakistan Test fast bowler SHOAIB AKHTAR
1976	Ecuadorian tennis player NICHOLAS LAPENTTI
1977	Australian swimmer MICHAEL KLIM
1982	American speed skater SHANI DAVIS
1992	Brazilian soccer midfielder LUCAS MOURA

⑭ AUGUST

1948 – Excruciating last 'duck' for Bradman
Needing to score only 4 runs to reach 7,000 Test runs and an average of 100, Don Bradman was bowled second ball by Eric Hollies at the Oval. England was dismissed for just 52 and lost the fifth Test by an innings, so 'The Don' didn't get a second chance in his final Test. His Test average finished at 99.94.

1977 – Sudden-death for first time at the PGA
In the first sudden-death playoff in PGA Championship history, Lanny Wadkins parred the third extra hole to defeat Gene Littler at Pebble Beach. Littler had held a 4-stroke lead but his game fell apart on the final 9 with 5 bogeys. On the third playoff hole, Littler missed a 12ft putt for Wadkins to win his first major title.

1994 – Dream Team II takes World title
US basketball's Dream Team II beat Russia 137-91 to win the world championships in Toronto. Shaquille O'Neal was tournament MVP. The United States finished with a perfect 8–0 record.

2004 – Back-to-back 400m titles for Thorpe
Ian Thorpe successfully defended his Olympic 400m freestyle title when he beat teammate Grant Hackett in Athens. Thorpe swam 3:43.1, 0.26 seconds ahead of Hackett. The champion only qualified for the event when teammate Craig Stevens sportingly withdrew after Thorpe had been disqualified in the trials.

2007 – Cranky Cox
Atlanta Braves manager Bobby Cox was ejected by umpire Ted Barrett for arguing a strike call against Atlanta's Chipper Jones. It was Cox's 132nd career MLB ejection, breaking the record held for over 70 years by the legendary John McGraw.

2010 – Baze wins #11,000
Canadian jockey Russell Baze rode his unprecedented 11,000th career winner. The 52-year-old Baze guided first-time starter Separate Forest to victory in the fourth race at the Sonoma County Fair in Santa Rosa, California to beat his big rival, South American champion rider Jorge Ricardo to the milestone.

The greatest Test batsman of all-time, Sir Donald Bradman, near the end of his career in 1948.

2011 – All in the Bradley family
Twenty-five-year-old Keegan Bradley, nephew of LPGA Hall of Famer Pat Bradley, won the PGA Championship after staging an amazing comeback to force a 3-hole playoff and beat Jason Dufner at Atlanta Athletic Club in Georgia. Bradley trailed Dufner by 5 strokes but then rallied. Dufner collapsed with 3 straight bogeys and Bradley won the playoff by a stroke. The players were tied at 8-under 272 at the end of regulation.

BIRTHDATES
1895	Australian Test all-rounder JACK GREGORY – died 1973
1929	Nigerian boxer DICK TIGER – died 1971.
1949	Danish soccer midfielder/manager MORTEN OLSEN
1952	American swimmer DEBBIE MEYER
1956	American auto racer RUSTY WALLACE
1959	Basketball Hall of Fame forward ERVIN 'MAGIC' JOHNSON
1962	Pakistan Test batsman RAMEEZ RAJA
1963	Argentine golfer JOSÉ CÓCERES
1965	English golfer PAUL BROADHURST
1968	Irish golfer DARREN CLARKE
1968	Indian Test batsman PRAVIN AMRE
1968	England rugby union prop JASON LEONARD
1973	Australian swimmer KIEREN PERKINS
1984	Swedish tennis player ROBIN SÖDERLING

⑮ AUGUST

1903 – All Blacks win first against Wallabies
The first international rugby union match between Australia and New Zealand was played at the Sydney Cricket Ground. The All Blacks won 22-3.

1948 – Babe easily takes her third Open
Babe Zaharias fired an even par 300 total to win the first of her 3 US Women's Open titles at the Atlantic City CC at Northfield, New Jersey – 8 strokes ahead of Betty Hicks.

1964 – 'Fiery Fred' first to 300
England fast bowler Fred Trueman became the first bowler to take 300 Test wickets when he had Australian tail-ender Neil Hawke caught in the slips by Colin Cowdrey during the fifth Test at the Oval. Trueman's career total of 307 wickets remained the world record until 1975–76.

1999 – Brilliant Garcia recovery not enough
Spaniard Sergio Garcia hit arguably the greatest recovery shot in major championship golf but lost the PGA Championship by a stroke to Tiger Woods at the Medinah CC in Illinois. On the par-4, 452-yard 16th, Garcia pushed a 3-wood 189 yards from the green in the exposed roots behind a large tree. His amazing recovery shot to within 60ft of the pin prompted his famous sprint and scissor-kick leap to see the green. He 2-putted for par. Woods hung on with a final par round 72 for an 11-under total 277.

2004 – Schumacher's flurry of records
German Formula 1 world champion Michael Schumacher scored his seventh straight victory in the Hungarian Grand Prix at the Hungaroring. It was his record 12th win of the year. The victory also gave him a record career total of 82 GP wins. Schumacher's teammate, Rubens Barrichello, finished second to help Ferrari clinch its record 14th and sixth consecutive Constructors' Championship.

2004 – South Africa's record relay victory
South Africa broke the world record for the prestigious men's 4 x 100m freestyle relay at the Athens Olympics. Roland Schoeman, Lyndon Ferns, Darian Townsend and Ryk Neethling swam a time of 3:13.17 seconds to beat the time set by Australia at the Sydney Games by 0.5 seconds.

2005 – Mickelson's major #2
Phil Mickelson flopped a chip out of deep rough to 2ft for birdie on the final hole to win the PGA Championship at Baltusrol CC in Springfield, New Jersey. He beat Steve Elkington and Thomas Bjørn by a stroke for his second major championship.

2008 – Phelps dominates in Beijing
Michael Phelps made it 6-for-6 in Beijing with another world-record triumph, this time in the 200m IM in a time of 1:54.23. Phelps was already the most successful athlete in Olympic history with 12 gold medals.

2008 – Liukin at last
American gymnast Nastia Liukin achieved what her father and coach Valeri could not, winning the Olympic all-around title, 20 years after her dad's narrow loss to fellow Soviet Vladimir Artemov in Seoul. Liukin edged out US favourite Shawn Johnson to become the third American, after Mary Lou Retton and Carly Patterson, to win the Olympic all-around gold.

BIRTHDATES
1886	Australian Test fast bowler BILL WHITTY – died 1974
1945	English equestrian rider/Princess ANNE WINDSOR
1945	NFL guard/players association leader GENE UPSHAW
1950	MLB manager TOM KELLY
1961	NFL coach GARY KUBIAK
1963	England Test wicketkeeper JACK RUSSELL
1966	MLB third baseman SCOTT BROSIUS
1976	Dutch soccer midfielder BOUDEWIJN ZENDEN
1979	American auto racer CARL EDWARDS
1981	American swimmer BRENDAN HANSEN

1936 – Equestrian heroics

German rider Konrad von Wangenheim became one of the heroes of Olympic history during the 3-day team event in Berlin. Von Wangenheim broke his collarbone when thrown in the endurance run, remounted, and completed the remaining 32 obstacles without fault. The following day, he was again thrown from his horse, and again recovered to complete the course without further penalty and win gold.

1948 – Baseball legend Babe Ruth dead at 53

NY Yankees home run king Babe Ruth died of throat cancer in New York. He was 53. Ruth set longstanding home-run records for a season (60) and career (714). 100,000 fans filed by his coffin as he lay in state in Yankee Stadium.

1969 – Player endures protests

The PGA Championship at the NCR Country Club in Kettering, Ohio, was disrupted by anti-apartheid protesters. During the third round, South African Gary Player and American Jack Nicklaus were verbally abused, balls were tossed onto greens while Player putted, and ice was thrown in his face. Despite the distractions, Player finished just a stroke behind winner Raymond Floyd.

1981 – Ella brothers make history

Gary, Glen and Mark Ella became the first set of 3 brothers to be selected on an Australian international rugby tour, when they were named in the squad for the British Isles. Mark Ella became the first player to score a try in each Test against the home nations, as the Wallabies claimed the first ever Grand Slam.

1992 – Price is right

Nick Price of Zimbabwe became the eighth foreign-born PGA Champion, when he scored a 3-stroke victory over John Cook, Gene Sauers, Nick Faldo and Jim Gallagher Jr at the Bellerive CC near St Louis, Missouri.

2000 – First cricket indoors

In the first international match to be played indoors, Australia beat South Africa by 94 runs at Melbourne's Colonial Stadium. Steve Waugh, with 114 not out, and Michael Bevan, with 106, put on 222 in Australia's 94-run win.

2003 – All Blacks' Tri Nations sweep

New Zealand completed the first Tri Nations clean sweep for 5 years with a 21-17 win over Australia at a rainswept Eden Park in Auckland. Doug Howlett scored 2 tries and Carlos Spencer kicked 3 penalties and a conversion for NZ, whilst George Smith crossed for the Wallabies and Elton Flatley landed 4 penalties.

2008 – Close call for Phelps

Michael Phelps finished brilliantly, tying Mark Spitz with his seventh gold medal by the narrowest of margins in the 100m butterfly at the Beijing Olympics. Phelps edged out Milorad avi of Serbia by just one-hundredth of a second. The finish was so close the Serbian delegation filed a protest and FINA reviewed the tape down to the 10-thousandth of a second. Phelps' time was 50.58 seconds.

2009 – Coventry's record to no avail

Zimbabwe batsman Charles Coventry's 194 off 154 balls against Bangladesh in Bulawayo equalled the then-highest score in an ODI. Tamim Iqbal's match-winning 154, however, guided Bangladesh to a comfortable win.

BIRTHDATES

1912	England soccer striker TED DRAKE – died 1995
1930	NFL running back/broadcaster FRANK GIFFORD
1930	American tennis player TONY TRABERT
1934	Australian Test batsman SAM TRIMBLE
1942	Australian tennis player LESLEY BOWREY
1946	Pro Football Hall of Fame tackle RON YARY
1950	Australian Test fast bowler JEFF THOMSON
1956	American golfer COLLEEN WALKER
1960	Trinidadian sprinter HASELY CRAWFORD
1958	Argentine tennis player JOSÉ LUIS CLERC
1964	England rugby union lock NIGEL REDMAN
1964	American tennis player JIMMY ARIAS
1974	Hungarian swimmer KRISZTINA EGERSZEGI
1974	West Indian Test batsman SHIVNARINE CHANDERPAUL
1978	Chinese diver FU MINGXA
1981	Paraguayan soccer striker ROQUE SANTA CRUZ

1919 – Ederle breaks world mark at 12
American Gertrude Ederle became the youngest world-record holder in any sport when she set a new world record of 13:19.0 for the 880 yards freestyle in Indianapolis. Ederle was 12 years, 298 days old. In 1926 she was the first woman to swim the English Channel.

1920 – MLB's only death
Cleveland Indians shortstop Ray Chapman became MLB's only fatality when he was hit by a pitch that fractured his skull at the Polo Grounds in New York.

1933 – Gehrig reaches consecutive game mark
New York Yankee first baseman Lou Gehrig played in his 1,308th consecutive game, breaking Everett Scott's former record at Sportsman's Park III in St Louis. Gehrig's streak eventually went to 2,130 games, a mark only broken by Cal Ripken Jr in 1995.

1938 – Three titles to Armstrong
Henry Armstrong became the first and only fighter to hold 3 titles simultaneously when he beat lightweight champion Lou Ambers in a controversial split decision in New York. Armstrong, featherweight and welterweight champion at the time, floored Ambers in the fifth and sixth rounds, but suffered severe cuts. He won despite losing 3 rounds on fouls, with both eyes cut and needing 37 stitches for a mouth wound.

1957 – Where's her glove?
Phillies centre fielder Richie Ashburn hit spectator Alice Roth with foul balls twice in the same at-bat at Shibe Park in Philadelphia. The first foul ball broke her nose and the second hit her while she was being taken away on a stretcher. Mrs. Roth was the wife of Earl Roth, the sports editor of the *Philadelphia Bulletin*.

1966 – Mays moves past Foxx in HR stakes
San Francisco Giants centre fielder Willie Mays moved to second on the all-time home-run list of the time, after passing Jimmie Foxx (534). Mays' #535 came in the Giants 4-3 home win over St Louis. The only man ahead of Mays was Babe Ruth (714). Mays retired in 1973 with 660 homers, 54 short of 'the Babe.'

1976 – 'Whispering Death' dominates
Fast bowler Michael Holding became the only West Indian to take 14 wickets in a Test during the fifth Test against England at the Oval. Holding captured 8 for 92 and 6 for 57 to wrap up a 231-run victory and a 3-0 series win.

1990 – Fantastic Fisk
Chicago White Sox catcher Carlton Fisk hit a homer off Charlie Hough in a 4-2 win over the Texas Rangers, setting 2 records. It made him the all-time home run leader among catchers with 328 and the all-time White Sox leader with 187 home runs.

2008 – Phelps overtakes golden Spitz
Michael Phelps eclipsed Mark Spitz's performance at the 1972 Munich Games when he won his eighth gold medal as part of the US 4 x 100m medley relay team at the Beijing Olympics. Together with Aaron Peirsol, Brendan Hansen and Jason Lezak, Phelps swam a world record time of 3:29.34 – his seventh world record in his personal 'Great Haul of China.'

BIRTHDATES

1878	Australian Test batsman REGGIE DUFF – died 1911
1880	South African Test wicketkeeper PERCY SHERWELL – died 1948
1909	England soccer midfielder WILFRED COPPING – died 1980
1922	England Test spinner ROY TATTERSALL – died 2011
1946	South African golfer HUGH BAIOCCHI
1952	Brazilian auto racer NELSON PIQUET
1952	Argentine tennis player GUILLERMO VILAS
1953	Australian AFL defender/coach MICHAEL MALTHOUSE
1955	American golfer SCOTT SIMPSON
1957	English figure skater ROBIN COUSINS
1963	NFL coach/analyst JON GRUDEN
1965	American golfer DOTTIE PEPPER
1970	American tennis player JIM COURIER
1970	Norwegian soccer striker ØYVIND LEONHARDSEN
1977	French soccer striker THIERRY HENRY

⑱ AUGUST

1922 – Sarazen youngest PGA winner
Twenty-year-old Gene Sarazen became the youngest winner in PGA Championship history when he beat Emmer French, 4 & 3 at Oakmont CC near Pittsburgh. Sarazen also became the first player to win the PGA Championship and US Open title in the same year.

1934 – Patient Ponsford's fond Test farewell
In his last Test, Australian opener Bill Ponsford scored 266 in a memorable 5-hour stand of 451 with Don Bradman during the fifth Test against England at the Oval. Somewhat overshadowed, Bradman hit 244. It was the biggest stand for any wicket in Test cricket at the time, and remains in the top 4 of all-time. England lost by 562 runs in a match they only needed to draw to retain the Ashes.

1992 – Brilliant Bird calls it a day
Star Boston Celtics forward Larry Bird announced his retirement from the NBA because of chronic back problems. He is the only non-centre to win 3 consecutive MVP awards (1984–86). Bird led the Celtics to 3 NBA titles, winning Finals MVP twice. He averaged 24.3 points, 10 rebounds and 6.3 assists in his 13-year career. He appeared in 10 All-Star Games. Bird later coached and undertook a management role with the Indiana Pacers.

1994 – Australia retakes rugby cup
Australia regained the Bledisloe Cup, defeating New Zealand 20-16 at the Sydney Football Stadium. The match featured Wallabies halfback George Gregan's famous try-saving tackle on NZ winger Jeff Wilson.

2000 – Woeful Windies
In the first two-day Test in over 50 years, England beat the West Indies by an innings for the first time since 1966 at Headingley. Trailing by 100 runs, the struggling Windies were dismissed in 26.2 overs for a paltry 61 – their second double-figure score in 3 Tests.

2004 – Greeks withdraw from home Games
Greek sprinters Kostas Kenteris and Katerina Thanou, both medallists at the Sydney Games, withdrew from the Athens Olympics after missing doping controls at the Olympic Village on the eve of the opening ceremony. The pair spent 4 days in hospital, claiming they were injured in a motorcycle crash. Despite denials, the IAAF suspended them.

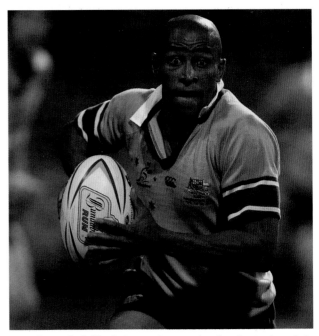

Australian rugby halfback George Gregan, who played a starring role in the 1994 Bledisloe Cup.

2004 – Oldest swim mark beaten by US
The US team of Natalie Coghlan, Carly Piper, Dana Vollmer and Kaitlin Sandino broke the oldest existing world record in swimming when they took the gold medal in the 4 x 200m freestyle relay at the Athens Olympics. The Americans sizzled at 7:53.42, smashing the world mark by 2.05 seconds. The previous record, set by drug-assisted East German athletes, had lasted 17 years to the day.

BIRTHDATES
1920	England Test wicketkeeper GODFREY EVANS – died 1999
1933	French soccer striker JUST FONTAINE
1934	Baseball Hall of Fame outfielder ROBERTO CLEMENTE – died 1972
1935	American decathlete RAFER JOHNSON
1943	Italian soccer midfielder GIANNI RIVERA
1952	Argentine soccer midfielder RICKY VILLA
1956	Indian Test batsman SANDEEP PATIL
1980	Argentine soccer midfielder ESTEBAN CAMBIASSO

⑲ AUGUST

1933 – Wills-Moody streak halted by injury
American Helen Wills Moody had her 7-year winning streak halted in the final of the US Nationals at Forest Hills against compatriot Helen Jacobs. After losing the first set 8-6, Wills Moody, wearing a back brace for her injured right hip and leg, levelled the match, taking the second set 6-3. With Jacobs leading the third set 3-0, Wills Moody forfeited due to her injuries. It was the first time Jacobs had beaten Wills Moody in their 8 matches.

1948 – Thousands honour 'The Babe'
In intermittent heavy rain, 6,000 mourners attended George Herman 'Babe' Ruth's funeral mass and there were another 75,000 outside St Patrick's Cathedral in midtown Manhattan. Among those attending were Joe DiMaggio, Jack Dempsey, Connie Mack, Hank Greenberg, Leo Durocher, Mel Ott, New York Governor Thomas Dewey and New York City Mayor Bill O'Dwyer. Ruth had passed away 3 days earlier as a result of throat cancer at the age of 53.

1976 – Wadsworth passes away at 29
New Zealand Test wicket keeper Ken Wadsworth died as a result of skin cancer, aged just 29. Wadsworth had played 33 Tests, making 96 dismissals. He averaged 59.00 against the West Indies in the Caribbean in 1971–72, when the Kiwis drew all 5 Tests.

1984 – Sizzling 4 rounds for 'Supermex'
Lee Trevino became the first PGA Champion to win with 4 rounds in the 60s (69-68-67-69) when he beat Lanny Wadkins and Gary Player by 4 strokes at the Shoal Creek CC in Birmingham, Alabama. He accomplished the same feat in the 1968 US Open but hadn't won a major in 10 years. It was his 27th and last win before he joined the Senior PGA Tour.

1985 – Gower's best
England cricket captain David Gower hit a career best 215 in a blistering partnership of 331 in 343 minutes, with opener Tim Robinson (148), in the fifth Test at Edgbaston. It was the highest score by an England captain against Australia since Wally Hammond's 240 at Lord's in 1938.

1992 – SL defeat despite three tons
Three players hit centuries on the same day before Sri Lanka declared at 547 for 8 in the first Test against Australia in Colombo. Asanka Gurusinha made 137, captain Arjuna Ranatunga 127 and Romesh Kaluwitharana 132 not out. In the second innings, SL's last 8 wickets fell for just 37 and they crashed to a 16-run defeat.

2006 – Teddy Oldest in Premier League
At 40 years and 139 days of age, Teddy Sheringham became the oldest player to take the field in a Premiership match when he came on as an 82nd-minute substitute in West Ham's 3-1 victory over Charlton at Upton Park. It was the former England forward's 699th league appearance.

2008 – Wrestling upset
Twenty-one-year-old wrestling prodigy Henry Cejudo, who had competed in only one world-level senior tournament before the Beijing Olympics, won the freestyle 55kg wrestling gold medal. Cejudo, from the US, defeated Tomohiro Matsunaga of Japan 2-2 on tiebreaker and 3-0 in the best-of-three match. He had been 31st in the previous year's world championships, his only prior tournament at the highest level.

BIRTHDATES
1909 New Zealand rugby union number 8 RON KING – died 1988
1931 American jockey WILLIE SHOEMAKER – died 2003
1934 American tennis player RENEE RICHARDS
1943 New Zealand rugby union halfback SID GOING
1958 Scottish golfer GORDON BRAND JR.
1960 NFL kicker MORTEN ANDERSON
1965 Australian rower JAMES TOMKINS
1971 American tennis player MARY JO FERNADEZ
1971 Portuguese soccer forward JOAO PINTO
1973 Italian soccer defender MARCO MATERAZZI
1985 American snowboarder LINDSEY JACOBELLIS

1920 – American Football Conference formed

The American Professional Football Conference, the forerunner of the NFL, was formed in Canton, Ohio. Charter members were Cleveland, Dayton, Akron, Canton, Buffalo, Hammond and Rochester, all of whom had previously played in the Ohio League or New York Pro Football League (NYPFL). The league went on to become the NFL in 1922.

1922 – IOC's hand forced by women

A one-day track meet labelled the first 'Women's Olympic Games' was conducted in Paris. The IOC were forced to add women's track and field events to the 1928 Olympic program in Amsterdam.

1938 – Gehrig's final Grand Slam

Lou Gehrig hit a grand slam home run in the first inning off Buck Ross in the New York Yankees' 11-3 win over the Philadelphia A's at Shibe Park. It was the 23rd and last of his career and remains an MLB record.

1944 – Hamilton upsets favourite in PGA

In the only major to be played that year, due to WWII, qualifier Bob Hamilton won the PGA Championship, beating heavily favoured Byron Nelson 1-up at the Manito CC in Spokane, Washington. In the final, he birdied the 19th hole to grab a 1-up lead, and held the advantage.

1995 – Non-member Webb takes Open

Australian golfer Karrie Webb won the first of her 3 British Open titles, before she had even become a member of the LPGA Tour. The Australian posted a total 278 as she cruised to a 6-stroke victory over Annika Sörenstam and Jill McGill at the Woburn CC. She won the Open again in 1997 and 2002.

2006 – First Cricket Test forfeit

Darrell Hair became the first umpire in the 129-year history of Test cricket to declare a match over by forfeiture, when Pakistan refused to take the field for the final session of the fourth day's play in the fourth Test against England at the Oval. Hair, an Australian, and the West Indian official Billy Doctrove, accused Inzamam ul-Haq's team of ball tampering. After tea, when the Pakistanis refused to end their protest, Hair and Doctrove awarded the Test to England. Thirty minutes later, the Pakistanis announced they were ready to play, with England also anxious to resume. Having already announced the forfeit, however, the umpires refused the offer. The ICC charged ul-Haq with bringing the game into disrepute.

2006 – Another Woods record

Tiger Woods became the first player in history to go consecutive years winning at least 2 majors when he scored an easy win in the PGA Championship at Medinah, Illinois. One month after an emotional victory in the British Open, Woods closed with a 4-under 68 for an 18-under 270 total and a 5-shot win over countryman Shaun Micheel. It was his third PGA Championship and his 12th career major.

2008 – 'Lightning' Bolt

Jamaican sprinter Usain Bolt took out the first Olympic sprint double since Carl Lewis in 1984, when he ran a world record in the 200m at the Beijing Games. Bolt's time of 19.30 seconds was 0.02 better than Michael Johnson's old world mark, topping off the 9.69 seconds in which he ran the 100m 4 nights earlier.

BIRTHDATES

1869	England Test batsman JACK BROWN – died 1904
1906	English tennis player HENRY 'BUNNY' AUSTIN – died 2000
1931	American boxing promoter DON KING
1952	England Test spinner JOHN EMBUREY
1956	West Indies Test batsman ALVIN GREENIDGE
1957	Scottish rugby flanker FINLAY CALDER
1960	MLB pitcher MARK LANGSTON
1962	American golfer DUFFY WALDORF
1968	French rugby union number 8 ABDELATIF BENAZZI
1968	Swedish soccer midfielder KLAS INGESSON
1972	Welsh rugby union number 8 SCOTT QUINNELL

㉑ AUGUST

1914 – Hagan leads Open wire-to-wire
Twenty-one-year-old Walter Hagen became the first man to lead the US Open from start to finish at the Midlothian CC in Blue Island, near Chicago. Hagen shot rounds of 68-74-75-73 for a 2-over 290, 1 stroke better than charging amateur Chick Evans.

1931 – 'The Babe' – 600 homers
Babe Ruth hit the 600th home run of his career off George Blaeholder of the St Louis Browns in the NY Yankees' 11-7 win at Sportsman's Park III. Lou Gehrig homered immediately after Ruth's historic blow. In their 10 years as teammates, they hit home runs in the same inning 19 times, and in the same game 72 times.

1982 – 300 saves for Fingers
Milwaukee closer Rollie Fingers became the first pitcher to save 300 games, concluding the Brewers' 3-2 win over the Seattle Mariners. Fingers retired after the 1985 season with 341 saves in 17 seasons and was inducted into the Hall of Fame in 1992.

1986 – Botham returns with record
Champion England all-rounder Ian Botham broke the world record for Test wickets in the drawn third Test against New Zealand at the Oval. Botham had just been reinstated to the England side after a ban for admitting to the use of marijuana, and equalled the record (355) with his first ball, trapping Jeff Crowe lbw.

1993 – Wallabies series win over Boks
In rugby union, Tim Horan scored a try and Marty Roebuck kicked 4 penalties and a conversion in Australia's 19-12 win over South Africa at the Sydney Football Stadium. The victory capped the Wallabies' first series win against the Springboks since an anti-apartheid boycott was imposed in the early 1970s.

1999 – Expensive Keane transfer
Nineteen-year-old Wolverhampton Wanderers' striker Robbie Keane became the most expensive teenager in British football when he transferred to Coventry City for a fee of £6 million. Keane has made several more big money moves since, playing for EPL juggernauts such as Tottenham Hotspur, Liverpool and West Ham.

American super-swimmer Michael Phelps in his gold medal winning swim in the 100m butterfly at the 2004 Athens Olympics.

2004 – Eighth swim medal to Phelps
American Michael Phelps won a record-equalling eighth medal, tying Russian gymnast Alexsander Dityatin's 1980 feat, at the Athens Olympics, as the US team swam a world record (3:30.68) in the 4 x 100m medley relay. Phelps swam in the heats but handed his place in the final to Ian Crocker. Phelps won individual gold medals in the 200m/400m IMs, the 100m/200m butterfly and as part of the 4 x 200m freestyle relay. The swimmer also collected bronze medals in the 200m freestyle and 4 x 100m relay.

2008 – Three from 4 for US soccer
The US made it 3 Olympic women's soccer gold medals in 4 attempts, with a 1-0 overtime win over Brazil in Beijing. Carli Lloyd scored in the sixth minute of extra time to seal the US gold medal. The US made it 4 golds in a row at the London Olympics in 2012.

BIRTHDATES
1936 Basketball Hall of Fame centre WILT CHAMBERLAIN – died 2000
1938 England rugby union captain MIKE WESTON
1945 Pro Football Hall of Fame linebacker WILLIE LANIER
1955 South African surfer SHAUN TOMSON
1959 NFL quarterback JIM McMAHON
1964 Australian surfer GARY ELKERTON
1969 Australian jockey GLEN BOSS
1970 Dutch road cyclist ERIK DEKKER
1971 Australian AFL midfielder ROBERT HARVEY
1975 Australian Test batsman SIMON KATICH
1986 Jamaican sprinter USAIN BOLT

1851 – 'America's Cup' born

The yacht *America* beat 14 boats from the Royal Yacht Squadron of Great Britain in a race around the Isle of Wight to win the Hundred Guinea Cup. The crew donated the trophy to the New York Yacht Club and in 1870 it was offered as challenge prize under the name of 'The America's Cup', now the best-known trophy in international yachting.

1939 – Harsh penalties cost title

World lightweight champion Henry Armstrong was penalised 5 rounds by referee Arthur Donovan for punching low in his unanimous points defeat to Lou Ambers at Yankee Stadium in New York. The penalties cost him the fight; 2 officials had Ambers winning 8-7.

1950 – Gibson breaks down the barriers

Althea Gibson became the first black tennis player to compete in the US national hampionship. She later became the first black player to compete in the French Open and Wimbledon. Gibson won both the US and Wimbledon singles titles in 1957 and 1958.

1951 – Globetrotters draw German crowd

The Harlem Globetrotters set a basketball attendance record during their 50th anniversary world tour, playing before a record 75,052 fans at Berlin's Olympic Stadium.

1965 – Giants/Dodgers rivalry erupts

One of baseball's bitter rivalries erupted into a 14-minute brawl after a nasty incident between LA Dodgers pitcher John Roseboro and Juan Marichal of the San Francisco Giants. After a Roseboro pitch went close to his face, Marichal went berserk, hitting him across the forehead with a bat. An all-in melee followed. Marichal was suspended for 8 games and fined a then-record $1,750.

1998 – Boks take Tri Nations

South Africa won the Tri Nations rugby trophy for the first time when they beat Australia 29-15 in Johannesburg. The Springboks' fullback Percy Montgomery was in spectacular kicking form, landing 5 penalties and 2 conversions.

2007 – Rangers score 30

The Texas Rangers became the first team in 110 years to score 30 runs in a game, setting an American League record in a 30-3 rout of the Baltimore Orioles at Camden Yards. It was the ninth time a major league team had scored 30 runs, and the first since the Chicago Colts set the major league mark in a 36-7 rout of Louisville in 1897. It was the most lopsided loss in Orioles franchise history

2008 – Distance double to Dibaba

Tirunesh Dibaba of Ethiopia became the first woman to win the distance double at the same Olympics when she sprinted away to win the 5,000m in 15:41.40 in Beijing. A week earlier, she won the 10,000m, setting a new Olympic record time of 29:54.66

2008 – Bolt's incredible treble

Usain Bolt wrapped up one of the most amazing performances in Olympic athletics history by leading Jamaica to a 4 x 100m relay victory in a world record 37.10 seconds at the Beijing Games. Bolt became the first sprinter to set 3 world records in the same Olympics after blitzing the 100m/200m double. Bolt joined Lewis, Bobby Morrow and Jesse Owens as only the fourth man to win the 100m, 200m and 4 x 100m relay at the Olympics.

BIRTHDATES

1897	Australian Test cricket captain BILL WOODFULL – died 1965
1930	Brazilian soccer goalkeeper GILMAR
1939	Baseball Hall of Fame outfielder CARL YASTRZEMSKI
1941	NFL coach BILL PARCELLS
1956	Australian Test spinner PETER TAYLOR
1956	MLB outfielder PAUL MOLITOR
1957	English snooker player STEVE DAVIS
1964	Swedish tennis player MATS WILANDER
1965	South African surfer WENDY BOTHA
1968	Kenyan middle distance runner PAUL ERENG
1968	Russian soccer midfielder ALEKSANDR MOSTOVOI
1974	Argentine rugby halfback AGUSTIN PICHOT

1936 – Pitching ace debut
At age 17, future Hall of Fame pitcher Bob Feller made his first MLB appearance for the Indians, striking out 15 St Louis Browns in a 4-1 win in Cleveland. After the season ended, Feller returned to Van Meter, Iowa, for his senior year in high school.

1938 – Hutton's record marathon innings
England batting icon Len Hutton amassed a record 364 against Australia in the fifth Test at the Oval. The record stood for 20 years until Gary Sobers made an unbeaten 365 in 1958. An injury-hit Australia lost by an innings and 579 runs. England captain Wally Hammond declared at a record 903 for 7, a mark that held for 59 years, until Sri Lanka scored 952 for 6 against India in 1997–98.

1971 – Two major firsts for Indian cricket
India scored its first ever Test victory in England, with a 4-wicket win in the third Test at the Oval. Leg spinner Bhagwat Chandrasekhar set up the historic win by taking 6 for 38, leaving England a moderate 173 to defend in the Indian second innings. The victory gave the Indians their first series on English soil 1-0.

1997 – Rugby's de Beer on target
Springbok five-eighth Jannie de Beer scored 26 points with a try, 6 conversions and 3 penalties in South Africa's record 61-22 thrashing of Australia in Pretoria. De Beer's points haul was a South African record and the Wallabies biggest-ever defeat.

2008 – Four hoops gold to Leslie
Lisa Leslie capped off her illustrious Olympic career with a fourth straight basketball gold medal, scoring 14 points in a 92-65 victory over Australia in Beijing. She joined former teammate Teresa Edwards as the only basketball players to have won 4 Olympic golds.

2008 – Relay double to US
The US captured the 4 x 400m relay Olympic gold medal double at the Beijing Games. Sanya Richards anchored her team to a come-from-behind victory in 3:18.54. It was the fourth consecutive Olympic win for the US in the women's event.

2009 – England regains Ashes
England beat Australia in 4 days at the Oval to regain the Ashes, winning the series 2-1. The 197-run defeat meant Ricky Ponting became the first Australian captain since Billy Murdoch in 1890 to lose the Ashes twice in England.

2010 – Celebrity divorce
Tiger Woods and wife Elin's divorce became final, their 6-year marriage ending after a massive sex scandal that enveloped the world's no. 1 golfer. Reports indicated Elin received between $100 million and $500 million in assets. The couple share custody of their 2 children, Sam Alexis, 3, and Charlie Axel, 1.

2012 – Armstrong stripped bare
Seven-time Tour de France winner Lance Armstrong said he wouldn't take the case to arbitration after the US Anti-Doping Agency officially charged him with doping and trafficking drugs, and suspended him from competition. His lawsuit against USADA in federal court in Texas had been dismissed and he was stripped of all results dating back to 1 August 1998 and banned from cycling for life. He later admitted to doping.

BIRTHDATES
1910	Italian soccer striker GIUSEPPE MEAZZA – died 1979
1911	Norwegian ski jumper BIRGER RUUD – died 1998
1929	Australian golfer PETER THOMSON
1933	Australian swim coach DON TALBOT
1934	Pro Football Hall of Fame quarterback SONNY JURGENSEN
1942	American tennis player NANCY RICHEY
1949	British strongman GEOFF CAPES
1961	England soccer midfielder GARY MABBUTT
1963	England Test fast bowler RICHARD ILLINGWORTH
1968	American golfer CHRIS DI MARCO
1971	Italian soccer midfielder DEMETRIO ALBERTINI
1972	England Test batsman MARK BUTCHER
1978	NBA forward KOBE BRYANT
1982	American swimmer NATALIE COGHLIN
1984	English soccer defender GLEN JOHNSON
1988	NBA point guard JEREMY LIN

1929 – Tommy's record total

Scotsman Tommy Armour broke Arthur Smith's 24-year-old scoring record by 5 when he won the Western Open at the Ozaukee CC in Mequon, Wisconsin, with a 273 total.

1972 – First ODI century

England opener Dennis Amiss scored the first century in any ODI with a sparkling 103 off 134 balls in a 6-wicket win over Australia at Old Trafford. Amiss also hit the first century in a World Cup match, against India at Lord's, in 1975.

1973 – Sobers, not sober!

West Indian captain Garry Sobers completed his 26th and final Test century during the third Test victory against England at Lord's. He scored 150 before retiring. He later admitted he had spent the previous night drinking port and brandy, so was in poor shape when he resumed his innings. He was worried about vomiting when he retired with a 'stomach virus'.

1984 – Bradley brilliant

Pat Bradley set an LPGA record, shooting 28 for 9 holes in the Columbia Savings Classic in Denver. The record was tied several times, and eventually broken by Jimin Kang in 2005 when she fired a 27 in the ShopRite LPGA Classic in a round of 62.

1989 – Troubled Rose suspended

All-time hits leader and Cincinnati manager Pete Rose and MLB Commissioner Bart Giamatti agreed to an indefinite suspension for betting on baseball, without a life suspension. The accord ended almost 6 months of legal wrangling.

1994 – Perkins' super swim

Kieran Perkins of Australia set new world records for the 800m and 1,500m in the same swim at the Commonwealth Games in Victoria, Canada. Perkins' time of 14:41.66 was 1.82 seconds faster than his own mark set at the 1992 Barcelona Olympics. The record stood for 7 years until fellow Australian Grant Hackett's 14:34.56 in 2001.

2004 – El Guerrouj breaks through for gold

Moroccan superstar Hicham El Guerrouj won a first Olympic gold medal when he took out the 1,500m in Athens. El Guerrouj stormed home in a time of 3:34.19 to beat Bernard Lagat of Kenya. Guerrouj later made it a double when he won the 5,000m.

2008 – Tragedy brings out best in US volleyball

The US won the men's volleyball gold at the Beijing Olympics with an upset 3-1 victory over defending champions Brazil. At the start of the Olympics, coach Hugh McCutcheon's father-in-law had been stabbed to death in Beijing. The US team, stirred by the tragedy, began an incredible undefeated run.

2008 – Spain challenges US in basketball

The US men's basketball team survived a huge challenge from Spain, winning 118-107 in the final at the Beijing Olympics. After overwhelming all comers for 7 games, the Americans led by only 4 points with less than 2 minutes to play. Dwyane Wade scored 27 points for the Americans and Kobe Bryant 20.

BIRTHDATES

1890	American-Hawaiian surfer DUKE KAHANAMOKU – died 1968
1940	England rugby union winger KEITH SAVAGE
1952	NFL coach MIKE SHANAHAN
1953	Scottish golfer SAM TORRANCE
1956	American heavyweight boxer GERRY COONEY
1959	South African Test batsman ADRIAN KUIPER
1960	Baseball Hall of Fame shortstop CAL RIPKEN JR
1963	England rugby union fullback JONATHAN WEBB
1965	Basketball Hall of Fame guard REGGIE MILLER
1966	Australian swimmer JON SIEBEN
1968	American boxer JAMES TONEY
1970	American golfer RICH BEEM
1973	Dutch swimmer INGE DE BRUIJN
1977	Dominican MLB shortstop RAFAEL FURCAL
1986	NFL running back ARIAN FOSTER

1875 – First English Channel success
Captain Matthew Webb became the first man to swim the English Channel, crossing from Dover on the English coast to Cape Gris Nez in France in 21 hours, 45 minutes. He relied mainly on breaststroke and swam an estimated 38 miles in covering the straight-line distance of 20 miles. During the swim in stormy seas, Webb sang, drank coffee and beer, ate steaks, and was stung by jellyfish.

1922 – MLB run-fest
The Chicago Cubs beat the Philadelphia Phillies 26-23 at Wrigley Field in the highest-scoring game in MLB history. The game featured 51 hits, 23 walks, 10 errors, and 25 runners left on base. The Cubs tied an MLB record with 14 runs in the fourth inning.

1946 – Hogan's first major
Ben Hogan captured his first major title when he won the PGA Championship in Portland, Oregon. In the 36-hole final, Ed Oliver built a 3-hole lead in the morning round, before Hogan regained his putting touch in the afternoon, posting a 30 on the front 9 for a 1-up lead. He then closed out Oliver 6 & 4.

1968 – McCabe dies
Flamboyant Australian batsman Stan McCabe died aged 58. McCabe played 2 of the most famous innings in Ashes history, hitting an explosive 187 not out in Sydney during the infamous 'Bodyline' series in 1932–33, and his 232 at Trent Bridge in 1938, one of the best innings of all-time. In 39 Tests, McCabe scored 1,543 runs at 48.21.

1986 – 24 runs off one over
England's Ian Botham equalled a Test-record 24 runs off an over by New Zealand's Derek Stirling during the third Test at the Oval. West Indian Andy Roberts scored 24 off Botham himself in 1980–81.

1991 – Best-ever 100m
In the greatest 100m race of all time, 6 runners went under 10 seconds in the same event for the first time at the World Championships in Tokyo. First to sixth were separated by just 0.1 seconds. Olympic champion Carl Lewis broke the world record to win in 9.86 seconds from Leroy Burrell in 9.88, with Dennis Mitchell in third place with 9.91. Englishman Linford Christie (9.92), Frankie Fredericks of Namibia (9.95) and Jamaican Raymond Stewart (9.96) were next.

1995 – Symonds sixes record
Australian Andrew Symonds hit a world record for first-class cricket with his 16 sixes in his unbeaten 254 for Gloucestershire against Glamorgan at Abergavenny. Symonds hit 4 sixes in the second innings to set a match record of 20.

1996 – Tiger wins three straight amateur titles
Twenty-year-old Stanford student Tiger Woods became the first player to win 3 consecutive US Amateur titles, after a dramatic comeback against Steve Scott in a 2-hole playoff at the Pumpkin Ridge GC in Cornelius, Oregon.

2005 – La Russa moves into third
St Louis skipper Tony La Russa, with his 2,195th career triumph – a 6-3 win against Pittsburgh at PNC Park – moved past Sparky Anderson for third place for most victories by a major league manager. Connie Mack (3,731) and John McGraw (2,763) were first and second on the all-time managerial list.

BIRTHDATES
1898	England Test wicketkeeper ARTHUR WOOD – died 1973
1925	England soccer striker NAT LOFTHOUSE – died 2011
1927	American tennis player ALTHEA GIBSON – died 2003
1927	Australian marathon swimmer DES RENFORD – died 1999
1944	Canadian NHL coach JACQUES DEMERS
1946	MLB pitcher ROLLIE FINGERS
1952	Sri Lankan Test captain DULEEP MENDIS
1965	NFL linebacker CORNELIUS BENNETT
1969	Scottish golfer CATRIONA MATTHEW
1970	NBA forward ROBERT HORRY
1972	NFL receiver MARVIN HARRISON
1975	Australian swimmer PETRIA THOMAS
1977	American boxer DIEGO CORRALES – died 2007

㉖ AUGUST

1920 – Swashbuckling fencing performance
Italian Nedo Nadi completed a spectacular performance in winning the sabre team event for an unprecedented 5 gold medals at the Antwerp Olympics. He was also part of the triumphant Italian foil and épée teams, and won the individual foil and épée titles.

1920 – Fastest century by the clock
England batsman Percy Fender scored the fastest first-class century in terms of time spent at the crease when he reached 100 in just 35 minutes for Surrey against Northamptonshire at Northampton.

1963 – Worrell bows out
West Indian captain Frank Worrell played his final Test match, an 8-wicket fifth Test victory over England, at the Oval. Worrell was the first black player to captain the West Indies on a regular basis. He played 51 Tests, scoring 3,860 runs at 49.48. He died in 1967 from leukaemia, aged just 42. The West Indies and Australia now play for the Sir Frank Worrell Trophy.

1999 – Back-to-back world titles for Freeman
Australian sprinter Cathy Freeman successfully defended her World 400m title in 49.67 seconds at Seville in Spain. Freeman first won the event in Athens in 1997. After lighting the flame at the spectacular opening ceremony at the Sydney Olympics, Freeman went on to win the gold medal over the distance. She retired from competition prior to the 2004 Athens Games.

2007 – Seven golfers in playoff
South African Senior PGA champion Denis Watson won a record 7-man playoff in the Boeing Classic at Snoqualmie in Seattle, Washington. He capped a wild finish by making an 18ft putt for eagle on the second playoff hole to win his second Champions Tour event of the season. The previous Champions Tour playoff record was five.

Australian sprinter Cathy Freeman during and after the 400m race at the 1999 World Athletics Championships in Seville, Spain

BIRTHDATES
1883	England soccer goalkeeper SAM HARDY – died 1966
1930	West Indian Test batsman JOE SOLOMON
1934	Basketball Hall of Fame forward TOM HEINSOHN
1952	American swimmer JOHN KINSELLA
1954	English golfer HOWARD CLARK
1959	NBA coach STAN VAN GUNDY
1962	American hurdler ROGER KINGDOM
1968	English track cyclist CHRIS BOARDMAN
1970	Australian rugby union centre JASON LITTLE
1970	South African Test fast bowler BRETT SCHULTZ
1977	Swedish swimmer THERESE ALSHAMMER

1908 – 'The Don' is born
Australia's greatest batsman, Sir Donald Bradman, was born in the New South Wales town of Cootamundra. No batsman in history comes close to Bradman's statistics in the Test and first-class arenas. In 52 Tests, he scored 6,996 runs at an average of 99.94. He made 29 Test centuries with a career best of 334. In 80 Test innings, he scored 50 or more on 42 occasions, an amazing 52.5%. In 234 first-class matches he amassed 28,067 runs at 95.14. He made 117 first-class centuries with a career high 452 not out. He died in February 2001, aged 90, as a beloved national treasure.

1956 – Unbeaten Rocky retires
World heavyweight champion Rocky Marciano announced his retirement from the ring as the only world champion to have completed his career undefeated. At 5ft 10in and 185lbs, Marciano was smaller and slower than most heavyweights but he was tough and had a powerful desire. He held the title from 1952 to 1956 and defended it on 6 occasions. He was troubled by chronic back problems and finished with a record of 49-0 with 43 knockouts. In 1969, he died in a plane crash near Newton, Iowa.

1973 – Sobers catching mark
West Indian captain Gary Sobers equalled the record for catches in a Test by a non-wicketkeeper, with 6, during the third Test against England at Lord's.

1979 – Proctor smashes 6-sixes
South African all-rounder Mike Proctor smashed 6 consecutive sixes, spread over 2 overs, off Somerset's Dennis Breakwell at Taunton. Proctor's feat equalled a world record that still stands.

1982 – Henderson become steals leader
In baseball, Rickey Henderson became the single-season steals record-holder, breaking Lou Brock's 1974 record of 118 in Oakland's 5-4 loss at Milwaukee.

1997 – Beachley takes first surfing crown
Australian Layne Beachley clinched her first ASP World Surfing title after winning her heat in France. Beachley won 5 events in an 11-tournament season. She won by the greatest points margin in the history of the sport (2,420 points) and capped a stellar year with a successful defence of her Hawaiian Triple Crown championship. Beachley went on to win a record 6 consecutive world titles before her run was broken in 2004.

2005 – 42 year-wait for England girls over
The England women's team survived a few scares and determined Australian bowling to win the second Test at Worcester by 6 wickets. It was their first victory over Australia since 1984, and after 42 years, they had regained the Ashes.

2006 – Bonds walked again, and again
Cincinnati Reds starter Kyle Lohse intentionally walked Barry Bonds in the first inning at AT&T Park, making it Bonds' 100th free pass of the year. It marked the San Francisco left fielder hitting the century mark for walks in 13 seasons to tie Babe Ruth's major league record. The Giants won 8-0.

BIRTHDATES
1908	Australian Test captain SIR DONALD BRADMAN – died 2001
1916	South African cricket/rugby player TONY HARRIS – died 1993
1925	English soccer striker NAT LOFTHOUSE – died 2011
1927	Australian swim coach JOHN CAREW – died 2008
1947	New Zealand Test batsman JOHN MORRISON
1954	English tennis player JOHN LLOYD
1954	British auto racer DERECK WARWICK
1957	German golfer BERNHARD LANGER
1959	Austrian auto racer GERHARD BERGER
1961	New Zealand rugby union STEVE McDOWELL
1968	New Zealand golfer MICHAEL LONG
1969	England Test all rounder MARK EALHAM
1970	Australian Test fast bowler ANDY BICHEL
1970	England Test fast bowler MARK ILOTT
1970	MLB outfielder JIM THOME
1971	New Zealand rugby union fullback GLEN OSBORNE
1974	Pakistan Test batsman YOUSUF YOUHANA
1976	Spanish tennis player CARLOS MOYÁ
1976	Australian auto racer MARK WEBBER
1977	Portuguese soccer midfielder DECO

㉘ AUGUST

1977 – Farewell to Pelé

Brazilian superstar footballer Pelé played his final match in the National American Soccer League, as the New York Cosmos beat the Seattle Sounders 2-1 to win the league championship in Soccer Bowl 77. A record crowd for an NASL title game, of 35,548 fans, turned up to Portland's Civic Stadium to see Pelé's last game. He is widely recognised as one of the greatest footballers of all time, and still holds numerous club and international records.

1981 – Coe breaks mile mark for third time

British runner Sebastian Coe broke the world mile record for the third and last time in his career. Coe ran a time of 3:47.33 in Brussels, 1.07 seconds faster than his countryman Steve Ovett's previous record. Coe's mark stood until 1985, when it was broken by another British runner, Steve Cram, in a time of 3:46.32 in Oslo.

1992 – Murali Test debut

Sri Lankan off-spinner Muttiah Muralitharan made his Test debut in the second Test against Australia in Colombo. Murali holds the world record for Test wickets with 800.

1995 – Highest score by losers

English county side Nottinghamshire compiled the highest score by a team who lost a first-class match by an innings. Playing at Northampton, Notts was dismissed for 527. Northamptonshire replied with a club record 781 for 7 declared. Indian Test spinner Anil Kumble then captured 5 for 43 as Notts crashed for 157.

2006 – Instant replay comes to the US Open ...

The US Open became the first Grand Slam tournament to use instant replay technology to oversee line calls in the main stadiums. American Mardy Fish ushered in the age of instant replay when he questioned a line call in his match against Simon Greul.

2008 – ... and in baseball too

Instant replay arrived in MLB at Wrigley Field in Chicago, as the Cubs beat Philadelphia 6-4. An umpiring crew chief could now phone a replay centre in New York to send him all available feeds so he could review boundary calls.

2010 – Cricket spot-fixing scandal

News broke that the ongoing Lord's Test was under investigation over spot-fixing allegations. Player agent Mazhar Majeed was filmed in a sting operation by English tabloid *News of the World*, claiming to have bribed Pakistan's bowlers to bowl no-balls on demand. Pakistan captain Salman Butt, Mohammad Amir and Mohammad Asif were suspended and ultimately jailed after the ICC's anti-corruption unit and Scotland Yard completed investigations.

BIRTHDATES

1913	Australian Test captain LINDSAY HASSETT – died 1993
1943	MLB manager LOU PINIELLA
1947	England soccer defender EMLYN HUGHES – died 2004
1953	Australian surfer MARK WARREN
1958	American figure skater SCOTT HAMILTON
1964	American golfer LEE JANZEN
1965	Australian rugby union front rower DAN CROWLEY
1969	Canadian NHL centre PIERRE TURGEON
1971	American swimmer JANET EVANS
1975	New Zealand rugby union lock ROYCE WILLIS
1981	Brazilian auto racer RAPHAEL MATOS
1983	Sri Lankan Test fast bowler LASITH MALINGA

Sri Lankan spin bowler Muttiah Muralitharan in action during the first Test against South Africa at Galle in 2000.

1882 – 'The Demon' strikes as Ashes born
Legendary fast bowler Frederick Spofforth took 7 for 44 to lead Australia to an amazing 7-run victory over England in the one-off Test at the Oval. Set only 85 to win, England crashed to be all out for 77. Spofforth had match figures of 14 for 90. The series between the 2 countries was thereafter coined 'The Ashes' after a mock obituary for English cricket appeared in *The Sporting Times*.

1920 – Bleibtrey's golden sweep
American Ethelda Bleibtrey completed a unique treble at the Antwerp Olympics when she won gold medals in all 3 women's events (100m/400m freestyle, and the 4 x 100 freestyle relay). In 5 races, including heats, Bleibtrey broke the world record in each one.

1960 – Italian cycling double
Reigning world sprint champion Sante Gaiardoni of Italy became the only cyclist to win both the Olympic 1,000m match sprint and the 1,000m time trial events. Having won the time trial 3 days earlier, Gaiardoni was never seriously challenged in the sprint.

1977 – Brock 'takes' steals record
St Louis Cardinals left-fielder Lou Brock broke Ty Cobb's MLB steals record of 892 with 2 during a 4-3 defeat in San Diego. Brock's 893 steals come in 2,376 games over 17 seasons, 7 less than Cobb.

1989 – British transfer record
Man United broke the transfer record between two British clubs when they signed England defender Gary Pallister. United paid Middlesbrough £2.3 million for Pallister's services. After earning winning medals in 4 League titles, 3 FA Cup Finals, 1 League Cup Final and 1 European Cup Winners Final, he moved back to Middlesbrough in 1998 for £2.5 million.

2004 – Marathon marred
With 3 miles to go in the Athens Olympic marathon, leader Vanderlei de Lima of Brazil was bundled into the crowd by Cornelius Horan, a public nuisance dressed as defrocked priest. De Lima lost about 15 to 20 seconds due to the interruption, and finished third in the event with a time of 2:12:11. He was awarded the prestigious Pierre de Coubertin Medal for sportsmanship, in addition to his bronze.

2004 – Schumacher's 7th F1 title
German Formula 1 driver Michael Schumacher clinched his record seventh world title with a second placing behind Finland's Kimi Räikkönen in the Belgian Grand Prix at the Circuit de Spa-Francorchamps. Through 14 races, he had an unassailable lead with 128 points. The win gave Schumacher a record fifth consecutive world title. Juan Manuel Fangio had won 4 straight (1954 to 1957).

2005 – Svetlana out on Round 1
Svetlana Kuznetsova of Russia became the first defending women's champion to lose a first-round match at the US Open in New York. Kuznetsova was upset by compatriot Ekaterina Bychkova, 6-3, 6-2.

2005 – Superdome damaged
Hurricane Katrina damaged the New Orleans Superdome with parts of the roof caving in. The damage was not serious enough to prevent to arena from being used as a shelter for hundreds of people affected by the storm.

BIRTHDATES
1842	England Test fast bowler Alfred Shaw – died 1907
1901	Canadian Hockey Hall of Fame wing AURÈLE JOLIAT – died 1986
1940	American land speed driver GARY GABELICH – died 1984
1945	American sprinter WYOMIA TYUS
1946	American long jumper BOB BEAMON
1947	British auto racer JAMES HUNT – died 1993
1953	England rugby union halfback RICHARD HARDING
1956	NFL kicker EDDIE MURRAY
1957	American jockey JERRY BAILEY
1962	NFL linebacker CARL BANKS
1970	Dutch tennis player JACCO ELTINGH

1937 – Farr goes distance with 'Bomber'

Welshman Tommy Farr went 15 rounds in heavyweight champion Joe Louis' first title defence Yankee Stadium in New York. Louis' points win was the first of a record 25 title defences.

1965 – Stengel retires

Seventy-five-year-old New York Mets manager Casey Stengel retired after suffering a broken hip. In a 56-year career in professional baseball, his best came as NY Yankees manager, when he won 10 pennants and 7 World Series (1949–60).

1972 – Inconsistent Korbut

Seventeen-year-old gymnast Olga Korbut had drawn attention with her spectacular performance in the teams event at the Munich Olympics. Expectation turned to disappointment when the 4ft 11in Korbut could only finish seventh in the individual all-around competition, but the following day she won gold medals in the floor exercises and the uneven parallel bars during the individual competition.

1972 – US springboard diving streak ends

After finishing eighth in 1964 and 11th in 1968, Russian diver Vladimir Vasin broke an amazing American winning streak in the 3-metre springboard event at the Munich Olympics. American divers had won the event in the last 11 Olympic Games. Viren scored the highest score of the competition on his second last dive to beat Italian Franco Giorgio Cagnotto.

1979 – Botham reaches double milestone

England all-rounder Ian Botham became the fastest player to score 1,000 runs and take 100 wickets in Tests when he scored 38 in the fourth Test against India at the Oval.

1991 – Powell breaks long-jump mark

Bob Beamon's famous 22-year-old world long jump record was smashed by fellow American Mike Powell's leap of 29ft 4¼in (8.95m) at the World Athletics Championships in Tokyo. He also broke Carl Lewis' 10-year undefeated streak in the event. Beamon's old mark of 29ft 2½in was the longest-standing track and field record.

1997 – Comets take first WNBA title

The Houston Comets beat the New York Liberty 65-51 in Houston to become the first WNBA champions. Season MVP Cynthia Cooper top-scored with 25 points to be Championship MVP.

2005 – 'A-Rod' joins 'Joltin' Joe'

In the long tradition of Bronx Bombers, Alex Rodriguez became only the second right-handed batter in Yankees history to hit 40 homers in a season. The Yankee's third baseman joined Joe DiMaggio, who hit 46 homers in 1937.

2007 – Sprint double to Gay

American sprinter Tyson Gay became the third man in history to complete a World Championship sprint double after winning the 200m in Osaka. Gay, who won the 100m the previous Sunday, romped to victory in 19.76 seconds to join Maurice Greene and Justin Gatlin in claiming gold in both events.

BIRTHDATES

1918	Baseball Hall of Famer TED WILLIAMS – died 2001
1923	American tennis player VIC SEIXAS
1937	New Zealand auto racer BRUCE McLAREN – died 1970
1942	Pakistan Test fast bowler PERVEZ SAJJAD
1943	French alpine skier JEAN-CLAUDE KILLY
1944	New Zealand rugby union flanker and coach ALEX WYLLIE
1952	Polish tennis player WOJTEK FIBAK
1953	Basketball Hall of Fame centre ROBERT PARISH
1962	NFL receiver RICKY SANDERS
1972	Czech soccer midfielder PAVEL NEDVĚD
1977	NFL running back SHAUN ALEXANDER
1978	MLB pitcher CLIFF LEE
1979	Argentine tennis player JUAN IGNACIO CHELA
1982	American tennis player ANDY RODDICK
1985	Australian swimmer LEISEL JONES
1985	Australian swimmer EAMON SULLIVAN

③① AUGUST

1904 – First African-American medallists
George Poage and Joseph Stadler became the first African-American athletes to win medals at a modern Olympic Games. Poage finished third in the Paris 440 yard hurdles, whilst on the same day Stadler finished second in the standing high jump, after a jump-off with compatriot Lawson Robertson.

1950 – Hodges bangs 4 HR's
Brooklyn first baseman Gil Hodges became the first national leaguer, and just the second player after Lou Gehrig, to hit 4 home runs in a 9-inning game during the Dodgers' 19-3 win over Boston at Ebbets Field.

1968 – Sobers' 6-sixes
Cricket superstar Garry Sobers became the first player to hit 6 sixes off a 6-ball over, while batting for Nottinghamshire against Glamorgan at Swansea. He was looking for quick runs and Glamorgan left-armer Malcolm Nash was experimenting with spin rather than his usual medium-pace. It was a recipe for runs.

1969 – Marciano killed in plane crash
Former world heavyweight champion Rocky Marciano was killed in a plane crash just one day short of his 46th birthday. He was travelling to a birthday party when his plane crashed in Iowa. Marciano was champion from 1952 to 1956, when back problems led to his retirement. He had a 49-0 record with 43 knockouts.

1972 – Virén's incredible gold
Twenty-three-year-old Fin Lasse Virén scored a remarkable victory in the 10,000m at the Munich Olympics. Running in fifth place, Virén stumbled and fell. He recovered in an instant and within 230m had moved into second place. He put on a withering sprint 600m from the finish to blow away the field and win by 5m, breaking Ron Clarke's 7-year-old world mark by a full second.

1990 – Griffeys turn out for Mariners
Forty-year-old Ken Griffey Sr. and 20-year-old Ken Jr became the first father and son tandem to play in an MLB game in the Seattle's 5-2 win over Kansas City.

Both singled and scored in the historic game.

2004 – Rooney transfers to United
Everton's teenage England international Wayne Rooney moved to Manchester United on transfer deadline day for a sum that would cost the Old Trafford club £30 million as Rooney saw out the full 6-year contract. It turned out to be a bargain.

2005 – Hermida HR in first AB
Jeremy Hermida became only the second player to hit a grand slam in his first major-league at-bat. The Marlin rookie pinch hitter joined Phillies hurler Bill Duggleby who accomplished the same feat in 1898.

2008 – Rare loss for beach volleyball champs
Olympic beach volleyball gold medallists Misty May-Treanor and Kerri Walsh lost for the first time in more than a year, dropping a 21-19, 10-21, 25-23 decision to Elaine Youngs and Nicole Branagh in The AVP Crocs Cup Shootout in Mason, Ohio. The loss ended their winning streak at 112 matches and 19 titles.

BIRTHDATES
1932	Canadian Hockey Hall of Fame forward JEAN BÉLIVEAU
1935	MLB outfielder/manager FRANK ROBINSON
1942	Japanese golfer ISAO AOKI
1944	West Indies Test captain CLIVE LLOYD
1946	NFL coach TOM COUGHLIN
1951	New Zealand rugby union winger GRANT BATTY
1955	American hurdler EDWIN MOSES
1958	French rugby union fullback SERGE BLANCO
1961	New Zealand rugby union fullback KIERAN COWLEY
1969	Indian Test fast bowler JAVAGAL SRINATH
1971	Irish golfer PÁDRAIG HARRINGTON
1974	Ukrainian tennis player ANDREI MEDVEDEV
1981	Welsh rugby halfback DWAYNE PEEL
1982	American swimmer IAN CROKER
1982	Spanish soccer goalie PEPE REINA
1983	NFL wide receiver LARRY FITZGERALD
1984	South African golfer CHARL SCHWARTZEL

SEPTEMBER

1 SEPTEMBER

1972 – Fischer wins chess challenge
Twenty-nine-year-old grandmaster Bobby Fischer became the first American to win the world championship when defending champion Boris Spassky of the Soviet Union resigned by telephone during the adjourned 21st game in Reykjavik, Iceland. Fischer combined 7 wins with 11 draws to total the 12½ points needed for victory in a controversial match that had started July 11. He earned $156,250 of the $250,000 purse, while Spassky $93,750. They had squabbled over television cameras, the chessboard, audience noise and late arrivals during the match.

1975 – Seaver so consistent
Thirty-year-old New York Mets starter Tom Seaver became the first pitcher to strike out at least 200 batters for 8 consecutive years during a 3-0 win over the Pittsburgh Pirates at Shea Stadium. Seaver finished with 10 strikeouts to become a 20-game winner for the fourth time. He extended his record to 9 seasons in 1976.

1981 – Alderman – swing is king
Australian fast bowler Terry Alderman took his 42nd wicket of the series on the last day of the drawn fifth Test against England at the Oval. The haul remains a record for an Australian bowler in England. It was also Mike Brearley's last day as England captain, maintaining his unbeaten home record with a 3-1 series win.

1987 – Teenage Chang into Open draw
At age 15 years 6 months, American teenager Michael Chang became the youngest male golfer to win a main draw match in the US Open, beating Australian Paul McNamee in the first round.

1989 – Deyna killed in car crash
Former Polish international Kazimierz Deyna was killed in a road accident at the age of 41. The former Manchester City striker was capped 102 times for Poland and was captain when the Poles upset England in the World Cup qualifiers in 1973.

2001 – Happy ending for rugby's Eales
Australian captain John Eales was given the perfect send off in his final game for the Wallabies with a last minute 29-26 win over New Zealand in Sydney. The home side was camped inside the All Blacks' quarter for the final 15 minutes and Eales spurned easy penalty opportunities in search of a match-winning try. It came via number 8 Toutai Kefu, who piled over in the final minute, for victory and a Tri Nations series win.

2006 – Basketball upset
The United States men's basketball team fell short at the World Basketball Championships in Japan, as the hot-shooting Greece pulled off a stunning 101-95 victory over the Americans in the semi-finals. The Greeks went on to fall to Spain, 70-47, in the final.

2007 – Three gold to Gay
Tyson Gay helped the US win the men's 4 x 100m relay at the World Athletics Championships in Osaka, Japan, joining Carl Lewis and Maurice Greene as the only men to have won 3 gold medals at one world meet.

BIRTHDATES
1866	American boxer JAMES J. CORBETT – died 1933
1914	American jockey JOHN ADAMS – died 1995
1916	American tennis player DOROTHY CHENEY
1919	South African Test batsman OSSIE DAWSON – died 2008
1923	American boxer ROCKY MARCIANO – died 1969.
1937	American golfer AL GEIBERGER
1941	Australian rugby league fullback GRAEME LANGLANDS
1951	England Test wicketkeeper DAVID BAIRSTOW
1959	American golfer KEITH CLEARWATER
1959	England soccer defender MICHAEL DUXBURY
1962	Dutch soccer player RUUD GULLIT
1962	English soccer striker TONY CASCARINO
1969	Norwegian soccer defender HENNING BERG
1972	American swimmer JOSH DAVIS
1973	England rugby union lock SIMON SHAW
1976	England Test captain CLAIR CONNOR
1976	Australian auto racer MARCOS AMBROSE
1977	Spanish soccer midfielder DAVID ALBELDA

② SEPTEMBER

1905 – First blood to All Blacks
The first international rugby match between Australia and New Zealand on Kiwi soil was played at Tahuna Park in Dunedin. In cold, wet conditions, New Zealand scored 4 tries to 1 to win 14-3 after the score was locked at 3-3 at halftime.

1946 – Three straight for Hogan makes 11
For the second time that year, Ben Hogan won 3 consecutive events when he took out the Golden State Open, his 11th title of the season. Earlier, Hogan had won successive tournaments – the Colonial Invitational, Western Open and Goodall Round Robin – and he then followed up with the Winnipeg Open, the PGA Championship and the Golden State event. Hogan is the only player to ever win 3 consecutive events twice in a season, although Byron Nelson won 11 consecutive events, and Hogan and Tiger Woods each won 6 straight tournaments.

1972 – Pole vault farce
The American monopoly on the Olympic pole vault competition was finally halted in Munich, but not before a series of farcical controversies. Americans had won all 16 pole vault gold medals since 1896. Eight days before Munich, the IAAF banned the use of a new model Cata-Pole. Four days prior to the event, the decision was reversed, but the following day it was re-imposed. All the top vaulters used the new poles and were adversely affected. The one competitor who had failed to adapt to the new poles was East German Wolfgang Nordwig, who went on to clear 5.5m for the gold medal.

1980 – Hughes bats in all 5 days
Australia's Kim Hughes, with 117 and 84, became only the third man to bat on all 5 days of a Test match during the Centenary Test against England at Lord's. It was also iconic commentator John Arlott's final stint behind the BBC microphone. He received a standing ovation from the crowd.

1992 – Déjà vu for Fischer
Twenty years after their famous world championship chess match in Iceland, American Bobby Fischer and Russian Boris Spassky were reunited for a challenge match in Yugoslavia. Fischer played despite UN sanctions against Yugoslavia. The prize purse was US$5m, with Fischer winning US$3.65m for his 17.5 to 12.5 victory.

1996 – Greenwell 9 – Seattle 8
Mike Greenwell of the Boston Red Sox set a major league record by driving in all of his team's runs in a 9-8 win over the Seattle Mariners. Greenwell's 7-hit day included a grand slam, a 2-run homer, a double, and a game-winning single.

2003 – Straight saves mark to Gagne
Los Angeles closer Eric Gagne established a major league record with his 55th consecutive save in the Dodgers 4-1 win over the Houston Astros at Dodger Stadium.

BIRTHDATES
1913	Scottish soccer midfielder/manager BILL SHANKLY – died 1981
1927	Austrian alpine skier TRUDE JOCHUM-BEISER
1935	American thoroughbred horse trainer D. WAYNE LUKAS
1937	Baseball executive PETER UEBERROTH
1941	Australian rugby league captain GRAHAM LANGLANDS
1941	College basketball coach JOHN THOMPSON JR
1943	Canadian Hockey hall of Fame executive GLEN SATHER
1947	New Zealand auto racer JIM RICHARDS
1948	Pro Football Hall of Fame quarterback TERRY BRADSHAW
1949	Basketball Hall of Fame guard NATE ARCHIBALD
1952	American tennis player JIMMY CONNERS
1953	England rugby union lock MAURICE COLCLOUGH – died 2006
1954	Australian horse trainer GAI WATERHOUSE
1960	Pro Football hall of Fame running back ERIC DICKERSON
1961	Columbian soccer striker CARLOS VALDERRAMA
1965	British boxer LENNOX LEWIS
1966	French auto racer OLIVIER PANIS
1967	German soccer midfielder ANDREAS MÖLLER
1969	Australian golfer SHANI WAUGH
1971	Norwegian alpine skier KJETIL ANDRÉ AAMODT
1988	Indian Test fast bowler ISHANT SHARMA

③ SEPTEMBER

1935 – Campbell's land speed record
Sir Malcolm Campbell became the first man to travel at 300mph on land when he powered his car *Bluebird* to a new land speed record on the Bonneville Salt Flats in Utah. Powered by a Rolls-Royce V-12 airplane engine, *Bluebird* reached the record speed of 301.129mph. Campbell soon became the only man to hold the land and water speed records at the same time. His son Donald took the land speed mark to over 400mph and also broke 7 water speed records before crashing to his death in 1964.

1950 – Farina first
Italian Alfa Romeo driver Nino Farina won the Italian Grand Prix at Monza to clinch the world title and become the first winner of the newly-instituted Driver's Championship. Farina finished with 30 championship points, 3 ahead of Juan Manuel Fangio. Alfa Romeo also took out the Constructors' Championship.

1960 – US eights' streak ends
The United States' rowing eights' amazing winning streak of 8 Olympic golds was ended by Germany in Rome. US crews had won every gold medal contested since 1920. The German eight, however, made up by oarsmen from 2 clubs from Ratzenburg and Ditmarsia Kiel, won by more than 4 seconds from Canada. The Americans finished a disappointing fifth.

1975 – 'The longest day/s'
England and Australia fought out the longest first-class match played in England – 32 hours 17 minutes in the drawn final Test at the Oval.

2006 – Leslie's MVP
Los Angeles Sparks centre Lisa Leslie won the WNBA's Most Valuable Player award, joining Sheryl Swoopes as the league's only three-time winners.

2006 – Agassi's career ends
Andre Agassi's career came to a close when he lost to 112th-ranked Benjamin Becker of Germany 7-5, 6-7, 6-4, 7-5 in the third round at the US Open. The 36-year-old eight-time Grand Slam winner finished with a competitive career match record of 870-274.

British land-speed record holder Malcolm Campbell posing in Bluebird in 1935

2008 – OKC is 'The Thunder'
Team officials announced that the team formerly known as the Seattle SuperSonics would be called the Oklahoma City Thunder. 'Thunder' was a reference to powerful storms in the area, known as Tornado Alley.

BIRTHDATES

1878	American tennis player DOROTHEA DOUGLASS CHAMBERS – died 1960
1882	England Test captain JOHNNY DOUGLAS – died 1930
1900	England Test captain PERCY CHAPMAN – died 1961
1905	New Zealand Test batsman JOHN 'JACKIE' MILLS – died 1972
1918	Australian horse trainer T.J.SMITH – died 1998
1921	England soccer defender JOHN ASTON – died 2003
1931	NBA coach DICK MOTTA
1933	West Indian Test batsman BASIL BUTCHER
1940	New Zealand rugby union flanker BRIAN LOCHORE
1943	American golfer DAVE EICHELBERGER
1947	French soccer manager GÉRARD HOULLIER
1965	British 400m runner DEREK REDMOND
1969	Swedish golfer ROBERT KARLSSON
1970	England soccer defender GARETH SOUTHGATE
1971	Australian swimmer GLEN HOUSMAN
1982	Canadian freestyle skier SARAH BURKE – died 2012

1951 – Sedgman first Aussie to win Open
Frank Sedgman became the first Australian to win the US Open when he beat Vic Seixas 6-4, 6-1, 6-1 at Forest Hills. In 1951–52 Sedgman was rated the world's no. 1 player having won the Australian Open (1949, 1950), Wimbledon (1952), US Open (1951, 1952), and leading Australia to Davis Cup wins (1950–53). He turned professional in 1953.

1972 – Magnificent 7 for Spitz
Twenty-two-year-old dental student Mark Spitz won his record seventh gold medal at the Munich Olympics when he swam the butterfly leg on the US 4 x 100m medley relay team. Spitz became the first athlete to win 7 gold medals in a single Olympiad. All 7 victories (4 individual and 3 relay) set world records. His other wins came in the 100/200 freestyle and butterfly, and the 4 x 100/200 freestyle relays.

1972 – Youngest athletics gold
Sixteen-year-old Cologne schoolgirl Ulrike Meyfarth became the youngest winner of an individual athletics event in Olympic history when she won the high jump in Munich. Meyfarth equalled the world record of 1.92m to win from Yordanka Blagoyeva of the Soviet Union. In 1984 in Los Angeles, Meyfarth became the oldest athlete to win the event, when she jumped a full 10cm higher than in Munich.

1994 – Back-to-back Worlds for Fu Mingxia
China's Fu Mingxia became the first woman to win consecutive 10m platform world titles in diving, beating countrywoman Chi Bin at the World Aquatics Championships in Rome.

2000 – Walsh's final farewell
West Indian fast bowler Courtney Walsh played his last Test innings at the Oval. It was also Walsh's last Test duck, giving England the match by 158 runs for their first series victory against the Windies since 1969. In 132 Tests, Walsh captured a then-record 519 wickets at 24.44 with a career-best 7-37 against New Zealand in 1994–95. He captained the Windies in 22 Tests.

2000 – Bankrupt Real on way back
European champions Real Madrid reported debts of £165 million. New club president Florentino Perez then signed some of the best players in the world – Luis Figo, Zinedine Zidane and David Beckham – and used their names to raise revenue via sponsorship, merchandise and internet rights. He also sold the club's city training ground to Madrid's City Council for US$310 million, as well as some high-priced talent, such as Nicolas Anelka and Fernando Redondo. As a result, Real's finances were back on track and the club remains the top football organisation in the world.

2002 – Pumas pull off basketball shock
Argentina pulled off one of the biggest upsets in basketball history, beating the US 87-80 in second-round action at the World Championships in Indianapolis. The US lost for the first time in 59 games since it started sending NBA players to international competitions in 1992.

2005 – Busch youngest NASCAR winner
At 20, Kyle Busch became the youngest driver to win a NASCAR Cup Series race when he out-duelled Greg Biffle in the Sony HD 500 at California Speedway.

BIRTHDATES
1937	Australian swimmer DAWN FRASER
1939	South African Test wicket keeper DENIS LINDSAY
1942	American golfer RAYMOND FLOYD
1949	American golfer TOM WATSON
1955	England rugby union fullback ALISTAIR HIGNELL
1955	South African Test fast bowler GARTH LE ROUX
1962	Indian Test wicketkeeper KIRAN MORE
1962	French rugby union winger PATRICE LAGISQUET
1963	American NHL goalie JOHN VANBIESBROUCK
1964	American golfer GUY BOROS
1966	Australian cyclist GARY NEIWAND
1968	MLB catcher MIKE PIAZZA
1969	Samoan, New Zealand rugby union winger INGA TUIGAMALA
1971	South African Test all rounder LANCE KLUSENER
1971	Danish soccer striker ALLAN NIELSEN
1985	Spanish soccer defender RA L ALBIOL

⑤ SEPTEMBER

1951 – Connolly youngest Open winner

Maureen Connolly became the youngest winner of the US Open at the age of 16 when she beat Shirley Fry 6-3, 1-6, 6-4 in the final. The youthful Connolly went on to beat Darlene Hart the next 2 years for an Open treble. In 1953 she became the first woman to win the Grand Slam of tennis, and in all, won 9 Grand Slam titles. In 1954 Connolly was thrown from a horse, suffering a leg injury that ended her brief but spectacular career.

1960 – Clay's boxing gold

Cassius Clay, aka Muhammad Ali, won a more famous than usual Olympic gold in a points decision over three-time European champion Zbigniew Pietrzykowski in the light-heavyweight final in Rome. After exalting the virtues of life for African-Americans in the US to the world's press, Clay threw his gold medal into the Ohio River after an experience with racism. The medal was reinstated at the Atlanta Olympics in 1996.

1970 – Rindt killed in crash

Austrian Formula 1 driver Jochen Rindt was killed during practice for the Italian Grand Prix at Monza. He had dominated the season to date, winning 4 races. Despite not competing in the last 4, he became the first driver to win the World Championship posthumously.

1972 – 'Munich massacre'

Arab terrorists invaded Israeli the athletes' quarters at the Olympic Village in Munich, murdering their wrestling coach Moshe Weinberg and weightlifter Yosef Romano, and taking 9 of the athletes hostage. The terrorists demanded the release of 234 Arab prisoners in Israel and 2 renowned German terrorists, plus an airplane to fly out of Germany. They were permitted to take the hostages via 2 helicopters to an airfield outside Munich, where police opened fire, killing 5 terrorists and capturing 3, but not before all 9 hostages were killed.

1989 – Chrissie retires

At age 34, Chris Evert announced her retirement from competition. In a 17-year career, Evert had won 18 Grand Slam singles titles, including 3 at Wimbledon, 6 US Opens, 2 Australian Opens and 7 French Opens. She was a finalist at the French Open for an incredible ten consecutive years (1972–83), and from August 1973 to May 1979, she won 125 consecutive matches on clay. Her 157 title victories comes second only to Martina Navratilova.

1989 – Johnson stripped of records

Disgraced Canadian sprinter Ben Johnson had all his track records declared void by the IAAF. After testing positive to performance-enhancing steroids at the Seoul Olympics in 1988, he was stripped of his gold medal and banned from competition for 2 years. Johnson returned to the track in 1991 but never recaptured form. In 1993, he again tested positive to steroids and was banned from competition for life.

1994 – Career TD mark to Rice

San Francisco 49ers wide receiver Jerry Rice caught 2 touchdown passes and ran for another score in a 44-14 victory over the Raiders at Candlestick Park to surpass Jim Brown as the NFL's career touchdowns leader with 127.

2004 – Singh takes over Woods mantle

Vijay Singh carded a 2-under 69 on to win the Deutsche Bank Championship and replace Tiger Woods as the top-ranked golfer in the world. Woods had held the no. 1 ranking for 264 consecutive weeks.

BIRTHDATES

1909	Australian Test batsman ARCHIE JACKSON – died 1933
1939	Swiss auto racer CLAY REGAZZONI – died 2006
1947	Australian Test spinner BRUCE YARDLEY
1951	German soccer defender PAUL BREITNER
1953	New Zealand rugby union number 8 MURRAY MEXTED
1959	American golfer TOM PERNICE JR.
1965	Australian auto racer DAVID BRABHAM
1967	German soccer sweeper MATTHIAS SAMMER
1969	England Test batsman MARK RAMPRAKASH
1969	Brazilian soccer defender/manager LEONARDO
1971	England Test batsman ADAM HOLLIOAKE
1972	Zimbabwe Test all-rounder GUY WHITTALL
1977	Spanish soccer winger JOSEBA ETXEBERRIA
1978	New Zealand rugby union lock CHRIS JACK
1989	English rugby halfback BEN YOUNGS

❻ SEPTEMBER

1880 – Grace scores first Test century
On the first day of Test cricket in England, 'the father of cricket' W. G. scored England's first Test century, a fine 152 against Australia at the Oval. The score was the foundation of England's total of 410 for 8. The home side won the match by 5 wickets.

1960 – Elliott wins gold, then bows out
Australian Herb Elliott ran a world record time of 3:35.6 to win the gold medal in the 1,500m at the Rome Olympics. He then retired from the sport at only 22. Elliott remained unbeaten in competition over the mile and 1,500m, having recorded 44 consecutive victories.

1975 – Martina moves to America
Czech tennis player Martina Navratilova, aged 18, requested US political asylum. Her request was granted and Navratilova represented the United States in Federation Cup competition on numerous occasions.

1989 – Irish record tied by Stapleton
Arsenal striker Frank Stapleton equalled Don Givens' Republic of Ireland goal-scoring record with his 19th against West Germany in Dublin. The match ended in a 1-1 draw. Stapleton took ownership of the record with his 20th and final international goal against Malta in 1990. The record lasted 20 years, until 2010, when Niall Quinn scored his 21st goal against Cyprus.

1995 – Ripken's amazing record
Baltimore shortstop Cal Ripken broke Lou Gehrig's 56-year-old record when he played in his 2,131st consecutive MLB game. The milestone took Ripken 13 years to reach and the streak reached 2,632 games before Ripken decided to sit out late in the 1998 season. The sell-out Camden Yard crowd included President Bill Clinton. Ripken hit a fourth inning homer and during his lap of honour the ovation lasted over 22 minutes.

1996 – Murray joins exclusive club
Baltimore's Eddie Murray hit his 500th career home run, in a 5-4 loss to the Detroit Tigers. Whilst only the 15th player to reach the 500 mark, Murray was the third player, after Willie Mays and Henry Aaron, to have 500 homers and 3,000 hits.

British tennis player Tim Henman during the 2004 Monte Carlo Masters.

2001 – No break of serve in 'classic'
At 12:14am, Pete Sampras and Andre Agassi completed one of the greatest tennis matches of all time as Sampras scored a 6-7(7), 7-6(2), 7-6(2), 7-6(5) victory in the quarterfinals. Neither player has his serve broken in the 3 hour, 32 minute match.

2008 – Serena's Open #3
Serena Williams outlasted Jelena Jankovic of Serbia 6-4, 7-5 for her third US Open championship and ninth Grand Slam title in a see-sawing match at Flushing Meadows. The win assured Williams' return to no. 1 in the rankings for the first time since August 2003, the longest gap at the top for a woman.

BIRTHDATES
1913	Brazilian soccer striker LEONIDAS – died 2004
1916	American golfer ED OLIVER – died 1961
1935	Scottish soccer manager JOCK WALLACE – died 1996
1942	England Test batsman RICHARD HUTTON
1947	English soccer midfielder/manager BRUCE RIOCH
1968	Pakistan Test batsman SAEED ANWAR
1969	Australian triathlete MICHELLIE JONES
1973	English tennis player GREG RUSEDSKI
1974	English tennis player TIM HENMAN
1980	Nigerian soccer defender JOSEPH YOBO
1984	Swedish biathlete HELENA JONSSON-EKHOLM

7 SEPTEMBER

1892 – 'Gentleman' Jim takes John L's title
An ageing John L. Sullivan lost the world heavyweight title in 21 rounds against Jim Corbett in New Orleans. Corbett was one of a new breed of gloved fighters who stressed skill and speed rather than brute force. He was a good all-round athlete and weighed in at 178lbs relative to Sullivan's 212lbs. Early in the fight Corbett moved, boxed and made Sullivan look slow. As the fight wore on, Corbett started fighting toe to toe. In the 20th round Sullivan almost went down and was knocked out the next round. He never challenged for the title again and went on the stage and lectured on the virtues of prohibition.

1953 – Connolly first to earn Grand Slam
Maureen Connolly became the first woman to achieve the Grand Slam of tennis when she beat Doris Hart 6-2, 6-4 to win the US singles championship at Forest Hills. Connolly had defeated Julia Sampson in the Australian Open final and Hart in the French Open and at Wimbledon to complete her Grand Slam.

1960 – Elvstrøm's four straight gold
Thirty-two-year-old Danish sailor Paul Elvstrøm won his fourth consecutive Olympic Finn class gold medal in Rome. Apart from his first success in 1948, Elvstrøm won each gold medal comfortably. In Rome (1960) he was so far ahead, he declined to sail the final race because of ill health.

1979 – ESPN born
The Entertainment and Sports Programming Network (ESPN) entered the homes of about 5 million cable TV viewers across the US. ESPN president William Rasmussen got the idea for a 24-hour all-sports network while stuck in a traffic jam. At first, he planned on a regional network, but when he learned his satellite fee would be the same if the telecast went to the entire country, he went nationwide and later international.

1980 – Mac prevails in 'greatest' US Open final
John McEnroe won the second of his 3 consecutive US Open titles when he beat Sweden's Björn Borg in an epic 5 set match at Flushing Meadows. The 21-year-old McEnroe fought off a typical Borg comeback to win

Danish yachting legend Paul Elvstrøm with his daughter Trine during the 1984 Los Angeles Olympics.

a memorable encounter 7-6, 6-1, 6-7, 5-7, 6-4 in the greatest US Open final in history.

2011 – Russian hockey air disaster
The opening of the Russian KHL's fourth season was marred after a passenger jet carrying members of the Lokomotiv Yaroslavl ice hockey team crashed near the Yaroslavl airport. There was only one survivor. Apart from Russian players, the renowned team consisted of international hockey stars including all-time Slovak legend Pavol Demitra, Czech stars Jan Marek, Karel Rachunek and Stanley Cup-winner Josef Vašicek, Robert Dietrich of Germany, Swedish goaltender Stefan Liv, Ukrainian Alexander Vyukhin, Karlis Skrastinš of Latvia and legendary Belarusian defender Ruslan Salei.

BIRTHDATES
1871	England Test all-rounder GEORGE HIRST – died 1954
1894	Australian Test batsman VICTOR RICHARDSON – died 1964
1908	NFL coach PAUL BROWN – died 1991
1923	American golfer LOUISE SUGGS
1929	English soccer defender JEFFREY HALL – died 1959
1944	England rugby union lock PETER LARTER
1945	New Zealand Test all rounder VIC POLLARD
1945	England soccer defender PETER STOREY
1951	American golfer MARK McCUMBER
1968	French soccer defender MARCEL DESAILLY
1971	American boxer 'SUGAR' SHANE MOSELEY
1975	Japanese motor cycle rider NORIFUMI ABE – died 2007
1980	Argentine soccer defender GABRIEL MILITO
1984	Russian tennis player VERA ZVONAREVA

⑧ SEPTEMBER

1957 – First African-American US Open win
Althea Gibson became the first African-American to win a US Open singles title, with a 6-3, 6-2 win over 4-time Wimbledon champion Louise Brough.

1968 – Ashe's US tennis title monopoly
The US national tennis tournament offered 2 championships in each division, the national championship, for amateurs only, and the open championship, for amateurs and professionals. Arthur Ashe became the first male black player to win a major title when he won both events. In the amateur section he beat Bob Lutz in 5 sets and in the professional division Ashe downed Dutchman Tom Okker, 14-12, 5-7, 6-3, 3-6, 6-3.

1969 – 'Rocket' takes second Grand Slam
Australian Rod Laver, with his second Grand Slam on the line, was given a giant scare by countryman Tony Roche before winning the US Open and completing the unique feat at Forest Hills. Roche took a tight first set 9-7, before Laver won comfortably 6-1, 6-3, 6-2. He remains the only player to have completed the Grand Slam twice. Laver won 11 Grand Slam tournaments: Wimbledon (1961, 1962, 1968, 1969); US Open (1962, 1969); Australian Open (1960, 1962, 1969); and French Open (1962, 1969). He was also a member of the winning Australian Davis Cup team in 1959–62 and 1973.

1979 – Austin youngest Open champ
At 16 years and 9 months, American Tracey Austin became the youngest ever winner of the US Open singles championship. Austin beat Chris Evert 6-4, 6-3 in the final.

1998 – 'Big Mac' hits homer #62
St Louis Cardinals slugger Mark McGwire made history at Busch Stadium when he blasted his 62nd home run of the season to break Roger Maris' record. McGwire scorched a low 341ft line drive off the Cubs' Steve Traschel for the record-breaking homer. McGwire finished the season with 70 home runs. He later admitted to taking performance-enhancing drugs.

2001 – Ashraful youngest centurian
Seventeen-year-old Bangladesh batsman Mohammad Ashraful became the youngest Test centurion when he made 114 in Bangladesh's second innings against Sri Lanka in Colombo.

2002 – Sampras' record 14th major
Pete Sampras won his record 14th and final Grand Slam title when he beat Andre Agassi in the final of the US Open in New York. Sampras won 6-3, 6-4, 5-7, 6-4 for his fifth US title. At 31, he was the Open's oldest champion since 1970, when Australia's Ken Rosewell claimed the title aged 35.

2008 – Popular Sox
The Boston Red Sox played before their 456th consecutive sell-out at Fenway Park, setting an MLB record. The streak began on May 15, 2003. Sox fans broke the previous record of 455 consecutive games set by the Cleveland Indians from June 12, 1995 through April 4, 2001.

BIRTHDATES
1929   English soccer defender ROGER BYRNE – died 1958
1930   English figure skater JEANETTE ALTWEGG
1934   New Zealand rugby union centre ROSS BROWN
1944   Australian Test spinner TERRY JENNER – died 2011
1945   Pro Football Hall of Fame defensive back LEM BARNEY
1951   American tennis player TIM GULLIKSON – died 1996
1951   American tennis player TOM GULLIKSON
1952   New Zealand rugby union flanker GRAHAM MOURIE
1956   NBA guard/coach MAURICE CHEEKS
1964   England rugby union prop VICTOR UBOGU
1969   Welsh soccer midfielder GARY SPEED – died 2011
1970   Australian rugby union lock JOHN WELBORN
1972   German soccer defender MARKUS BABBEL
1972   South African rugby prop OS DU RANDT
1975   Australian rugby union fullback CHRIS LATHAM
1975   Kazakhstan tennis player ELENA LIKHOVTSENA
1976   Dutch tennis player SJENG SCHALKEN
1983   Australian AFL midfielder CHRIS JUDD

⑨ SEPTEMBER

1916 – Evans' golf double
Chick Evans became the first golfer to ever win both the US Open and Amateur Championships in the same year, when he beat Bob Gardner 4 & 3 in the final match of the Amateur at the Merion Cricket Club in Ardmore, Pennsylvania.

1930 – Jersey Joe's pro debut
Jersey Joe Walcott made his professional debut with a first-round knockout of Frank 'Cowboy' Wallace in New Jersey. Walcott went on to become World Heavyweight Champion 21 years later in 1951, when he knocked out Ezzard Charles in the seventh round in Philadelphia.

1959 – 'Collie' killed in car crash
Twenty-six-year-old West Indies Test all-rounder O'Neil Gordon 'Collie' Smith was killed in a car crash in England. Smith played 26 Tests, scoring 4 centuries with a best of 168 against England in 1957. His close friend Garry Sobers was injured in the accident.

1960 – Indian field hockey streak ends
The Pakistan men's field hockey team upset India 1-0 in the Olympic final in Rome, breaking a long winning streak by their neighbour and arch-rival. The Indians had won 6 straight Olympic tournaments. Naseer Bunda scored the only goal of the match after 12 minutes.

1990 – Sampras youngest US Open champ
At 19 years 28 days, Pete Sampras became the youngest male US Open champion when he cruised to a 6-4, 6-3, 6-2 victory over Andre Agassi at Flushing Meadows for his first Grand Slam title.

2000 – Williams' first sisters to win Open
Venus Williams won her first US Open singles title, defeating Lindsay Davenport 6-4, 7-5 in the final. Combined with younger sister Serena's US Open title from 1999, the Williams sisters become the first set of sisters to win US Open singles titles.

2006 – Navratilova finale
Martina Navratilova played the final match of her

Pete Sampras on his way to the 1990 US Open at Flushing Meadows, New York

illustrious tennis career, winning the US Open Mixed Doubles championship with partner Bob Bryan, defeating Kveta Peschke and Martin Damm of the Czech Republic 6-2, 6-3. Navratilova, who would turn 50 on October 18, retired as arguably the best women's tennis player of all-time, having won 18 Grand Slam titles and 167 singles titles. She also racked up 178 doubles crowns, 41 coming in major tournaments (31 doubles, 10 mixed doubles).

2012 – 15 Grand Slams to Serena
Serena Williams regained her composure to come back and win the last 4 games, beating top-ranked Victoria Azarenka 6-2, 2-6, 7-5 for her fourth US Open title and 15th Grand Slam title overall.

BIRTHDATES
1853	Australian Test fast bowler FREDERICK SPOFFORTH – died 1926
1941	Indian Test all-rounder SYED ABID ALI
1949	British figure skater JOHN CURRY – died 1994
1949	NFL quarterback JOE THEISMANN
1963	England Test batsman NEIL FAIRBROTHER
1964	American golfer SKIP KENDALL
1966	German luge driver GEORGE HAKL
1966	Australian/Irish rugby union five-eighth BRIAN SMITH
1975	New Zealand rugby union hooker ANTON OLIVER
1985	Croatian soccer midfielder LUKA MODRIC
1987	German tennis player ANDREA PETKOVIC

1960 – Amazing sixth straight fencing gold
Fifty-year-old Hungarian Aladár Gerevich won his sixth consecutive Olympic gold medal in the sabre teams event in Rome. His winning streak started at the LA Games in 1932. In an illustrious career (1932–60), Gerevich won 7 gold, 1 silver and 2 bronze medals.

1961 – F1 carnage
In the worst incident in Formula 1 history, German driver Wolfgang von Trips' Ferrari ploughed into the crowd after colliding with Jim Clark's Lotus in the Italian Grand Prix at Monza. Along with von Trips himself, 15 spectators were killed.

1972 – 'Technicality' brings Russian upset
The United States' 62-game domination of basketball at the Olympics ended in Munich when the Soviet Union won the final 51-50. The game was ostensibly over with the US leading 50-49 on the buzzer, but the clock was ordered back 3 seconds after Soviet coach Vladimir Kondrashkin was ruled to have called a time out. Sasha Belov converted Ivan Edeshko's pass for a controversial victory.

1972 – Fittipaldi youngest F1 champ
Twenty-five-year-old Brazilian Emerson Fittipaldi, driving a Lotus-Ford, became the youngest Formula 1 World Champion when he won the Italian Grand Prix at Monza.

1974 – Brock 'steals' record
St Louis Cardinals left fielder Lou Brock stole 2 bases at Busch Stadium in an 8-2 loss against Philadelphia to give him 105 for the season, breaking Maury Wills' record.

1988 – Grand Slam to Graf
Steffi Graf of Germany clinched the Grand Slam of tennis when she beat Gabriela Sabatini of Argentina 6-3, 3-6, 6-1 to win the US Open at Flushing Meadow. Graf defeated Chris Evert in the Australian Open, Natalia Zvereva in the French Open and Martina Navratilova at Wimbledon. She also beat Sabatini to win the gold medal at the 1988 Seoul Olympics and complete the 'Golden' Slam.

2004 – USA smashed in cricket debut
The US lost its first ODI during the Champions Trophy in London. New Zealand's Nathan Astle (145 not out) and Craig McMillan (64 not out) smashed 13 sixes between them in the Black Caps' 4 for 347. After a promising start, with 52 for the first wicket, the Americans were rocked by Jacob Oram (5 for 36) and ended up losing 9 for 85.

2006 – Roger's double/treble
Swiss ace Roger Federer beat American Andy Roddick 6-2, 4-6, 7-5, 6-1 at Flushing Meadows to become the first player ever to double up at the US Open and Wimbledon for at least 3 consecutive years.

2006 – Manning v Manning
In the first battle between 2 quarterback brothers in NFL history, Peyton Manning's team came out on top as the Indianapolis Colts defeated Eli Manning and the New York Giants, 26-21 at Giants Stadium.

2012 – Andy's first major
Andy Murray became the first British man since Fred Perry in 1936 to win a Grand Slam singles title when he beat Novak Djokovic 7–6, 7–5, 2–6, 3–6, 6–2 in the final of the US Open in New York. Murray was also the first man to win both the US Open and the Olympic men's singles gold medal in the same year.

BIRTHDATES

1929	American golfer ARNOLD PALMER
1934	Baseball Hall of Fame slugger ROGER MARIS – died 1985
1946	American sprinter JIM HINES
1947	American golfer LARRY NELSON
1948	Basketball Hall of Fame centre BOB LANIER
1951	American golfer BILL ROGERS
1963	MLB pitcher RANDY JOHNSON
1966	Canadian NHL centre JOE NIEUWENDYK
1969	New Zealand rugby union/league centre CRAIG INNES
1970	French tennis player JULIE HALARD-DECUGIS
1972	Norwegian cross-country skier BENTE SKARI
1973	England rugby union fullback TIM STIMPSON
1974	NBA forward BEN WALLACE
1976	Brazilian tennis player GUSTAVO KUERTEN
1976	New Zealand rugby union flanker MARTY HOLAH
1977	New Zealand rugby union centre CALEB RALPH

⑪ SEPTEMBER

1951 – Chadwick swims Channel both ways
Florence Chadwick became the first woman to swim the English Channel in both directions. In 1950, she swam from France to England in a record 13 hours, 23 minutes. The England to France crossing was more difficult because of adverse tides and winds, and in 1951 it took her 16 hours, 22 minutes.

1978 – Peterson killed in crash
Swedish Formula 1 driver Ronnie Peterson was killed when his Lotus crashed in a multi-car pileup at the start of the Italian Grand Prix at Monza. As a result of the accident, it became compulsory for an ambulance to follow grand prix cars on the first lap, so that injured drivers could receive immediate medical help. In a 9-year Formula 1 career, Peterson gained 14 pole positions and won 10 Grand Prix.

1985 – Career hits record to Rose
Forty-four-year-old Reds player-manager Pete Rose broke Ty Cobb's 57-year-old MLB record for career hits in front of a sellout crowd during a 2-0 win against San Diego at Riverfront Stadium in Cincinnati. The 23-year veteran recorded his 4,192nd hit when he lined a single to left-centre in the first inning off the Padres' Eric Show.

1985 – First Test win for SL
After 14 matches as a nation with full Test-playing status, Sri Lanka won their first Test in Colombo. Inspired by 5-wicket hauls from Rumesh Ratnayake and Amal Silva, the Sri Lankans dismissed India for 198 to win by 149 runs. A draw in the next Test gave Sri Lanka a series for the first time.

1988 – Lendl's domination over ... for now
Ivan Lendl's 157-week reign as world no. 1 tennis player ended, when he was beaten by Sweden's Mats Wilander in the longest final in US Open history. Wilander prevailed 6-4, 4-6, 6-3, 5-7, 6-4 in a marathon match that lasted 4 hours, 55 minutes. Lendl had held the top ranking for nearly 3 years since September 1985. Wilander maintained the title for 20 weeks until Lendl regained the ranking for another lengthy stint of 80 weeks.

1998 – Fluctuating 'Fish' in Florida
With a 7-2 defeat to the Atlanta Braves, the Marlins lost their 100th game to become the first team that had gone from being World Series champions to a 100-game loser. The 'Fish' had the worst record in baseball, 48-100.

1999 – First major for Serena
Seventeen-year-old seventh-seeded Serena Williams won her first-ever Grand Slam title with a 6-3, 7-6 win over top-seeded Martina Hingis in the final at the US Open in New York. She became the first African-American woman to win a Grand Slam event since Althea Gibson won the US Open in 1958.

2009 – Jeter overtakes Gehrig
Derek Jeter broke the New York Yankees' hit record, held by Lou Gehrig for more than 7 decades, with a single in the third inning in a 10-4 loss to Baltimore at Yankee Stadium. The grounder gave Jeter 2,722 hits, 1 more than Gehrig, whose Hall of Fame career was cut short by illness in 1939.

BIRTHDATES
1911	Indian Test batsman LALA AMARNATH – died 2000
1913	College football coach PAUL 'BEAR' BRYANT – died 1983
1924	NFL coach TOM LANDRY – died 2000
1933	Italian tennis player NICOLA PIETRANGELI
1944	Brazilian soccer defender EVERALDO – died 1974
1945	West German Soccer captain FRANZ BECKENBAUER
1949	England rugby union flanker ROGER UTTLEY
1950	British motor cycle rider BARRY SHEENE – died 2003
1951	Argentine rugby fly-half HUGO PORTA
1957	American golfer JEFF SLUMAN
1959	South African golfer DAVID FROST
1959	American golfer ROBERT WRENN
1961	Argentine rugby union fly-half HUGO PORTA
1962	Spanish soccer forward JULIO SALINAS
1970	American boxer WILLIAM JOPPY
1977	British snooker player MATTHEW STEVENS
1976	Indian Test spinner MURALI KARTIK
1978	NFL free safety ED REED
1978	Serbian soccer midfielder DEJAN STANKOVI
1979	French soccer defender ERIC ABIDAL

1951 – 'Fight of the Century'

'Sugar' Ray Robinson regained his world middleweight title with a 10th-round TKO of Englishman Randy Turpin at the Polo Grounds in New York. In the 10th round, Robinson suffered a badly cut left eye and went for broke, catching Turpin with a flurry of power-packed punches. Referee Ruby Goldstein stopped the fight with 8 seconds remaining in the round. Turpin had upset Robinson earlier in the year by taking a 15-round points decision in London.

1979 – Yastrzemski reaches 3,000 hit/400 HR

Boston Red Sox left-fielder Carl Yastrzemski became the first American League player to reach 3,000 career hits and 400 home runs. The 40-year-old Yastrzemski achieved the milestone by grounding a single in the eighth inning of Boston's 9-2 win over the Yankees at Fenway Park. The only 3 players to have achieved the double were all National Leaguers – Stan Musial, Willie Mays and Hank Aaron.

1980 – Towering NBA star is born

Yao Ming, once the tallest active player in the NBA at an imposing 7ft 6in, was born on this day in Shanghai. One of China's most famous athletes, he played for the Shanghai Sharks and the Houston Rockets, and was selected to start in the NBA All-Star Game 8 times in his career.

2005 – England finally regains Ashes

An 18-year famine for English cricket ended when Kevin Pietersen smashed 158, enabling England to draw the fifth Test against Australia at the Oval for a 2-1 series win. England regained the Ashes after 8 one-sided series defeats

2006 – Longest NHL deal

Goalie Rick DiPietro re-signed with the New York Islanders, agreeing a record 15-year deal worth $67.5 million. The deal was designed to keep DiPietro in the fold until 2021, when he would be nearly 40. It was then the longest contract in NHL history, topping the 10-year $87.5 million agreement the Islanders gave enigmatic centre Alexei Yashin in 2001. In 2010, high-scoring Russian forward Ilya Kovalchuk signed a 17-year $102 million contract with the New Jersey Devils

2010 – Durant brilliant in US victory

Kevin Durant scored 28 points as the US silenced a raucous home crowd and beat Turkey 81-64 in Istanbul to win the gold medal at the World Basketball Championship for the first time in 16 years. With Kobe Bryant, LeBron James, Dwyane Wade and other stars skipping the tournament, the American group was labeled a 'B-Team.' But Durant led the team to its first world title since 1994 and fourth overall, to restore American prestige on the international stage.

BIRTHDATES

1913	American sprinter JESSE OWENS – died 1980
1916	American auto racer TONY BETTENHAUSEN – died 1961
1937	Canadian boxer GEORGE CHUVALO
1937	West Indian Test fast bowler WES HALL
1948	Australian Test fast bowler MAX WALKER
1949	Russian figure skater IRINA RODNINA
1951	Welsh rugby union centre RAY GRAVELL
1956	American golfer CHIP BECK
1959	American golfer CINDY FLOM
1969	Spanish golfer ANGEL CABRERA
1969	Japanese golfer SHIGEKI MARUYAMA
1971	Moroccan tennis player YOUNES EL AYNAOUI
1975	Australian swimmer BILL KIRBY
1977	Australian Test fast bowler NATHAN BRACKEN
1980	Chinese NBA centre YAO MING
1989	NFL quarterback ANDREW LUCK

The Houston Rockets' giant Chinese centre Yao Ming dunks during the 2005 NBA Western Conference playoffs in Dallas.

1936 – Feller ties strikeout mark

Cleveland starter Bob Feller broke the American League record and tied the Major League mark with 17 strikeouts in the Indians 5-2 win over Philadelphia at Cleveland Stadium. The future Hall of Fame pitcher was only 17 years of age when he achieved the feat.

1949 – LPGA born

The Women's Professional Golf Association became the Ladies Professional Golf Association. Patty Berg was elected LPGA president, while Betty Jameson, Babe Zaharias and several other top-line players joined the new association.

1965 – Mays reaches 500 homer mark

Thirty-four-year-old Willie Mays became only the fifth player to reach the 500 home run milestone with his 47th homer of the season. The San Francisco slugger slammed a pitch from Astros right-hander Don Nottebart 440ft into the centre-field bleachers in the fourth inning of the Giants 5-1 victory in Houston.

1970 – Court takes elusive Grand Slam

Margaret Court became only the second woman to claim the tennis Grand Slam when she beat Rosie Casals 6-2, 2-6, 6-1 in the final of the US Open. Smith had defeated Kerry Melville in the Australian Open final, Helga Niessen in the French Open and Billie Jean King at Wimbledon to complete her Grand Slam. Maureen Connolly had achieved the feat in 1953. Steffi Graf became the third female Grand Slammer in 1988.

1992 – No punts for Bills & 49ers.

The Buffalo Bills 34-31 victory over San Francisco at Candlestick Park was the only time in NFL history, a game was played without either team punting. The prime reason was that the teams combined for 1,086 yards in offence with 49ers quarterback Steve Young passing for 449 years and 3 touchdowns, and the Bills' Jim Kelly totalling 403 yards and 3 TDs.

1998 – Sosa second on all accounts

Chicago Cubs slugger Sammy Sosa became the second player to hit more than 61 home runs in a season, and also the second that season. Sosa crunched 2 drives over Wrigley Field's left-field bleachers in an 11-10 win against Milwaukee as he joined Mark McGwire with 62 homers. He finished the season with 66 HR's, second in history to McGwire's record 70.

2007 – Huge Formula 1 fine

The McLaren Formula 1 Racing Team was fined $100 million and stripped of all its constructors' points for using leaked secret data from its main rival Ferrari. A 780-page technical dossier on Ferrari cars was found at the home of McLaren's chief designer, Mike Coughlan. McLaren drivers Lewis Hamilton and Fernando Alonso escaped punishment.

2007 – Bill's harsh penalty for eves-dropping

New England coach Bill Belichick was fined $500,000 and the Patriots ordered to pay $250,000 for videotaping the New York Jets' offensive and defensive signals during the previous week's 38-14 win by New England. The NFL also ordered the team to give up their 2008 first-round draft choice if it reached the playoffs and second-and third-round picks if it didn't. It was the biggest fine ever for a coach and the first time in NFL history a first-round draft pick has been confiscated as a penalty.

2008 – Saves mark broken

Los Angeles Angels closer Francisco Rodríguez struck out Raúl Ibañez in a 5-2 win over Seattle and his 58th save of the season to break the MLB all-time saves record. Rodríguez topped Bobby Thigpen's mark with the 1990 Chicago White Sox.

BIRTHDATES

1931	Australian sprinter MARJORIE JACKSON-NELSON
1944	Australian surfer BERNARD 'MIDGET' FARRELLY
1957	American golfer MARK WIEBE
1962	American golfer NEAL LANCASTER
1963	England Test batsman ROBIN SMITH
1967	American sprinter MICHAEL JOHNSON
1969	Australian Test spin bowler SHANE WARNE
1971	Croatian tennis player GORAN IVANIŠEVI
1976	New Zealand Test batsman CRAIG McMILLAN

⑭ SEPTEMBER

1957 – Dual citizen Wessels born
Test opening batsman Kepler Wessels was born in Bloemfontein, but didn't play for South Africa until after he had represented Australia, the country he had emigrated to. Wessels is the only batsman to score Test centuries and 1,000 runs for 2 different countries. He also scored a century in his first Test innings – against England – while playing for both countries.

1963 – Best makes United debut
George Best made his debut for Manchester United against West Bromwich Albion at Old Trafford. Blessed with brilliant skills but a questionable work ethic, Best made 361 appearances for United, scoring 136 goals. He debuted for Northern Ireland in 1964 and in 37 appearances he scored 9 goals. He won League titles with United in 1965 and 1967, and the European Cup in 1968. In 1968 he was voted English and European Footballer of the Year.

1990 – Like father, like son
Ken Griffey and son Ken Jr hit back-to-back home runs in the Seattle Mariners 7-5 loss to the California Angels in Anaheim. Junior hit a 3-0 pitch from Kirk McCaskill over the centre-field wall, similar to his father's previous blast.

1997 – Doohan dominates
Australian Honda rider Michael Doohan set a new record of twelve 500cc Grand Prix motorcycle victories in a season when he won the Catalunya event in Spain. The win clinched the fourth of Doohan's 5 consecutive world titles. He also set a record for the most pole positions, consecutive pole positions and grand prix points in a season.

2003 – Rushing record to Lewis
Baltimore running back Jamal Lewis set the single-game rushing record when he rambled for 295 yards and 2 touchdowns on 30 carries in a 33-13 home victory over Cleveland. Lewis would have easily eclipsed 300 yards if not for a penalty that nullified a 60-yard TD run.

South African cricket captain Kepler Wessels on his way to 70 during a 1992 World Cup 7-wicket win against Zimbabwe.

2009 – Kim returns in triumph
Twenty-six-year-old Kim Clijsters of Belgium capped a comeback from 2 years out of tennis to become the first unseeded woman to win the US Open. Clijsters scored a 7-5, 6-3 victory over no. 9 seed Caroline Wozniacki of Denmark.

BIRTHDATES
1919   Australian Test wicketkeeper GIL LANGLEY – died 2001
1927   American golfer GARDNER DICKINSON – died 1998.
1934   New Zealand rugby union centre PAUL LITTLE – died 1993
1940   NBA coach LARRY BROWN
1944   German soccer midfielder GUNTER NETZER
1956   England soccer midfielder RAY WILKINS
1957   Australian/South African Test opener KEPLER WESSELS
1958   New Zealand Test batsman JEFF CROWE
1966   Pakistan Test batsman AAMER SOHAIL
1969   Great Britain rugby league captain DENIS BETTS
1972   American golfer NOTAH BEGAY
1974   Moroccan middle distance runner HICHAM EL GUERROUJ
1978   England rugby union winger BEN COHEN

1947 – Incomparable Compton
England Test batsman Denis Compton scored a world record 18th first-class century to complete his greatest summer. Compton made a slashing 246 for champion county Middlesex against The Rest in the annual end of season match at the Oval. The record still stands.

1978 – Ali takes title for third time
Muhammad Ali became the first man to win the heavyweight title 3 times when he scored a unanimous points decision over Leon Spinks in front of a capacity 63,350 at the New Orleans Superdome. In a disappointing contest, the 36-year-old Ali, now well past his best, avenged his loss to Spinks 7 months earlier.

1984 – Horse racing great
Champion English jockey Lester Piggott broke Frank Buckle's record of 27 Classic wins when he rode Commanche Run to victory in the St Leger. Piggott went on to win 30 Classic victories. In a career spanning 1948–95, Piggott rode over 5,300 winners in the UK and abroad. He won 9 Derbies; 3 Prix de l'Arc de Triomphes; 11 Championships (1960, 1964–71, 1981–82), 25 Centuries between 1955 and 1984; and 465 Group race wins. He became a trainer but served 12 months in prison for tax evasion. In 1990, at age 54, he made a comeback to riding and won the US Breeder's Cup Mile. Aged 56, he claimed the 2,000 Guineas in 1992 on Rodrigo de Triano. He finally retired in 1995.

1985 – Big Ryder Cup win for Europeans
The European team scored its largest winning margin in Ryder Cup history in beating the US by 5 points at The Belfry in Wishaw, Warwickshire, England. Captained by Tony Jacklin, Europe won 16½ to 11½ and regained the Cup for the first time in 18 years.

1988 – Surprise Olympic venue
The IOC announced the Norwegian town of Lillehammer had beaten Anchorage in Alaska for the right to host the 1994 Winter Olympics.

1999 – Another Maroney marathon
Australian Susie Maroney became the first person to swim from Jamaica to Cuba after a treacherous crossing through seas whipped up by Hurricane Floyd. The 24-year-old completed the gruelling 160km haul from Montego Bay, Jamaica to Marea del Portillo in Cuba in 36 hours. Her shark cage was designed and donated by her most famous fan, Cuban President Fidel Castro.

2001 – Zanardi crash
Alex Zanardi crashed in the American 500 CART race at the EuroSpeedway Lausitz in Germany, resulting in the loss of both legs below the knee. He made a miraculous comeback to racing less than 2 years after the accident, competing in the FIA World Touring Car Championship for BMW Team Italy-Spain between 2003 and 2009.

2007 – Slater sizzles in the surf
American surfer Kelly Slater passed countryman Tom Curren's long standing ASP tour record of 33 career victories, with his win at the Boost Mobile Pro at Lowers Trestles in California.

BIRTHDATES
1936   Australian tennis player ASHLEY COOPER
1937   West Indian Test batsman JOEY CAREW – died 2011
1938   Mexican tennis player RAFAEL OSUNA – died 1969
1938   Baseball Hall of fame pitcher GAYLORD PERRY
1940   Pro Football Hall of Fame defensive tackle MERLIN OLSEN
1946   South African Test all rounder MIKE PROCTOR
1951   Dutch soccer midfielder JOHANN NEESKENS
1951   NFL coach PETE CARROLL
1955   Pakistan Test spinner ABDUL QADIR
1957   South African golfer FULTON ALLEM
1961   NFL quarterback DAN MARINO
1961   West Indies Test fast bowler PATRICK PATTERSON
1967   Australian squash player RODNEY EYLES
1971   New Zealand Test batsman NATHAN ASTLE
1971   South African tennis player WAYNE FERREIRA
1975   American swimmer TOM DOLAN
1977   NBA guard JASON TERRY
1978   Icelandic soccer forward EIDUR GUDJOHNSEN

1978 – Triple Crown champs clash

For the first time in history, two Triple Crown winners met in a race, when 1977 winner Seattle Slew beat the 1978 champion Affirmed by 3 lengths in the Marlboro Cup at Belmont. The pair met again the following month in the Jockey Club Gold Cup at Belmont, but Affirmed's saddle slipped and Seattle Slew won comfortably. After the race, Seattle Slew was sold for $12 million to stand stud at Spendthrift Farm.

1979 – US beats all-European Ryder Cup team

The United States defeated the first all-Europe Ryder Cup team 17-11 at The Greenbrier in White Sulphur Springs, West Virginia. Previously, the Ryder Cup featured the US team against a team composed of players only from Great Britain and Ireland. The Americans triumphed on the strength of an 8½ to 3½ performance in the singles.

2000 – Thorpe stars in Sydney

Ian Thorpe of Australia thrilled the home crowd on the first day of the Sydney Olympics when he won the 400m freestyle at the Sydney International Aquatic Centre. He was also part of the 4 x 100 relay team (with Michael Klim, Chris Fydler and Ashley Callus) that smashed the world record and broke the US dominance of the event.

2007 – Lee's twenty20 hat-trick

Brett Lee claimed the first hat-trick in Twenty20 internationals as Australia's fast bowlers restricted Bangladesh to 123. Mathew Hayden and Adam Gilchrist then easily powered Australia to a 9-wicket win in Cape Town. Lee's 17th over hat-trick – Shakib edged a cut to the keeper, Mashrafe Mortaza was yorked and he trapped Alok Kapali lbw.

2007 – Tiger gets windfall

Tiger Woods won the biggest bonus in sports history as he ambled around Atlanta's storied East Lake GC in 23-under par to win the Tour Championship by a record 8 strokes from Zach Johnson and Mark Calcavecchia, and secure $10 million from FedEx. Woods broke the tournament scoring record by 6 shots in a total 257, matching the third-lowest score over 72 holes in tour history.

2007 – Full finish list in NASCAR event

All 43 cars finished the NASCAR Sylvania 300 at the New Hampshire International Speedway, the first time all starters completed a race since the series adopted the 43-car field in 1998. Clint Boyer led 222 of the 300 laps for his first career victory ahead of Jeff Gordon and Tony Stewart.

2007 – Mercury take WNBA title

Phoenix became the first team in the WNBA's 11-year history to claim the title on the road. The Mercury beat the Detroit Shock 108-92 and wrapped up their first league title in the deciding Game 5 of the WNBA Finals. Australian Penny Taylor scored 30 points and Diana Taurasi had 17 for Phoenix.

BIRTHDATES

1876	American boxer MARVIN HART – died 1931
1885	England cricket/soccer international DICK YOUNG – died 1968
1932	England Test batsman/coach MICKEY STEWART
1934	Basketball Hall of Fame forward ELGIN BAYLOR
1937	Russian wrestler ALEKSANDR MEDVED
1940	American tennis player EARL BUCHHOLZ
1942	American yachtsman DENNIS CONNOR
1948	American tennis player ROSIE CASALS
1951	Scotland rugby union fullback ANDY IRVINE
1953	American golfer JERRY PATE
1954	Australian Test wicket keeper ROGER WOOLLEY
1955	Baseball Hall of Fame infielder ROBIN YOUNT
1957	Irish soccer midfielder/manager DAVID McCREERY
1958	MLB pitcher OREL HERSHISER
1958	Welsh soccer goalkeeper NEVILLE SOUTHALL
1959	MLB outfielder TIM RAINES
1959	South African Test wicket keeper DAVE RICHARDSON
1965	German soccer striker KARL-HEINZ RIEDLE
1966	Sri Lankan Test batsman ASANKA GURUSINHA
1983	New Zealand rugby front rower JOHN AFOA
1983	Zimbabwean swimmer KIRSTY COVENTRY

⑰ SEPTEMBER

1977 – US scores in final UK player Ryder Cup
In the last Ryder Cup competition involving Great Britain and Ireland players alone, the United States scored a comfortable 5-point win at Royal Lytham & St Annes in England. After building a 7½-2½ lead on the first 2 days, the Americans won 12½-7½. The move to expand the competition to include Europeans with UK players was suggested by Jack Nicklaus to improve competitive balance.

1982 – 105 twice to Mendis
Sri Lanka batsman Duleep Mendis became the only batsman to hit identical hundreds in the same Test during the drawn inaugural Test between India and Sri Lanka in Madras. Mendis scored 105 in the Sri Lankan first innings and also 105 in the second innings.

1984 – Jackson reaches 500 HR's
California Angels' 38-year-old slugger Reggie Jackson became only the 13th player to reach the 500 home run milestone. Jackson hit a soaring drive off Kansas City left-hander Bud Black into the right field terrace at Anaheim Stadium, the same venue and 17 years before to the day, he hit his first MLB homer when, ironically, he was playing for Kansas City.

1989 – 200 TDs for Marino
Miami Dolphins quarterback Dan Marino reached the 200th touchdown pass milestone in a 24-10 win at New England. The feat was achieved in his 89th game in the NFL, faster than any other quarterback in history.

1994 – Gerulaitis dead at 40
American star Vitas Gerulaitis died of accidental carbon monoxide poisoning while on holiday in Long Island. The shaggy-haired Gerulaitis was one of the international tennis circuit's most visible personalities. He was ranked among the top 10 professional players from 1977 to 1982 but won only one Grand Slam event, the 1977 Australian Open singles title.

2000 – All the way NASCAR victory for Burton
Jeff Burton led all 300 laps in his win in the Dura Lube 300 at the New Hampshire International Speedway. Burton became the first driver to lead every lap in

Vitas Gerulaitis in 1978. Photo: Suyk, Koen / Anefo [CC-BY-SA-3.0], via Wikimedia Commons.

a superspeedway event since Fireball Roberts at Hanford, California in 1961.

2004 – Bonds has 700 homers
San Francisco slugger Barry Bonds became only the third player to hit 700 career home runs when he connected off Jake Peavy in the third inning of the Giants' 4-1 win over San Diego at SBC Park. It was Bonds' 42nd homer of the season. He became the first player to reach the 700 homers milestone since Hank Aaron on July 21, 1973. Aaron finished his career with a record 755 homers, with Babe Ruth second on 714.

BIRTHDATES
1901	British yachtsman SIR FRANCIS CHICHESTER – died 1971
1927	Pro Football Hall of Fame quarterback GEORGE BLANDA – died 2010
1929	British auto racer STIRLING MOSS
1934	American tennis player MAUREEN CONNOLLY – died 1969
1937	Puerto Rican Baseball Hall of Fame first baseman ORLANDO CEPEDA
1940	England Test fast bowler PETER LEVER
1945	NBA coach PHIL JACKSON
1946	England soccer defender BILLY BONDS
1952	American tennis player HAROLD SOLOMON
1955	American golfer SCOTT SIMPSON
1960	British auto racer DAMON HILL
1962	Australian golfer WAYNE RILEY
1971	England rugby union centre MIKE CATT
1974	Australian golfer CRAIG SPENCE
1975	American auto racer JIMMIE JOHNSON
1977	Italian soccer midfielder SIMONE PERROTTA
1985	Czech tennis player TOMÁŠ BERDYCH

1931 – Grove reaches 30 wins

Thirty-year-old Philadelphia Athletics pitcher Lefty Grove became the only left-hander to win 30 games in a season in the 20th century with his 3-1 victory over the Chicago White Sox at Shibe Park. Grove allowed only 5 hits as his record improved to 30-3. He finished the season 31-4 with a 2.06 ERA.

1972 – First black MLB umpire

Art Williams became the National League's first black umpire, working at third base during the Dodgers' 3-2 win in San Diego.

1996 – Clemens' 20 K's

Boston Red Sox pitcher Roger Clemens became the only major leaguer to record 20 strikeouts in a 9-inning game, when he held the Detroit Tigers to 4 hits in a 4-0 victory at Tiger Stadium. The win tied Clemens with the legendary Cy Young for both victories by a Red Sox pitcher (192) and most shutouts (38). It was Clemens' final win for Boston. He signed with Toronto as a free agent after the season.

1997 – Three sets of bros for Zimbabwe

For the first time in Test cricket history, 3 pairs of brothers played in the one Test team. Andy and Grant Flower, Bryan and Paul Strang, and Gavin and John Rennie lined up for Zimbabwe against New Zealand at Harare. Guy Whittall was also in the Zimbabwe team. His cousin Andy was 12th man. Grant Flower made a century in each innings of a drawn match.

1999 – First defeat for 'Golden Boy'

Puerto Rican IBF champion Felix Trinidad beat Oscar de la Hoya on points to win the WBC welterweight title in Las Vegas. It was De La Hoya's first defeat in 32 pro fights. Trinidad trailed in the first 8 rounds but won 3 of the last 4 rounds on 2 official cards and all 4 rounds on the third, to pull out a majority victory. Trinidad took his imposing record to 36-0.

2004 – Another beating for De la Hoya

Bernard Hopkins successfully defended his title as middleweight champion of the world, as he knocked out Oscar De La Hoya with a body punch in the ninth round at the MGM Grand at Las Vegas.

2005 – Favre passes for 50,000 yards

Green Bay quarterback Brett Favre connected with RB Ahman Green on a 17-yard pass play in the second quarter of the Packers' 26-24 loss to the Cleveland Browns at Lambeau Field to become the third player in history to reach 50,000 yards. Dan Marino first achieved the feat in 1996 with John Elway joining the elite club in 1998.

2011 – Thompson youngest LPGA winner

Sixteen-year-old Floridian Lexi Thompson scored a 5-stroke victory in the Navistar LPGA Classic in Prattville, Ala., making her the youngest ever LPGA tournament winner. Thompson, who still had 2 more stages of qualifying school to go through, closed with a 2-under 70 for a total 17-under 271 to beat Tiffany Joh. She shattered the age record for winning a multiple-round tournament held by Paula Creamer, who won in 2005 at 18.

BIRTHDATES

1933	NHL coach SCOTTY BOWMAN
1935	English snooker player JOHN SPENCER – died 2006
1942	England soccer goalkeeper ALEX STEPNEY
1949	England soccer goalkeeper PETER SHILTON
1950	Canadian Hockey Hall of Fame centre DARRYL SITTLER
1952	NBA/College basketball coach RICK PITINO
1954	Basketball Hall of Fame guard DENNIS JOHNSON – died 2007
1956	Slovak Hockey Hall of Fame centre PETER ŠTASTNÝ
1958	England Test fast bowler DEREK PRINGLE
1958	West Indian Test fast bowler WINSTON DAVIS
1959	Baseball Hall of Fame infielder RYNE SANDBERG
1968	Croatian NBA forward TONI KUKO
1968	Australian triathlete BRAD BEVEN
1970	England Test fast bowler DARREN GOUGH
1971	American road cyclist LANCE ARMSTRONG
1973	Australian wheelchair champion LOUISE SAUVAGE
1974	England soccer defender SOL CAMPBELL
1976	Brazilian soccer striker RONALDO

⑲ SEPTEMBER

1965 – 18 straight games with TD for Moore
Baltimore Colts running back Lenny Moore extended his NFL record when he scored a touchdown for the 18th consecutive game in the season opener against Minnesota in Baltimore. Moore's 1-yard run was the Colts' first score as they rallied from a 10-0 deficit to defeat the Vikings 35-16.

1988 – Armstrong upsets Gross
Australian coach Lawrie Lawrence engineered a second major upset of West German superstar Michael Gross, when Duncan Armstrong swam a world record to win the 200m freestyle final at the Seoul Olympics. Armstrong swam in American Matt Biondi's wash from his lane rope and sprinted home in 1:47.25. Gross had held the world mark for the past 5 years. Lawrence had previously guided Jon Sieben to a shock win over Gross in the 200m butterfly final at the LA Olympics in 1984.

1997 – Fleming's sticky hands
New Zealand captain Stephen Fleming took his fifth catch of Zimbabwe's first innings in Harare, equalling a Test record set by Australia's Victor Richardson in 1935–36. Fleming held another 2 catches in the second innings to equal another Test record, set by Richardson's grandson Greg Chappell in 1974–75 with 7 catches in a match.

1998 – 40-40 double to 'A-Rod'
Seattle Mariners shortstop Alex Rodriguez became the third player to have 40 home runs and 40 stolen bases in the same season. 'A-Rod' hit his 40th home run in a 5-3 loss to the Angels. He finished the season with 46 steals and 42 homers.

2004 – Europe in a canter
The Bernhard Langer-captained Europe routed the United States, 18½ to 9½ to retain the Ryder Cup at Oakland Hills, Michigan. It was the largest margin of victory by a European team, who won for the fourth time in the last 5 competitions.

2007 – Six sixes to Yuvraj
Yuvraj Singh became the second batsman to hit six

Ghana's Azumah Nelson, considered to be the greatest African boxer of all time, was born on this day.

sixes in international cricket during a World Twenty20 match against England in Durban. The unlucky bowler at the other end was Stuart Broad. Yuvraj's 12-ball half-century is a record in all forms of international cricket. Herschelle Gibbs was first to achieve the feat.

BIRTHDATES
1922	American boxer/referee WILLIE PEP – died 2006
1922	Czech distance runner EMILE ZÁTOPEK – died 2000
1936	American discus thrower AL OERTER – died 2007
1943	Baseball Hall of fame second baseman/analyst JOE MORGAN
1945	American golfer JANE BLALOCK
1953	Australian Test fast bowler WAYNE CLARK
1958	Ghanaian boxer AZUMAH NELSON
1963	England soccer goalkeeper DAVID SEAMAN
1965	Australian rugby union fullback ANDREW LEEDS
1969	Russian-Australian boxer KOSTYA TSZYU
1972	Australian rugby union back rower MATT COCKBAIN
1972	American tennis player AMY FRAZIER
1974	Bangladesh Test captain NAIMUR RAHMAN
1980	French rugby halfback DIMITRI YACHVILI
1981	American NHL goaltender RICK DiPIETRO
1985	Welsh rugby back-rower ALUN-WYN JONES

1913 – Amateur wins Open
Francis Ouimet became the first amateur to win the US Open, comfortably beating Harry Vardon and Ted Ray in a playoff at The Country Club in Brookline, Massachusetts.

1969 – Nicklaus shows sportsmanship
Jack Nicklaus, playing in his first Ryder Cup, performed a famous sporting gesture in the final and deciding match at Royal Birkdale in Southport, England. Knowing the United States would retain the Cup with a 16-16 tie, Nicklaus made a 4ft par putt on the 18th hole of his singles match with Tony Jacklin, then conceded Jacklin's 3ft par putt to halve the match. Nicklaus' gesture was not well received by US captain Sam Snead and some in his team.

1973 – 'Battle of the Sexes'
In the tennis 'Battle of the Sexes' Billie Jean King took on self-proclaimed male chauvinist Bobby Riggs at the Houston Astrodome. The match proved to be a one-sided contest with the 29-year-old King accounting for the 55-year-old Riggs in straight sets 6-4, 6-3, 6-3 to claim the $100,000 winner-take-all prize. The match was played in front of largest crowd (30,492) to ever attend a tennis match. Earlier in the year Riggs, the 1939 Wimbledon champion, had beaten Australian Grand Slam winner Margaret Court.

1987 – Payton's TD record
The NFL's career rushing leader Walter Payton scored his first touchdown of his final season to break Jim Brown's record for most rushing TDs. It was the Chicago running back's 107th career rushing touchdown, helping the Bears to a 20-3 win over Tampa Bay at Soldier Field. Payton scored 3 more rushing TDs to give him a career total of 110.

1998 – Ripken consecutive game streak ends
After a record 2,632 consecutive games in 16 years, Cal Ripken stood down from the Baltimore Orioles starting lineup. Ripken had broken Lou Gehrig's record of 2,130 in 1995.

2007 – Landis has title no more
American cyclist Floyd Landis was formally stripped of his 2006 Tour de France title. Two of three arbitrators upheld the results of a test that showed Landis used synthetic testosterone to fuel his spectacular comeback victory. He was also subject to a 2-year ban, retroactive to January 2007.

2007 – Back-to-back holes-in-one
Moments after Thomas Brady scored a hole-in-one on the 179-yard seventh hole, a downhill par-3, Dennis Gerhart stepped to the tee and matched it at Forsgate CC in Monroe Township, New Jersey. Neither Brady nor Gerhart had ever made a hole-in-one before. The odds of a golfer scoring an ace are about 12,000-to-1. But the odds of 2 players in a foursome doing it are 17 million to 1.

2009 – Warner tops in completions
Arizona Cardinals quarterback Kurt Warner set an NFL single-game mark for completion percentage, breaking Vinny Testaverde's mark set 1993. Testaverde went 21 of 23 for a 91.3% completion rate, and Warner one-upped him by going 24 of 26 (92.3%). Warner hit 9 different receivers in Arizona's 31-17 win over the Jaguars in Jacksonville.

BIRTHDATES
1917	Basketball Hall of Fame coach ARNOLD 'RED' AUERBACH – died 2006
1917	Uruguayan soccer captain OBDULIO VARELA – died 1996
1944	England soccer defender PAUL MADELEY
1951	Canadian Hockey Hall of Fame winger GUY LAFLEUR
1951	New Zealand Test spinner STEPHEN BOOCK
1953	Australian boxer ROCKY MATTIOLI
1955	Spanish golfer JOSÉ RIVERO
1963	Pakistan Test wicketkeeper ANIL DALPAT
1968	Pakistan Test batsman IJAZ AHMED
1971	New Zealand rugby union lock TODD BLACKADDER
1971	Swedish soccer striker HENRIK LARSSON
1975	Columbian auto racer JUAN PABLO MONTOYA
1975	Australian rugby union winger JOE ROFF
1990	Canadian NHl centre JOHN TAVARES

21 SEPTEMBER

1969 – 98-yard NFL punt
The New York Jets rookie Steve O'Neal kicked an NFL record 98-yard punt in a 21-19 defeat against the Denver Broncos at Mile High Stadium. The Jets were facing fourth down on their own 1-yard line and O'Neal's kick sailed over Floyd Little's head, took a great roll, and came to a stop on the Denver 1-yard line for the unlikely record.

1970 – MNF debuts
Monday Night Football went on the air on the ABC Network for the first time, when the Cleveland Browns beat the New York Jets, 31-21. Keith Jackson called the play-by-play action while Howard Cosell and Don Meredith did analysis.

1985 – Spinks moves up to win title
Michael Spinks became the first light-heavyweight to defeat a reigning heavyweight champion when he beat Larry Holmes in a unanimous points decision in Las Vegas. Both fighters were previously undefeated. Spinks immediately vacated the light-heavyweight title after the fight and went on to beat Holmes in a 1986 rematch on a split decision. He made 2 more title defences before being knocked out in his last fight in 1988, by Mike Tyson.

1986 – Marino's 6 TD passes not enough
Miami Dolphins quarterback Dan Marino threw 6 touchdown passes, but it wasn't enough to beat the New York Jets, who won 51-45 in overtime at East Rutherford, New Jersey. The teams combined for an NFL record 884 passing yards.

1998 – 'Flo Jo' dead at 38
American sprinter Florence Griffith Joyner died of an epileptic seizure, aged 38. Affectionately known as 'Flo Jo,' the flamboyant sprinter was the star of the 1988 Seoul Olympics where she won 3 gold medals and set 2 world records. She remains the fastest woman in history with her 100m mark of 10.49 seconds, set in the 1988 US Olympic trials. Her muscular physique and history-making performance made her a target for sceptics and speculation of steroid use followed her abrupt retirement. She never failed a drug test.

American sprinter Florence Griffith-Joyner on her way to a gold medal in the 100m at the 1988 Seoul Olympic Games.

2008 – Easy American Ryder Cup win
The United States won the Ryder Cup for the first time in 9 years with a 16½-11½ win over Europe at Valhalla in Louisville, Kentucky. It was the largest margin of victory for the US since an 18½-9½ thumping of the Europeans at Walton Heath in 1981. Playing without an injured Tiger Woods, the rookies stepped up for the US, combining for a 4-1-1 record in the final singles matches.

BIRTHDATES
1929   Hungarian soccer forward SÁNDOR KOCSIS – died 1979
1935   England soccer defender JIMMY ARMFIELD
1945   South African golfer JOHN BLAND
1949   NBA centre ARTIS GILMORE
1951   American jockey EDDIE DELAHOUSSAYE
1953   Dutch auto racer ARI LUYENDYK
1957   NBA forward SIDNEY MONCRIEF
1959   England Test fast bowler RICHARD ELLISON
1963   West Indies Test fast bowler CURTLEY AMBROSE
1963   England soccer midfielder TREVOR STEVEN
1971   England Test batsman JOHN CRAWLEY
1978   New Zealand rugby union winger DOUG HOWLETT
1979   West Indian Test batsman CHRIS GAYLE
1980   South African auto racer TOMAS SCHECKTER

㉒ SEPTEMBER

1904 – O'Rourke oldest
Fifty-four-year-old outfielder Jim O'Rourke became the oldest player in MLB as the New York Giants clinched the pennant in a 7-5 win over Cincinnati.

1927 – Boxing's 'Long Count'
More than 100,000 people paid a record $2,658,600 to see the second Gene Tunney – Jack Dempsey world heavyweight title fight at Soldier's Field, Chicago. In the seventh round Dempsey caught Tunney with a left hook, followed up with a flurry of punches and floored the champion. In the famous 'long count,' Dempsey forgot to go to a neutral corner. The referee properly stopped the count until Dempsey moved. The champion received an additional 5 seconds to clear his head before rising at the count of 9. He avoided Dempsey's rushes and lasted out the round. Tunney recovered to win a comfortable points decision and collect a then-massive $990,000 for the fight. Fight promoter Tex Rickard and Tunney wanted a third Tunney-Dempsey confrontation, but Dempsey refused.

1969 – Mays reaches 600 HR milestone
SF Giants outfielder Willie Mays became the second player, after Babe Ruth, to record 600 major league homers when he went deep as a pinch-hitter against Mike Corkins in San Diego. The Giants won the game 4-2. Mays went on to hit 660 career home runs.

1986 – Second tied Test
India and Australia completed only the second tied Test in cricket history in the first Test in Madras. Needing 348 to win in a minimum 87 overs, India looked comfortable at 330 for 6, with just 18 required from 5 overs. But Australian spinner Ray Bright captured 3 quick wickets before Ravi Shastri took 2 from the second ball and a single off the third ball of the final over, to tie the match. Australian spinner Greg Matthews then trapped Maninder Singh lbw with just 1 ball to spare. The first tied Test match took place in Brisbane in the first Test between Australia and the West Indies in 1960.

1988 – Evans invincible
Diminutive 17-year-old American Janet Evans swam

American swimmer Janet Evans in training after winning the 400m/800m double at the 1988 Seoul Olympics.

a freakish time to smash her own 400m world record and win the gold medal at the Seoul Olympic. Using her famous and unorthodox windmill freestyle stroke, Evans swam a time of 4:03.85, 1.6 seconds better than her existing mark. She beat 15-year-old East German Heike Friedrich, who was unbeaten in 13 consecutive finals in international competition. Evans also won the 800m and 400 IM in Seoul, and went on to win the 800 in 1992 in Barcelona.

1991 – Shula second to 300 NFL wins
Don Shula won his 300th game as an NFL head coach when Miami beat Green Bay at home 16-13. Shula was only the second after George Halas (324) to reach the milestone.

BIRTHDATES
1927	MLB manager TOMMY LASORDA
1932	Swedish boxer INGEMAR JOHANSSON – died 2009
1937	England rugby union fullback DON RUTHERFORD
1942	NBA commissioner DAVID STERN
1943	Australian AFL midfielder/coach BARRY CABLE
1962	New Zealand Test captain MARTIN CROWE
1967	Cuban boxer FÉLIX SAVÓN
1969	Australian tennis player NICOLE BRADTKE
1970	French soccer midfielder EMANUEL PETIT
1970	MLB catcher/manager MIKE METHENY
1972	England rugby union number 8 TONY DIPROSE
1978	Australian soccer striker HARRY KEWELL
1979	Australian rugby union flanker PHIL WAUGH
1982	Japanese swimmer KOSUKE KITAJIMA
1989	German tennis player SABINE LISICKI

1926 – Tunney takes Dempsey's title

Gene Tunney upset champion Jack Dempsey for the world heavyweight title in Philadelphia. Dempsey was rusty from inactivity over the past 3 years and never caught up to the much faster challenger, Tunney winning all 10 rounds. After the fight, Tunney was fresh and unmarked, while Dempsey was exhausted with his face cut to ribbons.

1952 – Rocky hits canvass but wins title

Twenty-nine-year-old Rocky Marciano suffered his first knockdown in 42 undefeated fights when heavyweight champion Jersey Joe Walcott floored him with a short left hook in the first round at Philadelphia's Municipal Stadium. After 12 rounds the 38-year-old Walcott was well ahead on all 3 officials' scorecards but early in the 13th round Marciano delivered one of the most devastating punches in history, a short right to Walcott's chin, for his 38th knockout victory and first heavyweight title.

1988 – Canseco 40-40 double

Oakland first baseman José Canseco stole his 39th and 40th bases of the season, to become the first player in MLB history to have 40 homers and 40 steals. Canseco also belted his 41st home run in the 14-inning 9-8 win at Milwaukee.

1993 – Olympics to Sydney via smart lobbying

The IOC announced Sydney had beaten Beijing for the rights to host the 2000 Summer Olympics. The conduct of the lobbying process for IOC votes was then brought into question and the system altered for the choice of future host cities.

1994 – Quinnell moves to league

Welsh rugby union number 8 Scott Quinnell moved to English rugby league club Wigan, in a deal worth an estimated £400,000. Quinnell returned to union in 1997.

2000 – Rowing star medals in five Games

Britain's Steven Redgrave became the first rower to win a gold medal at 5 consecutive Olympics as part of the winning coxless fours crew in Sydney. The British crew led from start to finish but beat Italy by just 0.38 seconds. The 38-year-old Redgrave also became only the fourth athlete to earn a gold medal at 5 different Games.

2006 – Bonds takes NL HR record

San Francisco slugger Barry Bonds broke Hank Aaron's National League home run record with his 734th career homer in the struggling Giants 10-8 loss to the Brewers in Milwaukee. The seven-time MVP hit a solo shot off Chris Capuano over the right-centre fence in the third inning. Bonds was 21 homers shy of Aaron's career mark of 755.

2006 – Gibbons' foul ball hits wife!

In the ninth inning of Baltimore's 8-5 home loss against Minnesota, Jay Gibbons fouled a ball straight back over the screen and into the ribcage of his wife, Laura. Mrs Gibbons suffered bruised ribs. Long before the matter became personal, Gibbons had asked team officials to do something about making it safer to sit in the seats behind the plate.

2010 – Suzuki's 200 hits for 10 straight

Seattle outfielder Ichiro Suzuki became the first player with 10 straight 200-hit MLB seasons, breaking his own record with a fifth-inning single as the Mariners were beaten 1-0 by the Blue Jays in Toronto.

BIRTHDATES

1936	England soccer forward GEORGE EASTHAM
1939	English cricket commentator HENRY BLOFELD
1942	Australian Test fast bowler DAVID RENNEBERG
1943	NFL coach MARTY SCHOTTENHEIMER
1945	England rugby union fly-half ALAN OLD
1949	American golfer FORREST FEZLER
1952	Indian Test batsman ANSHUMAN GAEKWAD
1956	Italian soccer striker PAOLO ROSSI
1956	Australian Test spinner TOM HOGAN
1958	American golfer LARRY MIZE
1958	NFL coach MARVIN LEWIS
1965	Australian tennis player MARK WOODFORDE
1969	Australian golfer ROD PAMPLING
1971	Pakistan Test wicketkeeper MOIN KHAN
1972	Zimbabwe Test captain ALISTAIR CAMPBELL
1979	Australian rugby union/league winger LOTE TUQIRI

1776 – St Leger run for the first time
The St Leger Stakes, the oldest of Britain's 5 'classic' races, was run for the first time at Cantley Common, Doncaster. In a 5-horse field, 2-1 favourite Allabaculia was the inaugural winner.

1938 – Budge claims tennis Grand Slam
Don Budge completed the first-ever Grand Slam by beating Gene Mako 6-3, 6-8, 6-2, 6-1 in the final of the US Open. Budge had dominated amateur tennis that year, defeating John Bromwich in the Australian Open, Roderick Menzel in the French Open, and Henry Austin at Wimbledon. He turned professional after winning the Grand Slam.

1982 – Crowd trouble in Karachi
Australian captain Kim Hughes twice led his team from the field in an eventful third day of the first Test against Pakistan in Karachi. The crowd responded to several decisions against the home team by throwing rubbish onto the field near players.

1988 – Johnson 'wins' Seoul 100m
Canadian sprinter Ben Johnson ran an unbelievable 'world record' time of 9.79 to cross the line first in the 100m at the Seoul Olympics. Johnson beat American Carl Lewis, Linford Christie of Great Britain and Calvin Smith of the US, but that trio were awarded the medals after Johnson tested positive to the banned anabolic steroid stanozolol. He was disqualified and suspended for 2 years, and returned to the track in 1991, but could not rediscover his form. He again tested positive to steroids in 1993 and was banned for life.

1994 – McCall shocks Lewis
American Oliver McCall scored a major upset by knocking out British champion Lennox Lewis in the second round in London to win the WBC heavyweight title. He lost a bizarre rematch with Lewis in Las Vegas in 1997 when he suffered an apparent emotional breakdown in the fifth round and refused to fight.

2006 – Hoffman new saves leader
San Diego Padres 38-year-old closer Trevor Hoffman pitched a 1-2-3 ninth inning in front of a roaring crowd to become baseball's career saves leader in a memorable 2-1 win over the Pittsburgh Pirates. It was Hoffman's 479th career save, breaking Lee Smith's record of 478 saves compiled between 1980–97.

2007 – India takes first Twenty20 title
India won the first Twenty20 world title, defeating Pakistan by 5 runs in Johannesburg. The Indians, restricted to 157-5 after electing to bat in good conditions, fought back to bowl out Pakistan for 152 with 3 balls to spare before a sell-out crowd of 32,000. Misbah-ul Haq gave the Indians a scare with a late charge of 43 off 38 balls holed out to fine-leg.

BIRTHDATES
1871	English tennis player LOTTE DODD – died 1960
1895	Scottish golfer TOMMY ARMOUR – died 1968.
1908	England soccer defender EDRIS HAPGOOD – died 1973
1921	American sports caster JIM McKAY – died 2008
1946	American golfer GIL MORGAN
1950	Indian Test batsman MOHINDER AMARNATH
1956	NBA coach HUBIE BROOKS
1964	Cuban MLB slugger RAFAEL PALMEIRO
1965	Swedish soccer midfielder ANDERS LIMPAR
1973	NFL running back EDDIE GEORGE
1980	English track cyclist VICTORIA PENDLETON
1980	Norwegian soccer defender JOHN ARNE RIISE
1981	Australian auto racer RYAN BRISCOE

Ben Johnson beats Carl Lewis across the line in the 100m final at the 1988 Seoul Olympics; he was later disqualified after failing a drug test.

㉕ SEPTEMBER

1949 – Suggs' US Open
American golfer Louise Suggs won her first major title as a professional as she blitzed the field in the US Women's Open at the Prince Georges CC at Landover, Maryland. Suggs posted a total 291 to beat Babe Zaharias by a massive 14 strokes for the fourth major victory of her career. She had previously captured 3 majors as an amateur.

1962 – Listen lifts heavyweight title
It took challenger Sonny Liston just 2:05 of the first round to capture Floyd Patterson's world heavyweight title in Chicago. Liston, who was infamous for a long criminal record, had a 25lb advantage and landed heavy combinations to the body before decking Patterson with a powerful left hook. It was several minutes before Patterson could be helped to his corner.

1982 – Unwanted streak over
The longest losing streak in major college football history ended at 34 when Northwestern beat Northern Illinois 31-6 at Dyche Stadium. Northwestern's debut senior running back Ricky Edwards scored 4 touchdowns in his first start.

1988 – Biondi takes fifth gold
American sprinter Matt Biondi swam the freestyle leg of the winning US 4 x 100m medley relay team to earn his fifth gold medal of the Seoul Olympics. Biondi had already won gold medals in the 50m/100m freestyle and the 4 x 100m/200m freestyle relays.

1988 – Otto wins sixth gold medal
East German powerhouse Kristen Otto won an unprecedented sixth Olympic gold medal when she took out the 50m sprint in Seoul in 25.49 seconds. She had already won the 100m freestyle, butterfly and backstroke, and the 4 x 100m freestyle and medley relays. Unfortunately, like many of her teammates, 1994 East German documents revealed that her performance had been enhanced by drugs.

East German swimmer Kristen Otto takes a fifth gold medal at the 1988 Seoul Olympics in the 4 x 100m relay.

2005 – Presidents Cup to US
Chris Di Marco rolled in a 12ft birdie putt at the last hole to defeat Stuart Appleby and win The Presidents Cup 18½–15½ for the United States at the Robert Trent Jones GC in Gainsville, Virginia.

2005 – Great start for 'Cadillac'
Tampa Bay Buccaneers running back Carnell 'Cadillac' Williams rushed for 158 yards in a 17-16 win at Green Bay to become the first player in NFL history to start his career with 3 consecutive 100-yard rushing games.

BIRTHDATES
1933	NBA coach HUBIE BROWN
1942	New Zealand Test spinner PETER PETHERICK
1942	Argentine boxer OSCAR BONAVENA – died 1976
1946	Indian Test spinner BISHAN BEDI
1946	American golfer GIL MORGAN
1949	West Indian Test spinner INSHAN ALI – died 1995
1951	Basketball Hall of Fame forward BOB McADOO
1954	Spanish soccer manager JUANDE RAMOS
1955	German soccer striker KARL-HEINZ RUMMENIGGE
1961	Australian Test wicketkeeper TIM ZOEHRER
1965	NBA player SCOTTIE PIPPEN
1968	Australian AFL defender/coach JOHN WORSFOLD
1969	South African Test captain HANSIE CRONJE – died 2002

1908 – Two shutouts in one day!
Chicago Cubs right-hander Ed Reulbach became the only major league pitcher to ever throw 2 shutouts in the same day. In a doubleheader at Washington Park, Reulbach pitched a 5-0 shutout against Brooklyn and with the Cubs pitching staff fatigued he pitched in the late game for a 3-0 shutout. Reulbach's eyesight was so poor his catchers used white-painted gloves.

1965 – 'Der Kaiser' debut
Franz Beckenbauer made his international debut for Germany in a 2-1 win over Sweden in a World Cup qualifier in Stockholm. The defender went on to become Germany's most famous captain, winning 102 caps. He captained Germany to a European Championship in 1972 and World Cup in 1974. With his club Bayern Munich, he won 3 consecutive European Cups (1974–76), a European Cup Winners Cup (1967), 4 League titles and 4 Cups. As a manager he guided Germany to the World Cup in 1990.

1983 – America's Cup goes down-under
The Ben Lexon designed *Australia II* became the first challenger to win the America's Cup in the event's 132-year history. The Australian yacht, skippered by John Bertrand and sporting a winged keel, defeated Dennis Connor's *Liberty* 4-3 in the waters off Rhode Island Sound.

1988 – Johnson loses gold
Two days after the Olympic 100m final in Seoul, Canadian race winner Ben Johnson was advised by the IOC that he had tested positive for the anabolic steroid stanozolol in the 'A' sample of his urine. The finding was confirmed when Johnson's 'B' sample was tested before members of the Canadian Olympic Association. He was stripped of the gold medal and world record.

1999 – Premature celebrations sour win
Justin Leonard and the American team were widely criticised for their premature celebrations on the final day of the Ryder Cup at The Country Club in Brookline, Massachusetts. Leonard sank a 45ft birdie putt to win the 17th hole to go 1-up against Spain's José Maria Olazábal, thus securing at least a tie and an overall US victory 14½-13½.

2004 – Rubens wins first Chinese GP
Brazilian Ferrari driver Rubens Barrichello won the inaugural Chinese Formula 1 Grand Prix in Shanghai. Barrichello started from pole and beat Englishman Jenson Button and Kimi Räikkönen of Finland. World champion Michael Schumacher failed to finish.

2006 – 'Lord Byron' passes on
Golf legend Byron Nelson passed away aged 94. Nelson had one of the greatest seasons in golf history when he won 18 times in 1945, including 11 in a row, a record that still stands. He visited the winner's circle 52 times, sixth on the PGA Tour's all-time wins list. Nelson won 5 major titles – the 1937 and 1942 Masters, the 1939 US Open and the 1940 and 1945 PGA Championships.

BIRTHDATES
1931	Indian Test batsman VIJAY MANJREKAR – died 1983
1934	English golfer NEIL COLES
1935	England Test batsman BOB BARBER
1943	Australian Test captain IAN CHAPPELL
1947	American swimmer DICK ROTH
1950	New Zealand rugby union lock ANDY HADEN
1958	England soccer defender KENNY SANSOM
1959	American golfer TREVOR DODDS
1966	New Zealand jockey SHANE DYE
1967	American NHL centre CRAIG JANNEY
1970	Australian motorcycle rider DARYL BEATTIE
1974	American swimmer GARY HALL JR
1976	German soccer midfielder MICHAEL BALLACK
1978	Kenyan marathon runner ROBERT KIPKOECH CHERUIYOT
1980	Swedish NHL left wing DANIEL SEDIN
1980	Swedish NHL centre HENRIK SEDIN
1981	American tennis player SERENA WILLIAMS

㉗ SEPTEMBER

1930 – Grand Slam first for Jones
Bobby Jones easily accounted for Eugene Homans 8 & 7 to win the US Amateur Championship at Merion Cricket Club in Ardmore, Pennsylvania and become the first man to complete the Grand Slam of Golf. Earlier in the year, Jones had won the British Amateur, British and US Opens. He ended the historic season with 13 major titles in an 8-year career. He then retired from competition to practice law, but helped design a golf course in Augusta, Georgia that became the permanent site of The Masters in 1934.

1946 – Famous boxing slugfest
Middleweight champion Tony Zale returned to the ring after 5 years Naval service to knock out Rocky Graziano in the sixth round at Yankee Stadium in New York. In a slugfest, both fighters scored knockdowns, before Zale unleashed a blistering right to the body and fight ending left hook. Graziano won the rematch in 1947, but Zale regained the title with a third round knockout in 1948.

1971 – Billie Jean in the money
Billie Jean King became the first professional female athlete to win $100,000 in one year by taking out the Virginia Slims Thunderbird Classic in Phoenix, Arizona. King beat her doubles partner Rosie Casals 7-5, 6-1 in the final.

1973 – Ryan breaks Koufax strikeout record
California Angels right-hander Nolan Ryan broke Sandy Koufax's major league strikeout record when he fanned 16 Minnesota Twins at Anaheim Stadium. Ryan pitched an incredible 11 innings to get the elusive record 383rd strikeout in a 5-4 Angels win.

1988 – Louganis double double
American Greg Louganis became the first man to take the Olympic platform/springboard double twice, when he edged China's Xiong Ni to win the platform event in Seoul. Louganis needed a high score on his dangerous final dive, a reverse 3½, to win. The dive's high 3.4 degree of difficulty was enough for a 1.14 point winning margin.

In a famous incident from the 1988 Seoul Olympic Games, American diver Greg Louganis hits his head on the board during the 3-metre springboard event, which he went on to win.

1992 – Mansell magnificent
British World Formula 1 drivers champion Nigel Mansell set a single season record of 9 victories after leading from start to finish in the Portuguese Grand Prix at Estoril. In a stellar season, Mansell started all but 2 races from pole and easily beat Italian Riccardo Patrese by 52 points for the world title with a then record 108 Championship points.

2006 – 4 rookies win 10
Florida pitcher Aníbal Sánchez beat the Cincinnati Reds, 7-2 in Miami as the Marlins became the first team in MLB history to have 4 rookie pitchers with ten wins – Sánchez (10-3), Scott Olsen (12-9), Josh Johnson (12-7) and Ricky Nolasco (11-10). Dontrelle Willis (12-12) gave the Marlins 5 ten-game winners for the first time in franchise history.

BIRTHDATES
1927	American golfer GARDNER DICKINSON – died 1998
1939	American golfer KATHY WHITWORTH
1941	English soccer goalkeeper PETER BONETTI
1949	Baseball Hall of Fame infielder MIKE SCHMIDT
1957	England Test batsman BILL ATHEY
1961	American golfer CHRIS PERRY
1962	New Zealand Test all rounder GAVIN LARSON
1965	NBA guard STEVE KERR
1981	New Zealand Test captain BRENDON McCULLUM
1982	Swedish soccer forward MARKUS ROSENBERG

1941 – Williams hits .406 for the season

Twenty-three-year-old Boston Red Sox cleanup-hitter Ted Williams risked his .400 season batting average to play in a season ending double-header against the Philadelphia Athletics and became the last player to hit .400 in a season. In the opening game, Williams raised his average to .404 with a homer and 3 singles in 5 at-bats. In the night game he hit a double and single in 3 at-bats to finish the season at .406. Williams also led the majors with 120 RBI, 135 runs and 145 walks while striking out just 27 times.

1951 – 500+ yard game for Van Brocklin

Los Angeles Rams quarterback Norm Van Brocklin became the first NFL player to pass for more than 500 yards in a game when he threw for a still-standing record 554 yards against the New York Yanks in Los Angeles. Van Brocklin connected for 5 touchdowns, 4 to Elroy Hirsch, in a 54-14 Rams victory. He also ran for one himself from a yard out. Van Brocklin broke Johnny Lujack's mark of 468 yards.

1969 – Kapp throws 7 TDs

Minnesota Viking quarterback Joe Kapp tied the NFL record by throwing 7 touchdown passes in a 52-14 home win over the Baltimore Colts. Kapp joined Sid Luckman, Adrian Burk, George Blanda and Y.A. Tittle to share the single game touchdown record.

1996 – Dettori aboard record 7 winners

Jockey Lanfranco 'Frankie' Dettori won 7-of-7 races at Ascot, a single-day wins record in England. His win streak was estimated to have cost English bookmakers £30 million and caused the closing of as many as 40 bookmaking shops.

1997 – Europe wins at home

In the first Ryder Cup in continental Europe, the European team won for the second time in a row, 14½-13½ at Valderrama in Sotogrande, Spain. Led by 5 rookies (Denmark's Thomas Bjørn, Northern Ireland's Darren Clarke, Spain's Ignacio Garrido, Sweden's Jesper Parnevik and England's Lee Westwood), Europe built a 10½-5½ advantage after 2 days. The US took the final day singles 7-3-2 to fall short.

2000 – Walker DQ'ed in sight of gold

Australian Jane Saville was disqualified while leading in the 20km walk at the Sydney Olympics, just as she was about to enter Stadium Australia. She went on to earn a bronze medal in the event at the Athens Olympics in 2004.

2001 – A-Rod first shortstop to 50 HR mark

Rangers' infielder Alex Rodriguez became the 20th player and first shortstop in major league history to hit 50 home runs in a season. The milestone blast is given up by Angel pitcher Ismael Valdes in the first inning at Edison Field in an 11-2 Texas win.

2004 – Rooney's hat-trick in United debut

High-priced teen signing Wayne Rooney made a spectacular debut for Man United at Old Trafford. The £30 million forward scored a hat-trick in a 6-2 Champions League win against Turkey's Fenerbahce.

BIRTHDATES

1887	IOC president AVERY BRUNDAGE – died 1975
1905	German boxer MAX SCHMELING – died 2005
1913	American tennis player ALICE MARBLE – died 1990
1935	Australian golfer BRUCE CRAMPTON
1943	English auto racer WIN PERCY
1944	American golfer RICHIE KARL
1945	French alpine skier MARIELLE GOITSCHEL
1946	Pakistan Test batsman MAJID KHAN
1954	England rugby union number 8 JOHN SCOTT
1954	Pro Football Hall of Fame receiver STEVE LARGENT
1960	West Indies Test batsman GUS LOGIE
1960	American golfer TOM BYRUM
1962	Hockey Hall of Fame goalie GRANT FUHR
1962	American golfer LAURIE RINKER
1968	Finnish auto racer MIKA HÄKKINEN
1971	South African rugby union centre BRAAM VAN STRAATEN
1975	Australian Test fast bowler/executive STUART CLARK
1975	American swimmer LENNY KRAYZELBURG
1977	Korean golfer SE RI PAK
1981	Ecuadorian soccer defender JORGE GUAGUA
1982	Russian soccer defender ALEKSANDR ANYUKOV
1988	Croatian tennis player MARIN ILI

㉙ SEPTEMBER

1937 – Ewry dead at 63
American athlete Ray Ewry died aged 63. He won a career total of 8 gold medals in individual events. Ewry won the standing high jump, long jump and triple jump in 1900 and 1904, and also the standing long and high jump double in 1908. He contracted polio as a small boy, but regained the use of his legs to become a superb athlete, specialising in the standing events.

1954 – Mays' classic catch
New York Giants outfielder Willie Mays took a brilliant catch during the first game of the World Series against the Cleveland Indians at the Polo Grounds in NY. It's been called the greatest defensive play in baseball history. With the game tied 2-2 in the eighth inning, Don Wertz hit a drive to deep centre-field far over Mays' head. He showed lighting speed and superb judgement, and with his back to the infield, made the incredible catch facing the right-centre field bleachers, an estimated 450ft from home plate. The play still makes baseball highlight reels. The Giants won the game 5-2 on their way to a World Series sweep.

1988 – Sisters-in-law each take second gold
American sisters-in-law Florence Griffith Joyner and Jackie Joyner-Kersee each won their second gold medals of the Seoul Olympics. 'Flo Jo' had already won the 100m sprint and Joyner-Kersee had taken out the heptathlon. 'Flo Jo' won the 200m with a record 21.34 seconds. Joyner-Kersee took gold in the long jump, with an Olympic record. Flo Jo won her third gold medal 2 days later, in the 4 x 100m relay.

1995 – Elahi's ODI century debut
Saleem Elahi of Pakistan with 102 not out became the fourth batsman to score a century on his ODI debut in a 9-wicket win over Sri Lanka in Gujranwala. It was also his first-class debut.

2002 – Rice NFL record
In a 52-25 home victory against the Tennessee Titans, Oakland wide receiver Jerry Rice had 151 yards from scrimmage, bringing his total to 21,281 to pass Walter Payton as the all-time leader. Rice finished the season with 22,242 yards from scrimmage.

The great Willie Mays taking an outfield catch for the New York Giants in the 1954 World Series against the Cleveland Indians.

2002 – McGinley to the rescue
Paul McGinley of Ireland holed a 10ft par save at the 18th hole to halve his match with Jim Furyk and give the Europeans the necessary 14½ points to reclaim the Ryder Cup. They went on to win 15½ to 12½ at the Belfry, Brabazon Course.

2004 – MLB back to D.C.
Major League Baseball announced the Montreal Expos would be relocated to Washington D.C. in 2005. The new franchise would be the Washington Nationals.

BIRTHDATES

1934	West Indies Test spinner LANCE GIBBS
1934	Australian Test spinner LINDSAY KLINE
1939	Scottish soccer midfielder JIM BAXTER – died 2001
1940	England rugby union coach JOHN DAWES
1941	England Test batsman DAVID STEELE
1943	German soccer midfielder WOLFGANG OVERATH
1945	Russian shot putter NADEZHDA CHIZHOVA
1951	Australian hurdler MAUREEN CAIRD
1955	Welsh rugby union fly-half GARETH DAVIES
1955	American golfer VICKI FERGON
1956	English middle distance runner SEBASTIAN COE
1957	England Test batsman/umpire CHRIS BROAD
1969	American golfer KELLY ROBBINS
1976	Ukrainian soccer forward ANDRIY SHEVCHENKO
1982	English skeleton racer AMY WILLIAMS
1985	NFL wide receiver CALVIN JOHNSON
1988	NBA power forward KEVIN DURANT

③⓪ SEPTEMBER

1927 – Babe breaks 60 HR barrier
After cracking 9 homers in the last 15 games Babe Ruth broke the 60 home run barrier during the next-to-last game of the season against Washington at Yankee Stadium. Ruth's 2-run homer gave the Yankees a 4-2 win. His 60 homers were more than any of the other 7 American League teams hit that season.

1972 – Clemente reaches 3,000 hits
Pittsburgh Pirates right-fielder Roberto Clemente became the 11th major leaguer to reach 3,000 hits in his last regular season appearance at the plate. Three months later, the 4-time batting champion was killed when his flight from Puerto Rico to Nicaragua crashed. He was the first Hispanic player to be inducted into the Hall of Fame.

1979 – First Springbok F1 champ
Jody Scheckter became the first South African to win a World Formula 1 Drivers' Championship when he finished fourth in the Canadian Grand Prix. Scheckter finished the season with 51 points, 4 ahead of Gilles Villeneuve of Canada. In 8 seasons, Scheckter drove in 113 Grand Prix for 10 wins and 22 podium finishes.

2000 – Johnson's final run at Olympics
Michael Johnson's Olympic career came to a triumphant end when he led the US 4 x 400m relay team to the gold medal in Sydney. In all, Johnson won 5 Olympic gold medals – the 200m/400m double in Atlanta, the 400m/400m relay in Sydney, and the 400 relay in Barcelona.

2000 – Cycling giants upset by Ekimov
Two giants of world road racing, Lance Armstrong and Germany's Jan Ullrich were upset in the road time trial at the Sydney Olympics. The gold medal was won by Armstrong's Russian teammate in the US Postal team, Vyacheslav Ekimov. Ullrich finished 8 seconds behind to take silver, and Armstrong was 26 seconds back for bronze. Armstrong was stripped of his bronze because of doping charges.

2007 – Favre breaks another Marino mark
Thirty-seven-year-old Green Bay Packers quarterback

Russian road cyclist Viatcheslav Ekimov on his way to a gold medal in the time trial at the 2000 Sydney Olympics.

Brett Favre broke Dan Marino's NFL record for career touchdown passes zipping no. 421 to Greg Jennings in the first quarter of a 23-16 win against the Minnesota Vikings at the Metrodome. Marino had held the record since 1995.

2012 – European recovery in Ryder Cup
Team Europe wiped out a 4-point deficit by sweeping the first 5 matches of the final singles and then outdueled their US counterparts over the final nail-biting matches to celebrate a 14½ to 13½ Ryder Cup triumph at Medinah CC in Illinois. German Martin Kaymer provided the clinching point by finishing off with a 1-up victory over Steve Stricker.

BIRTHDATES
1944	Scottish midfielder JIMMY JOHNSTONE – died 2006
1946	German auto racer JOCHEN MASS
1946	Australian Test batsman PAUL SHEAHAN
1952	Australian Test cricket umpire DARRELL HAIR
1962	Dutch soccer player FRANK RIJKAARD
1964	Australian rower MIKE McKAY
1966	Scotland rugby union halfback GARY ARMSTRONG
1972	NFL running back JAMAL ANDERSON
1980	Swiss tennis player MARTINA HINGIS
1981	American gymnast DOMINIQUE MOCEANU
1985	Uruguayan soccer winger CRISTIAN RODRIGUEZ

OCTOBER

1 OCTOBER

1921 – Hagan cracks a PGA Championship
Walter Hagen beat Jim Barnes 3 & 2 to win the PGA Championship at the Inwood CC in Far Rockaway, New York. It was Hagen's first PGA Championship and third major overall. After not entering in 1922 and losing the final in 1923, Hagen won 4 consecutive PGA Championships, starting in 1924.

1932 – Ruth points the finger
Babe Ruth's legendary call, pointing to centre-field before smashing a homer into the Wrigley Field bleachers in Game 3 of the World Series was alleged to have taken place. Ruth had hit a 3-run homer in the first inning and when he came to the plate in the fifth inning, he was unmercifully sledged by the Cubs dugout. Ruth held up 2 fingers after strike 2 and pointed to centre field. Charlie Root's next pitch was sent soaring to deep centre, in one of the most prodigious homers ever seen at Wrigley. The solo homer broke a 4-4 tie on the way to a 7-5 Yankees win.

1950 – Babe's scoring record
Babe Zaharias tied the US Women's Open scoring record of 291 to beat Betsy Rawls by 9 strokes at Rolling Hills in Wichita, Kansas.

1975 – 'The Thrilla in Manila'
In one of boxing's truly classic fights, Muhammad Ali beat arch-rival Joe Frazier in a 14th-round TKO for the heavyweight title. Frazier's corner threw in the towel prior to the bell for the 15th round. It was Ring Magazine's 'Fight of the Year'. The bout actually took place in the Philippine capital, Quezon City.

1988 – Steffi's golden slam
Germany's Steffi Graf finished off her Grand Slam year by beating Argentina's Gabriela Sabatini 6-3, 6-3 for the Olympic gold medal at the Seoul Games, the first tennis event contested since 1924.

1993 – All-Brit title bout
Lennox Lewis scored a seventh-round TKO win over Frank Bruno to retain his WBC heavyweight title at Cardiff Arms Park in Wales. It was Lewis' first defence of his title and the first all-British heavyweight title bout.

2000 – Super kayaker
Thirty-eight-year-old German Birgit Fischer became the first woman to win 2 or more medals at 4 Summer Games when she won the K2 500 with Katrin Wagner in Sydney. Fischer won 7 career gold medals and with American swimmer Jenny Thompson, was the only non-gymnast to win ten Olympic medals.

2004 – Suzuki breaks hits record
Seattle's Japanese outfielder Ichiro Suzuki singled in each of his first 2 at-bats to break George Sisler's record for hits in a season. The historic hit surpassed Sisler's 84-year-old mark of 257 hits established in 1920 with the St Louis Browns. Sisler set the old mark in 154 games during the 1920 season. Ichiro broke the record in 159 games.

BIRTHDATES
1900	England Test spinner TOM GODDARD – died 1966
1936	England soccer striker DUNCAN EDWARDS – died 1958
1937	Pakistan Test batsman SAEED AHMED
1939	American golfer GEORGE ARCHER – died 2005
1942	French auto racer JEAN-PIERRE JABOUILLE
1953	Norwegian marathon runner GRETA WAITZ
1961	Australian AFL forward GARY ABLETT
1963	Baseball slugger MARK McGWIRE
1968	England rugby union captain PHIL DE GLANVILLE
1970	Kenyan steeplechaser MOSES KIPTANUI
1970	Russian NHL centre ALEXEI ZHAMNOV
1981	Brazilian soccer forward JULIO BAPTISTA
1983	Serbian soccer forward MIRKO VUCINIC

Germans Birgit Fischer and Carolin Leonhardt compete in the K4 500m in Athens 2004.

❷ OCTOBER

1916 – 16 shutouts for Alexander
The Philadelphia Phillies started 29-year-old right-handed pitcher Grover Cleveland Alexander for the third time in 5 days in the home game against the Boston Braves. Alexander pitched his 20th century record 16th shutout of the season, allowing the Boston Braves just 3 hits in a 2-0 win. He improved his season record to 33-12.

1960 – First Vare for Wright
Mickey Wright won her first Vare Trophy after a season average of 73.25 strokes per tournament round. Wright became the first player in LPGA history to average fewer than 74 strokes per round. She won 5 consecutive Vare Trophies (1960–64) with a career low season average of 72.46 in 1964.

1966 – 'Nat' Young wins surf title
Australian Robert 'Nat' Young claimed the world surfing championship with a dominating performance at Ocean Beach, San Diego. It was Young's only world title, but he did win 4 world long board titles in the 1980s and 1990s.

1980 – Ali return unsuccessful
At age 38, Muhammad Ali came out of a 2-year retirement to challenge undefeated heavyweight champion Larry Holmes at Caesars Palace in Las Vegas. Ali was the only 3-time World Heavyweight Champion in history but proved no match for the 30-year-old Holmes who pounded him unmercifully for 10 rounds. With only courage keeping him standing, Ali's corner threw in the towel before the 11th round. It was Ali's 25th and final heavyweight title fight.

1988 – Lennox wins boxing gold
Future World Heavyweight Champion Lennox Lewis, representing Canada, won the Olympic super-heavyweight gold medal when he stopped American Riddick Bowe in the second round in Seoul. Lewis was in the ring for only 10:16 for the whole tournament. He became an excellent world champion, retiring in 2004 when he still held the title. Bowe had a successful pro career, highlighted by 3 fights with Evander Holyfield, winning 2 of them.

1994 – Pakis win Test on last gasp partnership
Pakistan batsmen Inzamam-ul-Haq and Mushtaq Ahmed put on 57 runs in 8 overs for the highest last-wicket partnership ever to win a Test, as the home team beat Australia in the first Test in Karachi. At 310 for 9, and needing 314 to win, Australian wicketkeeper Ian Healy missed a difficult stumping chance and the ball went for 4 byes for Pakistan to win by 1 wicket.

1999 – Guerrero's double
Vladimir and Wilton Guerrero of the Montreal Expos both hit home runs in the same game, a 13-3 win in Philadelphia. The brothers joined Hank and Tommie Aaron, Matty and Jesus Alou, Aaron and Bret Boone, Billy and Tony Conigliaro, Al and Tony Cuccinello, Rick and Wes Farrell, Graig and Jim Nettles, Cal and Billy Ripken, Jason and Jeremy Giambi, and Paul and Lloyd Waner as siblings who have homered in the same game.

BIRTHDATES
1873	England Test batsman PELHAM 'PLUM' WARNER – died 1963
1939	Indian Test all-rounder BUDHI KUNDERAN
1948	England soccer midfielder TREVOR BROOKING
1957	England rugby union lock WADE DOOLEY
1957	American golfer JOHN COOK
1962	Canadian NFL quarterback MARK RYPIEN
1965	Australian tennis player/coach DARREN CAHILL
1965	Australian Test all rounder TOM MOODY
1967	Austrian tennis player THOMAS MUSTER
1967	Namibian sprinter FRANKIE FREDERICKS
1968	Czech tennis player JANA NOVOTNÁ
1971	Kenyan runner MOSES KIPTANUI
1984	French tennis player MARION BARTOLI
1987	American racing driver RICKY STENHOUSE JR

③ OCTOBER

1920 – 'NFL' first game
The Dayton Triangles beat the Columbus Panhandles 14-0 in the first meeting of teams belonging to the American Professional Football Association. This was considered the NFL's first game as the APFA became the National Football League in 1922. Dayton fullback Lou Partlow scored the league's first touchdown on a short plunge after setting it up with a 40-yard run.

1965 – Jockey Glennon has the touch
Dual Melbourne Cup winning Australian jockey, Pat Glennon, rode champion colt, Sea Bird to victory in the Prix de l'Arc De Triomphe in Paris for an impressive double. Sea Bird defeated the previously unbeaten French Derby and Grand Prix de Paris winner Reliance by 6 lengths. Glennon had also ridden Sea Bird to an English Derby victory earlier that year.

1974 – First African-American MLB manager
Thirty-nine-year-old Frank Robinson became MLB's first African-American manager when he was signed as player-manager by the Cleveland Indians. The former MVP agreed to a 1-year contract estimated to be worth $180,000. The signing came 27 years after Jackie Robinson broke the colour line in MLB.

1989 – Shell NFL's first black coach
The Oakland Raiders promoted Art Shell as the first African-American NFL head coach in modern times. The 42-year-old Shell was an outstanding offensive tackle for 15 years with the Raiders and was hired after Raiders boss Al Davis fired Mike Shanahan.

1995 – O.J. innocent?
Former NFL champion running back O.J. Simpson was found innocent of murder charges relating to the death of his ex-wife Nicole and friend Ronald Goldman. The jury took less than 4 hours to reach a unanimous decision in a trial that lasted an entire year. Nicole Brown Simpson and Ronald Goldman were stabbed to death outside her Brentwood townhouse on June 12 1994.

1999 – Huge Chelsea upset
Chelsea scored the upset of the EPL season when they humbled Premiership champions Manchester United 5-0 at Stamford Bridge. Gustavo Poyet set the tone for the afternoon when he scored for Chelsea after just 27 seconds. The Red Devils recovered from the setback to win the Premiership by a whopping 18 points. Chelsea finished fifth.

2008 – Surf king Slater wins title #9
Kelly Slater clinched his record ninth world surfing championship after round 3 of the Billabong Pro in Mundaka, Spain. Dominating 5 of the season's first 8 events, Slater accrued enough points to win the title with 2 scheduled ASP Tour contests to be surfed. Slater's ninth world championship came 16 years after his first, in 1992. The Florida native was the youngest (aged 20), and the oldest (aged 36) competitor to win the biggest prize in surfing.

2012 – Cabrera takes rare Triple Crown
Detroit Tigers slugger Miguel Cabrera won the American League Triple Crown, leading the AL in batting average (.330), home runs (44) and RBI (139). No one had won a league Triple Crown since Carl Yastrzemski in 1967.

BIRTHDATES
1862	England Test fast bowler JOHNNY BRIGGS – died 1902
1921	Australian Test fast bowler RAY LINDWALL – died 1996
1932	South African golfer HAROLD HENNING
1933	Australian tennis player/Davis Cup captain NEALE FRASER
1940	American swimmer MIKE TROY
1950	New Zealand rugby union winger BRYAN WILLIAMS
1951	Baseball Hall of Fame outfielder DAVE WINFIELD
1952	New Zealand Test fast bowler GARY TROUP
1954	Baseball Hall of Fame pitcher DENNIS ECKERSLEY
1959	American golfer FRED COUPLES
1963	American tennis player DAN GOLDIE
1974	Dutch speed skater MARIANNE TIMMER
1975	England rugby union hooker PHIL GREENING
1978	Peruvian soccer striker CLAUDIO PIZARRO
1980	NFL wide receiver ANQUAN BOLDIN
1981	Swedish soccer striker ZLATAN IBRAHIMOVI
1981	Swedish soccer goalkeeper ANDREAS ISAKSSON

➍ OCTOBER

Australian wicketkeeper Ian Healy on his way to 82 during the first Test against Pakistan at Rawalpindi in 1998. Australia won by an innings and 99 runs.

1955 – Dodgers' first World Series after 8 tries
After losing their previous 7 World Series, the Brooklyn Dodgers won their first world championship with a 2-0 victory in Game 7 against archrivals the New York Yankees. The Dodgers had dropped 5 Series to the Yankees since 1941.

1989 – Secretariat dies
Outstanding American racehorse Secretariat died at the age of 19. Affectionately known as 'Big Red,' Secretariat won the 1973 Triple Crown. In 21 starts, Secretariat won 16 and was placed 4 times with earnings of $1.3 million.

1992 – Hulme dead at 56
The 1967 World Formula 1 drivers champion, Denny Hulme of New Zealand, died after suffering a massive heart attack following a race crash at Bathurst in Australia. He was 56. Hulme drove in 112 Grand Prix for 8 victories.

1996 – Youthful Afridi on fire
Pakistan batsman Shahid Afridi hit he fastest ODI century in history against Sri Lanka in the KCA Centenary Tournament in Nairobi. The 16-year-old was also the youngest player to score a ODI hundred. He took only 37 balls to reach 3 figures, comfortably beating Sanath Jayasuriya's existing record of 48 balls. Afridi also hit 11 sixes to equal Jayasuriya's one-day record.

1998 – Doohan earns fifth world title
Michael Doohan clinched his fifth consecutive world 500cc motor-cycle title with victory in the Australian Grand Prix at Phillip Island. Doohan won all 5 of his titles with Honda, and trailed only Italian rider Giacomo Agostini who won 7 consecutive world championships (1966–72).

1998 – Healy top 'keeper
Australian Ian Healy broke the world record for the number of Test dismissals by a wicket keeper with his 356th victim in the first Test against Pakistan in Rawlpindi. Healy overtook countryman Rod Marsh on 355, and finished his career with 366 catches and 29 stumpings in 119 Tests.

2001 – Rickey takes 'runs scored' record
Forty-two-year-old San Diego Padres outfielder Rickey Henderson passed the legendary Ty Cobb for the all-time runs scored record (2,246) with a home run in the third inning in a 6-3 home win against the Los Angeles Dodgers.

2010 – Europeans regain Ryder Cup
Europe defeated the US, 14½ to 13½, to win the Ryder Cup at Celtic Manor in Wales. The Americans trailed by 3 going into the final singles round of 12 matches and provided a gutsy comeback. US Open champion Graeme McDowell was the hero for the Europeans, holding his nerve to close out a 3 & 1 victory over Hunter Mahan amid joyous scenes. The win avenged Europe's defeat at Valhalla 2 years before.

BIRTHDATES
1931	England Test batsman BASIL D'OLIVEIRA – died 2011
1934	Pro Football Hall of Fame linebacker SAM HUFF
1940	Argentine soccer defender SILVIO MARZOLINI
1943	Australian tennis player OWEN DAVIDSON
1944	MLB player and manager TONY LA RUSSA
1955	Scotland rugby union fly-half JOHN RUTHERFORD
1955	Argentine soccer forward/manager JORGE VALDANO
1956	American golfer SHERRI TURNER
1963	NBA power forward A.C. GREEN
1964	American swimmer TOM JAGER
1965	American boxer MICKY WARD
1967	Australian rower NICK GREEN
1969	Australian golfer LUCAS PARSONS
1980	Czech soccer winger TOMÁŠ ROSICKÝ
1988	NBA guard DERRICK ROSE

⑤ OCTOBER

1921 – First radio World Series call
Radio station WJZ in Newark was the first to broadcast a World Series game, when the New York Yankees took on the New York Giants. A Newark sportswriter arranged for a telephone hook-up from the Polo Grounds in Manhattan and phoned in balls and strikes to the radio announcer who repeated them on-air.

1946 – Geordies blitz
Newcastle United equalled the Football League record for the biggest winning margin when they thrashed Newport County, 13-0, in a Division 2 match.

1949 – Jones ill
It was first reported that golfing great Bobby Jones's rare spinal disease would prevent him playing again. Afflicted with syringomyelia, Jones played his final Masters in 1948 and was then forced into a wheelchair. Finally succumbing to his illness, Jones died on 18 December 1971 at the age of 69.

1950 – Union star makes switch to league
Australian rugby union captain Trevor Allen was offered a record signing-on fee of £6,000 with English rugby league club Leigh. After playing 14 Tests for the Wallabies, Allen was one of the first post-World War II union stars to move to England to play rugby league. He was a big hit, scoring 52 tries in 99 games.

1994 – 3-point distance shortened
The NBA shortened the 3-point distance to a uniform 22ft to help offensive players score more. The new line was just inside the outer rim of Michael Jordan's reasonable shooting range. The' superstar (who had a career 3-point percentage in the mid-20s before) shot 43% from 3-point range in 1995–96. He set career highs in 3-point attempts and converted 3-point field goals at nearly double his previous career best.

2007 – Jones comes clean
After years of angry denials, celebrated American sprinter Marion Jones admitted she used steroids. The triple Olympic gold medallist from the Sydney Games in 2000 pleaded guilty to lying to federal investigators when she denied using performance-enhancing

Chicago Bulls superstar Michael Jordan in an NBA game against the Pacers in Indianapolis.

drugs, and then announced her retirement in a tearful apology outside the US District Court.

BIRTHDATES

1922	Scottish soccer manager JOCK STEIN – died 1985
1922	Argentine auto racer JOSE FROILÁN GONZÁLES
1937	NFL coach BARRY SWITZER
1940	Australian Test batsman BOB COWPER
1946	England soccer defender DAVE WATSON
1953	Scotland rugby union halfback ROY LAIDLAW
1960	Brazilian soccer striker CARECA
1960	New Zealand rugby union captain DAVID KIRK
1962	American auto racer MICHAEL ANDRETTI
1963	English golfer LAURA DAVIES
1963	Australian Test all rounder TONY DODEMAIDE
1965	Canadian Hockey Hall of Fame centre MARIO LEMIEUX
1965	American tennis player RICHIE RENEBERG
1965	Canadian Hockey Hall of Fame goalie PATRICK ROY
1967	England rugby union hooker DORIAN WEST
1972	NBA forward GRANT HILL
1983	German tennis player FLORIAN MAYER

❻ OCTOBER

1926 – Ruth's World Series records
New York Yankees slugger Babe Ruth hit 3 home runs against the Cardinals in Game 4 of the World Series at Sportsman's Park in St Louis. He was the first player to accomplish the feat in a Series game. The first 2 pitches from Cardinals right-hander Flint Rhem resulted in 2 solo homers and his third came in the sixth inning. Ruth went 3-for-3 and set a World Series record with 4 runs scored in the Yankees' 10-5 win that tied the Series 2-2.

1927 – 24-hour cycling record
Australian Hubert Opperman smashed the world record for 24-hour cycling by completing 416 miles, beating the previous record by 13.5 miles. The course ran from Mt Gambier in South Australia to the Victorian capital of Melbourne. Through the 1920s and 1930s, Opperman won over 50 major road races in Australia, England and Europe.

1969 – Golfing icon Hagan dies
Walter Hagen, the world's top golfer during the 1920s, died aged 76. He won 11 major titles: 2 US Opens, 4 British Opens, and 5 PGA Championships (4 straight from 1924 to 1927). He also won 40 PGA Tour events.

1973 – Stewart retires from F1
Scottish triple World Formula 1 Driver's champion Jackie Stewart announced his retirement from racing immediately after teammate François Cevert was killed in qualifying for the US Grand Prix at Watkins Glen. In 8 seasons, Stewart drove in 99 Grand Prix for 27 victories. He won the World Championship in 1969, 1971 and 1973.

1993 – MJ's first retirement
After leading the Chicago Bulls to 3 consecutive NBA titles, Michael Jordan announced his retirement. He had a short-lived career in minor league baseball before making a comeback with the Bulls and another 3 NBA Championships. After a second retirement, he played 2 seasons with the Washington Wizards.

2009 – Favre beats the League
Brett Favre became the first quarterback in history to

The great Walter Hagan in a promotional shoot on the roof of London's Savoy Hotel in 1922.

beat all 32 NFL teams as the Minnesota Vikings beat the Green Bay Packers 30-23 in Minneapolis. Favre connected for 3 touchdown passes and 271 yards in his first game against his former team.

2010 – Rare post-season no-no
Roy Halladay threw the second no-hitter in MLB postseason history, leading the Philadelphia Phillies over the Cincinnati Reds 4-0 in Game 1 of the NL Division Series in Philadelphia. Don Larsen was the only other pitcher to throw a postseason no-hitter, tossing a perfect game for the New York Yankees in the 1956 World Series against Brooklyn.

BIRTHDATES
1905	American tennis player HELEN WILLS MOODY – died 1998
1919	England soccer striker TOMMY LAWTON – died 1996
1930	Australian cricket captain/broadcaster RICHIE BENAUD
1944	Brazilian auto racer CARLOS PACE – died 1977
1946	England Test captain TONY GREIG – died 2012
1947	Italian diver KLAUS DIBIASI
1955	NFL coach TONY DUNGY
1959	American pro bowler WALTER RAY WILLIAMS JR
1964	American swimmer TOM JAGER
1966	Irish soccer striker NIALL QUINN
1967	Swedish soccer forward KENNET ANDERSSON
1968	American golfer BOB MAY
1969	Zimbabwean tennis player BYRON BLACK
1972	Australian golfer JARROD MOSELEY
1978	English boxer RICKY HATTEN
1981	Ecuadorian soccer defender JOSÉ PERLAZA
1984	South African Test fast bowler MORNÉ MORKEL

1945 – Happy Hutson

Green Bay's Hall of Fame wide receiver Don Hutson scored 29 points in one quarter when he caught 4 TD passes and kicked 5 extra points in the Packers' league-record 41 point second quarter against Detroit at Fair Park in Milwaukee. Hutson then retired to the bench except to kick 2 more extra points, giving him 31 points in the Packers' 57-21 win.

1962 – 'Golden Bear' wins first of 5 WS titles

Twenty-two-year-old PGA Tour rookie Jack Nicklaus won the first of his 5 World Series of Golf titles, posting a 135 total for 36 holes to beat Arnold Palmer and Gary Player at the Firestone CC in Akron, Ohio.

1965 – Second longest hole-in-one

Robert Mitera recorded the second longest ever hole-in-one – a gale assisted 447 yard effort on the 10th hole at the Miracle Hills GC in Omaha, Nebraska. Michael J. Crean broke Matera's mark in 2002 at the 517-yard ninth hole of the Green Valley GC in Ohio.

1983 – Newton returns

Jack Newton returned to a golf course for an informal hit-out less than 3 months after suffering shocking injuries when he accidentally walked into a single engine aeroplane propeller. The 1975 British Open and 1980 Masters runner-up lost his right arm and eye and suffered severe abdominal injuries. Now an accomplished television commentator, writer and course designer, he operates the Jack Newton Junior Academy for promising young golfers.

1984 – Payton tops 2 Brown marks

Chicago Bears running back Walter Payton broke 2 of Jim Brown's rushing records in the Bears 20-7 win over the New Orleans Saints at Soldier Field. A 6-yard run took him past Brown's career record of 12,312 yards and he finished with over 100 yards for a record 59th time in his career.

1999 – Ultra Marathon record to Farmer

Australian Pat Farmer broke the world record for a 10,000km marathon during his 14,662k Centenary of Federation run. He ran 10,000k in 129 days and completed the around Australia run in Canberra in 191 days.

2001 – Bonds record 73 homers

San Francisco Giants slugger Barry Bonds completed the greatest hitting season ever with his record 73rd home run in a 2-1 home win against the rival LA Dodgers. The 37-year-old Bonds' final home run of the year came in the first inning off Dennis Springer and shattered the slugging percentage record that Babe Ruth had held since 1920.

2004 – Clark's exciting debut

Michael Clark made the best-ever Australian Test debut on foreign soil, and became only the sixth Australian to score 150 on debut, when he compiled 151 in the first Test against India in Bangalore.

2012 – It's a Brees for Drew

Drew Brees broke Hall of Fame quarterback Johnny Unitas' half-century-old NFL record by throwing a touchdown pass in his 48th consecutive game, as the Saints defeated the San Diego Chargers 31-24 in New Orleans.

BIRTHDATES

1876	South African Test batsman LOUIS TANCRED – died 1934
1887	England Test batsman CHARLES RUSSELL – died 1961
1914	American golfer HERMAN KEISER – died 2003
1938	British tennis player ANN HAYDON-JONES
1950	NFL coach DICK JAURON
1952	Australian Test captain GRAHAM YALLOP
1956	England rugby union lock STEVE BAINBRIDGE
1957	British ice dancer JAYNE TORVIL
1967	English golfer PETER BAKER
1973	Finnish soccer defender SAMI HYYPIÄ
1976	Brazilian soccer midfielder GILBERTO SILVA
1978	Indian Test fast bowler ZAHEER KHAN
1982	American tennis player ROBBIE GINEPRI

⑧ OCTOBER

1915 – Ruth struggles early but ...
The Philadelphia Phillies, playing in their first World Series, beat Boston 3-1 in Game 1 at Baker Bowl in Philadelphia. 20-year-old Red Sox rookie Babe Ruth grounded out in the ninth inning as a pinch hitter and sat out the remainder of the series. The Red Sox went on to win the next 4 games and the World Series 4-1.

1956 – World Series perfect game
New York Yankees right-handed starting pitcher Don Larsen, known more for his partying than pitching, hurled the only perfect game in World Series history in a 2-0 victory over the Dodgers in Game 5 at Yankee Stadium. The Yankees won the Series in 7 games.

1961 – Ruth loses records
Babe Ruth's second MLB record was broken in the same season when Whitey Ford bettered his 43-year-old record for consecutive scoreless innings in the World Series. Ford hurled 5 scoreless innings in a 7-0 win over Cincinnati to take his streak to 32, beating Ruth's 29.2 in 1916/18. During the regular season, Roger Maris blasted 61 home runs, one better than Ruth's 1927 mark.

1978 – Warby's water speed record
Ken Warby became the fastest man on water guiding his jet hydroplane, *Spirit of Australia* to speeds of 511 kph at the Blowering Dam near Tumut in NSW, Australia. The Warby designed and built boat was powered by a 6,000 horsepower Westinghouse jet engine. The record has stood for more than 25 years.

1997 – Debutant double
Pakistan batsman Ali Naqvi (115) and Azhar Mahmood (128) became the first pair of debutants to score centuries in the same innings in the first Test against South Africa at Rawalpindi. Azhar also added 151 for the last wicket with Mushtaq Ahmed (59), equalling the Test record set by Kiwis Brian Hastings and Richard Collinge in 1973.

1999 – Chip off the old block
Laila Ali, the 21-year-old daughter of Muhammad Ali, made her professional debut by knocking out

Water speed record holder Ken Warby after breaking the 300mph and 500kph barriers in 1978.

April Flower 31 seconds into the first round at the Turning Stone Casino in Verona, New York. In 2004, Ali won the IWBF light-heavyweight title, knocking out Gwendolyn O'Neil in the third round in Atlanta.

BIRTHDATES
1875	English tennis player LAWRENCE DOHERTY – died 1919
1917	American boxer BILLY CONN – died 1993
1928	Australian Test batsman NEIL HARVEY
1928	Brazilian soccer midfielder DIDI – died 2001
1932	Welsh snooker player RAY REARDEN
1936	England soccer midfielder PETER SWAN
1938	Australian tennis player FRED STOLLE
1955	American auto racer BILL ELLIOTT
1957	Italian soccer defender ANTONIO CABRINI
1959	American golfer TOMMY ARMOUR III
1960	England rugby union flanker MIKE TEAGUE
1965	American swimmer MATT BIONDI
1974	Irish rugby union player MICK O'DRISCOLL

1919 – 'Black Sox' drama looms

The Chicago White Sox lost the decisive Game 8 in the World Series 10-5 to Cincinnati in Chicago, firing rumours the Series had been fixed. The Reds took the best-of-nine Series 5-3. Chicago's Lefty Williams (23-11) had lost his first 2 Series starts and was removed in the first inning after allowing 2 singles and 2 doubles. In 1921, Williams was one of 8 White Sox players banned from MLB for throwing the Series.

1938 – Three more WS dingers for 'the Babe'

Nearly 2 years to the day after becoming the first player to hit 3 home runs in a World Series game, Ruth repeated the performance in Game 4 against St Louis at Sportsmen Park. Ruth finished the game 3-for-5 and had 3 RBIs as all 3 shots were solo homers. The Yankees won 7-3 completing a 4-game sweep.

1958 – Yogi's 10th World Series

Yogi Berra equalled Babe Ruth and Joe Di Maggio in completing his tenth World Series with a Game 7, 6-2 win against the Milwaukee Braves at Yankee Stadium. Berra eventually made a record 13 World Series appearances. The Yankees became the first American League team to overcome a 3-1 deficit to win the World Series, 4-3.

1976 – Miandad/Petherick star

Nineteen-year-old Pakistan debutant Javed Miandad scored 163 in the first Test against New Zealand at Lahore. Also making his Test debut was 34-year-old Kiwi spinner Peter Petherick, who dismissed Miandad, Wasim Raja and Intikhab Alam with consecutive deliveries to complete a famous hat-trick. Petherick was only the second bowler to take a hat-trick on debut after England's Maurice Allom in 1929–30.

1989 – Shell, first black NFL coach – wins

Art Shell, the first African-American head coach in the NFL, won in his first game, guiding the LA Raiders to a 14-7 win over the New York Jets on national TV on *Monday Night Football*.

2005 – Longest postseason MLB game

In the longest game in MLB postseason history, Chris Burke hit a game-winning home run with one out in the bottom of the 18th inning, as Houston beat Atlanta 7-6 at Minute Maid Park. The Astros advanced to the National League Championship Series for a second straight year.

BIRTHDATES

1953	American tennis player HANK PFISTER
1955	British athlete STEVE OVETT
1958	NFL linebacker/coach MIKE SINGLETARY
1962	Argentine soccer midfielder JORGE LUIS BURRUCHAGA
1967	Canadian tennis player CARLING BASSETT-SEGUSO
1970	Swedish golfer ANNIKA SÖRENSTAM
1975	Australian soccer striker MARK VIDUKA
1980	Swedish NHL centre HENRIK ZETTERBERG
1986	French swimmer LAURE MANAUDOU

The Chicago 'Black Sox' team of 1919.

⑩ OCTOBER

1951 – Baseball manager' bribe offer

New York Giants baseball manager Leo Durocher received a bribe for his team to throw the World Series against cross-town rivals, the Yankees. Durocher handed a letter to authorities offering him the then massive sum of $15,000. The Yankees went on the win the Series 4-2.

1964 – First Asian Olympics

The first summer Olympic Games to be conducted in Asia opened in Tokyo. The Japanese wished to express their successful post World War II reconstruction by selecting Yoshinori Sakai as final torchbearer. Sakai was born in Hiroshima on the day the city was destroyed by an atomic bomb in 1945.

1976 – Match Play to Graham

David Graham beat Hale Irwin 1-up at the 38th hole to become the first Australian to win the Piccadilly World Match Play title at Wentworth in England. Graham went on to win 8 PGA Tour events including the 1979 PGA Championship and the 1980 US Open.

1987 – Houghton heroics not enough

Zimbabwe captain Dave Houghton scored a brilliant 142 off 137 balls, with 13 fours and 6 sixes in a World Cup match against New Zealand in Hyderabad. Chasing a winning target of 243, Zimbabwe was dismissed for 239.

1993 – Marino's streak stalled by injury

Miami quarterback Dan Marino ruptured his Achilles tendon in the Dolphins' 24-14 win in Cleveland ending his season and also his NFL leading streak of 145 consecutive starts. Marino made an immediate impact when he returned the following season, throwing for 473 yards and 5 touchdowns in a 39-35 win over New England in Miami.

2003 – 'Haydos' Test best

Matthew Hayden bludgeoned his way to 380 in the first Test against Zimbabwe in Perth, to break Brian Lara's record for the highest individual score in Test cricket. Hayden clobbered 38 fours and 11 sixes in 10 hours at the crease. Adam Gilchrist, with an 84-ball

Miami Dolphins quarterback Dan Marino during a 24-14 win against the Browns in Cleveland in 1993.

century, played a good support role.

2004 – 19 straight wins for Pats

The Super Bowl champion New England Patriots beat the Miami Dolphins 24-10 in Boston to win their NFL record 19th consecutive match. The Patriots record streak ended at 21, when they were beaten 34-20 at Pittsburgh on October 31.

BIRTHDATES

1919 West Indies Test all-rounder GERRY GOMEZ – died 1996
1922 New Zealand Test captain HARRY CAVE – died 1989
1923 English sports caster MURRAY WALKER
1937 Australian golfer BRUCE DEVLIN
1945 West Indies Test fast bowler VANBURN HOLDER
1953 NBA guard GUS WILLIAMS
1963 Norwegian cross-country skier VEGARD ULVANG
1966 England soccer defender TONY ADAMS
1969 NFL quarterback BRETT FAVRE
1970 British rower MATTHEW PINSENT
1974 American auto racer DALE EARNHARDT JR

1890 – Owens' sub-10 second 100 yards
John Owens Jr became the first man to break the 10-second barrier in the 100-yard dash. Owens was timed at 9.8 seconds when he won the event at an Amateur Athletic Union meet in Washington, DC.

1956 – Pakistan wins in inaugural Test
In a record day for the lowest run total, Australia was dismissed for 80 and Pakistan finished at 2 for 15 on the first day of the first Test in Karachi. In the first Test between the 2 countries, Pakistan spinner Fazal Mahmood had match figures of 13 for 114 as Pakistan went on to win by 9 wickets after Australia was dismissed for 187 in their second innings.

1980 – Mavs first NBA win
The Dallas Mavericks opened their first season in the NBA with a 103-92 victory at home against interstate rival the San Antonio Spurs. The Mavs won the NBA Championship in 2011.

1981 – Punt return record
LeRoy Irvin of the Los Angeles Rams set an NFL record by returning punts for 207 yards in a 37-35 win over the Atlanta Falcons. On a stellar day, Irvin had 6 returns, including 2 touchdowns, a 75-yarder in the first quarter and an 84-yarder in the fourth.

1999 – First £1m Testimonial
Manchester United manager Sir Alex Ferguson drew the first £1 million testimonial match when 54,842 paid to see a Rest of the World team beat Manchester United 4-2 at Old Trafford. A large portion of the receipts went to charity.

2004 – Great all-rounder Miller passes away
Outstanding Australian all-rounder Keith Miller passed away on Victoria's Mornington Peninsula after a long illness – he was 84. Miller played 55 Tests and scored 2,958 runs at an average of 36.97 with 7 centuries. He took 170 Test wickets at 22.97

2009 – Woods dominates Presidents Cup win
Tiger Woods beat Y. E. Yang 6 & 5 to wrap up a 19½-14½ victory for the United States over the International

A stand at Manchester United's Old Trafford stadium is named after legendary manager Sir Alex Ferguson. Photo: Duncan Hull (Flickr: Sir Alex Ferguson Stand) [CC-BY-2.0], via Wikimedia Commons.

team in the Presidents Cup at Harding Park in San Francisco. The US team maintained their unbeaten home record in the competition that began in 1994. Woods went 5-0 for the week, joining Mark O'Meara (1996) and Shigeki Maruyama (1998) as the only players to win all 5 matches in the Presidents Cup.

2010 – Favre first to 500 TDs and 70,000 yards
Forty-one-year-old Brett Favre became the first quarterback in NFL history to throw at least 500 touchdown passes as his Minnesota Viking lost 29-20 to the New York Jets at the Meadowlands. Earlier on the same drive, he became the first to amass 70,000 career passing yards. The historic 37-yard touchdown pass to Randy Moss came in the third quarter.

BIRTHDATES
1937	England soccer captain SIR BOBBY CHARLTON
1939	Brazilian tennis player MARIA BUENO
1943	West Indian Test batsman KEITH BOYCE
1946	Japanese gymnast SAWAO KATO
1959	Australian motorcycle rider WAYNE GARDNER
1961	NFL quarterback STEVE YOUNG
1963	Israeli soccer winger RONNIE ROSENTHAL
1973	Australian golfer GREG CHALMERS
1974	Norwegian snowboarder TERJE HÅKONSEN
1989	American golfer MICHELLE WIE

⑫ OCTOBER

1920 – Man o' War beats Sir Barton
In his final race after winning 19 of 20 races, 3-year-old Man o' War beat 1919 Triple Crown winner Sir Barton in a match race at Kenilworth Park in Windsor, Ontario. Man o' War took control early to beat the older Canadian-owned horse by 7 lengths in the 1¼ mile race to earn connections the $80,000 purse.

1929 – A's World Series comeback
The Philadelphia Athletics registered the greatest comeback in World Series history when they beat the Chicago Cubs 10-8 after trailing by 8 runs in the seventh inning in Game 4 in Philadelphia. All the scoring was completed in the record 10-run seventh inning, highlighted by a 3-run, inside-the-park homer by Mule Haas to make it 8-7.

1979 – First 3-pointer
Chris Ford of the Boston Celtics scored the first 3-point basket in NBA history with 3:48 left in the first quarter of a 114-106 victory over Houston at Boston Garden. The game also marked the debut of Boston rookie Larry Bird.

1989 – Famous Walker NFL trade
In then the biggest trade in history, star running back Herschel Walker was traded from the Dallas Cowboys to the Minnesota Vikings, in an agreement involving 18 players and draft picks. The trade was a disaster for the Vikings. It decimated their powerful squad and Walker was released in 1992. He was picked up by Philadelphia and later, ironically, went back to Dallas.

1991 – Beck breaks 60
Chip Beck became only the second player to fire a sub-60 round in a PGA round when he posted a 59 in the third round of the Las Vegas Invitational at the Sunrise Golf Club. Beck went out on the back 9 in 29 and came home in 30, carding 13 birdies for the record equalling round. Al Geiberger first achieved the feat in 1977, whilst David Duval also broke 60 in 1999.

1998 – 'Swiss Miss' on top for 80 weeks only
Martina Hingis' 80-week reign at the top of the women's rankings ended when Lindsay Davenport claimed the no. 1 spot. She regained the top ranking on another 4 occasions before retiring with injury in 2003 at age 22. Hingis won 76 singles and doubles titles, including 5 Grand Slam singles events during her career.

1999 – Chamberlain dead at 63
NBA Hall of Fame centre Wilt Chamberlain died of a heart attack at his home in Bel-Air, California, aged 63. Chamberlain's 14-year career included a string of MVP awards (1959, 1966–68), the only 100-point game in NBA history, 7 straight scoring titles (1960–66) and over 31,000 points (second in NBA history).

2004 – First Aussies to a WNBA title
Lauren Jackson and Tully Bivalaqua became the first Australians to play in a WNBA Championship team when the Seattle Storm beat the Connecticut Sun 74-60 in the Finals deciding Game 3 in Seattle. Jackson, who was the WNBA MVP in 2003, contributed 13 points and 7 rebounds. Seattle coach Anne Donovan made history by becoming the first female coach to guide a team to the WNBA title.

BIRTHDATES

1906	Italian auto racer PIERO TARUFFI – died 1988
1911	Indian Test batsman VIJAY MERCHANT – died 1987
1917	Uruguayan soccer goalkeeper ROQUE MÁSPOLI – died 2004
1921	Czech tennis player JAROSLAV DROBNÝ – died 2001
1923	American boxing trainer/manager GOODY PETRONELLI – died 2012
1932	American auto racer NED JARRETT
1935	England soccer defender DON HOWE
1946	Pakistan Test batsman ASHOK MANKAD – died 2008
1951	South African golfer SALLY LITTLE
1960	American golfer STEVE LOWERY
1966	Dutch soccer midfielder WIM JONK
1967	American golfer BECKY IVERSON
1968	NLF defensive back LEON LETT
1973	England rugby union flanker MARTIN CORRY
1975	American sprinter MARION JONES
1977	American golfer CRISTIE KERR
1977	American alpine skier BODE MILLER
1979	England rugby union lock STEVE BORTHWICK
1981	New Zealand rugby centre CONRAD SMITH
1988	New Zealand rugby lock SAM WHITELOCK

1964 – Three consecutive golds to Fraser

Twenty-seven-year-old Australian Dawn Fraser won her third consecutive Olympic 100m freestyle title, when she took the gold medal at the Tokyo Games. Fraser swam a time of 59.5 seconds to beat 15-year-old American Sharon Stouder (59.9). After her swimming commitments had been finalised, Fraser led a playful night raid on the Emperor's Palace, stealing a souvenir flag. She was banned for ten years over the incident by the Australian Swimming Union.

1982 – Thorpe medals reinstated

The IOC agreed to posthumously restore the 2 gold medals won by American athlete Jim Thorpe in 1912. Thorpe won the pentathlon and decathlon at the 1912 Games in Stockholm, but was stripped of the medals when it was found that he'd played semi-professional minor league baseball in North Carolina in 1909 and 1910. The Thorpe family had petitioned to have the medals returned after Thorpe's death in 1953, but IOC president Avery Brundage, whom Thorpe had badly beaten in 1912 in both events, blocked the move.

1986 – Baseball enters the Olympic arena

The IOC announced baseball would become a full medal sport at the 1992 Barcelona Olympics. Baseball was the only sport to be included as an exhibition or demonstration sport before achieving full medal status. Cuba beat Thailand 11-1 to win the inaugural gold medal. In 2005, the IOC removed baseball and softball from the 2012 London Games schedule.

1987 – Richards dominates

West Indian master batsman Vivian Richards smashed 181 from 125 balls against Sri Lanka in a World Cup match in Karachi. Richards' last 81 runs came off 27 deliveries as the West Indies made 360-4, the highest ODI total at the time, cruising to a 191-run win.

1993 – Ducks get first NHL victory

Newly formed franchise the Anaheim Mighty Ducks – owned by the Disney Corporation – recorded their first NHL win, a 4-3 home victory against the Edmonton Oilers. Anaheim won a record 33 games in their inaugural season.

American footballer and athlete Jim Thorpe crosses the finish line to win the 1,500m even in the pentathlon at the 1912 Stockholm Olympics.

2006 – Slater wins record eighth surf crown

Florida native Kelly Slater won an unprecedented eighth world surfing championship after beating Australian Joel Parkinson in the semi finals of the ASP World Championship Tour Billabong Pro in Mundaka, Spain. After claiming the title Slater was beaten by fellow American Bobby Martinez in the final.

BIRTHDATES

1931	Baseball Hall of Fame second baseman EDDIE MATHEWS
1941	England Test fast bowler JOHN SNOW
1942	Dallas Cowboys owner JERRY JONES
1944	American golfer BUDDY ALLIN
1950	German sprinter ANNEGRET RICHTER
1953	American jockey PAT DAY
1961	NBA coach DOC RIVERS
1962	NFL receiver JERRY RICE
1964	South African Test fast bowler FANIE DE VILLIERS
1967	Cuban high jumper JAVIER SOTOMAYOR
1967	MLB pitcher TREVOR HOFFMAN
1969	American figure skater NANCY KERRIGAN
1970	Welsh rugby halfback ROB HOWLEY
1972	American swimmer SUMMER SANDERS
1978	NBA forward JERMAINE O'NEAL
1982	Australian swimmer IAN THORPE

⑭ OCTOBER

1902 – Hill's century before lunch
Clem Hill (142) hit a century before lunch on the final day in the drawn first Test between Australia and South Africa in Johannesburg.

1908 – Cubs' last World Series win
Chicago right-hander Orval Overall pitched a 3-hitter in a 2-0 shutout in the Game 5 clincher in Detroit as the Cubs won their second consecutive World Series over the Tigers. It was the last time the much-maligned Cubs won baseball's biggest prize. It was Overall's second complete-game victory in 4 days, striking out 10 in the process. The paltry crowd of 6,210 in Detroit remains the lowest attendance for a World Series game.

1916 – Guest wins first PGA title
Englishman Jim Barnes became the first PGA champion, winning the inaugural event at the Siwanoy Country Club in Bronxville, New York. Barnes made a 5ft par putt on the 36th hole to score a 1-up victory over American Jock Hutchison.

1964 – Favourite upset in Olympic 10,000m
In one of the most exciting finishes in Olympic track and field history, American Billy Mills and Tunisia's Mohamed Gammoudi improved their personal best times by more than 45 seconds to upset the Australian world record holder Ron Clarke in the 10,000m in Tokyo. After a see-sawing struggle, Mills flashed home past Gammoudi and Clarke to win by 3 yards.

1989 – Corner kick feast
The record for corner-kicks (29) in a Football League match was set in the Division 2 clash between Sheffield United and West Ham at Bramall Lane. The Blades took 28 corners to the Hammers 1, but lost 2-0.

1989 – Akram's ODI hat-trick
Outstanding left-handed quick Wasim Akram bowled West Indian trio Jeff Dujon, Malcolm Marshall and Curtly Ambrose with consecutive deliveries during Pakistan's 11-run ODI win in Sharjah.

2005 – ICC Super Test to Australia
Australia scored an easy win in the ICC's Super Test

American runner Billy Mills in the 10,000m at the 1964 Tokyo Olympics.

against a star-studded World XI in Sydney. Australia took 4 days to wrap up a 210-run win over a team that included Rahul Dravid, Brian Lara, Muttiah Muralitharan, Virender Sehwag, Inzamam-ul-Haq and Jacques Kallis. Australia's 2 leg spinners, Stuart MacGill and Shane Warne accounted for 15 of the 20 World XI wickets.

BIRTHDATES
1872	English tennis player REGINALD DOHERTY – died 1910
1873	American jumper RAY EWRY – died 1937
1918	Australian Test spinner DOUG RING – died 2003
1940	American golfer J. C. SNEAD
1940	South African snooker player PERRIE MANS
1941	Australian swim coach LAURIE LAWRENCE
1942	England rugby union fullback BOB HILLER
1947	Pro Football Hall of Fame receiver CHARLIE JOINER
1952	Russian gymnast NIKOLAI ANDRIANOV
1956	American golfer BETH DANIEL
1960	English middle distance runner STEVE CRAM
1968	England soccer striker MATTHEW LE TISSIER
1971	Portuguese soccer defender JORGE COSTA
1975	New Zealand rugby union fly-half CARLOS SPENCER
1975	American road cyclist FLOYD LANDIS
1976	Sri Lankan Test batsman TILLAKARATNE DILSHAN
1981	Indian Test batsman GAUTAM GAMBHIR

1961 – Third major of the season for Mickey
Mickey Wright won her third major title of the year, the LPGA Championship at the Stardust Country Club in Las Vegas. She finished 9 stokes ahead of Louise Suggs with a 287 total. It was her second consecutive LPGA Championship and third overall.

1964 – Russian sculler takes three straight
Russian Vyacheslav Ivanov won his third consecutive Olympic single sculls gold medal in Tokyo. He gained an incredible eleven seconds over the final 500m on German runner-up Achim Hill. Ivanov blacked out before the finish line, but still won by 3.73 seconds.

1966 – Russell first black NBA coach
Bill Russell became the NBA's first black head coach signing as player-coach of the Boston Celtics. In his three seasons he led Boston to NBA titles in 1968 and 1969.

1968 – Oerter wins 4 straight discus gold
Thirty-two-year-old American Al Oerter became the first track and field athlete to take 4 gold medals in the same event when he won the discus at the Mexico City Olympics. Trailing after the second round, Oerter unleashed a winning throw of 212ft 6in, a personal best by an amazing 5ft.

1989 – 'The Great One' is leading scorer
Wayne Gretzky passed his childhood idol Gordie Howe as the NHL's leading scorer playing for the LA Kings against his former team the Oilers in Edmonton. Gretzky tied Howe's record of 1,850 with an assist early and broke it with just 53 seconds remaining. He scored in overtime to give the Kings a 5-4 victory.

1997 – Green cracks sound barrier for record
British driver Andy Green became the first man to set a land speed record exceeding the speed of sound. Green averaged 763.035mph on 2 runs across Black Rock Desert, Nevada. The speed of sound on the day was calculated at 748.111mph.

2004 – Warne overtakes Murali ... for now
Australian leg-spinner Shane Warne broke Muttiah

Andy Green, driving Richard Noble's Thrust Scc, breaks the sound barrier in setting a new land-speed record of 763.036mph at Black Rock Desert, Nevada.

Muralitharan's world record for Test wickets when he captured 3 for 95, taking his total to 534 on the second day of the second Test against India in Chennai.

2005 – McGrath greatest quick
Australia's Glenn McGrath passed former West Indian captain Courtney Walsh as the greatest wicket-taking fast bowler in history during the ICC World XI Test match in Sydney. McGrath had West Indian batsman Brian Lara trapped lbw for 5 to reach the 520 wicket mark, one ahead of Walsh's career total of 519.

BIRTHDATES
1858	American boxer JOHN L.SULLIVAN – died 1918.
1937	American swimmer SHELLEY MANN
1940	Great Britain rugby league halfback/coach TOMMY BISHOP
1945	West Indian Test batsman STEVE CAMACHO
1945	MLB pitcher JIM PALMER
1951	American tennis player ROSCOE TANNER
1956	American swimmer MELISSA BELOTE
1958	England Test batsman CHRIS SMITH
1968	French soccer midfielder/manager DIDIER DESCHAMPS
1969	Portuguese soccer goalkeeper VITOR BAÍA
1971	England soccer striker ANDY COLE
1973	Swedish golfer MARIA HJORTH
1977	French soccer striker DAVID TREZEGUET
1979	English soccer goalkeeper PAUL ROBINSON
1981	Russian tennis player ELENA DEMENTIEVA
1981	Chinese diver GUO JINGJING
1986	Swiss alpine skier CARLO JANKA

⑯ OCTOBER

1909 – Johnson overpowers Ketchel
Middleweight champion Stanley Ketchel's attempt to take Jack Johnson's heavyweight title ended in the 12th round in San Francisco when he decked Johnson with a right. Johnson immediately went after Ketchel and caught him with 2 lefts and a powerful right uppercut to end the fight. The last punch was so powerful that several of Ketchel's teeth were found embedded in Johnson's glove.

1968 – Infamous 'Black Power' salute
The famous 'Black Power' salute by American sprinters Tommie Smith and John Carlos at the 200m victory ceremony caused a stir at the 1968 Olympics in Mexico City. On the insistence of the IOC, Smith and Carlos were banned from any further participation at the Games and were sent home.

1995 – Lara's ODI best
Brian Lara made his highest ODI score in a Champions Trophy match against Sri Lanka at Sharjah. Lara smashed 169 off 129 balls with 15 fours and 4 sixes in the Windies 5-run victory.

1998 – Taylor equals 'The Don'
Mark Taylor equalled Sir Don Bradman's highest Test score by an Australian, declaring at 334 not out in the second Test against Pakistan. His declaration was a noble gesture, so as not to beat a cricket icon's long-standing record (1930 v England at Leeds).

2004 – Burnett's break of 148?
Scotsman Jamie Burnett made the highest break in snooker history during the UK Championship qualifiers at Prestatyn. During their second round match, Leo Fernandez fouled before any reds had been potted. Burnett then sank the brown as the 'extra' red, brown again, then the 15 reds, 12 blacks, 2 pinks, a blue and all the colours to clear the table with a break of 148. Burnett won the match, 9-8.

2005 – LT: 18 games and running
San Diego Chargers running back LaDainian Tomlinson tied an NFL record by scoring a touchdown in his 18th consecutive game. Tomlinson came out of

The infamous 'Black Power salute' at the 1968 Mexico City Olympics. Australian silver medallist Peter Norman stands by, wearing a human rights badge in support. Years later, Smith and Carlos carried Norman's coffin at his funeral.

the backfield to catch a pass from Drew Brees on the Chargers' second drive of their 27-14 win over the Oakland Raiders at McAfee Stadium, tying the record set by Baltimore's Lenny Moore in 1965.

BIRTHDATES
1861	American tennis player RICHARD SEARS – died 1943
1876	South African Test batsman JIMMY SINCLAIR – died 1913
1900	MLB outfielder LEON 'GOOSE' GOSLIN – died 1971
1941	American sports caster TIM McCARVER
1947	Welsh snooker player TERRY GRIFFITHS
1948	American golfer BRUCE FLEISHER
1953	Brazilian soccer midfielder/manager PAULO ROBERTO FALCÃO
1959	England rugby union captain JAMIE SALMON
1962	American alpine skier TAMARA McKINNEY
1972	Russian NHL defenseman DARIUS KASPARAITIS
1974	Canadian NHL left wing PAUL KARIYA
1975	South African Test all rounder JACQUES KALLIS
1975	Icelandic soccer midfielder BRYNJAR GUNNARSSON
1980	American WNBA guard SUE BIRD
1981	French rugby union fly-half FRÉDÉRIC MICHALAK
1983	German tennis player PHILIPP KOHLSCHREIBER
1985	Australian motorcycle rider CASEY STONER
1992	MLB outfielder BRYCE HARPER

1860 – Park wins first British Open
The inaugural British Open Championship was played at Prestwick in Scotland. A meagre field of 8 competitors played 3 rounds over the then 12-hole Prestwick course. Willie Park Snr. posted a 174 to beat Old Tom Morris by 2 strokes to be the inaugural winner.

1954 – Burk throws 7 TDs
Philadelphia quarterback Adrian Burk tied Sid Luckman's NFL record of 7 touchdown passes in a game as the Eagles beat the Redskins 49-21 in Washington. With 33 seconds remaining, Burk came off the bench after assistant coach Charley Gauer reminded head coach Jim Trimble that he had a chance at the record. Burk responded with a low pass to end Pete Pihos in the end zone for number 7.

1959 – Gasnier scores three in GB debut
Australian rugby league 'immortal' Reg Gasnier scored 3 tries in his first Test against Great Britain, a 22-14 victory at Station Road in Swinton. A brilliant centre with the all-conquering St George club in Sydney, Gasnier went on to play 36 Tests (1959–67) and appeared in 3 Kangaroo tours, 2 tours of New Zealand and one World Cup.

1989 – Quake interrupts World Series
The World Series between Bay Area rivals, the San Francisco Giants and Oakland Athletics, was interrupted when the massive Loma Prieta earthquake, measuring 6.9 on the Richter scale, struck just prior to Game 3. The earthquake cut off power and caused concrete to fall from some sections of Candlestick Park. A half-hour later, MLB Commissioner Fay Vincent postponed the game. The Series resumed after 10 days, with Oakland completing a 4-0 sweep.

1991 – Cordero rides 7,000th winner
American Hall of Fame jockey Angel Cordero rode his 7,000th winner on Don't Cross the Law at Belmont Park. Cordero retired in 1992 with 7,057 winners, ranking fourth all-time amongst US riders. He was Jockey of the Year in 1982–3 and won 6 Triple Crown races.

1991 – Richardson leads from in front
In his first match as West Indian captain, Richie Richardson made 106 not out in a 1-wicket victory over Pakistan at Sharjah. With the Windies facing almost-certain defeat at 158 for 8, Richardson took them to 217 for 9 with 15 balls to spare.

1999 – Marino goes over 60,000 yards
Miami Dolphins quarterback Dan Marino completed his first pass for 8 yards to Tony Martin to go over 60,000 yards for his career. The Dolphins defeated the New England Patriots, 31-30 at Foxboro Stadium.

2000 – Roy overtakes Sawchuck
Colorado Avalanche goalie Patrick Roy won his 448th game and became the all-time winningest goalie in NHL history. Roy passed Terry Sawchuck as the record holder for career victories as the Avalanche beat the Capitals, 4-3 in Washington.

2005 – Colts duo reach record 86 TDs
Indianapolis Colts quarterback Peyton Manning and wide receiver Marvin Harrison combined for a classic 6-yard touchdown pass with 9:25 left against St Louis to give the duo an NFL record 86 touchdown passes and breaking the mark set by San Francisco's Steve Young and Jerry Rice. The Colts won the game 45-28.

BIRTHDATES
1908	Australian rugby league forward WALLY PRIGG – died 1980
1917	New Zealand Test cricketer MARTIN DONNELLY – died 1999
1924	NFL coach DON CORYELL – died 2010
1934	England soccer forward JOHNNY HAYNES – died 2005
1938	American stunt rider EVEL KNIEVEL – died 2007
1940	New Zealand rugby union winger MAC HEREWINI
1946	American pole-vaulter BOB SEAGREN
1957	NFL defensive tackle STEVE McMICHAEL
1963	Argentine soccer goalie SERGIO GOYCOCHEA
1965	Sri Lanka Test batsman ARAVINDA DE SILVA
1967	French tennis player NATHALIE TAUZIAT
1968	England soccer defender GRAEME LE SAUX
1969	South African golfer ERNIE ELS
1970	Indian Test spinner ANIL KUMBLE
1976	Uruguayan soccer striker SEBASTIÁN ABREU
1977	Portuguese soccer manager ANDRÉ VILLAS-BOAS
1978	Irish rugby hooker JERRY FLANNERY
1979	Finnish auto racer KIMI RÄIKKÖNEN
1980	Pakistan Test all-rounder MOHAMMAD HAFEEZ

⑱ OCTOBER

1964 – Schollander swims to 4 gold in Tokyo
Eighteen-year-old American Don Schollander became the first swimmer to win 4 gold medals at a single Olympics when the US 4 x 200m freestyle relay team won in Tokyo. He had earlier won the 100 and 400m freestyle, and was a member of the 4 x 100m freestyle relay team.

1964 – Berry on front in Robie rivalry
Australian Kevin Berry broke his own world record in upsetting American race favourite Carl Robie in the final of the 200m butterfly at the Tokyo Olympics. Berry's time of 2:06.6 shaved 0.3 seconds off his old time. Robie came back to win the gold medal in 1968 in Mexico City.

1968 – Famous Beamon long jump mark
American long jumper Bob Beamon smashed the world record with a freakish jump of 29ft 2½in at the Mexico City Olympics. Beamon bettered Ralph Boston and Igor Ter-Ovanesyan's previous world mark by an incredible 1ft 9¾in. He never got near his super-leap again. Beamon's record stood for over 20 years.

1969 – Just not cricket
In some of the worst crowd behaviour seen in Test cricket, police were stoned, bonfires were lit in the stands and there was an attempt to set fire to thatched roofing when India was dismissed for a meagre 89 on the third day of the third Test against New Zealand at Hyderabad. The groundsman had forgotten to mow the pitch and the green-top was almost unplayable.

1969 – Kareem makes NBA debut
UCLA and future Hall of Fame centre Kareem Abdul-Jabbar (Lou Alcindor) made his NBA debut for the Milwaukee Bucks in a 119-110 home win against Detroit.

1974 – A rare quad-double
Chicago centre Nate Thurmond recorded the NBA's first quadruple-double, with 22 points, 14 rebounds, 13 assists and 12 blocks in the Bulls' 120-115 overtime win over Atlanta at Chicago Stadium. Alvin Robertson, Hakeem Olajuwon and David Robinson are the only other NBA players to have recorded quadruple-doubles.

1977 – Three first pitch HR's for Reggie
New York Yankees' slugger Reggie Jackson blasted 3 home runs on the first pitch from 3 LA Dodger pitchers in an 8-4 home win in Game 6 of the World Series. Only 4 players have hit 3 homers in a World Series game – Jackson; Babe Ruth – twice, in 1926 and 1938; Albert Pujols in 2011; and Pablo Sandoval in 2012.

1998 – Young throws for 300 yards x 6
San Francisco 49ers quarterback Steve Young set an NFL record with his sixth straight 300-yard game in a 34-31 win against Peyton Manning's Indianapolis Colts at Candlestick Park. He also ran for 2 touchdowns, his 39th and 40th of his career, tying him with Jack Kemp on the all-time list.

2005 – Steroid king goes to jail
Victor Conte, who founded the Bay Area Laboratory Co-Operative (BALCO), was sentenced to 8 months in jail for his role in a conspiracy to distribute illegal steroids and other performance enhancing drugs to athletes. He served 4 months and another 4 months in home confinement.

BIRTHDATES
1854	Australian Test batsman BILLY MURDOCH – died 1911
1875	England Test all-rounder LEN BRAUND – died 1955
1933	Pro Football Hall of Fame tackle/coach FORREST GREGG
1933	Italian auto racer LUDOVICO SCARFIOTTI – died 1968
1939	NFL coach MIKE DITKA
1952	Sri Lanka Test batsman ROY DIAS
1955	Zimbabwean golfer DENIS WATSON
1956	Tennis player MARTINA NAVRATILOVA
1958	American boxer THOMAS 'HITMAN' HEARNS
1961	Australian Test cricketer STEVE SMITH
1961	England Test fast bowler GLADSTONE SMALL
1968	Indian Test spinner NARENDA HIRWANI
1968	Australian Test batsman STUART LAW
1968	German tennis player MICHAEL STICH
1969	South African rugby union captain JAPIE MULDER
1971	Australian golfer NICK O'HERN
1973	Australian golfer STEPHEN ALLAN
1978	England rugby union captain MIKE TINDALL
1984	American alpine skier LINDSEY VONN

1940 – Vols' defensive streak over
Tennessee's NCAA record of 17 regular-season games without conceding a touchdown ended in Birmingham as Alabama scored twice. However the unbeaten Vols did score their 26th consecutive regular-season win, 27-12.

1957 – 'The Rocket' first to NHL 500
Maurice Richard of the Montreal Canadiens became the first NHL player to score 500 career goals. Richard put the puck past Chicago Blackhawks goalie Glenn Hill in the first period of a 3-1 win at the Montreal Forum.

1968 – Hurst's 6 for Hammers
West Ham United's England striker Geoff Hurst nailed a double hat-trick in the Hammers' 8-0 win over Sunderland at Upton Park. Hurst is the last player to have scored 6 goals in an English Division 1/Premier League match.

1968 – Wendon beats WR to win 100m
Eighteen-year-old Australian sprinter Michael Wenden swam a world record time of 52.2 seconds to win the blue ribband 100m freestyle at the Mexico City Olympics. Wendon broke Ken Walsh's world mark by 0.4 seconds. Walsh took the silver and Mark Spitz the bronze. Wendon went on to win the 200m freestyle for the sprint double.

1987 – Martin Yankees manager ... again
Billy Martin was appointed manager of the New York Yankees for a bizarre fifth time. Martin replaced Lou Piniella, who ironically, had replaced him. Martin's 5 terms at the Yankees tied a major league record. He won the World Series with the 'Bronx Bombers' in 1977–78.

1991 – Rugby union's brilliant Blanco
Playing for France in a 19-10 loss against England in Paris, champion fullback Serge Blanco became the most capped player in international rugby union, with a record 93rd international appearance. The record was broken in 1996 by Australian winger David Campese, against Wales in Sydney. Campese retired

NHL star Maurice Richard, pictured in 1945.

at the end of 1996 with 101 caps and a world record 64 tries for the Wallabies.

1999 – 'Occi' oldest world champ
At age 33, Australian veteran Mark Occhilupo became the oldest surfer to win his first world title when he clinched the championship with an event to spare, after winning in Mundaka in Spain. He had already won in Tahiti and Fiji, the other big lefts on the tour.

2004 – Red Sox meant to be
In an ALCS game featuring 2 reversed calls by the umpires, the Boston Red Sox become the first team in baseball history after trailing the series 0-3 to force a Game 7. Boston was 3 outs from being swept in Game 4, but got an outstanding pitching performance from Curt Schilling, playing with a dislocated ankle tendon, to beat the Yankees, 4-2. The Red Sox won Game 7, 10-3, and went on to sweep the Cardinals and win the World Series.

BIRTHDATES
1900   Australian Test opener BILL PONSFORD – died 1991
1933   Australian Test batsman BRIAN BOOTH
1937   Canadian marathon swimmer MARILYN BELL
1946   Australian Test spinner BOB HOLLAND
1960   Canadian golfer DAWN COE-JONES
1962   American boxer EVANDER HOLYFIELD
1962   American golfer BRIAN HENNINGER
1969   Bolivian soccer midfielder/manager ERWIN SÁNCHEZ
1973   Moroccan tennis player HICHAM ARAZI
1982   South African golfer LOUIS OOSTHUIZEN

1951 – Unbelievable international debut
Newcastle United's Billy Foulkes scored with his first kick in an international match. Foulkes scored for Wales 3 minutes into their 1-1 draw against England at Ninian Park in Cardiff.

1990 – All-in at Old Trafford
A 21-man brawl broke out after Arsenal's Nigel Winterburn and Anders Limpar had gang-tackled Denis Irwin of Manchester United in the Gunners' 1-0 victory at Old Trafford. Both clubs were fined £50,000. Arsenal was deducted 2 competition points and United 1. The Gunners went on to take the championship. United finished sixth.

1991 – Famous World Cup try to Lynagh
Australian five-eighth Michael Lynagh scored a famous try in injury time to clinch a memorable 19-18 victory over Ireland in a World Cup quarter final in Dublin. Ireland hit lead 18-15 with just 3 minutes remaining after a converted Gordon Hamilton try. But Lynagh's spectacular try not only set up the win, the Wallabies went on to win the Final 12-6 against England.

1994 – Age no barrier in harness racing
Eighty-three-year-old George McCandless became the oldest Harness Driver to win a parimutuel race when he guided Kehm's Scooter to victory in the fourth race at Freehold Raceway, New Jersey.

1996 – Akram's records
Pakistan's Wasim Akram smashed 257, the highest score by a number 8 batsman in Test history, in the first Test against Zimbabwe at Sheikhupura. Wasim also shared a record 323 partnership for the eighth wicket with Saqlain Mushtaq; and his 12 sixes beat Wally Hammond's record of 10 in his 336 against New Zealand in Auckland in 1932–33.

2004 – Red Sox greatest post-season comeback
The Boston Red Sox recovered from 3-0 down to complete the biggest comeback in post-season history when they beat the New York Yankees, 10-3 at Yankee Stadium to clinch the AL Championship 4-3. Boston outfielder Johnny Damon hit 2 home runs including a grand slam. The Red Sox went on to sweep the St Louis Cardinals 4-0 in the World Series.

Pakistan left-arm fast bowler Wasim Akram, pictured here in 1994.

BIRTHDATES
1920	English golfer HARRY WEETMAN – died 1972
1931	Baseball Hall of Fame outfielder MICKEY MANTLE – died 1995
1932	American Pro Football Hall of Fame linesman 'ROSEY' BROWN – died 2004
1937	Baseball Hall of Fame pitcher JUAN MARICHAL
1949	Russian sprinter VALERY BORZOV
1951	Italian soccer manager CLAUDIO RANIERI
1953	MLB first baseman KEITH HERNANDEZ
1955	American boxer AARON PRYOR
1957	England Test batsman CHRIS COWDREY
1961	Welsh soccer striker IAN RUSH
1963	Indian Test batsman NAVJOT SINGH SIDHU
1966	South African Test fast bowler ALLAN DONALD
1970	Australian rugby league captain LAURIE DALEY
1972	England rugby union centre WILL GREENWOOD
1978	Indian Test batsman VIRENDER SEHWAG
1979	Irish rugby second rower PAUL O'CONNELL

1961 – Arcaro's 10th Gold Cup

American jockey Eddie Arcaro won the Jockey Club Gold Cup at Belmont Park for a record 10th time. It was the second of 5 consecutive Gold Cup wins for his mount Kelso, a record for consecutive victories in a stakes race.

1964 – First back-to-back marathon gold

Ethiopia's defending champion Abebe Bikila became the first to win back-to-back Olympic marathon titles when he defeated British runner B. Basil Heatley by 4:08 seconds in Tokyo. Bikila achieved the feat only 6 weeks after an appendectomy. He was awarded a car by the Ethiopian government for the victory, but in 1969 suffered a spinal injury in a road accident, and was confined to a wheelchair for the remainder of his life. He died in 1973 aged 41.

1968 – Sundelin bros win yachting gold

The 3 Sundelin brothers, Ulf, Jörgen and Peter, from Sweden, easily won the 5.5m sailing gold medal at the Mexico City Olympics. The Sundelins won 5 of 7 races to win by a clear 24 points from the Swiss, whose crew included 66-year-old Louis Noverraz

1980 – Phillies first

For the first time in their 98-year history, the Phillies won the World Series with a 4-1 Game 6 win over Kansas City at Veterans Stadium. Mike Schmidt was named Series MVP.

1984 – Jones takes marathon mark

England's Steve Jones broke Robert de Castella's World marathon record in Chicago. Jones ran a time of 2.08:05 to beat de Castella's mark by 13 seconds. De Castella's record had stood for 3 years.

1989 – New owners for Nuggets

Bertram Lee and Peter Bynoe became the first African-American managing general partners of a major sports franchise in the US, when they bought the NBA's Denver Nuggets for $65 million. NBA commissioner David Stern, who was pushing for more minority ownership in the league, later had to bring in Comsat Video Enterprises to financially salvage the transaction.

1989 – Ware's huge first half

Houston University quarterback Andre Ware threw for 517 yards and 6 touchdowns – in the first half in a 95-21 destruction of SMU in the Astrodome. Ware sat out the second half.

1996 – Lloyd first Aussie in World Series

Graham Lloyd became the first Australian to play in an MLB World Series when he pitched relief for the New York Yankees in Game 2 against Atlanta. The Yankees lost the game 4-0, but won the series 4-2. Lloyd was credited with the win in Game 4 and pitched effectively in Games 3 and 6. He also earned a World Series ring with the Yankees in 1998.

2006 – Huge college recovery

In the biggest comeback in Division I-A football history Michigan State overcame Northwestern 41-38. After opening the scoring with a field goal, the Spartans watched their defense give up the next 38 points for a 38-3 Wildcat lead with just over 7 minutes to go in the third quarter. The Spartans then scored 5 straight touchdowns and kicked the game winning field goal with 0:13 remaining.

BIRTHDATES

1851	England Test all-rounder GEORGE ULYETT – died 1898
1926	American golfer BOB ROSBURG – died 2009
1928	Baseball Hall of Fame WHITEY FORD
1931	England Test wicket keeper JIM PARKS
1940	England Test opener GEOFF BOYCOTT
1942	Australian auto racer ALLAN GRICE
1949	Canadian NHL coach MIKE KEENAN
1952	Australian Test batsman TREVOR CHAPPELL
1959	MLB outfielder GEORGE BELL
1962	Australian rugby union winger DAVID CAMPESE
1966	Welsh golfer PHILLIP PRICE
1967	England soccer midfielder PAUL INCE
1971	Australian Test batsman DAMIEN MARTYN
1981	Serbian soccer defender NEMANJA VIDIC
1983	MLB pitcher ZACK GREINKE
1990	Spanish NBA guard RICKY RUBIO
1992	Australian tennis player BERNARD TOMIC

1933 – Carnera easily in Rome
Twenty-seven-year-old Italian Primo Carnera had an easy first defence of his world heavyweight title, when he won a 15 round decision over countryman Paulino Uzcudun in Rome. Carnera was 6ft 6in tall and weighed over 250lbs. His massive frame could take any punishment but he had a glass jaw. Unfortunately, racketeers had a great influence on his career results.

1939 – NFL on TV
The Brooklyn Dodgers beat the Philadelphia Eagles, 23-14 at Ebbets Field in the NFL's first televised game.

1967 – Hulme first Kiwi F1 champ
Denny Hulme became the first Kiwi to win a World Formula 1 Drivers Championship when he finished third in the season-ending Mexican Grand Prix in Mexico City. He finished on 51 points, 5 ahead of Jack Brabham. In a 9-year career, Hulme drove in 112 Grand Prix, winning 8 with another 25 podium finishes. He was killed in a race accident in 1992.

1983 – Malcolm in the middle – stump
West Indian fast bowler Malcolm Marshall scored a Test-best 92 and then produced a devastating opening spell of 4 for 9 off 8 overs, as India closed the second day of the first Test at Kanpur at 34 for 5. The Windies went on to win by an innings, with Marshall grabbing match figures of 8 for 66. Marshall played 81 Tests, taking 376 wickets at just 20.94. He died in 1999 at age 41.

1988 – Wallace trio of brothers feature
Danny, Rodney and Ray Wallace became the first trio of brothers to play in the same side together in an English Division 1 match when they appeared for Southampton in a 2-1 defeat to Sheffield Wednesday at The Dell. They played in another 24 games together for the Saints.

1995 – Waugh's big paying hit
Playing for New South Wales in a one-day match against Western Australia, Test batsman Steve Waugh hit Tom Moody for a 6, straight into a promotional Mercantile Mutual sign at the WACA Ground in Perth. Hitting the sign earned the N.S.W team a $140,000 bonus.

2002 – Celebrity marriage, anyone for tennis?
Tennis superstars Andre Agassi and Steffi Graf were married in a private ceremony in Las Vegas. The 31-year-old Agassi and Graf, 32, began dating after each won the French Open in 1999. Agassi was previously married to actress Brooke Shields.

2011 – Pujols blasts three homers in WS game
St Louis first baseman Albert Pujols connected for homers in 3 straight innings as the Cardinals earned a 16-7 World Series Game 3 win against the Texas Rangers at Arlington. Pujols finished 5-for-6, scored 4 times and drove in 6 runs. He joined Babe Ruth (twice in 1938) and Reggie Jackson (1977) as the only players to hit 3 homers in a World Series game. Pablo Sandoval achieved the feat in 2012.

2012 – Armstrong finally busted
Lance Armstrong was stripped of his 7 Tour de France titles and banned for life by cycling's governing body following a report from the US Anti-Doping Agency that accused him of leading a massive doping program on his teams including the use of steroids, the blood booster EPO and blood transfusions. The report included statements from eleven former teammates who testified against Armstrong, including testimony that he pressured them to take banned drugs. Armstrong initially denied doping, but came clean when interviewed by Oprah Winfrey in January 2013.

BIRTHDATES
1929	Russian soccer goalkeeper LEV YASHIN – died 1990
1939	England soccer defender GEORGE COHEN
1948	England Test fast bowler MIKE HENDRICK
1949	French soccer manager ARSENE WENGER
1961	American tennis player BARBARA POTTER
1963	American figure skater BRIAN BOITANO
1964	Croatian Basketball Hall of Fame guard DRAZEN PETROVIC – died 1993
1967	Austrian alpine skier ULRIKE MAIER – died 1994
1971	South African tennis player AMANDA COETZER
1973	Japanese MLB outfielder ICHIRO SUZUKI

1915 – 'Father of Cricket' passes on
W. G. Grace died aged 67, following a heart attack. Grace played 22 Tests, scoring 1,098 at 32.29, and over 44 seasons he scored a massive 54,211 first-class runs at 39.45 and captured 2,809 wickets at only 18.14.

1945 – Robinson first black MLB player
Jackie Robinson became the first black player to be hired by an MLB team, when the Brooklyn Dodgers announced he had signed for their farm club, the Montreal Royals of the International League. In 1946, Robinson batted a league-leading .349 and stole 40 bases. He led Montreal to the Little World Series championship before making his MLB debut with the Dodgers in 1947.

1964 – Gymnastics legend adds 6
Russian gymnast Larysa Latynina finished her Tokyo Olympic program with 6 medals (2 of each colour) to bring her career total to an unprecedented 18. In 3 Olympics, the 29-year-old had accumulated 9 gold, 5 silver and 4 bronze medals. Latynina served as head coach of the Soviet team from 1967 to 1977.

1988 – Marino magic
Miami Dolphins quarterback Dan Marino passed for 521 yards for 3 touchdowns and completed 35 of 60 against the New York Jets in Miami. It was considered the single-best passing day in NFL history, although the Dolphins lost 44-30.

1993 – Carter wins World Series with a HR
Joe Carter of the Toronto Blue Jays became only the second player to end the World Series with a home run. With one out and 2 men on in the bottom of the ninth, and the Blue Jays behind 6-5 against the Phillies in Game 6, Carter hit a Mitch Williams slider over the left field fence at the SkyDome in Toronto to win the game 8-6, and the Series, 4-2.

2009 – Blues take Twenty20 title
The Australian state of NSW beat Trinidad and Tobago to win the inaugural Champions League Twenty20 in Hyderabad. Local enthusiasm was dampened significantly by the capitulation of the IPL teams, none

Soviet gymnast Larissa Latynina in action during the compulsory floor exercises at the 1964 Tokyo Olympics.

of whom progressed beyond the second round.

2010 – UFC's bloody showdown
Cain Velasquez became the first fighter of Mexican heritage to claim a heavyweight title in either boxing or mixed martial arts when he beat Brock Lesnar into a bloody pulp to win the UFC heavyweight crown in the first round in Anaheim, CA. The biggest showdown in UFC history lasted just 4:12, before referee Herb Dean had seen enough of a pounding to step in.

BIRTHDATES
1900	England Test captain DOUGLAS JARDINE – died 1958
1905	American swimmer GERTRUDE EDERLE – died 2003
1931	Baseball Hall of Fame pitcher JIM BUNNNG
1935	American golfer JUAN 'CHI CHI' RODRIGUEZ
1940	Brazilian soccer striker PELÉ
1941	England Test opener COLIN MILBURN – died 1990
1957	England soccer midfielder GRAHAM RIX
1960	American motorcycle rider WAYNE RAINEY
1961	Spanish goalkeeper ANDONI ZUBIZARRETA
1962	NFL quarterback DOUG FLUTIE
1966	Italian auto racer ALEX ZINARDI
1977	Australian Test wicketkeeper BRAD HADDIN
1978	England Test fast bowler STEVE HARMISON

1965 – NFL's only negative passing game

In the only negative passing game in NFL history, Green Bay beat Dallas, 13-3 at Milwaukee County Stadium despite only 63 yards in total offence. Cowboys rookie quarterback Craig Morton and Packers' veteran Bart Starr were sacked 13 times.

1972 – Baseball race pioneer dead at 53

Hall of Fame infielder Jackie Robinson died aged 53, after suffering a heart attack in Stamford, Connecticut. Robinson arguably was America's most significant athlete, becoming the first African-American to play MLB in 1947 and leading a generation of black athletes in pro sports after World War II. The Brooklyn Dodgers second baseman challenged the prevailing social tide, almost single-handedly changing the face of baseball and American society.

1976 – Brotherly tons

Pakistan's Sadiq and Mushtaq Mohammad became only the second pair of brothers (after Australia's Greg and Ian Chappell) to score centuries in the same Test innings, during the second Test against New Zealand in Hyderabad. Sadiq made 103, and Mushtaq 101.

1977 – Cauthen first to $5m

Seventeen-year-old American jockey Steve Cauthen became the first rider to win $5 million in purses in a year. In a meteoric rise, he was the youngest jockey to win the Triple Crown in 1978 on Affirmed but after a lean spell he rode the rest of his career in England. Cauthen was English champion jockey (1984–5, 1987) and retired in 1993, aged 33.

1992 – World Series trophy goes to Canada

For the first time in baseball history, the World Series Championship banner flew in Canada, after the Toronto Blue Jays beat the Atlanta Braves 4 games to 2 for the title. Dave Winfield broke an 11th inning tie in Game 6 with a 2-run double and a 4-3 victory. Blue Jays catcher Pat Borders had a .450 series batting average to take MVP honours.

1999 – Five field goals to de Beer

South African rugby union fly-half Jannie de Beer set a world record for most dropped goals in an international, in the World Cup quarter-final against England in Paris. In a 34-point haul, De Beer kicked 5 second-half dropped goals in a 44-21 win. He also landed 2 conversions and 5 penalties.

2004 – Gunners' unbeaten streak broken

Arsenal had their record 49-game unbeaten streak broken when they lost to 2-0 by Manchester United at Old Trafford. Ruud Van Nistelrooy and Wayne Rooney scored for United. Arsenal's incredible streak started with 2 wins at the end of the 2002–03 season, through an unbeaten 2003–04, plus the first 9 matches of 2004–05.

2012 – Sandoval goes deep x 3 in WS

Pablo Sandoval joined Albert Pujols (2011), Reggie Jackson (1977) and Babe Ruth (twice, in 1926 and 1938) as the only men in baseball history to wallop 3 homers in one World Series game. The Giants third baseman dominated in the Giants 8-3 Game 1 win over Detroit in San Francisco. The Giants went on to sweep the series 4-0.

BIRTHDATES

1925	Australian Test batsman KEN 'SLASHER' MACKAY – died 1982
1926	Pro Football Hall of Fame quarterback Y.A. TITTLE
1934	Australian golfer MARGIE MASTERS
1943	Australian rugby union/league fly-half PHIL HAWTHORNE – died 1994
1948	Welsh rugby union fly-half PHIL BENNETT
1960	Australian golfer IAN BAKER-FINCH
1962	Welsh rugby union fly-half JONATHAN DAVIES
1965	American surfer FRIEDA ZAMBA
1967	New Zealand rugby union prop OLO BROWN
1967	West Indian Test fast bowler IAN BISHOP
1968	Spanish tennis player FRANCISCO CLAVET
1973	New Zealand rugby union winger JEFF WILSON
1977	Ecuadorian soccer striker IVAN KAVIEDES
1980	Australian jockey KERRIN McEVOY
1985	England soccer striker WAYNE ROONEY

1970 – Brabham retires

Australia's three-time World Formula 1 drivers champion, Jack Brabham, announced his retirement. Brabham was the first man to win a Formula One world title (1966) in a car of his own design. He also won the World Drivers' Championship in 1959–60 and the constructors title in 1967.

1979 – China's Olympic return

In the 'Nagoya Resolution', the IOC voted to readmit China to Olympic competition after a 21-year absence. In 1952, the IOC had invited teams from both mainland China and Taiwan. This led to decades of boycotting by the government of the People's Republic, which finally applied for readmission in 1980, for the Lake Placid Games.

1982 – Hookes' fastest ton

Australian Test batsman David Hookes scored the fastest-recorded authentic century in first-class history playing for South Australia against Victoria in Adelaide. Hookes smashed 100 from just 34 balls. The brash left-hander played 23 Tests, scoring 1,306 runs at 34.36. After retiring he went into coaching and had a successful career in the media. Hookes was tragically killed after an incident at a Melbourne hotel in 2004.

1983 – Hammers first to 10

West Ham United became the first team to score 10 goals in a League Cup match in their second-round tie against Bury. The Hammers won 10-0 in the second-leg match at Upton Park with striker Tony Cottee scoring four.

1999 – Stewart killed in plane crash

Golfer Payne Stewart, three-time Major champion, was killed in a plane crash along with five others. Stewart's Dallas-bound Learjet flew uncontrolled over part of the US for several hours before crashing in South Dakota. Stewart had won the 1991 and 1999 US Open and the 1989 PGA Championship. He was 42.

2003 – Rogers' kicking clinic

Matt Rogers kicked 16 conversions as Australia scored its biggest ever win, a 142-0 thrashing of Namibia in a Rugby World Cup match in Adelaide. Chris Latham crossed for 5 tries with Lote Tuqiri and Matt Giteau scoring 3 each and Rogers adding two.

2003 – Breeders Cup records

Trainer Richard Mandella set a single-day record by winning 4 Breeders' Cup World Thoroughbred Championship races at Santa Anita. Mandella saddled Halfbridled to victory in the Breeders' Cup Juvenile Fillies; Action This Day in the Bessemer Trust Breeders' Cup Juvenile; Johar to a dead-heat win in the John Deere Breeders' Cup Turf; and Pleasantly Perfect in the $4 million Breeders' Cup Classic. The Johar dead heat with High Chaparral in the Turf marked the first dead heat in Breeders' Cup history. In guiding Halfbridled to victory, jockey Julie Krone became the first woman to ride the winner of a Breeders' Cup flat race.

2005 – Sox win long time coming

After 5 hours, 41 minutes, former Astro Geoff Blum won the longest game in World Series history with a tiebreaking, 2-out solo homer in the 14th inning as the Chicago White Sox beat the Houston Astros 7-5 to move within a win of a sweep and its first title since 1917. Chicago went on to complete the sweep the following night for their first World Series win in 88 years.

BIRTHDATES

1904	American golfer DENNY SCHUTE – died 1974
1929	England Test fast bowler PETER LOADER – died 2011
1931	Irish soccer midfielder JIMMY McILROY
1940	American college basketball coach BOB KNIGHT
1944	Australian rugby league forward RON COOTE
1948	Basketball Hall of Fame forward DAVE COWENS
1948	Basketball Hall of Fame guard DAN ISSEL
1953	American golfer MUFFIN SPENCER DEVLIN
1953	Zimbabwean golfer MARK McNULTY
1958	East German swimmer KORNELIA ENDER
1958	New Zealand Test batsman DIPAK PATEL
1962	England soccer midfielder STEPHEN HODGE
1963	Australian rugby union five-eighth MICHAEL LYNAGH
1971	Scotland rugby union flanker MARTIN LESLIE

1951 – 'Brown Bomber' returns, briefly

In a short comeback, Joe Louis came out of retirement, to pay back taxes. He was favoured to beat solid contender Rocky Marciano at Madison Square Garden but suffered an eighth round knockout defeat. Marciano knocked Louis down with a left hook and then knocked him out with a right hand. Louis retired for good and within 11 months Marciano was the heavyweight champion.

1952 – First Paki Test win

Pakistan scored their first ever Test victory with an innings and 43-run win over India at Lucknow. Fast bowler Fazal Mahmood captured a career best 7 for 42 to follow up his 5 for 52 in the Indian first innings. India crashed for 106 and 182. Pakistan responded with 331. Nazar Mohammad became the first to be on the field throughout an entire Test match, anchoring Pakistan's first innings with an unbeaten 124.

1970 – Ali's successful comeback

After an enforced 3½ years out of the ring for failing to enlist in the army, Muhammad Ali scored a third round TKO win over Jerry Quarry in Atlanta. Ali had only 6 weeks to prepare for the fight. Referee Perez stopped the contest when Quarry suffered a badly cut eye. The fight was a lead-up to a 15 round points win over Oscar Bonavena and the long-awaited first title encounter with Joe Frazier, which Ali lost on points in New York.

1984 – MJ's NBA debut

Michael Jordan played his first NBA game for the Bulls, in a 109-93 win against the Washington Bullets in Chicago. He scored 16 points and was 5 for 16 from the field, and 6 of 7 from the line.

1991 – ODI bowling best

Pakistan fast bowler Aaquib Javed claimed ODI best bowling figures of 7 for 37 against India in the Sharjah Cup Final. Zahid Fazal (98 retired hurt) and Saleem Malik (87) starred in Pakistan's 262 for 6, before Aaquib almost single-handedly cleaned up India for 190.

1997 – Wildcard 'Fish' win World Series

The Florida Marlins became the first wild card team to win the World Series, defeating the Cleveland Indians, 3-2 in extra innings in Game 7 at Pro Player Stadium in Miami, Florida. The Marlins had only started as a franchise in 1993. This was their first of 2 world titles – they won again in 2003 as a wild card as well.

1998 – Aussies score rare win in Pakistan

Australia drew the third Test in Karachi to clinch their first series victory in Pakistan for 39 years. After taking a first-innings lead of 28, the Australians were happy to bat Pakistan out of the match with their second innings of 390 taking a laborious 142.3 overs. Mark Waugh scored 117 in 335 minutes and it took 222 minutes for Justin Langer to make just 51.

2006 – Kronk gym shut down

Detroit's famous Kronk Gym closed. Legendary trainer Emanuel Steward had worked with many world champions at the gym, including Evander Holyfield, Oscar De La Hoya, Alexis Arguello, Julio César Chávez, Thomas Hearns, Leon Spinks and Vitali Klitschko, but the cost of replacing stolen copper pipes and general repairs to the dilapidated building were too much for officials. Steward moved the gym elsewhere, but it too was closed after his death in 2012.

BIRTHDATES

1902	American boxer JACK SHARKEY – died 1994
1906	Italian boxer PRIMO CARNERA – died 1967
1911	Pro Football Hall of Fame coach SID GILLMAN – died 2003
1921	NBA forward JOE FULKS – died 1976
1965	New Zealand Test batsman KEN RUTHERFORD
1966	Russian gymnast OLGA BICHEROVA
1973	England rugby union winger AUSTIN HEALEY
1976	Finnish NHL goalie MIIKKA KIPRUSOFF
1980	Romanian soccer defender CRISTIAN CHIVU
1983	Russian soccer striker DMITRI SYCHEV
1984	Peruvian soccer winger JEFFERSON FARFAN
1985	New Zealand rugby back rower KIERAN READ

1961 – ABL starts play

The American Basketball League began its inaugural playing schedule. The league was designed to be a rival to the NBA but it lasted only one full season.

1990 – Big three beat Kangaroos

Great Britain scored a rare rugby league win over Australia, beating the Kangaroos 19-12 in the first Test at Wembley Stadium in front of 54,000 fans. Ellery Hanley, Andy Gregory and Gary Schofield crossed for second half tries for the home side.

1991 – World Series nail-biter

The Minnesota Twins beat the Atlanta Braves in only the second 1-0, Game 7 in World Series history (Yankees over the Giants, 1962, was the other). For the first time in 67 years, Game 7 went into extra innings as series MVP Jack Morris pitched 10 scoreless innings. The Twins and Braves, both of whom finished last in their divisions the previous season, put on an incredible World Series. For the first time in history, 3 games went into extra innings. Five games, all decided by 1 run, went down to the winning team's last at-bat.

1997 – Pollock, Symcox in form for Proteas

South African fast bowler Shaun Pollock took 4 top-order wickets in 7 deliveries to finish with 5 for 37 to inspire the Proteas to a 53-run victory over Pakistan in the third Test in Faisalabad. Pat Symcox scored a hard-hitting 81 and took 3 for 8 in the Pakistan second innings to win Man of the Match honours.

2002 – Emmitt is rushing king

Dallas Cowboys running back Emmitt Smith became the NFL all-time rushing leader when he extended his career yardage to 16,743 in a 17-14 home defeat to Seattle. He achieved the record in his 193rd game. He also scored his 150th career touchdown. Smith finished his career in 2004 with a record 18,355 rushing yards.

2004 – 'Curse of the Bambino' lifted

The famous curse was lifted when the Boston Red Sox beat the St Louis Cardinals 3-0 at Busch Stadium to complete a 4-0 World Series sweep. Boston starter Derek Lowe pitched 7 scoreless innings to set up the Red Sox triumph. The curse dated back to 1920 when Babe Ruth was traded from Boston to the New York Yankees.

2005 – First Sox title win since 1917

The Chicago White Sox scored a 1-0 win over the Houston Astros completed a remarkable run through October and give the franchise its first World Series title since 1917. Chicago won 16 of their final 17 games, starting with the final 5 games of the regular season. They swept Boston out of the first round, handled the LA Angels in 5 games in the ALCS and then swept away Houston. Little-used Willie Harris started the winning rally with a pinch-hit single and Jermaine Dye delivered with a run-scoring single, his third hit of the night.

2006 – Cards come good

The Cardinals beat the Detroit Tigers 4-2 in St Louis for a 4-1 series win and became the first World Series winner to have a regular-season winning percentage under .520. The Tony La Russa managed Cards finished .516 with an 83-78 record. In his 12th postseason La Russa became only the second manager to win a World Series in each league.

BIRTHDATES

1922	Baseball Hall of Fame outfielder RALPH KINER
1929	Pro Football Hall of Fame linebacker BILL GEORGE – died 1982
1931	English lawn bowler DAVID BRYANT
1932	Irish soccer goalkeeper/manager HARRY GREGG
1941	American auto racer DICK TRICKLE
1954	England Test batsman CHRIS TAVARE
1956	American golfer PATTY SHEEHAN
1957	England soccer midfielder/manager GLENN HODDLE
1958	England soccer midfielder GORDON COWANS
1959	NBA coach RICK CARLISLE
1963	Australian thoroughbred trainer DAVID HALL
1964	American swimmer MARY T. MEAGHER
1964	Australian cricket captain MARK TAYLOR
1971	Peruvian soccer midfielder JORGE SOTO
1972	Mozambique middle distance runner MARIA MUTOLA
1977	Sri Lanka Test wicketkeeper KUMAR SANGAKKARA
1984	Indian Test fast bowler IRFAN PATHAN
1986	Australian Test batsman DAVID WARNER

1967 – Smith 'Court'

Grand Slam winner Margaret Smith married Barry Court, the son of Western Australian Premier, Sir Charles Court, in Perth. Marriage did no harm to her form, with one Wimbledon title, 3 French, 4 Australian and 3 US Open titles still to come before she retired in 1977.

1973 – Secretariat off to stud after win

Secretariat won his final race by 6½ lengths in the Canadian International Stakes at Toronto's Woodbine Racetrack. The 1973 Triple Crown winner finished a 21-race career with sixteen wins, 4 places and $1.3 million in prize money.

1985 – Imran leads from in front

Despite a then-record 8 for 83 from spinner Ravi Ratnayeke, Sri Lanka crashed to an 8-wicket defeat to Pakistan in the second Test at Sialkot. Pakistan was inspired by skipper Imran Khan who took 5 for 40 as Sri Lanka was dismissed for 200. Imran's match figures were 9 for 95.

1995 – Atlanta's first

Behind the brilliant pitching of Tom Glavine, the Braves became the first Atlanta team to win a major pro sports championship when they edged the Cleveland Indians, 1-0 in Game 6 at Atlanta-Fulton County Stadium to capture the World Series 4-2. Glavine was named Series MVP after his second victory.

2002 – 'Junior' retires

After 128 Tests and 244 ODIs, Australian batsman Mark Waugh announced his retirement from international cricket. In a 12-year career, Waugh scored 8,029 Test runs at 41.81. He hit 20 Test centuries and took 59 wickets. An elegant and gifted stroke maker, Waugh is the twin brother of former Test captain Steve Waugh.

2011 – Cards add to trophy cabinet

The St Louis Cardinals defeated Texas 6-2 to capture the team's 11th World Series title as Allen Craig blasted a home run and Chris Carpenter scattered 6 hits over 6 innings in Game 7 at Busch Stadium in St Louis.

The great Secretariat at track work.

2012 – Giants sweep Tigers

The San Francisco Giants won the MLB World Series, defeating the Tigers 4-3 in 10 innings in Detroit to complete a 4-game sweep. It was the second title in 3 seasons for the Giants, who beat Texas in 2010, and the club's seventh all-time World Series crown.

2012 – Sixers win Champions League

The Sydney Sixers became the second Australian team to win the Champions League Twenty20 when they beat the Highveld Lions in the final in Johannesburg. The Big Bash League winners remained unbeaten, thanks to the leading run scorer, Michael Lumb (226) who made an unbeaten 82 in the one-sided final as the Sixers chased down 122 without losing a wicket.

BIRTHDATES

1880	England soccer defender WILLIAM WEDLOCK – died 1965
1933	Brazilian soccer winger GARRINCHA – died 1983
1937	Basketball Hall of Fame guard/coach LENNY WILKENS
1945	American golfer DON IVERSON
1946	Dutch soccer midfielder/manager WIM JANSEN
1949	American decathlete BRUCE JENNER
1965	British surfer MARTIN POTTER
1972	NFL running back TERRELL DAVIS
1981	Czech soccer striker MILAN BAROŠ

1960 – Clay's pro career starts

After winning the light-heavyweight gold medal at the Rome Olympics, Cassius Clay made his professional debut in Louisville, Kentucky, beating little known Tunney Hunsaker in a unanimous points decision over 6 rounds.

1967 – Thomson back with a win

After a 16-year break, Peter Thomson won his second Australian Open at the Commonwealth course in Melbourne. The 5-time British Open Champion posted a 281 total, 7 strokes ahead of Colin Johnston.

1983 – Rush, Woodcock hit 5 each

Liverpool's Welsh international striker Ian Rush scored 5 goals against Luton Town in their Division 1 clash at Anfield. The Reds won the match 6-0. On the same day Arsenal's Tony Woodcock hit 5 in the Gunners' 6-2 win against Aston Villa at Villa Park.

1983 – Sunny reaches 8,000 runs

Indian opener Sunil Gavaskar became only the third player to score 8,000 Test runs when he hit 121 on the first day of the drawn first Test against the West Indies in Delhi. The other batsmen to pass the 8,000-run mark to that stage were Garry Sobers and Geoff Boycott. Gavaskar went on to score 10,122 runs in 125 Tests at 51.12 with 34 centuries.

1984 – Watson's sixth award

PGA Tour leading money winner Tom Watson won his then record sixth PGA Player of the Year title.

1987 – 'Hitman' wins fourth title

Thomas Hearns moved down 15lbs to knock out Juan Roldan in the fourth round in Las Vegas and win the WBC middleweight title. It was Hearns' unprecedented fourth world title in a different weight division. In a 23-year career, he won world titles in welterweight, super welterweight, middleweight, super middleweight, cruiserweight and light-heavyweight divisions. His record reads 67 fights for 61 wins, 5 losses, 1 draw.

1989 – Steffi's lucky 13th

Steffi Graf won her 13th WTA tournament in a stellar

Amanda Beard on her way to a silver medal in the 200m IM at the 2004 Athens Olympics.

year, outclassing 15-year-old Monica Seles 7-5, 6-4 in the Brighton Indoor.

2000 – Jayasuriya ties Richards

Sri Lankan opener Sanath Jayasuriya smashed 189 off 161 balls with 21 fours and 4 sixes in his team's 245-run massacre of India in the Champions Trophy final in Sharjah. The big innings equalled the second-highest individual score in a ODI, made by West Indian batsman Vivian Richards against England in 1984.

2003 – LeBron debuts

LeBron James made his NBA debut for the Cleveland Cavaliers scoring 25 points, but it wasn't enough, as they lost to the Kings 106-92 in Sacramento.

BIRTHDATES

1877	England Test all-rounder WILFRED RHODES – died 1973
1897	England soccer forward BILLY WALKER – died 1964
1927	Australian tennis player FRANK SEDGMAN
1935	England Test all-rounder DAVID ALLEN
1935	England soccer goalkeeper EDWARD HOPKINSON – died 2004
1943	England soccer defender NORMAN HUNTER
1949	American pro wrestler PAUL ORNDORFF
1953	Canadian Hockey Hall of Fame defenseman DENIS POTVIN
1959	Canadian Hockey Hall of Fame right wing MIKE GARTNER
1968	Norwegian speed skater JOHAN KOSS
1970	Dutch soccer goalkeeper EDWIN van der SAR
1971	Australian Test batsman GREG BLEWETT
1971	Australian Test batsman MATTHEW HAYDEN
1973	South African Test batsman ADAM BACHER
1973	French soccer midfielder ROBERT PIRÈS
1974	England Test captain MICHAEL VAUGHAN
1981	American swimmer AMANDA BEARD

㉚ OCTOBER

1894 – Atlas born
Bodybuilder Charles Atlas was born. Atlas invented the 'dynamic tension' program of bodybuilding. Heavyweight boxing champions Max Baer, Rocky Marciano and Joe Louis all took his course.

1955 – First wicketkeeper double century
Pakistan's Imtiaz Ahmed became the first wicketkeeper to score a Test double century with a patient 209 in the second Test against New Zealand in Lahore. Imtiaz added a Pakistan-record 308 for the seventh wicket with Waqar Hassan (189) to lead the home team to a 4-wicket victory and an unassailable 2-0 lead in the series.

1973 – Seaver's 19 enough
Tom Seaver became the first to win a Cy Young award for the season's best pitcher without having won 20 games. In 36 starts the New York Mets pitcher had a 19-10 record with a 2.08 ERA. Seaver had won a World Series with the Mets in 1969, but in 1973 they were edged 4-3 by the Oakland Athletics.

1974 – 'Rumble in the Jungle'
Thirty-two-year-old Muhammad Ali regained the world heavyweight title by knocking out George Foreman in the eighth round of the classic fight at Kinshasa in the Congo Democratic Republic. The bout featured Ali's famous 'Rope a Dope' tactic whereby he covered up cleverly and let Foreman punch himself out before launching a furious attack on his fatigued opponent.

2001 – MJ back ... again
Michael Jordan returned to basketball after a 2½ year retirement to play for the Washington Wizards in a 93-91 defeat in New York. Jordan played 2 seasons with the Wizards, showing he could play with all his old flair, but the period was hampered by injuries.

2003 – Big fine for Gunners
The English Football Association fined Premier League club Arsenal £175,000 for failing to control their players in the League 0-0 draw with Manchester United at Old Trafford on September 21. Four Arsenal players – defenders Lauren Etame Mayer and Martin Keown,

Italian-born bodybuilder Charles Atlas in a typical pose.

captain Patrick Vieira, and fellow midfielder Ray Parlour – were all suspended and fined a cumulative 9 matches and £90,000. Arsenal's fine was then the second-largest handed out to a club in English football history; in 1994, Tottenham Hotspur had been fined £1.5 million for financial irregularities.

BIRTHDATES
1894	American bodybuilder CHARLES ATLAS – died 1972
1906	Italian auto racer NINO FARINA – died 1966
1917	French auto racer MAURICE TRINTIGNANT – died 2005
1936	NFL coach DICK VERMEIL
1936	Russian gymnast POLINA ASTAKHOVA – died 2005
1937	Welsh rugby union lock BRIAN PRICE
1951	American auto racer TONY BETTENHAUSEN JR – died 2000
1960	Argentine soccer captain DIEGO MARADONA
1961	Dutch soccer goalkeeper HANS SEGERS
1962	West Indies Test captain COURTNEY WALSH
1963	Australian Test batsman MIKE VELETTA
1986	Austrian alpine skier THOMAS MORGENSTERN

1950 – Lloyd breaks NBA race barrier

Earl Lloyd of the Washington Capitols became the NBA's first black player, with 6 points and 10 rebounds in a 78-70 loss to Rochester. Two other black players made their debuts the following day: Nat Clifton with the New York Knicks, and Chuck Cooper with the Boston Celtics.

1954 – Fütterer equals Owens' sprint mark

German sprinter Heinz Fütterer equalled Jesse Owens' 18-year-old world 100m record of 10.2 seconds in Yokohama, Japan. Out of the eleven sprinters who ran the time between June 1936 and June 1956, Fütterer was the only European in the group.

1987 – First WC hat-trick to Sharma

Indian spinner Chetan Sharma took the first ever hat-trick during a World Cup, against New Zealand in Nagpur. He bowled Ken Rutherford, Ian Smith and Ewen Chatfield with the last 3 balls of his sixth over as India hammered the Kiwis by 9 wickets

1997 – Shoemaker's second retirement

Bill Shoemaker retired from his second career in racing. After riding a record 8,833 winners as a jockey, he became a trainer in 1990. A car accident a year later left him paralysed from the neck down, but he returned to work after 5 months of rehabilitation, and trained 90 winners in 713 starts before his second retirement.

1999 – Tiger's third straight

In his third consecutive PGA Tour victory, Tiger Woods won the Tour Championship by 4 strokes from Davis Love III at the Champions GC in Houston. Woods finished at 15-under 269 in an emotion-charged tournament in the wake of the October 25 death of Payne Stewart in an airplane crash.

2004 – Patriots' streak undone

Super Bowl champions the New England Patriots had their NFL record 21-game winning streak halted when they were beaten 34-20 at Pittsburgh. The Steelers scored 21 points in the first quarter, rushed for 221 yards and sacked New England quarterback Tom Brady 4 times. The Patriots had not suffered a defeat since September 2003, when they lost to Washington Redskins (17-20).

2004 – Bumper season for Singh

Fijian golfer Vijay Singh became the first player to win $10 million in a year, when he took out the Chrysler Classic at Palm Harbour, Florida. Singh carded a final round 6-under par 65 to beat Jesper Parnevik and Tommy Armour III by 5 shots in his ninth tournament win of the season and his sixth in his last 8 starts.

2006 – Champion Heat smashed in opener

In by far the worst loss in NBA history for a defending champion on opening night, the Miami Heat was thrashed 108-66 by the Chicago Bulls after the Heat had received their 2005–06 NBA Championship rings in a glittering ceremony in Miami.

2010 – How the mighty fall

After nearly 5 years as golf's top-ranked player, Tiger Woods lost his world no. 1 status to Englishman Lee Westwood, who became the first European in 16 years to be no. 1 and only the fourth player to get there without having won a major. Woods lasted at no. 1 for a record 281 weeks. He had taken a 5-month break to cope with confessions of extramarital affairs, which ended in divorce, and his game had not been up to scratch.

BIRTHDATES

1883	New Zealand tennis player ANTHONY WILDING – died 1915
1895	Australian boxer LES DARCY – died 1916
1920	German soccer midfielder FRITZ WALTER – died 2002
1929	Australian snooker player EDDIE CHARLTON – died 2004
1941	British rally driver DEREK BELL
1947	American marathon runner FRANK SHORTER
1951	College/NFL coach NICK SABAN
1958	French cyclist JEANNIE LONGO-CIPRELLI
1963	Brazilian soccer midfielder/manager DUNGA
1964	Dutch soccer striker MARCO VAN BASTEN
1971	England soccer goalkeeper IAN WALKER
1971	New Zealand golfer PHIL TATAURANGI
1971	Scottish rugby prop TOM SMITH
1972	England rugby union halfback MATT DAWSON
1979	Portuguese soccer winger SIMÃO SABROSA

NOVEMBER

1 NOVEMBER

1938 – Classic match race
Seabiscuit, ridden by George Woolf, beat 1937 Triple Crown winner War Admiral by a full 3 lengths in Pimlico track record time to win $15,000 in one of the greatest match races in history. War Admiral was the 1-4 favourite but proved no match for the 5-year-old Seabiscuit in their mile and three-sixteenths (1,900m) race in Baltimore.

1959 – Facemasks in for goalies
Montreal Canadiens' goal tender Jacques Plante became the first NHL player to wear a protective facemask. After having 7 stitches inserted into his face, he modelled a mask made of fibreglass. Shortly thereafter, all NHL goalies were wearing masks.

1999 – NFL great Payton passes away
Legendary Chicago Bears running back Walter Payton died from cancer, aged 45. In his 13-year career with the Bears (1975–87), Payton rushed for a then-record 16,726 yards. He remains second all-time behind Emmitt Smith and ahead of Barry Sanders. He had ten 1,000-yard seasons, won 2 MVP awards and was voted to 9 Pro-Bowls. After carrying mediocre Chicago teams for most of his career, Payton saw the Bears finally win a Super Bowl (46-10 over New England) in 1985. He was elected to the Hall of Fame in 1993.

2001 – Burke kicks 10
In rugby union, Wallabies fullback Matt Burke kicked an Australian record 10 conversions and a penalty in the record 92-10 romp over Spain in Madrid. The Wallabies' previous highest result was a 76-0 win against England in 1998. It was Australia's 400th Test match in history.

2006 – Malkin scores in first six
Evgeni Malkin scored in the first period to become the first NHL player in 89 years with goals in his first 6 games, as the Pittsburgh Penguins scored a 4-3 OT win over the Kings in LA.

2007 – Hingis retires, not on a high
Five-time Grand Slam champion Martina Hingis announced her retirement for a second time after testing positive for cocaine at Wimbledon. The 27-year-old Swiss denied the accusations but didn't want to spend years fighting the case. She won 3 straight Australian Open titles from 1997–99, Wimbledon and the US Open championships in 1997.

2010 – Giants' first World Series since move
The San Francisco Giants clinched their first World Series since moving from New York in 1958, with a 3-1 win over the Texas Rangers in Game 5 at Arlington. Series MVP Edgar Renteria hit a seventh-inning 3-run homer for the Giants to take the series 4-1.

BIRTHDATES
1920	English sports caster 'WHISPERING' TED LOWE – died 2011
1932	Canadian Hockey Hall of Fame defenseman/coach AL ARBOUR
1935	South African golfer GARY PLAYER
1941	England rugby union hooker JOHN PULLIN
1947	Pro Football Hall of Fame linebacker TED HENDRICKS
1951	Australian Test batsman CRAIG SERJEANT
1957	New Zealand rugby union lock MURRAY PIERCE
1960	Mexican MLB pitcher FERNANDO VALENZUELA
1961	Basketball Hall of Fame centre/coach ANNE DONOVAN
1962	English swimmer SHARRON DAVIES
1963	Welsh soccer striker/manager MARK HUGHES
1974	Indian Test batsman V.V.S LAXMAN
1983	English rugby player JON WILKIN
1991	English footballer REECE BROWN

Pro Football Hall of Fame running back Walter Payton in full flight for the Chicago Bears.

② NOVEMBER

1946 – Auerbach arrives
Red Auerbach made his professional coaching debut for the Washington Capitols in a 50-33 road win over the Detroit Falcons. Auerbach went on to coach the Boston Celtics (1950–66), winning an unprecedented 8 consecutive NBA titles (1959–66). He retired as the winningest coach in NBA history with a 938-479 win-loss record in his 20-year career.

1947 – Ryder Cup renewed
The Ryder Cup was renewed after World War II, but not without the aid of Portland businessman Robert A. Hudson, a fruit grower and canner. The Americans routed the visiting Great Britain & Ireland team, 11-1, but the matches were saved thanks to Hudson's generosity in funding the visiting team's trip.

1958 – Rams' record crowd
The Los Angeles Rams beat the Chicago Bears 41-35 before 90,833 fans at the Los Angeles Coliseum. At the time it was the NFL single-game attendance record. The first game at Cowboys Stadium in 2009 set an NFL regular-season attendance record with a crowd of 105,121.

1972 – A 'Cy Young' from the basement
Philadelphia left-handed starting pitcher Steve Carlton became the first man to win the National League Cy Young Award on a last-place team. Carlton was the unanimous choice of 24 baseball writers after a 27-10 season, accounting for 46% of the Phillies' 59 victories. He led the NL in victories, earned run average (1.97), starts (41), complete games (30), innings pitched (346 1/3) and strikeouts (310

1990 – Pro sport goes abroad
In the first regular season game played outside North America by any major league sport, the Phoenix Suns defeated the Utah Jazz 119-96 at the Tokyo Metropolitan Gymnasium in Japan. The teams also met the following night in Tokyo, with the Jazz winning 102-101.

1991 – Wallabies first World Cup
Front rower Tony Daley scored the only try of the game as the Wallabies beat England 12-6 at Twickenham

Australian cricketer Victor Trumper.

to claim Australia's first Rugby World Cup. During the tournament, grand slam champions England had used their big, powerful pack and the right boot of fly-half Rob Andrew to win games, but in the final they unsuccessfully tried to run the ball through classy outside backs Jeremy Guscott, Will Carling and Rory Underwood.

2004 – Horse Racing
Makybe Diva became the first mare to win back-to-back Melbourne Cups in the race's 144-year history. The 6-year-old also set a weight carrying record for mares with 55.5kg and also was the first back-to-back winner with different trainers, David Hall (2003) and Lee Freedman (2004). Jockey Glen Boss rode Makybe Diva on both occasions.

BIRTHDATES
1877	Australian Test batsman VICTOR TRUMPER – died 1915
1908	England Test batsman FRED BAKEWELL – died 1983
1928	West Indies Test wicketkeeper GERRY ALEXANDER – died 2011
1934	Australian tennis player KEN ROSEWALL
1941	American golfer DAVE STOCKTON
1945	Pro Football Hall of Fame guard LARRY LITTLE
1946	Australian auto racer ALAN JONES
1966	South African tennis player ROSALYN FAIRBANK
1973	AFL forward/NFL punter BEN GRAHAM
1980	Uruguayan soccer defender DIEGO LUGANO
1986	Canadian basketballer ANDY RAUTINS

③ NOVEMBER

1962 – Wilt's 72 points
Wilt Chamberlain of the SF Warriors scored 72 points at the LA Lakers, the then fourth-highest point total in NBA history. Nine months earlier he had set the NBA record of 100 points against the NY Knicks.

1978 – Indian protest
Needing only 23 off 14 balls with 8 wickets in hand to win the third ODI against Pakistan at Sahiwal, Indian captain Bishan Bedi called his batsmen from the field in the first concession in international cricket history. It was a protest against the bowling of Sarfraz Nawaz, who had just sent down 4 consecutive bouncers, none of which was called a wide.

1989 – The Russians are coming!
Sarunas Marciulionis and Alexander Volkov became the first Russians to play in a regular season NBA game. Marciulionis scored 19 points as Golden State lost to Phoenix 136-106, and Volkov didn't score as Atlanta went down to Indiana 126-103.

1996 – Kobe's debut
Controversial LA Lakers superstar Kobe Bryant became the youngest player to make his NBA debut at that time, at the age of 18 years, 2 months, 11 days, when he played in a 91-85 home win against Minnesota.

2004 – Ruud's fabulous four
Striker Ruud van Nistelrooy scored all 4 goals as Manchester United thrashed Sparta Prague 4-1 in a Champions League match at Old Trafford. The Dutchman's clinical finishing included a first half penalty. The goal haul took van Nistelrooy's Champions League tally for United to an incredible 35 goals from 36 matches.

2011 – Match fixers sent to jail
Three Pakistan players were sentenced to jail for their involvement in spot-fixing during the Lord's Test in 2010. Salman Butt, who received 2½ years, Mohammad Asif (1 year), and Mohammad Amir (6 months), were serving ICC bans when they were tried by a London court, charged with accepting corrupt payments and conspiracy to cheat.

LA Lakers superstar Kobe Bryant, pictured in a 2005 NBA game against Dallas at the Staples Centre in Los Angeles.

2011 – Slater makes it 11
Kelly Slater was officially crowned surfing world champion for a history-making 11th time after winning his round 4 heat at the Rip Curl Search event in San Francisco. The American was prematurely awarded the world title the previous week due to a mathematical error in the rankings calculations.

BIRTHDATES
1899	American pocket billiards player RALPH GREENLEAF – died 1950
1908	Pro Football Hall of Fame fullback BRONCO NAGURSKI – died 1990
1918	Baseball Hall of Fame pitcher BOB FELLER – died 2010
1936	Australian tennis player ROY EMERSON
1945	German soccer striker GERD MÜLLER
1949	American boxer LARRY HOLMES
1955	NFL quarterback PHIL SIMMS
1956	MLB pitcher BOB WELCH
1960	American volleyball player KARCH KIRALY
1963	Tobagonian soccer striker IAN WRIGHT
1964	New Zealand Test batsman BRYAN YOUNG
1965	American golfer MIKE SPRINGER
1971	England soccer striker DWIGHT YORKE
1990	Australian soccer defender/cricket all-rounder ELLYSE PERRY

1923 – Team owner in the game
George Halas became the only team owner to ever set an NFL playing record when he returned a fumble 98 yards for a touchdown in the Chicago Bears' 26-0 victory over the Oorang Indians in Chicago. The record stood for 49 years. The 28-year-old Chicago Bears' founder also coached the Bears with Ed Sternaman. The man who fumbled was legendary athlete Jim Thorpe.

1951 – US prevail in Ryder Cup
The United States breezed past Great Britain and Ireland, 9½-2½, to win the Ryder Cup matches at Pinehurst, North Carolina. Skip Alexander, still suffering from injuries he suffered in a plane crash a year earlier, won his singles match for the Americans against in-form British champion John Panton.

1951 – Back-back kickoff returns
Touchdowns were scored on consecutive kick-off returns for the first time in NFL history, as the New York Giants beat the New York Yanks 37-31. Buddy Young of the Yanks returned a kick-off for a touchdown and the Giants' Emlen Tunnell also ran back the ensuing kick-off.

1961 – Another Wilt streak
Philadelphia Warriors' centre Wilt Chamberlain began an incredible streak of 65 consecutive games of scoring 30 or more points. The second-longest such streak in NBA history was also set by Chamberlain in 1962 with a streak of 31 games.

2000 – Scotland record
Glasgow Rangers striker Kenny Miller scored 5 goals in a 7-1 win against St Mirren at Ibrox Park, equalling a Scottish Premier League record for a single match. Dundee United's Paul Sturrock had scored 5 against Morton in 1984. Kris Boyd (twice) and Gary Hooper also have both equalled the mark.

1987 – NBA expansion
The NBA announced Charlotte, Miami, Minneapolis and Orlando would be granted expansion franchises at a price of $32.5 million each. Charlotte and Miami joined the league in 1988–89, and Minneapolis and Orlando in 1989–90.

2007 – NFL records
Minnesota running back Adrian Peterson rushed for 253 of his NFL single-game record 296 yards in the second half of the Viking's 35-17 victory over the San Diego Chargers in Minneapolis. Peterson scored on runs of 1, 64 and 46 yards and averaged a mind-boggling 9.9 yards per carry on 30 attempts. The game also featured San Diego cornerback Antonio Cromartie returning a missed field goal 109 yards for a touchdown as the first half ended – the longest play in NFL history.

2009 – Matsui stars for Yankees
The New York Yankees took their 27th World Series title with a 7-3 win over the defending champions, the Philadelphia Phillies in Game 6 at Yankee Stadium. Hideki Matsui drove in 6 of the Yankees' 7 runs. He hit a 2-run home run, a 2-run single, and a 2-run double. It was the first time the series MVP title had gone to a Japanese player or a full-time designated hitter.

BIRTHDATES
1912	New Zealand Test batsman GIFF VIVIAN – died 1983
1943	American tennis player CLARK GRAEBNER
1947	Australian Test wicketkeeper ROD MARSH
1947	Russian figure skater ALEXEI ULANOV
1961	Irish footballer and English soccer manager NIGEL WORTHINGTON
1963	West Indian Test wicketkeeper DAVID WILLIAMS
1967	Pakistan Test batsman ASIF MUJTABA
1968	New Zealand Test captain LEE GERMON
1972	Portuguese soccer winger LUÍS FIGO
1976	New Zealand rugby union lock TROY FLAVELL
1981	NFL defensive tackle VINCE WILFORK
1982	New Zealand rugby union number 8 JERRY COLLINS
1986	South African auto racer ADRIAN ZAUGG

1927 – Four straight PGA titles to Hagan

Walter Hagen became the first to win 4 consecutive US PGA titles when he recovered from 3-down halfway through the 36-hole match-play final at the Cedar Park CC in Dallas. Hagen took the lead at the 14th hole to record a 1-up victory over Joe Turnesa. It also was Hagen's fifth overall PGA triumph.

1932 – Next stop – 'Arsenal'

London Transport decided to change the name of the proposed new underground railway station near Arsenal's home ground to 'Arsenal.' Arsenal's manager Herbert Chapman persuaded authorities the proposed name 'Gillespie Road' was inappropriate.

1946 – Chuck makes his mark

Chuck Connors of the Boston Celtics shattered the first backboard in NBA history, during the warm-up before a Celtics game. Connors went on to become an actor, best known for his role in the television show *The Rifleman*.

1971 – Anne no 'princess'

Princess Anne was voted British Sportswoman of the Year after winning the European 3-day event at Burghley. The award was voted by the Sports Writers' Association, the Daily Express and the journal of the British Olympic Association. She competed in the 1976 Montreal Olympics and later became President of the British Olympic Association in 1983. In 1988 she became a UK delegate of the IOC.

1971 – Baylor bows out

Injury-prone Los Angeles Lakers star Elgin Baylor retired after a 14-year, 846-game career that included 23,149 points. In 1976, he was elected to the Basketball Hall of Fame.

1971 – Spain's first boxing world title

Pedro Carrasco became Spain's first ever world champion, beating Mando Ramos by an 11th round disqualification in Madrid to capture the vacant WBC lightweight title. Carrasco's next 2 fights were against Ramos, and he lost both by split points-decisions.

1994 – George oldest champ

At age 45, George Foreman became the oldest ever WBA/IBF heavyweight champion, after knocking out Michael Moorer in the 10th round in Las Vegas. Twenty years after losing for the first time, Foreman also broke the record for most time in between one world title run and the next.

2002 – Weld takes second Cup

Leading Irish trainer Dermott Weld won his second Melbourne Cup when Media Puzzle, ridden by Damien Oliver, won in one of the fastest ever run. Weld had first won the prestigious race in 1993, with Vintage Crop.

2003 – Goal feast

French club Monaco and Spain's Deportivo La Coruna scored 11 goals in the highest aggregate total in a Champions League match. Monaco won 8-3 at home.

2005 – Gregan's rugby record

Wallabies captain George Gregan became rugby union's most capped international player when he played his 115th Test in Australia's 26-16 defeat to France in Marseille. Gregan beat England prop Jason Leonard's record of 114 caps.

BIRTHDATES

1901	England Test batsman EDDIE PAYNTER – died 1979
1935	English jockey LESTER PIGGOTT
1936	German soccer forward UWE SEELER
1938	Argentine soccer manager CÉSAR LUIS MENOTTI
1950	American golfer DEBBIE MASSEY
1952	Basketball Hall of Fame centre BILL WALTON
1969	Australian jockey STEVEN KING
1972	South African rugby union flanker JOHAN ERASMUS
1973	MLB outfielder JOHNNY DAMON
1973	Russian NHL centre ALEXEI YASHIN
1974	New Zealand rugby union captain TAINE RANDELL
1977	Indian Test fast bowler SKIV SUNDER DAS
1986	Danish soccer goalkeeper KASPER SCHMEICHEL
1988	Indian cricketer VIRAT KOHLI

1934 – Second Cup for Peter Pan
Peter Pan joined Archer as only the second horse to win the Melbourne Cup twice. Peter Pan first won as a 3-year-old in 1932. He missed 1933 with injury but won by 3 lengths from Sarcherie in 1934. He had 38 career starts for 22½ wins, 6 seconds and one third.

1974 – 'Cy Young' to a reliever
Mike Marshall of the Los Angeles Dodgers became the first relief pitcher to win the Cy Young Award. Marshall appeared in an MLB record 106 games, recording 15 wins and 21 saves.

1992 – Parish's longevity
Robert Parish became only the second player to play in the NBA for 17 seasons when he scored 14 points and grabbed 12 rebounds in the host Boston Celtics' 113-92 win over Minnesota. Parish now holds the record with 21 seasons, passing Kareem (20) in the 1996–97.

1993 – Bizarre title bout delay
The seventh round of the Evander Holyfield-Riddick Bowe world heavyweight title fight in Las Vegas was delayed 22 minutes, when a man flying a propeller-powered parachute crashed into the ring. Holyfield eventually won in a majority-points decision.

1999 – Cardiff joy for Wallabies
Ben Tune and Owen Finnigan scored tries, and Matt Burke landed 7 penalties and 2 conversions as the Wallabies thrashed France 35-12 in Cardiff to claim Australia's second Rugby World Cup. The Wallabies had won their first World Cup in 1991.

2001 – First female Cup winning trainer
Welsh born Sheila Laxon became the first woman to train a Melbourne Cup winner when Ethereal completed the Caulfield-Melbourne Cup double. Ethereal's win, capped a remarkable recovery for Laxon who took up training in 1991 after she was almost killed in a race fall and spent 8 days in a coma.

2010 – Ten titles for Slater
Kelly Slater marked his unprecedented 10th world surfing title victory with a 10-out-of-10 wave score

The Holyfield-Bowe 1993 heavyweight title fight in Las Vegas was interrupted by a parachutist landing in the ring.

to also win the Rip Curl Pro Search event in Puerto Rico. The 38-year-old American saved his best for last against Australian Bede Durbidge in the final. In claiming his first championship in 1992 Slater became the youngest ever titleholder and his 2010 success also made him the oldest.

BIRTHDATES
1861	Basketball pioneer JAMES NAISMITH – died 1939
1887	MLB pitcher WALTER JOHNSON – died 1946
1908	American boxer TONY CANZONERI – died 1959
1921	New Zealand Test captain GEOFF RABONE – died 2006
1930	Sports management executive MARK McCORMACK – died 2003
1931	English auto racer PETER COLLINS – died 1958
1940	Irish soccer midfielder/manager JOHNNY GILES
1953	New Zealand Test fast bowler/RU fullback BRIAN MCKECHNIE
1955	New Zealand rugby union halfback MARK DONALDSON
1956	Australian Test spinner MURRAY BENNETT
1956	Australian Test opener GRAEME WOOD
1964	New Zealand rugby union flanker MIKE BREWER
1973	Australian rugby union lock DAVID GIFFIN
1987	Serbian tennis player ANNA IVANOVIC
1990	German soccer forward ANDRÉ SCHÜRRLE

⑦ NOVEMBER

1962 – Ice Hockey streak over
A bad back forced Chicago Blackhawks goaltender Glenn Hall out of the action in the first period of a 3-3 home tie against the Boston Bruins. That ended his NHL record streak of 502 consecutive complete games, stretching over 7 seasons.

1967 – Berenson not 'Blue' in St Louis
St Louis Blues centre Red Berenson tied the modern NHL record by scoring 6 goals in an 8-0 win over the Philadelphia Flyers. The record was 7 goals by Joe Malone of the Quebec Bulldogs in 1920. Berenson was tied on 6 goals with Newsy Lalonde, Joe Malone, Corb Denneny, Sid Howe and Darryl Sittler.

1985 – 'Hurricane' released
Former middleweight contender Rubin Carter, who had twice been convicted of a triple murder in New Jersey, was released after 19 years in prison. It was ruled Carter had been denied his civil rights during the 1967 and 1976 trials. He became a civil-rights cause celebrity and was immortalised in the Bob Dylan song 'Hurricane'.

1987 – Triple football treat
For only the third time in English League history, 3 members of a team scored hat-tricks in the same match, when Manchester City played Huddersfield Town in a Division 2 game at Maine Road. Paul Stewart, David White and Tony Adcock scored 3 goals each in City's 10-1 victory.

1991 – 'Magic' retires
Outstanding LA Lakers' point-guard Ervin 'Magic' Johnson announced his retirement because he had tested HIV positive. Johnson was advised that although he was healthy, any continued athletic involvement could harm his immune system. Johnson had led the Lakers to 5 NBA championships in 12 seasons. Today, he is an influential businessman and advocate for HIV/AIDS prevention and awareness.

1992 – Thomas third in all-time assists
Isiah Thomas earned 5 assists in Detroit's 89-87 win at Indiana to become only the third guard in NBA history

Ervin 'Magic' Johnson in 1991, playing for the Los Angeles Lakers.

(along with Magic Johnson and Oscar Robertson) to pass 8,000 career assists.

2007 – Modano top American in NHL
Mike Modano became the all-time American-born points leader in the National Hockey League. The Dallas captain scored a pair of goals in the Stars' 3-1 victory at San Jose to pass Phil Housely's mark of 1,288.

BIRTHDATES
1921	American golfer JACK FLECK
1944	Italian soccer striker LUIGI RIVA
1945	England rugby union centre BARRY CORLESS
1957	British auto racer JONATHAN PALMER
1961	England soccer striker MARK HATELEY
1963	England soccer midfielder JOHN CHARLES
1965	German middle distance runner SIGRUN WODARS
1966	American jockey CALVIN BOREL
1970	Swiss tennis player MARC ROSSET
1972	England rugby union lock DANNY GREWCOCK
1972	American boxer HASIM RAHMAN
1976	Australian tennis player MARK PHILIPPOUSSIS
1978	England soccer defender RIO FERDINAND
1980	New Zealand Test all-rounder JAMES FRANKLIN

❽ NOVEMBER

1966 – Robinson's unique double
Baltimore Orioles outfielder Frank Robinson became the only player to ever be voted MVP in both leagues when he was unanimous choice for the AL award. Robinson was NL MVP in 1961 with Cincinnati. In a Triple Crown season he batted .316 with 49 homers and 122 RBI, sparking Baltimore to its first pennant and a 4-0 World Series sweep of the LA Dodgers.

1970 – Longest field goal
Tom Dempsey kicked a record 63-yard field goal to give New Orleans a 19-17 home win over Detroit. He broke Bert Rechichar's 1953 record of 56 yards. Denver's Jason Elam equalled the mark in 1998.

1987 – Australia's first WC
David Boon top-scored with 75 and Mike Veletta smashed 45 off 31 balls as Australia won its first World Cup with a 7-run triumph over England at Eden Gardens in Calcutta. England was dismissed for 246 chasing 254 for victory.

1995 – Ferguson needs 'anger management'
Glasgow Rangers striker Duncan Ferguson lost an appeal against a 12-match suspension for his on-field attack on Raith Rovers' John McStay in April. Ferguson also served a 3-month prison sentence in Glasgow's tough Barlinnie jail for head-butting McStay.

1995 – Crenshaw 'blessed'
Ben Crenshaw holed a sand wedge on the final hole for an eagle to beat Steve Elkington and Corey Pavin by a stroke in the PGA Grand Slam of Golf at Poipu Bay in Kauai, Hawaii. Crenshaw was the only player to not walk over the sacred 'heiau' area near the 18th tee and local residents later said he was 'blessed' for honouring Hawaiian customs and a sacred site.

1999 – Indian pair's record partnership
Indian batsmen Sachin Tendulkar and Rahul Dravid put on a record ODI partnership of 331 against New Zealand in Hyderabad. Tendulkar scored 186 from 150 balls and Dravid hit a run-a-ball 153 as India finished at 376 for 2 to win by 174.

Snooker champion Eddie Charlton in action at the 1982 B & H Masters in London.

2004 – Irons' 3 straight titles
American Andy Irons became only the third surfer to ever win 3 consecutive world titles when Australian rival Joel Parkinson was eliminated in the third round of the Nova Shin event in Brazil. Others to achieve the feat are Australian Mark Richards (1979–82) and American Kelly Slater (1994–98). Irons died aged 32 in 2010 from a cardiac arrest. He remains the only surfer to win a title at every venue on the ASP calendar.

2004 – 'Steady Eddie' dead at 75
Australia's most successful snooker player, Eddie Charlton, died in New Zealand aged 75. Charlton won 3 prestigious Pot Black tournaments (1972, 1973 and 1980) and was runner-up in both the World Snooker and Billiards Championship on 3 occasions.

BIRTHDATES
1911　American golfer AL BROSCH – died 1975
1913　American boxer LOU AMBERS – died 1995
1929　College football coach BOBBY BOWDEN
1942　American jockey ANGEL CORDERO JR
1943　England soccer midfielder MARTIN PETERS
1945　Australian Test spinner TONY MANN
1946　Dutch soccer manager GUUS HIDDINK
1957　English soccer manager ALAN CURBISHLEY
1957　American swimmer TIM SHAW
1972　Australian swimmer CHRIS FYDLER
1974　South Africa swimmer PENNY HEYNS
1976　Australian Test fast bowler BRETT LEE
1980　Brazilian soccer forward LUÍS FABIANO
1981　England soccer midfielder JOE COLE
1986　Welsh rugby utility back JAMIE ROBERTS

1946 – College football stalemate
In a game regarded as among the best of the 20th century, the unbeaten Army and Notre Dame fought out a scoreless tie before 74,121 spectators at New York's Yankee Stadium. After the season, Notre Dame was ranked no. 1, barely ahead of Army.

1957 – Fast start in NHL
Claude Provost of the Montreal Canadiens scored the fastest goal from the start of an NHL period when he netted a goal after 4 seconds of the second period in the Canadiens' 4-2 home win over Boston. Chicago's Denis Savard equalled the record in 1986.

1963 – rugby league records tumble
Australia thrashed Great Britain 50-12 at Station Road, Swinton. It was the highest tally posted against the Lions; the biggest winning margin, and Graeme Langlands' tally of 20 points was the highest in any Test against Great Britain.

1985 – Hadlee's best
New Zealand fast bowler Richard Hadlee took a career best 9 for 52 in the first Test against Australia in Brisbane. Hadlee grabbed the first 8 wickets to fall, and then took a sharp catch to give Vaughan Brown a maiden Test wicket and spoiling his run at 10 wickets. Hadlee set up an innings victory with match figures of 15 for 123. It was the Kiwis' first ever Test success on Australian soil.

1985 – Youngest chess champion
Twenty-two-year-old Russian Garry Kasparov became the youngest world champion when he ended the 10-year reign of Anatoly Karpov, 13-11, in Moscow. Kasparov beat Karpov in another 3 world title matches over the next 4 years.

1993 – Williams' end from the line
Michael Williams of the Minnesota Timberwolves saw his record NBA consecutive free throw streak end at 97, when he missed in the second-quarter at San Antonio. Williams' mark of 97 eclipsed Calvin Murphy's previous record of 78, set during the 1980–81 season.

1996 – Tyson smashed
Evander Holyfield pounded Mike Tyson to win by TKO in round 11 in Las Vegas to capture the WBA heavyweight title. The following year the pair fought again in a bizarre contest when Tyson was disqualified after twice biting Holyfield's ear.

2010 – Suzuki ten Gold Gloves
Seattle outfielder Ichiro Suzuki won his 10th straight Gold Glove for a full season of fielding excellence, tying the AL record for an outfielder shared by Ken Griffey Jr and Al Kaline. The record for outfielders was held by Willie Mays and Roberto Clemente with 12 each.

2011 – Penn State disgrace
Legendary Penn State head football coach Joe Paterno, and President Graham Spanier, were fired amid questions about whether they did enough to stop, report or investigate what a grand jury report said was the continuous molestation of boys as young as 10 by former defensive coordinator Jerry Sandusky during the 1990s and 2000s.

BIRTHDATES
1918　American marathon swimmer FLORENCE CHADWICK – died 1995
1923　American high jumper ALICE COACHMAN
1931　MLB manager WHITEY HERZOG
1935　MLB pitcher BOB GIBSON
1942　American golfer TOM WEISKOPF
1948　American swimmer SHARON STOUDER
1949　American golfer TERRY DIEHL
1960　German soccer defender ANDREAS BREHME
1970　Canadian pro wrestler CHRIS JERICHO
1971　American golfer DAVID DUVAL
1975　New Zealand Test batsman MATTHEW SINCLAIR
1982　Australian hurdler JANA PITTMAN
1986　Swedish NHL defenseman CARL GUNNARSSON

1963 – Howe NHL's top scorer

Gordie Howe passed Maurice Richard as the NHL's all-time leading goal scorer when he notched his 545th score in the Red Wing's 3-0 win against Montreal in Detroit. In a 33-year NHL career (1947–80), Howe went on to score a record 975 goals.

1965 – 'Sugar' Ray retires

After a career spanning more than 25 years 'Sugar' Ray Robinson announced his retirement from the ring. Robinson first won the world welterweight title from Jimmy Doyle in 1947 and then the middleweight title from Jake La Motta in the famous 'Saint Valentine's Day Massacre' in 1951. His record read: 200 fights – won 173 (108 KOs), lost 19, drew 6.

1970 – Cooper's third Euro title

Englishman Henry Cooper won the European heavyweight title for the third time when he stopped Jose Manuel Urtain of Spain in the ninth round in London. Cooper was one of the few to knock down Muhammad Ali during a fight (1963).

1990 – Suns' NBA scoring mark

The Phoenix Suns shattered the NBA scoring record with 107 points in the first half during their 173-143 win at home over the Denver Nuggets. The Suns also tied with the 1959 Boston Celtics for most points scored in a non-overtime game. Suns coach Cotton Fitzsimmons also picked up his 700th career victory.

1991 – Proteas return

South Africa played its first international match in 21 years – a one-day international against India in Calcutta. Global opposition to apartheid had seen them ostracised since they beat Australia in 1969–70. India won by 3-wickets, although Proteas fast bowler Allan Donald announced himself to the world with 5 for 29.

1991 – Rivals in a tie

Martina Navratilova claimed her 157th title with a 6-3, 3-6, 6-3 win over Monica Seles in the California Virginia Slims event. The victory tied Navratilova with Chris Evert with most career titles.

1993 – O Canada

In a huge upset, rugby minnows Canada beat Wales 26-24 in Cardiff. Al Charron scored a try in the dying seconds for Gareth Rees to convert and seal the historic victory. In 2003 Charron, as the only remaining member of the 1993 team, went on to captain Canada in the Rugby World Cup.

1996 – Marino first to 50,000 yards

Miami Dolphins quarterback Dan Marino became the first player in NFL history to reach 50,000 passing yards with a 36-yard completion to O.J. McDuffie during a 37-13 win at home to Indianapolis. Only 3 other have achieved the feat – John Elway (1998), Brett Favre (2005) and Peyton Manning (2009).

1998 – Four tons in ODI match

Four batsmen made hundreds in a one-day international for the first time when Australia beat Pakistan by 6 wickets in Lahore. The centurions were Ijaz Ahmed (111) and Yousuf Youhana (100) for Pakistan, and Adam Gilchrist (103) and Ricky Ponting (124) for Australia.

2000 – Bangladesh arrives

Bangladesh became the 10th country to join cricket's top level, when they began their inaugural Test against India in Dhaka. For 3 days, they acquitted themselves admirably, before India stepped up for a 9-wicket win.

BIRTHDATES

1933	West Indian Test batsman SEYMOUR NURSE
1939	Canadian/Australian auto racer ALLAN MOFFAT
1963	American long jumper MIKE POWELL
1963	NFL coach MIKE McCARTHY
1965	Irish auto racer EDDIE IRVINE
1965	Welsh rugby union captain ROBERT JONES
1967	Australian triathlete JACKIE GALLAGHER
1969	Colombian soccer forward FAUSTINO ASPRILLA
1969	German soccer goalie JENS LEHMANN
1972	NFL wide receiver ISAAC BRUCE
1973	Czech soccer midfielder PATRIK BERGER
1976	Norwegian soccer striker STEFFEN IVERSEN

1969 – First series win to Kiwis
After 39 years of participation in top-class cricket, New Zealand clinched their first-ever series victory, with a drawn third Test against Pakistan in Dacca. Mark Burgess and Bob Cunis added a then-record 94 for the ninth wicket to set Pakistan an unlikely 184 in 37-overs. Bad light stopped play and a minor riot led to play being abandoned over an hour before close. The Kiwis had won the second Test in Lahore to take the series 1-0.

1984 – Oilers streak over
The Stanley Cup champion Edmonton Oilers had their NHL record 15-game season commencing unbeaten streak broken when beaten 7-5 by the Philadelphia Flyers at the Spectrum in Philadelphia. The Oilers had their revenge, whipping the Flyers in 5 games in the Stanley Cup finals.

1987 – One day, 2 games for Hughes
In the only occurrence of a player appearing in an international and an official club match on the same day, Mark Hughes was capped by Wales in a 0-2 European Championship loss to Czechoslovakia in Prague, then flew to Germany and came on as a substitute for Bayern Munich.

1990 – Thomas' QB sacks record
Kansas City Chiefs linebacker Derrick Thomas set an NFL record with 7 quarterback sacks against the Seattle Seahawks. He almost had 8 on the game's final play but Dave Krieg threw a touchdown for Seattle to win 17-16. Thomas suffered a severe spinal injury in a road accident in 2000 and died a month later in Miami. He was 33.

1995 – Hakeem joins 20,000 club
Houston centre Hakeem Olajuon scored 21 points in the Rockets' 119-97 victory over visiting Minnesota to became the ninth NBA player to collect 20,000 points and 10,000 career rebounds.

1995 – Sizzling Shane
Australia's record-breaking spinner Shane Warne took 7 for 23 as Pakistan was dismissed for a dismal 97 in

Welsh striker Mark Hughes during the 1987 European Championship qualifying match against Czechoslovakia in Prague. The Czechs won the match 2-0.

the first Test in Brisbane. Warne finished with match figures of 11 for 77.

2007 – Favre throws for 60,000 yards
Green Bay's Brett Favre joined Dan Marino as the only quarterbacks in NFL history to throw for more than 60,000 career yards during the Packers' 34-0 win over Minnesota at Lambeau Field.

BIRTHDATES
1924   Indian Test batsman RUSI MODI – died 1996
1937   Italian auto racer VITTORIO BRAMBILLA – died 2001
1942   West Indian Test batsman ROY FREDERICKS – died 2000
1943   Australian swim coach DOUG FROST
1949   American golfer KATHY POSTLEWAIT
1951   American golfer FRANK 'FUZZY' ZOELLER
1954   England rugby union hooker STEVE BRAIN
1967   Brazilian auto racer GIL DE FERRAN
1977   England Test all-rounder BEN HOLLIOAKE – died 2002.
1977   Portuguese soccer midfielder MANICHE
1986   French rugby player FRANÇOIS TRINH-DUC
1989   Scottish auto racer LEWIS WILLIAMSON

1920 – 'Czar of Baseball' hired

In the wake of the 'Black Sox Scandal' in 1919, Major League Baseball owners replaced the 3-man commission system by hiring a single commissioner, Judge Kenesaw Mountain Landis, to oversee the sport. Landis was given broad powers to police the sport's operation. He held the job until his death in 1944.

1921 – Gregory fires

Australian batsman Jack Gregory smashed the then fastest Test century by an Australian, off just 67 balls during the second Test against South Africa in Johannesburg. Gregory hit 19 fours and 2 sixes in his innings of 119 in just 85 minutes.

1985 – Kiwi first in Australia

New Zealand beat Australia by an innings and 41 runs for its first ever Test victory on Australian soil. Despite a battling 152 not out from Allan Border and 115 by Greg Matthews, the Kiwis' champion fast bowler Richard Hadlee captured 6 for 71 as Australia was dismissed for 333. New Zealand captain Martin Crowe earlier set up the win with a fine 188 after Hadlee took a brilliant 9 for 52 in the Aussie first innings.

1986 – NBA game with no head coaches

For the first time in NBA history, both head coaches were absent from a match. K.C. Jones of the Boston Celtics and Don Nelson of the Milwaukee Bucks were both too ill to attend the Celtics' 124-116 victory in Boston.

1988 – Sanders' College 5 TDs

Oklahoma State tailback Barry Sanders set a new NCAA season touchdown record by scoring 5 times against Kansas in a 63-24 thrashing in Stillwater, Oklahoma. Sanders' touchdown tally stood at 31 in 9 games, breaking the record of 29 set by Penn State's Lydell Mitchell in 1971 and Nebraska's Mike Rozier in 1983. Sanders' 312 yards on 37 carries made him only the third player in NCAA history to run for 2,000 yards in a season. He finished the season with 2,628 rushing yards and 39 touchdowns. He also won the Heisman Trophy in a landslide, then nominated for the NFL draft, to be picked up by the Detroit Lions.

1990 – Clubs fined after brawl

An FA disciplinary commission fined Arsenal and Manchester United £50,000 each for failure to control their players after a 21-man brawl erupted at Old Trafford during their October League Premiership match. Arsenal also had 2 premiership points deducted, and United 1.

2006 – Many happy Hester returns

Chicago Bears cornerback Devin Hester returned a missed field goal 108 yards against the New York Giants, tying the longest defensive touchdown run in the NFL, set on November 13, 2005 by Nathan Vasher, also of the Chicago Bears.

2011 – UFC officially arrives

The UFC's first fight on prime-time network television was an unqualified success as Junior Dos Santos stopped Cain Velasquez just 1:04 into their heavyweight title bout in Anaheim, California. It was a swift end to the mixed martial arts promotion's first show before millions of presumptive newcomers to the sport.

BIRTHDATES

1895	Spanish tennis player MANUEL ALONSO – died 1984
1910	South African Test batsman DUDLEY NOURSE – died 1981
1916	Pro Football Hall of Fame quarterback SID LUCKMAN – died 1998
1936	American golfer MARY RUTH JESSEN – died 2007
1943	Swedish rally driver BJÖRN WALDEGÅRD
1944	American sports caster AL MICHAELS
1944	Pro Football Hall of Fame safety KEN HOUSTON
1954	Australian tennis player PAUL McNAMEE
1957	England rugby union flanker NICK JEAVONS
1961	Rumanian gymnast NADIA COMANECI
1967	American boxer MICHAEL MOORER
1968	Dominican Republic baseball slugger SAMMY SOSA
1970	American figure skater TONYA HARDING
1975	American swimmer JASON LEZAK
1979	American golfer LUCAS GLOVER
1980	England rugby union fly-half CHARLIE HODGSON
1988	NBA guard RUSSELL WESTBROOKE

1963 – Sporting's Euro scoring record

Portuguese club Sporting Lisbon created a new record for the highest score in a major European club competition when they beat Cypriot club Apoel Nicosia 16-1 in Lisbon. The match was a European Cup Winners' Cup second round tie. Sporting went on to win the tournament.

1982 – Boxing tragedy

WBA lightweight champion Ray 'Boom Boom' Mancini scored a tragic TKO win over 23-year-old South Korean Deuk Koo Kim in the 14th round in Las Vegas. Moments after the fight, Kim collapsed and underwent surgery to relieve a blood clot in his brain. He never regained consciousness and died 5 days later. The fight was a catalyst to title bouts being reduced from 15 to 12 rounds.

1982 – Alderman's famous tackle

Australian fast bowler Terry Alderman dislocated his shoulder when tackling one of several spectators who invaded the WACA ground in Perth during the first Test against England. Alderman, who had taken 41 wickets in England in 1981, was thereafter persistently troubled by shoulder injuries but was still around for the 1989 Ashes Tour where he took another 41 scalps.

1985 – First female Globetrotter

US Olympic team captain Lynette Woodard became the first woman to play for the Harlem Globetrotters, scoring 7 points in at Spokane, Washington.

1990 – 'Magic' makes 9,000 assists

Ervin 'Magic' Johnson became only the second guard in NBA history to reach the 9,000 career assists mark (joining Oscar Robertson) in a 112-111 loss to Phoenix in LA.

1992 – Bowe takes Holyfield's title

Roddick Bowe won the undisputed world heavyweight title in Las Vegas with a unanimous points decision over Evander Holyfield. The 25-year-old Bowe landed 115 more punches in a one-sided contest. It was Holyfield's first defeat of his pro career. The following year, Holyfield beat Bowe in a close points decision to regain the title.

1999 – Lennox first Brit to win title

Lennox Lewis became the first British undisputed World Heavyweight Champion of the 20th century when he beat Evander Holyfield in a unanimous points decision in Las Vegas.

2004 – Record netball crowd

A world record crowd of 14,339 saw Australia beat New Zealand 54-49 at the Sydney SuperDome. The victory broke a 4-match NZ winning streak in internationals between the 2 leading netball nations.

2004 – Most goals in EPL game

Arsenal beat north London rivals Tottenham Hotspur 5-4 at White Hart Lane to equal what was then the largest aggregate number of goals scored in an Premier League match. Nine different players scored.

2005 – NFL return record

The Minnesota Vikings became the first team in NFL history to get touchdown returns on a punt, a kickoff and an interception, in their upset 24-21 win over the New York Giants at the Meadowlands. Safety Darren Sharper returned an interception for 92yards; Koren Robinson returned the second-half kickoff 86 yards; and Mewelde Moore ran a punt back 71 yards.

BIRTHDATES

1913	Australian AFL footballer JACK DYER – died 2003
1938	American golfer JACK RULE
1943	American golfer JAY SIGEL
1952	American golfer MARK LYE
1955	American golfer BILL BRITTON
1959	American golfer ROSIE JONES
1963	NFL quarterback VINNY TESTAVERDE
1972	Australian swimmer SAMANTHA RILEY
1973	French rugby union lock DAVID AURADOU
1974	New Zealand rugby union prop CARL HOEFT
1975	Portuguese soccer goalkeeper QUIM
1979	NBA forward METTA WORLD PEACE
1987	American swimmer DANA VOLLMER

1931 – Dixie heads a quick 3 from 5

Everton striker Dixie Dean scored the fastest hat-trick of headed goals, against Chelsea at Goodison Park. The headers came in a 10-minute period between the 5th and 15th minutes.

1934 – Seven Gunners get a go

Arsenal supplied a record 7 players in the England starting line up, in a 3-2 win against Italy at Highbury. The 7 Gunners were Cliff Bastin, Ted Drake, Frank Moss, George Male, Eddie Hapgood, Wilf Copping and Ray Bowden.

1943 – Luckman's record 7 TDs

Sid Luckman of the Chicago Bears threw a record 7 touchdown passes in a 56-7 rout of the New York Giants. He passed for 433 yards, becoming the first quarterback to surpass 400-yards. The record was later equalled by Adrian Burke (1954), George Blanda (1961), Y.A. Tittle (1962) and Joe Kapp (1969).

1943 – Baugh an incredible utility

Washington Redskins quarterback Sammy Baugh became the only NFL player to throw 4 interceptions and intercept 4 passes in a game, as the Redskins beat the Detroit Lions 42-20. Baugh also played safety in defence and in 1943 became the only player to lead the league in passing, interceptions and punting.

1947 – LaMotta stopped for first time

Jake LaMotta was stopped for the first time in 82 fights when Billy Fox scored a fourth-round TKO win in New York. Before the fight there was a huge betting plunge on Fox after La Motta had been the favourite. La Motta later alleged he had thrown the fight in exchange for a shot at the world middleweight title.

1970 – College Football plane tragedy

The plane carrying Marshall University's football team crashed on its approach to the runway at the Tri-State Airport in the Appalachian Mountains. All 75 aboard were killed, including 37 players and 5 coaches.

1973 – Moore's last for England

England legend Bobby Moore played his last international against Italy at Wembley. It was Moore's 108th England appearance. Italy won the match 1-0.

1993 – Schula coaching record

Don Shula surpassed George Halas as the NFL's all-time winningest coach, when his Miami Dolphins beat the Philadelphia Eagles 19-14 for his 325th career victory.

1998 – Celebrity Marriage:

NBA rebound champion Dennis Rodman married *Baywatch* beauty Carmen Electra in Las Vegas. After 9 days, Rodman filed papers to annul the marriage.

2005 – Webb youngest Hall of Famer

Thirty-year-old Australian golfer Karrie Webb became the youngest ever inductee into the World Golf Hall of Fame in St Augustine, Florida. Webb joined fellow Australians Peter Thomson and Greg Norman.

2012 – 'Best goal ever'

Sweden captain Zlatan Ibrahimovic scored 4 times to give his side a 4-2 win over England in Stockholm. The Paris St Germain striker had put the home side in front after 20 minutes, but goals from Danny Welbeck and Steven Caulker gave England the lead before the break. Ibrahimovic then found space to volley in an equaliser, before blasting home a free-kick from distance to restore Sweden's lead on the opening night at the new national stadium. He saved the best until last – an outrageous long-range overhead volley, after Joe Hart had failed to clear with his head.

BIRTHDATES

1877	Australian tennis player NORMAN BROOKES – died 1968
1904	England Test fast bowler HAROLD LARWOOD – died 1995.
1912	American golfer/designer GEORGE FAZIO – died 1986
1918	Australian tennis player JOHN BROMWICH – died 1999
1927	Australian horse trainer BART CUMMINGS
1947	Australian surfer NAT YOUNG
1954	French cyclist BERNARD HINAULT
1954	MLB pitcher WILLIE HERNANDEZ
1959	England soccer goalkeeper CHRIS WOODS
1966	MLB pitcher CURT SHILLING
1971	Australian Test wicketkeeper ADAM GILCHRIST
1979	New Zealand rugby union prop CARL HAYMAN
1985	Belgian soccer defender THOMAS VERMAELEN

1947 – Bradman's 100 centuries

Don Bradman cracked 172 for an Australian XI against India in Sydney for his 100th first-class century. In all, Bradman made 117 first-class centuries in 338 innings, a staggering ratio of a century every 2.88 innings.

1960 – Baylor's record 71 points

LA Lakers acrobatic forward Elgin Baylor broke his own NBA scoring record with 71 points in a 123-108 victory over the Knicks in New York. The 6ft 5in Baylor became the only NBA forward at that time to ever score more than 70 points, connecting on 28 field goals and 15 foul shots. His previous record was 64.

1965 – First over 600mph

Twenty-eight-year-old American Craig Breedlove set a new land-speed record of 600.601mph to become the first man to officially go faster than 600mph. Driving the Spirit of America at the Bonneville Salt Flats in Utah, Breedlove made 2 timed 1-mile runs at 593.178mph and 608.201mph to set the new mark.

1984 – Tasty quintet fight debut

Evander Holyfield, Pernell Whitaker, Meldrick Taylor, Mark Breland, and Virgil Hill made successful professional debuts on the same card at Madison Square Garden. All succeeded in winning multiple world titles.

1992 – Petty bows out in fiery crash

Champion NASCAR driver Richard Petty ended a 35-year career, crashing out of the Hooters 500 at Atlanta Motor Speedway. He was unhurt in the fiery accident. In 1,185 Winston Cup race appearances, Petty scored 200 victories. He was a 7-time NASCAR Winston Cup champion and also won the Daytona 500 7 times. He was Driver of the Year in 1967 and 1971.

1994 – Martina retires

Martina Navratilova announced her retirement after a disappointing first-round loss in the Virginia Slams Championships in New York. Navratilova ended her career with 167 titles, including 18 Grand Slam wins and $26.7 million in prize money.

Tennis champion Martina Navratilova.

2004 – Bonds' seventh NL MVP award

Forty-year-old San Francisco Giants left fielder Barry Bonds won his record seventh, and fourth consecutive, National League MVP award and became the oldest player to become the MVP of a major North American professional league. Among the 4 major league sports, Bonds was second in MVPs to the NHL's Wayne Gretzky, who won nine.

2011 – 'Coach K' tops all-time list

Mike Krzyzewski became the winningest coach in NCAA Division I men's basketball history thanks to Duke's 74-69 home win over Michigan State. It was his 903rd career victory in a 36 year career. He overtook Bob Knight's mark of 902 wins, achieved over 42 years.

BIRTHDATES

1903	New Zealand Test batsman STEWIE DEMPSTER – died 1974
1936	American NASCAR driver H. B. BAILEY – died 2003
1952	Pro wrestler 'Macho Man' RANDY SAVAGE – died 2011
1967	New Zealand rugby union halfback JON PRESTON
1967	Uruguayan soccer midfielder/manager GUS POYET
1970	Cameroon footballer PATRICK M'BOMA DEM
1981	Mexican golfer LORENA OCHOA
1983	Spanish tennis player FERNANDO VERDASCO
1988	French rugby halfback MORGAN PARRA

⑯ NOVEMBER

1938 – Fastest football treble
England striker Willie Hall scored the fastest ever hat-trick in an international match when he scored 5 goals against Ireland at Old Trafford. Hall's first 3 strikes came in a 3½ minute period during England's 7-0 victory.

1957 – Russell rebound king
Bill Russell of the Boston Celtics snared an NBA record 32 rebounds in one half in a 111-89 Celtics' home victory over Philadelphia. He finished the game with 49. In 1960 Russell grabbed 51 rebounds in a game against Syracuse. Only Wilt Chamberlain with 55 ever took more rebounds in a game.

1957 – Oklahoma streak over
The longest winning streak in college football history ended when Notre Dame upset Oklahoma 7-0 at Owen Field in Norman. The Sooners had won 47 consecutive games in a steak spanning 5 seasons 1953–7. Just a few days earlier, the Oklahoma team was featured on the cover of Sports Illustrated, with the headline, 'Why Oklahoma is Unbeatable.'

1981 – Famous cricket confrontation
There was controversy on the fourth afternoon of the first Test between Australia and Pakistan in Perth, when an angry Australian fast bowler Dennis Lillee deliberately impeded and aimed a kick at Pakistan batsman Javed Miandad, sparking a famous spat. Miandad threatened to hit Lillee with his bat, before umpire Tony Crafter intervened. As the initiator, Lillee was suspended from 2 ODIs.

1983 – Devastating Dev
India's Kapil Dev took 9 for 83 in the third Test against the West Indies in Ahmedabad to become the first captain to take 9 wickets in a Test innings. But in a low-scoring game India was blown away – dismissed for just 103, chasing 242.

1993 – Free throw streak ends
Denver Nuggets guard Mahmoud Abdul-Rauf had his consecutive free throw streak end at 81 in an 86-74 home loss against San Antonio. Abdul-Rauf's streak

Indian Test cricket captain Kapil Dev.

was the second longest in NBA history, trailing only the record 97 established by Minnesota's Michael Williams a week earlier.

2008 – Johnson takes third straight title
With a 15th place finish in the season-ending Ford 400, Jimmie Johnson won his third consecutive NASCAR Sprint Cup Series title, tying Cale Yarborough for that record.

BIRTHDATES
1862	Australian Test fast bowler CHARLIE TURNER – died 1944
1894	American golfer BOBBY CRUICKSHANK – died 1975
1906	American jockey CHARLES KURTSINGER – died 1946
1942	Scottish jockey WILLIE CARSON
1943	New Zealand rugby union halfback CHRIS LAIDLAW
1951	New Zealand rugby union hooker ANDY DALTON
1959	American golfer COREY PAVIN
1961	English boxer FRANK BRUNO
1963	American tennis player ZINA GARRISON
1964	MLB pitcher DWIGHT GOODEN
1971	Pakistan Test captain WAQAR YOUNIS
1971	Russian swimmer ALEX POPOV
1974	England soccer striker PAUL SCHOLES
1977	Ukrainian gymnast OKSANA BAIUL
1979	American surfer BRUCE IRONS
1982	South African rugby prop JANNIE DU PLESSIS
1983	German swimmer BRITTA STEFFEN
1986	French rugby player MAXIME MÉDARD

1956 – Brown's College Football record
Syracuse running back Jim Brown set an NCAA record by scoring 6 touchdowns and 7 conversions for 43 points in a 61-7 win over Colgate. Brown carried the ball 22 times for 197 yards and had touchdown runs of 50, 19, 15, and 8 yards, plus 2 one-yard plunges.

1963 – Four straight Vares to Mickey
Mickey Wright won her fourth consecutive Vare Trophy with a scoring average of 72.81, another LPGA record. Wright broke her record the following year with a 72.46 average and a still-standing record fifth consecutive Vare Trophy.

1993 – Fastest international score
San Marino's Davide Gualtieri scored the fastest ever goal in international football, when he nailed one in just 8.3 seconds against England in a World Cup match in Bologna, Italy. England won 7-1.

1993 – Heavyweights implode
The foursome of the year's major champions combined for 2 triple bogeys and 4 double bogeys, playing in the PGA Grand Slam of Golf at the PGA West course in La Quinta, California. Greg Norman finished at 1-over par 145 for 36 holes to win by 2 strokes over Paul Azinger, who earlier in the year had beaten him in a 2-hole playoff for the PGA title. Bernhard Langer and Lee Janzen shared third at 148.

1996 – Youthful solo yachting feat
Eighteen-year-old Australian David Dicks became the youngest person to circumnavigate the globe solo, non-stop, on the 10-metre sloop *Sea Flight*. The trip took 264 days. Californian Zac Sunderland, 17, took over Dicks' youthful mantle in 2009.

2000 – Kidd tops for turnover
Phoenix Suns guard Jason Kidd tied the NBA record for turnovers in a game with 14 in a 90-85 loss to New York. Kidd tied with John Drew of the Atlanta Hawks for the dubious record.

2001 – Lleyton youngest #1
Twenty-year-old Lleyton Hewitt of Australia became

At 20, the youngest WTA no. 1 ranked player, Lleyton Hewitt.

the youngest world no. 1 ranked player, when he beat countryman Patrick Rafter in straight sets in the Masters Cup in Sydney. Hewitt won the match 7-5, 6-2 and went on to beat Frenchman Sébastien Grosjean in the final.

2007 – 'Gilly' first to 100 sixes
During his unbeaten 67 against Sri Lanka in the second Test in Hobart, Australian wicketkeeper Adam Gilchrist hit his 99th and 100th career 6 over midwicket off consecutive deliveries from ace spinner Muttiah Muralitharan. He finished his career with an even 100.

BIRTHDATES
1901	English golfer JOYCE WETHERED – died 1997
1905	Australian Test batsman ARTHUR CHIPPERFIELD – died 1987
1922	England soccer midfielder JACK FROGGATT – died 1993
1923	New Zealand Test batsman BERT SUTCLIFFE – died 2001
1928	Australian Test opener COLIN McDONALD
1930	American decathlete BOB MATHIAS – died 2006
1930	Austrian alpine skier TONI SAILER – died 2009
1938	New Zealand middle distance runner PETER SNELL
1942	Australian marathon runner DEREK CLAYTON
1944	Baseball Hall of Fame pitcher TOM SEAVER
1945	Basketball Hall of Fame centre ELVIN HAYES
1949	Australian swimmer MICHAEL WENDEN
1950	German swimmer ROLAND MATTHES
1959	England soccer defender TERRY FENWICK
1965	Australian jockey DARREN BEADMAN
1977	South African swimmer RYK NEETHLING
1983	Australian swimmer JODIE HENRY
1986	Portuguese soccer winger NANI

🔞 NOVEMBER

1929 – Starting blocks legal
The Amateur Athletic Union decided to accept track world track records from races using starting blocks.

1959 – Outsider Baker plays for England
Hibernian striker Joe Baker became the first player outside the Football League to play for England. Baker scored in England's 2-1 win over Northern Ireland at Wembley Stadium. He went on to earn 8 England caps.

1970 – Frazier too strong for Foster
Joe Frazier knocked out world light-heavyweight champion Bob Foster in 2 rounds in Detroit to retain his heavyweight title. On the official tale of the tape, Frazier outweighed Foster by 21lbs. In the second round, Foster was tagged with 2 lefts and counted out.

1982 – 'First' retirement for Leonard
'Sugar' Ray Leonard made the first of 5 career retirement announcements, 5 months after retinal surgery on his left eye. In the 1980s Leonard won an unprecedented 5 world titles in 5 weight divisions and competed in some of the era's most memorable contests including his famous trilogy with tough Panamanian Roberto Duran (won 2, lost 1). In 40 fights, Leonard won 36 (25 KOs), lost 3 and drew 1.

1989 – Russian NBA confrontation
For the first time in NBA history, 2 players from the Soviet Union met on the court.

1988
Olympic gold medallists Alexander Volkov of the Atlanta Hawks and Golden State's Šarunas Marciulionis faced off as the Hawks downed the Warriors, 112-96.

1990 – Seles in five
Monica Seles captured the first official 5-set match in women's tennis since 1901 when she defeated Gabriela Sabatini in the final of the Virginia Slims Championships in New York. Seles won the match 6-4, 5-7, 3-6, 6-4, 6-2 in 3 hours 47 minutes.

1997 – Elegant Els
South African Ernie Els finished with a final-round 65

South African golfer Ernie Els during the 1997 PGA Grand Slam of Golf in Hawaii.

to set an event-record 11-under 133 to win the PGA Grand Slam of Golf at Poipu Bay in Kauai, Hawaii.

2007 – Federer in the money
Top-ranked Roger Federer won his fourth Masters Cup title in 5 years, overwhelming David Ferrer 6-2, 6-3, 6-2 in Shanghai. It was Federer's 53rd career title. Federer collected $1.2 million and a new car for the win, increasing his winnings in 2007 to over $10 million – a record for the ATP Tour.

BIRTHDATES
1900	American jockey ALBERT JOHNSON – died 1966
1901	American golfer CRAIG WOOD – died 1968
1941	American auto racer GARY BETTENHAUSEN
1956	NFL quarterback WARREN MOON
1963	Danish soccer goalkeeper PETER SCHMEICHEL
1968	MLB slugger GARY SHEFFIELD
1980	American auto racer DENNY HAMLIN
1985	American sprinter ALLYSON FELIX

1932 – 'Bodyline' here we come!
English fast bowler Harold Larwood hit Australian Test captain Bill Woodfull just above the heart with a vicious bouncer during the MCC's tour match against an Australian XI in Melbourne. The incident was a forerunner to England captain Douglas Jardine's infamous leg-theory tactic.

1961 – Blanda's magnificent seven
Houston's George Blanda tied an NFL record when he threw 7 touchdowns against the New York Titans. Blanda equalled the record first set by Sid Luckman (1943) and then Adrian Burk (1954).

1966 – Koufax retires
Los Angeles Dodgers pitcher Sandy Koufax announced his retirement after a season in which he won 27 games. The 30-year-old Koufax, who had won the Cy Young Award 3 times in 5 seasons, was troubled by an arthritic left elbow.

1969 – Pelé hits 1,000 mark
Pelé scored his 1,000th goal in senior football, a penalty in a 2-1 win for Santos against Vasco da Gama at the Maracanã Stadium in Rio de Janeiro. During a brilliant career, Pelé played 93 internationals for Brazil, scoring a record 97 goals. He also scored a remarkable 1,280 goals in 1,360 first-class games. He led Santos to 2 World Club championships and also holds the world record for hat-tricks (92).

1983 – Kareem reaches 30,000
Kareem Abdul-Jabbar of the LA Lakers became the second player in NBA history to score 30,000 points, joining Wilt Chamberlain at that plateau, as the Lakers won 117-110 at Portland. Kareem retired in 1989 as all-time points leader with 38,387.

2004 – NBA brawl
In one of the most disgraceful incidents in NBA history, players from the Detroit Pistons and Indiana Pacers were involved in a brawl with spectators at The Palace in Detroit. The melee was sparked by a clash between Pacers' guard Ron Artest and Ben Wallace of the Pistons, and spread into the stands. Nine players involved received a total of 143 match suspensions. Artest suffered the harshest penalty – a season suspension, encompassing 73 games and costing him $5.5 million.

2005 – Chelsea's world record youth signing
English Premier League champions Chelsea reached an agreement with OFK Belgrade to sign highly-rated 16-year-old Slobodan Rajkovi . The £3.5m deal for the young centre-half was a world record for a player under 18 years of age.

2006 – LT fastest to 100 TDs
San Diego running back LaDainian Tomlinson scored 4 times and reached 100 touchdowns faster than any player in NFL history, leading the Chargers past the Denver Broncos 35-27 in Denver. Tomlinson reached 100 TDs in his 89th game, 4 fewer than it took Hall of Famer Jim Brown and Emmitt Smith.

2006 – McCallum kicks in Canada
Paul McCallum tied a title game record, landing 6 field goals, while scoring 19 total points as the BC Lions posted a 25-14 win over the Montreal Alouettes in Winnipeg in the 94th Grey Cup game.

2009 – First-class catches
Wicketkeeper Peter McGlashan set the first-class world record for most catches in a match when he took 6 in each innings against Central Districts in Whangarei in New Zealand. Six of his catches came off the bowling of Graeme Aldrige, who took 11 wickets in the match.

BIRTHDATES
1921	MLB catcher ROY CAMPANELLA – died 1993
1938	Australian Test fast bowler FRANK MISSON
1938	Media /sports mogul TED TURNER
1942	American golfer LARRY GILBERT – died 1998
1949	English snooker player DENNIS TAYLOR
1955	England rugby union flanker DAVID H. COOKE
1965	French soccer defender/manager LAURENT BLANC
1966	American sprinter GAIL DEVERS
1976	Czech NHL right wing PETR SÝKORA
1977	American gymnast KERRI STRUG
1986	Australian swimmer JESSICAH SCHIPPER
1988	American NHL centre PATRICK KANE

1971 – L'Strange double
Centre Rex L'Estrange scored 2 tries on debut as Australia caused a massive upset in beating the highly rated French team 13-11 in the first international in Toulouse. France won the second game, 18-9 in Colombes to square the series.

1971 – MacDougall's FA Cup nine
Ted MacDougall scored 9 goals in Bournemouth's 11-0 thrashing of Margate in an FA Cup first-round match at Dean Court. The haul remains an FA Cup scoring record for one match.

1977 – Water speed mark
Ken Warby set a new world water speed record of just over 288.60mph at Blowering Dam, near Tumut, Australia in his jet boat *Spirit of Australia*. Warby went on to smash his record 11 months later, when he recorded a speed of 317mph at the same venue. The record still stands.

1977 – Payton's single game rushing record
Walter Payton of the Chicago Bears had a 58-yard run in the closing minutes of a 10-7 win over the Minnesota Vikings at Soldier Field, creating an NFL record 275 yards for the game. The record was broken by Cincinnati's Corey Dillon (278) in 2000 and by Baltimore's Jamal Lewis (295) in 2003.

1997 – Green's consecutive NBA game mark
A. C. Green of the Dallas Mavericks set an NBA record by playing in his 907th consecutive game when the Mavs lost 101-97 at home against Golden State. Green broke Randy Smith's record of 906 (1972–83). Green added to the record, playing in 1,192 games, still an NBA record.

2005 – Sörenstam another perfect 10
Annika Sörenstam closed another spectacular year with her 10th victory, holding off a spirited charge from Liselotte Neumann for a 2-stroke victory in the ADT Championshi p at West Palm Beach, Florida. She also captured her sixth Vare Trophy for the lowest scoring average, finishing at 69.3.

2009 – Sachin reaches 30,000 run milestone
Sachin Tendulkar became the first man to make 30,000 international runs, on the final day of the first Test between India and Sri Lanka in Ahmedabad. His 35th run meant the 12,777 Test runs, 17,178 one-day international runs and 10 from his lone Twenty20 game, added up to the record. He finished on 100 not out in the draw.

2011 – Furyk's fabulous five
Jim Furyk became the fourth player to win all 5 of his matches, as the Americans scored their fourth straight win in the President Cup golf competition in Melbourne, Australia. The US team held on the beat the Internationals 19-15.

2011 – Great drive for Stewart
In one of the greatest drives in NASCAR history, Tony Stewart won the Ford 400 at Homestead-Miami Speedway, holding off Carl Edwards for a tie in the final Sprint Cup Series standings – good enough to win his third title. It was the first tie in the points-standings in NASCAR history. Stewart drove from the back twice and passed 118 cars during the race.

2012 – NCAA record
Grinnell College's Jack Taylor scored an NCAA-record 138 points in a 179-104 Division III win over Faith Baptist Bible. The previous record was the 113-point performance from Rio Grande's Bevo Francis in 1954. David Larson scored 70 for Faith Baptist Bible.

BIRTHDATES
1866	MLB commissioner KENESAW MOUNTAIN LANDIS – died 1944
1917	South African golfer BOBBY LOCKE – died 1987
1929	American golfer DON JANUARY
1937	Finnish cross country skier EERO MÄNTYRANTA
1948	Swedish auto racer GUNNAR NILSSON – died 1978
1956	England rugby union prop GARETH CHILCOTT
1961	England soccer defender DAVE WATSON
1963	Australian rugby union number 8 TIM GAVIN
1965	American auto racer JIMMY VASSER
1968	American tennis player JEFF TARANGO
1971	New Zealand Test fast bowler DION NASH
1973	English motor cycle rider NEIL HODGSON
1974	Australian rower DREW GINN

1920 – 'Bloody Sunday'

After 11 British intelligence agents and 2 Auxiliaries were shot dead in their homes around Dublin on the morning of the Dublin-Tipperary friendly at Croke Park, a convoy of military lorries parked outside the venue and British troops fired from vantage points around the ground. Tipperary full-back Michael Hogan was shot dead together with 13 spectators.

1934 – DiMaggio trade

The New York Yankees acquired 19-year-old outfielder, Joe DiMaggio, from the San Francisco Seals for 5 players and $40,000 cash. DiMaggio remained with the Seals in 1935, and then hit .323 with 206 hits, 29 homers, 132 runs and 125 RBI as a rookie with the Yankees in 1936, helping them win the first of 4 consecutive World Series.

1977 – World Series Cricket launched

Media mogul Kerry Packer, as well as cricketers Sir Garfield Sobers, Richie Benaud and Ian Chappell, were in attendance as World Series Cricket was officially launched in Melbourne. Packer's failure to negotiate broadcasting rights with the Australian Cricket Board prompted him to sign 60 of the world's best players and start his own series. WSC lasted 18 months until Packer and the ACB came to an agreement.

1989 – First £1m goalie

Nigel Martyn became Britain's first £1 million goalkeeper when he was transferred from Bristol Rovers to Crystal Palace. Martyn became an England goalie and moved again in 1996 to Leeds United for another record fee of £2.25 million.

1990 – Long shot winner

At odds of 250-1, Equinoctial became the longest priced race winner in Britain with its win at Kelso.

2000 – Rio EPL transfer

English Premier League clubs Leeds United and West Ham United agreed on an £18 million transfer fee for Rio Ferdinand, making him the most expensive defender in the world. In 2002 Ferdinand moved to Man United for another record fee of £30 million.

Sinn Fein leader and Commander-in-Chief of the Irish Free State Army, Michael Collins, throws to start a hurling match at Croke Park, Dublin, scene of the 'Bloody Sunday' massacre the year before.

2010 – NASCAR title #5 for Johnson

Jimmie Johnson became the first driver in the 7-year history of the Chase for the Sprint Cup championship to overcome a points-deficit in the season finale at Homestead-Miami Speedway, finishing second to race winner Carl Edwards while winning his record fifth consecutive NASCAR title. The final margin was 39 points over Denny Hamlin.

BIRTHDATES

1870	England Test captain STANLEY JACKSON – died 1947
1870	Australian Test captain JOE DARLING – died 1946
1919	Swedish canoeist GERT FREDRIKSSON – died 2006
1934	Australian Test spinner PETER PHILPOTT
1943	French auto racer JACQUES LAFFITE
1944	Basketball Hall of Fame forward EARL MONROE
1952	American golfer GARY KOCH
1958	England Test batsman TIM ROBINSON
1959	Australian yachtsman COLIN BEASHEL
1960	England rugby union winger MARK BAILEY
1966	NFL quarterback TROY AIKMAN
1968	England Test fast bowler ANDY CADDICK
1968	American boxer ANTONIO TARVER
1969	MLB slugger KEN GRIFFEY JR
1969	New Zealand rugby union lock JAMIE JONES
1970	Australian Test batsman JUSTIN LANGER
1974	Australian Test captain KAREN ROLTON

1950 – Pistons keep the score down
Using a stall offence to keep the ball away from George Mikan, the Fort Wayne Pistons beat the Minneapolis Lakers 19-18 in the lowest scoring game in NBA history. Four years later, the 24-second shot clock was adopted to prevent any repeat of the tactic.

1965 – Clay KO's Patterson
World heavyweight champion Cassius Clay scored a 12th-round TKO win over former titleholder Floyd Patterson in Las Vegas. It was his second title defence after winning the championship from Sonny Liston in 1964 and then knocking him out in the first round of a farcical rematch in May 1965.

1972 – Ice hockey 5 in 2 minutes
Bryan Hextall, Jean Pronovost, Al McDonough, Ken Schinkel and Ron Schock of the Pittsburgh Penguins scored in a span of 2:07 in the third period of a 10-4 win over St Louis. The goal spree remains an NHL record for the fastest 5 goals.

1998 – Elway passes for 50,000 yards
Denver quarterback John Elway moved past 50,000 yards career passing in the Broncos' 40-14 win over Oakland at Mile High Stadium in Denver. Dan Marino was the first quarterback to achieve the feat in 1996. Brett Favre was added to the list in 2005 and Peyton Manning in 2009.

2000 – Zátopek dead at 78
All-time great Czech distance runner Emil Zátopek died aged 78. Zátopek won an unprecedented Olympic treble in Helsinki in 1952, winning the 5,000m, 10,000m, and the marathon. He also won the 10,000m in London in 1948. He broke the 10,000m world record on 5 occasions.

2003 – 'Jonny on the spot' England hero
Jonny Wilkinson landed a field goal in the final minute of extra time to give England a dramatic 20-17 win over Australia in the Rugby World Cup final in Sydney. The match was heading into sudden death after Wilkinson and Elton Flatley swapped penalties in extra-time, but Wilkinson's dropped goal sealed victory.

England fly-half Jonny Wilkinson kicking at goal during the 2003 World Cup final against Australia in Sydney. Wilkinson landed a dramatic field goal in the final minute of extra time to give England a 20-17 win.

2009 – NASCAR title #4 to Johnson, #12 to Hendrick
Jimmie Johnson clinched a record fourth consecutive NASCAR Championship with a fifth placing in the Ford 400 at Homestead-Miami Speedway. 25th place would have won him the title. In doing so, Johnson joined Richard Petty (7), Dale Earnhardt (7) and teammate Jeff Gordon (4) as the only drivers to win more than 3 titles. Johnson's title also gave a record 12th overall championship to team owner Rick Hendrick.

BIRTHDATES

1873	England Test batsman JOHNNY TYLDESLEY – died 1930
1911	American golfer RALPH GULDAHL – died 1987
1913	American tennis player GARDNAR MULLOY
1943	American tennis player BILLIE JEAN KING
1943	Pakistan Test batsman MUSHTAQ MOHAMMAD
1943	Canadian Hockey Hall of Fame forward YVAN COURNOYER
1953	England Test batsman WAYNE LARKINS
1967	German tennis player BORIS BECKER
1970	Sri Lankan Test batsman MARVIN ATAPATTU
1971	England rugby union halfback KYRAN BRACKEN
1972	French rugby union flanker OLIVIER BROUZET
1973	Australian rugby league/Union utility ANDREW WALKER
1974	Canadian pairs figure skater DAVID PELLETIER

1956 – Vinci sacrifice for gold
American bantamweight Charles Vinci set a world record by winning gold at the Melbourne Olympics. At the weigh-in, Vinci was 1½lbs over the limit, and was still 7oz overweight after an hour of running. He qualified by shaving off all his hair.

1963 – Breasley's fourth Premiership
Jockey Scobie Breasley won his fourth English Jockey's Premiership. Breasley rode 176 winners from 746 rides, beating Lester Piggott for the title by just 1 win.

1984 – Flutie first over 10,000 yards
Boston College quarterback Doug Flutie became the first to pass for more than 10,000 yards in a major-college career and also clinched the Heisman Trophy with a famous 'Hail Mary' at Miami's Orange Bowl. Boston trailed 45-41 with 6 seconds left when Flutie threw 64 yards to Gerard Phelan in the end zone, giving the Eagles an incredible 47-45 victory over the national champions. It was the first time college quarterbacks each surpassed 400 yards in one game – Flutie with 472 yards and Miami's Bernie Kosar 447.

1975 – Tarkenton breaks Unitas' mark
Thirty-five-year-old Minnesota Vikings quarterback Fran Tarkenton beat Johnny Unitas' NFL record for all-time pass completions during a 28-13 victory over San Diego in Bloomington, Minnesota. The 15-year veteran connected with Ed Marino for a 4-yard gain, the 2,831st completion of his career.

1991 – Football disgrace
Brazilian team America Tres Rios earned the unenviable record of the most dismissals by one team in a top-level match. Five players were sent off in the first 10 minutes after a disputed goal in the Cup-tie against Itaperuna in Rio de Janeiro. The game was abandoned and awarded to Itaperuna.

1994 – Hornacek hits 8 straight from the arc
Utah's Jeff Hornacek set an NBA record by sinking all 8 of his 3-point field goal attempts during the Jazz' 113-103 home win over Seattle. Hornacek broke the records of Terry Porter (1992) and Sam Perkins (1993), who both went 7-of-7. Perkins tied Hornacek's 8-for-8 performance in 1997.

1994 – Suns' 10 in double figures
The Phoenix Suns became the third NBA team to have 10 different players score double figures in the same game in their 140-109 home win over the LA Clippers. The Seattle SuperSonics achieved the feat twice, in 1980 and 1994.

2003 – Presidents Cup shared after tie
The Presidents Cup trophy was shared for the first time when bad light halted a playoff between Tiger Woods and Ernie Els after 3 holes at the Fancourt Hotel and Country Club in George, South Africa. Respective team captains Jack Nicklaus and Gary Player agreed a tie was the fairest result because of players' commitments if the playoff was to continue the following day. The US and International teams had tied 17-17.

BIRTHDATES

1928	Australian AFL full forward JOHN COLEMAN – died 1973
1930	MLB manager JACK McKEON
1934	Australian tennis player LEW HOAD – died 1994.
1935	Australian Test opener KEN EASTWOOD
1941	England soccer midfielder ALAN MULLERY
1953	Australian Test batsman MARTIN KENT
1956	New Zealand Test batsman BRUCE EDGAR
1956	Australian swimmer SHANE GOULD
1958	New Zealand Test fast bowler MARTIN SNEDDEN
1961	Australian Test fast bowler MERV HUGHES
1966	American golfer JERRY KELLY
1982	Jamaican sprinter ASAFA POWELL

Weightlifter Charles Vinci stands proudly at the no. 1 spot on the podium, having won gold at the 1956 Olympics.

㉔ NOVEMBER

1963 – Arnie's in the money ...
Arnold Palmer became first player to finish a PGA Tour season with earnings of more than $100,000, heading up the money list with $128,230 and 7 tournament victories.

1968 – ... Billy too
Billy Casper became the first player to top $200,000 in prize money on the PGA Tour in a single year, leading the money list with $205,168.

1984 – Rugby Grand Slam third leg complete
Australia beat Wales 28-9 at Cardiff Arms Park, the third leg of their Grand Slam tour of the British Isles. The Wallabies had already defeated England 19-3 and Ireland 16-9. They went on to down Scotland 37-12 at Murrayfield to complete the history-making undefeated tour.

1996 – Sensational Sanders
Detroit Lions running back Barry Sanders became the first NFL player to rush for over 1,000 yards in each of his first 8 seasons. In a stellar season, Sanders won the NFL rushing title, was selected to the Pro Bowl for the eighth time and became the first to rush for over 1,500 yards in 3 consecutive seasons.

1989 – Sachin youngest Test 50
At 16 years, 214 days, India's Sachin Tendulkar became the youngest batsman to make a Test 50 when he stroked 59 in the second Test against Pakistan in Faisalabad.

1996 – Webb first to $1m
Australian rookie Karrie Webb became the first female to earn $1 million in prize money in an LPGA season by winning the prestigious Tour Championship at the Desert Inn Golf Club in Nevada. Webb finished at 16-under 272, 4 ahead of Kelly Robbins, Nancy Lopez, and Emilee Klein.

2001 – Porter's unique treble
Terry Porter of the San Antonio Spurs had 3 assists in a 99-94 loss to Minnesota to achieve a unique record. He became the only player in NBA history to record

Spurs' guard Terry Porter in action during a 2001 NBA playoff game against Minnesota in San Antonio.

15,000 points, 7,000 assists, 1,000 steals and 1,000 3-pointers.

2011 – Harbaugh v Harbaugh
John and Jim Harbaugh became the first head-coaching brothers to meet in an NFL game, when John's Baltimore Ravens overpowered Jim's San Francisco 49ers, 16-6 in Baltimore. The pair would later square off in the 2013 Super Bowl, with similar results.

BIRTHDATES
1894	England Test batsman HERBERT SUTCLIFFE – died 1978.
1927	New Zealand rugby union prop KEVIN SKINNER
1930	England Test batsman KEN BARRINGTON – died 1981
1932	England Test spinner FRED TITMUS – died 2011
1938	Basketball Hall of Fame forward OSCAR ROBERTSON
1940	NFL Commissioner PAUL TAGLIABUE
1943	Basketball Hall of Fame guard DAVE BING
1951	Welsh rugby union prop GRAHAM PRICE
1955	England Test all rounder IAN BOTHAM
1955	England rugby union winger JOHN CARLETON
1962	Australian swimmer TRACEY WICKHAM
1969	Sri Lanka Test wicketkeeper ROMESH KALUWITHARANA
1955	American golfer SCOTT HOCH
1971	Kenyan marathon runner COSMAS NDETI
1984	German alpine skier MARIA HÖFL-RIESCH

1970 – Shilton era starts

Goalkeeper Peter Shilton made his international debut for England in a 3-1 win against East Germany at Wembley Stadium. He went on to make a record 125 appearances in an England career spanning 20 seasons.

1980 – 'Sugar' Ray exacts his revenge

After losing his welterweight crown to Roberto Duran in June, Sugar Ray Leonard changed his strategy in a famous re-match in New Orleans, with devastating results. Leonard avoided any brawling and boxed the tough Panamanian into submission with 16 seconds remaining in the eighth round.

2000 – Consecutive Test mark tied

Australia equalled the record of 11 successive Test wins set by the West Indies in 1984 when they beat the Windies in the first Test in Brisbane, the start of a 5-Test sweep. Australian fast bowler Glenn McGrath returned astonishing match figures of 10 for 27, with 4 for 10 and 6 for 17.

2000 – Paralympic cover-up

The Spanish Paralympic Committee opened an inquiry into allegations by basketballer, Carlos Ribagorda that up to 15 members of the team, including 10 from the basketball squad did not suffer from learning difficulties. The allegations were confirmed and the basketball team was forced to return their gold medals. Because of the difficulties of testing, all events for people with learning difficulties were abolished for the Athens Paralympics.

2005 – George Best dies

Former Manchester United and Northern Ireland football legend George Best died in London aged 59. Best passed away after multiple organ failure. Considered to be one of the most talented footballers of all-time, Best helped the Red Devils win the European Cup in 1968 while claiming the coveted European Player of the Year award. He won 37 caps for Northern Ireland but retired unexpectedly from Manchester United at the age of 28. He returned with stints at a number of clubs but before retiring in 1983.

'Sugar' Ray Leonard on his way to beating Roberto Duran in their famous 1980 welterweight title rematch in New Orleans.

2012 – Vettel youngest triple F1 champion

Red Bull's 25-year-old lead driver Sebastian Vettel became Formula One's youngest triple World Driver's champion after finishing sixth in a wet and chaotic Brazilian Grand Prix in São Paulo. Vettel joined the greats as the first driver to win his first 3 titles consecutively.

BIRTHDATES

1909	West Indian Test fast bowler MANNY MARTINDALE – died 1972
1914	Baseball Hall of Fame outfielder JOE DI MAGGIO – died 1999.
1923	American golfer ART WALL – died 2001.
1933	Pro Football Hall of Fame receiver LENNY MOORE
1940	NFL coach JOE GIBBS
1948	England rugby union flanker TONY NEARY
1949	Australian Test spinner KERRY O'KEEFFE
1951	Dutch soccer forward JOHNNY REP
1952	Pakistan Test captain IMRAN KHAN
1964	American golfer NOLAN HENKE
1965	NFL wide receiver/analyst CRIS CARTER
1967	Suriname swimmer ANTHONY NESTY
1977	Argentine tennis player GUILLERMO CAÑAS
1981	Spanish soccer midfielder XABI ALONSO
1984	Australian Test fast bowler PETER SIDDLE

1956 – Betty takes sprint gold
Betty Cuthbert ran 11.5 seconds to edge Germany's Christa Stubnick and fellow Australian Marlene Matthews in the 100m at the Melbourne Olympics. It was the first of 3 gold medals for the 18-year-old Cuthbert who also won the 200m and 4 x 100 relay.

1995 – Marino NFL TD leader
Miami Dolphins quarterback Dan Marino's threw his 343rd career touchdown pass to become the NFL's all-time leader. During the second quarter of a 36-28 loss at Indianapolis, Marino connected with a 6-yard TD pass to Keith Byars to break Fran Tarkenton's record.

1995 – Cricket tragedy
Nine people were killed and many seriously injured when the wall of a stand extension collapsed during lunch in the fifth ODI between India and New Zealand in Nagpur. The players were not told of the catastrophe and authorities continued the game, won by the Kiwis.

1998 – Sampras' 6-year domination
Pete Sampras became the first to top the rankings in 6 consecutive years. He was no. 1 from 1993 to 1998, playing in 15 or more tournaments in each year. His longest period as actual top-ranked player was 102 consecutive weeks from April 1996 to March 1998.

1999 – Green breaks Boone mark
A.C. Green of the Los Angeles Lakers played in his NBA record 1,042nd consecutive game in a 103-80 win at home over New Jersey. Green eclipsed the record of Ron Boone.

2000 – Stockton plays most for single team
Utah's John Stockton appeared in his 1,271st NBA game, a 94-79 win at Detroit, passing previous record-holder John Havlicek for most career games played for one team.

2005 – Lara's world record
West Indian batsman Brian Lara became Test cricket's highest run-scorer after scoring a magnificent 226 in the West Indies' first innings of 405 against Australia on day 2 of the third Test in Adelaide. Lara passed former Australian captain Allan Border's record aggregate of 11,174. When he was out, Lara had an aggregate of 11,187 at 54.04 in 121 Tests – 13 runs more than Border.

2005 – All Blacks' Slam
The New Zealand All Blacks beat Scotland 29-10 at Murrayfield to complete a second 'grand slam' of British Isles nations. New Zealand had previously beaten Wales 41-3, Ireland 45-7 and England 23-19 on the tour. The All Blacks became the first team since Australia in 1984, and the first All Blacks side since 1978, to complete the 'grand slam'.

2005 – Kangaroos finally lose a series
New Zealand kept Australia scoreless for the first time in 20 years to secure the 2005 Tri Nations rugby union title, with an emphatic 24-0 win in the final at Elland Road, Leeds. The Australians had not lost a Test series since 1978 in France, but were blown away by the Kiwis' enthusiastic first-half display.

BIRTHDATES
1874	Scottish golfer FRED HERD – died 1954
1898	Uruguayan soccer forward HÉCTOR SCARONE – died 1967
1924	Indian Test spinner JASUBHAI PATEL – died 1992
1942	Norwegian Pro Football Hall of Fame kicker JAN STENERUD
1946	NFL coach ART SHELL
1948	England rugby union hooker PETER WHEELER
1952	Australian tennis player WENDY TURNBULL
1956	American auto racer DALE JARRETT
1958	England rugby union flanker MICKEY SKINNER
1961	Australian surfer TOM CARROLL
1964	Swiss alpine skier VRENI SCHNEIDER
1965	England soccer defender DES WALKER
1967	West Indian Test wicketkeeper RIDLEY JACOBS
1971	American boxer RONALD 'WINKY' WRIGHT
1977	Italian road cyclist IVAN BASSO
1990	American basketballer AVERY BRADLEY

1940 – Bruce is born

Martial arts extraordinaire Bruce Lee was born. A pop culture icon of the 20th century, and one of the most influential proponents of martial arts in history, Lee appeared in a number of feature films. He began by training in Wing Chun, but eventually learned a number of different styles, and championed his own philosophy of mixed style, called Jeet Kune Do (The Way of the Intercepting Fist).

1947 – Dallmar's bad day

Philadelphia's Howie Dallmar set an NBA record for the most field goal attempts with none made, when he missed 15 against the New York Knicks. The record was not topped for 44 years, until Tim Hardaway of Golden State shot 0-for-17 in 1991.

1948 – Third Vardon to Hogan

Ben Hogan won his third Vardon Trophy beating out Byron Nelson and Sam Snead for golf's most prestigious award. Hogan had a scoring average of 69.30. He had previously won the award in 1940–41 when it was decided on a points scoring system.

1966 – NFL points feast

The Washington Redskins beat the New York Giants, 72-41 at home to score the most cumulative points (113) in an NFL match. Washington's 72 points were also the most scored by a team in a single game.

1971 – Forest first

Sammy Chapman ended Nottingham Forest's proud 32-year-old record of not having a player sent off when he was dismissed in a 2-0 Division 1 loss to Leeds United. Chapman was red-carded after an incident with Leeds striker Mick Jones. He was already under a 6 week suspended sentence but an FA disciplinary committee found the dismissal was sufficient penalty.

1973 – Ashe opens the door

Arthur Ashe became the first black tennis player to compete in the final of the South African Open, when he was beaten 6-4, 7-6, 6-3 by Jimmy Connors in Johannesburg. In 1970 Ashe had brought apartheid to world attention when he called for South Africa

Martial arts film star Bruce Lee.

to be expelled from the International Lawn Tennis Federation. To further make his point, Ashe applied for, and was denied a visa to travel there. The South African government yielded to pressure in 1973.

1997 – Sanders second all-time rusher

Detroit Lions running back Barry Sanders passed Eric Dickerson as second all-time NFL rushing leader with a dominating 167 yard, 3-touchdown performance against the Chicago Bears. Sanders finished his 10-year career in 1998 with a total of 15,269 yards behind Walter Payton's 16,726. The pair was overtaken by Emmitt Smith with 17,418 yards.

2009 – Woods accident starts slippery dip

Tiger Woods suffered facial lacerations in a car crash outside his Florida home, after colliding with a fire hydrant and a tree. This was the beginning of a far-reaching sex scandal that saw the end of Woods' marriage, a dramatic loss of form and his demise as the world's no. 1 ranked golfer.

BIRTHDATES

1935	American boxer WILLIE PASTRANO – died 1997
1940	American martial arts exponent BRUCE LEE – died 1973
1942	England soccer forward PETER THOMPSON
1958	MLB catcher/manager MIKE SCIOSCIA
1964	Italian soccer midfielder/manager ROBERTO MANCINI
1965	American golfer DANIELLE AMMACCAPANE
1971	NBA guard NICK VAN EXEL
1978	Czech tennis player RADEK ŠTEPÁNEK
1981	Portuguese soccer defender BRUNO ALVES

1929 – 6 TDs for Nevers

Chicago fullback Ernie Nevers became the only NFL player to ever run for 6 touchdowns in a game in the Cardinals' 40-6 Thanksgiving Day victory over the neighbouring Chicago Bears at Comiskey Park. He also kicked 4 extra points for a 40-point haul that remains the NFL's oldest standing record.

1939 – Basketball founder dies

James Naismith, the man credited with inventing basketball, died aged 78. As a gym teacher at the Springfield Christian Association Training School in 1891, the Canadian-born Naismith set out to develop a new indoor sport with a large ball and 2 suspended peach baskets, 10ft above the court at each end. His death came 3 years after basketball became an official Olympic sport.

1978 – Lights, action … cricket

Cricket was played under lights for the first time at the Sydney Cricket Ground, drawing a crowd of 44,000 for the WSC Australia-West Indies day/night clash. Australia won by 5 wickets, with man of the match Denis Lillee taking 4 for 13. Ian Davis scored a match-high 48 not out for the Australians.

1979 – Restrictions for ODIs

Fielding restrictions in one-day internationals were introduced after England beat the West Indies by 2 runs in a WSC match in Sydney. With the Windies needing 3 to win off the last ball, England captain Mike Brearley positioned all his fielders, including the wicketkeeper, on the boundary to the outrage of West Indies players and SCG patrons.

1992 – Lenny in the sport for 2,500 games

Cleveland head coach Lenny Wilkens made his 2,500th NBA appearance (in 29 seasons as a player and coach) in the Cavs' 95-93 road loss at Orlando. Wilkens joined Don Nelson as the only individuals to achieve the feat. In 1995 he passed Nelson as the NBA's all-time leader in game appearances, as a player or coach, with 2,737.

Record-breaking fullback Eddie Nevers.

1999 – Goalie scores hat-trick

National soccer goalkeeper José Luis Chilavert scored a hat-trick in a Paraguayan Division 1 match. Chilavert's Velez Sarsfield beat Ferro Carril Oeste 6-1.

2004 – NFL points feast

The Bengals outgunned the Cleveland Browns 58-48 in Cincinnati for the second most cumulative points total in an NFL game. The 106-point total was second only to the 113 scored when the Washington Redskins beat the New York Giants 72-41 in 1966.

BIRTHDATES

1907	American golfer HENRY PICARD – died 1997
1919	Australian Test all rounder KEITH MILLER – died 2004
1935	South African rugby union flanker FRIK du PREEZ
1948	England soccer forward MICK CHANNON
1955	Italian soccer striker ALESSANDRO ALTOBELLI
1958	MLB pitcher DAVE RIGHETTI
1959	Irish road cyclist STEPHEN ROCHE
1965	MLB third baseman MATT WILLIAMS
1967	Peruvian soccer midfielder JOSÉ DEL SOLAR
1977	New Zealand rugby union prop GREG SOMERVILLE
1983	Paraguayan soccer striker NELSON VALDEZ
1984	Australian NBA centre ANDREW BOGUT
1985	Uruguayan soccer midfielder ÁLVARO PEREIRA

1970 – Cowdrey passes Hammond

England batsman Colin Cowdrey passed Wally Hammond's then world record career aggregate of 7,249 when he reached 22 in the first innings of the drawn first Test against Australia in Brisbane. Cowdrey ended his Test career in 1975, having played 114 Tests and scoring 7,624 runs at 44.06 with 22 Test centuries.

1975 – Hill killed in plane crash

British World Formula 1 drivers champion Graham Hill was killed in an aeroplane crash aged 46. Hill was piloting a light aircraft when it went down on Arkley golf course near Elstree in Hertfordshire. He was a dual World Formula 1 champion (1962, 1968) and Indianapolis 500 winner (1966).

1984 – Twin tons for Javed

Pakistan master batsman Javed Miandad completed 'twin tons' during the second Test against New Zealand at Hyderabad. Miandad hit 104 and 103 as Pakistan eased to a 7-wicket victory on a slow turning pitch.

1991 – AB breaks Sunny Test mark

Allan Border broke the world record for the most Test appearances during the first Test against India in Brisbane. It was his 126th Test match eclipsing the record of former Indian captain Sunil Gavaskar.

1994 – 'Gabba' best

Shane Warne captured 8 for 71 in 50.2 overs in the first Test against England in Brisbane, in what was the best-ever Test bowling performance by an Australian at the 'Gabba' (Brisbane Cricket Ground). Set 508 to win in just over 5 sessions, the tourists were dismissed for 323 for a 184-run defeat.

1998 – Marino magic 400 TDs

Miami Dolphins quarterback Dan Marino became the first player in NFL history to throw 400 touchdown passes. Marino reached the milestone with his 7-yard TD pass to O.J. McDuffie in a 30-10 win against the New Orleans Saints in Miami. He retired in 1999 with a total of 420 touchdown passes.

British celebrity Formula 1 driver Graham Hill.

2000 – Flower power

Zimbabwe wicket keeper Andy Flower belted 30 fours and 2 sixes in a match-saving 232 not out in the second Test against India at Nagpur. The innings also took Flower's average above 50 for the first time.

BIRTHDATES

1952	England rugby union fullback DUSTY HARE
1962	Spanish golfer SANTIAGO LUNA
1969	MLB pitcher MARIANO RIVERA
1969	American soccer goalkeeper KASEY KELLER
1969	Dutch soccer striker PIERRE VAN HOOIJONK
1973	Welsh soccer forward RYAN GIGGS
1977	Pakistan Test batsman YOUNUS KHAN
1980	New Zealand rugby union centre AARON MAUGER
1988	NFL quarterback RUSSELL WILSON

1928 – Bradman makes Test debut

Twenty-year-old Don Bradman made his Test debut in Brisbane, scoring just 18 and 1 in Australia's 675-run first Test loss to England. Bradman was dropped for the second Test in Sydney, but returned for the remainder of the series, scoring 79 and 112 in Melbourne, 40 and 58 in Adelaide and 123 and 37 not out back in Melbourne.

1956 – Patterson youngest champ

Twenty-one-year-old Floyd Patterson became the youngest fighter to claim the world heavyweight crown when he knocked out Archie Moore in the fifth round in Chicago. He floored the 39-year-old world light-heavyweight champion with a fierce left-hook.

1990 – Bird hits 20,000

Boston forward Larry Bird scored his 20,000th career point, in the Celtics' 123-95 win over Washington at Boston Garden. Bird joined Kareem Abdul-Jabbar, John Havlicek, Oscar Robertson and Jerry West as the only players with both 20,000 points and 5,000 assists.

1991 – US takes first women's WC

The United States beat Norway 2-1 to win the inaugural women's World Cup at Guangzhou in China. Michelle Akers scored twice for the US, and teammate Carin Jennings was named the tournament's most outstanding player.

1996 – Jordan, onward & upward

Chicago superstar Michael Jordan became the 10th player in NBA history to reach 25,000 points after scoring 35 in the Bulls 97-88 win at San Antonio.

1999 – United world champs

Manchester United captain Roy Keane scored the match-winner as the Red Devils became the first British club to be crowned FIFA World Club champions after a 1-0 win over Brazilian side Palmeiras in Tokyo.

1999 – Sri Lankan first

Left-arm Sri Lankan seamer Nuwan Zoysa became the first bowler to take a Test hat-trick off his first 3 balls

History's best batsman, Don Bradman.

in a match, during the second Test against Zimbabwe in Harare. Zoysa also became the first Sri Lankan to capture a hat-trick when he dismissed Trevor Gripper, Neil Johnson and Murray Goodwin. Sri Lanka won the match by 6 wickets.

2006 – Yousif's calendar runs record

Pakistan batsman Mohammad Yousuf passed one of the longest-standing records in cricket – most runs in a calendar year. On the fourth day of the final Test between Pakistan and the West Indies at Karachi, Yousuf passed Vivian Richards' total of 1,710 runs made in 1976. His final tally for the year was 1,788 from 11 Tests.

BIRTHDATES

1931	NFL coach BILL WALSH – died 2007
1946	New Zealand Test wicketkeeper KEN WADSWORTH – died 1976
1950	NBA guard/coach PAUL WESTPHAL
1954	Australian surfer WAYNE BARTHOLOMEW
1955	Scotland soccer striker ANDY GRAY
1960	England soccer striker GARY LINEKER
1962	NFL/MLB player BO JACKSON
1966	Finnish auto racer MIKA SALO
1967	Australian rugby union front rower RICHARD HARRY
1976	England rugby union winger JOSH LEWSEY
1984	Dutch soccer midfielder NIGEL DE JONG

DECEMBER

1956 – Marathon runners follow the line

In the first Olympic marathon where runners followed a line painted on the course, 35-year-old Algerian-born Frenchman Alain Mimoun won his first gold medal at his third Olympics. He won by 1:32 from Yugoslav Franjo Mihali .

1973 – 'Golden Bear' hits pay-dirt

Jack Nicklaus became the first player to reach $2 million in PGA Tour career earnings when he won his third consecutive Walt Disney World Open. Nicklaus finished at 13-under 275 to win by 1 stroke over Mason Rudolph.

1981 – Kareem almost supreme

Kareem Abdul-Jabbar of the LA Lakers passed Oscar Robertson (26,710) to become the NBA's second all-time leading scorer, behind Wilt Chamberlain (31,419).

1989 – Comaneci asks US for asylum

Outstanding Romanian gymnast, Nadia Comaneci arrived in New York requesting political asylum after fleeing her homeland. Asylum was granted and Comaneci began a career as a model. She moved to Norman, Oklahoma, working as a gymnastics coach at her husband Bart Conner's Academy.

1991 – One win enough for Stewart in Skins

Payne Stewart won only 1 hole, but won the Skins Game and set a Skins Game record in the process. His 3ft birdie putt on the 14th hole earned him 8 skins worth $260,000, a record for most money won on 1 hole. Stewart beat John Daly (7 skins), Curtis Strange (3 skins) and Jack Nicklaus (0 skins).

1991 – Rare French tennis win

The Yannick Noah-captained French Davis Cup team beat the United States 3-1 in Lyon to lift the Cup for the first time since 1932. Guy Forget clinched the trophy with a 7-6, 3-6, 6-3, 6-4 win over Pete Sampras, who had been upset in his first singles rubber in straight sets by Henri Leconte.

2012 – Barca best start

Lionel Messi scored twice as Barcelona beat Athletic Bilbao 5-1 to set a new record start to a La Liga. Barca put together 13 wins and a draw from their first 14 matches to beat the previous best start in the Spanish top flight by Real Madrid in the 1991–92 season.

2006 – Baze is the best

Canadian jockey Russell Baze became North American horse racing's all-time win leader when Butterfly Belle won the fourth race at Bay Meadows in San Mateo, California. Baze overtook Laffit Pincay Jr when he posted career wins of 9,531.

2007 – First US Davis Cup in 12 years

The United States won its first Davis Cup since 1995, with a doubles victory over defending champion Russia in Portland, Oregon. Leading 2-0 in the best-of-5 final, twins Bob and Mike Bryan cruised past Nikolay Davydenko and Igor Andreev 7-6 (7-4), 6-4, 6-2 in under 2 hours to seal the tie. Andy Roddick and James Blake had won the first 2 singles rubbers.

2012 – Bon voyage Beckham

Former England captain David Beckham bowed out of the LA Galaxy with a second MLS Cup winner's medal. He helped the Galaxy to a 3-1 win over Houston Dynamo in his last game of a 6-year stint in the US.

BIRTHDATES

1871	England Test captain ARCHIE MacLAREN – died 1944
1912	England soccer forward CHARLES WILLINGHAM – died 1975
1939	Mexican golfer LEE TREVINO
1940	England Test batsman MIKE DENNESS
1942	Australian Test batsman ROSS EDWARDS
1947	Australian rugby league captain BOB FULTON
1947	England rugby union number 8 ANDY RIPLEY
1948	Pakistan Test fast bowler SARFRAZ NARWAZ
1955	Gaelic football half forward PAT SPILLANE
1959	Australian rugby league captain WALLY LEWIS
1962	Canadian speed skater SYLVIE DAIGLE
1963	Sri Lankan Test captain ARJUNA RANATUNGA
1965	South African rugby union fly-half HENRY HONIBALL
1968	Australian squash player SARAH FITZGERALD
1974	Portuguese soccer midfielder COSTINHA

❷ DECEMBER

1932 – 'Bodyline' begins
The controversial Bodyline Series between Australia and England began at the Sydney Cricket Ground. Fast bowler Harold Larwood took immediate advantage of England captain Douglas Jardine's leg-side theory capturing 5 for 96 in the Australian first innings. Australia played without Don Bradman who was out because of a contractual disagreement, and lost by 10 wickets.

1950 – Sullivan takes punishment
South African world bantamweight champion Vic Toweel set a record for knockdowns in a title fight against Englishman Danny Sullivan in Johannesburg. Towel floored Sullivan 14 times in 10 rounds before the fight was stopped.

1972 – Rare six against Irish
Southern Cal speedster Anthony Davis became the first player to score 6 touchdowns against Notre Dame in a 45-23 victory over the Fighting Irish in front of 75,000 fans at the Los Angeles Memorial Coliseum.

1973 – Laver returns for tennis whitewash
Australia, led by Rod Laver and John Newcombe, defeated the United States 5-0 in Cleveland to claim the 62nd Davis Cup. Laver had made a long-awaited return to the Australian team and the clean sweep ended the United States' 5-year stranglehold on the Cup.

1977 – Slow start for WSC
Barely 200 spectators attended the first day of the first World Series Cup match at VFL Park outside Melbourne to watch Australia take on West Indies. Crowds did improve. The West Indies won the first 3-day match by 3 wickets.

1979 – Quick round of golf
American 1,500m record-holder Steve Scott set a record for the fastest round played on a regulation course, posting a score of 95 in 29:33.05 in Anaheim.

1993 – Good start to Rockets' NBA season
The Houston Rockets recorded their 15th consecutive

Australia's double Grand Slam winner Rod Laver. Photo: NL-HaNA, ANEFO / neg. stroken, 1945–1989, 2.24.01.05, item number 922-4468 [CC-BY-SA-3.0-nl], via Wikimedia Commons.

win to start the season, tying the all-time NBA record set by the Washington Capitols at the start of the 1948–49 season. Inspired by Hakeem Olajuwon's 37 points and 13 rebounds, the Rockets scored a 94-85 victory over the Knicks in New York. The Rockets' streak ended the following evening.

2000 – England hold off 'Bocks
England held off a determined comeback by South Africa to notch up their third Southern Hemisphere scalp of the autumn with a 25-17 win at Twickenham. Super boot Jonny Wilkinson kicked 6 penalties and a conversion for England. His Springbok counterpart Braam van Straaten scored a try and landed 4 penalties for all of South Africa's points.

BIRTHDATES
1899   English land/water speed driver JOHN COBB – died 1952
1940   Pro Football Hall of Fame defensive back WILLIE BROWN
1945   Australian Test fast bowler ALAN THOMSON
1947   English auto racer ANDY ROUSE
1953   American golfer JAY HAAS
1955   NHL forward/coach PAUL HOLMGREN
1968   England soccer defender DAVID BATTY
1969   American golfer PAUL STANKOWSKI
1970   Czech golfer ALEX CEJKA
1971   Australian tennis player RACHEL McQUILLAN
1973   American tennis player MONICA SELES
1973   German road cyclist JAN ULLRICH
1979   Pakistan Test all rounder ABDUL RAZZAQ
1983   NFL quarterback AARON RODGERS

1950 – No pass Browns
The Cleveland Browns, playing in their first NFL season, became the only team ever to play a game without completing a pass. Playing on a muddy Cleveland field in torrential rain, the Browns rushed for just 68 yards but still managed to score a 13-7 victory over Philadelphia. The Browns scored on a 30-yard interception return and 2 field goals.

1967 – Clayton clicks at Fukuoka
Australia's Dereck Clayton took a massive 2:23 off Morio Shigematsu's world record when he won the prestigious Fukuoka Marathon in Japan. Clayton ran a time of 2.09:36.4. He took another 1:03 off the record in 1969, a record that stood for 12-years before broken by another Australian Robert de Castella at Fukuoka in 1981.

1986 – Walsh fires for Windies at Sharjah
Fast bowler Courtney Walsh helped West Indies rout Sri Lanka by 193 runs with the most economical 5-wicket haul in one-day international history. Walsh finished with the remarkable figures of 5 for 1 off 4.3 overs with 3 maidens. Sri Lanka crumbled to 55 all out, their lowest ODI score.

1993 – Win streak ends for Rockets
The Atlanta Hawks beat the Houston Rockets 133-111 at home, ending Houston's record-tying streak for the best start in NBA history at 15-0. The start tied the all-time NBA record set by the Washington Capitols at the start of the 1948–49 season.

1995 – Jack Russell no dog behind the stumps
England wicketkeeper Jack Russell took a Test record 11 catches in the second Test against South Africa in Johannesburg. Russell also scored 29 in 2 sessions with Mike Atherton to salvage a draw. Russell and Atherton shared the Man-of-the-Match award.

2000 – Record 12 straight wins
Australia scored their record 12th consecutive Test victory when they thrashed the West Indies by an innings and 27 runs in the second Test in Perth. Glenn McGrath took a hat-trick in the Windies' second innings. The victory broke the Windies world record of 11 consecutive Test wins set in the early 1980s. Australia went on to take the record streak to 16.

2007 – Murali passes Warne mark
Controversial Sri Lankan spinner Muttiah Muralitharan became the leading wicket-taker in Test cricket after breaking Shane Warne's record of 708 Test wickets during the first Test against England in Kandy. Murali dismissed Paul Collingwood during England's first innings to take his 709th wicket. He achieved the record in his 116th Test and on his home ground.

2012 – Final innings for 'Punter'
The decorated international career Australian cricket captain Ricky Ponting ended when he was out for 8 in his 168th and final Test. Ponting was caught at first slip before lunch on the fourth day of the third Test against South Africa in Perth. The soft dismissal was a sad way for Australia's greatest run-scorer to leave the game. Ponting scored 13,378 Test runs at 51.85.

BIRTHDATES
1905	England Test wicket keeper LES AMES – died 1990
1923	England Test all-rounder TREVOR BAILEY – died 2011
1937	American auto-racer BOBBY ALLISON
1942	Irish rugby union centre MIKE GIBSON
1950	Cuban middle distance runner ALBERTO JUANTORENA
1951	American auto-racer RICK MEARS
1953	Austrian alpine skier FRANZ KLAMMER
1959	American tennis player KATHY JORDAN
1960	Russian Hockey Hall of Fame centre IGOR LARIONOV
1965	German figure skater KATERINA WITT
1972	American skateboarder BUCKY LASEK
1976	South African Test wicketkeeper MARK BOUCHER
1976	New Zealand rugby union halfback BYRON KELLEHER
1981	Spanish soccer striker DAVID VILLA
1983	New Zealand rugby fly-half STEPHEN DONALD

4 DECEMBER

1948 – Capitals' best NBA start
The Washington Capitols beat Baltimore 83-82 to raise their record to 15-0, the best start in NBA history. The streak ended with a 94-78 loss at Indianapolis on December 7. The Capitols' streak was matched by the Houston Rockets at the outset of 1993–94.

1948 – Quick triple ton to Compton
England batsman Denis Compton scored 300 in just 181 minutes for the MCC against Northern Transvaal, the fastest triple century in first-class history. Compton smashed 42 fours and 5 sixes. His first hundred was scored in 66 minutes, the second in 78, and the third in 37.

1977 – Bucs lose – again
The Tampa Bay Buccaneers' record losing streak stretched to 26 in a 10-0 home defeat to the Chicago Bears. The run ended in the last 2 games of the season.

1980 – Mixed up sprinter shot dead
1932 Olympic women's 100m champion and 1936 silver medallist Stanislawa Walasiewicz (assumed name Stella Walsh) was shot dead in a robbery attempt in Cleveland, Ohio. An autopsy found she had a tiny penis and testes, and no female organs. Walsh, who had run eleven 'world records' for females, was a man.

1985 – Hadlee guides Kiwis to first series win
New Zealand captured their first series against Australia when they won the third Test in Perth by 6 wickets. Richard Hadlee had match figures of 11 for 155.

1987 – Kareem streak ends
Kareem Abdul-Jabbar's record run of double digit scoring in 787 consecutive regular-season games over 10 years ended in the Lakers' 85-83 loss in Milwaukee.

1988 – Merv hat-trick a long time coming
Australian fast bowler Merv Hughes captured the most convoluted hat-trick in Test history during the second Test against the West Indies in Perth. Hughes dismissed Curtly Ambrose with the last ball of his 36th over, Patrick Patterson with the first ball of his 37th over,

Disgraced American sprinter Marion Jones in action during the 2000 Sydney Olympics.

the last of the West Indies' first innings, and Gordon Greenidge with the first ball of their second innings.

1997 – Sprewell suspended over coach assault
All Star guard Latrell Sprewell was suspended for 1 year for choking and threatening to kill Golden State coach P.J. Carlisimo at practise.

2004 – Conte makes drug claims
BALCO founder Victor Conte appeared on US television claiming he had supplied sprinter Marion Jones with growth hormone, insulin, endurance-drug EPO and a designer steroid called 'the clear' in 2000–01. Conte indicated Jones was using banned drugs when she won 3 gold medals at the 2000 Sydney Olympics. He also claimed record-breaking baseball slugger Barry Bonds had used performance-enhancing drugs. Bonds acknowledged he had used drugs, but denied knowing they were steroids. Jones was later jailed for lying to a grand jury about the claims.

BIRTHDATES
1931 Canadian Hockey Hall of Fame centre ALEX DELVECCHIO
1941 American tennis player/coach MARTY RIESSEN
1956 Italian golfer CONSTANTINO ROCCA
1956 NBA forward BERNARD KING
1960 Australian heptathlete GLYNIS NUNN
1961 New Zealand rugby league halfback/coach GARY FREEMAN
1963 England rugby union winger NIGEL HESLOP
1963 Ukrainian pole-vaulter SERGEY BUBKA
1964 Scottish rugby centre SCOTT HASTINGS
1968 American swimmer MIKE BARROWMAN
1974 German tennis player ANKE HUBER
1977 Indian Test all-rounder AJIT AGARKAR

⑤ DECEMBER

1908 – Fast finish by 'Black Cats'
Sunderland scored 8 goals in the last 28 minutes to beat north-east rivals Newcastle United 9-1 in a First Division match. Five of the goals were scored in the final 8 minutes.

1931 – No corners
For the first time, not one corner-kick was taken in an English Division 1 match. The bizarre non-statistic occurred in the 0-0 draw between Newcastle United and Portsmouth at St James' Park.

1947 – Jersey Joe pushes 'Bomber'
Joe Louis edged Jersey Joe Walcott in a controversial 15-round split decision at Madison Square Garden to regain the world heavyweight title. Louis was floored in the first and fourth rounds and ringside observers thought Walcott had won the title, but two judges had Louis ahead (8-6-1 and 9-6). The decision was investigated, but authorities found nothing illegal. Louis won the rematch with an 11th-round knockout.

1951 – Famous 'Black Sox' dies
The legendary 'Shoeless' Joe Jackson died of a heart attack in Greenville, South Carolina, aged 64. As one of 8 'Black Sox' charged with throwing the 1919 World Series, Jackson and his cohorts were found innocent by a jury in 1921, but Commissioner Kenesaw Mountain Landis banned all 8 from baseball for life.

1964 – Ken scores against all
England's Ken Barrington became the first to score hundreds against 6 different Test-playing countries, with 148 not out against South Africa at Durban.

1970 – NHL trophies gone
The Stanley Cup, Con Smythe Trophy and the Bill Masterson Trophy were stolen from the NHL's Hall of Fame, and later recovered from a Toronto cleaning store.

2001 – Kiwi yachting guru murdered
It was reported that New Zealand helmsman Sir Peter Blake had been murdered by Brazilian pirates, who boarded his research vessel *Seamaster* at the mouth of

England Test batsman Ken Barrington in action for his County side Surry in 1966.

the Amazon River on 5 December. He was 53. Blake won all 6 legs of the 1989–90 Whitbread around the World Yacht Race and was the team leader when New Zealand's *Black Magic* won the America's Cup in 1996 and retained it in 2000.

2012 – Kobe youngest to 30,000
Kobe Bryant scored 29 points, making him the fifth player in NBA history to score 30,000, as the LA Lakers scored a 103-87 victory over the Hornets in New Orleans. He entered the game needing only 13 points to eclipse the scoring milestone and did so with a short jumper late in the first half. At age 34, Bryant was the youngest to reach the milestone. Wilt Chamberlain had been 35 when he hit the mark, Kareem Abdul-Jabbar and Karl Malone were each 36, and Michael Jordan was 38.

BIRTHDATES
1940	Australian Test cricket umpire TONY CRAFTER
1947	NFL quarterback JIM PLUNKETT
1949	American golfer LANNY WADKINS
1951	American golfer TOM PURTZER
1957	NFL receiver ART MONK
1964	American swimmer PABLO MORALES
1965	England soccer defender CARLTON PALMER
1971	Swedish golfer GABRIEL HJERTSTEDT
1975	English snooker player RONNIE O'SULLIVAN
1983	Australian rugby league halfback COOPER CRONK

❻ DECEMBER

1930 – Rockne's fond farewell
In his last game, coach Knute Rockne led Notre Dame to its second consecutive national championship with a 27-0 rout of USC before a crowd of 90,000 at the Coliseum. He coached the Irish for 13 years, compiling a record of 105-12-5, for a winning percentage of .881, the highest in NCAA history. In the off-season, the 42-year-old Rockne was killed in an airplane crash.

1956 – Blood in the water
The Olympic water polo match between Hungary and the Soviet Union became a political contest as well as a physical one in Melbourne. Soviet troops had put down a major revolt against Communist rule in Hungary in early November and feelings between the 2 nations' athletes ran high. In the most famous Water Polo match ever played, referees had to abandon the contest when they lost control as the play erupted into a series of brawls. Hungary was credited with the victory as they led 4-0 when play was halted. The Hungarians won the gold medal and the Soviets the bronze.

1981 – 'Deek' breaks Marathon record
Robert de Castella ran 2.08:18 seconds in Fukuoka, Japan, to break fellow Australian Dereck Clayton's 12-year-old world record by 16 seconds.

1984 – Martina's win streak over
Martina Navratilova lost to Helena Sukova 6-1, 3-6, 5-7 in the semi-finals of the Australian Open in Melbourne, ending the longest winning streak on the women's circuit. Navratilova had won 74 consecutive matches in an undefeated period lasting 10 months.

1987 – Montana magic
San Francisco 49ers quarterback Joe Montana, who completed his final 5 passes the previous week against the Cleveland Browns, connected on his first 17 passes against the Green Bay Packers to set an NFL record of 22 consecutive completions. The previous record was 20 by Cincinnati Bengals quarterback Ken Anderson in 1983.

1993 – All over for Fraser
After 23 years as Australian Davis Cup captain, Neale

Legendary Notre Dame coach Knute Rockne.

Fraser announced his retirement. Fraser succeeded the legendary non-playing captain Harry Hopman in 1970 and masterminded 4 victories.

2000 – 51-apiece
Antwan Jamison of Golden State and Kobe Bryant of the Los Angeles Lakers each scored 51 points in the Warriors' 125-122 overtime victory in Oakland.

2006 – Knight ties Rupp mark
Texas Tech coach Bobby Knight recorded his milestone 876th victory, as his Red Raiders posted a 66-59 victory over the Louisiana Tech Bulldogs. That victory tied him with Adolph Rupp for the second-most wins in Division I history.

BIRTHDATES
1882	Australian Test batsman WARREN BARDSLEY – died 1954
1909	American cricket broadcaster ALAN McGILVRAY – died 1996
1913	American swimmer ELEANOR HOLM – died 2004
1914	England Test batsman CYRIL WASHBROOK – died 1999
1921	Pro Football Hall of Fame quarterback OTTO GRAHAM – died 2003
1946	England Test batsman FRANK HAYES
1948	Finnish auto racer KEKE ROSBERG
1949	England Test batsman/umpire PETER WILLEY
1951	English soccer midfielder/manager GERRY FRANCIS
1955	England soccer striker TONY WOODCOCK
1966	Swedish golfer PER-ULRIK JOHANSSON
1970	American swimmer JEFF ROUSE
1971	Dutch tennis player RICHARD KRAJICEK
1977	England Test all-rounder ANDREW FLINTOFF
1979	Australian soccer midfielder TIM CAHILL

❼ DECEMBER

1948 – Basketball win streak ends
The Indianapolis Jets beat the Washington Capitols 94-78, ending the Capitols' NBA-record streak at 15 consecutive games won at the start of the season. The mark was tied by the 1993–94 Houston Rockets.

1948 – Bradman's testimonial
In his final innings, Don Bradman scored just 10 in his testimonial match against Lindsay Hassett's XI at the Melbourne Cricket Ground. The four-day match drew 94,000 fans and raised the then massive amount of £10,200.

1980 – Huge 49er comeback
The San Francisco 49ers erased a 35-7 halftime deficit against New Orleans to record the biggest comeback in NFL history. The 49ers rebounded to beat the Saints 38-35 in overtime on Ray Wersching's 36-yard field goal.

1996 – Sharp shooter Mills
Detroit's Terry Mills tied an NBA record for most consecutive 3-point field goals made with 13, after connecting on his first attempt during the Pistons' 95-69 win at New Jersey. Mills' streak, which stretched over 3 games, tied Brent Price's mark set in the 1995–96 season.

2002 – Gunners win streak no more
Arsenal's record scoring streak of 55 consecutive Premiership games ended with a 2-0 defeat by Manchester United at Old Trafford. The incredible streak started in the final match of the 2000–1 season, continued through all 38 games in their Championship season of 2001–2 and in the first 16 games of the 2002–3 season.

2003 – Smith is new sacks king
Forty-year-old defensive end Bruce Smith became the NFL's career sacks leader (199) when he tackled Jesse Palmer in the fourth quarter of the Washington Redskins 20-7 win over the New York Giants in New Jersey. Smith passed Reggie White, who had 198 sacks (1985–2000). He retired at the end of the season with 200 sacks.

Albert Pujols playing for the Cardinals in 2010. Photo: Herkie on Flickr (Original version) UCinternational (Crop) [CC-BY-SA-2.0], via Wikimedia Commons.

2011 – Pujols leaves Cardinals
After 11 years with the newly crowned world champion St Louis Cardinals, All Star first baseman Albert Pujols signed a 10-year contract with the Anaheim Angels. The former NL MVP's new contract was worth a reported $254 million.

BIRTHDATES
1928	American auto racer MICKEY THOMPSON – died 1988
1940	Canadian Hockey Hall of Fame goalie GERRY CHEEVERS
1947	Baseball Hall of Fame catcher JOHNNY BENCH
1956	Basketball Hall of Fame forward LARRY BIRD
1957	Australian Test fast bowler GEOFF LAWSON
1959	Pakistan Test wicket keeper SALEEM YOUSUF
1965	Scottish soccer defender COLIN HENDRY
1972	Austrian alpine skier HERMANN MAIER
1973	NFL wide receiver TERRELL OWENS
1973	French rugby union lock FABIAN PELOUS
1980	England soccer defender JOHN TERRY
1990	Polish tennis player URSZULA RADWA SKA

❽ DECEMBER

1906 – First Springboks
The first South African rugby union team abroad, and the first to wear the Springbok emblem, played a 3-3 draw with England at Crystal Palace. Freddie Brooks, who had been rejected in the Springbok trials, scored a try to level the scores for England.

1961 – Chamberlain's 78 points
Wilt Chamberlain scored 78 points in the Philadelphia Warriors' 151-147 loss to the LA Lakers in 3OT, the second highest scoring performance in NBA history. He broke his own record 6 months later, when he scored 100 points.

1984 – Wallabies' Grand Slam
Australia achieved the first ever rugby union Grand Slam when they beat Scotland 37-12 at Murryfield. The Wallabies won each match against the home nations, beating England 19-3; Ireland 16-9; and Wales 28-9. Mark Ella created a unique record of scoring a try in each of the 4 grand slam internationals.

1985 – All-Swedish affair
In an all-Swedish men's final at the Australian Open at Kooyong, Stefan Edberg scored a comfortable 6-4, 6-3, 6-3 win over defending champion Mats Wilander.

1990 – Lorenzo off in 10 seconds
Bologna's Giuseppe Lorenzo set a world record for fastest send-off in a top grade football match. Lorenzo was dismissed for striking an opponent after only 10 seconds of a Serie A match against Parma. The match ended 1-1.

1991 – Matthäus first Footballer of the Year
German captain Lothar Matthäus became the first official World Footballer of the Year following a poll of FIFA coaches. Matthäus beat Frenchman Jean-Pierre Papin and England's Gary Lineker for the coveted award.

1992 – Dominique's free throw delight
Atlanta forward Dominique Wilkins made a record 23 consecutive free throws in the Hawks' 123-114 home win against Chicago. Wilkins broke the existing NBA record of 19 set by Bill Cartwright, Bob Pettit and Adrian Dantley.

1999 – 'Sir Charles' forced to retire
Houston forward Charles Barkley's storied career came to an end when he tore the left quadriceps tendon away from the kneecap in the Rocket's 83-73 defeat at Philadelphia. Barkley scored 23,755 points (13th in NBA history) and grabbed 12,545 rebounds (14th).

2000 – Shaq misses from the line
Shaquille O'Neal of the Los Angeles Lakers broke an unwanted 40-year-old NBA record when he missed all 11 free throw attempts against Seattle. Wilt Chamberlain missed all 10 from the line against Detroit in 1960.

2007 – Mayweather still undefeated
Floyd Mayweather remained unbeaten and lived up to his claim of being the best pound-for-pound fighter in the world by stopping Englishman Ricky Hatton in the 10th round of their WBC Welterweight title fight in Las Vegas. It was the first loss for Hatton.

2011 – Sehwag's rare double ton
Indian opener Virender Sehwag smashed 219 in a one-day international against West Indies in Indore. The spectacular innings took 149 balls as he directed India towards their highest ever ODI total of 418. He didn't come out to field, even though he was the captain – the Windies never challenged at any stage during the chase.

BIRTHDATES
1914 Australian Test medium pace bowler ERNIE TOSHACK – died 2003
1917 Australian Test captain IAN JOHNSON – died 1998.
1936 England Test batsman PETER PARFITT
1941 England soccer striker GEOFF HURST
1951 England soccer forward TERRY McDERMOTT
1962 Australian golfer STEVE ELKINGTON
1966 England soccer striker LES FERDINAND
1975 American auto racer KEVIN HARVICK
1977 French rugby back rower SEBASTIEN CHABAL
1981 NFL quarterback PHILIP RIVERS

❾ DECEMBER

1936 – England easily
Australia was reduced to its lowest 20th century total at home when dismissed for 58 on a rain-affected wicket in the first Test against England in Brisbane. Pace men Gubby Allen and Bill Voce shared 18 of 19 wickets to fall in England 322-run victory.

1963 – Benaud double
Australian cricket captain Richie Benaud scored 43 and took 5 for 68 to become the first to score 2,000 runs and take 200 Test wickets during the drawn first Test against South Africa in Brisbane.

1978 – Forest beaten after 42
Nottingham Forest's English League record 42 match unbeaten streak ended in a 2-0 loss to Liverpool at Anfield. Terry McDermott scored both Reds' goals. Forest's undefeated sequence included 21 wins and 21 draws. The record was beaten by Arsenal in 2004–5.

1978 – All Black Grand Slam
The New Zealand rugby union team clinched a historic British Isles tour Grand Slam with an 18-9 win over Scotland at Murrayfield. The All Blacks scored 2 tries to 1 and dual cricket/rugby international Brian McKechnie landed 2 penalties and 2 conversions. New Zealand had beaten Ireland 10-6, Wales 13-12 and England 16-6 to claim the coveted Slam.

1984 – Dickerson dynamic
Los Angeles Rams running back Eric Dickerson rushed for 215 yards in a 27-16 win over Houston to break O.J. Simpson's single-season record of 2,003 yards. Dickerson ended the season with 2,105 yards from 379 carries.

1993 – Jan sues Heat
Glamour golfer Jan Stephenson sued NBA team the Miami Heat over career-threatening injuries she suffered during a 1990 assault in the parking lot after a Heat game. The matter was settled out of court. Stephenson won LPGA major titles – the Peter Jackson Classic in 1981, LPGA Championship in 1982 and the US Open in 1983.

John Force in action during the 2000 NHRA Nationals in Las Vegas.

1996 – John is a Force
Drag Racer John Force became the first driver from any discipline outside of NASCAR, Cart or Formula 1 to be named American Driver of the Year. In 1996 he won the NHRA Funny Car championship for the sixth time, reaching the finals 16 times in 19 races, and winning 13.

1997 – MJ third all-time
Chicago Bulls superstar Michael Jordan scored 29 points in a 100-82 win over New York to become the NBA's third-leading scorer with 27,432 in 13 seasons, moving ahead of Moses Malone.

BIRTHDATES
1912	American golfer JIM TURNESA – died 1971
1916	Australian Test all-rounder COLIN McCOOL – died 1986
1932	American jockey BILL HARTACK
1933	American golfer ORVILLE MOODY – died 2008
1938	Pro Football Hall of Fame defensive end DEACON JONES
1942	American sports caster DICK BUTKUS
1942	Scottish soccer midfielder BILLY BREMNER – died 1997
1949	American golfer TOM KITE
1969	French soccer defender BIXENTE LIZARAZU
1972	French tennis player FABRICE SANTORO
1978	Argentine tennis player GASTÓN GAUDIO
1981	American tennis player MARDY FISH

1949 – Hogan returns
Ben Hogan played his first round since his near-fatal February car accident, shooting 71 at the Colonial Country Club in Fort Worth, Texas. Hogan elected to be transported around the course in a motorcycle-like cart, a precursor to today's golf cart.

1977 – Cauthen first to $6m in a season
Steve Cauthen became the first jockey to win $6 million in a single US season when he rode Little Happiness to victory at Aqueduct. The feat was achieved in only Cauthen's second year of riding at the top level.

1982 – Title bout lasts a minute
In one of the shortest world heavyweight title fights on record, Michael Dokes won the WBA title by stopping defending champion Mike Weaver after just 63 seconds of their bout at Caesar's Palace, Las Vegas. Dokes became the first man since Sonny Liston knocked out Floyd Patterson in 1962 to win the title with a first-round stoppage.

1999 – Hawkins' game streak ends
Chicago Bulls guard Hersey Hawkins' streak of 527 consecutive games ended when he was unable to suit up for the Bulls' 71-69 win at home over New Jersey, with a torn left calf. His streak was the second-longest active sequence behind all-time leader A.C. Green.

1999 – Doohan retires
Five-time 500cc motorcycle world champion Michael Doohan retired from racing after suffering multiple injuries in a crash in practise for the Spanish Grand Prix in Jerez in May. In ten seasons, Doohan made 137 starts for 54 wins, second only to Italian Giacomo Agostini who had 68 wins.

2006 – Beachley's seventh World Surf Crown
Thirty-four-year-old Australian surfer Layne Beachley extended her own mark by claiming a record seventh world women's title in Hawaii after defending world champion Chelsea Georgeson was beaten in the quarter-finals of the Billabong Pro at Honolua Bay. Beachley had won 6 straight ASP Tour championships from 1998 to 2003.

Steve Cauthen aboard Reference Point prior to the 1987 L'Arc de Triomphe in Paris.

2006 – LT's TD record
San Diego running back LaDainian Tomlinson scored 3 touchdowns, including the final 2 in a span of 47 seconds late in the game, to break the NFL single-season record with 29 TDs in the Chargers 48-20 win over Denver in San Diego. Shaun Alexander had held the record 28, set in 2005.

2007 – Vick in jail
Michael Vick was sentenced to 23 months in prison for his role in a dog fighting conspiracy. Vick pleaded guilty, admitting he bankrolled the 'Bad Newz Kennels' dog fighting operation, and helped kill 6 to 8 dogs.

BIRTHDATES
1938	Australian golfer BILLY DUNK
1941	England Test fast bowler JEFF JONES
1950	New Zealand golfer SIMON OWEN
1959	NBA forward MARK AGUIRRE
1963	Pakistani squash player JAHANGIR KHAN
1963	American tennis player ROBIN WHITE
1966	New Zealand rugby union number 8 ROBIN BROOKE
1969	Canadian NHL defenseman ROB BLAKE
1978	Australian triathlete NICOLE HACKETT

1937 – Scottish record
East Fife beat Edinburgh City 13-2 for the biggest win in the Scottish League in the 20th century. East Fife later became the only Second Division team to win the Scottish FA Cup.

1965 – Inaugural Four-Ball
Butch Baird and Gay Brewer won the first PGA National Four-Ball Championship at the PGA National GC in Palm Beach Gardens, Florida. Brothers Lionel and Jay Hebert were runners-up. Tournament favourites Arnold Palmer and Jack Nicklaus finished seventh.

1977 – Record 8 points for a defenseman
Tom Bladon of the Philadelphia Flyers scored 8 points from 4 goals and 4 assists in an 11-1 win at home over Cleveland, the most by a defenseman in a single NHL game. The record was tied by Edmonton's Paul Coffey in 1986 (2 goals/6 assists) in a 12-3 home win against Detroit.

1981 – Ali's bows out with a loss
At age 39, an overweight Muhammad Ali lost his last fight, a unanimous 10-round decision to Trevor Berbick, at Nassau in the Bahamas. Ali was pounded by the lighter and younger Berbick. The former three-time heavyweight champion retired with a 56-5 record.

1983 – John Henry tops $4m
John Henry became the first racehorse to top $4 million in career earnings when he won the Hollywood Turf Cup at Hollywood Park. The late-maturing gelding dominated in handicap and turf stakes races, twice winning the Santa Anita Handicap and the Arlington Million Stakes. His record was 39 wins from 83 starts with $6.5m in earnings.

2000 – Spanish giants best club
Real Madrid FC was awarded 20th Century's Best Club award by FIFA.

2005 – Allenby's Aussie golf slam
Robert Allenby became the first winner of Australian golf's triple crown by taking the first playoff hole against American Bubba Watson in the Australian Masters at Huntingdale. The win secured an unprecedented sweep of the Australian Open, PGA and Masters titles.

2006 – Sloan reaches 1,000 wins
Utah head coach Jerry Sloan won his 1,000th career NBA game. The Jazz defeated the Dallas Mavericks, 101-79 in Salt Lake City.

2006 – Hester is return king
Rookie Devon Hester returned 2 kickoffs for touchdowns as Chicago Bears defeated the Rams, 42-27 in St Louis. The 2 scores gave the Hester 6 return touchdowns on the season, an NFL record.

2010 – Huge hockey crowd
Michigan beat Michigan State 5-0 and set a world record for attendance at a hockey game, playing in front of 113,411 at Michigan Stadium. The previous mark was 77,803 at the 2010 world championship in Germany.

2011 – Donald takes unique money double
World no. 1 ranked Englishman Luke Donald became the first golfer in history to win both the American and European money titles when he finished third, 3 strokes behind the winner Álvaro Quirós of Spain, in the Dubai World Championship.

BIRTHDATES
1929	Indian Test spinner SUBHASH GUPTE – died 2002
1931	Canadian Hockey Hall of Fame defenseman PIERRE PILOTE
1934	Indian Test all-rounder SALIM DURANI
1946	Australian Test opener RICK McCOSKER
1954	West Indian Test fast bowler SYLVESTER CLARKE – died 1999.
1958	Czech tennis player REGINA MARŠÍKOVÁ
1959	New Zealand jockey GRANT COOKSLEY
1963	New Zealand Test batsman MARK GREATBATCH
1963	German tennis player CLAUDIA KOHDE-KILSCH
1969	Norwegian soccer defender STIG INGE BJØRNEBYE
1972	Zimbabwe Test batsman MURRAY GOODWIN
1981	Argentine soccer striker JAVIER SAVIOLA
1988	New Zealand Test all-rounder TIM SOUTHEE

⓬ DECEMBER

1908 – First ever Anglo-Australian drawn Test
Dally Messenger captained Australia's rugby league team to a 22-22 draw against Great Britain at the Park Royal Ground in London in the first ever 'Ashes' rugby league Test match. North Sydney winger Jim Devereaux had the distinction of scoring Australia's first Test try. He crossed for 3 tries before England converted a last-minute penalty to snatch a draw.

1959 – McLaren youngest F1 winner
Twenty-two-year-old Kiwi Bruce McLaren, driving a Cooper T51, became the youngest winner of a Formula 1 Grand Prix when he won the US event at Sebring. Championship points leader Jack Brabham ran out of fuel on the last lap and had to push his Cooper across the line to finish fourth. It was enough to earn him the first of 3 World Drivers titles.

1965 – Sayers' six
Chicago Bears rookie running back Gale Sayers scored 6 touchdowns in a 61-20 rout of the San Francisco 49ers at Wrigley Field to tie the NFL record set by Ernie Nevers in 1929 and matched by Dub Jones in 1951.

1971 – Gould freestyle queen
Shane Gould of Australia smashed the world 1,500m record by a huge 18 seconds in Sydney, to become the first swimmer in history to simultaneously hold every freestyle world record. Gould swam a time of 17:06. She had equalled Dawn Fraser's 100m record of 58.9 seconds in April, and between July and December broke the 200, 400, 800 and 1,500m records. In January 1972, Gould made the feat all hers, when she broke the 100m record with a time of 58.5 seconds in Sydney.

1971 – Lakers hit 21 straight wins
The Los Angeles Lakers broke the NBA record of 20 consecutive wins when they beat Atlanta 104-95 at the Forum for their 21st straight victory. The 20-game mark was previously shared by the Washington Capitols and Milwaukee Bucks. The Lakers went on to win 33 consecutive games, the longest winning streak in NBA history.

1988 – The Heat's on Miami
The Miami Heat set an NBA record for the most consecutive defeats at the start of a season with 17, after a 110-94 road loss to Utah. The LA Clippers tied the mark when they opened the 1998–99 season with 17 straight defeats

1992 – McCoist reaches 200-goal mark
Ally McCoist became the first player to score 200 goals in the Scottish Premier Division when he netted Rangers' winner in a 2-1 victory at Falkirk. When he retired in 2001, McCoist had scored 281 Scottish League goals for StJohnstone, Rangers and Kilmarnock.

2006 – Tiger 'Player of the Year' ...again
Tiger Woods was named the PGA Tour Player of the Year for the eighth time in his career.

2007 – Jones officially outed
Marion Jones was erased from the Olympic records when the IOC formally stripped her of her 3 gold and 2 bronze medals after the former track and field star admitted to being a drug cheat. Jones won gold medals in the 100m, 200m and 4 x 100m relay in Sydney, and bronze in the long jump and 200m relay. She was the first female track and field athlete to 'win' 5 medals at a single Olympics.

BIRTHDATES
1912 American boxer HENRY ARMSTRONG – died 1988
1925 Indian Test all-rounder DATTU PHADKAR – died 1985
1925 Canadian Hockey Hall of Fame forward TEEDER KENNEDY – died 2009
1932 Basketball Hall of Fame forward BOB PETTIT
1946 Brazilian auto racer EMERSON FITTIPALDI
1948 England soccer defender COLIN TODD
1962 American tennis player TRACEY AUSTIN
1965 England rugby union captain WILL CARLING
1967 NFL defensive tackle JOHN RANDLE
1974 Peruvian soccer midfielder NOLBERTO SOLANO
1976 New Zealand rugby union halfback STEVE DEVINE
1981 Indian Test all-rounder YUVRAJ SINGH

1942 – 16 goals for Stanis
Racing Club Lens striker Stephan Stanis created a world record for scoring in a senior professional football match in a 32-0 French Cup win against Aubry-Asturies. Stanis netted 16 goals.

1983 – NBA records tumble
The Detroit Pistons beat the Denver Nuggets 186-184 in 3OT, setting several NBA records: most points scored in a game by one team (Detroit-186) and combined (370); most field goals by one team (Detroit-74) and combined (142); and combined assists (93).

1986 – Kangaroos unbeaten
The Australian rugby league team completed their 9-week tour of England and France undefeated, with a 52-0 thrashing of France in Carcassonne. The Kangaroos had beaten Great Britain in 3 Tests: 38-16 at Manchester; 34-4 at Leeds; and 24-15 at Wigan.

1989 – Quick Robson score
England midfielder Bryan Robson scored the then fastest goal in an international match at Wembley Stadium when he netted after just 38 seconds against Yugoslavia. England won 2-1 in their 100th victory at the famous venue.

2000 – Stockton sensational
John Stockton of the Utah Jazz collected his 14,000th career assist in a 111-102 loss to Milwaukee. When Stockton notched the assist, he increased his lead over no. 2 career assist man 'Magic' Johnson (10,141 assists) to 3,859 assists. He ended his career in 2003 as all-time assists leader with 15,806. He also led in steals with 3,265.

2006 – GDR Doping Victims Paid Out
An agreement was signed in Berlin resulting in former athletes who were victims of East Germany's systematic doping program getting a one-time payment as compensation for health problems whilst giving up any other legal action. A group of 167 recognised victims received $12,210. The agreement ended years of legal wrangling between the victims and German sports officials.

2007 – Rookie world champ
Australian surfer Stephanie Gilmore became the first in history to win the world title in her rookie year. Competing at the season-ending Billabong Pro at Honolua Bay on Maui, and locked in a three-way battle for the world crown with Peru's Sofia Mulanovich and Brazilian Silvana Lima, Gilmore's 2 title rivals succumbed on the final heat of the day.

2009 – NFL reception record
Denver wide receiver Brandon Marshall set an NFL single game reception record with 21 grabs in the Broncos 28-10 loss in Indianapolis. Terrell Owens set the previous mark of 17 in 2000.

2010 – Favre starts record ends
Brett Favre's NFL record streak of 297 straight starts ended when he failed to suit up in the Minnesota Vikings' 21-3 loss to the New York Giants in a re-scheduled game in Detroit. The 41-year-old Favre was suffering from a right shoulder injury. He stood on the sideline for the start of a game for the first time since 1992.

BIRTHDATES
1913	American boxer ARCHIE MOORE – died 1998
1918	American auto racer BILL VUKOVICH – died 1955
1923	Baseball Hall of Fame outfielder LARRY DOBY – died 2003
1935	Australian rugby union/league halfback ARTHUR SUMMONS
1938	American golfer TOM SHAW
1952	Pro wrestler JUNKYARD DOG – died 1998
1953	Canadian Hockey Hall of Fame forward BOB GAINEY
1960	NFL defensive end RICHARD DENT
1962	NFL coach REX RYAN
1969	Russian NHL centre SERGEI FEDOROV
1977	Irish rugby halfback PETER STRINGER
1983	Polish swimmer OTYLIA JEDRZEJCZAK
1988	American golfer RICKIE FOWLER

1935 – Drake's 7 for Gunners

Arsenal striker Ted Drake scored all of the Gunners goals in a 7-1 rout of Aston Villa at Villa Park. The haul equalled a First Division scoring record in one match. Preston North End's James Ross also scored 7 against Stoke City in 1888.

1941 – Typical 1-2-3

Defending titleholder Byron Nelson won the Miami Open at the Miami Springs Golf and Country Club, ahead of Ben Hogan and Sam Snead. It marked the second of 5 occasions on which the dominant trio finished in the sequence.

1960 – Famous 'Tied Test'

Australia and West Indies played out the first tied Test match after a sensational finish in Brisbane. Australia started the last over from Windies fast bowling great Wes Hall on 227 for 7, needing 6 runs to win. The final drama-charged over included a leg bye, a bye, a caught behind, a dropped catch by the bowler, and 2 run-outs. The last crucial run-out for the 10th wicket was a direct hit from Joe Solomon at square-leg to leave the match even.

1967 – Open Tennis at Wimbledon

The British Lawn Tennis Association voted 295-5 for open tennis, thus paving the way for professionals to play at Wimbledon. It was apparent that amateur rules were being flouted via appearance money won at several tournaments. The vote caused the International Lawn Tennis Federation to rethink their repeated rejection of open tennis proposals

1969 – Lombardi's last

Vince Lombardi directed his last win as an NFL coach as Washington scored a 17-14 home win over New Orleans. The Redskins finished with a 7-5-2 record, their first winning season in 14 years. The victory guaranteed Lombardi a winning season in all 10 years of his coaching career, the first 9 being with the Green Bay Packers. Lombardi died of cancer the following year, having finished with a career record of 105-36-5, including a 9-1 postseason record with the Packers.

1975 – Kareem supreme rebounder

Los Angeles Lakers centre Kareem Abdul-Jabbar created a still-standing NBA record for defensive rebounds in a game when he grabbed 29 in a 110-100 win over the Detroit Pistons.

1991 – Wheaton's rich tennis victory

American David Wheaton picked up the then richest prize in tennis when he won £1.2 million by beating Michael Chang 7-5, 6-2, 6-4 in the Grand Slam Cup in Munich.

2003 – Indian duo dominate

Indian batsmen VVS Laxman (148) and Rahul Dravid (233) put on 303 in a day in the second Test against Australia in Adelaide.

2005 – Sprinters banned after BALCO

In a landmark verdict, former world 100m record holder Tim Montgomery and Chryste Gaines, a member of the US women's 4x100m gold medal-winning team at the 1996 Atlanta Olympics, were banned for 2 years for doping offences. The athletes were implicated in the criminal investigation into the Bay Area Laboratory Co-Operative scandal in California.

BIRTHDATES

1901	French tennis player HENRI COCHET – died 1987
1929	New Zealand rugby union winger RON JARDEN – died 1977
1938	West Indian Test pace bowler CHARLIE GRIFFITH
1946	American tennis player STAN SMITH
1953	Indian tennis player VIJAY AMRITRAJ
1954	American auto racer ALAN KULWICKI – died 1993
1955	Australian golfer JANE CRAFTER
1956	Liechtenstein alpine skier HANNI WENZEL
1960	England soccer forward CHRIS WADDLE
1965	MLB utility CRAIG BIGGIO
1966	NHL goalie BILL RANFORD
1975	England rugby union lock BEN KAY
1978	Swiss tennis player PATTY SCHNYDER
1979	England soccer striker MICHAEL OWEN

ⓕ DECEMBER

1925 – Madison Square Garden opens
The first Madison Square Garden was officially opened with a hockey game. Before an enthusiastic and capacity crowd of 17,000, the New York Americans went down 3-1 to the Montreal Canadiens.

1930 – A wicket for 'The Don'
Australian batsman Don Bradman took his first of only 2 Test wickets, when he trapped West Indian batsman Ivan Barrow lbw for 27, during the first Test in Adelaide.

1961 – 'Golden Bear' arrives
Amidst unprecedented media attention, US Amateur champion Jack Nicklaus arrived in Miami to practice for his pro debut, an 18-hole exhibition against Arnold Palmer, Gary Player, and Sam Snead.

1982 – England 9-0
Watford striker Luther Blissett scored a hat-trick as England scored a then tournament record 9-0 win over Luxembourg in a European Championship qualifier at Wembley Stadium.

1982 – Zaheer's double ton
Pakistan batsman Zaheer Abbas smashed 215 off only 254 balls in the drawn first Test against India in Lahore. Zaheer hit 23 fours and 2 sixes in his 100th first-class century. In a 78-Test career he scored 5,062 at 44.79 with 12 centuries and a career high 274.

1995 – 'Bosman Rule' born
Jean-Marc Bosman won his lawsuit against FC Liege and UEFA on the basis of restriction of trade. The European Court of Justice ruled clubs had no right to demand transfer fees for out of contract players. The ruling irrevocably changed player-club relationships.

2004 – Drug drama
Track superstar Marion Jones filed a legal suit against BALCO founder Victor Conte for defamation, claiming he had lied on television when he supplied her with banned drugs before the 2000 Sydney Olympics. Jones said his accusations were likely to cost her $25 million in endorsement deals. She was later jailed for lying about drug-related activities.

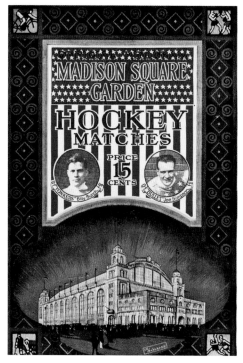

The cover of the program for the first NHL game at Madison Square Garden in 1925.

2012 – Slater denied by brave Kerr
Eleven-time world surfing champion Kelly Slater was beaten in the semi-finals of the Pipeline Masters to miss out on an unprecedented 12th title. Australian Josh Kerr was earlier taken to hospital for scans after being hammered by a 'Banzai bomb' in the heats. He returned to bravely beat Slater and reach the final against countryman Joel Parkinson, who won the Masters and world title, both for the first time.

BIRTHDATES
1899	English sprinter HAROLD ABRAHAMS – died 1978
1942	New Zealand rugby union centre BILL DAVIS
1944	MLB manager JIM LEYLAND
1951	Scottish soccer striker/manager JOE JORDAN
1959	New Zealand rugby union flanker ALAN WHETTON
1959	New Zealand rugby union lock GARY WHETTON
1959	Australian Test spinner GREG MATTHEWS
1962	England rugby union fullback SIMON HODGKINSON
1966	West Indian Test captain CARL HOOPER
1974	England rugby union lock GARETH ARCHER
1980	American tennis player ALEXANDRA STEVENSON
1981	Russian soccer striker ROMAN PAVLYUCHENKO

1945 – Nelson's 18th victory

Byron Nelson won the Glen Garden Invitational in Fort Worth, Texas to post his 18th win of the season, a PGA Tour record. Eleven of Nelson's victories were consecutive, another PGA record. Ben Hogan went on to win 13 times in 1946, but no one has come any closer to Nelson's 18 wins since.

1969 – Cricket in demand

Six people were killed when 20,000 fans stampeded for tickets in Calcutta, before the final day of the fourth Test between India and Australia. India trailed by 123 and resumed their second innings at 12 for 0 with great expectations. They were dismissed for a disappointing 161 and Australia won the match by 10 wickets.

1973 – O.J. first 2,000 yard rusher

Buffalo Bills running back O.J. Simpson ran through the New York Jets for 200 yards on the frozen turf at snow-covered Shea Stadium to become the NFL's first 2,000-yard rusher. Simpson finished with 2,003 yards to break Jim Brown's 10-year-old record of 1,863 yards. In 1984, L.A. Rams running back Eric Dickerson beat the mark, gaining 2,105 yards but Simpson remains the only running back in NFL history to better 2,000 yards in 14 games.

1984 – Monk passes 100 catches

Art Monk of the Washington Redskins became the first receiver to take more than 100 catches in an NFL season. Monk caught 11 passes in a 29-27 win over the St Louis Cardinals, giving him a record 106 for the season.

2005 – Chelsea clinches surf title

The 22-year-old Australian surfer Chelsea Georgeson became the only athlete in women's surfing history to have won the Billabong Pro Maui, the Vans Triple Crown of Surfing and the Women's World Championship in one swoop. She claimed her first world title by winning the season-ending event at Honolua Bay in Hawaii.

2006 – Gilchrist second fastest ton

Adam Gilchrist bludgeoned the second fastest century in Test history, and the fastest ever by an Australian, on day 3 of the third Test against England in Perth. He needed just 57 deliveries to reach his ton, narrowly missing out on Viv Richards' record set in 1985–86 when he faced just 56 balls against England at St John's, Antigua. Gilchrist's century consisted of 14 fours and 4 sixes.

2007 – Favre passes Marino

Brett Favre became the NFL career leader in yards passing, overtaking Dan Marino during the Packers 33-14 win over the Rams in St Louis. Marino passed for 61,361 yards in 17 seasons. Favre, who entered the game needing 184 yards, also was in his 17th season and enjoying a year comparable to his peak production.

2009 – Accolade for Tiger

Tiger Woods was named Athlete of the Decade for the period 2000 to 2009 by Associated Press sports editors. Woods won with 56 votes. Road-cyclist Lance Armstrong polled 33, tennis ace Roger Federer 25, swimmer Michael Phelps 13, and NFL quarterback Tom Brady 6. Woods has since suffered a loss of form after revelations of sexual affairs, while Armstrong has admitted to doping and been banned from cycling.

BIRTHDATES

1882	English Test batsman JACK HOBBS – died 1963
1910	England Test captain FREDDIE BROWN – died 1991
1952	West Indies Test fast bowler JOEL GARNER
1952	Italian soccer striker/manager FRANCESCO GRAZIANI
1962	NFL defensive lineman WILLIAM PERRY
1964	German long jumper HEIKE DRECHSLER
1964	New Zealand rugby union winger JOHN KIRWAN
1966	American golfer CATHY JOHNSTON-FORBES
1966	Irish golfer PAUL McGINLEY
1966	English soccer midfielder DENNIS WISE
1967	Canadian sprinter DONOVAN BAILEY
1968	Australian golfer WENDY DOOLAN
1969	Irish swimmer MICHELLE SMITH
1969	England Test all-rounder CRAIG WHITE
1979	South African golfer TREVOR IMMELMAN

1903 – 'Tip's Test debut treat
English batsman Reginald 'Tip' Foster scored 287 on debut in the first Test against Australia in Sydney. It remains the highest score by an Englishman in a Test in Australia.

1936 – Bing's racecourse plans
Crooner Bing Crosby and his celebrity friends Jimmy Durante and Pat O'Brien announced plans to construct a new racetrack in southern California, to be called the Del Mar Thoroughbred Club. The seaside track remains one of the top racecourses in North America.

1950 – Hogan is an official hero
Ben Hogan, who won the US Open just 16 months after a near-fatal road accident, was voted the PGA Player of the Year.

1984 – Mac's Davis Cup doubles streak ends
John McEnroe and Peter Fleming lost their first doubles match from 14 in Davis Cup competition when they were beaten 7-5, 5-7, 6-2, 7-5 by Swedish pair Anders Järryd and Stefan Edberg in Gothenburg. The win gave the Swedes an unassailable 3-0 lead. It was Sweden's second Davis Cup victory and the first since 1975.

1993 – Chávez boxing record
Julio César Chávez of Mexico retained his WBC light welterweight title with a fifth-round knockout of Britain's Andy Holligan at Puebla in Mexico. It was the 27th time Chávez had fought for a title without defeat, breaking Joe Louis' record of 26.

2000 – Reds end United home streak
Manchester United's 2-year unbeaten home record in the Premiership ended when the Red Devils were beaten by Liverpool at Old Trafford. Liverpool's Danny Murphy scored the winning goal as the Reds recorded a famous 1-0 victory over one of their fiercest rivals.

2000 – TO catches record 20 passes
Terrell Owens of the San Francisco 49ers caught an NFL-record 20 passes for 283 yards and a TD in a 17-0 win against the Chicago Bears at Candlestick Park. The previous record was held by Tom Fears of the LA Rams with 18 catches in 1950.

2005 – Another Warne record
Australian leg spinner Shane Warne claimed the world record for most wickets in a calendar year on the second day of the first Test against South Africa in Perth. Warne trapped Ashwell Prince lbw for 28, his 86th Test wicket in his 14th Test since January 1. He surpassed Dennis Lillee's record of 85 in 1981.

2005 – Valuev first Russian champ
Seven-foot (213cm) Nikolai Valuev became the first Russian to win any version of the world heavyweight title, and also the tallest champion in boxing history, by earning a majority decision over John Ruiz in Berlin to capture the WBA heavyweight belt.

2011 – Thompson youngest winner
American teenager Lexi Thompson shot a 5-under 67 to win the Dubai Masters and become the youngest pro winner on the Ladies European Tour. The 16-year-old beat Lee-Anne Pace of South Africa by 4 strokes. In September, she won her first event to become the youngest winner on the LPGA Tour.

BIRTHDATES
1881	South African Test all-rounder AUBREY FAULKNER – died 1930
1895	Australian tennis player GERALD PATTERSON – died 1967
1914	Indian Test batsman MUSHTAQ ALI – died 2005
1934	England soccer defender RAMON WILSON
1938	New Zealand middle distance runner PETER SNELL
1937	Media tycoon KERRY PACKER – died 2005
1951	Canadian NHL coach KEN HITCHCOCK
1962	American golfer ROCCO MEDIATE
1967	Canadian NHL centre VINCENT DAMPHOUSSE
1968	American auto-racer PAUL TRACEY
1973	British marathon runner PAULA RADCLIFFE
1973	French rugby union hooker RAPHAËL IBAÑEZ
1975	South African golfer TIM CLARK
1977	French tennis star ARNAUD CLEMENT
1978	Filipino boxer MANNY PACQUIAO

Golf balls are left at the grave of champion golfer Bobby Jones.

1910 – Freak Kiwi all-round sportsman born

Unique New Zealand all-round sportsman Eric Tindill was born. Tindill is the only man to play Test cricket and rugby union, as well as becoming a Test umpire and international rugby referee. He played one international for the All Blacks at Twickenham in 1936 and kept wicket for the Kiwi cricket team in a war interrupted career. He died aged 99 in 2010.

1927 – Perfect Ponsford

Bill Ponsford belted a world first-class record 437 runs for Victoria against Queensland in a Sheffield Shield match in Melbourne. The innings lasted 621 minutes and included 42 boundaries – leaving Ponsford's Shield average at 100.6 from 31 innings.

1932 – Famous NFL venue change

The NFL Championship game between the Chicago Bears and the Portsmouth Spartans was moved indoors to Chicago Stadium after Wrigley Field was ruled unplayable because of snow and extreme cold. Officials made an improvised 80-yard long dirt field flanked by walls. The Bears won 9-0.

1971 – Golf icon Jones dead at 69

Bobby Jones died aged 69 following a 20-year battle with a spinal ailment that gradually paralysed his limbs. Jones was the winner of 13 major championships and the only man to complete a single-season Grand Slam, achieved in 1930 when he won the British Amateur, British Open, US Open, and US Amateur. Although only 28, Jones then retired from competition, and several years later founded Augusta National and the Masters Tournament.

1983 – 'The Great One' reaches fastest 100

Edmonton Oilers' champion centre Wayne Gretzky had 2 goals and 2 assists in a 7-5 win at Winnipeg to give him 100 points in just 34 games. The feat remains the NHL record for the fastest 100 points.

2002 – First black sports ownership

The NBA awarded an expansion franchise to Robert L. Johnson, the founder of Black Entertainment Television, making him the first African-American to become the principal owner of a major professional sports team. Johnson paid a $300 million expansion fee for the new franchise in Charlotte, North Carolina, which began play in the 2004–5 season.

BIRTHDATES

1886	Baseball Hall of Fame infielder TY COBB – died 1961.
1910	New Zealand rugby rep/referee-Cricket rep/umpire – ERIC TINDILL – died 2010
1922	England soccer midfielder IVAN 'IVOR' BROADIS
1931	New Zealand Test batsman NOEL McGREGOR – died 2007
1932	Australian rugby league captain NORM PROVAN
1961	Canadian figure skater BRIAN ORSER
1963	American tennis player LORI McNEIL
1963	NBA forward CHARLES OAKLEY
1964	Pro wrestler 'STONE COLD' STEVE AUSTIN
1966	Italian soccer goalie GIANLUCA PAGLIUCA
1971	Spanish tennis player ARANTXA SÁNCHEZ VICARIO
1975	Dutch darts player VINCENT VAN DER VOORT
1987	Panamanian jockey FERNANDO JARA

1953 – Famous Welsh rugby victory

With 5 minutes remaining and scores locked at 8-8, Welsh flanker Clem Thomas set up a try for winger Ken Jones with a speculator kick to give Wales a famous 13-8 win over New Zealand at Cardiff Arms Park. An inspired All Black line-up had dominated play throughout the second half and appeared set for an upset victory before the dramatic finish.

1976 – Lever electric

England fast bowler John Lever took the new ball with immediate results as he captured 7 for 46 off 23 overs to dismiss India for 122 in the first Test in Delhi. Lever also hit 53 in his first Test innings as England won by an innings and 25 runs on their way to an unexpected series victory.

1982 – First unbeaten Kangaroos

Australia wrapped up the first undefeated rugby league tour of Britain and France with a 23-9 win over France at Narbonne. On the British leg of the tour the Kangaroos beat Great Britain 40-4 at Hull, 27-6 at Wigan and 32-8 at Leeds.

1989 – Bird begins famous free throw streak

Boston Celtics great Larry Bird started a phenomenal 71 game free throw streak. It was the second longest in NBA history behind Houston's Calvin Murphy (78). Denver's Mahmoud Abdul-Rauf (81) and Minnesota's Michael Williams (97) have since taken the record further.

2003 – Ferdinand's long suspension

A Football Association commission suspended Manchester United and England defender Rio Ferdinand for a record-equalling 8 months and fined him £50,000 for failing to take a random drug test at the club's training ground in September.

2010 – Tendulkar reaches 50 Test centuries

With India batting to save the first Test against South Africa in Centurian, Sachin Tendulkar hit an unprecedented 50th Test century. After conceding a 484-run first-innings lead, Tendulkar hit 111, bringing his 2010 tally to 7 centuries. Rahul Dravid also crossed the 12,000-run milestone. India lost the Test by an innings after Jacques Kallis scored his maiden double century.

BIRTHDATES

1922	Irish sports caster EAMMON ANDREWS – died 1987
1924	Hockey Hall of Fame defenseman DOUG HARVEY – died 1989
1926	Pro Football Hall of Fame quarterback BOBBY LAYNE – died 1986
1934	Baseball Hall of Fame outfielder AL KALINE
1949	American swimmer CLAUDIA KOLB
1957	Basketball Hall of Fame forward KEVIN McHALE
1961	Pro Football Hall of Fame defensive tackle REGGIE WHITE – died 2004
1964	Canadian golfer LORI KANE
1964	Lithuanian NBA centre ARVYDAS SABONIS
1966	Italian alpine skier ALBERTO TOMBA
1969	Indian Test wicketkeeper NAYAN MONGIA
1969	NBA forward TOM GUGLIOTTA
1972	NFL defensive tackle WARREN SAPP
1974	Australian Test captain RICKY PONTING
1988	Chilean soccer forward ALEXIS SÁNCHEZ

Indian cricketer Sachin Tandulkar in action.

1948 – England by 1

England beat South Africa by 1 run in the first Test in Durban in the only Test to be won off the last ball of the match. England's Alec Bedser and Cliff Gladwin began the final 8-ball over needing 8 runs to win with 2 wickets remaining. The equation came down to 1 run to win off 1 ball. Gladwin missed his stroke, the ball striking his thigh and bouncing a yard in front of him. Both batsmen sprinted home safely, enabling England to win the dramatic finish.

1959 – Patel's nine

India's Jasu Patel took 9 for 69 against Australia in the second Test in Kanpur. Patel's off-spin exploited a recently laid turf pitch to help win the match by 119 runs. His figures were a Test-best for India until Anil Kumble took all 10 against Pakistan at Delhi in 1998–99. Patel was the second bowler to take 9 wickets in a Test innings for India, after Subhash Gupte against West Indies on the same ground the previous winter.

1981 – Fastest Ice Hockey goal

Doug Smail of the Winnipeg Jets scored after 5 seconds of play to create the NHL record for the fastest goal from start of a game in the Jets' 5-4 home win over St Louis. The record was equalled by Bryan Trottier in 1984 and Alexander Mogilny in 1991

1988 – McLean does it all

Dundee United manager and Board member Jim McLean was also elected chairman of the Board. After 21 years of service, Scotland's longest serving manager resigned at the end of the 1992–3 season but remained chairman.

1991 – Expensive midfielder

Yugoslav midfielder Dejan Savicevic became the then world's most expensive player when he transferred from AC Milan to Atlético Madrid for a fee of £11.5 million. Savicevic's personal terms amounted to £7 million over 3 years.

1992 – Van Basten takes third award

AC Milan's Dutch international striker Marco van Basten was voted European Footballer of the Year for

Dutch forward Marco van Basten in action for AC Milan in 1990.

the third time in 5 years. The feat equalled countryman Johan Cruyff and French captain Michel Platini.

1996 – Middlesbrough cancel Premier League match

With manager Bryan Robson claiming he had 23 players unavailable through illness or injury, Middlesbrough cancelled their Premier League match against Blackburn Rovers. The Football Association later deducted 3 competition points from Middlesbrough after conducting an inquiry. Boro was relegated at the end of the season.

BIRTHDATES

1905 Australian Test spinner BILL O'REILLY – died 1992.
1928 Pro Football Hall of Fame safety JACK CHRISTIANSEN – died 1986
1942 American sprinter BOB HAYES – died 2002
1950 American rodeo rider TOM R. FERGUSON
1965 NFL quarterback RICH GANNON
1970 Zimbabwe Test batsman GRANT FLOWER
1979 Australian road cyclist MICHAEL ROGERS
1980 England soccer defender ASHLEY COLE
1982 Pakistan Test fast bowler MOHAMMAD ASIF
1982 MLB infielder DAVID WRIGHT
1983 West Indian Test fast bowler DARREN SAMMY

891 – Basketball's first game
Basketball is believed to have been played for the first time at Springfield College, Massachusetts. The game was played by 18 students who utilised 2 peach baskets and a soccer ball.

1975 – Davis Cup first for Sweden
Nineteen-year-old Björn Borg defeated Czech ace Jan Kodeš 6-4, 6-2, 6-2 in Stockholm to clinch Sweden's first ever Davis Cup title. Borg won both his singles and teamed with Ove Bengtson to win the doubles rubber.

1975 – Blanda first to 2,000 NFL points
Forty-eight-year-old Oakland Raiders quarterback George Blanda became the first player to reach 2,000 career points in the NFL when he kicked 4 extra points in Oakland's 28-20 win over the Kansas City Chiefs. The conversions lifted his scoring total to 2,002 points. Blanda scored 9 touchdowns, kicked 335 field goals and made 943 extra points in a 26-year pro career.

1983 – Spanish blitz
Needing to win by 11 clear goals to qualify for the European Championships the Spanish soccer team thrashed Malta 12-1 in Seville. It was a record for the highest score in the competition.

1990 – Wonderful Waughs
Steve Waugh with an unbeaten 216 and brother Mark 229 not out, established a world first-class record 464-run fifth wicket partnership for New South Wales in the Sheffield Shield match against Western Australia in Perth. The brothers hit 19 fours each.

1991 – A Russian rush
Russian forward Alexander Mogilny of the Buffalo Sabres scored a goal after only 5 seconds play in Buffalo's 4-1 away win over Toronto. Mogilny tied the record for fastest goal from start of an NHL game with Winnipeg's Doug Smail (1981) and Bryan Trottier of the NY Islanders (1984).

1997 – Sanders third to 2,000 yards
Champion Detroit Lions running back Barry Sanders became only the third player in history (after O.J. Simpson and Eric Dickerson) to rush for an amazing 2,000 yards in a season. Sanders ran for 184 yards in a 13-10 home win against the New York Jets in the final game of the regular season. He pushed his 1997 total to 2,053 yards.

1999 – British Boxing broke
The British Boxing Board of Control was placed into administration in a bid to ensure its long-term survival as the regulatory body of the sport in Britain. The development came after Michael Watson won a high profile and costly lawsuit against the Board.

2008 – LT makes three
LaDainian Tomlinson rushed for 90 yards in San Diego's 41-24 win at Tampa Bay to join Barry Sanders and Curtis Martin as the only players in NFL history to run for 1,000 in each of their first 8 seasons.

2010 – 89 straight for UConn girls
The no. 1-ranked University of Connecticut women's basketball team topped the 88-game winning streak set by John Wooden's UCLA men's team from 1971–74, beating no. 22 Florida State 93-62 in Hartford. Maya Moore had a career-high 41 points and 10 rebounds for the Huskies, who had not lost since April 2008 in the NCAA tournament semifinals. The famous win streak ended at 90 when UConn was beaten by Stanford on December 30.

BIRTHDATES
1892	American golfer WALTER HAGEN – died 1969
1926	College football coach JOE PATERNO – died 2012
1933	West Indian Test wicketkeeper JACKIE HENDRIKS
1934	Pakistan Test batsman HANIF MOHAMMAD
1935	Italian auto racer LORENZO BANDINI – died 1967
1945	Australian Test batsman DOUG WALTERS
1952	American swimmer STEVE FURNISS
1954	American tennis player CHRIS EVERT
1959	American sprinter FLORENCE GRIFFITH JOYNER – died 1998
1959	Indian Test batsman KRIS SRIKKANTH
1966	England rugby union lock MARTIN BAYFIELD
1972	Costa Rican swimmer CLAUDIA POLL
1974	Australian golfer KARRIE WEBB
1977	New Zealand rugby union centre LEON MacDONALD
1978	Italian swimmer EMILIANO BREMBILLA

1951 – Worrell worries home team
West Indies all-rounder Frank Worrell took 6 for 38 off 12.7 overs as Australia was dismissed for a meagre 82 in the third Test at the Adelaide Oval. The Windies went on to win by 6 wickets to trail the 5-Test series 2-1.

1971 – Lakers' pro sports record
The Los Angeles Lakers set a major-league professional sports record for consecutive victories with their 27th straight win, a 127-120 victory over the Bullets in Baltimore. Led by future Hall of Famers Jerry West, Wilt Chamberlain and Gail Goodrich, the Lakers had shared the record at 26 with the New York Giants, who had set the mark during the 1916 baseball season. The Lakers extended their record streak to 33 before losing to the Milwaukee Bucks.

1987 – English golfer passes away
Three-time British Open champion Henry Cotton died aged 80. Cotton won the Open Championship in 1934, 1937, and 1948 and was active on the European Continent in the 1930s. His best year was 1937, when he won the British, French and Czechoslovakian Opens and was selected for the Ryder Cup matches. Cotton served as captain of the Ryder Cup team in 1947 and 1953.

1999 – Spurs worst Cup defeat
Newcastle thrashed Tottenham Hotspur 6-1 in their FA Cup third round replay at St James' Park. It was the north London club's worst defeat in a competition they had won 8 times.

2004 – rugby union's rich TV deal
The SANZAR triumvirate of South Africa, New Zealand and Australia confirmed a new 5-year broadcasting deal with News Limited and South Africa's Supersport. The deal, worth US$323 million covered broadcast rights for the 3 SANZAR countries and the UK. The substantial increase was for an expanded Tri Nations tournament and a new Super 14 competition in 2006.

2010 – Sloan moves to third on NBA coaches list
The Utah Jazz scored a 112-107 victory over the Timberwolves in Minneapolis and coach Jerry Sloan picked up victory no. 1,211 to break a tie with Pat Riley for third on the NBA career list. Only Don Nelson (1,335) and Lenny Wilkens (1,332) had more victories in NBA history.

2012 – 'Megatron' beats Rice's record
Lions' wide receiver Calvin Johnson broke Jerry Rice's 17-year-old single-season yardage record of 1,848 yards against the Atlanta Falcons in Detroit, picking up 204 yards to give him 1,871 yards on the season and the record. Johnson also set the NFL record for passing 100 yards receiving in 8 consecutive games. It was the 11th time that season he surpassed 100 yards; that tied an NFL record held by Michael Irvin.

BIRTHDATES
1929	Pakistan Test batsman WAZIR MOHAMMAD
1934	American auto racer DAVID PEARSON
1944	Baseball Hall of Fame pitcher STEVE CARLTON
1947	Indian Test spinner DILIP DOSHI
1948	England Test fast bowler CHRIS OLD
1948	MLB first baseman STEVE GARVEY
1951	Australian golfer JAN STEPHENSON
1954	West Indian Test spinner DERICK PARRY
1959	German soccer midfielder/manager BERND SCHUSTER
1963	South African Test all-rounder BRIAN McMILLAN
1963	Italian soccer defender GIUSEPPE BERGOMI
1966	Russian gymnast DMITRY BILOZERCHEV
1967	Romanian defender DAN PETRESCU
1968	Mexican soccer striker LUIS HERNÁNDEZ
1969	Canadian biathlete MYRIAM BÉDARD
1970	Scottish darts player GARY ANDERSON
1988	Welsh rugby winger LEIGH HALFPENNY

West Indian Test captain Sir Frank Worrell in 1950.

1972 – Steelers' famous first playoff win

The Pittsburgh Steelers scored the first playoff victory in franchise history when they beat the Oakland Raiders 13-7 in an AFC Divisional Playoff Game. The game featured Franco Harris' famous 'Immaculate Reception' when quarterback Jack Tatum hit the intended receiver, 'Frenchy' Fuqua, who knocked the ball back to Harris who ran into the end zone.

1972 – Spinner's wicket

Indian spinner Bhagwat Chandrasekhar captured 8 for 79 against England in the first Test in Delhi. England won the match by 6 wickets, but lost the series 2-1.

1978 – Trottier's 6 points in a period

Bryan Trottier of the New York Islanders scored an NHL record 6 points in the second period of their 9-4 win against arch-rivals the New York Rangers at Madison Square Garden. Trottier scored 3 goals and made 3 assists in a blistering period.

1981 – Boring Boycott leading scorer

England opening batsman Geoff Boycott became the leading run scorer in Test cricket with a total of 8,033 during the third Test in Delhi. Boycott scored 105 in a typically lengthy 440-minute innings to pass Garry Sobers' Test record of 8,032 runs. It was Boycott's 22nd Test century.

1984 – Double ton to Viv

Swashbuckling West Indian batsman Vivian Richards belted 22 fours and 3 sixes in scoring a blistering 208 against Australia in the fourth Test against Australia in Melbourne. The match was drawn, putting to an end the West Indies' run of 11 consecutive Test victories.

1997 – Jackson reaches 500 win milestone

Chicago Bulls coach Phil Jackson reached 500 wins after coaching only 682 games with a 94-89 win at home against the LA Clippers. He achieved the feat faster than any other coach in NBA history. After guiding the Bulls to 6 NBA Championships and the Los Angeles Lakers to three, Jackson left LA in 2004, only to be rehired in 2005.

2000 – Kiwis win women's World Cup

New Zealand won the Women's World Cup final with a nail-biting 4-run win over Australia at Lincoln. After being dismissed for 184, tight Kiwi bowling by Katrina Keenan and Rachel Pullar helped to dismiss the favoured Australians for 180 in the last over to take the trophy.

2006 – Knight ties Smith's NCAA mark

Texas Tech basketball head coach Bob Knight tied the legendary Dean Smith for most career wins in NCAA Division I history after notching no. 879 in a 72-60 triumph over Bucknell.

2007 – Pats go 15 straight

The New England Patriots set an NFL record with their 15th win to start the season. Tom Brady threw 3 touchdown passes, 2 to Randy Moss, and the Patriots beat the Miami Dolphins 28-7 at Foxborough to improve to 15-0, the best start in league history. Miami's old mark was 14-0 in 1972 when the season lasted just 14 games.

2007 – Kobe youngest to 20,000

Kobe Bryant scored 39 points as the LA Lakers held off the Knicks 95-90 in New York to become the youngest player in NBA history to reach 20,000 points. He reached the milestone at 29 years, 122 days. Only Wilt Chamberlain and Michael Jordan had reached the mark before turning 30.

BIRTHDATES

1894	England Test captain ARTHUR GILLIGAN – died 1976
1924	Basketball Hall of fame centre BOB KURLAND
1929	American pro bowler DICK WEBER – died 2005
1935	Pro Football Hall of Fame utility PAUL HORNUNG
1936	Pro Football Hall of Fame safety WILLIE WOOD
1936	NFL coach BOBBY ROSS
1947	American marathon runner BILL RODGERS
1948	NFL linebacker JACK HAM
1950	Spanish soccer manager VICENTE DEL BOSQUE
1956	Italian auto racer MICHELE ALBORETO – died 2001
1963	NFL quarterback/coach JIM HARBAUGH
1970	Canadian speed skater CATRIONA LE MAY DOAN
1979	American NHL centre SCOTT GOMEZ
1979	Scottish soccer striker KENNY MILLER
1987	New Zealand rugby prop OWEN FRANKS

1932 – Cricket icon born

The late Lord Colin Cowdrey was born at Bangalore in India. Cowdrey was the first player to appear in 100 Tests, celebrating with a century against Australia at Edgbaston in 1968 despite pulling a leg muscle. At one stage, he'd scored more Test runs than any other batsman – 7,624 runs in 114 Tests for England at 44.06. Even at age 42, he commanded respect when he was recalled to face the venom of Lillee and Thomson in Australia in 1974–75. Having played for Kent in county cricket Cowdrey was elected president of the MCC in 1986. He was knighted in 1992, and in 1997 became a life peer, the second cricketer after Learie Constantine to be elevated to the House of Lords. He died in 2000, aged 67.

1950 – Browns an instant success

In their first NFL season, the Cleveland Browns beat the Los Angeles Rams, 30-28 with a last minute field goal in the NFL Championship game. It was the Browns' fifth consecutive championship after they had won all 4 titles in the All-American Football Conference. Down 28-20 in the fourth quarter, Rex Baumgardner scored and an Otto Graham engineered 57-yard drive led to Lou Groza's 16-yard winning field goal.

1967 – Joe first QB to 4,000 yards

New York Jets quarterback Joe Namath became the first player to throw for 4,000 yards in a season (4,007). Namath passed for 343 yards in a 42-32 win over the Chargers at San Diego's Jack Murphy Stadium.

2005 – Alexander ties touchdown record

Seattle Seahawks' running back Shaun Alexander ran for 139 yards and scored 3 TDs to tie Priest Holmes' NFL record of 27 TDs in a season. The Seahawks clinched NFC home-field advantage with a 28-13 victory over Indianapolis.

2006 – Colt throws for NCAA record

Colt Brennan broke the NCAA single-season record for touchdown passes with 58. He threw 5 in the second half to lead Hawaii to a 41-24 victory over Arizona State in the Hawaii Bowl. Brennan, 33-of-42

New York Jets quarterback Joe Namath in 1966 NFL action.

for 559 yards, broke the previous mark of 54 set by Houston's David Klingler in 1990.

2006 – Vick runs for 1,000

Atlanta's Michael Vick became the first NFL quarterback to rush for 1,000 yards in a season in the Falcons' 10–3 loss to Carolina in Atlanta. Vick, who needed only 10 yards to reach the mark, gained 17 on his first carry on the Falcons' opening possession. The drive ended with another milestone, Morten Andersen's 539th career field goal. He passed Gary Andersen for the career record.

2011 – New NFL field goal mark

David Akers made 4 field goals to give him 42 for the season, most in league history, as San Francisco beat the Seahawks 19-17 in Seattle. Akers passed the NFL mark set by Neil Rackers in 2005 with Arizona.

BIRTHDATES

1914	England soccer goalkeeper FRANK SWIFT – died 1958
1921	Pro Football Hall of Fame defensive back BILL DUDLEY – died 2010
1929	Swedish soccer winger LENNART SKOGLUND – died 1975
1932	England Test batsman COLIN COWDREY – died 2000
1944	German speed skater ERHARD KELLER
1944	Australian golfer BOB SHAW
1947	Australian AFL defender/coach KEVIN SHEEDY
1971	New Zealand Test fast bowler GEOFF ALLOTT
1974	Chilean soccer striker MARCELO SALAS

㉕ DECEMBER

1948 – Innovative football program

Chelsea published football's first-ever magazine style match programme for their Division 1 match against Portsmouth at Stamford Bridge. The 16-page issue cost sixpence.

1951 – Windies whitewash

The West Indies wrapped up the third Test against Australia in Adelaide in just 3 days after dismissing the home side for 82 and 255. Windies spinner Alf Valentine took 6 for 102 to follow-on from Frank Worrell's first innings 6 for 62. They were set a winning target of 233 and reached it in 73.5 overs for the loss of 4 wickets.

1971 – NFL's longest game

The Miami Dolphins and Kansas City Chiefs gave fans a Christmas present – the longest game in Pro Football history. Their AFC semi-final game was tied 24-24 at the end of regulation and the first overtime period. In the second overtime, Miami's Gary Yepremian hit a 37-yard field goal to win it, 27-24. The game lasted 82 minutes and 40 seconds.

1989 – Controversial MLB manager Martin dead at 61

Billy Martin, who had a 1,253–1,013 record as manager of 4 different teams, died in a truck crash, aged 61. Martin was a fine second baseman for the New York Yankees when they won the 1952 and 1953 World Series. His feisty nature transferred from the playing field to his managerial demeanour. After stints with Minnesota and Detroit, Martin returned to the Yankees as manager and won the 1977 and 1978 World Series despite a public feud with star slugger Reggie Jackson. He was then fired for the first of a record 5 times by the Yankees in a fiery career.

2008 – Kobe ends Celtics' streak

Kobe Bryant had 27 points, 9 rebounds and 5 assists, Paul Gascol scored 7 of his 20 points in the final 3 minutes, as the LA Lakers beat Boston 92-83 at the Staples Centre, snapping the Celtics' franchise-record 19-game winning streak.

Outstanding West Indies spin bowler Alf Valentine.

BIRTHDATES

1891	Australian Test spinner CLARRIE GRIMMETT – died 1980.
1927	Baseball Hall of Fame second baseman NELLIE FOX – died 1975
1934	Italian auto racer GIANCARLO BAGHETTI – died 1995
1942	French tennis star FRANÇOISE DÜRR
1944	Brazilian soccer winger JAIRZINHO
1944	New Zealand rugby union lock SAM STRAHAN
1945	NFL quarterback KEN STABLER
1946	Pro Football Hall of Fame running back LARRY CSONKA
1957	Pakistan Test batsman MANSOOR AKHTAR
1958	Baseball Hall of Fame outfielder RICKY HENDERSON
1964	England rugby union captain KEVIN SIMMS
1964	Scottish soccer midfielder GARY McALLISTER
1975	England Test batsman MARCUS TRESCOTHICK
1978	England Test fast bowler SIMON JONES
1981	England Test batsman ALASTAIR COOK

Indianapolis Colts quarterback Peyton Manning in 2004 NFL action.

㉖ DECEMBER

1908 – Johnson breaks boxing race barrier

Thirty-year-old Texan challenger Jack Johnson became the first African-American to win the world heavyweight title when he pounded Canadian champion Tommy Burns to a 14th round knockout in Sydney, Australia. Johnson weighed 192lbs – 24lbs more than Burns – and was also 7in taller. With his brute strength ,Johnson dominated, until police intervened to halt the one-sided fight. Burns received an extraordinary guarantee of $30,000 for the bout, whilst Johnson was paid $5,000.

1919 – 'The Babe' sold to Yankees

Cash-strapped Boston Red Sox owner Harry Frazee agreed to sell star slugger Babe Ruth to the New York Yankees. Ruth had broken the major league home run record with 29 and led the American League with 114 RBI and 103 runs. Frazee received $125,000 and a $300,000 loan in the transaction. Ruth had guided Boston to 3 World Series wins, but it was 85 years until 'The Curse of the Bambino' was broken in 2004, when they swept the St Louis Cardinals 4-0.

1963 – Fast Football hat-trick

Fulham's Graham Leggat scored the fastest hat-trick in Division 1 since World War II as the Cottagers thrashed Ipswich Town 10-1 at Craven Cottage. Leggat scored 3 goals in 3 minutes during the first half.

1999 – No Brits at Chelsea

Chelsea made history by starting their Premier League match against Southampton at The Dell without a single British player in the side. The Blues won the match 2-1.

2004 – 'Minister of Defence' passes away

Fearsome defensive end Reggie White died of respiratory failure. He was 43. The two-time NFL defensive player of the year and ordained minister played a 15-year career with Philadelphia, Green Bay and Carolina. He retired after the 2000 NFL season as the all-time sacks leader with 198.

2005 – Ponting breaks his own record

Australian captain Ricky Ponting smashed a vital century – his 26th in Test cricket – on the first day of the second Test against South Africa in Melbourne. He also broke his own Australian record for the number of Test runs scored in a calendar year. Ponting's 117 runs came off 198 balls and included 13 fours.

2011 – Brees overtakes Marino mark

Drew Brees set the NFL record for yards passing in a season, breaking a mark that Dan Marino had held for 27 years, as the New Orleans Saints clinched the NFC South title with a 45-16 victory over Atlanta at the Superdome. Brees threw for 307 yards and 4 TDs, for 5,087 yards passing – with one game still to play. Marino finished with 5,084 yards for Miami in 1984.

BIRTHDATES

1913	England soccer captain FRANK SWIFT – died 1958
1935	West Indies Test batsman ROHAN KANHAI
1947	Baseball Hall of Fame catcher CARLTON FISK
1954	Baseball Hall of Fame shortstop OZZIE SMITH
1963	Canadian NBA centre BILL WENNINGTON
1975	Chilean tennis player MARCELO RIOS
1982	Norwegian alpine skier AKSEL LUND SVINDAL
1989	Jamaican sprinter JOHAN BLAKE
1990	Welsh soccer midfielder AARON RAMSEY

㉗ DECEMBER

1967 – Powerful Australian team wins Cup
Australia won its fourth consecutive Davis Cup when John Newcombe and Tony Roche beat Spaniards Manuel Santana and Manuel Orantes in the doubles tie 6-4, 6-4, 6-4 for an unbeatable 3-0 lead in the final in Brisbane. Roy Emerson and Newcombe had won the opening singles rubbers.

1982 – Imran leads the way
Pakistan captain Imran Khan took a magnificent 8 for 60 to wrap up the second Test against India in Karachi by an innings and 86 runs. Imran followed up his 3 for 19 in the first innings to finish with a match haul of 11 wickets, taking 5 for 3 off his last 25 balls.

1985 – Tennis legend dies
Legendary tennis coach Harry Hopman died, aged 79, in Florida. Although Hopman won 7 major doubles titles as a player, he made his name as the most successful of all Davis Cup captains, guiding Australia to 16 Cups from 1939–67. He is famous for nurturing tennis champions like Rod Laver, Ken Rosewall, Lew Hoad, Roy Emerson, John Newcombe and Tony Roche in their informative years. Hopman emigrated to the US to become a highly successful teaching pro, counselling the likes of John McEnroe and Vitas Gerulaitis.

1987 – Rice records
San Francisco 49ers receiver Jerry Rice ended a stellar season catching 2 touchdown passes from quarterback Steve Young in a 48-0 rout of the Los Angeles Rams and clinching the NFC West title for San Francisco. Rice extended his NFL record of touchdown receptions to 13 consecutive games, counting back to the final game of the 1986 regular season and also finished with a record 22 touchdown receptions, and 23 touchdowns overall.

1991 – Hardaway can't buy a basket
Tim Hardaway of the Golden State Warriors set an NBA record for futility by missing all 17 of his shots. Nevertheless, the Warriors won 106-102, thanks to 36 points from Chris Mullin.

Australian tennis player Tony Roche at Wimbledon, 1968.

2009 – Manning makes an elite quartet
Indianapolis Colts quarterback Peyton Manning became the fourth player in NFL history to reach 50,000 passing yards when he completed a 24-yard pass to Austin Collie in the Colts 29-15 home defeat to the New York Jets.

BIRTHDATES
1920	English jockey/trainer BRUCE HOBBS – died 2005
1933	American golfer DAVE MARR – died 1997
1934	Ukrainian gymnast LARISSA LATYNINA
1936	England Test batsman PHIL SHARPE
1940	English Test cricket umpire DAVID SHEPHERD – died 2009
1950	Italian soccer striker ROBERTO BETTEGA
1953	Australian Test wicketkeeper KEVIN WRIGHT
1958	American golfer STEVE JONES
1959	Pro Football Hall of Fame wide receiver ANDRE TIPPETT
1960	Australian golfer TERRY PRICE
1962	American golfer SHERRI STEINHAUER
1966	American pro wrestler/NFL tackle/actor BILL GOLDBERG
1971	Scottish soccer striker DUNCAN FERGUSON
1972	Welsh rugby flanker COLIN CHARVIS
1973	Swedish golfer SOPHIE GUSTAFSON
1984	French tennis player GILLES SIMON
1990	Canadian tennis player MILOS RAONIC

1926 – Vics top 1,100 in an innings
Australian Test batsman Bill Ponsford scored 352 and Jack Ryder 295 as Victoria scored a world first-class record 1,107 runs in a Sheffield Shield match against New South Wales at the Melbourne Cricket Ground. Test leg-spinner Arthur Mailey took 4 wickets for NSW, but they cost him 362 runs from 64 overs and he didn't bowl a maiden.

1934 – First women's Test
England fast bowler Myrtle Maclagan took 7 for 10 as Australia was dismissed for 47 on the first day of the first ever women's Test in Brisbane. England went on to win by 9 wickets.

1954 – US Davis Cup victory
The United States won its first Davis Cup in 4 years when Tony Trabert and Vic Seixas beat Australia's Lew Hoad and Ken Rosewall in the doubles tie 6-2, 4-6, 6-2, 10-8 at White City in Sydney. The victory gave the US an unassailable 3-0 lead after Trabert and Seixas had beaten Hoad and Rosewall respectively in the opening singles.

1958 – Hail Ameche
Harry Ameche scored on a famous 1-yard run to give the Baltimore Colts a 23-17 overtime win over the New York Giants in what has been labelled 'the greatest game ever played' and the first overtime NFL Championship match.

1983 – Demaret passes away at 73
Three-time Masters champion Jimmy Demaret died aged 73, suffering a heart attack getting into a golf cart. In a career between 1935–57, Demaret won 31 events and was the first three-time Masters winner (1940, 1947 and 1950). He reached his peak in the late 1940s when he won in the Masters and the Vardon Trophy, and was leading money winner in 1947. Known for his colourful outfits, Demaret was the original television host of *Shell's Wonderful World of Golf* in the early 1960s.

1983 – Sunny passes Bradman's century mark
Indian opener Sunil Gavaskar broke Don Bradman's record for career Test centuries during the drawn sixth Test against the West Indies in Madras. Gavaskar completed 30 hundreds to break Bradman's mark of 29, set in 1948. By the end of his career Gavaskar had taken the record to 34 centuries.

2006 – Zito in the money
Barry Zito became the highest paid pitcher in MLB history when he agreed to a $126 million 7-year contract with the San Francisco Giants. The Cy Young winner's deal was also the largest ever in Giants history, supplanting the $90 million contract Barry Bonds signed after the 2001 season.

2008 – Losing Lions
The Detroit Lions lost 31-21 to the Packers in Green Bay, making them the first team to go winless through a 16-game NFL season. The 1976 expansion Tampa Bay Buccaneers (0-14) were the last team to complete a season without a victory.

BIRTHDATES
1920	South African Test spin bowler NORMAN 'TUFTY' MANN – died 1952
1929	Canadian Hockey Hall of Fame goalie TERRY SAWCHUK – died 1970
1932	Canadian Hockey Hall of Fame defenseman HARRY HOWELL
1936	Pro Football Hall of Fame linebacker RAY NITSCHKE – 1998
1941	Pakistan Test captain INTIKHAB ALAM
1946	American golfer HUBERT GREEN
1946	Panamanian jockey LAFFIT PINCAY JR
1957	Australian netball captain ANNE SARGEANT
1958	England soccer defender TERRY BUTCHER
1958	American golfer CURT BYRUM
1959	Swedish speed skater TOMAS GUSTAFSON
1960	Canadian Hockey Hall of Fame defenseman RAY BOURQUE
1960	Australian Davis Cup player/captain JOHN FITZGERALD
1961	Danish soccer defender/manager KENT NIELSEN
1972	Australian tennis player PATRICK RAFTER
1972	Peruvian soccer midfielder ROBERTO PALACIOS
1972	NFL kicker ADAM VINATIERI
1976	Australian rugby union winger BEN TUNE
1979	American tennis player JAMES BLAKE

1978 – College Football fisticuffs

In a bizarre incident, Ohio State coach Woody Hayes came to blows with an opposition player. Ohio State was losing 17-15 with less than 2 minutes remaining in the Gator Bowl when Clemson's Charlie Bauman intercepted a pass and was run out of bounds. A frustrated Hayes threw a punch at Bauman and then had to be restrained by his own players. He was fired the next day.

1979 – Perry's 4 interceptions

Houston Oilers' safety Vernon Perry set an NFL playoff record with 4 interceptions in the Oilers' 17-14 victory over San Diego. The regular season record is also 4 interceptions, held by many players.

1994 – Warne Ashes hat-trick

Australian spinner Shane Warne took the first hat-trick in an Ashes Test since 1903–04 during the second Test against England in Melbourne. Warne dismissed Phil DeFreitas, Darren Gough and Devon Malcolm with consecutive balls as Australia won by 295 runs for a 2-0 series lead. Warne followed on his 6 for 64 in the first innings with a super economical 3 for 16 off 13 overs that included his hat-trick.

2001 – 800 NBA wins for Sloan

Jerry Sloan earned his 800th career victory as an NBA coach when his Utah Jazz beat the Philadelphia 76ers 89-81. Karl Malone had 20 points and 17 rebounds for the Jazz. That took Sloan to equal ninth on the all-time list together with Larry Brown.

2004 – Aussies invincible

Australia beat Pakistan by 9 wickets in the second Test in Melbourne to clinch the 3-Test series and become the first team to score 5 Test series victories in a calendar year. During 2004 the Australians had beaten Sri Lanka, Zimbabwe, India, New Zealand and Pakistan in Test series.

2007 – Patriots' record season

The New England Patriots became the first NFL team since the 1972 Dolphins (14-0) to win every game on the schedule (16-0) with a 38-35 win over the New York Giants at Giants Stadium. Tom Brady-engineered a comeback from a 12-point deficit and smashed the Patriots' league mark for consecutive victories, their 19th straight regular season win over 2 seasons. New England went on top on Brady's NFL record 50th touchdown pass of the year and Randy Moss' NFL record 23rd TD reception. Brady beat Peyton Manning's mark of 49 TD passes and Moss broke Jerry Rice's record of 22 TD receptions. The Pats also finished with an incredible 589 points, another single-season record as well as a league mark of 75 TDs.

2010 – England score rare Ashes win in Oz

England retained the Ashes in Australia for the first time in 24 years, taking the fourth Test in Melbourne behind a brilliant bowling performance with Australia out for 98 in the first innings. Then they piled on 513 – Jonathan Trott was unbeaten on 168 – and dismissed Australia to win with a day to spare by an innings-and-157-runs.

2012 – Grieg passes away

Former England Test captain Tony Grieg died aged 66 after a short battle with lung cancer. Grieg was in hospital when he suffered cardiac arrest. The tall South African-born all-rounder was pivotal in the establishment of World Series Cricket. In 58 Tests he scored 3,599 runs at 40.43. He also took 141 wickets. After retiring as a player he became a popular television commentator around the world.

BIRTHDATES

1881	American boxer JESS WILLARD – died 1968.
1944	New Zealand Test batsman RODNEY REDMOND
1949	Indian Test wicket keeper SYED KIRMANI
1949	Great Britain rugby league five-eighth DAVID TOPLISS – died 2008
1957	Scotland rugby union number 8 IAIN PAXTON
1960	Australian Test batsman DAVID BOON
1960	Australian Test fast bowler DAVE GILBERT
1962	New Zealand soccer player WYNTON RUFER
1963	NFL coach SEAN PAYTON
1966	Great Britain rugby league winger MARTIN OFFIAH
1976	Pakistan Test spinner SAQLAIN MUSHTAQ
1981	Japanese figure skater SHIZUKA ARAKAWA

1961 – Wilt's freakish streak

Wilt Chamberlain of the Philadelphia Warriors completed an incredible streak of 14 consecutive games in which he scored 40 or more points. The streak commenced December 8. He began another similar 14 game streak on January 11.

1970 – Sonny Liston found dead

Former World Heavyweight Champion Sonny Liston died at his Las Vegas home. His body was found by his wife on January 5. Officially, Liston died of heart failure and lung congestion, but needle marks found in his arm suggest he may have died of a heroin overdose. It has been speculated he was murdered for demanding a bigger stake in a loan-sharking ring. Liston had a 50-4 ring record, including 39 knockouts. His ties to organized crime always put into question the validity of his results.

1981 – Fast 50 for 'The Great One'

Wayne Gretzky of the Edmonton Oilers reached the 50-goal mark faster than any other player in NHL history with 5 goals in a 7-5 home win against the Philadelphia Flyers. Gretzky took just 39 games to reach the mark.

1990 – Skiles' assists record

Orlando Magic guard Scott Skiles set an NBA record with 30 assists in a 155-116 win over the Denver Nuggets in Orlando. Stiles broke the record of 29 by New Jersey's Kevin Porter set in 1978. Stiles' record remains the NBA mark.

1995 – Shearer's Premier League first

Alan Shearer became the first player to score 100 goals in the English Premier League. The England striker was on target in Blackburn's 2-1 win over Tottenham at Ewood Park.

1997 – Woods award

On his 22nd birthday, Tiger Woods was named the Associated Press Male Athlete of the Year after his first year on the PGA Tour. Woods was only the fifth golfer to ever win the prestigious award. In his first PGA Tour season, Woods won The Masters by a record 12

'The Great One' Wayne Gretzky.

strokes with a record score of 18-under par 270.

1999 – 'King of the Channel' dead at 72

Australian marathon swimmer Des Renford died in Sydney aged 72. Renford swam the English Channel on 19 occasions and never failed in any Channel attempt.

2007 – Return specialist

Chicago wide receiver Devin Hester recorded an NFL-record sixth kick runback for a score to break his own mark as the Bears beat the New Orleans Saints 33-25 at Soldier Field. Hester sprinted 64 yards for a TD for the record and also caught a 55-yard touchdown pass from Kyle Orton. The Bears missed the playoffs after being part of the Super Bowl in 2006.

BIRTHDATES

1883	Canadian hockey defenseman LESTER PATRICK – died 1960
1919	England Test wicket keeper DICK SPOONER – died 1997
1935	Baseball Hall of Fame pitcher SANDY KOUFAX
1937	England soccer goalkeeper GORDON BANKS
1946	German soccer defender BERTI VOGTS
1957	English darts player/analyst ROD HARRINGTON
1968	Australian Test fast bowler ADAM DALE
1969	American golfer MICHELLE McGANN
1973	Trinidadian sprinter ATO BOLDEN
1975	American golfer TIGER WOODS
1977	American boxer LAILA ALI
1984	NBA forward LeBRON JAMES
1989	American skateboarder RYAN SHECKLER

1927 – Ponsford in form

Bill Ponsford scored 336 for Victoria against South Australia in Adelaide, taking his run tally for the month to 1,146. Ponsford had an outstanding Test batting average of 48.22, but relished playing for Victoria in the Sheffield Shield competition. In 162 first-class matches, Ponsford scored 13,819 runs, at a staggering average of 65.18 with 47 centuries.

1950 – Teenage riders pass record

At the age of 19, Bill Shoemaker and Italian rider Joe Culmone became the first jockeys to ride 388 winners in a US racing season. That total equalled a 44-year-old world record set by Walter Miller in 1906. Eight years later to the day, Shoemaker became the first jockey to win the national riding premiership in the US for a fourth time.

1953 – Famous Davis Cup win

Ken Rosewall beat Vic Seixas 6-2, 2-6, 6-3, 6-4 to clinch Australia's 3-2 Davis Cup Final win over the US in Melbourne. Lew Hoad had won both his singles rubbers for Australia whilst Seixas lost both of his, although he teamed with Tony Trabert to win the doubles. It was the tenth consecutive year the 2 nations had contested the Davis Cup final and it was Australia's fourth consecutive victory (1950–53).

1973 – All-Australian Tennis final at the Open

In an all-Australian final in the Australian Open, Margaret Court beat Evonne Goolagong in straight sets in Melbourne. Court won 6-4, 7-5 for the last of her amazing eleven home titles. It was Goolagong's third of 6 straight final appearances; she won the next three (1974–76).

1967 – Packers win 'The Ice Bowl'

The Green Bay Packers became the first NFL team to win 3 consecutive league championship games when they beat the visiting Dallas Cowboys 21-17 at Lambeau Field. With 4:50 remaining, the temperature at -13° and the wind blowing at 14mph, Dallas led 17-14. Packers quarterback Bart Starr then moved them 67 yards and completed a last play touchdown rush for a memorable Green Bay victory.

1988 – 5 for 'Super Mario'

Mario Lemieux of the Pittsburgh Penguins scored 5 goals in an 8-6 win against the New Jersey Devils, one in each possible way. Lemieux scored goals short-handed, on the power play, at even strength, penalty shot, and an empty net.

1995 – Two centuries in one day

Australian Test opener Matthew Elliott achieved the rare feat of completing 2 first-class hundreds on the same day for Victoria in a Sheffield Shield match against Western Australia in Perth. Elliott scored an unbeaten 104, and 135 in Victoria's follow-on.

2007 – Maddison makes his mark

Robbie Maddison shot to international prominence in Las Vegas by breaking the world motorcycle distance jumping record of 322ft, soaring more than the length of a football field. Maddison's jump beat Ryan Capes' 2005 effort of 310ft. The spectacular footage, complete with the raucous atmosphere, was shown globally.

BIRTHDATES

1902	England soccer defender ROY GOODALL – died 1982
1929	England Test batsman PETER MAY – died 1994
1941	Scottish soccer manager SIR ALEX FERGUSON
1946	Irish soccer midfielder BRYAN HAMILTON
1946	American tennis player CLIFF RICHEY JR
1950	England rugby union prop PHIL BLAKEWAY
1950	American golfer BOB GILDER
1951	American motor cycle rider KENNY ROBERTS
1952	French rugby union flanker JEAN-PIERRE RIVES
1958	Australian Test batsman GEOFF MARSH
1960	English soccer manager STEVE BRUCE
1964	West Indies Test fast bowler WINSTON BENJAMIN
1965	Indian Test spinner LAXMAN SIVARAMAKRISHNAN
1973	Canadian swimmer CURTIS MYDEN
1976	England Test fast bowler MATTHEW HOGGARD
1980	New Zealand rugby union flanker RICHIE McCAW
1981	Australian AFL forward MATTHEW PAVLICH
1982	Scottish soccer goalkeeper CRAIG GORDON
1995	American gymnast GABBY DOUGLAS

UK £14.99
US $19.99